CAMBRIDGE
UNIVERSITY PRESS

University Printing House, Cambridge CB2 8BS, United Kingdom

One Liberty Plaza, 20th Floor, New York, NY 10006, USA

477 Williamstown Road, Port Melbourne, VIC 3207, Australia

314-321, 3rd Floor, Plot 3, Splendor Forum, Jasola District Centre, New Delhi - 110025, India

79 Anson Road, #06-04/06, Singapore 079906

Cambridge University Press is part of the University of Cambridge.

It furthers the University's mission by disseminating knowledge in the pursuit of education, learning and research at the highest international levels of excellence.

www.cambridge.org
Information on this title: www.cambridge.org/9781108486828
DOI: 10.1017/9781108571401

First published 2020

A catalogue record for this publication is available from the British Library

Library of Congress Cataloging in Publication data
Names: Lattimore, Tor, 1987- author. | Szepesvári, Csaba, author.
Title: Bandit algorithms / Tor Lattimore and Csaba Szepesvári.
Description: Cambridge ; New York, NY : Cambridge University Press, 2020. |
    Includes bibliographical references and index.
Identifiers: LCCN 2019053276 (print) | LCCN 2019053277 (ebook) |
    ISBN 9781108486828 (hardback) | ISBN 9781108571401 (epub)
Subjects: LCSH: Mathematical optimization. | Probabilities. |
    Decision making–Mathematical models. | Resource allocation–Mathematical
    models. | Algorithms.
Classification: LCC QA402.5 .L367 2020 (print) | LCC QA402.5 (ebook) |
    DDC 519.3–dc23
LC record available at https://lccn.loc.gov/2019053276
LC ebook record available at https://lccn.loc.gov/2019053277

ISBN 978-1-108-48682-8 Hardback

Bandit Algorithms

Decision-making in the face of uncertainty is a significant challenge in machine learning, and the multi-armed bandit model is a commonly used framework to address it. This comprehensive and rigorous introduction to the multi-armed bandit problem examines all the major settings, including stochastic, adversarial and Bayesian frameworks. A focus on both mathematical intuition and carefully worked proofs makes this an excellent reference for established researchers and a helpful resource for graduate students in computer science, engineering, statistics, applied mathematics and economics. Linear bandits receive special attention as one of the most useful models in applications, while other chapters are dedicated to combinatorial bandits, ranking, non-stationary problems, Thompson sampling and pure exploration. The book ends with a peek into the world beyond bandits with an introduction to partial monitoring and learning in Markov decision processes.

TOR LATTIMORE is a research scientist at DeepMind. His research is focused on decision-making in the face of uncertainty, including bandit algorithms and reinforcement learning. Before joining DeepMind, he was an assistant professor at Indiana University and a postdoctoral fellow at the University of Alberta.

CSABA SZEPESVÁRI is a professor at the Department of Computing Science of the University of Alberta and a principal investigator at the Alberta Machine Intelligence Institute. He also leads the Foundations team at DeepMind. He has co-authored a book on nonlinear approximate adaptive controllers and authored a book on reinforcement learning, in addition to publishing over 200 journal and conference papers. He is an action editor of the *Journal of Machine Learning Research*.

Bandit Algorithms

Tor Lattimore
DeepMind

Csaba Szepesvári
University of Alberta

CAMBRIDGE
UNIVERSITY PRESS

Contents

Preface

Multi-armed bandits have now been studied for nearly a century. While research in the beginning was quite meandering, there is now a large community publishing hundreds of articles every year. Bandit algorithms are also finding their way into practical applications in industry, especially in on-line platforms where data is readily available and automation is the only way to scale.

We had hoped to write a comprehensive book, but the literature is now so vast that many topics have been excluded. In the end we settled on the more modest goal of equipping our readers with enough expertise to explore the specialised literature by themselves, and to adapt existing algorithms to their applications. This latter point is important. Problems in theory are all alike; every application is different. A practitioner seeking to apply a bandit algorithm needs to understand which assumptions in the theory are important and how to modify the algorithm when the assumptions change. We hope this book can provide that understanding.

What is covered in the book is covered in some depth. The focus is on the mathematical analysis of algorithms for bandit problems, but this is not a traditional mathematics book, where lemmas are followed by proofs, theorems and more lemmas. We worked hard to include guiding principles for designing algorithms and intuition for their analysis. Many algorithms are accompanied by empirical demonstrations that further aid intuition.

We expect our readers to be familiar with basic analysis and calculus and some linear algebra. The book uses the notation of measure-theoretic probability theory, but does not rely on any deep results. A dedicated chapter is included to introduce the notation and provide intuitions for the basic results we need. This chapter is unusual for an introduction to measure theory in that it emphasises the reasons to use σ-algebras beyond the standard technical justifications. We hope this will convince the reader that measure theory is an important and intuitive tool. Some chapters use techniques from information theory and convex analysis, and we devote a short chapter to each.

Most chapters are short and should be readable in an afternoon or presented in a single lecture. Some components of the book contain content that is not really about bandits. These can be skipped by knowledgeable readers, or otherwise referred to when necessary. They are marked with a ($\lefttail$) because 'Skippy the Kangaroo' skips things. [1] The same mark is used for those parts that contain useful, but perhaps overly specific information for the first-time reader. Later parts will not build on these chapters in any substantial way. Most chapters end with a list of notes and exercises. These are intended to deepen intuition and highlight

---

[1] Taking inspiration from Tor's grandfather-in-law, John Dillon [Anderson et al., 1977].

the connections between various subsections and the literature. There is a table of notation at the end of this preface.

Thanks

We're indebted to our many collaborators and feel privileged that there are too many of you to name. The University of Alberta, Indiana University and DeepMind have all provided outstanding work environments and supported the completion of this book. The book has benefited enormously from the proofreading efforts of a large number of our friends and colleagues. We're sorry for all the mistakes introduced after your hard work. Alphabetically, they are: Aaditya Ramdas, Abbas Mehrabian, Aditya Gopalan, Ambuj Tewari, András György, Arnoud den Boer, Branislav Kveton, Brendan Patch, Chao Tao, Christoph Dann, Claire Vernade, Emilie Kaufmann, Eugene Ji, Gellért Weisz, Gergely Neu, Johannes Kirschner, Julian Zimmert, Kwang-Sung Jun, Lalit Jain, Laurent Orseau, Marcus Hutter, Michal Valko, Omar Rivasplata, Pierre Menard, Ramana Kumar, Roman Pogodin, Ronald Ortner, Ronan Fruit, Ruihao Zhu, Shuai Li, Toshiyuki Tanaka, Wei Chen, Yoan Russac, Yufei Yi and Zhu Xiaohu. We are especially grateful to Gábor Balázs and Wouter Koolen, who both read almost the entire book. Thanks to Lauren Cowles and Cambridge University Press for providing free books for our proofreaders, tolerating the delays and for supporting a freely available PDF version. Réka Szepesvári is responsible for converting some of our school figures to their current glory. Last of all, our families have endured endless weekends of editing and multiple false promises of 'done by Christmas'. Rosina and Beáta, it really is done now!

Notation

Some sections are marked with special symbols, which are listed and described below.

 This symbol is a note. Usually this is a remark that is slightly tangential to the topic at hand.

 A warning to the reader.

 Something important.

 An experiment.

Nomenclature and Conventions

A sequence $(a_n)_{n=1}^{\infty}$ is **increasing** if $a_{n+1} \geq a_n$ for all $n \geq 1$ and **decreasing** if $a_{n+1} \leq a_n$. When the inequalities are strict, we say **strictly increasing/decreasing**. The same terminology holds for functions. We will not be dogmatic about what is the range of argmin/argmax. Sometimes they return sets, sometimes arbitrary elements of those sets and, where stated, specific elements of those sets. We will be specific when it is non-obvious/matters. The infimum of the empty set is $\inf \emptyset = \infty$ and the supremum is $\sup \emptyset = -\infty$. The empty sum is $\sum_{i \in \emptyset} a_i = 0$ and the empty product is $\prod_{i \in \emptyset} a_i = 1$.

Landau Notation

We make frequent use of the Bachmann–Landau notation. Both were nineteenth century mathematicians who could have never expected their notation to be adopted so enthusiastically by computer scientists. Given functions $f, g : \mathbb{N} \to [0, \infty)$, define

$$f(n) = O(g(n)) \Leftrightarrow \limsup_{n \to \infty} \frac{f(n)}{g(n)} < \infty,$$

$$f(n) = o(g(n)) \Leftrightarrow \lim_{n \to \infty} \frac{f(n)}{g(n)} = 0,$$

$$f(n) = \Omega(g(n)) \Leftrightarrow \liminf_{n \to \infty} \frac{f(n)}{g(n)} > 0,$$

$$f(n) = \omega(g(n)) \Leftrightarrow \liminf_{n \to \infty} \frac{f(n)}{g(n)} = \infty,$$

$$f(n) = \Theta(g(n)) \Leftrightarrow f(n) = O(g(n)) \text{ and } f(n) = \Omega(g(n)).$$

We make use of the (Bachmann–)Landau notation in two contexts. First, in proofs where limiting arguments are made, we sometimes write lower-order terms using Landau notation. For example, we might write that $f(n) = \sqrt{n} + o(\sqrt{n})$, by which we mean that $\lim_{n \to \infty} f(n)/\sqrt{n} = 1$. In this case we use the mathematical definitions as envisaged by Bachmann and Landau. The second usage is to informally describe a result without the clutter of uninteresting constants. For better or worse, this usage is often a little imprecise. For example, we will often write expressions of the form: $R_n = O(m\sqrt{dn})$. Almost always what is meant by this is that there exists a **universal constant** $c > 0$ (a constant that does not depend on either of the quantities involved) such that $R_n \leq cm\sqrt{dn}$ for all (reasonable) choices of m, d and n. In this context we are careful *not* to use Landau notation to hide large lower-order terms. For example, if $f(x) = x^2 + 10^{100}x$, we will not write $f(x) = O(x^2)$, although this would be true.

Bandits

A_t	action in round t
k	number of arms/actions
n	time horizon
X_t	reward in round t
Y_t	loss in round t
π	a policy
ν	a bandit
μ_i	mean reward of arm i

Sets

$\emptyset$	empty set
$\mathbb{N}, \mathbb{N}^+$	natural numbers, $\mathbb{N} = \{0, 1, 2, \ldots\}$ and $\mathbb{N}^+ = \mathbb{N} \setminus \{0\}$
$\mathbb{R}$	real numbers
$\bar{\mathbb{R}}$	$\mathbb{R} \cup \{-\infty, \infty\}$
$[n]$	$\{1, 2, 3, \ldots, n-1, n\}$
2^A	the power set of set A (the set of all subsets of A)
A^*	set of finite sequences over A, $A^* = \bigcup_{i=0}^{\infty} A^i$
B_2^d	d-dimensional unit ball, $\{x \in \mathbb{R}^d : \|x\|_2 \leq 1\}$
$\mathcal{P}_d$	probability simplex, $\{x \in [0,1]^{d+1} : \|x\|_1 = 1\}$
$\mathcal{P}(A)$	set of distributions over set A
$\mathfrak{B}(A)$	Borel σ-algebra on A
$[x, y]$	convex hull of vectors or real values x and y

Functions, Operators and Operations

$|A|$	the cardinality (number of elements) of the finite set A
$(x)^+$	$\max(x, 0)$

$a \bmod b$	remainder when natural number a is divided by b
$\lfloor x \rfloor, \lceil x \rceil$	floor and ceiling functions of x
$\mathrm{dom}(f)$	domain of function f
$\mathbb{E}$	expectation
$\mathbb{V}$	variance
Supp	support of distribution or random variable
$\nabla f(x)$	gradient of f at x
$\nabla_v f(x)$	directional derivative of f at x in direction v
$\nabla^2 f(x)$	Hessian of f at x
$\vee, \wedge$	maximum and minimum, $a \vee b = \max(a,b)$ and $a \wedge b = \min(a,b)$
$\mathrm{erf}(x)$	$\frac{2}{\sqrt{\pi}} \int_0^x \exp(-y^2) dy$
$\mathrm{erfc}(x)$	$1 - \mathrm{erf}(x)$
$\Gamma(z)$	Gamma function, $\Gamma(z) = \int_0^\infty x^{z-1} \exp(-x) dx$
$\phi_A(x)$	support function $\phi_A(x) = \sup_{y \in A} \langle x, y \rangle$
$f^*(y)$	convex conjugate, $f^*(y) = \sup_{x \in A} \langle x, y \rangle - f(x)$
$\binom{n}{k}$	binomial coefficient
$\mathrm{argmax}_x f(x)$	maximiser or maximisers of f
$\mathrm{argmin}_x f(x)$	minimiser or minimisers of f
$\mathbb{I}\phi$	indicator function: converts Boolean ϕ into binary
$\mathbb{I}_B$	indicator of set B
$D(P, Q)$	Relative entropy between probability distributions P and Q
$d(p, q)$	Relative entropy between $\mathcal{B}(p)$ and $\mathcal{B}(q)$

Linear Algebra

$e_1, \ldots, e_d$	standard basis vectors of the d-dimensional Euclidean space
$\mathbf{0}, \mathbf{1}$	vectors whose elements are all zeros and all ones, respectively
$\det(A)$	determinant of matrix A
$\mathrm{trace}(A)$	trace of matrix A
$\mathrm{im}(A)$	image of matrix A
$\ker(A)$	kernel of matrix A
$\mathrm{span}(v_1, \ldots, v_d)$	span of vectors $v_1, \ldots, v_d$
$\lambda_{\min}(G)$	minimum eigenvalue of matrix G
$\langle x, y \rangle$	inner product, $\langle x, y \rangle = \sum_i x_i y_i$
$\|x\|_p$	p-norm of vector x
$\|x\|_G^2$	$x^\top G x$ for positive definite $G \in \mathbb{R}^{d \times d}$ and $x \in \mathbb{R}^d$
$\prec, \preceq$	Loewner partial order of positive semidefinite matrices: $A \preceq B$ $(A \prec B)$ if $B - A$ is positive semidefinite (respectively, definite).

Distributions

$\mathcal{N}(\mu, \sigma^2)$	Normal distribution with mean μ and variance σ^2
$\mathcal{B}(p)$	Bernoulli distribution with mean p
$\mathcal{U}(a, b)$	uniform distribution supported on $[a, b]$
$\mathrm{Beta}(\alpha, \beta)$	Beta distribution with parameters $\alpha, \beta > 0$
δ_x	Dirac distribution with point mass at x

Topological

cl(A)	closure of set A
int(A)	interior of set A
∂A	boundary of a set A, $\partial A = \text{cl}(A) \setminus \text{int}(A)$
co(A)	convex hull of A
aff(A)	affine hull of A
ri(A)	relative interior of A

Part I

Bandits, Probability and Concentration

1 Introduction

Bandit problems were introduced by William R. Thompson in an article published in 1933 in *Biometrika*. Thompson was interested in medical trials and the cruelty of running a trial blindly, without adapting the treatment allocations on the fly as the drug appears more or less effective. The name comes from the 1950s, when Frederick Mosteller and Robert Bush decided to study animal learning and ran trials on mice and then on humans. The mice faced the dilemma of choosing to go left or right after starting in the bottom of a T-shaped maze, not knowing each time at which end they would find food. To study a similar learning setting in humans, a 'two-armed bandit' machine was commissioned where humans could choose to pull either the left or the right arm of the machine, each giving a random pay-off with the distribution of pay-offs for each arm unknown to the human player. The machine was called a 'two-armed bandit' in homage to the one-armed bandit, an old-fashioned name for a lever-operated slot machine ('bandit' because they steal your money).

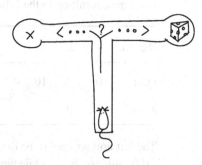

Figure 1.1 Mouse learning a T-maze.

There are many reasons to care about bandit problems. Decision-making with uncertainty is a challenge we all face, and bandits provide a simple model of this dilemma. Bandit problems also have practical applications. We already mentioned clinical trial design, which researchers have used to motivate their work for 80 years. We can't point to an example where bandits have actually been used in clinical trials, but adaptive experimental design is gaining popularity and is actively encouraged by the US Food and Drug Administration, with the justification that not doing so can lead to the withholding of effective drugs until long after a positive effect has been established.

While clinical trials are an important application for the future, there are applications where bandit algorithms are already in use. Major tech companies use bandit algorithms for configuring web interfaces, where applications include news recommendation, dynamic pricing and ad placement. A bandit algorithm plays a role in Monte Carlo Tree Search, an algorithm made famous by the recent success of AlphaGo.

Finally, the mathematical formulation of bandit problems leads to a rich structure with connections to other branches of mathematics. In writing this book (and previous papers), we have read books on convex analysis/optimisation, Brownian motion, probability theory, concentration analysis, statistics, differential geometry, information theory, Markov chains, computational complexity and more. What fun!

A combination of all these factors has led to an enormous growth in research over the last two decades. Google Scholar reports less than 1000, then 2700 and 7000 papers when searching for the phrase 'bandit algorithm' for the periods of 2001–5, 2006–10, and 2011–15, respectively, and the trend just seems to have strengthened since then, with 5600 papers coming up for the period of 2016 to the middle of 2018. Even if these numbers are somewhat overblown, they are indicative of a rapidly growing field. This could be a fashion, or maybe there is something interesting happening here. We think that the latter is true.

A Classical Dilemma

Imagine you are playing a two-armed bandit machine and you already pulled each lever five times, resulting in the following pay-offs (in dollars):

ROUND	1	2	3	4	5	6	7	8	9	10
LEFT	0		10	0		0				10
RIGHT		10			0		0	0	0	

Figure 1.2 Two-armed bandit

The left arm appears to be doing slightly better. The average pay-off for this arm is $4, while the average for the right arm is only $2. Let's say you have 10 more trials (pulls) altogether. What is your strategy? Will you keep pulling the left arm, ignoring the right? Or would you attribute the poor performance of the right arm to bad luck and try it a few more times? How many more times? This illustrates one of the main interests in bandit problems. They capture the fundamental dilemma a learner faces when choosing between uncertain options. Should one explore an option that looks inferior or exploit by going with the option that looks best currently? Finding the right balance between exploration and exploitation is at the heart of all bandit problems.

1.1 The Language of Bandits

A bandit problem is a sequential game between a **learner** and an **environment**. The game is played over n rounds, where n is a positive natural number called the **horizon**. In each round $t \in [n]$, the learner first chooses an action A_t from a given set $\mathcal{A}$, and the environment then reveals a reward $X_t \in \mathbb{R}$.

In the literature, actions are often also called 'arms'. We talk about k-**armed bandits** when the number of actions is k, and about **multi-armed bandits** when the number of arms is at least two and the actual number is immaterial to the discussion. If there are multi-armed bandits, there are also **one-armed bandits**, which are really two-armed bandits where the pay-off of one of the arms is a known fixed deterministic number.

Of course the learner cannot peek into the future when choosing their actions, which means that A_t should only depend on the **history** $H_{t-1} = (A_1, X_1, \ldots, A_{t-1}, X_{t-1})$. A **policy** is a mapping from histories to actions: A learner adopts a policy to interact with an environment. An environment is a mapping from history sequences ending in actions to rewards. Both the learner and the environment may randomise their decisions, but this detail is not so important for now. The most common objective of the learner is to choose actions that lead to the largest possible cumulative reward over all n rounds, which is $\sum_{t=1}^{n} X_t$.

The fundamental challenge in bandit problems is that the environment is unknown to the learner. All the learner knows is that the true environment lies in some set $\mathcal{E}$ called the **environment class**. Most of this book is about designing policies for different kinds of environment classes, though in some cases the framework is extended to include side observations as well as actions and rewards.

The next question is how to evaluate a learner. We discuss several performance measures throughout the book, but most of our efforts are devoted to understanding the **regret**. There are several ways to define this quantity. To avoid getting bogged down in details, we start with a somewhat informal definition.

DEFINITION 1.1. The regret of the learner relative to a policy π (not necessarily that followed by the learner) is the difference between the total expected reward using policy π for n rounds and the total expected reward collected by the learner over n rounds. The regret relative to a set of policies Π is the maximum regret relative to any policy $\pi \in \Pi$ in the set.

The set Π is often called the **competitor class**. Another way of saying all this is that the regret measures the performance of the learner relative to the best policy in the competitor class. We usually measure the regret relative to a set of policies Π that is large enough to include the optimal policy for all environments in $\mathcal{E}$. In this case, the regret measures the loss suffered by the learner relative to the optimal policy.

EXAMPLE 1.2. Suppose the action set is $\mathcal{A} = \{1, 2, \ldots, k\}$. An environment is called a **stochastic Bernoulli bandit** if the reward $X_t \in \{0, 1\}$ is binary valued and there exists a vector $\mu \in [0, 1]^k$ such that the probability that $X_t = 1$ given the learner chose action $A_t = a$ is μ_a. The class of stochastic Bernoulli bandits is the set of all such bandits, which are characterised by their mean vectors. If you knew the mean vector associated with the environment, then the optimal policy is to play the fixed action $a^* = \mathrm{argmax}_{a \in \mathcal{A}} \mu_a$. This means that for this problem the natural competitor class is the set of k constant polices $\Pi = \{\pi_1, \ldots, \pi_k\}$, where π_i chooses action i in every round. The regret over n rounds becomes

$$R_n = n \max_{a \in \mathcal{A}} \mu_a - \mathbb{E}\left[\sum_{t=1}^{n} X_t\right],$$

where the expectation is with respect to the randomness in the environment and policy. The first term in this expression is the maximum expected reward using any policy. The second term is the expected reward collected by the learner.

For a fixed policy and competitor class, the regret depends on the environment. The environments where the regret is large are those where the learner is behaving worse. Of course the ideal case is that the regret be small for all environments. The **worst-case regret** is the maximum regret over all possible environments.

One of the core questions in the study of bandits is to understand the growth rate of the regret as n grows. A good learner achieves sublinear regret. Letting R_n denote the regret over n rounds, this means that $R_n = o(n)$ or equivalently that $\lim_{n\to\infty} R_n/n = 0$. Of course one can ask for more. Under what circumstances is $R_n = O(\sqrt{n})$ or $R_n = O(\log(n))$? And what are the leading constants? How does the regret depend on the specific environment in which the learner finds itself? We will discover eventually that for the environment class in Example 1.2, the worst-case regret for any policy is at least $\Omega(\sqrt{n})$ and that there exist policies for which $R_n = O(\sqrt{n})$.

> A large environment class corresponds to less knowledge by the learner. A large competitor class means the regret is a more demanding criteria. Some care is sometimes required to choose these sets appropriately so that *(a)* guarantees on the regret are meaningful and *(b)* there exist policies that make the regret small.

The framework is general enough to model almost anything by using a rich enough environment class. This cannot be bad, but with too much generality it becomes impossible to say much. For this reason, we usually restrict our attention to certain kinds of environment classes and competitor classes.

A simple problem setting is that of **stochastic stationary bandits**. In this case the environment is restricted to generate the reward in response to each action from a distribution that is specific to that action and independent of the previous action choices and rewards. The environment class in Example 1.2 satisfies these conditions, but there are many alternatives. For example, the rewards could follow a Gaussian distribution rather than Bernoulli. This relatively mild difference does not change the nature of the problem in a significant way. A more drastic change is to assume the action set $\mathcal{A}$ is a subset of $\mathbb{R}^d$ and that the mean reward for choosing some action $a \in \mathcal{A}$ follows a linear model, $X_t = \langle a, \theta \rangle + \eta_t$ for $\theta \in \mathbb{R}^d$ and η_t a standard Gaussian (zero mean, unit variance). The unknown quantity in this case is θ, and the environment class corresponds to its possible values ($\mathcal{E} = \mathbb{R}^d$).

For some applications, the assumption that the rewards are stochastic and stationary may be too restrictive. The world mostly appears deterministic, even if it is hard to predict and often chaotic looking. Of course, stochasticity has been enormously successful in explaining patterns in data, and this may be sufficient reason to keep it as the modelling assumption. But what if the stochastic assumptions fail to hold? What if they are violated for a single round? Or just for one action, at some rounds? Will our best algorithms suddenly perform poorly? Or will the algorithms developed be robust to smaller or larger deviations from the modelling assumptions?

An extreme idea is to drop all assumptions on how the rewards are generated, except that they are chosen without knowledge of the learner's actions and lie in a bounded set. If these are the only assumptions, we get what is called the setting of **adversarial bandits**. The trick to say something meaningful in this setting is to restrict the competitor class. The learner is not expected to find the best sequence of actions, which may be like finding a needle in a haystack. Instead, we usually choose Π to be the set of constant policies and demand that the learner is not much worse than any of these. By defining the regret in this way, the stationarity assumption is transported into the definition of regret rather than constraining the environment.

Of course there are all shades of grey between these two extremes. Sometimes we consider the case where the rewards are stochastic, but not stationary. Or one may analyse the robustness of an algorithm for stochastic bandits to small adversarial perturbations. Another idea is to isolate exactly which properties of the stochastic assumption are really exploited by a policy designed for stochastic bandits. This kind of inverse analysis can help explain the strong performance of policies when facing environments that clearly violate the assumptions they were designed for.

1.1.1   Other Learning Objectives

We already mentioned that the regret can be defined in several ways, each capturing slightly different aspects of the behaviour of a policy. Because the regret depends on the environment, it becomes a multi-objective criterion: ideally, we want to keep the regret small across all possible environments. One way to convert a multi-objective criterion into a single number is to take averages. This corresponds to the Bayesian viewpoint where the objective is to minimise the average cumulative regret with respect to a prior on the environment class.

Maximising the sum of rewards is not always the objective. Sometimes the learner just wants to find a near-optimal policy after n rounds, but the actual rewards accumulated over those rounds are unimportant. We will see examples of this shortly.

1.1.2   Limitations of the Bandit Framework

One of the distinguishing features of all bandit problems studied in this book is that the learner never needs to plan for the future. More precisely, we will invariably make the assumption that the learner's available choices and rewards tomorrow are not affected by their decisions today. Problems that do require this kind of long-term planning fall into the realm of **reinforcement learning**, which is the topic of the final chapter. Another limitation of the bandit framework is the assumption that the learner observes the reward in every round. The setting where the reward is not observed is called **partial monitoring** and is the topic of Chapter 37. Finally, often, the environment itself consists of strategic agents, which the learner needs to take into account. This problem is studied in game theory and would need a book on its own.

1.2   Applications

After this short preview, and as an appetiser before the hard work, we briefly describe the formalisations of a variety of applications.

A/B Testing

The designers of a company website are trying to decide whether the 'buy it now' button should be placed at the top of the product page or at the bottom. In the old days, they would commit to a trial of each version by splitting incoming users into two groups of 10 000. Each group would be shown a different version of the site, and a statistician would examine the data at the end to decide which version was better. One problem with this approach is the non-adaptivity of the test. For example, if the effect size is large, then the trial could be stopped early.

One way to apply bandits to this problem is to view the two versions of the site as actions. Each time t a user makes a request, a bandit algorithm is used to choose an action $A_t \in \mathcal{A} = \{\text{SiteA}, \text{SiteB}\}$, and the reward is $X_t = 1$ if the user purchases the product and $X_t = 0$ otherwise.

> In traditional A/B testing, the objective of the statistician is to decide which website is better. When using a bandit algorithm, there is no need to end the trial. The algorithm automatically decides when one version of the site should be shown more often than another. Even if the real objective is to identify the best site, then adaptivity or early stopping can be added to the A/B process using techniques from bandit theory. While this is not the focus of this book, some of the basic ideas are explained in Chapter 33.

Advert Placement

In advert placement, each round corresponds to a user visiting a website, and the set of actions $\mathcal{A}$ is the set of all available adverts. One could treat this as a standard multi-armed bandit problem, where in each round a policy chooses $A_t \in \mathcal{A}$, and the reward is $X_t = 1$ if the user clicked on the advert and $X_t = 0$ otherwise. This might work for specialised websites where the adverts are all likely to be appropriate. But for a company like Amazon, the advertising should be targeted. A user that recently purchased rock-climbing shoes is much more likely to buy a harness than another user. Clearly an algorithm should take this into account.

The standard way to incorporate this additional knowledge is to use the information about the user as **context**. In its simplest formulation, this might mean clustering users and implementing a separate bandit algorithm for each cluster. Much of this book is devoted to the question of how to use side information to improve the performance of a learner.

This is a good place to emphasise that the world is messy. The set of available adverts is changing from round to round. The feedback from the user can be delayed for many rounds. Finally, the real objective is rarely just to maximise clicks. Other metrics such as user satisfaction, diversity, freshness and fairness, just to mention a few, are important too. These are the kinds of issues that make implementing bandit algorithms in the real world a challenge. This book will not address all these issues in detail. Instead we focus on the foundations and hope this provides enough understanding that you can invent solutions for whatever peculiar challenges arise in your problem.

Recommendation Services

Netflix has to decide which movies to place most prominently in your 'Browse' page. Like in advert placement, users arrive at the page sequentially, and the reward can be measured as some function of (a) whether or not you watched a movie and (b) whether or not you rated it positively. There are many challenges. First of all, Netflix shows a long list of movies, so the set of possible actions is combinatorially large. Second, each user watches relatively few movies, and individual users are different. This suggests approaches such as low-rank matrix factorisation (a popular approach in 'collaborative filtering'). But notice this is not an offline problem. The learning algorithm gets to choose what users see and this affects the data. If the users are never recommended the AlphaGo movie, then few users will watch it, and the amount of data about this film will be scarce.

Network Routing

Another problem with an interesting structure is network routing, where the learner tries to direct internet traffic through the shortest path on a network. In each round the learner receives the start/end destinations for a packet of data. The set of actions is the set of all paths starting and ending at the appropriate points on some known graph. The feedback in this case is the time it takes for the packet to be received at its destination, and the reward is the negation of this value. Again the action set is combinatorially large. Even relatively small graphs have an enormous number of paths. The routing problem can obviously be applied to more physical networks such as transportation systems used in operations research.

Dynamic Pricing

In dynamic pricing, a company is trying to automatically optimise the price of some product. Users arrive sequentially, and the learner sets the price. The user will only purchase the product if the price is lower than their valuation. What makes this problem interesting is (a) the learner never actually observes the valuation of the product, only the binary signal that the price was too low/too high, and (b) there is a monotonicity structure in the pricing. If a user purchased an item priced at \$10, then they would surely purchase it for \$5, but whether or not it would sell when priced at \$11 is uncertain. Also, the set of possible actions is close to continuous.

Waiting Problems

Every day you travel to work, either by bus or by walking. Once you get on the bus, the trip only takes 5 minutes, but the timetable is unreliable, and the bus arrival time is unknown and stochastic. Sometimes the bus doesn't come at all. Walking, on the other hand, takes 30 minutes along a beautiful river away from the road. The problem is to devise a policy for choosing how long to wait at the bus stop before giving up and walking to minimise the time to get to your workplace. Walk too soon, and you miss the bus and gain little information. But waiting too long also comes at a price.

While waiting for a bus is not a problem we all face, there are other applications of this setting. For example, deciding the amount of inactivity required before putting a hard drive into sleep mode or powering off a car engine at traffic lights. The statistical part of the waiting problem concerns estimating the cumulative distribution function of the bus arrival times from data. The twist is that the data is censored on the days you chose to walk before the bus arrived, which is a problem analysed in the subfield of statistics called survival analysis. The interplay between the statistical estimation problem and the challenge of balancing exploration and exploitation is what makes this and the other problems studied in this book interesting.

Resource Allocation

A large part of operations research is focussed on designing strategies for allocating scarce resources. When the dynamics of demand or supply are uncertain, the problem has elements reminiscent of a bandit problem. Allocating too few resources reveals only partial information about the true demand, but allocating too many resources is wasteful. Of course, resource allocation is broad, and many problems exhibit structure that is not typical of bandit problems, like the need for long-term planning.

Tree Search

The UCT algorithm is a tree search algorithm commonly used in perfect-information game-playing algorithms. The idea is to iteratively build a search tree where in each iteration the algorithm takes three steps: *(1)* chooses a path from the root to a leaf; *(2)* expands the leaf (if possible); *(3)* performs a Monte Carlo roll-out to the end of the game. The contribution of a bandit algorithm is in selecting the path from the root to the leaves. At each node in the tree, a bandit algorithm is used to select the child based on the series of rewards observed through that node so far. The resulting algorithm can be analysed theoretically, but more importantly has demonstrated outstanding empirical performance in game-playing problems.

1.3   Notes

1 The reader may find it odd that at one point we identified environments with maps from histories to rewards, while we used the language that a learner 'adopts a policy' (a map from histories to actions). The reason is part historical and part because policies and their design are at the center of the book, while the environment strategies will mostly be kept fixed (and relatively simple). On this note, strategy is also a word that sometimes used interchangeably with policy.

1.4   Bibliographic Remarks

As we mentioned in the very beginning, the first paper on bandits was by Thompson [1933]. The experimentation on mice and humans that led to the name comes from the paper by Bush and Mosteller [1953]. Much credit for the popularisation of the field must go to famous mathematician and statistician, Herbert Robbins, whose name appears on many of the works that we reference, with the earliest being: [Robbins, 1952]. Another early pioneer is Herman Chernoff, who wrote papers with titles like 'Sequential Decisions in the Control of a Spaceship' [Bather and Chernoff, 1967].

Besides these seminal papers, there are already a number of books on bandits that may serve as useful additional reading. The most recent (and also most related) is by Bubeck and Cesa-Bianchi [2012] and is freely available online. This is an excellent book and is warmly recommended. The main difference between their book and ours is that *(a)* we have the benefit of seven years of additional research in a fast-moving field and *(b)* our longer page limit permits more depth. Another relatively recent book is *Prediction, Learning and Games* by Cesa-Bianchi and Lugosi [2006]. This is a wonderful book, and quite comprehensive. But its scope is 'all of' online learning, which is so broad that bandits are not covered in great depth. We should mention there is also a recent book on bandits by Slivkins [2019]. Conveniently it covers some topics not covered in this book (notably Lipschitz bandits and bandits with knapsacks). The reverse is also true, which should not be surprising since our book is currently 400 pages longer. There are also four books on sequential design and multi-armed bandits in the Bayesian setting, which we will address only a little. These are based on relatively old material, but are still useful references for this line of work and are well worth reading [Chernoff, 1959, Berry and Fristedt, 1985, Presman and Sonin, 1990, Gittins et al., 2011].

Without trying to be exhaustive, here are a few articles applying bandit algorithms; a recent survey is by Bouneffouf and Rish [2019]. The papers themselves will contain more useful pointers to the vast literature. We mentioned AlphaGo already [Silver et al., 2016]. The tree search algorithm that drives its search uses a bandit algorithm at each node [Kocsis and Szepesvári, 2006]. Le et al. [2014] apply bandits to wireless monitoring, where the problem is challenging due to the large action space. Lei et al. [2017] design specialised contextual bandit algorithms for just-in-time adaptive interventions in mobile health: in the typical application the user is prompted with the intention of inducing a long-term beneficial behavioural change. See also the article by Greenewald et al. [2017]. Rafferty et al. [2018] apply Thompson sampling to educational software and note the trade-off between knowledge and reward. Sadly, by 2015, bandit algorithms still have not been used in clinical trials, as explicitly mentioned by Villar et al. [2015]. Microsoft offers a 'Decision Service' that uses bandit algorithms to automate decision-making [Agarwal et al., 2016].

2 Foundations of Probability (🐪)

This chapter covers the fundamental concepts of measure-theoretic probability, on which the remainder of this book relies. Readers familiar with this topic can safely skip the chapter, but perhaps a brief reading would yield some refreshing perspectives. Measure-theoretic probability is often viewed as a necessary evil, to be used when a demand for rigour combined with continuous spaces breaks the simple approach we know and love from high school. We claim that measure-theoretic probability offers more than annoying technical machinery. In this chapter we attempt to prove this by providing a non-standard introduction. Rather than a long list of definitions, we demonstrate the intuitive power of the notation and tools. For those readers with little prior experience in measure theory this chapter will no doubt be a challenging read. We think the investment is worth the effort, but a great deal of the book can be read without it, provided one is willing to take certain results on faith.

2.1 Probability Spaces and Random Elements

The thrill of gambling comes from the fact that the bet is placed on future outcomes that are uncertain at the time of the gamble. A central question in gambling is the fair value of a game. This can be difficult to answer for all but the simplest games. As an illustrative example, imagine the following moderately complex game: I throw a dice. If the result is four, I throw two more dice; otherwise I throw one dice only. Looking at each newly thrown dice (one or two), I repeat the same, for a total of three rounds. Afterwards, I pay you the sum of the values on the faces of the dice. How much are you willing to pay to play this game with me?

Many examples of practical interest exhibit a complex random interdependency between outcomes. The cornerstone of modern probability as proposed by Kolmogorov aims to remove this complexity by separating the randomness from the mechanism that produces the outcome.

Instead of rolling the dice one by one, imagine that sufficiently many dice were rolled before the game has even started. For our game we need to roll seven dice, because this is the maximum number that might be required (one in the first round, two in the second round and four in the third round. See Fig. 2.1). After all the dice are rolled, the game can be emulated by ordering the dice and revealing the outcomes sequentially. Then the value of the first dice in the chosen ordering is the outcome of the dice in the first round. If we see a four, we look at the next two dice in the ordering; otherwise we look at the single next dice.

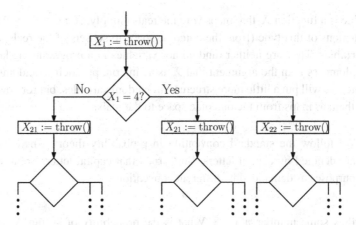

Figure 2.1 The initial phase of a gambling game with a random number of dice rolls. Depending on the outcome of a dice roll, one or two dice are rolled for a total of three rounds. The number of dice used will then be random in the range of three to seven.

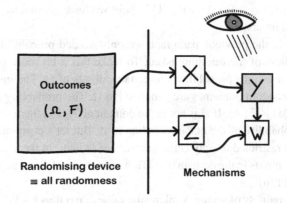

Figure 2.2 A key idea in probability theory is the separation of sources of randomness from game mechanisms. A mechanism creates values from the elementary random outcomes, some of which are visible for observers, while others may remain hidden.

By taking this approach, we get a simple calculus for the probabilities of all kinds of **events**. Rather than directly calculating the likelihood of each pay-off, we first consider the probability of any single outcome of the dice. Since there are seven dice, the set of all possible outcomes is $\Omega = \{1, \ldots, 6\}^7$. Because all outcomes are equally probable, the probability of any $\omega \in \Omega$ is $(1/6)^7$. The probability of the game pay-off taking value v can then be evaluated by calculating the total probability assigned to all those outcomes $\omega \in \Omega$ that would result in the value of v. In principle, this is trivial to do thanks to the separation of everything that is probabilistic from the rest. The set Ω is called the **outcome space**, and its elements are the **outcomes**. Fig. 2.2 illustrates this idea. Random outcomes are generated on the left, while on the right, various mechanisms are used to arrive at values; some of these values may be observed and some not.

There will be much benefit from being a little more formal about how we come up with the value of our artificial game. For this, note that the process by which the game gets its value is a function X that maps Ω to the reals (simply, $X : \Omega \to \mathbb{R}$). We find it ironic that functions of this type (from the outcome space to subsets of the reals) are called **random variables**. They are neither random nor variables in a programming language sense. The randomness is in the argument that X is acting on, producing randomly changing results. Later we will put a little more structure on random variables, but for now it suffices to think of them as maps from the outcome space to the reals.

> We follow the standard convention in probability theory where random variables are denoted by capital letters. Be warned that capital letters are also used for other purposes as demanded by different conventions.

Pick some number $v \in \mathbb{N}$. What is the probability of seeing $X = v$? As described above, this probability is $(1/6)^7$ times the size of the set $X^{-1}(v) = \{\omega \in \Omega : X(\omega) = v\}$. The set $X^{-1}(v)$ is called the **preimage** of v under X. More generally, the probability that X takes its value in some set $A \subseteq \mathbb{N}$ is given by $(1/6)^7$ times the cardinality of $X^{-1}(A) = \{\omega \in \Omega : X(\omega) \in A\}$, where we have overloaded the definition of X^{-1} to set-valued inputs.

Notice in the previous paragraph we only needed probabilities assigned to subsets of Ω, regardless of the question asked. To make this a bit more general, let us introduce a map $\mathbb{P}$ that assigns probabilities to certain subsets of Ω. The intuitive meaning of $\mathbb{P}$ is as follows. Random outcomes are generated in Ω. The probability that an outcome falls into a set $A \subset \Omega$ is $\mathbb{P}(A)$. If A is not in the domain of $\mathbb{P}$, then there is no answer to the question of the probability of the outcome falling in A. But let's postpone the discussion of why $\mathbb{P}$ should be restricted to only certain subsets of Ω later. In the above example with the dice, the set of subsets in the domain of $\mathbb{P}$ is not restricted and, in particular, for any subset $A \subseteq \Omega$, $\mathbb{P}(A) = (1/6)^7 |A|$.

The probability of seeing X taking the value of v is thus $\mathbb{P}\left(X^{-1}(v)\right)$. To minimise clutter, the more readable notation for this is $\mathbb{P}(X = v)$. But always keep in mind that this familiar form is just a shorthand for $\mathbb{P}\left(X^{-1}(v)\right)$. More generally, we also use

$$\mathbb{P}(\text{predicate}(U, V, \dots)) = \mathbb{P}(\{\omega \in \Omega : \text{predicate}(U(\omega), V(\omega), \dots) \text{ is true}\})$$

with any predicate (an expression evaluating to true or false) where $U, V, \dots$ are functions with domain Ω.

What properties should $\mathbb{P}$ satisfy? Since Ω is the set of all possible outcomes, it seems reasonable to expect that $\mathbb{P}$ is defined for Ω and $\mathbb{P}(\Omega) = 1$ and since $\emptyset$ contains no outcomes, $\mathbb{P}(\emptyset) = 0$ is also expected to hold. Furthermore, probabilities should be non-negative so $\mathbb{P}(A) \geq 0$ for any $A \subset \Omega$ on which $\mathbb{P}$ is defined. Let $A^c = \Omega \setminus A$ be the **complement** of A. Then we should expect that $\mathbb{P}$ is defined for A exactly when it is defined for A^c and $\mathbb{P}(A^c) = 1 - \mathbb{P}(A)$ (negation rule). Finally, if A, B are disjoint so that $A \cap B = \emptyset$ and $\mathbb{P}(A), \mathbb{P}(B)$ and $\mathbb{P}(A \cup B)$ are all defined, then $\mathbb{P}(A \cup B) = \mathbb{P}(A) + \mathbb{P}(B)$. This is called the **finite additivity property**.

Let $\mathcal{F}$ be the set of subsets of Ω on which $\mathbb{P}$ is defined. It would seem silly if $A \in \mathcal{F}$ and $A^c \notin \mathcal{F}$, since $\mathbb{P}(A^c)$ could simply be defined by $\mathbb{P}(A^c) = 1 - \mathbb{P}(A)$. Similarly, if $\mathbb{P}$ is defined on disjoint sets A and B, then it makes sense if $A \cup B \in \mathcal{F}$. We will also require the additivity property to hold *(i)* regardless of whether the sets are disjoint and *(ii)* even for **countably infinitely many** sets. If $\{A_i\}_i$ is a collection of sets and $A_i \in \mathcal{F}$ for all $i \in \mathbb{N}$, then $\cup_i A_i \in \mathcal{F}$, and if these sets are pairwise disjoint, $\mathbb{P}(\cup_i A_i) = \sum_i \mathbb{P}(A_i)$. A set of subsets that satisfies all these properties is called a σ-**algebra**, which is pronounced 'sigma-algebra' and sometimes also called a σ-field (see Note 1).

DEFINITION 2.1 (σ-algebra and probability measures). A set $\mathcal{F} \subseteq 2^\Omega$ is a σ-algebra if $\Omega \in \mathcal{F}$ and $A^c \in \mathcal{F}$ for all $A \in \mathcal{F}$ and $\cup_i A_i \in \mathcal{F}$ for all $\{A_i\}_i$ with $A_i \in \mathcal{F}$ for all $i \in \mathbb{N}$. That is, it should include the whole outcome space and be closed under complementation and countable unions. A function $\mathbb{P} : \mathcal{F} \to \mathbb{R}$ is a **probability measure** if $\mathbb{P}(\Omega) = 1$ and for all $A \in \mathcal{F}$, $\mathbb{P}(A) \geq 0$ and $\mathbb{P}(A^c) = 1 - \mathbb{P}(A)$ and $\mathbb{P}(\cup_i A_i) = \sum_i \mathbb{P}(A_i)$ for all countable collections of disjoint sets $\{A_i\}_i$ with $A_i \in \mathcal{F}$ for all i. If $\mathcal{F}$ is a σ-algebra and $\mathcal{G} \subset \mathcal{F}$ is also a σ-algebra, then we say $\mathcal{G}$ is a **sub-σ-algebra** of $\mathcal{F}$. If $\mathbb{P}$ is a measure defined on $\mathcal{F}$, then the **restriction** of $\mathbb{P}$ to $\mathcal{G}$ is a measure $\mathbb{P}_{|\mathcal{G}}$ on $\mathcal{G}$ defined by $\mathbb{P}_{|\mathcal{G}}(A) = \mathbb{P}(A)$ for all $A \in \mathcal{G}$.

At this stage, the reader may rightly wonder about why we introduced the notion of sub-σ-algebras. The answer should become clear quite soon. The elements of $\mathcal{F}$ are called **measurable sets**. They are measurable in the sense that $\mathbb{P}$ assigns values to them. The pair $(\Omega, \mathcal{F})$ alone is called a **measurable space**, while the triplet $(\Omega, \mathcal{F}, \mathbb{P})$ is called a **probability space**. If the condition that $\mathbb{P}(\Omega) = 1$ is lifted, then $\mathbb{P}$ is called a **measure**. If the condition that $\mathbb{P}(A) \geq 0$ is also lifted, then $\mathbb{P}$ is called a **signed measure**. For measures and signed measures, it would be unusual to use the symbol $\mathbb{P}$, which is mostly reserved for probabilities. Probability measures are also called **probability distributions**, or just **distributions**.

Random variables lead to new probability measures. In particular, in the example above $\mathbb{P}_X(A) = \mathbb{P}\left(X^{-1}(A)\right)$ is a probability measure defined for all the subsets A of $\mathbb{R}$ for which $\mathbb{P}\left(X^{-1}(A)\right)$ is defined. More generally, for a random variable X, the probability measure $\mathbb{P}_X$ is called the **law** of X, or the **push-forward** measure of $\mathbb{P}$ under X.

The significance of the push-forward measure $\mathbb{P}_X$ is that any probabilistic question concerning X can be answered from the knowledge of $\mathbb{P}_X$ alone. Even Ω and the details of the map X are not needed. This is often used as an excuse to not even mention the underlying probability space $(\Omega, \mathcal{F}, \mathbb{P})$.

If we keep X fixed but change $\mathbb{P}$ (for example, by switching to loaded dice), then the measure induced by X changes. We will often use arguments that do exactly this, especially when proving lower bounds on the limits of how well bandit algorithms can perform.

The astute reader would have noticed that we skipped over some details. Measures are defined as functions from a σ-algebra to $\mathbb{R}$, so if we want to call $\mathbb{P}_X$ a measure, then its domain $\{A \subset \mathbb{R} : X^{-1}(A) \in \mathcal{F}\}$ better be a σ-algebra. This holds in great generality. You will show in Exercise 2.3 that for functions $X : \Omega \to \mathcal{X}$ with $\mathcal{X}$ arbitrary, the collection $\{A \subset \mathcal{X} : X^{-1}(A) \in \mathcal{F}\}$ is a σ-algebra.

It will be useful to generalise our example a little by allowing X to take on values in sets other than the reals. For example, the range could be vectors or abstract objects like sequences. Let $(\Omega, \mathcal{F})$ be a measurable space, $\mathcal{X}$ be an arbitrary set and $\mathcal{G} \subseteq 2^{\mathcal{X}}$. A function $X : \Omega \to \mathcal{X}$ is called an $\mathcal{F}/\mathcal{G}$-**measurable map** if $X^{-1}(A) \in \mathcal{F}$ for all $A \in \mathcal{G}$. Note that $\mathcal{G}$ need not be a σ-algebra. When $\mathcal{F}$ and $\mathcal{G}$ are obvious from the context, X is called a **measurable map**. What are the typical choices for $\mathcal{G}$? When X is real-valued, it is usual to let $\mathcal{G} = \{(a, b) : a < b \text{ with } a, b \in \mathbb{R}\}$ be the set of all open intervals. The reader can verify that if X is $\mathcal{F}/\mathcal{G}$-measurable, then it is also $\mathcal{F}/\sigma(\mathcal{G})$-measurable, where $\sigma(\mathcal{G})$ is the smallest σ-algebra that contains $\mathcal{G}$. This smallest σ-algebra can be shown to exist. Furthermore, it contains exactly those sets A that are in every σ-algebra that contains $\mathcal{G}$ (see Exercise 2.5). When $\mathcal{G}$ is the set of open intervals, $\sigma(\mathcal{G})$ is usually denoted by $\mathfrak{B}$ or $\mathfrak{B}(\mathbb{R})$ and is called the **Borel σ-algebra** of $\mathbb{R}$. This definition is extended to $\mathbb{R}^k$ by replacing open intervals with open rectangles of the form $\prod_{i=1}^{k}(a_i, b_i)$, where $a < b \in \mathbb{R}^k$. If $\mathcal{G}$ is the set of all such open rectangles, then $\sigma(\mathcal{G})$ is the Borel σ-algebra: $\mathfrak{B}(\mathbb{R}^k)$. More generally, the Borel σ-algebra of a topological space $\mathcal{X}$ is the σ-algebra generated by the open sets of $\mathcal{X}$.

DEFINITION 2.2 (Random variables and elements). A **random variable** (**random vector**) on measurable space $(\Omega, \mathcal{F})$ is a $\mathcal{F}/\mathfrak{B}(\mathbb{R})$-measurable function $X : \Omega \to \mathbb{R}$ (respectively $\mathcal{F}/\mathfrak{B}(\mathbb{R}^k)$-measurable function $X : \Omega \to \mathbb{R}^k$). A **random element** between measurable spaces $(\Omega, \mathcal{F})$ and $(\mathcal{X}, \mathcal{G})$ is a $\mathcal{F}/\mathcal{G}$-measurable function $X : \Omega \to \mathcal{X}$.

Thus, random vectors are random elements where the range space is $(\mathbb{R}^k, \mathfrak{B}(\mathbb{R}^k))$, and random vectors are random variables when $k = 1$. Random elements generalise random variables and vectors to functions that do not take values in $\mathbb{R}^k$. The push-forward measure (or law) can be defined for any random element. Furthermore, random variables and vectors work nicely together. If $X_1, \ldots, X_k$ are k random variables on the same domain $(\Omega, \mathcal{F})$, then $X(\omega) = (X_1(\omega), \ldots, X_k(\omega))$ is an $\mathbb{R}^k$-valued random vector, and vice versa (Exercise 2.2). Multiple random variables $X_1, \ldots, X_k$ from the same measurable space can thus be viewed as a random vector $X = (X_1, \ldots, X_k)$.

Given a map $X : \Omega \to \mathcal{X}$ between measurable spaces $(\Omega, \mathcal{F})$ and $(\mathcal{X}, \mathcal{G})$, we let $\sigma(X) = \{X^{-1}(A) : A \in \mathcal{G}\}$ be the σ-**algebra generated by** X. The map X is $\mathcal{F}/\mathcal{G}$-measurable if and only if $\sigma(X) \subseteq \mathcal{F}$. By checking the definitions one can show that $\sigma(X)$ is a sub-σ-algebra of $\mathcal{F}$ and in fact is the smallest sub-σ-algebra for which X is measurable. If $\mathcal{G} = \sigma(\mathcal{A})$ itself is generated by a set system $\mathcal{A} \subset 2^{\mathcal{X}}$, then to check the $\mathcal{F}/\mathcal{G}$-measurability of X, it suffices to check whether $X^{-1}(\mathcal{A}) = \{X^{-1}(A) : A \in \mathcal{A}\}$ is a subset of $\mathcal{F}$. The reason this is sufficient is because $\sigma(X^{-1}(\mathcal{A})) = X^{-1}(\sigma(\mathcal{A}))$, and by definition the latter is $\sigma(X)$. In fact, to check whether a map is measurable, either one uses the composition rule or checks $X^{-1}(\mathcal{A}) \subset \mathcal{F}$ for a 'generator' $\mathcal{A}$ of $\mathcal{G}$.

Random elements can be combined to produce new random elements by composition. One can show that if f is $\mathcal{F}/\mathcal{G}$-measurable and g is $\mathcal{G}/\mathcal{H}$-measurable for σ-algebras $\mathcal{F}, \mathcal{G}$ and $\mathcal{H}$ over appropriate spaces, then their composition $g \circ f$ is $\mathcal{F}/\mathcal{H}$-measurable (Exercise 2.1). This is used most often for **Borel functions**, which is a special name for $\mathfrak{B}(\mathbb{R}^m)/\mathfrak{B}(\mathbb{R}^n)$-measurable functions from $\mathbb{R}^m$ to $\mathbb{R}^n$. These functions are also called **Borel measurable**. The reader will find it pleasing that all familiar functions are Borel. First and foremost, all continuous functions are Borel, which includes elementary operations such as addition and multiplication. Continuity is far from essential, however. In fact one is hard-pressed to construct a function that is not Borel. This means the usual operations are 'safe' when working with random variables.

Indicator Functions

Given an arbitrary set Ω and $A \subseteq \Omega$, the **indicator function** of A is $\mathbb{I}_A : \Omega \to \{0,1\}$ given by

$$\mathbb{I}_A(\omega) = \begin{cases} 1, & \text{if } \omega \in A; \\ 0, & \text{otherwise.} \end{cases}$$

Sometimes A has a complicated description, and it becomes convenient to abuse notation by writing $\mathbb{I}\{\omega \in A\}$ instead of $\mathbb{I}_A(\omega)$. Similarly, we will often write $\mathbb{I}\{predicate(X, Y, \ldots)\}$ to mean the indicator function of the subset of Ω on which the predicate is true. It is easy to check that an indicator function $\mathbb{I}_A$ is a random variable on $(\Omega, \mathcal{F})$ if and only if A is measurable: $A \in \mathcal{F}$.

Why So Complicated?

You may be wondering why we did not define $\mathbb{P}$ on the power set of Ω, which is equivalent to declaring that all sets are measurable. In many cases this is a perfectly reasonable thing to do, including the example game where nothing prevents us from defining $\mathcal{F} = 2^\Omega$. However, beyond this example, there are two justifications not to have $\mathcal{F} = 2^\Omega$, the first technical and the second conceptual.

The technical reason is highlighted by the following surprising theorem according to which there does not exist a uniform probability distribution on $\Omega = [0,1]$ if $\mathcal{F}$ is chosen to be the power set of Ω (a uniform probability distribution over $[0,1]$, if existed, would have the property of assigning its length to every interval). In other words, if you want to be able to define the uniform measure, then $\mathcal{F}$ cannot be too large. By contrast, the uniform measure can be defined over the Borel σ-algebra, though proving this is not elementary.

THEOREM 2.3. *Let $\Omega = [0,1]$, and $\mathcal{F}$ be the power set of Ω. Then there does not exist a measure $\mathbb{P}$ on $(\Omega, \mathcal{F})$ such that $\mathbb{P}([a,b]) = b - a$ for all $0 \le a \le b \le 1$.*

The main conceptual reason of why not to have $\mathcal{F} = 2^\Omega$ is because then we can use σ-algebras represent information. This is especially useful in the study of bandits where the learner is interacting with an environment and is slowly gaining knowledge. One useful way to represent this is by using a sequence of nested σ-algebras, as we explain in the next section. One might also be worried that the Borel σ-algebra does not contain enough measurable sets. Rest assured that this is not a problem and you will not easily find a non-measurable set. For completeness, an example of a non-measurable set will still be given in the notes, along with a little more discussion on this topic.

A second technical reason to prefer the measure-theoretic approach to probabilities is that this approach allows for the unification of distributions on discrete spaces and densities on continuous ones (the uninitiated reader will find the definitions of these later). This unification can be necessary when dealing with random variables that combine elements of both, e.g. a random variable that is zero with probability $1/2$ and otherwise behaves like a standard Gaussian. Random variables like this give rise to so-called "mixed continuous and discrete distributions", which seem to require special treatment in a naive approach to probabilities, yet dealing with random variables like these are nothing but ordinary under the measure-theoretic approach.

From Laws to Probability Spaces and Random Variables

A big 'conspiracy' in probability theory is that probability spaces are seldom mentioned in theorem statements, despite the fact that a measure cannot be defined without one. Statements are instead given in terms of random elements and constraints on their joint probabilities. For example, suppose that X and Y are random variables such that

$$\mathbb{P}(X \in A, Y \in B) = \frac{|A \cap [6]|}{6} \cdot \frac{|B \cap [2]|}{2} \qquad \text{for all } A, B \in \mathfrak{B}(\mathbb{R}), \qquad (2.1)$$

which represents the joint distribution for the values of a dice ($X \in [6]$) and coin ($Y \in [2]$). The formula describes some constraints on the probabilistic interactions between the outputs of X and Y, but says nothing about their domain. In a way, the domain is an unimportant detail. Nevertheless, one *must* ask whether or not an appropriate domain exists at all. More generally, one may ask whether an appropriate probability space exists given some constraints on the joint law of a collection $X_1, \ldots, X_k$ of random variables. For this to make sense, the constraints should not contradict each other, which means there is a probability measure μ on $\mathfrak{B}(\mathbb{R}^k)$ such that μ satisfies the postulated constraints. But then we can choose $\Omega = \mathbb{R}^k$, $\mathcal{F} = \mathfrak{B}(\mathbb{R}^k)$, $\mathbb{P} = \mu$ and $X_i : \Omega \to \mathbb{R}$ to be the ith coordinate map: $X_i(\omega) = \omega_i$. The push-forward of $\mathbb{P}$ under $X = (X_1, \ldots, X_k)$ is μ, which by definition is compatible with the constraints.

A more specific question is whether for a particular set of constraints on the joint law there exists a measure μ compatible with the constraints. Very often the constraints are specified for elements of the cartesian product of finitely many σ-algebras, like in Eq. (2.1). If $(\Omega_1, \mathcal{F}_1), \ldots, (\Omega_n, \mathcal{F}_n)$ are measurable spaces, then the cartesian product of $\mathcal{F}_1, \ldots \mathcal{F}_n$ is

$$\mathcal{F}_1 \times \cdots \times \mathcal{F}_n = \{A_1 \times \cdots \times A_n : A_1 \in \mathcal{F}_1, \ldots, A_n \in \mathcal{F}_n\} \subseteq 2^{\Omega_1 \times \cdots \times \Omega_n}.$$

Elements of this set are known as **measurable rectangles** in $\Omega_1 \times \cdots \times \Omega_n$.

THEOREM 2.4 (Carathéodory's extension theorem). *Let* $(\Omega_1, \mathcal{F}_1), \ldots, (\Omega_n, \mathcal{F}_n)$ *be measurable spaces and* $\bar{\mu} : \mathcal{F}_1 \times \cdots \times \mathcal{F}_n \to [0, 1]$ *be a function such that*

(a) $\bar{\mu}(\Omega_1 \times \cdots \times \Omega_n) = 1$; *and*
(b) $\bar{\mu}(\cup_{k=1}^{\infty} A_k) = \sum_{k=1}^{\infty} \bar{\mu}(A_k)$ *for all sequences of disjoint sets with* $A_k \in \mathcal{F}_1 \times \cdots \times \mathcal{F}_n$.

Let $\Omega = \Omega_1 \times \cdots \times \Omega_n$ *and* $\mathcal{F} = \sigma(\mathcal{F}_1 \times \cdots \times \mathcal{F}_n)$. *Then there exists a unique probability measure* μ *on* $(\Omega, \mathcal{F})$ *such that* μ *agrees with* $\bar{\mu}$ *on* $\mathcal{F}_1 \times \cdots \times \mathcal{F}_n$.

The theorem is applied by letting $\Omega_k = \mathbb{R}$ and $\mathcal{F}_k = \mathfrak{B}(\mathbb{R})$. Then the values of a measure on all cartesian products uniquely determines its value everywhere.

It is not true that $\mathcal{F}_1 \times \mathcal{F}_2 = \sigma(\mathcal{F}_1 \times \mathcal{F}_2)$. Take, for example, $\mathcal{F}_1 = \mathcal{F}_2 = 2^{\{1,2\}}$. Then, $|\mathcal{F}_1 \times \mathcal{F}_2| = 1 + 3 \times 3 = 10$ (because $\emptyset \times X = \emptyset$), while, since $\mathcal{F}_1 \times \mathcal{F}_2$ includes the singletons of $2^{\{1,2\} \times \{1,2\}}$, $\sigma(\mathcal{F}_1 \times \mathcal{F}_2) = 2^{\{1,2\} \times \{1,2\}}$. Hence, six sets are missing from $\mathcal{F}_1 \times \mathcal{F}_2$. For example, $\{(1,1), (2,2)\} \in \sigma(\mathcal{F}_1 \times \mathcal{F}_2) \setminus \mathcal{F}_1 \times \mathcal{F}_2$.

The σ-algebra $\sigma(\mathcal{F}_1 \times \cdots \times \mathcal{F}_n)$ is called the **product σ-algebra** of $(\mathcal{F}_k)_{k \in [n]}$ and is also denoted by $\mathcal{F}_1 \otimes \cdots \otimes \mathcal{F}_n$. The product operation turns out to be associative: $(\mathcal{F}_1 \otimes \mathcal{F}_2) \otimes$

$\mathcal{F}_3 = \mathcal{F}_1 \otimes (\mathcal{F}_2 \otimes \mathcal{F}_3)$, which justifies writing $\mathcal{F}_1 \otimes \mathcal{F}_2 \otimes \mathcal{F}_3$. As it turns out, things work out well again with Borel σ-algebras: for $p, q \in \mathbb{N}^+$, $\mathfrak{B}(\mathbb{R}^{p+q}) = \mathfrak{B}(\mathbb{R}^p) \otimes \mathfrak{B}(\mathbb{R}^q)$. Needless to say, the same holds when there are more than two terms in the product. The n-fold product σ-algebra of $\mathcal{F}$ is denoted by $\mathcal{F}^{\otimes n}$.

2.2 σ-Algebras and Knowledge

One of the conceptual advantages of measure-theoretic probability is the relationship between σ-algebras and the intuitive idea of 'knowledge'. Although the relationship is useful and intuitive, it is regrettably not quite perfect. Let $(\Omega, \mathcal{F})$, $(\mathcal{X}, \mathcal{G})$ and $(\mathcal{Y}, \mathcal{H})$ be measurable spaces and $X : \Omega \to \mathcal{X}$ and $Y : \Omega \to \mathcal{Y}$ be random elements. Having observed the value of X ('knowing X'), one might wonder what this entails about the value of Y. Even more simplistically, under what circumstances can the value of Y be determined exactly having observed X? The situation is illustrated in Fig. 2.3. As it turns out, with some restrictions, the answer can be given in terms of the σ-algebras generated by X and Y. Except for a technical assumption on $(\mathcal{Y}, \mathcal{H})$, the following result shows that Y is a measurable function of X if and only if Y is $\sigma(X)/\mathcal{H}$-measurable. The technical assumption mentioned requires $(\mathcal{Y}, \mathcal{H})$ to be a Borel space, which is true of all probability spaces considered in this book, including $(\mathbb{R}^k, \mathfrak{B}(\mathbb{R}^k))$. We leave the exact definition of Borel spaces to the next chapter.

LEMMA 2.5 (Factorisation lemma). *Assume that $(\mathcal{Y}, \mathcal{H})$ is a Borel space. Then Y is $\sigma(X)$-measurable ($\sigma(Y) \subseteq \sigma(X)$) if and only if there exists a $\mathcal{G}/\mathcal{H}$-measurable map $f : \mathcal{X} \to \mathcal{Y}$ such that $Y = f \circ X$.*

In this sense $\sigma(X)$ contains all the information that can be extracted from X via measurable functions. This is not the same as saying that Y can be deduced from X if and only if Y is $\sigma(X)$-measurable because the set of $\mathcal{X} \to \mathcal{Y}$ maps can be much larger than the set of $\mathcal{G}/\mathcal{H}$-measurable functions. When $\mathcal{G}$ is coarse, there are not many $\mathcal{G}/\mathcal{H}$-measurable functions with the extreme case occurring when $\mathcal{G} = \{\mathcal{X}, \emptyset\}$. In cases like this, the intuition that $\sigma(X)$ captures all there is to know about X is not true anymore (Exercise 2.6). The issue is that $\sigma(X)$ does not only depend on X, but also on the σ-algebra of $(\mathcal{X}, \mathcal{G})$ and that if $\mathcal{G}$ is coarse-grained, then $\sigma(X)$ can also be coarse-grained and not many functions will be $\sigma(X)$-measurable. If X is a random variable, then by definition $\mathcal{X} = \mathbb{R}$ and $\mathcal{G} = \mathfrak{B}(\mathbb{R})$, which is relatively fine-grained, and the requirement that f be measurable is less restrictive. Nevertheless, even in the nicest setting where $\Omega = \mathcal{X} = \mathcal{Y} = \mathbb{R}$ and

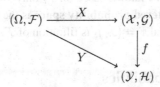

Figure 2.3 The factorisation problem asks whether there exists a (measurable) function f that makes the diagram commute.

$\mathcal{F} = \mathcal{G} = \mathcal{H} = \mathfrak{B}(\mathbb{R})$, it can still occur that $Y = f \circ X$ for some non-measurable f. In other words, all the information about Y exists in X but cannot be extracted in a measurable way. These problems only occur when X maps measurable sets in Ω to non-measurable sets in $\mathcal{X}$. Fortunately, while such random variables exist, they are never encountered in applications, which provides the final justification for thinking of $\sigma(X)$ as containing all that there is to know about any random variable X that one may ever expect to encounter.

Filtrations

In the study of bandits and other online settings, information is revealed to the learner sequentially. Let $X_1, \ldots, X_n$ be a collection of random variables on a common measurable space $(\Omega, \mathcal{F})$. We imagine a learner is sequentially observing the values of these random variables. First X_1, then X_2 and so on. The learner needs to make a prediction, or act, based on the available observations. Say, a prediction or an act must produce a real-valued response. Then, having observed $X_{1:t} \doteq (X_1, \ldots, X_t)$, the set of maps $f \circ X_{1:t}$ where $f : \mathbb{R}^t \to \mathbb{R}$ is Borel, captures all the possible ways the learner can respond. By Lemma 2.5, this set contains exactly the $\sigma(X_{1:t})/\mathfrak{B}(\mathbb{R})$-measurable maps. Thus, if we need to reason about the set of $\Omega \to \mathbb{R}$ maps available after observing $X_{1:t}$, it suffices to concentrate on the σ-algebra $\mathcal{F}_t = \sigma(X_{1:t})$. Conveniently, $\mathcal{F}_t$ is independent of the space of possible responses, and being a subset of $\mathcal{F}$, it also hides details about the range space of $X_{1:t}$. It is easy to check that $\mathcal{F}_0 \subseteq \mathcal{F}_1 \subseteq \mathcal{F}_2 \subseteq \cdots \subseteq \mathcal{F}_n \subseteq \mathcal{F}$, which means that more and more functions are becoming $\mathcal{F}_t$-measurable as t increases, which corresponds to increasing knowledge (note that $\mathcal{F}_0 = \{\emptyset, \Omega\}$, and the set of $\mathcal{F}_0$-measurable functions is the set of constant functions on Ω).

Bringing these a little further, we will often find it useful to talk about increasing sequences of σ-algebras without constructing them in terms of random variables as above. Given a measurable space $(\Omega, \mathcal{F})$, a **filtration** is a sequence $(\mathcal{F}_t)_{t=0}^n$ of sub-σ-algebras of $\mathcal{F}$ where $\mathcal{F}_t \subseteq \mathcal{F}_{t+1}$ for all $t < n$. We also allow $n = \infty$, and in this case we define

$$\mathcal{F}_\infty = \sigma\left(\bigcup_{t=0}^\infty \mathcal{F}_t\right)$$

to be the smallest σ-algebra containing the union of all $\mathcal{F}_t$. Filtrations can also be defined in continuous time, but we have no need for that here. A sequence of random variables $(X_t)_{t=1}^n$ is **adapted** to filtration $\mathbb{F} = (\mathcal{F}_t)_{t=0}^n$ if X_t is $\mathcal{F}_t$-measurable for each t. We also say in this case that $(X_t)_t$ is $\mathbb{F}$-adapted. The same nomenclature applies if n is infinite. Finally, $(X_t)_t$ is $\mathbb{F}$-**predictable** if X_t is $\mathcal{F}_{t-1}$-measurable for each $t \in [n]$. Intuitively we may think of an $\mathbb{F}$-predictable process $X = (X_t)_t$ as one that has the property that X_t can be known (or 'predicted') based on $\mathcal{F}_{t-1}$, while a $\mathbb{F}$-adapted process is one that has the property that X_t can be known based on $\mathcal{F}_t$ only. Since $\mathcal{F}_{t-1} \subseteq \mathcal{F}_t$, a predictable process is also adapted. A **filtered probability space** is the tuple $(\Omega, \mathcal{F}, \mathbb{F}, \mathbb{P})$, where $(\Omega, \mathcal{F}, \mathbb{P})$ is a probability space and $\mathbb{F} = (\mathcal{F}_t)_t$ is filtration of $\mathcal{F}$.

2.3   Conditional Probabilities

Conditional probabilities are introduced so that we can talk about how probabilities should be updated when one gains some partial knowledge about a random outcome. Let $(\Omega, \mathcal{F}, \mathbb{P})$

be a probability space, and let $A, B \in \mathcal{F}$ be such that $\mathbb{P}(B) > 0$. The **conditional probability** $\mathbb{P}(A \mid B)$ of A given B is defined as

$$\mathbb{P}(A \mid B) = \frac{\mathbb{P}(A \cap B)}{\mathbb{P}(B)}.$$

We can think about the outcome $\omega \in \Omega$ as the result of throwing a many-sided dice. The question asked is the probability that the dice landed so that $\omega \in A$ given that it landed with $\omega \in B$. The meaning of the condition $\omega \in B$ is that we focus on dice rolls when $\omega \in B$ is true. All dice rolls when $\omega \in B$ does not hold are discarded. Intuitively, what should matter in the conditional probability of A given B is how large the portion of A is that lies in B, and this is indeed what the definition means.

> The importance of conditional probabilities is that they define a calculus of how probabilities are to be updated in the presence of extra information.

The probability $\mathbb{P}(A \mid B)$ is also called the **a posteriori** ('after the fact') probability of A given B. The **a priori** probability is $\mathbb{P}(A)$. Note that $\mathbb{P}(A \mid B)$ is defined for every $A \in \mathcal{F}$ as long as $\mathbb{P}(B) > 0$. In fact, $A \mapsto \mathbb{P}(A \mid B)$ is a probability measure over the measure space $(\Omega, \mathcal{F})$ called the a posteriori probability measure given B (see Exercise 2.7). In a way the temporal characteristics attached to the words 'a posteriori' and 'a priori' can be a bit misleading. Probabilities are concerned with predictions. They express the degrees of uncertainty one assigns to future events. The conditional probability of A given B is a prediction of certain properties of the outcome of the random experiment that results in ω given a certain condition. Everything is related to a future hypothetical outcome. Once the dice is rolled, ω gets fixed, and either $\omega \in A, B$ or not. There is no uncertainty left: predictions are trivial after an experiment is done.

Bayes rule states that provided events $A, B \in \mathcal{F}$ both occur with positive probability,

$$\mathbb{P}(A \mid B) = \frac{\mathbb{P}(B \mid A)\, \mathbb{P}(A)}{\mathbb{P}(B)}. \tag{2.2}$$

Bayes rule is useful because it allows one to obtain $\mathbb{P}(A \mid B)$ based on information about the quantities on the right-hand side. Remarkably, this happens to be the case quite often, explaining why this simple formula has quite a status in probability and statistics. Exercise 2.8 asks the reader to verify this law.

2.4   Independence

Independence is another basic concept of probability that relates to knowledge/information. In its simplest form, independence is a relation that holds between events on a probability space $(\Omega, \mathcal{F}, \mathbb{P})$. Two events $A, B \in \mathcal{F}$ are **independent** if

$$\mathbb{P}(A \cap B) = \mathbb{P}(A)\, \mathbb{P}(B). \tag{2.3}$$

How is this related to knowledge? Assuming that $\mathbb{P}(B) > 0$, dividing both sides by $\mathbb{P}(B)$ and using the definition of conditional probability, we get that the above is equivalent to

$$\mathbb{P}(A \mid B) = \mathbb{P}(A). \tag{2.4}$$

Of course, we also have that if $\mathbb{P}(A) > 0$, (2.3) is equivalent to $\mathbb{P}(B \mid A) = \mathbb{P}(B)$. Both of the latter relations express that A and B are independent if the probability assigned to A (or B) remains the same regardless of whether it is known that B (respectively, A) occurred.

We hope our readers will find the definition of independence in terms of a 'lack of influence' to be sensible. The reason not to use Eq. (2.4) as the definition is mostly for the sake of convenience. If we started with (2.4), we would need to separately discuss the case of $\mathbb{P}(B) = 0$, which would be cumbersome. A second reason is that (2.4) suggests an asymmetric relationship, but intuitively we expect independence to be symmetric.

Uncertain outcomes are often generated part by part with no interaction between the processes, which naturally leads to an independence structure (think of rolling multiple dice with no interactions between the rolls). Once we discover some independence structure, calculations with probabilities can be immensely simplified. In fact, independence is often used as a way of constructing probability measures of interest (cf. Eq. (2.1), Theorem 2.4 and Exercise 2.9). Independence can also appear serendipitously in the sense that a probability space may hold many more independent events than its construction may suggest (Exercise 2.10).

You should always carefully judge whether assumptions about independence are really justified. This is part of the modelling and hence is not mathematical in nature. Instead you have to think about the physical process being modelled.

A collection of events $\mathcal{G} \subset \mathcal{F}$ is said to be **pairwise independent** if any two distinct elements of $\mathcal{G}$ are independent of each other. The events in $\mathcal{G}$ are said to be **mutually independent** if for any $n > 0$ integer and $A_1, \ldots, A_n$ distinct elements of $\mathcal{G}$, $\mathbb{P}(A_1 \cap \cdots \cap A_n) = \prod_{i=1}^{n} \mathbb{P}(A_i)$. This is a stronger restriction than pairwise independence. In the case of mutually independent events, the knowledge of joint occurrence of any finitely many events from the collection will not change our prediction of whether some other event in the collection happens. But this may not be the case when the events are only pairwise independent (Exercise 2.10). Two collections of events $\mathcal{G}_1, \mathcal{G}_2$ are said to be **independent of each other** if for any $A \in \mathcal{G}_1$ and $B \in \mathcal{G}_2$ it holds that A and B are independent. This definition is often applied to σ-algebras.

When the σ-algebras are induced by random variables, this leads to the definition of **independence between random variables**. Two random variables X and Y are independent if $\sigma(X)$ and $\sigma(Y)$ are independent of each other. The notions of pairwise and mutual independence can also be naturally extended to apply to collections of random variables. All these concepts can be and are in fact extended to random elements.

The default meaning of independence when multiple events or random variables are involved is mutual independence.

When we say that $X_1, \ldots, X_n$ are independent random variables, we mean that they are mutually independent. Independence is always relative to some probability measure, even when a probability measure is not explicitly mentioned. In such cases the identity of the probability measure should be clear from the context.

2.5 Integration and Expectation

A key quantity in probability theory is the **expectation** of a random variable. Fix a probability space $(\Omega, \mathcal{F}, \mathbb{P})$ and random variable $X : \Omega \to \mathbb{R}$. The expectation X is often denoted by $\mathbb{E}[X]$. This notation unfortunately obscures the dependence on the measure $\mathbb{P}$. When the underlying measure is not obvious from context, we write $\mathbb{E}_\mathbb{P}$ to indicate the expectation with respect to $\mathbb{P}$. Mathematically, we define the expected value of X as its Lebesgue integral with respect to $\mathbb{P}$:

$$\mathbb{E}[X] = \int_\Omega X(\omega) \, d\mathbb{P}(\omega).$$

The right-hand side is also often abbreviated to $\int X \, d\mathbb{P}$. The integral on the right-hand side is constructed to satisfy the following two key properties:

(a) The integral of indicators is the probability of the underlying event. If $X(\omega) = \mathbb{I}\{\omega \in A\}$ is an indicator function for some $A \in \mathcal{F}$, then $\int X d\mathbb{P} = \mathbb{P}(A)$.

(b) Integrals are linear. For all random variables X_1, X_2 and reals α_1, α_2 such that $\int X_1 d\mathbb{P}$ and $\int X_2 d\mathbb{P}$ are defined, $\int (\alpha_1 X_1 + \alpha_2 X_2) d\mathbb{P}$ is defined and satisfies

$$\int_\Omega (\alpha_1 X_1 + \alpha_2 X_2) \, d\mathbb{P} = \alpha_1 \int_\Omega X_1 \, d\mathbb{P} + \alpha_2 \int_\Omega X_2 \, d\mathbb{P}. \tag{2.5}$$

These two properties together tell us that whenever $X(\omega) = \sum_{i=1}^n \alpha_i \mathbb{I}\{\omega \in A_i\}$ for some n, $\alpha_i \in \mathbb{R}$ and $A_i \in \mathcal{F}$, $i = 1, \ldots, n$, then

$$\int_\Omega X d\mathbb{P} = \sum_i \alpha_i \mathbb{P}(A_i). \tag{2.6}$$

Functions of the form X are called **simple functions**.

In defining the Lebesgue integral of some random variable X, we use (2.6) as the definition of the integral when X is a simple function. The next step is to extend the definition to non-negative random variables. Let $X : \Omega \to [0, \infty)$ be measurable. The idea is to approximate X from below using simple functions and take the largest value that can be obtained this way:

$$\int_\Omega X d\mathbb{P} = \sup \left\{ \int_\Omega h \, d\mathbb{P} : h \text{ is simple and } 0 \leq h \leq X \right\}. \tag{2.7}$$

The meaning of $U \leq V$ for random variables U, V is that $U(\omega) \leq V(\omega)$ for all $\omega \in \Omega$. The supremum on the right-hand side could be infinite, in which case we say the integral of X is not defined. Whenever the integral of X is defined, we say that X is **integrable** or, if the identity of the measure $\mathbb{P}$ is unclear, that X is integrable with respect to $\mathbb{P}$.

Integrals for arbitrary random variables are defined by decomposing the random variable into positive and negative parts. Let $X : \Omega \to \mathbb{R}$ be any measurable function. Then define $X^+(\omega) = X(\omega)\mathbb{I}\{X(\omega) > 0\}$ and $X^-(\omega) = -X(\omega)\mathbb{I}\{X(\omega) < 0\}$ so that $X(\omega) = X^+(\omega) - X^-(\omega)$. Now X^+ and X^- are both non-negative random variables called the **positive** and **negative** parts of X. Provided that both X^+ and X^- are integrable, we define

$$\int_\Omega X\,d\mathbb{P} = \int_\Omega X^+\,d\mathbb{P} - \int_\Omega X^-\,d\mathbb{P}.$$

Note that X is integrable if and only if the non-negative-valued random variable $|X|$ is integrable (Exercise 2.12).

> None of what we have done depends on $\mathbb{P}$ being a probability measure. The definitions hold for any measure, though for signed measures it is necessary to split Ω into disjoint measurable sets on which the measure is positive/negative, an operation that is possible by the **Hahn decomposition theorem**. We will never need signed measures in this book, however.

A particularly interesting case is when $\Omega = \mathbb{R}$ is the real line, $\mathcal{F} = \mathfrak{B}(\mathbb{R})$ is the Borel σ-algebra and the measure is the **Lebesgue measure** λ, which is the unique measure on $\mathfrak{B}(\mathbb{R})$ such that $\lambda((a, b)) = b - a$ for any $a \leq b$. In this scenario, if $f : \mathbb{R} \to \mathbb{R}$ is a Borel-measurable function, then we can write the Lebesgue integral of f with respect to the Lebesgue measure as

$$\int_\mathbb{R} f\,d\lambda.$$

Perhaps unsurprisingly, this almost always coincides with the improper Riemann integral of f, which is normally written as $\int_{-\infty}^\infty f(x)\,dx$. Precisely, if $|f|$ is both Lebesgue integrable and Riemann integrable, then the integrals are equal.

> There exist functions that are Riemann integrable and not Lebesgue integrable, and also the other way around (although examples of the former are more exotic than the latter).

The Lebesgue measure and its relation to Riemann integration is mentioned because when it comes to actually calculating the value of an expectation or integral, this is often reduced to calculating integrals over the real line with respect to the Lebesgue measure. The calculation is then performed by evaluating the Riemann integral, thereby circumventing the need to rederive the integral of many elementary functions. Integrals (and thus expectations) have a number of important properties. By far the most important is their linearity, which was postulated above as the second property in (2.5). To practice using the notation with expectations, we restate the first half of this property. In fact, the statement is slightly more general than what we demanded for integrals above.

PROPOSITION 2.6. *Let* $(X_i)_i$ *be a (possibly infinite) sequence of random variables on the same probability space and assume that* $\mathbb{E}[X_i]$ *exists for all* i *and furthermore that* $X = \sum_i X_i$ *and* $\mathbb{E}[X]$ *also exist. Then*

$$\mathbb{E}[X] = \sum_i \mathbb{E}[X_i].$$

This exchange of expectations and summation is the source of much magic in probability theory because it holds even if X_i are not independent. This means that (unlike probabilities) we can very often decouple the expectations of dependent random variables, which often proves extremely useful (a collection of random variables is dependent if they are not independent). You will prove Proposition 2.6 in Exercise 2.14. The other requirement for linearity is that if $c \in \mathbb{R}$ is a constant, then $\mathbb{E}[cX] = c\mathbb{E}[X]$ (Exercise 2.15).

Another important statement is concerned with independent random variables.

PROPOSITION 2.7. *If* X *and* Y *are independent, then* $\mathbb{E}[XY] = \mathbb{E}[X]\mathbb{E}[Y]$.

In general $\mathbb{E}[XY] \neq \mathbb{E}[X]\mathbb{E}[Y]$ (Exercise 2.18). Finally, an important simple result connects expectations of non-negative random variables to their tail probabilities.

PROPOSITION 2.8. *If* $X \geq 0$ *is a non-negative random variable, then*

$$\mathbb{E}[X] = \int_0^\infty \mathbb{P}(X > x)\,dx.$$

The integrand in Proposition 2.8 is called the **tail probability function** $x \mapsto \mathbb{P}(X > x)$ of X. This is also known as the complementary cumulative distribution function of X. The **cumulative distribution function** (CDF) of X is defined as $x \mapsto \mathbb{P}(X \leq x)$ and is usually denoted by F_X. These functions are defined for all random variables, not just non-negative ones. One can check that $F_X : \mathbb{R} \to [0,1]$ is increasing, right continuous and $\lim_{x \to -\infty} F_X(x) = 0$ and $\lim_{x \to \infty} F_X(x) = 1$. The CDF of a random variable captures every aspect of the probability measure $\mathbb{P}_X$ induced by X, while still being just a function on the real line, a property that makes it a little more human friendly than $\mathbb{P}_X$. One can also generalise CDFs to random vectors: if X is an $\mathbb{R}^k$-valued random vector, then its CDF is defined as the $F_X : \mathbb{R}^k \to [0,1]$ function that satisfies $F_X(x) = \mathbb{P}(X \leq x)$, where, in line with our conventions, $X \leq x$ means that all components of X are less than or equal to the respective component of x. The pushforward $\mathbb{P}_X$ of a random element is an alternative way to summarise the distribution of X. In particular, for any real-valued, $f : \mathcal{X} \to \mathbb{R}$ measurable function,

$$\mathbb{E}[f(X)] = \int_{\mathcal{X}} f(x)d\mathbb{P}_X(x)$$

provided that either the right-hand side, or the left-hand side exist.

2.6 Conditional Expectation

Conditional expectation allows us to talk about the expectation of a random variable given the value of another random variable, or more generally, given some σ-algebra.

EXAMPLE 2.9. Let $(\Omega, \mathcal{F}, \mathbb{P})$ model the outcomes of an unloaded dice: $\Omega = [6]$, $\mathcal{F} = 2^{\Omega}$ and $\mathbb{P}(A) = |A|/6$. Define two random variables X and Y by $Y(\omega) = \mathbb{I}\{\omega > 3\}$ and $X(\omega) = \omega$. Suppose we are interested in the expectation of X given a specific value of Y. Arguing intuitively, we might notice that $Y = 1$ means that the unobserved X must be either 4, 5 or 6, and that each of these outcomes is equally likely, and so the expectation of X given $Y = 1$ should be $(4 + 5 + 6)/3 = 5$. Similarly, the expectation of X given $Y = 0$ should be $(1 + 2 + 3)/3 = 2$. If we want a concise summary, we can just write that 'the expectation of X given Y' is $5Y + 2(1 - Y)$. Notice how this is a random variable itself.

The notation for this conditional expectation is $\mathbb{E}[X \mid Y]$. Using this notation, in Example 2.9 we can concisely write $\mathbb{E}[X \mid Y] = 5Y + 2(1 - Y)$. A little more generally, if $X : \Omega \to \mathcal{X}$ and $Y : \Omega \to \mathcal{Y}$ with $\mathcal{X}, \mathcal{Y} \subset \mathbb{R}$ and $|\mathcal{X}|, |\mathcal{Y}| < \infty$, then $\mathbb{E}[X \mid Y] : \Omega \to \mathbb{R}$ is the random variable given by $\mathbb{E}[X \mid Y](\omega) = \mathbb{E}[X \mid Y = Y(\omega)]$, where

$$\mathbb{E}[X \mid Y = y] = \sum_{x \in \mathcal{X}} x\, \mathbb{P}(X = x \mid Y = y) = \sum_{x \in \mathcal{X}} \frac{x\, \mathbb{P}(X = x, Y = y)}{\mathbb{P}(Y = y)}. \qquad (2.8)$$

This is undefined when $\mathbb{P}(Y = y) = 0$ so that $\mathbb{E}[X \mid Y](\omega)$ is undefined on the measure zero set $\{\omega : \mathbb{P}(Y = Y(\omega)) = 0\}$.

Eq. (2.8) does not generalise to continuous random variables because $\mathbb{P}(Y = y)$ in the denominator might be zero for all y. For example, let Y be a random variable taking values on $[0, 1]$ according to a uniform distribution and $X \in \{0, 1\}$ be Bernoulli with bias Y. This means that the joint measure on X and Y is $\mathbb{P}(X = 1, Y \in [p, q]) = \int_p^q x\, dx$ for $0 \le p < q \le 1$. Intuitively it seems like $\mathbb{E}[X \mid Y]$ should be equal to Y, but how to define it? The mean of a Bernoulli random variable is equal to its bias so the definition of conditional probability shows that for $0 \le p < q \le 1$,

$$\begin{aligned}
\mathbb{E}[X = 1 \mid Y \in [p, q]] &= \mathbb{P}(X = 1 \mid Y \in [p, q]) \\
&= \frac{\mathbb{P}(X = 1, Y \in [p, q])}{\mathbb{P}(Y \in [p, q])} \\
&= \frac{q^2 - p^2}{2(q - p)} \\
&= \frac{p + q}{2}.
\end{aligned}$$

This calculation is not well defined when $p = q$ because $\mathbb{P}(Y \in [p, p]) = 0$. Nevertheless, letting $q = p + \varepsilon$ for $\varepsilon > 0$ and taking the limit as ε tends to zero seems like a reasonable way to argue that $\mathbb{P}(X = 1 \mid Y = p) = p$. Unfortunately this approach does not generalise to abstract spaces because there is no canonical way of taking limits towards a set of measure zero, and different choices lead to different answers.

Instead we use Eq. (2.8) as the starting point for an abstract definition of conditional expectation as a random variable satisfying two requirements. First, from Eq. (2.8) we see that $\mathbb{E}[X \mid Y](\omega)$ should only depend on $Y(\omega)$ and so should be measurable with respect to $\sigma(Y)$. The second requirement is called the 'averaging property'. For measurable $A \subseteq \mathcal{Y}$, Eq. (2.8) shows that

$$\mathbb{E}[\mathbb{I}_{Y^{-1}(A)}\mathbb{E}[X\,|\,Y]] = \sum_{y\in A}\mathbb{P}(Y=y)\,\mathbb{E}[X\,|\,Y=y]$$
$$= \sum_{y\in A}\sum_{x\in\mathcal{X}} x\,\mathbb{P}(X=x,Y=y)$$
$$= \mathbb{E}[\mathbb{I}_{Y^{-1}(A)}X].$$

This can be viewed as putting a set of linear constraints on $\mathbb{E}[X\,|\,Y]$ with one constraint for each measurable $A\subseteq\mathcal{Y}$. By treating $\mathbb{E}[X\,|\,Y]$ as an unknown $\sigma(Y)$-measurable random variable, we can attempt to solve this linear system. As it turns out, this can always be done: the linear constraints and the measurability restriction on $\mathbb{E}[X\,|\,Y]$ completely determine $\mathbb{E}[X\,|\,Y]$ except for a set of measure zero. Notice that both conditions only depend on $\sigma(Y)\subseteq\mathcal{F}$. The abstract definition of conditional expectation takes these properties as the definition and replaces the role of Y with a sub-σ-algebra.

DEFINITION 2.10 (Conditional expectation). Let $(\Omega,\mathcal{F},\mathbb{P})$ be a probability space and $X:\Omega\to\mathbb{R}$ be random variable and $\mathcal{H}$ be a sub-σ-algebra of $\mathcal{F}$. The conditional expectation of X given $\mathcal{H}$ is denoted by $\mathbb{E}[X\,|\,\mathcal{H}]$ and defined to be any $\mathcal{H}$-measurable random variable on Ω such that for all $H\in\mathcal{H}$,

$$\int_H \mathbb{E}[X\,|\,\mathcal{H}]\mathrm{d}\mathbb{P} = \int_H X\mathrm{d}\mathbb{P}. \tag{2.9}$$

Given a random variable Y, the conditional expectation of X given Y is $\mathbb{E}[X\,|\,Y] = \mathbb{E}[X\,|\,\sigma(Y)]$.

THEOREM 2.11. *Given any probability space* $(\Omega,\mathcal{F},\mathbb{P})$, *a sub-$\sigma$-algebra* $\mathcal{H}$ *of* $\mathcal{F}$ *and a* $\mathbb{P}$-*integrable random variable* $X:\Omega\to\mathbb{R}$, *there exists an* $\mathcal{H}$-*measurable function* $f:\Omega\to\mathbb{R}$ *that satisfies* (2.9). *Further, any two* $\mathcal{H}$-*measurable functions* $f_1,f_2:\Omega\to\mathbb{R}$ *that satisfy* (2.9) *are equal with probability one:* $\mathbb{P}(f_1=f_2)=1$.

When random variables X and Y agree with $\mathbb{P}$-probability one, we say they are $\mathbb{P}$-**almost surely** equal, which is often abbreviated to '$X=Y$ $\mathbb{P}$-a.s.', or '$X=Y$ a.s.' when the measure is clear from context. A related useful notion is the concept of **null sets**: $U\in\mathcal{F}$ is a null set of $\mathbb{P}$, or a $\mathbb{P}$-null set if $\mathbb{P}(U)=0$. Thus, $X=Y$ $\mathbb{P}$-a.s. if and only if $X=Y$ agree except on a $\mathbb{P}$-null set.

The reader may find it odd that $\mathbb{E}[X\,|\,Y]$ is a random variable on Ω rather than the range of Y. Lemma 2.5 and the fact that $\mathbb{E}[X\,|\,\sigma(Y)]$ is $\sigma(Y)$-measurable shows there exists a measurable function $f:(\mathbb{R},\mathfrak{B}(\mathbb{R}))\to(\mathbb{R},\mathfrak{B}(\mathbb{R}))$ such that $\mathbb{E}[X\,|\,\sigma(Y)](\omega) = (f\circ Y)(\omega)$ (see Fig. 2.4). In this sense $\mathbb{E}[X\,|\,Y](\omega)$ only depends on $Y(\omega)$, and occasionally we write $\mathbb{E}[X\,|\,Y](y)$.

Returning to Example 2.9, we see that $\mathbb{E}[X\,|\,Y] = \mathbb{E}[X\,|\,\sigma(Y)]$ and $\sigma(Y) = \{\{1,2,3\},\{4,5,6\},\emptyset,\Omega\}$. Denote this set-system by $\mathcal{H}$ for brevity. The condition that

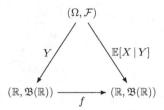

Figure 2.4 Factorisation of conditional expectation. When there is no confusion, we occasionally write $\mathbb{E}[X \mid Y](y)$ in place of $f(y)$.

$\mathbb{E}[X \mid \mathcal{H}]$ is $\mathcal{H}$-measurable can only be satisfied if $\mathbb{E}[X \mid \mathcal{H}](\omega)$ is constant on $\{1, 2, 3\}$ and $\{4, 5, 6\}$. Then (2.9) immediately implies that

$$\mathbb{E}[X \mid \mathcal{H}](\omega) = \begin{cases} 2, & \text{if } \omega \in \{1, 2, 3\}; \\ 5, & \text{if } \omega \in \{4, 5, 6\}. \end{cases}$$

While the definition of conditional expectations given above is non-constructive and $\mathbb{E}[X \mid \mathcal{H}]$ is uniquely defined only up to events of $\mathbb{P}$-measure zero, none of this should be of a significant concern. First, we will rarely need closed-form expressions for conditional expectations, but we rather need how they relate to other expectations, conditional or not. This is also the reason why it should not be concerning that they are only determined up to zero probability events: usually, conditional expectations appear in other expectations or in statements that are concerned with how probable some event is, making the difference between the different 'versions' of conditional expectations disappear.

We close the section by summarising some additional important properties of conditional expectations. These follow from the definition directly, and the reader is invited to prove them in Exercise 2.20.

THEOREM 2.12. *Let $(\Omega, \mathcal{F}, \mathbb{P})$ be a probability space, $\mathcal{G}, \mathcal{G}_1, \mathcal{G}_2 \subset \mathcal{F}$ be sub-σ-algebras of $\mathcal{F}$ and X, Y integrable random variables on $(\Omega, \mathcal{F}, \mathbb{P})$. The following hold true:*

1 *If $X \geq 0$, then $\mathbb{E}[X \mid \mathcal{G}] \geq 0$ almost surely.*
2 $\mathbb{E}[1 \mid \mathcal{G}] = 1$ *almost surely.*
3 $\mathbb{E}[X + Y \mid \mathcal{G}] = \mathbb{E}[X \mid \mathcal{G}] + \mathbb{E}[Y \mid \mathcal{G}]$ *almost surely.*
4 $\mathbb{E}[XY \mid \mathcal{G}] = Y\mathbb{E}[X \mid \mathcal{G}]$ *almost surely if $\mathbb{E}[XY]$ exists and Y is $\mathcal{G}$-measurable.*
5 *If $\mathcal{G}_1 \subset \mathcal{G}_2$, then $\mathbb{E}[X \mid \mathcal{G}_1] = \mathbb{E}[\mathbb{E}[X \mid \mathcal{G}_2] \mid \mathcal{G}_1]$ almost surely.*
6 *If $\sigma(X)$ is independent of $\mathcal{G}_2$ given $\mathcal{G}_1$, then $\mathbb{E}[X \mid \sigma(\mathcal{G}_1 \cup \mathcal{G}_2)] = \mathbb{E}[X \mid \mathcal{G}_1]$ almost surely.*
7 *If $\mathcal{G} = \{\emptyset, \Omega\}$ is the trivial σ-algebra, then $\mathbb{E}[X \mid \mathcal{G}] = \mathbb{E}[X]$ almost surely.*

Properties 1 and 2 are self-explanatory. Property 3 generalises the linearity of expectation. Property 4 shows that a measurable quantity can be pulled outside of a conditional expectation and corresponds to the property that for constants c, $\mathbb{E}[cX] = c\mathbb{E}[X]$. Property 5 is called the **tower rule** or the **law of total expectations**. It says that the fineness of $\mathbb{E}[X \mid \mathcal{G}_2]$ is obliterated when taking the conditional expectation with respect to $\mathcal{G}_1$. Property 6 relates independence and conditional expectations, and it says that conditioning on independent quantities does not give further information on expectations. Here, the two event systems

$\mathcal{A}$ and $\mathcal{B}$ are said to be **conditionally independent** of each other given a σ-algebra $\mathcal{F}$ if for all $A \in \mathcal{A}$ and $B \in \mathcal{B}$, $\mathbb{P}(A \cap B \mid \mathcal{F}) = \mathbb{P}(A \mid \mathcal{F})\mathbb{P}(B \mid \mathcal{F})$ holds almost surely. We also often say that $\mathcal{A}$ is conditionally independent of $\mathcal{B}$ given $\mathcal{F}$, but of course, this relation is symmetric. This property is often applied with random variables: X is said to be conditionally independent of Y given Z, if $\sigma(X)$ is conditionally independent of $\sigma(Y)$ given $\sigma(Z)$. In this case, $\mathbb{E}[X \mid Y, Z] = \mathbb{E}[X \mid Z]$ holds almost surely. Property 7 states that conditioning on no information gives the same expectation as not conditioning at all.

> The above list of abstract properties will be used over and over again. We encourage the reader to study the list carefully and convince yourself that all items are intuitive. Playing around with discrete random variables can be invaluable for this. Eventually it will all become second nature.

2.7 Notes

1 The Greek letter σ is often used by mathematicians in association with countable infinities. Hence the term σ-algebra (and σ-field). Note that countable additivity is often called σ-additivity. The requirement that additivity should hold for systems of countably infinitely many sets is made so that probabilities of (interesting) limiting events are guaranteed to exist.

2 **Measure theory** is concerned with measurable spaces, measures and with their properties. An obvious distinction between probability theory and measure theory is that in probability theory, one is (mostly) concerned with probability measures. But the distinction does not stop here. In probability theory, the emphasis is on the probability measures and their relations to each other. The measurable spaces are there in the background, but are viewed as part of the technical toolkit rather than the topic of main interest. Also, in probability theory, independence is often at the center of attention, while independence is not a property measure-theorists care much about.

3 In our toy example, instead of $\Omega = [6]^7$, we could have chosen $\Omega = [6]^8$ (considering rolling eight dice instead of seven, one dice never used). There are many other possibilities. We can consider coin flips instead of dice rolls (think about how this could be done). To make this easy, we could use weighted coins (for example, a coin that lands on heads with probability 1/6), but we don't actually need weighted coins (this may be a little tricky to see). The main point is that there are many ways to emulate one randomisation device by using another. The difference between these is the set Ω. What makes a choice of Ω viable is if we can emulate the game mechanism on the top of Ω so that in the end the probability of seeing any particular value remains the same. But the main point is that the choice of Ω is far from unique. The same is true for the way we calculate the value of the game! For example, the dice could be reordered, if we stay with the first construction. This was noted already, but it cannot be repeated frequently enough: the biggest conspiracy in all probability theory is that we first make a big fuss about introducing Ω, and then it turns out that the actual construction of Ω does not matter.

4 All Riemann-integrable functions on a bounded domain are Lebesgue integrable. Difficulties only arise when taking improper integrals. A standard example is $\int_0^\infty \frac{\sin(x)\,dx}{x}$, which is an improper Riemann integrable function, but is not Lebesgue integrable because $\int_{(0,\infty)} |\sin(x)/x|\,dx = \infty$. The situation is analogous to the difference between conditionally and absolutely convergent series, with the Lebesgue integral only defined in the latter case.

5 Can you think of a set that is not Borel measurable? Such sets exist, but do not arise naturally in applications. The classic example is the **Vitali set**, which is formed by taking the quotient group $G = \mathbb{R}/\mathbb{Q}$ and then applying the axiom of choice to choose a representative in $[0, 1]$ from each equivalence class in G. Non-measurable functions are so unusual that you do not have to worry much about whether or not functions $X : \mathbb{R} \to \mathbb{R}$ are measurable. With only a few exceptions, questions of measurability arising in this book are not related to the fine details of the Borel σ-algebra. Much more frequently they are related to filtrations and the notion of knowledge available having observed certain random elements.

6 There is a lot to say about why the sum, or the product of random variables are also random variables. Or why $\inf_n X_n$, $\sup_n X_n$, $\liminf_n X_n$, $\limsup_n X_n$ are measurable when X_n are. The key point is to show that the composition of measurable maps is a measurable map and that continuous maps are measurable and then apply these results (Exercise 2.1). For $\limsup_n X_n$, just rewrite it as $\lim_{m \to \infty} \sup_{n \geq m} X_n$; note that $\sup_{n \geq m} X_n$ is decreasing (we take suprema of smaller sets as m increases), hence $\limsup_n X_n = \inf_m \sup_{n \geq m} X_n$, reducing the question to studying $\inf_n X_n$ and $\sup_n X_n$. Finally, for $\inf_n X_n$ note that it suffices if $\{\omega : \inf_n X_n \geq t\}$ is measurable for any t real. Now, $\inf_n X_n \geq t$ if and only if $X_n \geq t$ for all n. Hence, $\{\omega : \inf_n X_n \geq t\} = \cap_n \{\omega : X_n \geq t\}$, which is a countable intersection of measurable sets, hence measurable (this latter follows by the elementary identity $(\cap_i A_i)^c = \cup_i A_i^c$).

7 The factorisation lemma, Lemma 2.5, is attributed to Joseph Doob and Eugene Dynkin. The lemma sneakily uses the properties of real numbers (think about why), which is another reason why what we said about σ-algebras containing all information is not entirely true. The lemma has extensions to more general random elements [Taraldsen, 2018, for example]. The key requirement in a way is that the σ-algebra associated with the range space of Y should be rich enough.

8 We did not talk about basic results like Lebesgue's dominated/monotone convergence theorems, Fatou's lemma or Jensen's inequality. We will definitely use the last of these, which is explained in a dedicated chapter on convexity (Chapter 26). The other results can be found in the texts we cite. They are concerned with infinite sequences of random variables and conditions under which their limits can be interchanged with Lebesgue integrals. In this book we rarely encounter problems related to such sequences and hope you forgive us on the few occasions they are necessary (the reason is simply because we mostly focus on finite time results or take expectations before taking limits when dealing with asymptotics).

9 You might be surprised that we have not mentioned **densities**. For most of us, our first exposure to probability on continuous spaces was by studying the normal distribution and its density

$$p(x) = \frac{1}{\sqrt{2\pi}} \exp(-x^2/2), \tag{2.10}$$

which can be integrated over intervals to obtain the probability that a Gaussian random variable will take a value in that interval. The reader should notice that $p : \mathbb{R} \to \mathbb{R}$ is Borel measurable and that the Gaussian measure associated with this density is $\mathbb{P}$ on $(\mathbb{R}, \mathfrak{B}(\mathbb{R}))$ defined by

$$\mathbb{P}(A) = \int_A p \, d\lambda.$$

Here the integral is with respect to the Lebesgue measure λ on $(\mathbb{R}, \mathfrak{B}(\mathbb{R}))$. The notion of a density can be generalised beyond this simple setup. Let P and Q be measures (not necessarily probability measures) on arbitrary measurable space $(\Omega, \mathcal{F})$. The **Radon–Nikodym derivative** of P with respect to Q is an $\mathcal{F}$-measurable random variable $\frac{dP}{dQ} : \Omega \to [0, \infty)$ such that

$$P(A) = \int_A \frac{dP}{dQ} \, dQ \qquad \text{for all } A \in \mathcal{F}. \tag{2.11}$$

We can also write this in the form $\int \mathbb{I}_A dP = \int \mathbb{I}_A \frac{dP}{dQ} dQ$, $A \in \mathcal{F}$, from which we may realise that for any X P-integrable random variable, $\int X dP = \int X \frac{dP}{dQ} dQ$ must also hold. This is often called the **change-of-measure formula**. Another word for the Radon–Nikodym derivative $\frac{dP}{dQ}$ is the **density** of P with respect to Q. It is not hard to find examples where the density does not exist. We say that P is **absolutely continuous** with respect to Q if $Q(A) = 0 \implies P(A) = 0$ for all $A \in \mathcal{F}$. When $\frac{dP}{dQ}$ exists, it follows immediately that P is absolutely continuous with respect to Q by Eq. (2.11). Except for some pathological cases, it turns out that this is both necessary and sufficient for the existence of dP/dQ. The measure Q is σ-finite if there exists a countable covering $\{A_i\}$ of Ω with $\mathcal{F}$-measurable sets such that $Q(A_i) < \infty$ for each i.

THEOREM 2.13. *Let P, Q be measures on a common measurable space $(\Omega, \mathcal{F})$ and assume that Q is σ-finite. Then the density of P with respect to Q, $\frac{dP}{dQ}$, exists if and only if P is absolutely continuous with respect to Q. Furthermore, $\frac{dP}{dQ}$ is uniquely defined up to a Q-null set so that for any f_1, f_2 satisfying (2.11), $f_1 = f_2$ holds Q-almost surely.*

Densities work as expected. Suppose that Z is a standard Gaussian random variable. We usually write its density as in Eq. (2.10), which we now know is the Radon–Nikodym derivative of the Gaussian measure with respect to the Lebesgue measure. The densities of 'classical' continuous distributions are almost always defined with respect to the Lebesgue measure.

10 In line with the literature, we will use $P \ll Q$ to denote that P is absolutely continuous with respect to Q. When P is absolutely continuous with respect to Q, we also say that Q **dominates** P.

11 A useful result for Radon–Nikodym derivatives is the **chain rule**, which states that if $P \ll Q \ll S$, then $\frac{dP}{dQ} \frac{dQ}{dS} = \frac{dP}{dS}$. The proof of this result follows from our earlier observation that $\int f dQ = \int f \frac{dQ}{dS} dS$ for any Q-integrable f. Indeed, the chain rule is obtained from this by taking $f = \mathbb{I}_A \frac{dP}{dQ}$ with $A \in \mathcal{F}$ and noting that this is indeed Q-integrable and $\int \mathbb{I}_A \frac{dP}{dQ} dQ = \int \mathbb{I}_A dQ$. The chain rule is often used to reduce the calculation of densities to calculation with known densities.

12 The Radon–Nikodym derivative unifies the notions of distribution (for discrete spaces) and density (for continuous spaces). Let Ω be discrete (finite or countable) and let ρ be the **counting measure** on $(\Omega, 2^\Omega)$, which is defined by $\rho(A) = |A|$. For any P on $(\Omega, \mathcal{F})$, it is easy to see that $P \ll \rho$ and $\frac{dP}{d\rho}(i) = P(\{i\})$, which is sometimes called the distribution function of P.

13 The Radon–Nikodym derivative provides another way to define the conditional expectation. Let X be an integrable random variable on $(\Omega, \mathcal{F}, \mathbb{P})$ and $\mathcal{H} \subset \mathcal{F}$ be a sub-σ-algebra and $\mathbb{P}|_\mathcal{H}$ be the restriction of $\mathbb{P}$ to $(\Omega, \mathcal{H})$. Define measure μ on $(\Omega, \mathcal{H})$ by $\mu(A) = \int_A X d\mathbb{P}|_\mathcal{H}$. It is easy to check that $\mu \ll \mathbb{P}|_\mathcal{H}$ and that $\mathbb{E}[X \mid \mathcal{H}] = \frac{d\mu}{d\mathbb{P}|_\mathcal{H}}$ satisfies Eq. (2.9). We note that the proof of the Radon–Nikodym theorem is nontrivial and that the existence of conditional expectations are more easily guaranteed via an 'elementary' but abstract argument using functional analysis.

14 The **Fubini–Tonelli theorem** is a powerful result that allows one to exchange the order of integrations. This result is needed for example for proving Proposition 2.8 (Exercise 2.19). To state it, we need to introduce **product measures**. These work as expected: given two probability spaces, $(\Omega_1, \mathcal{F}_1, \mathbb{P}_1)$ and $(\Omega_2, \mathcal{F}_2, \mathbb{P}_2)$, the product measure $\mathbb{P}$ of $\mathbb{P}_1$ and $\mathbb{P}_2$ is defined as any measure on $(\Omega_1 \times \Omega_2, \mathcal{F}_1 \otimes \mathcal{F}_2)$ that satisfies $\mathbb{P}(A_1, A_2) = \mathbb{P}_1(A_1)\mathbb{P}_2(A_2)$ for all $(A_1, A_2) \in \mathcal{F}_1 \times \mathcal{F}_2$ (recall that $\mathcal{F}_1 \otimes \mathcal{F}_2 = \sigma(\mathcal{F}_1 \times \mathcal{F}_2)$ is the product σ-algebra of $\mathcal{F}_1$ and $\mathcal{F}_2$). Theorem 2.4 implies that this product measure, which is often denoted by $\mathbb{P}_1 \times \mathbb{P}_2$ (or $\mathbb{P}_1 \otimes \mathbb{P}_2$) is uniquely defined. (Think about what this product measure has to do with independence.) The Fubini–Tonelli theorem (often just 'Fubini') states the following: let $(\Omega_1, \mathcal{F}_1, \mathbb{P}_1)$ and $(\Omega_2, \mathcal{F}_2, \mathbb{P}_2)$

be two probability spaces and consider a random variable X on the product probability space $(\Omega, \mathcal{F}, \mathbb{P}) = (\Omega_1 \times \Omega_2, \mathcal{F}_1 \otimes \mathcal{F}_2, \mathbb{P}_1 \times \mathbb{P}_2)$. If any of the three integrals $\int |X(\omega)| \, d\mathbb{P}(\omega)$, $\int (\int |X(\omega_1, \omega_2)| \, d\mathbb{P}_1(\omega_1)) \, d\mathbb{P}_2(\omega_2)$, $\int (\int |X(\omega_1, \omega_2)| \, d\mathbb{P}_2(\omega_2)) \, d\mathbb{P}_1(\omega_1)$ is finite, then

$$\int X(\omega) \, d\mathbb{P}(\omega) = \int \left(\int X(\omega_1, \omega_2) \, d\mathbb{P}_1(\omega_1) \right) d\mathbb{P}_2(\omega_2)$$

$$= \int \left(\int X(\omega_1, \omega_2) \, d\mathbb{P}_2(\omega_2) \right) d\mathbb{P}_1(\omega_1).$$

15 For topological space X, the **support** of a measure μ on $(X, \mathfrak{B}(X))$ is

$$\text{Supp}(\mu) = \{x \in X : \mu(U) > 0 \text{ for all neighborhoods } U \text{ of } x\}.$$

When X is discrete, this reduces to $\text{Supp}(\mu) = \{x : \mu(\{x\}) > 0\}$.

16 Let X be a topological space. The weak* topology on the space of probability measures $\mathcal{P}(X)$ on $(X, \mathfrak{B}(X))$ is the coarsest topology such that $\mu \mapsto \int f \, d\mu$ is continuous for all bounded continuous functions $f : X \to \mathbb{R}$. In particular, a sequence of probability measures $(\mu_n)_{n=1}^{\infty}$ converges to μ in this topology if and only if $\lim_{n \to \infty} \int f \, d\mu_n = \int f \, d\mu$ for all bounded continuous functions $f : X \to \mathbb{R}$.

THEOREM 2.14. *When X is compact and Hausdorff and $\mathcal{P}(X)$ is the space of regular probability measures on $(X, \mathfrak{B}(X))$ with the weak* topology, then $\mathcal{P}(X)$ is compact.*

17 Mathematical terminology can be a bit confusing sometimes. Since $\mathbb{E}$ maps (certain) functions to real values, it is also called the **expectation operator**. 'Operator' is just a fancy name for a function. In **operator theory**, the study of operators, the focus is on operators whose domain is infinite dimensional, hence the distinct name. However, most results of operator theory do not hinge upon this property. If the image space is the set of reals, we talk about **functionals**. The properties of functionals are studied in yet another subfield of mathematics, **functional analysis**. The expectation operator is a functional that maps the set of $\mathbb{P}$-integrable functions (often denoted by $L^1(\Omega, \mathbb{P})$ or $L^1(\mathbb{P})$) to reals. Its most important property is linearity, which was stated as a requirement for integrals that define the expectation operator (Eq. (2.5)). In line with the previous comment, when we use $\mathbb{E}$, more often than not, the probability space remains hidden. As such, the symbol $\mathbb{E}$ is further abused.

2.8   Bibliographic Remarks

Much of this chapter draws inspiration from David Pollard's *A user's guide to measure theoretic probability* [Pollard, 2002]. We like this book because the author takes a rigorous approach, but still explains the 'why' and 'how' with great care. The book gets quite advanced quite fast, concentrating on the big picture rather than getting lost in the details. Other useful references include the book by Billingsley [2008], which has many good exercises and is quite comprehensive in terms of its coverage of the 'basics'. These books are both quite detailed. For an outstanding shorter introduction to measure-theoretic probability, see the book by Williams [1991], which has an enthusiastic style and a pleasant bias towards martingales. We also like the book by Kallenberg [2002], which is recommended for the mathematically inclined readers who already have a good understanding of the basics. The author has put a major effort into organising the material so that redundancy is minimised and generality is maximised. This reorganisation resulted in quite a few original proofs, and the book is comprehensive. The factorisation lemma (Lemma 2.5) is stated in the book by Kallenberg [2002]

(Lemma 1.13 there). Kallenberg calls this lemma the 'functional representation' lemma and attributes it to Joseph Doob. Theorem 2.4 is a corollary of Carathéodory's extension theorem, which says that probability measures defined on semi-rings of sets have a unique extension to the generated σ-algebra. The remaining results can be found in either of the three books mentioned above. Theorem 2.14 appears as theorem 8.9.3 in the two-volume book by Bogachev [2007]. Finally, for something older and less technical, we recommend the philosophical essays on probability by Pierre Laplace, which was recently reprinted [Laplace, 2012].

2.9   Exercises

2.1 (COMPOSING RANDOM ELEMENTS) Show that if f is $\mathcal{F}/\mathcal{G}$-measurable and g is $\mathcal{G}/\mathcal{H}$-measurable for sigma algebras $\mathcal{F}, \mathcal{G}$ and $\mathcal{H}$ over appropriate spaces, then their composition, $g \circ f$ (defined the usual way: $(g \circ f)(\omega) = g(f(\omega))$, $\omega \in \Omega$), is $\mathcal{F}/\mathcal{H}$-measurable.

2.2 Let $X_1, \ldots, X_n$ be random variables on $(\Omega, \mathcal{F})$. Prove that $(X_1, \ldots, X_n)$ is a random vector.

2.3 (RANDOM VARIABLE INDUCED σ-ALGEBRA) Let $\mathcal{U}$ be an arbitrary set and $(\mathcal{V}, \Sigma)$ a measurable space and $X : \mathcal{U} \to \mathcal{V}$ an arbitrary function. Show that $\Sigma_X = \{X^{-1}(A) : A \in \Sigma\}$ is a σ-algebra over $\mathcal{U}$.

2.4 Let $(\Omega, \mathcal{F})$ be a measurable space and $A \subseteq \Omega$ and $\mathcal{F}_{|A} = \{A \cap B : B \in \mathcal{F}\}$.

(a) Show that $(A, \mathcal{F}_{|A})$ is a measurable space.
(b) Show that if $A \in \mathcal{F}$, then $\mathcal{F}_{|A} = \{B : B \in \mathcal{F}, B \subseteq A\}$.

2.5 Let $\mathcal{G} \subseteq 2^\Omega$ be a non-empty collection of sets and define $\sigma(\mathcal{G})$ as the smallest σ-algebra that contains $\mathcal{G}$. By 'smallest' we mean that $\mathcal{F} \in 2^\Omega$ is smaller than $\mathcal{F}' \in 2^\Omega$ if $\mathcal{F} \subset \mathcal{F}'$.

(a) Show that $\sigma(\mathcal{G})$ exists and contains exactly those sets A that are in every σ-algebra that contains $\mathcal{G}$.
(b) Suppose $(\Omega', \mathcal{F})$ is a measurable space and $X : \Omega' \to \Omega$ be $\mathcal{F}/\mathcal{G}$-measurable. Show that X is also $\mathcal{F}/\sigma(\mathcal{G})$-measurable. (We often use this result to simplify the job of checking whether a random variable satisfies some measurability property).
(c) Prove that if $A \in \mathcal{F}$ where $\mathcal{F}$ is a σ-algebra, then $\mathbb{I}\{A\}$ is $\mathcal{F}$-measurable.

2.6 (KNOWLEDGE AND σ-ALGEBRAS: A PATHOLOGICAL EXAMPLE) In the context of Lemma 2.5, show an example where $Y = X$ and yet Y is not $\sigma(X)$ measurable.

HINT   As suggested after the lemma, this can be arranged by choosing $\Omega = \mathcal{Y} = \mathcal{X} = \mathbb{R}$, $X(\omega) = Y(\omega) = \omega$, $\mathcal{F} = \mathcal{H} = \mathfrak{B}(\mathbb{R})$ and $\mathcal{G} = \{\emptyset, \mathbb{R}\}$ to be the trivial σ-algebra.

2.7 Let $(\Omega, \mathcal{F}, \mathbb{P})$ be a probability space, $B \in \mathcal{F}$ be such that $\mathbb{P}(B) > 0$. Prove that $A \mapsto \mathbb{P}(A \mid B)$ is a probability measure over $(\Omega, \mathcal{F})$.

2.8 (BAYES LAW) Verify (2.2).

2.9 Consider the standard probability space $(\Omega, \mathcal{F}, \mathbb{P})$ generated by two standard, unbiased, six-sided dice that are thrown independently of each other. Thus, $\Omega = \{1, \ldots, 6\}^2$, $\mathcal{F} = 2^\Omega$ and $\mathbb{P}(A) = |A|/6^2$ for any $A \in \mathcal{F}$ so that $X_i(\omega) = \omega_i$ represents the outcome of throwing dice $i \in \{1, 2\}$.

(a) Show that the events '$X_1 < 2$' and 'X_2 is even' are independent of each other.

(b) More generally, show that for any two events, $A \in \sigma(X_1)$ and $B \in \sigma(X_2)$, are independent of each other.

2.10 (SERENDIPITOUS INDEPENDENCE) The point of this exercise is to understand independence more deeply. Solve the following problems:

(a) Let $(\Omega, \mathcal{F}, \mathbb{P})$ be a probability space. Show that $\emptyset$ and Ω (which are events) are independent of any other event. What is the intuitive meaning of this?

(b) Continuing the previous part, show that any event $A \in \mathcal{F}$ with $\mathbb{P}(A) \in \{0, 1\}$ is independent of any other event.

(c) What can we conclude about an event $A \in \mathcal{F}$ that is independent of its complement, $A^c = \Omega \backslash A$? Does your conclusion make intuitive sense?

(d) What can we conclude about an event $A \in \mathcal{F}$ that is independent of itself? Does your conclusion make intuitive sense?

(e) Consider the probability space generated by two independent flips of unbiased coins with the smallest possible σ-algebra. Enumerate all pairs of events A, B such that A and B are independent of each other.

(f) Consider the probability space generated by the independent rolls of two unbiased three-sided dice. Call the possible outcomes of the individual dice rolls 1, 2 and 3. Let X_i be the random variable that corresponds to the outcome of the ith dice roll ($i \in \{1, 2\}$). Show that the events $\{X_1 \leq 2\}$ and $\{X_1 = X_2\}$ are independent of each other.

(g) The probability space of the previous example is an example when the probability measure is uniform on a finite outcome space (which happens to have a product structure). Now consider any n-element, finite outcome space with the uniform measure. Show that A and B are independent of each other if and only if the cardinalities $|A|, |B|, |A \cap B|$ satisfy $n|A \cap B| = |A| \cdot |B|$.

(h) Continuing with the previous problem, show that if n is prime, then no non-trivial events are independent (an event A is **trivial** if $\mathbb{P}(A) \in \{0, 1\}$).

(i) Construct an example showing that pairwise independence does not imply mutual independence.

(j) Is it true or not that A, B, C are mutually independent if and only if $\mathbb{P}(A \cap B \cap C) = \mathbb{P}(A) \mathbb{P}(B) \mathbb{P}(C)$? Prove your claim.

2.11 (INDEPENDENCE AND RANDOM ELEMENTS) Solve the following problems:

(a) Let X be a constant random element (that is, $X(\omega) = x$ for any $\omega \in \Omega$ over the outcome space over which X is defined). Show that X is independent of any other random variable.

(b) Show that the above continues to hold if X is almost surely constant (that is, $\mathbb{P}(X = x) = 1$ for an appropriate value x).

(c) Show that two events are independent if and only if their indicator random variables are independent (that is, A, B are independent if and only if $X(\omega) = \mathbb{I}\{\omega \in A\}$ and $Y(\omega) = \mathbb{I}\{\omega \in B\}$ are independent of each other).

(d) Generalise the result of the previous item to pairwise and mutual independence for collections of events and their indicator random variables.

2.12 Our goal in this exercise is to show that X is integrable if and only if $|X|$ is integrable. This is broken down into multiple steps. The first issue is to deal with the measurability of $|X|$. While a direct calculation can also show this, it may be worthwhile to follow a more general path:

(a) Any $f : \mathbb{R} \rightarrow \mathbb{R}$ continuous function is Borel measurable.

(b) Conclude that for any random variable X, $|X|$ is also a random variable.

(c) Prove that for any random variable X, X is integrable if and only if $|X|$ is integrable. (The statement makes sense since $|X|$ is a random variable whenever X is).

HINT   For (b) recall Exercise 2.1. For (c) examine the relationship between $|X|$ and $(X)^+$ and $(X)^-$.

2.13 (INFINITE-VALUED INTEGRALS) Can we consistently extend the definition of integrals so that for non-negative random variables, the integral is always defined (it may be infinite)? Defend your view by either constructing an example (if you are arguing against) or by proving that your definition is consistent with the requirements we have for integrals.

2.14 Prove Proposition 2.6.

HINT   You may find it useful to use Lebesgue's dominated/monotone convergence theorems.

2.15 Prove that if $c \in \mathbb{R}$ is a constant, then $\mathbb{E}[cX] = c\mathbb{E}[X]$ (as long as X is integrable).

2.16 Prove Proposition 2.7.

HINT   Follow the 'inductive' definition of Lebesgue integrals, starting with simple functions, then non-negative functions and finally arbitrary independent random variables.

2.17 Suppose that $\mathcal{G}_1 \subset \mathcal{G}_2$ and prove that $\mathbb{E}[X \mid \mathcal{G}_1] = \mathbb{E}[\mathbb{E}[X \mid \mathcal{G}_1] \mid \mathcal{G}_2]$ almost surely.

2.18 Demonstrate using an example that in general, for dependent random variables, $\mathbb{E}[XY] = \mathbb{E}[X]\mathbb{E}[Y]$ does not hold.

2.19 Prove Proposition 2.8.

HINT   Argue that $X(\omega) = \int_{[0,\infty)} \mathbb{I}\{[0, X(\omega)]\}(x)\,dx$ and exchange the integrals. Use the Fubini–Tonelli theorem to justify the exchange of integrals.

2.20 Prove Theorem 2.12.

3 Stochastic Processes and Markov Chains (🦘)

The measure-theoretic probability in the previous chapter covers almost all the definitions required. Occasionally, however, infinite sequences of random variables arise, and for these a little more machinery is needed. We expect most readers will skip this chapter on the first reading, perhaps referring to it when necessary.

Before one can argue about the properties of infinite sequences of random variables, it must be demonstrated that such sequences exist under certain constraints on their joint distributions. For example, does there exist an infinite sequence of random variables such that any finite subset of the random variables are independent and distributed like a standard Gaussian? The first theorem provides conditions under which questions like this can be answered positively. This allows us to write, for example, 'let $(X_n)_{n=1}^{\infty}$ be an infinite sequence of independent standard Gaussian random variables' and be comfortable knowing there exists a probability space on which these random variables can be defined. To state the theorem, we need the concept of Borel spaces.

Two measurable spaces $(\mathcal{X}, \mathcal{F})$ and $(\mathcal{Y}, \mathcal{G})$ are said to be **isomorphic** if there exists a bijective function $f : \mathcal{X} \to \mathcal{Y}$ such that f is $\mathcal{F}/\mathcal{G}$-measurable and f^{-1} is $\mathcal{G}/\mathcal{F}$-measurable. A **Borel space** is a measurable space $(\mathcal{X}, \mathcal{F})$ that is isomorphic to $(A, \mathfrak{B}(A))$ with $A \in \mathfrak{B}(\mathbb{R})$ a Borel measurable subset of the reals. This is not a very strong assumption. For example, $(\mathbb{R}^n, \mathfrak{B}(\mathbb{R}^n))$ is a Borel space, along with all of its measurable subsets.

THEOREM 3.1. *Let μ be a probability measure on a Borel space S and λ be the Lebesgue measure on $([0, 1], \mathfrak{B}([0, 1]))$. Then there exists a sequence of independent random elements $X_1, X_2, \ldots$ on $([0, 1], \mathfrak{B}([0, 1]), \lambda)$ such that the law $\lambda_{X_t} = \mu$ for all t.*

We give a sketch of the proof because, although it is not really relevant for the material in this book, it illustrates the general picture and dispels some of the mystic about what is really going on. Exercise 3.1 asks you to provide the missing steps from the proof.

Proof sketch of Theorem 3.1 For simplicity we consider only the case that $S = ([0, 1], \mathfrak{B}([0, 1]))$ and μ is the Lebesgue measure. For any $x \in [0, 1]$, let $F_1(x), F_2(x), \ldots$ be the binary expansion of x, which is the unique binary-valued infinite sequence such that

$$x = \sum_{t=1}^{\infty} F_t(x) 2^{-t}.$$

We can view $F_1, F_2, \ldots$ as (binary-valued) random variables over the probability space $([0, 1], \mathfrak{B}([0, 1]), \lambda)$. Viewed as such, a direct calculation shows that $F_1, F_2, \ldots$ are independent. From this we can create an infinite sequence of uniform random variables by reversing the process. To do this, we rearrange the $(F_t)_{t=1}^{\infty}$ sequence into a grid. For example:

$$F_1, F_2, F_4, F_7, \cdots$$
$$F_3, F_5, F_8, \cdots$$
$$F_6, F_9, \cdots$$
$$F_{10}, \cdots$$
$$\vdots$$

Letting $X_{m,t}$ be the tth entry in the mth row of this grid, we define $X_m = \sum_{t=1}^{\infty} 2^{-t} X_{m,t}$, and again one can easily check that with this choice the sequence $X_1, X_2, \ldots$ is independent and $\lambda_{X_t} = \mu$ is uniform for each t. $\qquad\square$

3.1 Stochastic Processes

Let $\mathcal{T}$ be an arbitrary set. A **stochastic process** on probability space $(\Omega, \mathcal{F}, \mathbb{P})$ is a collection of random variables $\{X_t : t \in \mathcal{T}\}$. In this book $\mathcal{T}$ will always be countable, and so in the following we restrict ourselves to $\mathcal{T} = \mathbb{N}$. The first theorem is not the most general, but suffices for our purposes and is more easily stated than more generic alternatives.

THEOREM 3.2. *For each $n \in \mathbb{N}^+$, let $(\Omega_n, \mathcal{F}_n)$ be a Borel space and μ_n be a measure on $(\Omega_1 \times \cdots \times \Omega_n, \mathcal{F}_1 \otimes \cdots \otimes \mathcal{F}_n)$ and assume that μ_n and μ_{n+1} are related through*

$$\mu_{n+1}(A \times \Omega_{n+1}) = \mu_n(A) \qquad \text{for all } A \in \Omega_1 \otimes \cdots \otimes \Omega_n. \tag{3.1}$$

Then there exists a probability space $(\Omega, \mathcal{F}, \mathbb{P})$ and random elements $X_1, X_2, \ldots$ with $X_t : \Omega \to \Omega_t$ such that $\mathbb{P}_{X_1, \ldots, X_n} = \mu_n$ for all n.

 Sequences of measures $(\mu_n)_n$ satisfying Eq. (3.1) are called **projective**.

Theorem 3.1 follows immediately from Theorem 3.2. By assumption a random variable takes values in $(\mathbb{R}, \mathfrak{B}(\mathbb{R}))$, which is Borel. Then let $\mu_n = \otimes_{t=1}^n \mu$ be the n-fold product measure of μ with itself. That this sequence of measures is projective is clear, and the theorem does the rest.

3.2 Markov Chains

A Markov chain is an infinite sequence of random elements $(X_t)_{t=1}^{\infty}$ where the conditional distribution of X_{t+1} given $X_1, \ldots, X_t$ is the same as the conditional distribution of X_{t+1} given X_t. The sequence has the property that given the last element, the history is irrelevant to 'predict' the future. Such random sequences appear throughout probability theory and have many applications besides. The theory is too rich to explain in detail, so we give the basics and point towards the literature for more details at the end. The focus here is mostly on the definition and existence of Markov chains.

Let $(\mathcal{X}, \mathcal{F})$ and $(\mathcal{Y}, \mathcal{G})$ be measurable spaces. A **probability kernel** or **Markov kernel** from $(\mathcal{X}, \mathcal{F})$ to $(\mathcal{Y}, \mathcal{G})$ is a function $K : \mathcal{X} \times \mathcal{G} \to [0, 1]$ such that

(a) $K(x, \cdot)$ is a measure for all $x \in \mathcal{X}$; and
(b) $K(\cdot, A)$ is $\mathcal{F}$-measurable for all $A \in \mathcal{G}$.

The idea here is that K describes a stochastic transition. Having arrived at x, a process's next state is sampled $Y \sim K(x, \cdot)$. Occasionally, we will use the notation $K_x(A)$ or $K(A \,|\, x)$ rather than $K(x, A)$.

If K_1 is a $(\mathcal{X}, \mathcal{F}) \to (\mathcal{Y}, \mathcal{G})$ probability kernel and K_2 is a $(\mathcal{Y}, \mathcal{G}) \to (\mathcal{Z}, \mathcal{H})$ probability kernel, then the **product kernel** $K_1 \otimes K_2$ is the probability kernel from $(\mathcal{X}, \mathcal{F}) \to (\mathcal{Y} \times \mathcal{Z}, \mathcal{G} \otimes \mathcal{H})$ defined by

$$(K_1 \otimes K_2)(x, A) = \int_{\mathcal{Y}} \int_{\mathcal{Z}} \mathbb{I}_A((y, z)) K_2(y, dz) K_1(x, dy).$$

When P is a measure on $(\mathcal{X}, \mathcal{F})$ and K is a kernel from $\mathcal{X}$ to $\mathcal{Y}$, then $P \otimes K$ is a measure on $(\mathcal{X} \times \mathcal{Y}, \mathcal{F} \otimes \mathcal{G})$ defined by

$$(P \otimes K)(A) = \int_{\mathcal{X}} \int_{\mathcal{Y}} \mathbb{I}_A((x, y)) K(x, dy) dP(x).$$

There operations can be composed. When P is a probability measure on $\mathcal{X}$ and K_1 a kernel from $\mathcal{X}$ to $\mathcal{Y}$ and K_2 a kernel from $\mathcal{X} \times \mathcal{Y}$ to $\mathcal{Z}$, then $P \otimes K_1 \otimes K_2$ is a probability measure on $\mathcal{X} \times \mathcal{Y} \times \mathcal{Z}$. The following provides a counterpart of Theorem 3.2.

Theorem 3.3 (Ionescu–Tulcea). *Let $(\Omega_n, \mathcal{F}_n)_{n=1}^{\infty}$ be a sequence of measurable spaces and K_1 be a probability measure on $(\Omega_1, \mathcal{F}_1)$. For $n \geq 2$, let K_n be a probability kernel from $\prod_{t=1}^{n-1} \Omega_t$ to Ω_n. Then there exists a probability space $(\Omega, \mathcal{F}, \mathbb{P})$ and random elements $(X_t)_{t=1}^{\infty}$ with $X_t : \Omega \to \Omega_t$ such that $\mathbb{P}_{X_1, \ldots, X_n} = \bigotimes_{t=1}^{n} K_t$ for all $n \in \mathbb{N}^{+}$.*

A **homogeneous Markov chain** is a sequence of random elements $(X_t)_{t=1}^{\infty}$ taking values in **state space** $\mathcal{S} = (\mathcal{X}, \mathcal{F})$ and with

$$\mathbb{P}(X_{t+1} \in \cdot \,|\, X_1, \ldots, X_t) = \mathbb{P}(X_{t+1} \in \cdot \,|\, X_t) = \mu(X_t, \cdot) \qquad \text{almost surely,}$$

where μ is a probability kernel from $(\mathcal{X}, \mathcal{F})$ to $(\mathcal{X}, \mathcal{F})$ and we assume that $\mathbb{P}(X_1 \in \cdot) = \mu_0(\cdot)$ for some measure μ_0 on $(\mathcal{X}, \mathcal{F})$.

The word 'homogeneous' refers to the fact that the probability kernel does not change with time. Accordingly, sometimes one writes 'time homogeneous' instead of homogeneous. The reader can no doubt see how to define a Markov chain where μ depends on t, though doing so is purely cosmetic since the state space can always be augmented to include a time component.

Note that if $\mu(x \,|\, \cdot) = \mu_0(\cdot)$ for all $x \in \mathcal{X}$, then Theorem 3.3 is yet another way to prove the existence of an infinite sequence of independent and identically distributed random variables. The basic questions in Markov chains resolve around understanding the evolution of X_t in terms of the probability kernel. For example, assuming that $\Omega_t = \Omega_1$ for all $t \in \mathbb{N}^+$, does the law of X_t converge to some fixed distribution as $t \to \infty$, and if so, how fast is this convergence? For now we make do with the definitions, but in the special case that $\mathcal{X}$ is finite, we will discuss some of these topics much later in Chapters 37 and 38.

3.3 Martingales and Stopping Times

Let $X_1, X_2, \ldots$ be a sequence of random variables on $(\Omega, \mathcal{F}, \mathbb{P})$ and $\mathbb{F} = (\mathcal{F}_t)_{t=1}^n$ a filtration of $\mathcal{F}$ and where we allow $n = \infty$. Recall that the sequence $(X_t)_{t=1}^n$ is $\mathbb{F}$-adapted if X_t is $\mathcal{F}_t$-measurable for all $1 \leq t \leq n$.

DEFINITION 3.4. A $\mathbb{F}$-adapted sequence of random variables $(X_t)_{t\in\mathbb{N}_+}$ is a $\mathbb{F}$-adapted **martingale** if

(a) $\mathbb{E}[X_t \mid \mathcal{F}_{t-1}] = X_{t-1}$ almost surely for all $t \in \{2, 3, \ldots\}$; and
(b) X_t is integrable.

If the equality is replaced with a less-than (greater-than), then we call $(X_t)_t$ a **supermartingale** (respectively, a **submartingale**).

> The time index t need not run over $\mathbb{N}^+$. Very often t starts at zero instead.

EXAMPLE 3.5. A gambler repeatedly throws a coin, winning a dollar for each heads and losing a dollar for each tails. Their total winnings over time is a martingale. To model this situation, let $Y_1, Y_2, \ldots$ be a sequence of independent Rademacher distributions, which means that $\mathbb{P}(Y_t = 1) = \mathbb{P}(Y_t = -1) = 1/2$. The winnings after t rounds is $S_t = \sum_{s=1}^t Y_s$, which is a martingale adapted to the filtration $(\mathcal{F}_t)_{t=1}^\infty$ given by $\mathcal{F}_t = \sigma(Y_1, \ldots, Y_t)$. The definition of super/sub-martingales (the direction of inequality) can be remembered by remembering that the definition favors the casino, not the gambler.

Can a gambler increase its expected winning by stopping cleverly? Precisely, the gambler at the end of round t can decide to stop ($\delta_t = 1$) or continue ($\delta_t = 0$) based on the information available to them. Denoting by $\tau = \min\{t : \delta_t = 1\}$ the time when the gambler stops, the question is whether by a clever choice of $(\delta_t)_{t\in\mathbb{N}}$, $\mathbb{E}[S_\tau]$ can be made positive. Here, $(\delta_t)_{t\in\mathbb{N}}$, a sequence of binary, $\mathbb{F}$-adapted random variables, is called a **stopping rule**, while τ is a stopping time with respect $\mathbb{F}$.

> Note that the stopping rule is not allowed to inject additional randomness beyond what is already there in $\mathbb{F}$.

DEFINITION 3.6. Let $\mathbb{F} = (\mathcal{F}_t)_{t\in\mathbb{N}}$ be a filtration. A random variable τ with values in $\mathbb{N} \cup \{\infty\}$ is a **stopping time** with respect to $\mathbb{F}$ if $\mathbb{I}\{\tau \leq t\}$ is $\mathcal{F}_t$-measurable for all $t \in \mathbb{N}$. The σ-algebra at stopping time τ is

$$\mathcal{F}_\tau = \{A \in \mathcal{F}_\infty : A \cap \{\tau \leq t\} \in \mathcal{F}_t \text{ for all } t\}.$$

The filtration is usually indicated by writing 'τ is a $\mathbb{F}$-stopping time'. When the underlying filtration is obvious from context, it may be omitted. This is also true for martingales.

Using the interpretation of σ-algebras encoding information, if $(\mathcal{F}_t)_t$ is thought of as the knowledge available at time t, $\mathcal{F}_\tau$ is the information available at the random time τ. Exercise 3.7 asks you to explore properties of stopped σ-algebras; amongst other things, it asks you to show that $\mathcal{F}_\tau$ is in fact a σ-algebra.

EXAMPLE 3.7. In the gambler example, the first time when the gambler's winnings hits 100 is a stopping time: $\tau = \min\{t : S_t = 100\}$. On the other hand, $\tau = \min\{t : S_{t+1} = -1\}$ is not a stopping time because $\mathbb{I}\{\tau = t\}$ is not $\mathcal{F}_t$-measurable.

Whether or not $\mathbb{E}[S_\tau]$ can be made positive by a clever choice of a stopping time τ is answered in the negative by a fundamental theorem of Doob:

THEOREM 3.8 (Doob's optional stopping). *Let $\mathbb{F} = (\mathcal{F}_t)_{t\in\mathbb{N}}$ be a filtration and $(X_t)_{t\in\mathbb{N}}$ be an $\mathbb{F}$-adapted martingale and τ an $\mathbb{F}$-stopping time such that at least one of the following holds:*

(a) *There exists an $n \in \mathbb{N}$ such that $\mathbb{P}(\tau > n) = 0$.*
(b) *$\mathbb{E}[\tau] < \infty$, and there exists a constant $c \in \mathbb{R}$ such that for all $t \in \mathbb{N}$, $\mathbb{E}[|X_{t+1} - X_t| \,|\, \mathcal{F}_t] \le c$ almost surely on the event that $\tau > t$.*
(c) *There exists a constant c such that $|X_{t\wedge\tau}| \le c$ almost surely for all $t \in \mathbb{N}$.*

Then X_τ is almost surely well defined, and $\mathbb{E}[X_\tau] = \mathbb{E}[X_0]$. Furthermore, when (X_t) is a super/sub-martingale rather than a martingale, then equality is replaced with less/greater-than, respectively.

The theorem implies that if S_τ is almost-surely well defined then either $\mathbb{E}[\tau] = \infty$ or $\mathbb{E}[S_\tau] = 0$. Gamblers trying to outsmart the casino would need to live a very long life! One application of Doob's optional stopping theorem is a useful and a priori surprising generalisation of Markov's inequality to non-negative supermartingales.

THEOREM 3.9 (Maximal inequality). *Let $(X_t)_{t=0}^\infty$ be a supermartingale with $X_t \ge 0$ almost surely for all t. Then for any $\varepsilon > 0$,*

$$\mathbb{P}\left(\sup_{t\in\mathbb{N}} X_t \ge \varepsilon\right) \le \frac{\mathbb{E}[X_0]}{\varepsilon}.$$

Proof   Let A_n be the event that $\sup_{t\le n} X_t \ge \varepsilon$ and $\tau = (n+1) \wedge \min\{t \le n : X_t \ge \varepsilon\}$, where the minimum of an empty set is assumed to be infinite so that $\tau = n+1$ if $X_t < \varepsilon$ for all $0 \le t \le n$. Clearly τ is a stopping time and $\mathbb{P}(\tau \le n+1) = 1$. Then by Theorem 3.8 and elementary calculation,

$$\mathbb{E}[X_0] \ge \mathbb{E}[X_\tau] \ge \mathbb{E}[X_\tau\mathbb{I}\{\tau \le n\}] \ge \mathbb{E}[\varepsilon\mathbb{I}\{\tau \le n\}] = \varepsilon\mathbb{P}(\tau \le n) = \varepsilon\mathbb{P}(A_n),$$

where the second inequality uses the definition of the stopping time and the non-negativity of the supermartingale. Rearranging shows that $\mathbb{P}(A_n) \le \mathbb{E}[X_0]/\varepsilon$ for all $n \in \mathbb{N}$. Since $A_1 \subseteq A_2 \subseteq \ldots$, it follows that $\mathbb{P}(\sup_{t\in\mathbb{N}} X_t \ge \varepsilon) = \mathbb{P}(\cup_{n\in\mathbb{N}} A_n) \le \mathbb{E}[X_0]/\varepsilon$.   □

Markov's inequality (which we will cover in the next chapter) combined with the definition of a supermartingale shows that

$$\mathbb{P}(X_n \geq \varepsilon) \leq \frac{\mathbb{E}[X_0]}{\varepsilon}. \qquad (3.2)$$

In fact, in the above we have effectively applied Markov's inequality to the random variable X_τ (the need for the proof arises when the conditions of Doob's optional sampling theorem are *not* met). The maximal inequality is a strict improvement over Eq. (3.2) by replacing X_n with $\sup_{t \in \mathbb{N}} X_t$ at no cost whatsoever.

A similar theorem holds for submartingales. You will provide a proof in Exercise 3.8.

THEOREM 3.10. *Let* $(X_t)_{t=0}^n$ *be a submartingale with* $X_t \geq 0$ *almost surely for all* t. *Then for any* $\varepsilon > 0$,

$$\mathbb{P}\left(\max_{t \in \{0,1,\ldots,n\}} X_t \geq \varepsilon\right) \leq \frac{\mathbb{E}[X_n]}{\varepsilon}.$$

3.4 Notes

1 Some authors include in the definition of a stopping time τ that $\mathbb{P}(\tau < \infty) = 1$ and call random times without this property **Markov times**. We do *not* adopt this convention and allow stopping times to be infinite with non-zero probability. Stopping times are also called **optional times**.

2 There are several notations for probability kernels depending on the application. The following are commonly seen and equivalent: $K(x, A) = K(A \mid x) = K_x(A)$. For example, in statistics a parametric family is often given by $\{\mathbb{P}_\theta : \theta \in \Theta\}$, where Θ is the parameter space and $\mathbb{P}_\theta$ is a measure on some measurable space $(\Omega, \mathcal{F})$. This notation is often more convenient than writing $\mathbb{P}(\theta, \cdot)$. In Bayesian statistics the posterior is a probability kernel from the observation space to the parameter space, and this is often written as $\mathbb{P}(\cdot \mid x)$.

3 There is some disagreement about whether or not a Markov chain on an uncountable state space should instead be called a **Markov process**. In this book we use Markov chain for arbitrary state spaces and discrete time. When time is continuous (which it never is in this book), there is general agreement that 'process' is more appropriate. For more history on this debate, see [Meyn and Tweedie, 2012, preface].

4 A topological space $\mathcal{X}$ is **Polish** if it is separable and there exists a metric d that is compatible with the topology that makes $(\mathcal{X}, d)$ a complete metric space. All Polish spaces are Borel spaces. We follow Kallenberg [2002], but many authors use **standard Borel space** rather than Borel space, and define it as the σ-algebra generated by the open sets of a Polish space.

5 In Theorem 3.2 it was assumed that each μ_n was defined on a Borel space. No such assumption was required for Theorem 3.3, however. One can derive Theorem 3.2 from Theorem 3.3 by using the existence of regular conditional probability measures when conditioning on random elements taking values in a Borel space (see the next note). Topological assumptions often creep into foundational questions relating to the existence of probability measures satisfying certain conditions, and pathological examples show these assumptions cannot be removed completely. Luckily, in this book we have no reason to consider random elements that do not take values in a Borel space.

6 The fact that conditional expectation is only unique almost surely can be problematic when you want a conditional distribution. Given random elements X and Y on the same probability space, it seems reasonable to hope that $\mathbb{P}(X \in \cdot \mid Y)$ is a probability kernel from the space of Y to that of X. A version of the conditional distributions that satisfies this is called a **regular version**. In general, there is no guarantee that such a regular version exist. The basic properties of conditional expectation only guarantee that for any fixed measurable A, $\mathbb{P}(X \in A \mid Y)$ is unique up to a set of measure zero. The set of measure zero can depend on A, which causes problems when there are 'too many' measurable sets in the space of X. Assuming X lives in a Borel space, the following theorem guarantees the existence of a conditional distribution.

THEOREM 3.11 (Regular conditional distributions). *Let X and Y be random elements on the same probability space $(\Omega, \mathcal{F}, \mathbb{P})$ taking values in measurable spaces $\mathcal{X}$ and $\mathcal{Y}$, and assume that $\mathcal{X}$ is Borel. Then there exists a probability kernel K from $\mathcal{Y}$ to $\mathcal{X}$ such that $K(\cdot \mid Y) = \mathbb{P}(X \in \cdot \mid Y)$ $\mathbb{P}$-almost surely. Furthermore, K is unique in the sense that for any kernels K_1 and K_2 satisfying this condition, it holds that $K_1(\cdot \mid y) = K_2(\cdot \mid y)$ for all y in some set of $\mathbb{P}_Y$-measure one.*

The theorem implies the useful relation that $\mathbb{P}_{X,Y} = \mathbb{P}_Y \otimes K$ (cf. Exercise 3.9) where recall that for a random variable Z, $\mathbb{P}_Z$ denotes its pushforward under $\mathbb{P}$. To make the origin K clear, we often write $\mathbb{P}_{X|Y}$ instead of K. With this, the above equality becomes $\mathbb{P}_{X,Y} = \mathbb{P}_Y \otimes \mathbb{P}_{X|Y}$, which can be viewed as the converse of the Ionescu–Tulcea theorem (Theorem 3.3). Sometimes this is called the **chain rule of probabilities measures**.

You can also condition on a σ-algebra $\mathcal{G} \subset \mathcal{F}$, in which case K is a probability kernel from $(\Omega, \mathcal{G})$ to $\mathcal{X}$. The condition that $\mathcal{X}$ be Borel is sufficient, but not necessary. Some conditions are required, however. An example where no regular version exists can be found in [Halmos, 1976, p210]. Regular versions play a role in the following useful theorem for decomposing random variables on product spaces.

THEOREM 3.12 (Disintegration). *Let X and Y be random elements on the same probability space taking values in measurable spaces $\mathcal{X}$ and $\mathcal{Y}$. Let f be a random variable on $\mathcal{X} \times \mathcal{Y}$ so that $\mathbb{E}[|f(X,Y)|] < \infty$. Suppose that K is a regular version of $\mathbb{P}(X \in \cdot \mid \mathcal{G})$ and Y is $\mathcal{G}$-measurable. Then,*

$$\mathbb{E}[f(X,Y) \mid \mathcal{G}] = \int_{\mathcal{X}} f(x,Y) K(dx \mid \cdot) \text{ almost surely.}$$

In many applications $\mathcal{G} = \sigma(Y)$, in which case the theorem says that $\mathbb{E}[f(X,Y) \mid Y] = \int_{\mathcal{X}} f(x,Y) K(dx \mid Y)$ almost surely. Proofs of both theorems appear in chapter 6 of Kallenberg [2002].

3.5   Bibliographic Remarks

There are many places to find the construction of a stochastic process. Like before, we recommend Kallenberg [2002] for readers who want to refresh their memory and Billingsley [2008] for a more detailed account. For Markov chains the recent book by Levin and Peres [2017] provides a wonderful introduction. After reading that, you might like the tome by Meyn and Tweedie [2012]. Theorem 3.1 can be found as theorem 3.19 in the book by Kallenberg [2002], where the reader can also find its proof. Theorem 3.2 is credited to Percy John Daniell by Kallenberg [2002] (see Aldrich 2007). More general versions of this theorem exist. Readers looking for these should look up **Kolmogorov's** extension theorem [Kallenberg, 2002, theorem 6.16]. The theorem of Ionescu–Tulcea (Theorem 3.3) is attributed to him [Tulcea, 1949–50] with a modern proof in the book by Kallenberg [2002, theorem 6.17]. There are lots of minor variants of the optional stopping theorem, most of which can be found in any probability book featuring martingales. The most historically notable source is by the man himself [Doob, 1953]. A more modern book that also gives the maximal inequalities is the book on optimal stopping by Peskir and Shiryaev [2006].

3.6   Exercises

3.1 Fill in the details of Theorem 3.1:

(a) Prove that $F_t \in \{0, 1\}$ is a Bernoulli random variable for all $t \geq 1$.

(b) In what follows, equip S with $\mathbb{P} = \lambda$, the uniform probability measure. Show that for any $t \geq 1$, F_t is uniformly distributed: $\mathbb{P}(F_t = 0) = \mathbb{P}(F_t = 1) = 1/2$.

(c) Show that $(F_t)_{t=1}^{\infty}$ are independent.

(d) Show that $(X_{m,t})_{t=1}^{\infty}$ is an independent sequence of Bernoulli random variables that are uniformly distributed.

(e) Show that $X_t = \sum_{t=1}^{\infty} X_{m,t} 2^{-t}$ is uniformly distributed on $[0, 1]$.

(f) Show that $(X_t)_{t=1}^{\infty}$ are independent.

3.2 (MARTINGALES AND OPTIONAL STOPPING) Let $(X_t)_{t=1}^{\infty}$ be an infinite sequence of independent Rademacher random variables and $S_t = \sum_{s=1}^{t} X_s 2^{s-1}$.

(a) Show that $(S_t)_{t=0}^{\infty}$ is a martingale.

(b) Let $\tau = \min\{t : S_t = 1\}$ and show that $\mathbb{P}(\tau < \infty) = 1$.

(c) What is $\mathbb{E}[S_\tau]$?

(d) Explain why this does not contradict Doob's optional stopping theorem.

3.3 (MARTINGALES AND OPTIONAL STOPPING (II)) Give an example of a martingale $(S_n)_{n=0}^{\infty}$ and stopping time τ such that

$$\lim_{n \to \infty} \mathbb{E}[S_{\tau \wedge n}] \neq \mathbb{E}[S_\tau].$$

3.4 (MAXIMAL INEQUALITY FAILS WITHOUT NON-NEGATIVITY) Show that Theorem 3.9 does not hold in general for supermartingales if the assumption that it be non-negative is dropped.

3.5 Let $(\Omega, \mathcal{F})$ and $(\mathcal{X}, \mathcal{G})$ be measurable spaces, $X : \mathcal{X} \to \mathbb{R}$ be a random variable and $K : \Omega \times \mathcal{G} \to [0, 1]$ a probability kernel from $(\Omega, \mathcal{F})$ to $(\mathcal{X}, \mathcal{G})$. Define function $U : \Omega \to \mathbb{R}$ by $U(\omega) = \int_{\mathcal{X}} X(x) K(\omega, dx)$ and assume that $U(\omega)$ exists for all ω. Prove that U is $\mathcal{F}$-measurable.

3.6 (LIMITS OF INCREASING STOPPING TIMES ARE STOPPING TIMES) Let $(\tau_n)_{n=1}^{\infty}$ be an almost surely increasing sequence of $\mathbb{F}$-stopping times on probability space $(\Omega, \mathcal{F}, \mathbb{P})$ with filtration $\mathbb{F} = (\mathcal{F}_n)_{n=1}^{\infty}$, which means that $\tau_n(\omega) \leq \tau_{n+1}(\omega)$ for all $n \geq 1$ almost surely. Prove that $\tau(\omega) = \lim_{n \to \infty} \tau_n(\omega)$ is a $\mathbb{F}$-stopping time.

3.7 (PROPERTIES OF STOPPING TIMES) Let $\mathbb{F} = (\mathcal{F}_t)_{t \in \mathbb{N}}$ be a filtration, and τ, τ_1, τ_2 be stopping times with respect to $\mathbb{F}$. Show the following:

(a) $\mathcal{F}_\tau$ is a σ-algebra.

(b) If $\tau = k$ for some $k \geq 1$, then $\mathcal{F}_\tau = \mathcal{F}_k$.

(c) If $\tau_1 \leq \tau_2$, then $\mathcal{F}_{\tau_1} \subset \mathcal{F}_{\tau_2}$.

(d) τ is $\mathcal{F}_\tau$-measurable.

(e) If (X_t) is $\mathbb{F}$-adapted, then X_τ is $\mathcal{F}_\tau$-measurable.

(f) $\mathcal{F}_\tau$ is the smallest σ-algebra such that all $\mathbb{F}$-adapted sequences (X_t) satisfy X_τ is $\mathcal{F}_\tau$-measurable.

3.8 Prove Theorem 3.10.

3.9 (DECOMPOSING JOINT DISTRIBUTIONS) Let X and Y be random elements on the same probability space $(\Omega, \mathcal{F}, \mathbb{P})$ taking values in measurable spaces $\mathcal{X}$ and $\mathcal{Y}$ respectively and assume that $\mathcal{X}$ is Borel. Show that $\mathbb{P}_{(X,Y)} = \mathbb{P}_Y \otimes \mathbb{P}_{X|Y}$ where $\mathbb{P}_{X|Y}$ denotes a regular conditional distribution of X and Y (the existence of which is guaranteed by Theorem 3.11).

4 Stochastic Bandits

The goal of this chapter is to formally introduce stochastic bandits. The model introduced here provides the foundation for the remaining chapters that treat stochastic bandits. While the topic seems a bit mundane, it is important to be clear about the assumptions and definitions. The chapter also introduces and motivates the learning objectives, and especially the regret. Besides the definitions, the main result in this chapter is the regret decomposition, which is presented in Section 4.5.

4.1 Core Assumptions

A **stochastic bandit** is a collection of distributions $v = (P_a : a \in \mathcal{A})$, where $\mathcal{A}$ is the set of available actions. The learner and the environment interact sequentially over n rounds. In each round $t \in \{1, \ldots, n\}$, the learner chooses an action $A_t \in \mathcal{A}$, which is fed to the environment. The environment then samples a reward $X_t \in \mathbb{R}$ from distribution P_{A_t} and reveals X_t to the learner. The interaction between the learner (or policy) and environment induces a probability measure on the sequence of outcomes $A_1, X_1, A_2, X_2, \ldots, A_n, X_n$. Usually the horizon n is finite, but sometimes we allow the interaction to continue indefinitely ($n = \infty$). The sequence of outcomes should satisfy the following assumptions:

(a) The conditional distribution of reward X_t given $A_1, X_1, \ldots, A_{t-1}, X_{t-1}, A_t$ is P_{A_t}, which captures the intuition that the environment samples X_t from P_{A_t} in round t.

(b) The conditional law of action A_t given $A_1, X_1, \ldots, A_{t-1}, X_{t-1}$ is $\pi_t(\cdot \,|\, A_1, X_1, \ldots, A_{t-1}, X_{t-1})$, where $\pi_1, \pi_2, \ldots$ is a sequence of probability kernels that characterise the learner. The most important element of this assumption is the intuitive fact that the learner cannot use the future observations in current decisions.

A mathematician might ask whether there even exists a probability space carrying these random elements such that (a) and (b) hold. Specific constructions showing this in the affirmative are given in Section 4.6. These constructions are also valuable because they teach us important lessons about equivalent models. For now, however, we move on.

4.2 The Learning Objective

The learner's goal is to maximise the total reward $S_n = \sum_{t=1}^{n} X_t$, which is a random quantity that depends on the actions of the learner and the rewards sampled by the environment. This is not an optimisation problem for three reasons:

1 What is the value of n for which we are maximising? Occasionally prior knowledge of the horizon is reasonable, but very often the learner does not know ahead of time how many rounds are to be played.
2 The cumulative reward is a random quantity. Even if the reward distributions were known, then we require a measure of utility on distributions of S_n.
3 The learner does not know the distributions that govern the rewards for each arm.

Of these points, the last is fundamental to the bandit problem and is discussed in the next section. The lack of knowledge of the horizon is usually not a serious issue. Generally speaking it is possible to first design a policy assuming the horizon is known and then adapt it to account for the unknown horizon while proving that the loss in performance is minimal. This is almost always quite easy, and there exist generic approaches for making the conversion.

Assigning a utility to distributions of S_n is more challenging. Suppose that S_n is the revenue of your company. Fig. 4.1 shows the distribution of S_n for two different learners; call them A and B. Suppose you can choose between learners A and B. Which one would you choose? One choice is to go with the learner whose reward distribution has the larger expected value. This will be our default choice for stochastic bandits, but it bears remembering that there are other considerations, including the variance or tail behaviour of the cumulative reward, which we will discuss occasionally. In particular, in the situation shown on in Fig. 4.1, learner B achieves a higher expected reward than A. However B has a reasonable probability of earning less than the least amount that A can earn, so a risk-sensitive user may prefer learner A.

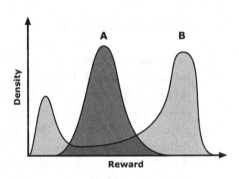

Figure 4.1 Alternative revenue distributions

4.3   Knowledge and Environment Classes

Even if the horizon is known in advance and we commit to maximising the expected value of S_n, there is still the problem that the bandit instance $v = (P_a : a \in \mathcal{A})$ is unknown. A policy that maximises the expectation of S_n for one bandit instance may behave quite badly on another. The learner usually has partial information about v, which we represent by defining a set of bandits $\mathcal{E}$ for which $v \in \mathcal{E}$ is guaranteed. The set $\mathcal{E}$ is called the **environment class**. We distinguish between **structured** and **unstructured** bandits.

Unstructured Bandits
An environment class $\mathcal{E}$ is unstructured if $\mathcal{A}$ is finite and there exist sets of distributions $\mathcal{M}_a$ for each $a \in \mathcal{A}$ such that

$$\mathcal{E} = \{v = (P_a : a \in \mathcal{A}) : P_a \in \mathcal{M}_a \text{ for all } a \in \mathcal{A}\},$$

Table 4.1 Typical environment classes for stochastic bandits. Supp(P) is the (topological) support of distribution P. The kurtosis of a random variable X is a measure of its tail behaviour and is defined by $\mathbb{E}[(X - \mathbb{E}[X])^4]/\mathbb{V}[X]^2$. Subgaussian distributions have similar properties to the Gaussian and will be defined in Chapter 5.

Name	Symbol	Definition
Bernoulli	$\mathcal{E}_B^k$	$\{(\mathcal{B}(\mu_i))_i : \mu \in [0,1]^k\}$
Uniform	$\mathcal{E}_U^k$	$\{(\mathcal{U}(a_i, b_i))_i : a, b \in \mathbb{R}^k \text{ with } a_i \leq b_i \text{ for all } i\}$
Gaussian (known var.)	$\mathcal{E}_N^k(\sigma^2)$	$\{(\mathcal{N}(\mu_i, \sigma^2))_i : \mu \in \mathbb{R}^k\}$
Gaussian (unknown var.)	$\mathcal{E}_N^k$	$\{(\mathcal{N}(\mu_i, \sigma_i^2))_i : \mu \in \mathbb{R}^k \text{ and } \sigma^2 \in [0, \infty)^k\}$
Finite variance	$\mathcal{E}_V^k(\sigma^2)$	$\{(P_i)_i : \mathbb{V}_{X \sim P_i}[X] \leq \sigma^2 \text{ for all } i\}$
Finite kurtosis	$\mathcal{E}_{\mathrm{Kurt}}^k(\kappa)$	$\{(P_i)_i : \mathrm{Kurt}_{X \sim P_i}[X] \leq \kappa \text{ for all } i\}$
Bounded support	$\mathcal{E}_{[a,b]}^k$	$\{(P_i)_i : \mathrm{Supp}(P_i) \subseteq [a, b]\}$
Subgaussian	$\mathcal{E}_{\mathrm{SG}}^k(\sigma^2)$	$\{(P_i)_i : P_i \text{ is } \sigma\text{-subgaussian for all } i\}$

or, in short, $\mathcal{E} = \times_{a \in \mathcal{A}} \mathcal{M}_a$. The product structure means that by playing action a the learner cannot deduce anything about the distributions of actions $b \neq a$.

Some typical choices of unstructured bandits are listed in Table 4.1. Of course, these are not the only choices, and the reader can no doubt find ways to construct more, e.g. by allowing some arms to be Bernoulli and some Gaussian, or have rewards being exponentially distributed, or Gumbel distributed, or belonging to your favourite (non-)parametric family.

The Bernoulli, Gaussian and uniform distributions are often used as examples for illustrating some specific property of learning in stochastic bandit problems. The Bernoulli distribution is actually a natural choice. Think of applications like maximising click-through rates in a web-based environment. A bandit problem is often called a 'distribution bandit', where 'distribution' is replaced by the underlying distribution from which the pay-offs are sampled. Some examples are: Gaussian bandit, Bernoulli bandit or subgaussian bandit. Similarly we say 'bandits with X', where 'X' is a property of the underlying distribution from which the pay-offs are sampled. For example, we can talk about bandits with finite variance, meaning the bandit environment where the a priori knowledge of the learner is that all pay-off distributions are such that their underlying variance is finite.

Some environment classes, like Bernoulli bandits, are **parametric**, while others, like subgaussian bandits, are **non-parametric**. The distinction is the number of degrees of freedom needed to describe an element of the environment class. When the number of degrees of freedom is finite, it is parametric, and otherwise it is non-parametric. Of course, if a learner is designed for a specific environment class $\mathcal{E}$, then we might expect that it has good performance on all bandits $\nu \in \mathcal{E}$. Some environment classes are subsets of other classes. For example, Bernoulli bandits are a special case of bandits with a finite variance, or bandits with bounded support. Something to keep in mind is that we expect that it will be harder to achieve a good performance in a larger class. In a way, the theory of finite-armed stochastic bandits tries to quantify this expectation in a rigourous fashion.

Structured Bandits

Environment classes that are not unstructured are called structured. Relaxing the requirement that the environment class is a product set makes structured bandit problems much richer than the unstructured set-up. The following examples illustrate the flexibility.

EXAMPLE 4.1. Let $\mathcal{A} = \{1, 2\}$ and $\mathcal{E} = \{(\mathcal{B}(\theta), \mathcal{B}(1 - \theta)) : \theta \in [0, 1]\}$. In this environment class, the learner does not know the mean of either arm, but can learn the mean of both arms by playing just one. The knowledge of this structure dramatically changes the difficulty of learning in this problem.

EXAMPLE 4.2 (Stochastic linear bandit). Let $\mathcal{A} \subset \mathbb{R}^d$ and $\theta \in \mathbb{R}^d$ and

$$v_\theta = (\mathcal{N}(\langle a, \theta \rangle, 1) : a \in \mathcal{A}) \qquad \text{and } \mathcal{E} = \{v_\theta : \theta \in \mathbb{R}^d\}.$$

In this environment class, the reward of an action is Gaussian, and its mean is given by the inner product between the action and some unknown parameter. Notice that even if $\mathcal{A}$ is extremely large, the learner can deduce the true environment by playing just d actions that span $\mathbb{R}^d$.

EXAMPLE 4.3. Consider an undirected graph G with vertices $V = \{1, \ldots, |V|\}$ and edges $E = \{1, \ldots, |E|\}$. In each round the learner chooses a path from vertex 1 to vertex $|V|$. Then each edge $e \in [E]$ is removed from the graph with probability $1 - \theta_e$ for unknown $\theta \in [0, 1]^{|E|}$. The learner succeeds in reaching their destination if all the edges in their chosen path are present. This problem can be formalised by letting $\mathcal{A}$ be the set of paths and

$$v_\theta = \left(\mathcal{B}\left(\prod_{e \in a} \theta_e \right) : a \in \mathcal{A} \right) \qquad \text{and} \qquad \mathcal{E} = \{v_\theta : \theta \in [0, 1]^{|E|}\}.$$

An important feature of structured bandits is that the learner can often obtain information about some actions while never playing them.

4.4   The Regret

In Chapter 1 we informally defined the regret as being the deficit suffered by the learner relative to the optimal policy. Let $v = (P_a : a \in \mathcal{A})$ be a stochastic bandit and define

$$\mu_a(v) = \int_{-\infty}^{\infty} x \, dP_a(x).$$

Then let $\mu^*(v) = \max_{a \in \mathcal{A}} \mu_a(v)$ be the largest mean of all the arms.

We assume throughout that $\mu_a(v)$ exists and is finite for all actions and that $\operatorname{argmax}_{a \in \mathcal{A}} \mu_a(v)$ is non-empty. The latter assumption could be relaxed by carefully adapting all arguments using nearly optimal actions, but in practice this is never required.

The regret of policy π on bandit instance v is

$$R_n(\pi, v) = n\mu^*(v) - \mathbb{E}\left[\sum_{t=1}^{n} X_t \right], \tag{4.1}$$

where the expectation is taken with respect to the probability measure on outcomes induced by the interaction of π and v. Minimising the regret is equivalent to maximising the expectation of S_n, but the normalisation inherent in the definition of the regret is useful when stating results, which would otherwise need to be stated relative to the optimal action.

> If the context is clear, we will often drop the dependence on v and π in various quantities. For example, by writing $R_n = n\mu^* - \mathbb{E}[\sum_{t=1}^n X_t]$. Similarly, the limits in sums and maxima are abbreviated when we think you can work out ranges of symbols in a unique way, e.g. $\mu^* = \max_i \mu_i$.

The regret is always non-negative, and for every bandit v, there exists a policy π for which the regret vanishes.

LEMMA 4.4. *Let v be a stochastic bandit environment. Then,*

(a) $R_n(\pi, v) \geq 0$ *for all policies π;*
(b) *the policy π choosing $A_t \in \mathrm{argmax}_a \, \mu_a$ for all t satisfies $R_n(\pi, v) = 0$; and*
(c) *if $R_n(\pi, v) = 0$ for some policy π, then $\mathbb{P}(\mu_{A_t} = \mu^*) = 1$ for all $t \in [n]$.*

We leave the proof for the reader (Exercise 4.1). Part (b) of Lemma 4.4 shows that for every bandit v, there exists a policy for which the regret is zero (the best possible outcome). According to Part (c), achieving zero is possible if and only if the learner knows which bandit it is facing (or at least, what is the optimal arm). In general, however, the learner only knows that $v \in \mathcal{E}$ for some environment class $\mathcal{E}$. So what can we hope for? A relatively weak objective is to find a policy π with sublinear regret on all $v \in \mathcal{E}$. Formally, this objective is to find a policy π such that

$$\text{for all } v \in \mathcal{E}, \qquad \lim_{n \to \infty} \frac{R_n(\pi, v)}{n} = 0.$$

If the above holds, then at least the learner is choosing the optimal action almost all of the time as the horizon tends to infinity. One might hope for much more, however, for example, that for some specific choice of $C > 0$ and $p < 1$ that

$$\text{for all } v \in \mathcal{E}, \qquad R_n(\pi, v) \leq Cn^p. \tag{4.2}$$

Yet another alternative is to find a function $C : \mathcal{E} \to [0, \infty)$ and $f : \mathbb{N} \to [0, \infty)$ such that

$$\text{for all } n \in \mathbb{N}, \, v \in \mathcal{E}, \qquad R_n(\pi, v) \leq C(v)f(n). \tag{4.3}$$

This factorisation of the regret into a function of the instance and a function of the horizon is not uncommon in learning theory and appears in particular in supervised learning.

We will spend a lot of time in the following chapters finding policies satisfying Eq. (4.2) and Eq. (4.3) for different choices of $\mathcal{E}$. The form of Eq. (4.3) is quite general, so much time is also spent discovering what are the possibilities for f and C, both of which should be 'as small as possible'. All of the policies are inspired by the simple observation that in order to make the regret small, the algorithm must discover the action/arm with the largest mean. Usually this means the algorithm should play each arm some number of times to form an estimate of the mean of that arm, and subsequently play the arm with the largest estimated mean. The question essentially boils down to discovering exactly how often the learner must play each arm in order to have reasonable statistical certainty that it has found the optimal arm.

There is another candidate objective called the **Bayesian regret**. If Q is a prior probability measure on $\mathcal{E}$ (which must be equipped with a σ-algebra $\mathcal{F}$), then the Bayesian regret is the average of the regret with respect to the prior Q.

$$BR_n(\pi, Q) = \int_{\mathcal{E}} R_n(\pi, v) \, dQ(v), \tag{4.4}$$

which is only defined by assuming (or proving) that the regret is a measurable function with respect to $\mathcal{F}$. An advantage of the Bayesian approach is that having settled on a prior and horizon, the problem of finding a policy that minimises the Bayesian regret is just an optimisation problem. Most of this book is devoted to analyzing the 'frequentist' regret in Eq. (4.1), which does not integrate over all environments as Eq. (4.4) does. Bayesian methods are covered in Chapters 34 to 36, where we also discuss the strengths and weaknesses of the Bayesian approach.

4.5   Decomposing the Regret

We now present a lemma that forms the basis of almost every proof for stochastic bandits. Let $v = (P_a : a \in \mathcal{A})$ be a stochastic bandit and define $\Delta_a(v) = \mu^*(v) - \mu_a(v)$, which is called the **suboptimality gap** or **action gap** or **immediate regret** of action a. Further, let

$$T_a(t) = \sum_{s=1}^{t} \mathbb{I}\{A_s = a\}$$

be the number of times action a was chosen by the learner after the end of round t. In general, $T_a(n)$ is random, which may seem surprising if we think about a deterministic policy that chooses the same action for any fixed history. So why is $T_a(n)$ random in this case? The reason is because for all rounds t except for the first, the action A_t depends on the rewards observed in rounds $1, 2, \ldots, t - 1$, which are random, hence A_t will also inherit their randomness. We are now ready to state the second and last lemmas of the chapter. In the statement of the lemma, we use our convention that the dependence of the various quantities involved on the policy π and the environment v is suppressed.

LEMMA 4.5 (Regret decomposition lemma). *For any policy π and stochastic bandit environment v with $\mathcal{A}$ finite or countable and horizon $n \in \mathbb{N}$, the regret R_n of policy π in v satisfies*

$$R_n = \sum_{a \in \mathcal{A}} \Delta_a \mathbb{E}\left[T_a(n)\right]. \tag{4.5}$$

The lemma decomposes the regret in terms of the loss due to using each of the arms. It is useful because it tells us that to keep the regret small, the learner should try to minimise the weighted sum of expected action counts, where the weights are the respective suboptimality gaps, $(\Delta_a)_{a \in \mathcal{A}}$.

Lemma 4.5 tells us that a learner should aim to use an arm with a larger suboptimality gap proportionally fewer times.

Note that the suboptimality gap for optimal arm(s) is zero.

Proof of Lemma 4.5 Since R_n is based on summing over rounds, and the right-hand side of the lemma statement is based on summing over actions, to convert one sum into the other one, we introduce indicators. In particular, note that for any fixed t we have $\sum_{a \in \mathcal{A}} \mathbb{I}\{A_t = a\} = 1$. Hence $S_n = \sum_t X_t = \sum_t \sum_a X_t \mathbb{I}\{A_t = a\}$, and thus

$$R_n = n\mu^* - \mathbb{E}[S_n] = \sum_{a \in \mathcal{A}} \sum_{t=1}^{n} \mathbb{E}\left[(\mu^* - X_t)\mathbb{I}\{A_t = a\}\right]. \tag{4.6}$$

The expected reward in round t conditioned on A_t is μ_{A_t}, which means that

$$
\begin{aligned}
\mathbb{E}\left[(\mu^* - X_t)\mathbb{I}\{A_t = a\} \mid A_t\right] &= \mathbb{I}\{A_t = a\}\mathbb{E}\left[\mu^* - X_t \mid A_t\right] \\
&= \mathbb{I}\{A_t = a\}(\mu^* - \mu_{A_t}) \\
&= \mathbb{I}\{A_t = a\}(\mu^* - \mu_a) \\
&= \mathbb{I}\{A_t = a\}\Delta_a.
\end{aligned}
$$

The result is completed by plugging this into Eq. (4.6) and using the definition of $T_a(n)$. □

The argument fails when $\mathcal{A}$ is uncountable because you cannot introduce the sum over actions. Of course the solution is to use an integral, but for this we need to assume $(\mathcal{A}, \mathcal{G})$ is a measurable space. Given a bandit ν and policy π define measure G on $(\mathcal{A}, \mathcal{G})$ by

$$G(U) = \mathbb{E}\left[\sum_{t=1}^{n} \mathbb{I}\{A_t \in U\}\right],$$

where the expectation is taken with respect to the measure on outcomes induced by the interaction of π and ν.

LEMMA 4.6. *Provided that everything is well defined and appropriately measurable,*

$$R_n = \mathbb{E}\left[\sum_{t=1}^{n} \Delta_{A_t}\right] = \int_{\mathcal{A}} \Delta_a \, dG(a).$$

For those worried about how to ensure everything is well defined, see Section 4.7.

4.6 The Canonical Bandit Model (✦)

In most cases the underlying probability space that supports the random rewards and actions is never mentioned. Occasionally, however, it becomes convenient to choose a specific probability space, which we call the **canonical bandit model**.

Finite Horizon

Let $n \in \mathbb{N}$ be the horizon. A policy and bandit interact to produce the outcome, which is the tuple of random variables $H_n = (A_1, X_1, \ldots, A_n, X_n)$. The first step towards constructing a probability space that carries these random variables is to choose the measurable space. For each $t \in [n]$, let $\Omega_t = ([k] \times \mathbb{R})^t \subset \mathbb{R}^{2t}$ and $\mathcal{F}_t = \mathfrak{B}(\Omega_t)$. The random variables $A_1, X_1, \ldots, A_n, X_n$ that make up the outcome are defined by their coordinate projections:

$$A_t(a_1, x_1, \ldots, a_n, x_n) = a_t \quad \text{and} \quad X_t(a_1, x_1, \ldots, a_n, x_n) = x_t.$$

The probability measure on $(\Omega_n, \mathcal{F}_n)$ depends on both the environment and the policy. Our informal definition of a policy is not quite sufficient now.

DEFINITION 4.7. A **policy** π is a sequence $(\pi_t)_{t=1}^n$, where π_t is a probability kernel from $(\Omega_{t-1}, \mathcal{F}_{t-1})$ to $([k], 2^{[k]})$. Since $[k]$ is discrete, we adopt the notational convention that for $i \in [k]$,

$$\pi_t(i \mid a_1, x_1, \ldots, a_{t-1}, x_{t-1}) = \pi_t(\{i\} \mid a_1, x_1, \ldots, a_{t-1}, x_{t-1}).$$

Let $v = (P_i)_{i=1}^k$ be a stochastic bandit where each P_i is a probability measure on $(\mathbb{R}, \mathfrak{B}(\mathbb{R}))$. We want to define a probability measure on $(\Omega_n, \mathcal{F}_n)$ that respects our understanding of the sequential nature of the interaction between the learner and a stationary stochastic bandit. Since we only care about the law of the random variables (X_t) and (A_t), the easiest way to enforce this is to directly list our expectations, which are

(a) the conditional distribution of action A_t given $A_1, X_1, \ldots, A_{t-1}, X_{t-1}$ is $\pi_t(\cdot \mid A_1, X_1, \ldots, A_{t-1}, X_{t-1})$ almost surely.

(b) the conditional distribution of reward X_t given $A_1, X_1, \ldots, A_t$ is P_{A_t} almost surely.

The sufficiency of these assumptions is asserted by the following proposition, which we ask you to prove in Exercise 4.2.

PROPOSITION 4.8. *Suppose that $\mathbb{P}$ and $\mathbb{Q}$ are probability measures on an arbitrary measurable space $(\Omega, \mathcal{F})$ and $A_1, X_1, \ldots, A_n, X_n$ are random variables on Ω, where $A_t \in [k]$ and $X_t \in \mathbb{R}$. If both $\mathbb{P}$ and $\mathbb{Q}$ satisfy (a) and (b), then the law of the outcome under $\mathbb{P}$ is the same as under $\mathbb{Q}$:*

$$\mathbb{P}_{A_1, X_1, \ldots, A_n, X_n} = \mathbb{Q}_{A_1, X_1, \ldots, A_n, X_n}.$$

Next we construct a probability measure on $(\Omega_n, \mathcal{F}_n)$ that satisfies (a) and (b). To emphasise that what follows is intuitively not complicated, imagine that $X_t \in \{0, 1\}$ is Bernoulli, which means the set of possible outcomes is finite and we can define the measure in terms of a distribution. Let $p_i(0) = P_i(\{0\})$ and $p_i(1) = 1 - p_i(0)$ and define

$$p_{v\pi}(a_1, x_1, \ldots, a_n, x_n) = \prod_{t=1}^n \pi(a_t \mid a_1, x_1, \ldots, a_{t-1}, x_{t-1}) p_{a_t}(x_t).$$

The reader can check that $p_{v\pi}$ is a distribution on $([k] \times \{0, 1\})^n$ and that the associated measure satisfies (a) and (b) above. Making this argument rigourous when (P_i) are not discrete requires the use of Radon–Nikodym derivatives. Let λ be a σ-finite measure on $(\mathbb{R}, \mathfrak{B}(\mathbb{R}))$ for which P_i is absolutely continuous with respect to λ for all i. Next, let $p_i = dP_i/d\lambda$ be the Radon–Nikodym derivative of P_i with respect to λ, which is a function

$p_i : \mathbb{R} \to \mathbb{R}$ such that $\int_B p_i \, d\lambda = P_i(B)$ for all $B \in \mathfrak{B}(\mathbb{R})$. Letting ρ be the counting measure with $\rho(B) = |B|$, the density $p_{v\pi} : \Omega \to \mathbb{R}$ can now be defined with respect to the product measure $(\rho \times \lambda)^n$ by

$$p_{v\pi}(a_1, x_1, \ldots, a_n, x_n) = \prod_{t=1}^{n} \pi(a_t \mid a_1, x_1, \ldots, a_{t-1}, x_{t-1}) p_{a_t}(x_t). \tag{4.7}$$

The reader can again check (more abstractly) that (a) and (b) are satisfied by the probability measure $\mathbb{P}_{v\pi}$ defined by

$$\mathbb{P}_{v\pi}(B) = \int_B p_{v\pi}(\omega)(\rho \times \lambda)^n(d\omega) \qquad \text{for all } B \in \mathcal{F}_n.$$

It is important to emphasise that this choice of $(\Omega_n, \mathcal{F}_n, \mathbb{P}_{v\pi})$ is not unique. Instead, all that this shows is that a suitable probability space does exist. Furthermore, if some quantity of interest depends on the law of H_n, by Proposition 4.8, there is no loss in generality in choosing $(\Omega_n, \mathcal{F}_n, \mathbb{P}_{v\pi})$ as the probability space.

A choice of λ such that $P_i \ll \lambda$ for all i always exists since $\lambda = \sum_{i=1}^{k} P_i$ satisfies this condition. For direct calculations, another choice is usually more convenient, e.g. the counting measure when (P_i) are discrete and the Lebesgue measure for continuous (P_i).

There is another way to define the probability space, which can be useful. Define a collection of independent random variables $(X_{si})_{s \in [n], i \in [k]}$ such that the law of X_{ti} is P_i. By Theorem 2.4 these random variables may be defined on $(\Omega, \mathcal{F})$, where $\Omega = \mathbb{R}^{nk}$ and $\mathcal{F} = \mathfrak{B}(\mathbb{R}^{nk})$. Then let $X_t = X_{tA_t}$, where the actions A_t are $\mathcal{F}_{t-1}$-measurable with $\mathcal{F}_{t-1} = \sigma(A_1, X_1, \ldots, A_{t-1}, X_{t-1})$. We call this the **random table model**. Yet another way is to define $(X_{si})_{s,i}$ as above but let $X_t = X_{T_{A_t}(t), A_t}$. This corresponds to sampling a **stack of rewards** for each arm at the beginning of the game, giving rise to the reward-stack model. Each time the learner chooses an action, they receive the reward on top of the stack. All of these models are convenient from time to time. The important thing is that it does not matter which model we choose because the quantity of ultimate interest (usually the regret) only depends on the law of $A_1, X_1, \ldots, A_n, X_n$, and this is the same for all choices.

Infinite Horizon

We never need the canonical bandit model for the case that $n = \infty$. It is comforting to know, however, that there does exist a probability space $(\Omega, \mathcal{F}, \mathbb{P}_{v\pi})$ and infinite sequences of random variables $X_1, X_2, \ldots$ and $A_1, A_2, \ldots$ satisfying (a) and (b). The result follows directly from the theorem of Ionescu–Tulcea (Theorem 3.3).

4.7 The Canonical Bandit Model for Uncountable Action Sets (✦)

For uncountable action sets, a little more machinery is necessary to make things rigorous. The first requirement is that the action set must be a measurable space $(\mathcal{A}, \mathcal{G})$ and the collection of distribution $\nu = (P_a : a \in \mathcal{A})$ that defines a bandit environment must be a probability kernel from $(\mathcal{A}, \mathcal{G})$ to $(\mathbb{R}, \mathfrak{B}(\mathbb{R}))$. A policy is a sequence $(\pi_t)_{t=1}^n$, where π_t is a probability kernel from $(\Omega_{t-1}, \mathcal{F}_{t-1})$ to $(\mathcal{A}, \mathcal{G})$ with

$$\Omega_t = \prod_{s=1}^t (\mathcal{A} \times \mathbb{R}) \qquad \text{and} \qquad \mathcal{F}_t = \bigotimes_{s=1}^t (\mathcal{G} \otimes \mathfrak{B}(\mathbb{R})).$$

The canonical bandit model is the probability measure $\mathbb{P}_{\nu\pi}$ on $(\Omega_n, \mathcal{F}_n)$ obtained by taking the product of the probability kernels $\pi_1, P_1, \ldots \pi_n, P_n$ and using Ionescu–Tulcea (Theorem 3.3), where P_t is the probability kernel from $(\Omega_{t-1} \times \mathcal{A}, \mathcal{F}_t \otimes \mathcal{G})$ to $(\mathbb{R}, \mathfrak{B}(\mathbb{R}))$ given by $P_t(\cdot \,|\, a_1, x_1, \ldots, a_{t-1}, x_{t-1}, a_t) = P_{a_t}(\cdot)$.

> We did not define $\mathbb{P}_{\nu\pi}$ in terms of a density because there may not exist a common dominating measure for either $(P_a : a \in \mathcal{A})$ or the policy. When such measures exist, as they usually do, then $\mathbb{P}_{\nu\pi}$ may be defined in terms of a density in the same manner as the previous section.

You will check in Exercise 4.5 that the assumptions on ν and π in this section are sufficient to ensure the quantities in Lemma 4.6 are well defined and that Proposition 4.8 continues to hold in this setting without modification. Finally, in none of the definitions above do we require that n be finite.

4.8 Notes

1 It is not obvious why the expected value is a good summary of the reward distribution. Decision makers who base their decisions on expected values are called risk-neutral. In the example shown on the figure above, a risk-averse decision maker may actually prefer the distribution labelled as A because occasionally distribution B may incur a very small (even negative) reward. Risk-seeking decision makers, if they exist at all, would prefer distributions with occasional large rewards to distributions that give mediocre rewards only. There is a formal theory of what makes a decision maker rational (a decision maker in a nutshell is rational if they do not contradict themself). Rational decision makers compare stochastic alternatives based on the alternatives' expected utilities, according to the von-Neumann–Morgenstern utility theorem. Humans are known not to do this. We are irrational. No surprise here.

2 The study of utility and risk has a long history, going right back to (at least) the beginning of probability [Bernoulli, 1954, translated from the original Latin, 1738]. The research can broadly be categorised into two branches. The first deals with describing how people actually make choices (**descriptive theories**), while the second is devoted to characterising how a rational decision maker should make decisions (**prescriptive theories**). A notable example of the former type is 'prospect theory' [Kahneman and Tversky, 1979], which models how people handle probabilities (especially small ones) and earned Daniel Khaneman a Nobel Prize (after the death of his long-time collaborator, Amos Tversky). Further descriptive theories concerned with alternative aspects of human decision-making include bounded rationality, choice strategies, recognition-primed decision-making and image theory [Adelman, 2013].

3 The most famous example of a prescriptive theory is the von Neumann–Morgenstern expected utility theorem, which states that under (reasonable) axioms of rational behaviour under uncertainty,
a rational decision maker must choose amongst alternatives by computing the expected utility
of the outcomes [Neumann and Morgenstern, 1944]. Thus, rational decision makers, under the
chosen axioms, differ only in terms of how they assign utility to outcomes (i.e. rewards). Finance
is another field where attitudes towards uncertainty and risk are important. Markowitz [1952]
argues against expected return as a reasonable metric that investors would use. His argument is
based on the (simple) observation that portfolios maximising expected returns will tend to have a
single stock only (unless there are multiple stocks with equal expected returns, a rather unlikely
outcome). He argues that such a complete lack of diversification is unreasonable. He then proposes
that investors should minimise the variance of the portfolio's return subject to a constraint on
the portfolio's expected return, leading to the so-called **mean-variance optimal portfolio choice
theory**. Under this criteria, portfolios will indeed tend to be diversified (and in a meaningful way:
correlations between returns are taken into account). This theory eventually won him a Nobel
Prize in economics (shared with two others). Closely related to the mean-variance criterion are the
'value-at-risk' (VaR) and the 'conditional value-at-risk', the latter of which has been introduced
and promoted by Rockafellar and Uryasev [2000] due to its superior optimisation properties. The
distinction between the prescriptive and descriptive theories is important: human decision makers
are in many ways violating rules of rationality in their attitudes towards risk.

4 We defined the regret as an expectation, which makes it unusable in conjunction with measures of
risk because the randomness has been eliminated by the expectation. When using a risk measure
in a bandit setting, we can either base this on the **random regret** or **pseudo-regret** defined by

$$\hat{R}_n = n\mu^* - \sum_{t=1}^{n} X_t. \qquad \text{(random regret)}$$

$$\bar{R}_n = n\mu^* - \sum_{t=1}^{n} \mu_{A_t}. \qquad \text{(pseudo-regret)}$$

While $\hat{R}_n$ is influenced by the noise $X_t - \mu_{A_t}$ in the rewards, the pseudo-regret filters this out,
which arguably makes it a better basis for measuring the 'skill' of a bandit policy. As these random
regret measures tend to be highly skewed, using variance to assess risk suffers not only from the
problem of penalising upside risk, but also from failing to capture the skew of the distribution.

5 What happens if the distributions of the arms are changing with time? Such bandits are unimagina-
tively called **non-stationary** bandits. With no assumptions, there is not much to be done. Because
of this, it is usual to assume the distributions change infrequently or drift slowly. We'll eventually
see that techniques for stationary bandits can be adapted to this set-up (see Chapter 31).

6 The rigourous models introduced in Sections 4.6 and 4.7 are easily extended to more sophisticated
settings. For example, the environment sometimes produces side information as well as rewards
or the set of available actions may change with time. You are asked to formalise an example in
Exercise 4.6.

4.9   Bibliographical Remarks

There is now a huge literature on stochastic bandits, much of which we will discuss in detail in the
chapters that follow. The earliest reference that we know of is by Thompson [1933], who proposed an
algorithm that forms the basis of many of the currently practical approaches in use today. Thompson

was a pathologist who published broadly and apparently did not pursue bandits much further. Sadly his approach was not widely circulated, and the algorithm (now called Thompson sampling) did not become popular until very recently. Two decades after Thompson, the bandit problem was formally restated in a short but influential paper by Robbins [1952], an American statistician now most famous for his work on empirical Bayes. Robbins introduced the notion of regret and minimax regret in his 1952 paper. The regret decomposition (Lemma 4.5) has been used in practically every work on stochastic bandits, and its origin is hard to pinpoint. All we can say for sure is that it does *not* appear in the paper by Robbins [1952], but does appear in the work of Lai and Robbins [1985]. Denardo et al. [2007] considers risk in a (complicated) Bayesian setting. Sani et al. [2012] consider a mean-variance approach to risk, while Maillard [2013] considers so-called coherence risk measures (CVaR, is one example of such a risk measure), and with an approach where the regret itself is redefined. VaR is considered in the context of a specific bandit policy family by Audibert et al. [2007, 2009].

4.10   Exercises

4.1 (POSITIVITY OF THE REGRET) Prove Lemma 4.4.

4.2 (UNIQUENESS OF LAW) Prove Proposition 4.8.

4.3 (DEFINITION OF CANONICAL PROBABILITY MEASURE) Prove that the measure defined in terms of the density in Eq. (4.7) satisfies the conditions (a) and (b) in Section 4.6.

HINT   Use the properties of the Radon–Nikodym derivative in combination with Fubini's theorem.

4.4 (MIXING POLICIES) Fix a horizon n and k. Let Π be a finite set of policies for k-armed bandits on horizon n and $p \in \mathcal{P}(\Pi)$ be a distribution over Π. Show there exists a policy π° such that for any k-armed stochastic bandit ν,

$$\mathbb{P}_{\nu\pi^\circ} = \sum_{\pi\in\Pi} p(\pi)\mathbb{P}_{\nu\pi}.$$

Proof   For action/reward sequence $a_1, x_1, \ldots, a_n, x_n$, syntactically abbreviate $h_t = a_1, x_1, \ldots, a_t, x_t$. Then define

$$\pi_t^\circ(a_t \mid h_{t-1}) = \frac{\sum_{\pi\in\Pi} p(\pi) \prod_{s=1}^t \pi_s(a_s \mid h_{s-1})}{\sum_{\pi\in\Pi} p(\pi) \prod_{s=1}^{t-1} \pi_s(a_s \mid h_{s-1})}.$$

By the definition of the canonical probability space and the product of probability kernels,

$$\mathbb{P}_{\nu\pi^\circ}(B) = \sum_{a_1=1}^k \int_{\mathbb{R}} \cdots \sum_{a_n=1}^k \int_{\mathbb{R}} \mathbb{I}_B(h_n)\nu_{a_n}(dx_n)\pi_n^\circ(a_n \mid h_{n-1}) \cdots \nu_{a_1}(dx_1)\pi_1^\circ(a_1)$$

$$= \sum_{\pi\in\Pi} p(\pi) \sum_{a_1=1}^k \int_{\mathbb{R}} \cdots \sum_{a_n=1}^k \int_{\mathbb{R}} \mathbb{I}_B(h_n)\nu_{a_n}(dx_n)\pi_n(a_n \mid h_{n-1}) \cdots \nu_{a_1}(dx_1)\pi_1(a_1)$$

$$= \sum_{\pi\in\Pi} p(\pi)\mathbb{P}_{\nu\pi}(B),$$

where the second equality follows by substituting the definition of π° and induction. $\square$

4.5 (REGRET DECOMPOSITION AND CANONICAL MODEL FOR LARGE ACTION SPACES) Let ν be a bandit on measurable action space $(\mathcal{A}, \mathcal{G})$ and $\pi_1, \ldots, \pi_n$ be a policy satisfying the conditions in Section 4.7.

(a) Show that all quantities in Lemma 4.6 are appropriately defined and measurable.

(b) Prove Lemma 4.6.

(c) Prove that Proposition 4.8 continues to hold.

4.6 (CANONICAL MODEL FOR CONTEXTUAL BANDIT) Let $\mathcal{A}$ and $\mathcal{C}$ be finite sets. A stochastic contextual bandit is like a normal stochastic bandit, but in each round the learner first observes a context $C_t \in \mathcal{C}$. They then choose an action $A_t \in \mathcal{A}$ and receive a reward $X_t \sim P_{A_t, C_t}$.

(a) Suppose that $C_1, \ldots, C_n$ is sampled independently from distribution ξ on $\mathcal{C}$. Construct the canonical probability space that carries $C_1, A_1, X_1, \ldots, C_n, A_n, X_n$.

(b) What changes when C_t is allowed to depend on $C_1, A_1, X_1, \ldots, C_{t-1}, A_{t-1}, X_{t-1}$?

4.7 (BERNOULLI ENVIRONMENT IMPLEMENTATION) Implement a Bernoulli bandit environment in Python using the code snippet below (or adapt to your favourite language).

```
class BernoulliBandit:
    # accepts a list of K >= 2 floats, each lying in [0,1]
    def __init__(self, means):
        pass

    # Function should return the number of arms
    def K(self):
        pass

    # Accepts a parameter 0 <= a <= K-1 and returns the
    # realisation of random variable X with P(X = 1) being
    # the mean of the (a+1)th arm.
    def pull(self, a):
        pass

    # Returns the regret incurred so far.
    def regret(self):
        pass
```

4.8 (FOLLOW-THE-LEADER IMPLEMENTATION) Implement the following simple algorithm called 'follow-the-leader', which chooses each action once and subsequently chooses the action with the largest average observed so far. Ties should be broken randomly.

```
def FollowTheLeader(bandit, n):
    # implement the Follow-the-Leader algorithm by replacing
    # the code below that just plays the first arm in every
        round
    for t in range(n):
        bandit.pull(0)
```

 Depending on the literature you are reading, follow-the-leader may be called 'stay with the winner' or the 'greedy algorithm'.

4.9 Suppose ν is a finite-armed stochastic bandit and π is a policy such that

$$\lim_{n \to \infty} \frac{R_n(\pi, \nu)}{n} = 0.$$

Let $T^*(n) = \sum_{t=1}^{n} \mathbb{I}\{\mu_{A_t} = \mu^*\}$ be the number of times an optimal arm is chosen. Prove or disprove each of the following statements:

(a) $\lim_{n\to\infty} \mathbb{E}[T^*(n)]/n = 1$.

(b) $\lim_{n\to\infty} \mathbb{P}(\Delta_{A_t} > 0) = 0$.

4.10 (ONE-ARMED BANDITS) Let $\mathcal{M}_1$ be a set of distributions on $(\mathbb{R}, \mathfrak{B}(\mathbb{R}))$ with finite means and $\mathcal{M}_2 = \{\delta_{\mu_2}\}$ be the singleton set with a Dirac at $\mu_2 \in \mathbb{R}$. The set of bandits $\mathcal{E} = \mathcal{M}_1 \times \mathcal{M}_2$ is called a **one-armed bandit** because, although there are two arms, the second arm always yields a known reward of μ_2. A policy $\pi = (\pi_t)_t$ is called a **retirement policy** if once action 2 has been played once, it is played until the end of the game. Precisely, if $a_t = 2$, then

$$\pi_{t+1}(2 \mid a_1, x_1, \ldots, a_t, x_t) = 1 \text{ for all } (a_s)_{s=1}^{t-1} \text{ and } (x_s)_{s=1}^{t}.$$

(a) Let n be fixed and $\pi = (\pi_t)_{t=1}^{n}$ be any policy. Prove there exists a retirement policy $\pi' = (\pi'_t)_{t=1}^{n}$ such that for all $\nu \in \mathcal{E}$.

$$R_n(\pi', \nu) \le R_n(\pi, \nu).$$

(b) Let $\mathcal{M}_1 = \{\mathcal{B}(\mu_1) : \mu_1 \in [0, 1]\}$ and suppose that $\pi = (\pi_t)_{t=1}^{\infty}$ is a retirement policy. Prove there exists a bandit $\nu \in \mathcal{E}$ such that

$$\limsup_{n\to\infty} \frac{R_n(\pi, \nu)}{n} > 0.$$

4.11 (FAILURE OF FOLLOW-THE-LEADER (I)) Consider a Bernoulli bandit with two arms and means $\mu_1 = 0.5$ and $\mu_2 = 0.6$.

(a) Using a horizon of $n = 100$, run 1000 simulations of your implementation of follow-the-leader on the Bernoulli bandit above and record the (random) pseudo regret, $n\mu^* - \sum_{t=1}^{n} \mu_{A_t}$, in each simulation.

(b) Plot the results using a histogram. Your figure should resemble Fig. 4.2.

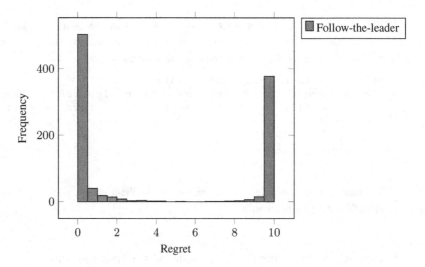

Figure 4.2 Histogram of regret for follow-the-leader over 1000 trials on a Bernoulli bandit with means $\mu_1 = 0.5$, $\mu_2 = 0.6$

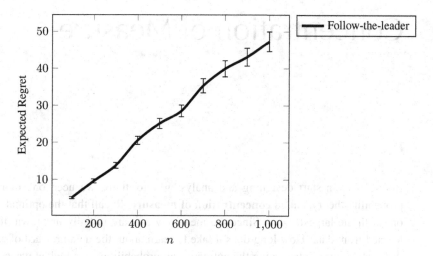

Figure 4.3 The regret for Follow-the-leader over 1000 trials on Bernoulli bandit with means $\mu_1 = 0.5$, $\mu_2 = 0.6$ and horizons ranging from $n = 100$ to $n = 1000$.

(c) Explain the results in the figure.

4.12 (FAILURE OF FOLLOW-THE-LEADER (II)) Consider the same Bernoulli bandit as used in the previous question.

(a) Run 1000 simulations of your implementation of follow-the-leader for each horizon $n \in \{100, 200, 300, \ldots, 1000\}$.

(b) Plot the average regret obtained as a function of n (see Fig. 4.3). Because the average regret is an estimator of the expected regret, you should generally include error bars to indicate the uncertainty in the estimation.

(c) Explain the plot. Do you think follow-the-leader is a good algorithm? Why/why not?

5 Concentration of Measure

Before we can start designing and analysing algorithms, we need one more tool from probability theory, called **concentration of measure**. Recall that the optimal action is the one with the largest mean. Since the mean pay-offs are initially unknown, they must be learned from data. How long does it take to learn about the mean reward of an action? In this section, after introducing the notion of tail probabilities, we look at ways of obtaining upper bounds on them. The main point is to introduce subgaussian random variables and the Cramér–Chernoff exponential tail inequalities, which will play a central role in the design and analysis of the various bandit algorithms.

5.1 Tail Probabilities

Suppose that $X, X_1, X_2, \ldots, X_n$ is a sequence of independent and identically distributed random variables, and assume that the mean $\mu = \mathbb{E}[X]$ and variance $\sigma^2 = \mathbb{V}[X]$ exist. Having observed $X_1, X_2, \ldots, X_n$, we would like to estimate the common mean μ. The most natural estimator is

$$\hat{\mu} = \frac{1}{n} \sum_{i=1}^{n} X_i,$$

which is called the **sample mean** or **empirical mean**. Linearity of expectation (Proposition 2.6) shows that $\mathbb{E}[\hat{\mu}] = \mu$, which means that $\hat{\mu}$ is an **unbiased** estimator of μ. How far from μ do we expect $\hat{\mu}$ to be? A simple measure of the spread of the distribution of a random variable Z is its variance, $\mathbb{V}[Z] = \mathbb{E}\left[(Z - \mathbb{E}[Z])^2\right]$. A quick calculation using independence shows that

$$\mathbb{V}[\hat{\mu}] = \mathbb{E}\left[(\hat{\mu} - \mu)^2\right] = \frac{\sigma^2}{n}, \tag{5.1}$$

which means that we expect the squared distance between μ and $\hat{\mu}$ to shrink as n grows large at a rate of $1/n$ and scale linearly with the variance of X. While the expected squared error is important, it does not tell us very much about the distribution of the error. To do this we usually analyse the probability that $\hat{\mu}$ overestimates or underestimates μ by more than some value $\varepsilon > 0$. Precisely, how do the following quantities depend on ε?

$$\mathbb{P}(\hat{\mu} \geq \mu + \varepsilon) \quad \text{and} \quad \mathbb{P}(\hat{\mu} \leq \mu - \varepsilon).$$

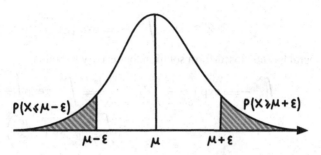

Figure 5.1 The figure shows a probability density, with the tails shaded indicating the regions where X is at least ε away from the mean μ.

The expressions above (as a function of ε) are called the **tail probabilities** of $\hat{\mu} - \mu$ (Fig. 5.1). Specifically, the first is called the upper tail probability and the second the lower tail probability. Analogously, $\mathbb{P}\left(|\hat{\mu} - \mu| \geq \varepsilon\right)$ is called a two-sided tail probability.

5.2 The Inequalities of Markov and Chebyshev

The most straightforward way to bound the tails is by using **Chebyshev's inequality**, which is itself a corollary of **Markov's inequality**. The latter is one of the golden hammers of probability theory, and so we include it for the sake of completeness.

LEMMA 5.1. *For any random variable X and $\varepsilon > 0$, the following holds:*

(a) *(Markov):* $\mathbb{P}\left(|X| \geq \varepsilon\right) \leq \dfrac{\mathbb{E}\left[|X|\right]}{\varepsilon}.$

(b) *(Chebyshev):* $\mathbb{P}\left(|X - \mathbb{E}\left[X\right]| \geq \varepsilon\right) \leq \dfrac{\mathbb{V}\left[X\right]}{\varepsilon^2}.$

We leave the proof of Lemma 5.1 as an exercise for the reader. By combining (5.1) with Chebyshev's inequality, we can bound the two-sided tail directly in terms of the variance by

$$\mathbb{P}\left(|\hat{\mu} - \mu| \geq \varepsilon\right) \leq \frac{\sigma^2}{n\varepsilon^2}. \tag{5.2}$$

This result is nice because it was so easily bought and relied on no assumptions other than the existence of the mean and variance. The downside is that when X is well behaved, the inequality is rather loose. By assuming that higher moments of X exist, Chebyshev's inequality can be improved by applying Markov's inequality to $|\hat{\mu} - \mu|^k$, with the positive integer k to be chosen so that the resulting bound is optimised. This is a bit cumbersome, and thus instead we present the continuous analog of this, known as the Cramér-Chernoff method.

To calibrate our expectations on what improvement to expect relative to Chebyshev's inequality, let us start by recalling the **central limit theorem** (CLT). Let $S_n = \sum_{t=1}^{n}(X_t - \mu)$. The CLT says that under no additional assumptions than the existence of the variance, the limiting distribution of $S_n/\sqrt{n\sigma^2}$ as $n \to \infty$ is a Gaussian with mean zero and unit variance. If $Z \sim \mathcal{N}(0, 1)$, then

$$\mathbb{P}\left(Z \geq u\right) = \int_u^\infty \frac{1}{\sqrt{2\pi}} \exp\left(-\frac{x^2}{2}\right) dx.$$

The integral has no closed-form solution, but is easy to bound:

$$\int_u^\infty \frac{1}{\sqrt{2\pi}} \exp\left(-\frac{x^2}{2}\right) dx \leq \frac{1}{u\sqrt{2\pi}} \int_u^\infty x \exp\left(-\frac{x^2}{2}\right) dx$$

$$= \sqrt{\frac{1}{2\pi u^2}} \exp\left(-\frac{u^2}{2}\right), \tag{5.3}$$

which gives

$$\mathbb{P}\left(\hat{\mu} \geq \mu + \varepsilon\right) = \mathbb{P}\left(S_n/\sqrt{\sigma^2 n} \geq \varepsilon\sqrt{n/\sigma^2}\right) \approx \mathbb{P}\left(Z \geq \varepsilon\sqrt{n/\sigma^2}\right)$$

$$\leq \sqrt{\frac{\sigma^2}{2\pi n \varepsilon^2}} \exp\left(-\frac{n\varepsilon^2}{2\sigma^2}\right). \tag{5.4}$$

This is usually much smaller than what we obtained with Chebyshev's inequality (Exercise 5.3). In particular, the bound on the right-hand side of (5.4) decays slightly faster than the negative exponential of $n\varepsilon^2/\sigma^2$, which means that $\hat{\mu}$ rapidly concentrates around its mean.

> An oft-taught rule of thumb is that the CLT provides a reasonable approximation for $n \geq 30$. We advise caution. Suppose that $X_1, \ldots, X_n$ are independent Bernoulli with bias $p = 1/n$. As n tends to infinity the distribution of $\sum_{t=1}^n X_t$ converges to a Poisson distribution with parameter 1, which does not look Gaussian at all.

The asymptotic nature of the CLT makes it unsuitable for designing bandit algorithms. In the next section, we derive finite-time analogs, which are only possible by making additional assumptions.

5.3   The Cramér-Chernoff Method and Subgaussian Random Variables

For the sake of moving rapidly towards bandits, we start with a straightforward and relatively fundamental assumption on the distribution of X, known as the **subgaussian** assumption.

DEFINITION 5.2 (Subgaussianity). A random variable X is σ-subgaussian if for all $\lambda \in \mathbb{R}$, it holds that $\mathbb{E}\left[\exp(\lambda X)\right] \leq \exp\left(\lambda^2 \sigma^2/2\right)$.

An alternative way to express the subgaussianity condition uses the **moment-generating function** of X, which is a function $M_X : \mathbb{R} \to \mathbb{R}$ defined by $M_X(\lambda) = \mathbb{E}\left[\exp(\lambda X)\right]$. The condition in the definition can be written as

$$\psi_X(\lambda) = \log M_X(\lambda) \leq \frac{1}{2}\lambda^2 \sigma^2 \qquad \text{for all } \lambda \in \mathbb{R}.$$

The function ψ_X is called the **cumulant-generating function**. It is not hard to see that M_X (or ψ_X) need not exist for all random variables over the whole range of real numbers. For example, if X is exponentially distributed and $\lambda \geq 1$, then

$$\mathbb{E}\left[\exp(\lambda X)\right] = \int_0^\infty \underbrace{\exp(-x)}_{\text{density of exponential}} \times \exp(\lambda x)dx = \infty.$$

The moment-generating function of $X \sim \mathcal{N}(0, \sigma^2)$ satisfies $M_X(\lambda) = \exp(\lambda^2 \sigma^2/2)$, and so X is σ-subgaussian.

A random variable X is **heavy tailed** if $M_X(\lambda) = \infty$ for all $\lambda > 0$. Otherwise it is **light tailed**.

The following theorem explains the origin of the term 'subgaussian'. The tails of a σ-subgaussian random variable decay approximately as fast as that of a Gaussian with zero mean and the same variance.

THEOREM 5.3. *If X is σ-subgaussian, then for any $\varepsilon \geq 0$,*

$$\mathbb{P}\left(X \geq \varepsilon\right) \leq \exp\left(-\frac{\varepsilon^2}{2\sigma^2}\right). \tag{5.5}$$

Proof We take a generic approach called the **Cramér–Chernoff method**. Let $\lambda > 0$ be some constant to be tuned later. Then

$$\begin{aligned}
\mathbb{P}\left(X \geq \varepsilon\right) &= \mathbb{P}\left(\exp\left(\lambda X\right) \geq \exp\left(\lambda \varepsilon\right)\right) & \\
&\leq \mathbb{E}\left[\exp\left(\lambda X\right)\right]\exp\left(-\lambda \varepsilon\right) & \text{(Markov's inequality)} \\
&\leq \exp\left(\frac{\lambda^2 \sigma^2}{2} - \lambda \varepsilon\right). & \text{(Def. of subgaussianity)}
\end{aligned}$$

Choosing $\lambda = \varepsilon/\sigma^2$ completes the proof. $\qquad\qquad\square$

A similar inequality holds for the left tail. By using the union bound $\mathbb{P}\left(A \cup B\right) \leq \mathbb{P}\left(A\right) + \mathbb{P}\left(B\right)$, we also find that $\mathbb{P}\left(|X| \geq \varepsilon\right) \leq 2\exp(-\varepsilon^2/(2\sigma^2))$. An equivalent form of these bounds is

$$\mathbb{P}\left(X \geq \sqrt{2\sigma^2 \log(1/\delta)}\right) \leq \delta \qquad \mathbb{P}\left(|X| \geq \sqrt{2\sigma^2 \log(2/\delta)}\right) \leq \delta.$$

This form is often more convenient and especially the latter, which for small δ shows that with overwhelming probability X takes values in the interval

$$\left(-\sqrt{2\sigma^2 \log(2/\delta)}, \ \sqrt{2\sigma^2 \log(2/\delta)}\right).$$

To study the tail behaviour of $\hat{\mu} - \mu$, we need one more lemma.

LEMMA 5.4. *Suppose that X is σ-subgaussian and X_1 and X_2 are independent and σ_1 and σ_2-subgaussian, respectively, then:*

(a) $\mathbb{E}[X] = 0$ *and* $\mathbb{V}\left[X\right] \leq \sigma^2$.
(b) cX *is* $|c|\sigma$-subgaussian for all $c \in \mathbb{R}$.
(c) $X_1 + X_2$ *is* $\sqrt{\sigma_1^2 + \sigma_2^2}$-subgaussian.

The proof of the lemma is left to the reader (Exercise 5.7). Combining Lemma 5.4 and Theorem 5.3 leads to a straightforward bound on the tails of $\hat{\mu} - \mu$.

COROLLARY 5.5. *Assume that $X_i - \mu$ are independent, σ-subgaussian random variables. Then for any $\varepsilon \geq 0$,*

$$\mathbb{P}(\hat{\mu} \geq \mu + \varepsilon) \leq \exp\left(-\frac{n\varepsilon^2}{2\sigma^2}\right) \quad and \quad \mathbb{P}(\hat{\mu} \leq \mu - \varepsilon) \leq \exp\left(-\frac{n\varepsilon^2}{2\sigma^2}\right),$$

where $\hat{\mu} = \frac{1}{n}\sum_{t=1}^{n} X_t$.

Proof By Lemma 5.4, it holds that $\hat{\mu} - \mu = \sum_{i=1}^{n}(X_i - \mu)/n$ is $\sigma/\sqrt{n}$-subgaussian. Then apply Theorem 5.3.   □

For $x > 0$, it holds that $\exp(-x) \leq 1/(ex)$, which shows that the above inequality is stronger than what we obtained via Chebyshev's inequality except when ε is very small. It is exponentially smaller if $n\varepsilon^2$ is large relative to σ^2. The deviation form of the above result says that under the conditions of the result, for any $\delta \in [0, 1]$, with probability at least $1 - \delta$,

$$\mu \leq \hat{\mu} + \sqrt{\frac{2\sigma^2 \log(1/\delta)}{n}}. \tag{5.6}$$

Symmetrically, it also follows that with probability at least $1 - \delta$,

$$\mu \geq \hat{\mu} - \sqrt{\frac{2\sigma^2 \log(1/\delta)}{n}}. \tag{5.7}$$

Again, one can use a union bound to derive a two-sided inequality.

EXAMPLE 5.6. The following random variables are subgaussian:

(a) If X is Gaussian with mean zero and variance σ^2, then X is σ-subgaussian.
(b) If X has mean zero and $|X| \leq B$ almost surely for $B \geq 0$, then X is B-subgaussian.
(c) If X has mean zero and $X \in [a, b]$ almost surely, then X is $(b-a)/2$-subgaussian.

If X is exponentially distributed with rate $\lambda > 0$, then X is not σ-subgaussian for any $\sigma \in \mathbb{R}$.

> For random variables that are not **centred** ($\mathbb{E}[X] \neq 0$), we abuse notation by saying that X is σ-subgaussian if the **noise** $X - \mathbb{E}[X]$ is σ-subgaussian. A distribution is called σ-subgaussian if a random variable drawn from that distribution is σ-subgaussian. Subgaussianity is really a property of both a random variable and the measure on the space on which it is defined, so the nomenclature is doubly abused.

5.4   Notes

1 The Berry–Esseen theorem (independently discovered by Berry [1941] and Esseen [1942]) quantifies the speed of convergence in the CLT. It essentially says that the distance between the Gaussian and the actual distribution decays at a rate of $1/\sqrt{n}$ under some mild assumptions (see Exercise 5.5). This is known to be tight for the class of probability distributions that appear in the

Berry–Esseen result. However, this is a vacuous result when the tail probabilities themselves are much smaller than $1/\sqrt{n}$. Hence the need for concrete finite-time results.

2 Theorem 5.3 shows that subgaussian random variables have tails that decay almost as fast as a Gaussian. A version of the converse is also possible. That is, if a centered random has tails that behave in a similar way to a Gaussian, then it is subgaussian. In particular, the following holds: let X be a centered random variable ($\mathbb{E}[X] = 0$) with $\mathbb{P}(|X| \geq \varepsilon) \leq 2\exp(-\varepsilon^2/2)$. Then X is $\sqrt{5}$-subgaussian:

$$\mathbb{E}[\exp(\lambda X)] = \mathbb{E}\left[\sum_{i=0}^{\infty} \frac{\lambda^i X^i}{i!}\right] \leq 1 + \sum_{i=2}^{\infty} \mathbb{E}\left[\frac{\lambda^i |X|^i}{i!}\right]$$

$$\leq 1 + \sum_{i=2}^{\infty} \int_0^{\infty} \mathbb{P}\left(|X| \geq \frac{i!^{1/i}}{\lambda} x^{1/i}\right) dx \qquad \text{(Exercise 2.19)}$$

$$\leq 1 + 2\sum_{i=2}^{\infty} \int_0^{\infty} \exp\left(-\frac{i!^{2/i} x^{2/i}}{2\lambda^2}\right) dx \qquad \text{(by assumption)}$$

$$= 1 + \sqrt{2\pi}\lambda\left(\exp(\lambda^2/2)\left(1 + \text{erf}\left(\frac{\lambda}{\sqrt{2}}\right)\right) - 1\right) \qquad \text{(by Mathematica)}$$

$$\leq \exp\left(\frac{5\lambda^2}{2}\right).$$

This bound is surely loose. At the same time, there is little room for improvement: if X has density $p(x) = |x|\exp(-x^2/2)/2$, then $\mathbb{P}(|X| \geq \varepsilon) = \exp(-\varepsilon^2/2)$. And yet X is at best $\sqrt{2}$-subgaussian, so some degree of slack is required (see Exercise 5.4).

3 We saw in (5.4) that if $X_1, X_2, \ldots, X_n$ are independent standard Gaussian random variables and $\hat{\mu} = \frac{1}{n}\sum_{t=1}^{n}$, then

$$\mathbb{P}(\hat{\mu} \geq \varepsilon) \leq \sqrt{\frac{\sigma^2}{2\pi n\varepsilon^2}} \exp\left(-\frac{n\varepsilon^2}{2\sigma^2}\right).$$

If $n\varepsilon^2/\sigma^2$ is relatively large, then this bound is marginally stronger than $\exp(-n\varepsilon^2/(2\sigma^2))$, which follows from the subgaussian analysis. One might ask whether or not a similar improvement is possible more generally. And Talagrand [1995] will tell you: yes! At least for bounded random variables (details in the paper).

4 Hoeffding's lemma states that for a zero-mean random variable X such that $X \in [a, b]$ almost surely for real values $a < b$, then $M_X(\lambda) \leq \exp(\lambda^2(b-a)^2/8)$. Applying the Cramér–Chernoff method shows that if $X_1, X_2, \ldots, X_n$ are independent and $X_t \in [a_t, b_t]$ almost surely with $a_t < b_t$ for all t, then

$$\mathbb{P}\left(\frac{1}{n}\sum_{t=1}^{n}(X_t - \mathbb{E}[X_t]) \geq \varepsilon\right) \leq \exp\left(\frac{-2n^2\varepsilon^2}{\sum_{t=1}^{n}(b_t - a_t)^2}\right). \tag{5.8}$$

The above is called **Hoeffding's inequality**. For details see Exercise 5.11. There are many variants of this result that provide tighter bounds when X satisfies certain additional distributional properties like small variance (see Exercise 5.14).

5 The Cramér–Chernoff method is applicable beyond the subgaussian case, even when the moment-generating function is not defined globally. One example where this occurs is when $X_1, X_2, \ldots, X_n$ are independent standard Gaussian and $Y = \sum_{i=1}^{n} X_i^2$. Then Y has a χ^2-distribution with n degrees of freedom. An easy calculation shows that $M_Y(\lambda) = (1 - 2\lambda)^{-n/2}$ for $\lambda \in [0, 1/2)$ and $M_Y(\lambda)$ is undefined for $\lambda \geq 1/2$. By the Cramér–Chernoff method, we have

$$\mathbb{P}(Y \geq n + \varepsilon) \leq \inf_{\lambda \in [0,1/2)} M_\lambda(Y) \exp(-\lambda(n + \varepsilon))$$

$$\leq \inf_{\lambda \in [0,1/2)} \left(\frac{1}{1 - 2\lambda}\right)^{\frac{n}{2}} \exp(-\lambda(n + \varepsilon))$$

Choosing $\lambda = \frac{1}{2} - \frac{n}{2(n+\varepsilon)}$ leads to $\mathbb{P}(Y \geq n + \varepsilon) \leq \left(1 + \frac{\varepsilon}{n}\right)^{\frac{n}{2}} \exp\left(-\frac{\varepsilon}{2}\right)$, which turns out to be about the best you can do [Laurent and Massart, 2000].

6 The subgaussian concept provides a large class of distributions for which concentration is easily analysed. As mentioned, however, many distributions are not subgaussian, like the exponential and χ^2-distribution. There are other general notions based on bounds on the moment generating function that generalise these kinds of distributions. For more on these ideas, you should look for keywords **subexponential** and **subgamma**.

5.5   Bibliographical Remarks

We return to concentration of measure many times, but note here that it is an interesting (and still active) topic of research. What we have seen is only the tip of the iceberg. Readers who want to learn more about this exciting field might enjoy the book by Boucheron et al. [2013]. For matrix versions of many standard results, there is a recent book by Tropp [2015]. The survey of McDiarmid [1998] has many of the classic results. There is a useful type of concentration bound that are 'self-normalised' by the variance. A nice book on this is by de la Peña et al. [2008]. Another tool that is occasionally useful for deriving concentration bounds in more unusual set-ups is called **empirical process theory**. There are several references for this, including those by van de Geer [2000] or Dudley [2014].

5.6   Exercises

There are too many candidate exercises to list. We heartily recommend *all* the exercises in chapter 2 of the book by Boucheron et al. [2013].

5.1 (VARIANCE OF AVERAGE) Let $X_1, X_2, \ldots, X_n$ be a sequence of independent and identically distributed random variables with mean μ and variance $\sigma^2 < \infty$. Let $\hat{\mu} = \frac{1}{n} \sum_{t=1}^n X_t$ and show that $\mathbb{V}[\hat{\mu}] = \mathbb{E}[(\hat{\mu} - \mu)^2] = \sigma^2/n$.

5.2 (MARKOV'S INEQUALITY) Prove Markov's inequality (Lemma 5.1).

5.3 Compare the Gaussian tail probability bound on the right-hand side of (5.4) and the one on (5.2). What values of ε make one smaller than the other? Discuss your findings.

5.4 Let X be a random variable on $\mathbb{R}$ with density with respect to the Lebesgue measure of $p(x) = |x| \exp(-x^2/2)/2$. Show the following:

(a) $\mathbb{P}(|X| \geq \varepsilon) = \exp(-\varepsilon^2/2)$.
(b) X is not $\sqrt{(2 - \varepsilon)}$-subgaussian for any $\varepsilon > 0$.

5.5 (BERRY–ESSEEN INEQUALITY) Let $X_1, X_2, \ldots, X_n$ be a sequence of independent and identically distributed random variables with mean μ, variance σ^2 and bounded third absolute moment:

$$\rho = \mathbb{E}[|X_1 - \mu|^3] < \infty.$$

Let $S_n = \sum_{t=1}^{n}(X_t - \mu)/\sigma$. The Berry–Esseen theorem shows that

$$\sup_x \left| \mathbb{P}\left(\frac{S_n}{\sqrt{n}} \le x\right) - \underbrace{\frac{1}{\sqrt{2\pi}}\int_{-\infty}^{x}\exp(-y^2/2)dy}_{\Phi(x)} \right| \le \frac{C\rho}{\sqrt{n}},$$

where $C < 1/2$ is a universal constant.

(a) Let $\hat\mu_n = \frac{1}{n}\sum_{t=1}^{n} X_t$ and derive a tail bound from the Berry–Esseen theorem. That is, give a bound of the form $\mathbb{P}(\hat\mu_n \ge \mu + \varepsilon)$ for positive values of ε.

(b) Compare your bound with the one that can be obtained from the Cramér–Chernoff method. Argue pro- and contra- for the superiority of one over the other.

5.6 (CENTRAL LIMIT THEOREM) We mentioned that invoking the CLT to approximate the distribution of sums of independent Bernoulli random variables using a Gaussian can be a bad idea. Let $X_1, \ldots, X_n \sim \mathcal{B}(p)$ be independent Bernoulli random variables with common mean $p = p_n = \lambda/n$, where $\lambda \in (0,1)$. For $x \in \mathbb{N}$ natural number, let $P_n(x) = \mathbb{P}(X_1 + \cdots + X_n = x)$.

(a) Show that $\lim_{n\to\infty} P_n(x) = e^{-\lambda}\lambda^x/(x!)$, which is a Poisson distribution with parameter λ.

(b) Explain why this does not contradict the CLT, and discuss the implications of the Berry–Esseen.

(c) In what way does this show that the CLT is indeed a poor approximation in some cases?

(d) Based on Monte Carlo simulations, plot the distribution of $X_1 + \cdots + X_n$ for $n = 30$ and some well-chosen values of λ. Compare the distribution to what you would get from the CLT. What can you conclude?

5.7 (PROPERTIES OF SUBGAUSSIAN RANDOM VARIABLES (I)) Prove Lemma 5.4.

HINT   Use Taylor series.

5.8 (PROPERTIES OF SUBGAUSSIAN RANDOM VARIABLES (II)) Let X_i be σ_i-subgaussian for $i \in \{1, 2\}$ with $\sigma_i \ge 0$. Prove that $X_1 + X_2$ is $(\sigma_1 + \sigma_2)$-subgaussian. Do *not* assume independence of X_1 and X_2.

5.9 (PROPERTIES OF MOMENT/CUMULATIVE-GENERATING FUNCTIONS) Let X be a real-valued random variable and let $M_X(\lambda) = \mathbb{E}[\exp(\lambda X)]$ be its moment-generating function defined over $\mathrm{dom}(M_X) \subset \mathbb{R}$, where the expectation takes on finite values. Show that the following properties hold:

(a) M_X is convex, and in particular $\mathrm{dom}(M_X)$ is an interval containing zero.

(b) $M_X(\lambda) \ge e^{\lambda \mathbb{E}[X]}$ for all $\lambda \in \mathrm{dom}(M_X)$.

(c) For any λ in the interior of $\mathrm{dom}(M_X)$, M_X is infinitely many times differentiable.

(d) Let $M_X^{(k)}(\lambda) = \frac{d^k}{d\lambda^k}M_X(\lambda)$. Then, for λ in the interior of $\mathrm{dom}(M_X)$, $M^{(k)}(\lambda) = \mathbb{E}[X^k \exp(\lambda X)]$.

(e) Assuming 0 is in the interior of $\mathrm{dom}(M_X)$, $M_X^{(k)}(0) = \mathbb{E}[X^k]$ (hence the name of M_X).

(f) ψ_X is convex (that is, M_X is log-convex).

HINT   For part (a), use the convexity of $x \mapsto e^x$.

5.10 (LARGE DEVIATION THEORY) Let $X, X_1, X_2, \ldots, X_n$ be a sequence of independent and identically distributed random variables with zero mean and moment-generating function M_X with $\mathrm{dom}(M_X) = \mathbb{R}$. Let $\hat\mu_n = \frac{1}{n}\sum_{t=1}^{n} X_t$.

(a) Show that for any $\varepsilon > 0$,

$$\frac{1}{n} \log \mathbb{P} \left(\hat{\mu}_n \geq \varepsilon \right) \leq -\psi_X^*(\varepsilon) = -\sup_{\lambda} \left(\lambda \varepsilon - \log M_X(\lambda) \right). \tag{5.9}$$

(b) Show that when X is a Rademacher variable ($\mathbb{P}(X = -1) = \mathbb{P}(X = 1) = 1/2$), $\psi_X^*(\varepsilon) = \frac{1+\varepsilon}{2} \log(1 + \varepsilon) + \frac{1-\varepsilon}{2} \log(1 - \varepsilon)$ when $|\varepsilon| < 1$ and $\psi_X^*(\varepsilon) = +\infty$, otherwise.

(c) Show that when X is a centered Bernoulli random variable with parameter p (that is, $\mathbb{P}(X = -p) = 1 - p$ and $\mathbb{P}(X = 1 - p) = p$) then $\psi_X^*(\varepsilon) = \infty$ when ε is such that $p + \varepsilon > 1$ and $\psi_X^*(\varepsilon) = d(p + \varepsilon, p)$ otherwise, where $d(p, q) = p \log(p/q) + (1 - p) \log((1 - p)/(1 - q))$ is the relative entropy between the distributions $\mathcal{B}(p)$ and $\mathcal{B}(q)$.

(d) Show that when $X \sim \mathcal{N}(0, \sigma^2)$ then $\psi_X^*(\varepsilon) = \varepsilon^2/(2\sigma^2)$.

(e) Let $\sigma^2 = \mathbb{V}[X]$. The (strong form of the) central limit theorem says that

$$\lim_{n \to \infty} \sup_{x \in \mathbb{R}} \left| \mathbb{P} \left(\hat{\mu}_n \sqrt{\frac{n}{\sigma^2}} \geq x \right) - (1 - \Phi(x)) \right| = 0,$$

where $\Phi(x) = \frac{1}{\sqrt{2\pi}} \int_{-\infty}^{x} \exp(-y^2/2) dy$ is the cumulative distribution of the standard Gaussian. Let Z be a random variable distributed like a standard Gaussian. A careless application of this result might suggest that

$$\lim_{n \to \infty} \frac{1}{n} \log \mathbb{P} \left(\hat{\mu}_n \geq \varepsilon \right) \stackrel{?}{=} \lim_{n \to \infty} \frac{1}{n} \log \mathbb{P} \left(Z \geq \varepsilon \sqrt{\frac{n}{\sigma^2}} \right).$$

Evaluate the right-hand side. In light of the previous parts, what can you conclude about the validity of the question-marked equality? What goes wrong with the careless application of the central limit theorem? What do you conclude about the accuracy of this theorem?

HINT For Part ((e)), consider using Eq. (13.4).

As it happens, the inequality in (5.9) may be replaced by an equality as $n \to \infty$. The assumption that the moment-generating function exists everywhere may be relaxed significantly. We refer the interested reader to the classic text by Dembo and Zeitouni [2009]. The function ψ_X^* is called the **Legendre transform, convex conjugate** or **Fenchel dual** of the convex function ψ_X. In probability theory, ψ_X^* is also called the **Cramér transform** and is also known as a **rate function**. Convexity and the Fenchel dual will play a role in some of the later chapters and will be discussed in more detail in Chapter 26 and later.

The name "large deviation" originates from rewriting the tail probabilities in terms of the partial sum $S_n = X_1 + \cdots + X_n$, we see that the inequality in (5.9) bounds the probability of the deviation of S_n from its mean (which is zero by assumption) at a scale of $\Theta(n)$: $\mathbb{P}(\hat{\mu}_n \geq \varepsilon) = \mathbb{P}(S_n \geq n\varepsilon)$. In contrast, the central-limit theorem (CLT) gives the (limiting) probability of the deviation of S_n from its mean at the scales of $\Theta(\sqrt{n})$: $\mathbb{P}(\hat{\mu}_n \sqrt{n} \geq \varepsilon) = \mathbb{P}(S_n \geq \sqrt{n}\varepsilon)$. Compared to $\sqrt{n}\varepsilon$, $n\varepsilon$ is thought of as a "large" deviation. The deviation probabilities at this scale can decay to zero faster than what the CLT predicts, as also showcased in the last part of the last exercise. But what happens at intermediate scales? That is, when deviations are of size $n^\alpha \varepsilon$ with $1/2 < \alpha < n$? This is studied on the formulaic name of moderate deviations. As it turns out, in this case, the ruthless use of the large deviation formula gives correct answers. The reader who wants to learn more about large deviation theory can check out the lecture notes by Swart [2017].

5.11 (HOEFFDING'S LEMMA) Suppose that X is zero mean and $X \in [a, b]$ almost surely for constants $a < b$.

(a) Show that X is $(b - a)/2$-subgaussian.
(b) Prove Hoeffding's inequality (5.8).

HINT   For part (a), it suffices to prove that $\psi_X(\lambda) \leq \lambda^2(b-a)^2/4$. By Taylor's theorem, for some λ' between 0 and λ, $\psi_X(\lambda) = \psi_X(0) + \psi'_X(0)\lambda + \psi''_X(\lambda')\lambda^2/2$. To bound the last term, introduce the distribution P_λ for $\lambda \in \mathbb{R}$ arbitrary: $P_\lambda(dz) = e^{-\psi_X(\lambda)}e^{\lambda z}P(dz)$. Show that $\Psi''_X(\lambda) = \mathbb{V}[Z]$, where $Z \sim P_\lambda$. Now, since $Z \in [a, b]$ with probability one, argue (without relying on $\mathbb{E}[Z]$) that $\mathbb{V}[Z] \leq (b-a)^2/4$.

5.12 (SUBGAUSSIANITY OF BERNOULLI DISTRIBUTION) Let X be a random variable with Bernoulli distribution with mean p. That is $X \sim \mathcal{B}(p)$: $\mathbb{P}(X = 1) = p$ and $\mathbb{P}(X = 0) = 1 - p$.

(a) Show that X is $1/2$-subgaussian for all p.
(b) Let $Q : [0, 1] \to [0, 1/2]$ be the function given by $Q(p) = \sqrt{\frac{1-2p}{2\ln((1-p)/p)}}$ where undefined points are defined in terms of their limits. Show that X is $Q(p)$-subgaussian.
(c) The subgaussianity constant of a random variable X is the smallest value of σ such that X is σ-subgaussian. Show that the subgaussianity constant of $X \sim \mathcal{B}(p)$ is $Q(p)$.
(d) Plot $Q(p)$ as a function of p. How does it compare to $\sqrt{\mathbb{V}[X]} = \sqrt{p(1-p)}$?
(e) Show that for $\lambda \geq 0$ and $p \geq 1/2$, $\mathbb{E}\exp(\lambda X) \leq \exp(p(1-p)\lambda^2/2)$. Think of how these inequalities are used for bounding tails. What do you conclude?

Readers looking for a hint to parts (b), (c) and (e) in the previous exercise might like to look at the papers by Berend and Kontorovich [2013] and Ostrovsky and Sirota [2014]. The result that the subgaussianity constant of $X \sim \mathcal{B}(p)$ is upper bounded by $Q(p)$ is known as the Kearn-Saul inequality and is due to Kearns and Saul [1998].

5.13 (CENTRAL LIMIT THEOREM FOR SUMS OF BERNOULLI RANDOM VARIABLES) In this question we try to understand the concentration of the empirical mean for Bernoulli random variables. Let $X_1, X_2, \ldots, X_n$ be independent Bernoulli random variables with mean $p \in [0, 1]$ and $\hat{p}_n = \sum_{t=1}^{n} X_t/n$. Let Z_n be normally distributed random variable with mean p and variance $p(1-p)/n$.

(a) Write down expressions for $\mathbb{E}[\hat{p}_n]$ and $\mathbb{V}[\hat{p}_n]$.
(b) What does the central limit theorem say about the relationship between $\hat{p}_n$ and Z_n as n gets large?
(c) For each $p \in \{1/10, 1/2\}$ and $\delta = 1/100$ and $\Delta = 1/10$, find the minimum n such that $\mathbb{P}(\hat{p}_n \geq p + \Delta) \leq \delta$.
(d) Let $p = 1/10$ and $\Delta = 1/10$ and

$$n_{\text{Ber}}(\delta, p, \Delta) = \min\{n : \mathbb{P}(\hat{p}_n \geq p + \Delta) \leq \delta\},$$
$$n_{\text{Gauss}}(\delta, p, \Delta) = \min\{n : \mathbb{P}(Z_n \geq p + \Delta) \leq \delta\}.$$

(i) Evaluate analytically the value of

$$\lim_{\delta \to 0} \frac{n_{\text{Ber}}(\delta, 1/10, 1/10)}{n_{\text{Gauss}}(\delta, 1/10, 1/10)}.$$

(ii) In light of the central limit theorem, explain why the answer you got in (i) was not 1.

HINT For Part (d.i) use large deviation theory (Exercise 5.10).

5.14 (BERNSTEIN'S INEQUALITY) Let $X_1, \ldots, X_n$ be a sequence of independent random variables with $X_t - \mathbb{E}[X_t] \leq b$ almost surely and $S = \sum_{t=1}^{n}(X_t - \mathbb{E}[X_t])$ and $v = \sum_{t=1}^{n} \mathbb{V}[X_t]$.

(a) Show that $g(x) = \frac{1}{2} + \frac{x}{3!} + \frac{x^2}{4!} + \cdots = (\exp(x) - 1 - x)/x^2$ is increasing.

(b) Let X be a random variable with $\mathbb{E}[X] = 0$ and $X \leq b$ almost surely. Show that $\mathbb{E}[\exp(X)] \leq 1 + g(b)\mathbb{V}[X]$.

(c) Prove that $(1 + \alpha)\log(1 + \alpha) - \alpha \geq \frac{3\alpha^2}{6+2\alpha}$ for all $\alpha \geq 0$. Prove that this is the best possible approximation in the sense that the 2 in the denominator cannot be increased.

(d) Let $\varepsilon > 0$ and $\alpha = b\varepsilon/v$ and prove that

$$\mathbb{P}(S \geq \varepsilon) \leq \exp\left(-\frac{v}{b^2}\left((1+\alpha)\log(1+\alpha) - \alpha\right)\right) \tag{5.10}$$

$$\leq \exp\left(-\frac{\varepsilon^2}{2v\left(1 + \frac{b\varepsilon}{3v}\right)}\right). \tag{5.11}$$

(e) Use the previous result to show that

$$\mathbb{P}\left(S \geq \sqrt{2v\log\left(\frac{1}{\delta}\right)} + \frac{2b}{3}\log\left(\frac{1}{\delta}\right)\right) \leq \delta.$$

(f) Let be $X_1, X_2, \ldots, X_n$ be a sequence of random variables adapted to filtration $\mathbb{F} = (\mathcal{F}_t)_t$. Abbreviate $\mathbb{E}_t[\cdot] = \mathbb{E}[\cdot \mid \mathcal{F}_t]$ and $\mu_t = \mathbb{E}_{t-1}[X_t]$. Define $S = \sum_{t=1}^{n} X_t - \mu_t$ and let $V = \sum_{t=1}^{n} \mathbb{E}_{t-1}[(X_t - \mu_t)^2]$ be the predictable variation of $(\sum_{t=1}^{p} X_t - \mu_t)_p$. Show that if $X_t - \mu_t \leq b$ holds almost surely for all $t \in [n]$ then with $\alpha = b\varepsilon/v$,

$$\mathbb{P}(S \geq \varepsilon, V \leq v) \leq \exp\left(-\frac{v}{b^2}\left((1+\alpha)\log(1+\alpha) - \alpha\right)\right).$$

Note that the right-hand side of this inequality is the same as that shown in Eq. (5.10).

The bound in Eq. (5.10) is called **Bennett's inequality** and the one in Eq. (5.11) is called **Bernstein's inequality**. There are several generalisations, the most notable of which is the martingale version that slightly relaxes the independence assumption and which was presented in Part (f). Martingale techniques appear in Chapter 20. Another useful variant (under slightly different conditions) replaces the actual variance with the empirical variance. This is useful when the variance is unknown. For more, see the papers by Audibert et al. [2007], Mnih et al. [2008], Maurer and Pontil [2009].

5.15 (ANOTHER BERNSTEIN-TYPE INEQUALITY) Let $X_1, X_2, \ldots, X_n$ be a sequence of random variables adapted to the filtration $\mathbb{F} = (\mathcal{F}_t)_t$. Abbreviate $\mathbb{E}_t[\cdot] = \mathbb{E}[\cdot \mid \mathcal{F}_t]$ and $\mu_t = \mathbb{E}_{t-1}[X_t]$. Prove the following

(a) If $\eta > 0$ and $\eta(X_t - \mu_t) \leq 1$ almost surely, then

$$\mathbb{P}\left(\sum_{t=1}^{n}(X_t - \mu_t) \geq \eta \sum_{t=1}^{n} \mathbb{E}_{t-1}[(X_t - \mu_t)^2] + \frac{1}{\eta}\log\left(\frac{1}{\delta}\right)\right) \leq \delta.$$

(b) If $\eta > 0$ and $\eta X_t \le 1$ almost surely, then

$$\mathbb{P}\left(\sum_{t=1}^{n}(X_t - \mu_t) \ge \eta \sum_{t=1}^{n} \mathbb{E}_{t-1}[X_t^2] + \frac{1}{\eta} \log\left(\frac{1}{\delta}\right)\right) \le \delta.$$

HINT   Use the Cramér–Chernoff method and the fact that $\exp(x) \le 1 + x + x^2$ for all $x \le 1$ and $\exp(x) \ge 1 + x$ for all x.

Let (M_t) be the martingale defined by $M_t = \sum_{s=1}^{t}(X_s - \mu_s)$. The inequalities in Exercise 5.15 can be viewed as a kind of Bernstein's inequality because they bound the tail of the martingale (M_t) in terms of the **predictable variation** of the martingale (M_t), which is $V = \sum_{t=1}^{n} \mathbb{E}_{t-1}[(X_t - \mu_t)^2]$. The main difference relative to well-known results is that the analysis has stopped early. The next step is usually to choose η to minimise the bound in some sense. Either by assuming bounds on the predictable variation, union bounding or using the method of mixtures [de la Peña et al., 2008]. These techniques are covered in Chapter 20. Note, optimising η directly is not possible because the bounds hold for any fixed η, but minimising the right-hand side inside the probability with respect to η would lead to a random η. For more martingale results with this flavour, see the notes by McDiarmid [1998].

5.16 Let $X_1, \ldots, X_n$ be independent random variables with $\mathbb{P}(X_t \le x) \le x$ for each $x \in [0, 1]$ and $t \in [n]$. Prove for any $\varepsilon > 0$ that

$$\mathbb{P}\left(\sum_{t=1}^{n} \log(1/X_t) \ge \varepsilon\right) \le \left(\frac{\varepsilon}{n}\right)^n \exp(n - \varepsilon).$$

5.17 (CONCENTRATION FOR CATEGORICAL DISTRIBUTIONS) Let $X_1, \ldots, X_n$ be an independent and identically distributed sequence taking values in $[m]$. For $i \in [m]$, let $p(i) = \mathbb{P}(X_1 = i)$ and $\hat{p}(i) = \frac{1}{n}\sum_{t=1}^{n} \mathbb{I}\{X_t = i\}$. Show that for any $\delta \in (0, 1)$,

$$\mathbb{P}\left(\|p - \hat{p}\|_1 \ge \sqrt{\frac{2\left[\log\left(\frac{1}{\delta}\right) + m \log(2)\right]}{n}}\right) \le \delta. \tag{5.12}$$

HINT   Use the fact that $\|p - \hat{p}\|_1 = \max_{\lambda \in \{-1,1\}^m} \langle \lambda, p - \hat{p}\rangle$.

5.18 (EXPECTATION OF MAXIMUM) Let $X_1, \ldots, X_n$ be a sequence of σ-subgaussian random variables (possibly dependent) and $Z = \max_{t \in [n]} X_t$. Prove that

(a) $\mathbb{E}[Z] \le \sqrt{2\sigma^2 \log(n)}$.
(b) $\mathbb{P}\left(Z \ge \sqrt{2\sigma^2 \log(n/\delta)}\right) \le \delta$ for any $\delta \in (0, 1)$.

HINT   Use Jensen's inequality to show that $\exp(\lambda \mathbb{E}[Z]) \le \mathbb{E}[\exp(\lambda Z)]$, and then provide a naive bound on the moment-generating function of Z.

5.19 (ALMOST SURELY BOUNDED SUMS) Let $X_1, X_2, \ldots, X_n$ be a sequence of non-negative random variables adapted to filtration $(\mathcal{F}_t)_{t=0}^{n}$ such that $\sum_{t=1}^{n} X_t \le 1$ almost surely. Prove that for all $x > 1$,

$$\mathbb{P}\left(\sum_{t=1}^{n} \mathbb{E}[X_t \mid \mathcal{F}_{t-1}] \ge x\right) \le f_n(x) \doteq \begin{cases} \left(\frac{n-x}{n-1}\right)^{n-1}, & \text{if } x < n; \\ 0, & \text{if } x \ge n, \end{cases}$$

where the equality serves as the definition of $f_n(x)$.

HINT   This problem does not use the techniques introduced in the chapter. Prove that Bernoulli random variables are the worst case and use backwards induction. Although this result is new to our knowledge, a weaker version was derived by Kirschner and Krause [2018] for the analysis of information-directed sampling. The bound is tight in the sense that there exists a sequence of random variables and filtration for which equality holds.

Part II
Stochastic Bandits with Finitely Many Arms

Over the next few chapters, we introduce the fundamental algorithms and tools of analysis for unstructured stochastic bandits with finitely many actions. The keywords here are finite, unstructured and stochastic. The first of these just means that the number of actions available is finite. The second is more ambiguous, but roughly means that choosing one action yields no information about the mean pay-off of the other arms. A bandit is stochastic if the sequence of rewards associated with each action is independent and identically distributed according to some distribution. This latter assumption will be relaxed in Part III.

There are several reasons to study this class of bandit problems. First, their simplicity makes them relatively easy to analyse and permits a deep understanding of the trade-off between exploration and exploitation. Second, many of the algorithms designed for finite-armed bandits, and the principle underlying them, can be generalised to other settings. Finally, finite-armed bandits already have applications – notably as a replacement to A/B testing, as discussed in the introduction.

6 The Explore-Then-Commit Algorithm

The first bandit algorithm of the book is called **explore-then-commit** (ETC), which explores by playing each arm a fixed number of times and then exploits by committing to the arm that appeared best during exploration.

> For this chapter, as well as Chapters 7 to 9, we assume that all bandit instances are in $\mathcal{E}_{SG}^{k}(1)$, which means the reward distribution for all arms is 1-subgaussian.

The focus on subgaussian distributions is mainly for simplicity. Many of the techniques in the chapters that follow can be applied to other stochastic bandits such as those listed in Table 4.1. The key difference is that new concentration analysis is required that exploits the different assumptions. The Bernoulli case is covered in Chapter 10, where other situations are discussed along with references to the literature. Notice that the subgaussian assumption restricts the subgaussian constant to $\sigma = 1$, which saves us from endlessly writing σ. All results hold for other subgaussian constants by scaling the rewards (see Lemma 5.4). Two points are obscured by this simplification:

(a) All the algorithms that follow rely on the knowledge of σ.

(b) It may happen that P_i is subgaussian for all arms, but with a different subgaussian constant for each arm. Algorithms are easily adapted to this situation if the subgaussian constants are known, as you will investigate in Exercise 7.2. The situation is more complicated when the subgaussian constant is unknown (Exercise 7.7).

6.1 Algorithm and Regret Analysis

ETC is characterised by the number of times it explores each arm, denoted by a natural number m. Because there are k actions, the algorithm will explore for mk rounds before choosing a single action for the remaining rounds. Let $\hat{\mu}_i(t)$ be the average reward received from arm i after round t, which is written formally as

$$\hat{\mu}_i(t) = \frac{1}{T_i(t)} \sum_{s=1}^{t} \mathbb{I}\{A_s = i\} X_s,$$

where $T_i(t) = \sum_{s=1}^{t} \mathbb{I}\{A_s = i\}$ is the number of times action i has been played after round t. The ETC policy is given in Algorithm 1 below.

1: **Input** m.
2: In round t choose action

$$A_t = \begin{cases} (t \bmod k) + 1, & \text{if } t \leq mk; \\ \text{argmax}_i \ \hat{\mu}_i(mk), & t > mk. \end{cases}$$

(ties in the argmax are broken arbitrarily)

Algorithm 1: Explore-then-commit.

Recall that μ_i is the mean reward when playing action i and $\Delta_i = \mu^* - \mu_i$ is suboptimality gap between the mean of action i and the optimal action.

THEOREM 6.1. *When ETC is interacting with any 1-subgaussian bandit and $1 \leq m \leq n/k$,*

$$R_n \leq m \sum_{i=1}^{k} \Delta_i + (n - mk) \sum_{i=1}^{k} \Delta_i \exp\left(-\frac{m\Delta_i^2}{4}\right).$$

Proof Assume without loss of generality that the first arm is optimal, which means that $\mu_1 = \mu^* = \max_i \mu_i$. By the decomposition given in Lemma 4.5, the regret can be written as

$$R_n = \sum_{i=1}^{k} \Delta_i \mathbb{E}\left[T_i(n)\right]. \tag{6.1}$$

In the first mk rounds, the policy is deterministic, choosing each action exactly m times. Subsequently it chooses a single action maximising the average reward during exploration. Thus,

$$\mathbb{E}\left[T_i(n)\right] = m + (n - mk)\mathbb{P}\left(A_{mk+1} = i\right)$$

$$\leq m + (n - mk)\mathbb{P}\left(\hat{\mu}_i(mk) \geq \max_{j \neq i} \hat{\mu}_j(mk)\right). \tag{6.2}$$

The probability on the right-hand side is bounded by

$$\mathbb{P}\left(\hat{\mu}_i(mk) \geq \max_{j \neq i} \hat{\mu}_j(mk)\right) \leq \mathbb{P}\left(\hat{\mu}_i(mk) \geq \hat{\mu}_1(mk)\right)$$

$$= \mathbb{P}\left(\hat{\mu}_i(mk) - \mu_i - (\hat{\mu}_1(mk) - \mu_1) \geq \Delta_i\right).$$

The next step is to check that $\hat{\mu}_i(mk) - \mu_i - (\hat{\mu}_1(mk) - \mu_1)$ is $\sqrt{2/m}$-subgaussian, which by the properties of subgaussian random variables follows from the definitions of $(\hat{\mu}_j)_j$ and the algorithm. Hence by Corollary 5.5,

$$\mathbb{P}\left(\hat{\mu}_i(mk) - \mu_i - \hat{\mu}_1(mk) + \mu_1 \geq \Delta_i\right) \leq \exp\left(-\frac{m\Delta_i^2}{4}\right). \tag{6.3}$$

Substituting Eq. (6.3) into Eq. (6.2) and the regret decomposition (Eq. (6.1)) gives the result.
□

The bound in Theorem 6.1 illustrates the trade-off between exploration and exploitation. If m is large, then the policy explores for too long, and the first term will be large. On the other hand, if m is too small, then the probability that the algorithm commits to the wrong arm will grow, and the second term becomes large. The question is how to choose

m. Assume that $k = 2$ and that the first arm is optimal so that $\Delta_1 = 0$, and abbreviate $\Delta = \Delta_2$. Then the bound in Theorem 6.1 simplifies to

$$R_n \leq m\Delta + (n - 2m)\Delta \exp\left(-\frac{m\Delta^2}{4}\right) \leq m\Delta + n\Delta \exp\left(-\frac{m\Delta^2}{4}\right). \qquad (6.4)$$

For large n the quantity on the right-hand side of Eq. (6.4) is minimised up to a possible rounding error by

$$m = \max\left\{1, \left\lceil \frac{4}{\Delta^2} \log\left(\frac{n\Delta^2}{4}\right) \right\rceil\right\}, \qquad (6.5)$$

and for this choice and any n, the regret is bounded by

$$R_n \leq \min\left\{n\Delta, \Delta + \frac{4}{\Delta}\left(1 + \max\left\{0, \log\left(\frac{n\Delta^2}{4}\right)\right\}\right)\right\}. \qquad (6.6)$$

In Exercise 6.2 you will show that Eq. (6.6) implies that

$$R_n \leq \Delta + C\sqrt{n}, \qquad (6.7)$$

where $C > 0$ is a universal constant. In particular, when $\Delta \leq 1$ as is often assumed, we get

$$R_n \leq 1 + C\sqrt{n},$$

Bounds of this type are called **worst-case, problem free** or **problem independent** (see Eq. (4.2) or Eq. (4.3)). The reason is that the bound only depends on the horizon and class of bandits for which the algorithm is designed, and not the specific instance within that class. Because the suboptimality gap does not appear, bounds like this are sometimes called **gap-free**. In contrast, bounds like the one in Eq. (6.6) are called **gap/problem/distribution/instance dependent**.

Note that without the condition $\Delta \leq 1$, the worst-case bound for ETC is infinite. In fact, without a bound on the reward range, the worst-case bound of all reasonable algorithms (that try each action at least once) will also be infinite. With the understanding that Eq. (6.7) gives rise to a meaningful worst-case bound for bandits with bounded reward range, we take the liberty and will also call bounds like that in Eq. (6.7) a worst-case bound.

The bound in (6.6) is close to optimal (see Part IV), but there is a caveat. The choice of m that defines the policy and leads to this bound depends on both the suboptimality gap and the horizon. While the horizon is sometimes known in advance, it is seldom reasonable to assume knowledge of the suboptimality gap. You will show in Exercise 6.5 that there is a choice of m depending only on n, for which $R_n = O(n^{2/3})$ regardless of the value of Δ. Alternatively, the number of plays before commitment can be made data dependent, which means the learner plays arms alternately until it decides based on its observations to commit to a single arm for the remainder (Exercise 6.5). ETC also has the property that its immediate expected regret per time step is monotonically decreasing as time goes by, though not in a nice smooth fashion. This monotone decreasing property is a highly desirable property. In later chapters we will see policies where the decrease is smoother.

 EXPERIMENT 6.1   Fig. 6.1 shows the expected regret of ETC when playing a Gaussian bandit with $k = 2$ and means $\mu_1 = 0$ and $\mu_2 = -\Delta$. The horizon is set to $n = 1000$, and the suboptimality gap Δ is varied between 0 and 1. Each data point is the average of

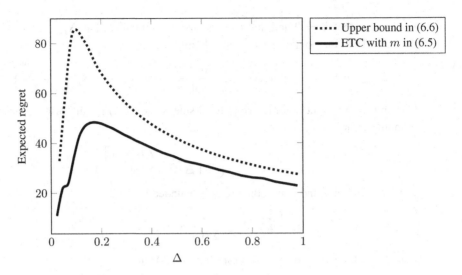

Figure 6.1   The expected regret of ETC and the upper bound in Eq. (6.6).

10^5 simulations, which makes the error bars invisible. The results show that the theoretical upper bound provided by Theorem 6.1 is quite close to the actual performance.

6.2   Notes

1 An algorithm is called **anytime** if it does not require advance knowledge of the horizon n. ETC is not anytime because the choice of commitment time depends on the horizon. This limitation can be addressed by the **doubling trick**, which is a simple way to convert a horizon-dependent algorithm into an anytime algorithm (Exercise 6.6).

2 By allowing the exploration time m to be a data-dependent random variable, it is possible to recover near-optimal regret without knowing the suboptimality gap. For more details see Exercise 6.5. Another idea is to use an **elimination algorithm** that acts in phases and eliminates arms using increasingly sensitive hypothesis tests (Exercise 6.8). Elimination algorithms are often easy to analyse and can work well in practice, but they also have inherent limitations, just like ETC algorithms, as will be commented on later.

3 The ε-greedy algorithm is a randomised relative of ETC that in round t plays the empirically best arm with probability $1 - \varepsilon_t$ and otherwise explores uniformly at random. You will analyse this algorithm in Exercise 6.7.

6.3   Bibliographical Remarks

ETC has a long history. Robbins [1952] considered 'certainty equivalence with forcing', which chooses the arm with the largest sample mean except at a fixed set of times $T_i \subset \mathbb{N}$ when arm i is chosen for $i \in [k]$. By choosing the set of times carefully, it is shown that this policy enjoys sublinear regret. While ETC performs all the exploration at the beginning, Robbins's policy spreads the exploration over time. This is advantageous if the horizon is not known, but disadvantageous otherwise. Anscombe [1963] considered exploration and commitment in the context of medical trials or other experimental set-ups. He already largely solves the problem in the Gaussian case and highlights many of the important considerations. Besides this, the article is beautifully written and well worth reading. Strategies based on exploration and commitment are simple to implement and analyse. They can also generalise well to more complex settings. For example, Langford and Zhang [2008] consider this style of policy under the name 'epoch-greedy' for contextual bandits (the idea of exploring then exploiting in epochs, or intervals, is essentially what Robbins [1952] suggested). We'll return to contextual bandits in Chapter 18. Abbasi-Yadkori et al. [2009], Abbasi-Yadkori [2009b] and Rusmevichientong and Tsitsiklis [2010] consider ETC-style policies under the respective names of 'forced exploration' and 'phased exploration and greedy exploitation' (PEGE) in the context of linear bandits (which we shall meet in Chapter 19). Other names include 'forced sampling', 'explore-first', 'explore-then-exploit'. Garivier et al. [2016b] have shown that ETC policies are necessarily suboptimal in the limit of infinite data in a way that is made precise in Chapter 16. This comment also applies to elimination-based strategies, which are described in Exercise 6.8. The history of ε-greedy is unclear, but it is a popular and widely used and known algorithm in reinforcement learning [Sutton and Barto, 1998]. Auer et al. [2002a] analyse the regret of ε-greedy with slowly decreasing exploration probabilities. There are other kinds of randomised exploration as well, including Thompson sampling [1933] and Boltzmann exploration analysed recently by Cesa-Bianchi et al. [2017].

6.4 Exercises

6.1 (SUBGAUSSIAN EMPIRICAL ESTIMATES) Let π be the policy of ETC and $P_1, \ldots, P_k$ be the 1-subgaussian distributions associated with the k arms. Provide a fully rigourous proof of the claim that

$$\hat{\mu}_i(mk) - \mu_i - \hat{\mu}_1(mk) + \mu_1$$

is $\sqrt{2/m}$-subgaussian. You should only use the definitions and the interaction protocol, which states that

(a) $\mathbb{P}(A_t \in \cdot \mid A_1, X_1, \ldots, A_{t-1}, X_{t-1}) = \pi(\cdot \mid A_1, X_1, \ldots, A_{t-1}, X_{t-1})$ a.s.
(b) $\mathbb{P}(X_t \in \cdot \mid A_1, X_1, \ldots, A_{t-1}, X_{t-1}, A_t) = P_{A_t}(\cdot)$ a.s.

6.2 (MINIMAX REGRET) Show that Eq. (6.6) implies the regret of an optimally tuned ETC for subgaussian two-armed bandits satisfies $R_n \leq \Delta + C\sqrt{n}$ where $C > 0$ is a universal constant.

6.3 (HIGH-PROBABILITY BOUNDS (I)) Assume that $k = 2$, and let $\delta \in (0,1)$. Modify the ETC algorithm to depend on δ and prove a bound on the pseudo-regret $\bar{R}_n = n\mu^* - \sum_{t=1}^{n} \mu_{A_t}$ of ETC that holds with probability $1 - \delta$. The algorithm is allowed to use the action suboptimality gaps.

6.4 (HIGH-PROBABILITY BOUNDS (II)) Repeat the previous exercise, but now prove a high probability bound on the random regret: $\hat{R}_n = n\mu^* - \sum_{t=1}^{n} X_t$. Compare this to the bound derived for the pseudo-regret in the previous exercise. What can you conclude?

6.5 (ADAPTIVE COMMITMENT TIMES) Suppose that ETC interacts with a two-armed 1-subgaussian bandit $\nu \in \mathcal{E}$ with means $\mu_1, \mu_2 \in \mathbb{R}$ and $\Delta_\nu = |\mu_1 - \mu_2|$.

(a) Find a choice of m that only depends on the horizon n and not Δ such that there exists a constant $C > 0$ such that for any n and for any $\nu \in \mathcal{E}$, the regret $R_n(\nu)$ of Algorithm 1 is bounded by

$$R_n(\nu) \leq (\Delta_\nu + C)n^{2/3}.$$

Furthermore, show that there is no $C > 0$ such that for any problem instance v and $n \geq 1$, $R_n(v) \leq \Delta_v + Cn^{2/3}$ holds.

(b) Now suppose the commitment time is allowed to be data dependent, which means the algorithm explores each arm alternately until some condition is met and then commits to a single arm for the remainder. Design a condition such that the regret of the resulting algorithm can be bounded by

$$R_n(v) \leq \Delta_v + \frac{C \log n}{\Delta_v}, \tag{6.8}$$

where C is a universal constant. Your condition should only depend on the observed rewards and the time horizon. It should not depend on μ_1, μ_2 or Δ_v.

(c) Show that any algorithm for which (6.8) holds also satisfies $R_n(v) \leq \Delta_v + C\sqrt{n \log(n)}$ for any $n \geq 1$ and $v \in \mathcal{E}$ and a suitably chosen universal constant $C > 0$.

(d) As for (b), but now the objective is to design a condition such that for any $n \geq 1$ and $v \in \mathcal{E}$, the regret of the resulting algorithm is bounded by

$$R_n(v) \leq \Delta_v + \frac{C \log \max\left\{e, n\Delta_v^2\right\}}{\Delta_v}. \tag{6.9}$$

(e) Show that any algorithm for which (6.9) holds also satisfies that for any $n \geq 1$ and $v \in \mathcal{E}$, $R_n(v) \leq \Delta_v + C\sqrt{n}$ for suitably chosen universal constant $C > 0$.

HINT   For (a) start from $R_n \leq m\Delta + n\Delta \exp(-m\Delta^2/2)$ and show an upper bound on the second term which is independent of Δ. Then, choose m. For (b) think about the simplest stopping policy and then make it robust by using confidence intervals. Tune the failure probability. For (c) note that the regret can never be larger than $n\Delta$.

6.6 (DOUBLING TRICK) The purpose of this exercise is to analyse a meta-algorithm based on the so-called **doubling trick** that converts a policy depending on the horizon to a policy with similar guarantees that does not. Let $\mathcal{E}$ be an arbitrary set of bandits. Suppose you are given a policy $\pi = \pi(n)$ designed for $\mathcal{E}$ that accepts the horizon n as a parameter and has a regret guarantee of

$$\max_{1 \leq t \leq n} R_t(\pi(n), v) \leq f_n(v), \qquad \forall v \in \mathcal{E},$$

where $f_n : \mathcal{E} \to [0, \infty)$ is a sequence of functions. Let $n_1 < n_2 < n_3 < \cdots$ be a fixed sequence of integers and consider the policy that runs π with horizon n_1 until round $t = \min\{n, n_1\}$, then runs π with horizon n_2 until $t = \min\{n, n_1 + n_2\}$, and then restarts again with horizon n_3 until $t = \min\{n, n_1 + n_2 + n_3\}$ and so-on. Note that t is the real-time counter and is not reset on each restart. Let π^* be the resulting policy. When $n_{\ell+1} = 2n_\ell$, the length of periods when π is used double with each phase, hence the name 'doubling trick'.

(a) Let $n > 0$ be arbitrary, $\ell_{\max} = \min\{\ell : \sum_{i=1}^{\ell} n_i \geq n\}$. Prove that for any $v \in \mathcal{E}$, the n-horizon regret of π^{dbl} on v is at most

$$R_n(\pi^*, v) \leq \sum_{\ell=1}^{\ell_{\max}} f_{n_\ell}(v). \tag{6.10}$$

(b) Suppose that $f_n(v) \leq \sqrt{n}$. Show that if $n_\ell = 2^{\ell-1}$, then for any $v \in \mathcal{E}$ and horizon n the regret of π^{dbl} is at most

$$R_n(\pi^*, v) \leq C\sqrt{n},$$

where $C > 0$ is a carefully chosen universal constant.

(c) Suppose that $f_n(v) = g(v) \log(n)$ for some function $g : \mathcal{E} \to [0, \infty)$. What is the regret of π^* if $n_\ell = 2^{\ell-1}$? Can you find a better choice of $(n_\ell)_\ell$?

(d) In light of this idea, should we bother trying to design algorithms that do not depend on the horizon? Are there any disadvantages to using the doubling trick? If so, what are they? Write a short summary of the pros and cons of the doubling trick.

According to Besson and Kaufmann [2018], the doubling trick was first applied to bandits by Auer et al. [1995]. Note, nowhere in this exercise did we use that the bandit is stochastic. Nothing changes in the adversarial or contextual settings studied later in the book.

6.7 (ε-GREEDY) For this exercise assume the rewards are 1-subgaussian and there are $k \geq 2$ arms. The ε-greedy algorithm depends on a sequence of parameters $\varepsilon_1, \varepsilon_2, \dots$. First it chooses each arm once and subsequently chooses $A_t = \operatorname{argmax}_i \hat\mu_i(t-1)$ with probability $1 - \varepsilon_t$ and otherwise chooses an arm uniformly at random.

(a) Prove that if $\varepsilon_t = \varepsilon > 0$, then $\displaystyle\lim_{n\to\infty} \frac{R_n}{n} = \frac{\varepsilon}{k} \sum_{i=1}^{k} \Delta_i$.

(b) Let $\Delta_{\min} = \min \{\Delta_i : \Delta_i > 0\}$ and let $\varepsilon_t = \min \left\{1, \frac{Ck}{t\Delta_{\min}^2}\right\}$, where $C > 0$ is a sufficiently large universal constant. Prove that there exists a universal $C' > 0$ such that

$$R_n \leq C' \sum_{i=1}^{k} \left(\Delta_i + \frac{\Delta_i}{\Delta_{\min}^2} \log \max \left\{e, \frac{n\Delta_{\min}^2}{k}\right\}\right).$$

6.8 (ELIMINATION ALGORITHM) A simple way to generalise the ETC policy to multiple arms and overcome the problem of tuning the commitment time is to use an elimination algorithm. The algorithm operates in phases and maintains an active set of arms that could be optimal. In the ℓth phase, the algorithm aims to eliminate from the active set all arms i for which $\Delta_i \geq 2^{-\ell}$.

1: **Input:** k and sequence $(m_\ell)_\ell$
2: $A_1 = \{1, 2, \dots, k\}$
3: **for** $\ell = 1, 2, 3, \dots$ **do**
4: Choose each arm $i \in A_\ell$ exactly m_ℓ times
5: Let $\hat\mu_{i,\ell}$ be the average reward for arm i from this phase only
6: Update active set:

$$A_{\ell+1} = \left\{i : \hat\mu_{i,\ell} + 2^{-\ell} \geq \max_{j \in A_\ell} \hat\mu_{j,\ell}\right\}$$

7: **end for**

Algorithm 2: Phased elimination for finite-armed bandits

Without loss of generality, assume that arm 1 is an optimal arm. You may assume that the horizon n is known.

(a) Show that for any $\ell \geq 1$,

$$\mathbb{P}\left(1 \notin A_{\ell+1}, 1 \in A_\ell\right) \leq k \exp\left(-\frac{m_\ell\, 2^{-2\ell}}{4}\right).$$

(b) Show that if $i \in [k]$ and $\ell \geq 1$ are such that $\Delta_i \geq 2^{-\ell}$, then

$$\mathbb{P}\left(i \in A_{\ell+1}, \ 1 \in A_\ell, \ i \in A_\ell\right) \leq \exp\left(-\frac{m_\ell (\Delta_i - 2^{-\ell})^2}{4}\right).$$

(c) Let $\ell_i = \min\{\ell \geq 1 : 2^{-\ell} \leq \Delta_i/2\}$. Choose m_ℓ in such a way that $\mathbb{P}\left(\text{exists } \ell : 1 \notin A_\ell\right) \leq 1/n$ and $\mathbb{P}\left(i \in A_{\ell_i+1}\right) \leq 1/n$.

(d) Show that your algorithm has regret at most

$$R_n \leq C \sum_{i:\Delta_i>0} \left(\Delta_i + \frac{1}{\Delta_i} \log(n)\right),$$

where $C > 0$ is a carefully chosen universal constant.

(e) Modify your choice of m_ℓ and show that the regret of the resulting algorithm satisfies

$$R_n \leq C \sum_{i:\Delta_i>0} \left(\Delta_i + \frac{1}{\Delta_i} \log \max\left\{e, n\Delta_i^2\right\}\right).$$

(f) Show that with an appropriate universal constant $C' > 0$, the regret satisfies

$$R_n \leq \sum_i \Delta_i + C' \sqrt{nk \log(k)}.$$

Algorithm 2 is due to Auer and Ortner [2010]. The $\log(k)$ term in Part (f) can be removed by modifying the algorithm to use the refined confidence intervals in Chapter 9, but we would not recommend this for the reasons discussed in Section 9.2 of that chapter. You could also use a more sophisticated confidence level [Lattimore, 2018].

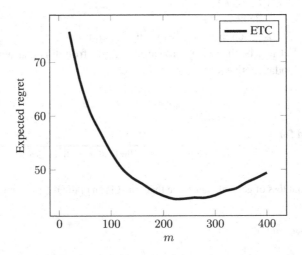

Figure 6.2   Expected regret for ETC over 10^5 trials on a Gaussian bandit with means $\mu_1 = 0$, $\mu_2 = -1/10$

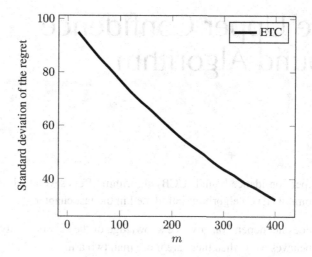

Figure 6.3 Standard deviation of the regret for ETC over 10^5 trials on a Gaussian bandit with means $\mu_1 = 0, \mu_2 = -1/10$

6.9 (EMPIRICAL STUDY) In this exercise you will investigate the empirical behaviour of ETC on a two-armed Gaussian bandit with means $\mu_1 = 0$ and $\mu_2 = -\Delta$. Let

$$\bar{R}_n = \sum_{t=1}^{n} \Delta_{A_t},$$

which is chosen so that $R_n = \mathbb{E}[\bar{R}_n]$. Complete the following:

(a) Using programming language of your choice, write a function that accepts an integer n and $\Delta > 0$ and returns the value of m that exactly minimises the expected regret.

(b) Reproduce Fig. 6.1.

(c) Fix $\Delta = 1/10$ and plot the expected regret as a function of m with $n = 2000$. Your plot should resemble Fig. 6.2.

(d) Plot the standard deviation $\mathbb{V}[\bar{R}_n]^{1/2}$ as a function of m for the same bandit as above. Your plot should resemble Fig. 6.3.

(e) Explain the shape of the curves you observed in Parts (b), (c) and (d) and reconcile what you see with the theoretical results.

(f) Think, experiment and plot. Is it justified to plot $\mathbb{V}[\bar{R}_n]^{1/2}$ as a summary of how $\bar{R}_n$ is distributed? Explain your thinking.

7 The Upper Confidence Bound Algorithm

The upper confidence bound (UCB) algorithm offers several advantages over the explore-then-commit (ETC) algorithm introduced in the last chapter.

(a) It does not depend on advance knowledge of the suboptimality gaps.

(b) It behaves well when there are more than two arms.

(c) The version introduced here depends on the horizon n, but in the next chapter, we will see how to eliminate that as well.

The algorithm has many different forms, depending on the distributional assumptions on the noise. Like in the previous chapter, we assume the noise is 1-subgaussian. A serious discussion of other options is delayed until Chapter 10.

7.1 The Optimism Principle

The UCB algorithm is based on the principle of **optimism in the face of uncertainty**, which states that one should act as if the environment is as nice as **plausibly possible**. As we shall see in later chapters, the principle is applicable beyond the finite-armed stochastic bandit problem.

Imagine visiting a new country and making a choice between sampling the local cuisine or visiting a well-known multinational chain. Taking an optimistic view of the unknown local cuisine leads to exploration because without data, it could be amazing. After trying the new option a few times, you can update your statistics and make a more informed decision. On the other hand, taking a pessimistic view of the new option discourages exploration, and you may suffer significant regret if the local options are delicious. Just how optimistic you should be is a difficult decision, which we explore for the rest of the chapter in the context of finite-armed bandits.

For bandits, the optimism principle means using the data observed so far to assign to each arm a value, called the **upper confidence bound** that with high probability is an overestimate of the unknown mean. The intuitive reason why this leads to sublinear regret is simple. Assuming the upper confidence bound assigned to the optimal arm is indeed an overestimate, then another arm can only be played if its upper confidence bound is larger than that of the optimal arm, which in turn is larger than the mean of the optimal arm. And yet this cannot happen too often because the additional data provided by playing a suboptimal arm means that the upper confidence bound for this arm will eventually fall below that of the optimal arm.

In order to make this argument more precise, we need to define the upper confidence bound. Let $(X_t)_{t=1}^n$ be a sequence of independent 1-subgaussian random variables with mean μ and $\hat{\mu} = \frac{1}{n}\sum_{t=1}^n X_t$. By Eq. (5.6),

$$\mathbb{P}\left(\mu \geq \hat{\mu} + \sqrt{\frac{2\log(1/\delta)}{n}}\right) \leq \delta \qquad \text{for all } \delta \in (0,1). \tag{7.1}$$

When considering its options in round t, the learner has observed $T_i(t-1)$ samples from arm i and received rewards from that arm with an empirical mean of $\hat{\mu}_i(t-1)$. Then a reasonable candidate for 'as large as plausibly possible' for the unknown mean of the ith arm is

$$\mathrm{UCB}_i(t-1,\delta) = \begin{cases} \infty & \text{if } T_i(t-1) = 0 \\ \hat{\mu}_i(t-1) + \sqrt{\frac{2\log(1/\delta)}{T_i(t-1)}} & \text{otherwise.} \end{cases} \tag{7.2}$$

Great care is required when comparing (7.1) and (7.2) because in the former the number of samples is the constant n, but in the latter it is a random variable $T_i(t-1)$. By and large, however, this is merely an annoying technicality, and the intuition remains that δ is approximately an upper bound on the probability of the event that the above quantity is an underestimate of the true mean. More details are given in Exercise 7.1.

At last we have everything we need to state a version of the UCB algorithm, which takes as input the number of arms and the error probability δ.

1: **Input** k and δ
2: **for** $t \in 1, \ldots, n$ **do**
3:     Choose action $A_t = \operatorname{argmax}_i \mathrm{UCB}_i(t-1,\delta)$
4:     Observe reward X_t and update upper confidence bounds
5: **end for**

Algorithm 3: UCB(δ).

Although there are many versions of the UCB algorithm, we often do not distinguish them by name and hope the context is clear. For the rest of this chapter, we'll usually call UCB(δ) just UCB.

The value inside the argmax is called the **index** of arm i. Generally speaking, an **index algorithm** chooses the arm in each round that maximises some value (the index), which usually only depends on the current time step and the samples from that arm. In the case of UCB, the index is the sum of the empirical mean of rewards experienced so far and the **exploration bonus**, which is also known as the **confidence width**.

Besides the slightly vague 'optimism guarantees optimality or learning' intuition we gave before, it is worth exploring other intuitions for the choice of index. At a very basic level, an algorithm should explore arms more often if they are (a) promising because $\hat{\mu}_i(t-1)$ is large or (b) not well explored because $T_i(t-1)$ is small. As one can plainly see, the definition in Eq. (7.2) exhibits this behaviour. This explanation is not completely satisfying, however, because it does not explain why the form of the functions is just so.

A more refined explanation comes from thinking of what we expect of any reasonable algorithm. Suppose at the start of round t the first arm has been played much more frequently than the rest. If we did a good job designing our algorithm, we would hope this is the optimal arm, and because it has been played so often, we expect that $\hat{\mu}_1(t-1) \approx \mu_1$. To confirm the hypothesis that arm 1 is optimal, the algorithm had better be highly confident that other arms are indeed worse. This leads quite naturally to the idea of using upper confidence bounds. The learner can be reasonably certain that arm i is worse than arm 1 if

$$\hat{\mu}_i(t-1) + \sqrt{\frac{2\log(1/\delta)}{T_i(t-1)}} \le \mu_1 \approx \hat{\mu}_1(t-1) + \sqrt{\frac{2\log(1/\delta)}{T_1(t-1)}}, \tag{7.3}$$

where δ is called the **confidence level** and quantifies the degree of certainty. This means that choosing the arm with the largest upper confidence bound leads to a situation where arms are only chosen if their true mean could reasonably be larger than those of arms that have been played often. That this rule is indeed a good one depends on two factors. The first is whether the width of the confidence interval at a given confidence level can be significantly decreased, and the second is whether the confidence level is chosen in a reasonable fashion. For now, we will take a leap of faith and assume that the width of confidence intervals for subgaussian bandits cannot be significantly improved from what we use here (we shall see that this holds in later chapters), and concentrate on choosing the confidence level now.

Choosing the confidence level is a delicate problem, and we will analyse a number of choices in future chapters. The basic difficulty is that δ should be small enough to ensure optimism with high probability, but not so large that suboptimal arms are explored excessively.

Nevertheless, as a first cut, the choice of this parameter can be guided by the following considerations. If the confidence interval fails and the index of an optimal arm drops below its true mean, then it could happen that the algorithm stops playing the optimal arm and suffers linear regret. This suggests we might choose $\delta \approx 1/n$ so that the contribution to the regret of this failure case is relatively small. Unfortunately things are not quite this simple. As we have already alluded to, one of the main difficulties is that the number of samples $T_i(t-1)$ in the index (7.2) is a random variable, and so our concentration results cannot be immediately applied. For this reason we will see that (at least naively) δ should be chosen a bit smaller than $1/n$.

THEOREM 7.1. *Consider UCB as shown in Algorithm 3 on a stochastic k-armed 1-subgaussian bandit problem. For any horizon n, if $\delta = 1/n^2$, then*

$$R_n \le 3\sum_{i=1}^{k} \Delta_i + \sum_{i:\Delta_i>0} \frac{16\log(n)}{\Delta_i}.$$

Before the proof we need a little more notation. Let $(X_{ti})_{t\in[n],i\in[k]}$ be a collection of independent random variables with the law of X_{ti} equal to P_i. Then define

$\hat{\mu}_{is} = \frac{1}{s}\sum_{u=1}^{s} X_{ui}$ to be the empirical mean based on the first s samples. We make use of the third model in Section 4.6 by assuming that the reward in round t is

$$X_t = X_{T_{A_t}(t)A_t}.$$

Then we define $\hat{\mu}_i(t) = \hat{\mu}_{iT_i(t)}$ to be the empirical mean of the ith arm after round t. The proof of Theorem 7.1 relies on the basic regret decomposition identity,

$$R_n = \sum_{i=1}^{k} \Delta_i \mathbb{E}\left[T_i(n)\right]. \hspace{2cm} \text{(Lemma 4.5)}$$

The theorem will follow by showing that $\mathbb{E}\left[T_i(n)\right]$ is not too large for suboptimal arms i. The key observation is that after the initial period where the algorithm chooses each action once, action i can only be chosen if its index is higher than that of an optimal arm. This can only happen if at least one of the following is true:

(a) The index of action i is larger than the true mean of a specific optimal arm.
(b) The index of a specific optimal arm is smaller than its true mean.

Since with reasonably high probability the index of any arm is an upper bound on its mean, we don't expect the index of the optimal arm to be below its mean. Furthermore, if the suboptimal arm i is played sufficiently often, then its exploration bonus becomes small and simultaneously the empirical estimate of its mean converges to the true value, putting an upper bound on the expected total number of times when its index stays above the mean of the optimal arm. The proof that follows is typical for the analysis of algorithms like UCB, and hence we provide quite a bit of detail so that readers can later construct their own proofs.

Proof of Theorem 7.1   Without loss of generality, we assume the first arm is optimal so that $\mu_1 = \mu^*$. As noted above,

$$R_n = \sum_{i=1}^{k} \Delta_i \mathbb{E}\left[T_i(n)\right]. \hspace{2cm} (7.4)$$

The theorem will be proven by bounding $\mathbb{E}[T_i(n)]$ for each suboptimal arm i. We make use of a relatively standard idea, which is to decouple the randomness from the behaviour of the UCB algorithm. Let G_i be the 'good' event defined by

$$G_i = \left\{\mu_1 < \min_{t\in[n]} \text{UCB}_1(t,\delta)\right\} \cap \left\{\hat{\mu}_{iu_i} + \sqrt{\frac{2}{u_i}\log\left(\frac{1}{\delta}\right)} < \mu_1\right\},$$

where $u_i \in [n]$ is a constant to be chosen later. So G_i is the event when μ_1 is never underestimated by the upper confidence bound of the first arm, while at the same time the upper confidence bound for the mean of arm i after u_i observations are taken from this arm is below the pay-off of the optimal arm. We will show two things:

1 If G_i occurs, then arm i will be played at most u_i times: $T_i(n) \leq u_i$.
2 The complement event G_i^c occurs with low probability (governed in some way yet to be discovered by u_i).

Because $T_i(n) \leq n$ no matter what, this will mean that

$$\mathbb{E}\left[T_i(n)\right] = \mathbb{E}\left[\mathbb{I}\left\{G_i\right\}T_i(n)\right] + \mathbb{E}\left[\mathbb{I}\left\{G_i^c\right\}T_i(n)\right] \leq u_i + \mathbb{P}\left(G_i^c\right)n. \tag{7.5}$$

The next step is to complete our promise by showing that $T_i(n) \leq u_i$ on G_i and that $\mathbb{P}\left(G_i^c\right)$ is small. Let us first assume that G_i holds and show that $T_i(n) \leq u_i$, which we do by contradiction. Suppose that $T_i(n) > u_i$. Then arm i was played more than u_i times over the n rounds, and so there must exist a round $t \in [n]$ where $T_i(t-1) = u_i$ and $A_t = i$. Using the definition of G_i,

$$\mathrm{UCB}_i(t-1, \delta) = \hat{\mu}_i(t-1) + \sqrt{\frac{2\log(1/\delta)}{T_i(t-1)}} \qquad \text{(definition of } \mathrm{UCB}_i(t-1,\delta))$$

$$= \hat{\mu}_{iu_i} + \sqrt{\frac{2\log(1/\delta)}{u_i}} \qquad \text{(since } T_i(t-1) = u_i)$$

$$< \mu_1 \qquad \text{(definition of } G_i)$$

$$< \mathrm{UCB}_1(t-1, \delta). \qquad \text{(definition of } G_i)$$

Hence $A_t = \mathrm{argmax}_j \, \mathrm{UCB}_j(t-1, \delta) \neq i$, which is a contradiction. Therefore if G_i occurs, then $T_i(n) \leq u_i$. Let us now turn to upper bounding $\mathbb{P}\left(G_i^c\right)$. By its definition,

$$G_i^c = \left\{\mu_1 \geq \min_{t \in [n]} \mathrm{UCB}_1(t, \delta)\right\} \cup \left\{\hat{\mu}_{iu_i} + \sqrt{\frac{2\log(1/\delta)}{u_i}} \geq \mu_1\right\}. \tag{7.6}$$

The first of these sets is decomposed using the definition of $\mathrm{UCB}_1(t, \delta)$,

$$\left\{\mu_1 \geq \min_{t \in [n]} \mathrm{UCB}_1(t, \delta)\right\} \subset \left\{\mu_1 \geq \min_{s \in [n]} \hat{\mu}_{1s} + \sqrt{\frac{2\log(1/\delta)}{s}}\right\}$$

$$= \bigcup_{s \in [n]} \left\{\mu_1 \geq \hat{\mu}_{1s} + \sqrt{\frac{2\log(1/\delta)}{s}}\right\}.$$

Then using a union bound and the concentration bound for sums of independent subgaussian random variables in Corollary 5.5, we obtain:

$$\mathbb{P}\left(\mu_1 \geq \min_{t \in [n]} \mathrm{UCB}_1(t, \delta)\right) \leq \mathbb{P}\left(\bigcup_{s \in [n]} \left\{\mu_1 \geq \hat{\mu}_{1s} + \sqrt{\frac{2\log(1/\delta)}{s}}\right\}\right)$$

$$\leq \sum_{s=1}^{n} \mathbb{P}\left(\mu_1 \geq \hat{\mu}_{1s} + \sqrt{\frac{2\log(1/\delta)}{s}}\right) \leq n\delta. \tag{7.7}$$

The next step is to bound the probability of the second set in (7.6). Assume that u_i is chosen large enough that

$$\Delta_i - \sqrt{\frac{2\log(1/\delta)}{u_i}} \geq c\Delta_i \tag{7.8}$$

for some $c \in (0, 1)$ to be chosen later. Then, since $\mu_1 = \mu_i + \Delta_i$, and using Corollary 5.5,

$$\mathbb{P}\left(\hat{\mu}_{iu_i} + \sqrt{\frac{2\log(1/\delta)}{u_i}} \geq \mu_1\right) = \mathbb{P}\left(\hat{\mu}_{iu_i} - \mu_i \geq \Delta_i - \sqrt{\frac{2\log(1/\delta)}{u_i}}\right)$$

$$\leq \mathbb{P}\left(\hat{\mu}_{iu_i} - \mu_i \geq c\Delta_i\right) \leq \exp\left(-\frac{u_i c^2 \Delta_i^2}{2}\right).$$

Taking this together with (7.7) and (7.6), we have

$$\mathbb{P}(G_i^c) \leq n\delta + \exp\left(-\frac{u_i c^2 \Delta_i^2}{2}\right).$$

When substituted into Eq. (7.5), we obtain

$$\mathbb{E}[T_i(n)] \leq u_i + n\left(n\delta + \exp\left(-\frac{u_i c^2 \Delta_i^2}{2}\right)\right). \tag{7.9}$$

It remains to choose $u_i \in [n]$ satisfying (7.8). A natural choice is the smallest integer for which (7.8) holds, which is

$$u_i = \left\lceil \frac{2\log(1/\delta)}{(1-c)^2 \Delta_i^2} \right\rceil.$$

This choice of u_i can be larger than n, but in this case Eq. (7.9) holds trivially since $T_i(n) \leq n$. Then, using the assumption that $\delta = 1/n^2$ and this choice of u_i leads via (7.9) to

$$\mathbb{E}[T_i(n)] \leq u_i + 1 + n^{1-2c^2/(1-c)^2} = \left\lceil \frac{2\log(n^2)}{(1-c)^2 \Delta_i^2} \right\rceil + 1 + n^{1-2c^2/(1-c)^2}. \tag{7.10}$$

All that remains is to choose $c \in (0, 1)$. The second term will contribute a polynomial dependence on n unless $2c^2/(1-c)^2 \geq 1$. However, if c is chosen too close to 1, then the first term blows up. Somewhat arbitrarily we choose $c = 1/2$, which leads to

$$\mathbb{E}[T_i(n)] \leq 3 + \frac{16\log(n)}{\Delta_i^2}.$$

The result follows by substituting the above display in Eq. (7.4).   □

As we saw for the ETC strategy, the regret bound in Theorem 7.1 depends on the reciprocal of the gaps, which may be meaningless when even a single suboptimal action has a very small suboptimality gap. As before, one can also prove a sublinear regret bound that does not depend on the reciprocal of the gaps.

THEOREM 7.2. *If $\delta = 1/n^2$, then the regret of UCB, as defined in Algorithm 3, on any $v \in \mathcal{E}_{SG}^k(1)$ environment, is bounded by*

$$R_n \leq 8\sqrt{nk\log(n)} + 3\sum_{i=1}^{k}\Delta_i.$$

Proof Let $\Delta > 0$ be some value to be tuned subsequently, and recall from the proof of Theorem 7.1 that for each suboptimal arm i, we can bound

$$\mathbb{E}[T_i(n)] \leq 3 + \frac{16 \log(n)}{\Delta_i^2}.$$

Therefore, using the basic regret decomposition again (Lemma 4.5), we have

$$R_n = \sum_{i=1}^{k} \Delta_i \mathbb{E}[T_i(n)] = \sum_{i:\Delta_i < \Delta} \Delta_i \mathbb{E}[T_i(n)] + \sum_{i:\Delta_i \geq \Delta} \Delta_i \mathbb{E}[T_i(n)]$$

$$\leq n\Delta + \sum_{i:\Delta_i \geq \Delta} \left(3\Delta_i + \frac{16 \log(n)}{\Delta_i} \right) \leq n\Delta + \frac{16k \log(n)}{\Delta} + 3 \sum_i \Delta_i$$

$$\leq 8\sqrt{nk \log(n)} + 3 \sum_{i=1}^{k} \Delta_i,$$

where the first inequality follows because $\sum_{i:\Delta_i < \Delta} T_i(n) \leq n$ and the last line by choosing $\Delta = \sqrt{16k \log(n)/n}$. $\square$

The additive $\sum_i \Delta_i$ term is unavoidable because no reasonable algorithm can avoid playing each arm once (try to work out what would happen if it did not). In any case, this term does not grow with the horizon n and is typically negligible. As it happens, Theorem 7.2 is close to optimal. We will see in Chapter 15 that no algorithm can enjoy regret smaller than $O(\sqrt{nk})$ over all problems in $\mathcal{E}_{\mathrm{SG}}^k(1)$. In Chapter 9 we will also see a more complicated variant of Algorithm 3 that shaves the logarithmic term from the upper bound given above.

EXPERIMENT 7.1   We promised that UCB would overcome the limitations of ETC by achieving the same guarantees but without prior knowledge of the suboptimality gaps. The theory supports this claim, but just because two algorithms have similar theoretical guarantees does not mean they perform the same empirically. The theoretical analysis might be loose for one algorithm and maybe not the other, or by a different margin. For this reason it is always wise to prove lower bounds (which we do later) and compare the empirical performance, which we do (very briefly) now.

The set-up is the same as in Fig. 6.1, which has $n = 1000$ and $k = 2$ and unit variance Gaussian rewards with means 0 and $-\Delta$ respectively. The plot in Fig. 7.1 shows the expected regret of UCB relative to ETC for a variety of choices of commitment time m. The expected regret of ETC with the optimal choice of m (which depends on the knowledge of Δ and that the pay-offs are Gaussian, cf. Fig. 6.1) is also shown.

The results demonstrate a common phenomenon. If ETC is tuned with the optimal choice of commitment time for each choice of Δ, then it outperforms the parameter-free UCB, though only by a relatively small margin. If, however, the commitment time must be chosen without the knowledge of Δ, then ETC will usually not outperform UCB. As it happens, a variant of UCB introduced in the next chapter actually outperforms even the optimally tuned ETC.

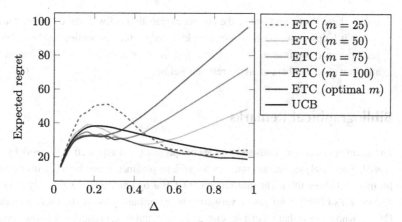

Figure 7.1 Experiment showing universality of UCB relative to fixed instances of ETC

7.2   Notes

1 The choice of $\delta = 1/n^2$ led to an easy analysis, but comes with two disadvantages. First of all, it turns out that a slightly smaller value of δ improves the regret (and empirical performance). Secondly, the dependence on n means the horizon must be known in advance, which is often not reasonable. Both of these issues are resolved in the next chapter, where δ is chosen to be smaller and to depend on the current round t rather than n. Nonetheless – as promised – Algorithm 3 with $\delta = 1/n^2$ does achieve a regret bound similar to the ETC strategy, but without requiring knowledge of the gaps.

2 The assumption that the rewards generated by each arm are independent can be relaxed significantly. All of the results would go through by assuming there exists a mean reward vector $\mu \in \mathbb{R}^k$ such that

$$\mathbb{E}[X_t \mid X_1, A_1, \ldots, A_{t-1}, X_{t-1}, A_t] = \mu_{A_t} \text{ a.s..} \tag{7.11}$$

$$\mathbb{E}[\exp(\lambda(X_t - \mu_{A_t})) \mid X_1, A_1, \ldots, A_{t-1}, X_{t-1}, A_t] \leq \exp(\lambda^2/2) \text{ a.s..} \tag{7.12}$$

Eq. (7.11) is just saying that the conditional mean of the reward in round t only depends on the chosen action. Eq. (7.12) ensures that the tails of X_t are conditionally subgaussian. That everything still goes through is proven using martingale techniques, which we develop in detail in Chapter 20.

3 So is the optimism principle universal? Does it always lead to policies with strong guarantees in more complicated settings? Unfortunately the answer turns out to be no. The optimism principle usually leads to reasonable algorithms when *(i)* any action gives feedback about the quality of that action and *(ii)* no action gives feedback about the value of other actions. When *(i)* is violated, even sublinear regret may not be guaranteed. When *(ii)* is violated, an optimistic algorithm may avoid actions that lead to large information gain and low reward, even when this trade-off is optimal. An example where this occurs is provided in Chapter 25 on linear bandits. Optimism can work in more complex models as well, but sometimes fails to appropriately balance exploration and exploitation.

4 When thinking about future outcomes, humans and some animals often have higher expectations than are warranted by past experience or conditions of the environment. This phenomenon, a form of **cognitive bias**, is known as the **optimism bias** in the psychology and behavioural economics literature and is in fact 'one of the most consistent, prevalent, and robust biases documented in psychology and behavioral economics' [Sharot, 2011a]. While much has been written about this

bias in these fields, and one of the current explanations of why the optimism bias is so prevalent is that it helps exploration, to our best knowledge, the connection to the deeper mathematical justification of optimism, pursued here and in other parts of this book, has so far escaped the attention of researchers in all the relevant fields.

7.3   Bibliographical Remarks

The use of confidence bounds and the idea of optimism first appeared in the work by Lai and Robbins [1985]. They analysed the asymptotics for various parametric bandit problems (see the next chapter for more details on this). The first version of UCB is by Lai [1987]. Other early work is by Katehakis and Robbins [1995], who gave a very straightforward analysis for the Gaussian case, and Agrawal [1995], who noticed that all that was needed is an appropriate sequence of upper confidence bounds on the unknown means. In this way, their analysis is significantly more general than what we have done here. These researchers also focused on the asymptotics, which at the time was the standard approach in the statistics literature. The UCB algorithm was independently discovered by Kaelbling [1993], although with no regret analysis or clear advice on how to tune the confidence parameter. The version of UCB discussed here is most similar to that analysed by Auer et al. [2002a] under the name UCB1, but that algorithm used t rather than n in the confidence level (see the next chapter). Like us, they prove a finite-time regret bound. However, rather than considering 1-subgaussian environments, Auer et al. [2002a] considers bandits where the pay-offs are confined to the $[0, 1]$ interval, which are ensured to be $1/2$-subgaussian. See Exercise 7.2 for hints on what must change in this situation. The basic structure of the proof of our Theorem 7.1 is essentially the same as that of theorem 1 of Auer et al. [2002a]. The worst-case bound in Theorem 7.2 appeared in the book by Bubeck and Cesa-Bianchi [2012], which also popularised the subgaussian set-up. We did not have time to discuss the situation where the subgaussian constant is unknown. There have been several works exploring this direction. If the variance is unknown, but the noise is bounded, then one can replace the subgaussian concentration bounds with an empirical Bernstein inequality [Audibert et al., 2007]. For details, see Exercise 7.6. If the noise has heavy tails, then a more serious modification is required, as discussed in Exercise 7.7 and the note that follows.

   We found the article by Sharot [2011a] on optimism bias from the psychology literature quite illuminating. Readers looking to dive deeper into this literature may enjoy the book by the same author [Sharot, 2011b]. Optimism bias is also known as 'unrealistic optimism', a term that is most puzzling to us – what bias is ever realistic? The background of this is explained by Jefferson et al. [2017].

7.4   Exercises

7.1 (Concentration for sequences of random length) In this exercise, we investigate one of the more annoying challenges when analyzing sequential algorithms. Let $X_1, X_2, \ldots$ be a sequence of independent standard Gaussian random variables defined on probability space $(\Omega, \mathcal{F}, \mathbb{P})$. Suppose that $T : \Omega \to \{1, 2, 3, \ldots\}$ is another random variable, and let $\hat{\mu} = \sum_{t=1}^{T} X_t / T$ be the empirical mean based on T samples.

(a) Show that if T is independent from X_t for all t, then

$$\mathbb{P}\left(\hat{\mu} - \mu \geq \sqrt{\frac{2 \log(1/\delta)}{T}} \right) \leq \delta.$$

(b) Now relax the assumption that T is independent from $(X_t)_t$. Let $E_t = \mathbb{I}\{T = t\}$ be the event that $T = t$ and $\mathcal{F}_t = \sigma(X_1, \ldots, X_t)$ be the σ-algebra generated by the first t samples. Let $\delta \in (0, 1)$ and show there exists a T such that for all $t \in \{1, 2, 3, \ldots\}$ it holds that E_t is $\mathcal{F}_t$-measurable and

$$\mathbb{P}\left(\hat{\mu} - \mu \geq \sqrt{\frac{2\log(1/\delta)}{T}}\right) = 1.$$

(c) Show that

$$\mathbb{P}\left(\hat{\mu} - \mu \geq \sqrt{\frac{2\log(T(T+1)/\delta)}{T}}\right) \leq \delta. \tag{7.13}$$

HINT   For part (b) above, you may find it useful to apply the law of the iterated logarithm, which says if $X_1, X_2, \ldots$ is a sequence of independent and identically distributed random variables with zero mean and unit variance, then

$$\limsup_{n \to \infty} \frac{\sum_{t=1}^n X_t}{\sqrt{2n \log \log n}} = 1 \qquad \text{almost surely.}$$

This result is especially remarkable because it relies on no assumptions other than zero mean and unit variance. You might wonder if Eq. (7.13) might continue to hold if $\log(T(T+1)/\delta)$ were replaced by $\log(\log(T)/\delta)$. It almost does, but the proof of this fact is more sophisticated. For more details, see the paper by Garivier [2013] or Exercise 20.9.

7.2 (RELAXING THE SUBGAUSSIAN ASSUMPTION) In this chapter, we assumed the pay-off distributions were 1-subgaussian. The purpose of this exercise is to relax this assumption.

(a) First suppose that $\sigma^2 > 0$ is a known constant and that $v \in \mathcal{E}^k_{\text{SG}}(\sigma^2)$. Modify the UCB algorithm and state and prove an analogue of Theorems 7.1 and 7.2 for this case.

(b) Now suppose that $v = (P_i)_{i=1}^k$ is chosen so that P_i is σ_i-subgaussian where $(\sigma_i^2)_{i=1}^k$ are known. Modify the UCB algorithm and state and prove an analogue of Theorems 7.1 and 7.2 for this case.

(c) If you did things correctly, the regret bound in the previous part should not depend on the values of $\{\sigma_i^2 : \Delta_i = 0\}$. Explain why not.

7.3 (HIGH-PROBABILITY BOUNDS) Recall from Chapter 4 that the pseudo-regret is defined to be the random variable

$$\bar{R}_n = \sum_{t=1}^n \Delta_{A_t}.$$

The UCB policy in Algorithm 3 depends on confidence parameter $\delta \in (0, 1]$ that determines the level of optimism. State and prove a bound on the pseudo-regret of this algorithm that holds with probability $1 - f(n, k)\delta$, where $f(n, k)$ is a function, that depends on n and k only. More precisely show that for bandit $v \in \mathcal{E}^k_{\text{SG}}(1)$ that

$$\mathbb{P}\left(\bar{R}_n \geq g(n, v, \delta)\right) \leq f(n, k)\delta,$$

where g and f should be as small as possible (there are trade-offs – try and come up with a natural choice).

7.4 (PHASED UCB (I)) Fix a 1-subgaussian k-armed bandit environment and a horizon n. Consider the version of UCB that works in phases of exponentially increasing length of $1, 2, 4, \ldots$. In each phase, the algorithm uses the action that would have been chosen by UCB at the beginning of the phase (see Algorithm 4 below).

(a) State and prove a bound on the regret for this version of UCB.

(b) Compare your result with Theorem 7.1.

(c) How would the result change if the ℓth phase had a length of $\lceil \alpha^{\ell} \rceil$ with $\alpha > 1$?

1: **Input** k and δ
2: Choose each arm once
3: **for** $\ell = 1, 2, \ldots$ **do**
4:     Compute $A_{\ell} = \text{argmax}_i \, \text{UCB}_i(t-1, \delta)$
5:     Choose arm A_{ℓ} exactly 2^{ℓ} times
6: **end for**

Algorithm 4: A phased version of UCB.

7.5 (PHASED UCB (II)) Let $\alpha > 1$ and consider the version of UCB that first plays each arm once. Thereafter it operates in the same way as UCB, but rather than playing the chosen arm just once, it plays it until the number of plays of that arm is a factor of α larger (see Algorithm 5 below).

(a) State and prove a bound on the regret for version of UCB with $\alpha = 2$ (doubling counts).

(b) Compare with the result of the previous exercise and with Theorem 7.1. What can you conclude?

(c) Repeat the analysis for $\alpha > 1$. What is the role of α?

(d) Implement these algorithms and compare them empirically to UCB(δ).

1: **Input** k and δ
2: Choose each arm once
3: **for** $\ell = 1, 2, \ldots$ **do**
4:     Let $t_{\ell} = t$
5:     Compute $A_{\ell} = \text{argmax}_i \, \text{UCB}_i(t_{\ell} - 1, \delta)$
6:     Choose arm A_{ℓ} until round t such that $T_i(t) \geq \alpha T_i(t_{\ell} - 1)$
7: **end for**

Algorithm 5: A phased version of UCB.

The algorithms of the last two exercises may seem ridiculous. Why would you wait before updating empirical estimates and choosing a new action? There are at least two reasons:

(a) It can happen that the algorithm does not observe its rewards immediately, but rather they appear asynchronously after some delay. Alternatively many bandits algorithms may be operating simultaneously and the results must be communicated at some cost.

(b) If the feedback model has a more complicated structure than what we examined so far, then even computing the upper confidence bound just once can be quite expensive. In these circumstances, it's comforting to know that the loss of performance by updating the statistics only rarely is not too severe.

7.6 (ADAPTING TO REWARD VARIANCE IN BANDITS WITH BOUNDED REWARDS) Let $X_1, X_2, \dots, X_n$ be a sequence of independent and identically distributed random variables with mean μ and variance σ^2 and bounded support so that $X_t \in [0, b]$ almost surely. Let $\hat{\mu} = \sum_{t=1}^{n} X_t / n$ and $\hat{\sigma}^2 = \sum_{t=1}^{n} (\hat{\mu} - X_t)^2 / n$. The **empirical Bernstein** inequality says that for any $\delta \in (0, 1)$,

$$\mathbb{P}\left(|\hat{\mu} - \mu| \geq \sqrt{\frac{2\hat{\sigma}^2}{n} \log\left(\frac{3}{\delta}\right)} + \frac{3b}{n} \log\left(\frac{3}{\delta}\right)\right) \leq \delta.$$

(a) Show that $\hat{\sigma}^2 = \frac{1}{n}\sum_{t=1}^{n}(X_t - \mu)^2 - (\hat{\mu} - \mu)^2$.
(b) Show that $\mathbb{V}[(X_t - \mu)^2] \leq b^2\sigma^2$.
(c) Use Bernstein's inequality (Exercise 5.14) to show that

$$\mathbb{P}\left(\hat{\sigma}^2 \geq \sigma^2 + \sqrt{\frac{2b^2\sigma^2}{n}\log\left(\frac{1}{\delta}\right)} + \frac{2b^2}{3n}\log\left(\frac{1}{\delta}\right)\right) \leq \delta.$$

(d) Suppose that $\nu = (\nu_i)_{i=1}^{k}$ is a bandit where $\text{Supp}(\nu_i) \subset [0, b]$ and the variance of the ith arm is σ_i^2 (with our earlier notation, $\nu \in \mathcal{E}_{[0,b]}^{k}$). Design a policy that depends on b, but not on σ_i^2 such that

$$R_n \leq C \sum_{i:\Delta_i > 0} \left(\Delta_i + \left(b + \frac{\sigma_i^2}{\Delta_i}\right)\log(n)\right), \tag{7.14}$$

where $C > 0$ is a universal constant.

If you did things correctly, then the policy you derived in Exercise 7.6 should resemble UCB-V by Audibert et al. [2007]. The proof of the empirical Bernstein also appears there or (with slightly better constants) in the papers by Mnih et al. [2008] and Maurer and Pontil [2009].

It is worth comparing (7.14) to the result of Theorem 7.1. In particular, recall that if the rewards are bounded by b, the reward distributions are b-subgaussian. The regret of UCB which adjusts the confidence intervals accordingly can then be shown to be $R_n = O(\sum_{i:\Delta_i > 0} \frac{b\log(n)}{\Delta_i})$. Thus, the main advantage of the policy of the previous exercise is the replacement of b/Δ_i in this bound with $b + \frac{\sigma_i^2}{\Delta_i}$. In Exercise 16.7, you will show that this is essentially unimprovable.

7.7 (MEDIAN OF MEANS AND BANDITS WITH KNOWN FINITE VARIANCE) Let $n \in \mathbb{N}^+$ and $(A_i)_{i=1}^{m}$ be a partition of $[n]$ so that $\cup_{i=1}^{m} A_i = [n]$ and $A_i \cap A_j = \emptyset$ for all $i \neq j$. Suppose that $\delta \in (0, 1)$ and $X_1, X_2, \dots, X_n$ is a sequence of independent random variables with mean μ and variance σ^2. The **median-of-means estimator** $\hat{\mu}_M$ of μ is the median of $\hat{\mu}_1, \hat{\mu}_2, \dots, \hat{\mu}_m$, where $\hat{\mu}_i = \sum_{t \in A_i} X_t / |A_i|$ is the mean of the data in the ith block.

(a) Show that if $m = \left\lfloor \min\left\{ \frac{n}{2}, 8\log\left(\frac{e^{1/8}}{\delta}\right) \right\} \right\rfloor$ and A_i are chosen as equally sized as possible, then

$$\mathbb{P}\left(\hat{\mu}_M + \sqrt{\frac{192\sigma^2}{n} \log\left(\frac{e^{1/8}}{\delta}\right)} \le \mu \right) \le \delta.$$

(b) Use the median-of-means estimator to design an upper confidence bound algorithm such that for all $v \in \mathcal{E}_V^k(\sigma^2)$,

$$R_n \le C \sum_{i:\Delta_i>0} \left(\Delta_i + \frac{\sigma^2 \log(n)}{\Delta_i} \right),$$

where $C > 0$ is a universal constant.

This exercise shows that the subgaussian assumption can be relaxed to requiring only finite variance at the price of increased constant factors. The result is only possible by replacing the standard empirical estimator with something more robust. The median-of-means estimator is only one way to do this. In fact, the empirical estimator can be made robust by truncating the observed rewards and applying the empirical Bernstein concentration inequality. The disadvantage of this approach is that choosing the location of truncation requires prior knowledge about the approximate location of the mean. Another approach is **Catoni's estimator**, which also exhibits excellent asymptotic properties [Catoni, 2012]. Yet another idea is to minimise the Huber loss [Sun et al., 2017]. This latter paper is focussing on linear models, but the results still apply in one dimension. The application of these ideas to bandits was first made by Bubeck et al. [2013a], where the reader will find more interesting results. Most notably, that things can still be made to work even if the variance does not exist. In this case, however, there is a price to be paid in terms of the regret. The median-of-means estimator is due to Alon et al. [1996]. In case the variance is also unknown, then it may be estimated by assuming a known bound on the **kurtosis**, which covers many classes of bandits (Gaussian with arbitrary variance, exponential and many more), but not some simple cases (Bernoulli). The policy that results from this procedure has the benefit of being invariant under the transformations of shifting or scaling the losses [Lattimore, 2017].

7.8 (EMPIRICAL COMPARISON)

(a) Implement Algorithm 3.

(b) Reproduce Fig. 7.1.

(c) Explain the shape of the curves for ETC. In particular, when $m = 50$, we see a bump, a dip and then a linear asymptote as Δ grows. Why does the curve look like this?

(d) Design an experiment to determine the practical effect of the choice of δ.

(e) Explain your results.

8 The Upper Confidence Bound Algorithm: Asymptotic Optimality

The algorithm analysed in the previous chapter is not anytime. This shortcoming is resolved via a slight modification and a refinement of the analysis. The improved analysis leads to constant factors in the dominant logarithmic term that match a lower bound provided later in Chapter 16.

8.1 Asymptotically Optimal UCB

The algorithm studied is shown in Algorithm 6. It differs from the one analysed in the previous section (Algorithm 3) only by the choice of the confidence level, the choice of which is dictated by the analysis of its regret.

1: **Input** k
2: Choose each arm once
3: Subsequently choose

$$A_t = \operatorname{argmax}_i \left(\hat{\mu}_i(t-1) + \sqrt{\frac{2 \log f(t)}{T_i(t-1)}} \right)$$

where $f(t) = 1 + t \log^2(t)$

Algorithm 6: Asymptotically optimal UCB.

The regret bound for Algorithm 6 is more complicated than the bound for Algorithm 3 (see Theorem 7.1). The dominant terms in the two results have the same order, but the gain here is that in this result the leading constant, governing the asymptotic rate of growth of regret, is smaller.

THEOREM 8.1. *For any 1-subgaussian bandit, the regret of Algorithm 6 satisfies*

$$R_n \leq \sum_{i:\Delta_i>0} \inf_{\varepsilon \in (0,\Delta_i)} \Delta_i \left(1 + \frac{5}{\varepsilon^2} + \frac{2 \left(\log f(n) + \sqrt{\pi \log f(n)} + 1 \right)}{(\Delta_i - \varepsilon)^2} \right). \tag{8.1}$$

Furthermore,

$$\limsup_{n \to \infty} \frac{R_n}{\log(n)} \leq \sum_{i:\Delta_i>0} \frac{2}{\Delta_i}. \tag{8.2}$$

Choosing $\varepsilon = \Delta_i/2$ inside the sum shows that

$$R_n \leq \sum_{i:\Delta_i>0} \left(\Delta_i + \frac{1}{\Delta_i} \left(8 \log f(n) + 8\sqrt{\pi \log f(n)} + 28 \right) \right). \qquad (8.3)$$

Even more concretely, there exists some universal constant $C > 0$ such that

$$R_n \leq C \sum_{i:\Delta_i>0} \left(\Delta_i + \frac{\log(n)}{\Delta_i} \right),$$

which by the same argument as in the proof of Theorem 7.2 leads a worst-case bound of $R_n \leq C \sum_{i=1}^{k} \Delta_i + 2\sqrt{Cnk \log(n)}$.

Taking the limit of the ratio of the bound in (8.3) and $\log(n)$ does not result in the same constant as in the theorem, which is the main justification for introducing the more complicated regret bound. You will see in Chapter 15 that the asymptotic bound on the regret given in (8.2) is unimprovable in a strong sense.

We start with a useful lemma to bound the number of times the index of a suboptimal arm will be larger than some threshold above its mean.

LEMMA 8.2. *Let* $X_1, \ldots, X_n$ *be a sequence of independent 1-subgaussian random variables,* $\hat{\mu}_t = \frac{1}{t}\sum_{s=1}^{t} X_s$, $\varepsilon > 0$, $a > 0$ *and*

$$\kappa = \sum_{t=1}^{n} \mathbb{I}\left\{ \hat{\mu}_t + \sqrt{\frac{2a}{t}} \geq \varepsilon \right\}, \qquad \kappa' = u + \sum_{t=\lceil u \rceil}^{n} \mathbb{I}\left\{ \hat{\mu}_t + \sqrt{\frac{2a}{t}} \geq \varepsilon \right\},$$

where $u = 2a\varepsilon^{-2}$. *Then it holds* $\mathbb{E}[\kappa] \leq \mathbb{E}[\kappa'] \leq 1 + \frac{2}{\varepsilon^2}(a + \sqrt{\pi a} + 1)$.

The intuition for this result is as follows. Since the X_i are 1-subgaussian and independent we have $\mathbb{E}[\hat{\mu}_t] = 0$, so we cannot expect $\hat{\mu}_t + \sqrt{2a/t}$ to be smaller than ε until t is at least $2a/\varepsilon^2$. The lemma confirms that this is the right order as an estimate for $\mathbb{E}[\kappa]$.

Proof By Corollary 5.5 we have

$$\mathbb{E}[\kappa] \leq \mathbb{E}[\kappa'] = u + \sum_{t=\lceil u \rceil}^{n} \mathbb{P}\left(\hat{\mu}_t + \sqrt{\frac{2a}{t}} \geq \varepsilon \right) \leq u + \sum_{t=\lceil u \rceil}^{n} \exp\left(-\frac{t\left(\varepsilon - \sqrt{\frac{2a}{t}}\right)^2}{2} \right)$$

$$\leq 1 + u + \int_{u}^{\infty} \exp\left(-\frac{t\left(\varepsilon - \sqrt{\frac{2a}{t}}\right)^2}{2} \right) dt = 1 + \frac{2}{\varepsilon^2}(a + \sqrt{\pi a} + 1),$$

where the final equality follows by making the substitution $s = \varepsilon\sqrt{t} - \sqrt{2a}$ and substituting the value of u from the lemma statement. $\qquad \square$

Proof of Theorem 8.1 As usual, the starting point is the fundamental regret decomposition (Lemma 4.5),

$$R_n = \sum_{i:\Delta_i > 0} \Delta_i \mathbb{E}[T_i(n)].$$

The rest of the proof revolves around bounding $\mathbb{E}[T_i(n)]$. Let i be a suboptimal arm. The main idea is to decompose $T_i(n)$ into two terms. The first measures the number of times the index of the optimal arm is less than $\mu_1 - \varepsilon$. The second term measures the number of times that $A_t = i$ and its index is larger than $\mu_1 - \varepsilon$.

$$T_i(n) = \sum_{t=1}^{n} \mathbb{I}\{A_t = i\} \leq \sum_{t=1}^{n} \mathbb{I}\left\{ \hat{\mu}_1(t-1) + \sqrt{\frac{2 \log f(t)}{T_1(t-1)}} \leq \mu_1 - \varepsilon \right\}$$

$$+ \sum_{t=1}^{n} \mathbb{I}\left\{ \hat{\mu}_i(t-1) + \sqrt{\frac{2 \log f(t)}{T_i(t-1)}} \geq \mu_1 - \varepsilon \text{ and } A_t = i \right\}. \qquad (8.4)$$

The proof of the first part of the theorem is completed by bounding the expectation of each of these two sums. Starting with the first, we again use Corollary 5.5:

$$\mathbb{E}\left[\sum_{t=1}^{n} \mathbb{I}\left\{ \hat{\mu}_1(t-1) + \sqrt{\frac{2 \log f(t)}{T_1(t-1)}} \leq \mu_1 - \varepsilon \right\} \right]$$

$$\leq \sum_{t=1}^{n} \sum_{s=1}^{n} \mathbb{P}\left(\hat{\mu}_{1s} + \sqrt{\frac{2 \log f(t)}{s}} \leq \mu_1 - \varepsilon \right)$$

$$\leq \sum_{t=1}^{n} \sum_{s=1}^{n} \exp\left(-\frac{s\left(\sqrt{\frac{2 \log f(t)}{s}} + \varepsilon \right)^2}{2} \right)$$

$$\leq \sum_{t=1}^{n} \frac{1}{f(t)} \sum_{s=1}^{n} \exp\left(-\frac{s\varepsilon^2}{2} \right) \leq \frac{5}{\varepsilon^2}.$$

The first inequality follows from the union bound over all possible values of $T_1(t-1)$. The last inequality is an algebraic exercise (Exercise 8.1). The function $f(t)$ was chosen precisely so this bound would hold. For the second term in (8.4) we use Lemma 8.2 to get

$$\mathbb{E}\left[\sum_{t=1}^{n} \mathbb{I}\left\{ \hat{\mu}_i(t-1) + \sqrt{\frac{2 \log f(t)}{T_i(t-1)}} \geq \mu_1 - \varepsilon \text{ and } A_t = i \right\} \right]$$

$$\leq \mathbb{E}\left[\sum_{t=1}^{n} \mathbb{I}\left\{ \hat{\mu}_i(t-1) + \sqrt{\frac{2 \log f(n)}{T_i(t-1)}} \geq \mu_1 - \varepsilon \text{ and } A_t = i \right\} \right]$$

$$\leq \mathbb{E}\left[\sum_{s=1}^{n} \mathbb{I}\left\{ \hat{\mu}_{is} + \sqrt{\frac{2 \log f(n)}{s}} \geq \mu_1 - \varepsilon \right\} \right]$$

$$= \mathbb{E}\left[\sum_{s=1}^{n} \mathbb{I}\left\{\hat{\mu}_{is} - \mu_i + \sqrt{\frac{2\log f(n)}{s}} \geq \Delta_i - \varepsilon\right\}\right]$$

$$\leq 1 + \frac{2}{(\Delta_i - \varepsilon)^2}\left(\log f(n) + \sqrt{\pi \log f(n)} + 1\right).$$

The first part of the theorem follows by substituting the results of the previous two displays into (8.4). The second part follows by choosing $\varepsilon = \log^{-1/4}(n)$ and taking the limit as n tends to infinity. $\square$

8.2   Notes

1 The improvement to the constants comes from making the confidence interval slightly smaller, which is made possible by a more careful analysis. The main trick is the observation that we do not need to show that $\hat{\mu}_{1s} \geq \mu_1$ for all s with high probability, but instead that $\hat{\mu}_{1s} \geq \mu_1 - \varepsilon$ for small ε.

2 The choice of $f(t) = 1 + t\log^2(t)$ looks quite odd. With a slightly messier calculation we could have chosen $f(t) = t\log^\alpha(t)$ for any $\alpha > 0$. If the rewards are actually Gaussian, then a more careful concentration analysis allows one to choose $f(t) = t$ or even some slightly slower-growing function [Katehakis and Robbins, 1995, Lattimore, 2016a, Garivier et al., 2016b].

3 The asymptotic regret is often indicative of finite-time performance. The reader is advised to be cautious, however. The lower-order terms obscured by the asymptotics can be dominant in all practical regimes.

8.3   Bibliographic Remarks

Lai and Robbins [1985] designed policies for which Eq. (8.2) holds. They also proved a lower bound showing that no 'reasonable' policy can improve on this bound for any problem, where 'reasonable' means that they suffer subpolynomial regret on all problems (see Part IV). The policy proposed by Lai and Robbins [1985] was based on upper confidence bounds, but was not a variant of UCB. The asymptotics for variants of the policy presented here were given first by Lai [1987], Katehakis and Robbins [1995] and Agrawal [1995]. None of these articles gave finite-time bounds like what was presented here. When the reward distributions lie in an exponential family, then asymptotic and finite-time bounds with the same flavor to what is presented here are given by Cappé et al. [2013]. There are now a huge variety of asymptotically optimal policies in a wide range of settings. Burnetas and Katehakis [1996] study the general case and give conditions for a version of UCB to be asymptotically optimal. Honda and Takemura [2010, 2011] analyse an algorithm called DMED, proving asymptotic optimality for noise models where the support is bounded or semi-bounded. Kaufmann et al. [2012b] prove asymptotic optimality for Thompson sampling (see Chapter 36) when the rewards are Bernoulli, which is generalised to single-parameter exponential families by Korda et al. [2013]. Kaufmann [2018] proves asymptotic optimality for the BayesUCB class of algorithms for single-parameter exponential families. Ménard and Garivier [2017] prove asymptotic optimality and minimax optimality for exponential families (more discussion in Chapter 9).

8.4   Exercises

8.1 Do the algebra needed at the end of the proof of Theorem 8.1. Precisely, show that

$$\sum_{t=1}^{n} \frac{1}{f(t)} \sum_{s=1}^{n} \exp\left(-\frac{s\varepsilon^2}{2}\right) \le \frac{5}{\varepsilon^2},$$

where $f(t) = 1 + t \log^2(t)$.

HINT   First bound $F = \sum_{s=1}^{n} \exp(-s\varepsilon^2/2)$ using a geometric series. Then show that $\exp(-a)/(1 - \exp(-a)) \le 1/a$ holds for any $a > 0$ and conclude that $F \le \frac{2}{\varepsilon^2}$. Finish by bounding $\sum_{t=1}^{n} 1/f(t)$ using the fact that $1/f(t) \le 1/(t \log(t)^2)$ and bounding a sum by an integral.

8.2 (ONE-ARMED BANDITS) Consider the one-armed bandit problem: $\mathcal{E} = \{\mathcal{N}(\mu_1, 1) : \mu_1 \in \mathbb{R}\} \times \{\mathcal{N}(0,1)\}$. Suppose that $\nu = (P_1, P_2) \in \mathcal{E}$ and P_1 has mean $\mu_1 = 1$. Evaluate

$$\limsup_{n\to\infty} \frac{R_n(\pi, \nu)}{\log(n)},$$

where π is the policy of Algorithm 6.

8.3 (ONE-ARMED BANDITS (II)) Consider the setting of Exercise 8.2 and define a policy by

$$A_t = \begin{cases} 1 & \text{if } \hat{\mu}_1(t-1) + \sqrt{\frac{2\log f(t)}{T_1(t-1)}} \ge 0 \\ 2 & \text{otherwise.} \end{cases} \tag{8.5}$$

Suppose that $\nu = (P_1, P_2)$ where $P_1 = \mathcal{N}(\mu_1, 1)$ and $P_2 = \mathcal{N}(0, 1)$. Prove that for the modified policy,

$$\limsup_{n\to\infty} \frac{R_n(\nu)}{\log(n)} \le \begin{cases} 0 & \text{if } \mu_1 \ge 0 \\ \frac{2}{\mu_1^2} & \text{if } \mu_1 < 0. \end{cases}$$

HINT   Follow the analysis for UCB, but carefully adapt the proof by using the fact that the index of the second arm is always zero.

 The strategy proposed in the above exercise is based on the idea that optimism is used to overcome uncertainty in the estimates of the quality of an arm, but for one-armed bandits the mean of the second arm is known in advance.

8.4 (ONE-ARMED BANDITS (III)) The purpose of this question is to compare UCB and the modified version in (8.5).

(a) Implement a simulator for the one-armed bandit problem and two algorithms: UCB and the modified version analysed in Exercise 8.3.

(b) Use your simulator to estimate the expected regret of each algorithm for a horizon of $n = 1000$ and $\mu_1 \in [-1, 1]$.

(c) Plot your results with μ_1 on the x-axis and the estimated expected regret on the y-axis. Don't forget to label the axis and include error bars and a legend.

(d) Explain the results. Why do the curves look the way they do?

(e) In your plot, for what values of μ_1 does the worst-case expected regret for each algorithm occur? What is the worst-case expected regret for each algorithm?

8.5 (DIFFERENT SUBGAUSSIAN CONSTANTS) Let $\sigma^2 \in [0, \infty)^k$ be known and suppose that the reward is $X_t \sim \mathcal{N}(\mu_{A_t}, \sigma^2_{A_t})$. Design an algorithm (that depends on σ^2) for which the asymptotic regret is

$$\limsup_{n \to \infty} \frac{R_n}{\log(n)} = \sum_{i : \Delta_i > 0} \frac{2\sigma_i^2}{\Delta_i}.$$

9 The Upper Confidence Bound Algorithm: Minimax Optimality ()

We proved that the variants of UCB analysed in the last two chapters have a worst-case regret of $R_n = O(\sqrt{kn \log(n)})$. Further, in Exercise 6.8 you showed that an elimination algorithm achieves $R_n = O(\sqrt{kn \log(k)})$. By modifying the confidence levels of the algorithm it is possible to remove the log factor entirely. Building on UCB, the directly named 'minimax optimal strategy in the stochastic case' (MOSS) algorithm was the first to make this modification and is presented below. MOSS again depends on prior knowledge of the horizon, a requirement that may be relaxed, as we explain in the notes.

> The term **minimax** is used because, except for constant factors, the worst-case bound proven in this chapter cannot be improved on by any algorithm. The lower bounds are deferred to Part IV.

9.1 The MOSS Algorithm

Algorithm 7 shows the pseudocode of MOSS, which is again an instance of the UCB family. The main novelty is that the confidence level is chosen based on the number of plays of the individual arms, as well as n and k.

1: **Input** n and k
2: Choose each arm once
3: Subsequently choose

$$A_t = \operatorname{argmax}_i \hat{\mu}_i(t-1) + \sqrt{\frac{4}{T_i(t-1)} \log^+\left(\frac{n}{kT_i(t-1)}\right)},$$

where $\log^+(x) = \log \max\{1, x\}$.

Algorithm 7: MOSS.

THEOREM 9.1. *For any 1-subgaussian bandit, the regret of Algorithm 7 satisfies*

$$R_n \le 39\sqrt{kn} + \sum_{i=1}^{k} \Delta_i.$$

Before the proof we state and prove a strengthened version of Corollary 5.5.

THEOREM 9.2. *Let $X_1, X_2, \ldots, X_n$ be a sequence of independent σ-subgaussian random variables and $S_t = \sum_{s=1}^{t} X_s$. Then, for any $\varepsilon > 0$,*

$$\mathbb{P}\left(\text{exists } t \leq n : S_t \geq \varepsilon\right) \leq \exp\left(-\frac{\varepsilon^2}{2n\sigma^2}\right). \tag{9.1}$$

The bound in Eq. (9.1) is the same as the bound on $\mathbb{P}(S_n \geq \varepsilon)$ that appears in a simple reformulation of Corollary 5.5, so this new result is strictly stronger.

Proof From the definition of subgaussian random variables and Lemma 5.4,

$$\mathbb{E}\left[\exp\left(\lambda S_n\right)\right] \leq \exp\left(\frac{n\sigma^2\lambda^2}{2}\right).$$

Then, choosing $\lambda = \varepsilon/(n\sigma^2)$ leads to

$$\mathbb{P}\left(\text{exists } t \leq n : S_t \geq \varepsilon\right) = \mathbb{P}\left(\max_{t \leq n} \exp\left(\lambda S_t\right) \geq \exp\left(\lambda\varepsilon\right)\right)$$

$$\leq \frac{\mathbb{E}\left[\exp\left(\lambda S_n\right)\right]}{\exp\left(\lambda\varepsilon\right)} \leq \exp\left(\frac{n\sigma^2\lambda^2}{2} - \lambda\varepsilon\right) = \exp\left(-\frac{\varepsilon^2}{2n\sigma^2}\right).$$

The novel step is the first inequality, which follows from Doob's submartingale inequality (Theorem 3.10) and the fact that that $\exp(\lambda S_t)$ is a submartingale with respect to the filtration generated by $X_1, X_2, \ldots, X_n$ (Exercise 9.1). □

Before the proof of Theorem 9.1, we need one more lemma to bound the probability that the index of the optimal arm ever drops too far below the actual mean of the optimal arm. The proof of this lemma relies on a tool called the **peeling device**, which is an important technique in probability theory and has many applications beyond bandits. For example, it can be used to prove the celebrated law of the iterated logarithm.

LEMMA 9.3. *Let $\delta \in (0, 1)$ and $X_1, X_2, \ldots$ be independent and 1-subgaussian and $\hat{\mu}_t = \frac{1}{t}\sum_{s=1}^{t} X_s$. Then, for any $\Delta > 0$,*

$$\mathbb{P}\left(\text{exists } s \geq 1 : \hat{\mu}_s + \sqrt{\frac{4}{s}\log^+\left(\frac{1}{s\delta}\right)} + \Delta \leq 0\right) \leq \frac{15\delta}{\Delta^2}.$$

Proof Let $S_t = t\hat{\mu}_t$. Then

$$\mathbb{P}\left(\text{exists } s \geq 1 : \hat{\mu}_s + \sqrt{\frac{4}{s}\log^+\left(\frac{1}{s\delta}\right)} + \Delta \leq 0\right)$$

$$= \mathbb{P}\left(\text{exists } s \geq 1 : S_s + \sqrt{4s\log^+\left(\frac{1}{s\delta}\right)} + s\Delta \leq 0\right)$$

$$\leq \sum_{j=0}^{\infty} \mathbb{P}\left(\text{exists } s \in [2^j, 2^{j+1}] : S_s + \sqrt{4s\log^+\left(\frac{1}{s\delta}\right)} + s\Delta \leq 0\right)$$

$$\leq \sum_{j=0}^{\infty} \mathbb{P}\left(\text{exists } s \leq 2^{j+1} : S_s + \sqrt{4 \cdot 2^j \log^+\left(\frac{1}{2^{j+1}\delta}\right)} + 2^j \Delta \leq 0 \right)$$

$$\leq \sum_{j=0}^{\infty} \exp\left(-\frac{\left(\sqrt{2^{j+2} \log^+\left(\frac{1}{2^{j+1}\delta}\right)} + 2^j \Delta \right)^2}{2^{j+2}} \right).$$

The first inequality follows from a union bound over a geometric grid. The second step is straightforward but important because it sets up to apply Theorem 9.2. The rest is purely algebraic:

$$\sum_{j=0}^{\infty} \exp\left(-\frac{\left(\sqrt{2^{j+2} \log^+\left(\frac{1}{2^{j+1}\delta}\right)} + 2^j \Delta \right)^2}{2^{j+2}} \right) \leq \delta \sum_{j=0}^{\infty} 2^{j+1} \exp\left(-\Delta^2 2^{j-2} \right)$$

$$\leq \frac{8\delta}{e\Delta^2} + \delta \int_0^{\infty} 2^{s+1} \exp\left(-\Delta^2 2^{s-2} \right) ds \leq \frac{15\delta}{\Delta^2}.$$

Above, the first inequality follows since $(a+b)^2 \geq a^2 + b^2$ for $a, b \geq 0$, and the second last step follows by noting that the integrand is unimodal and has a maximum value of $8\delta/(e\Delta^2)$. For such functions f, one has the bound $\sum_{j=a}^{b} f(j) \leq \max_{s \in [a,b]} f(s) + \int_a^b f(s) ds$. □

Proof of Theorem 9.1   As usual, we assume without loss of generality that the first arm is optimal, so $\mu_1 = \mu^*$. Arguing that the optimal arm is sufficiently optimistic with high probability is no longer satisfactory because in this refined analysis, the probability that an arm is played linearly often needs to depend on its suboptimality gap. A way around this difficulty is to make an argument in terms of the expected amount of optimism. Define a random variable Δ that measures how far below the index of the optimal arm drops below its true mean.

$$\Delta = \left(\mu_1 - \min_{s \leq n} \left(\hat{\mu}_{1s} + \sqrt{\frac{4}{s} \log^+\left(\frac{n}{ks}\right)} \right) \right)^+.$$

Arms with suboptimality gaps much larger than Δ will not be played too often, while arms with suboptimality gaps smaller than Δ may be played linearly often, but Δ is sufficiently small in expectation that this price is small. Using the basic regret decomposition (Lemma 4.5) and splitting the actions based on whether or not their suboptimality gap is smaller or larger than 2Δ leads to

$$R_n = \sum_{i:\Delta_i>0} \Delta_i \mathbb{E}[T_i(n)]$$

$$\leq \mathbb{E}\left[2n\Delta + \sum_{i:\Delta_i>2\Delta} \Delta_i T_i(n) \right]$$

$$\leq \mathbb{E}\left[2n\Delta + 8\sqrt{kn} + \sum_{i:\Delta_i>\max\{2\Delta, 8\sqrt{k/n}\}} \Delta_i T_i(n) \right].$$

The first term is easily bounded using Proposition 2.8 and Lemma 9.3:

$$\mathbb{E}[2n\Delta] = 2n\mathbb{E}[\Delta] = 2n\int_0^\infty \mathbb{P}(\Delta \geq x)\,dx \leq 2n\int_0^\infty \min\left\{1, \frac{15k}{nx^2}\right\}dx \leq 16\sqrt{kn}.$$

For suboptimal arm i, define

$$\kappa_i = \sum_{s=1}^n \mathbb{I}\left\{\hat{\mu}_{is} + \sqrt{\frac{4}{s}\log^+\left(\frac{n}{ks}\right)} \geq \mu_i + \Delta_i/2\right\}.$$

The reason for choosing κ_i in this way is that for arms i with $\Delta_i > 2\Delta$, it holds that the index of the optimal arm is always larger than $\mu_i + \Delta_i/2$, so κ_i is an upper bound on the number of times arm i is played, $T_i(n)$. If $\Delta_i \geq 8(k/n)^{1/2}$, then the expectation of $\Delta_i \kappa_i$ is bounded using Lemma 8.2 by

$$\Delta_i \mathbb{E}[\kappa_i] \leq \frac{1}{\Delta_i} + \Delta_i \mathbb{E}\left[\sum_{s=1}^n \mathbb{I}\left\{\hat{\mu}_{is} + \sqrt{\frac{4}{s}\log^+\left(\frac{n\Delta_i^2}{k}\right)} \geq \mu_i + \Delta_i/2\right\}\right]$$

$$\leq \frac{1}{\Delta_i} + \Delta_i + \frac{8}{\Delta_i}\left(2\log^+\left(\frac{n\Delta_i^2}{k}\right) + \sqrt{2\pi\log^+\left(\frac{n\Delta_i^2}{k}\right)} + 1\right)$$

$$\leq \frac{1}{8}\sqrt{\frac{n}{k}} + \Delta_i + \sqrt{\frac{n}{k}}\left(4\log 8 + 2\sqrt{\pi\log 8} + 1\right) \leq \Delta_i + 15\sqrt{\frac{n}{k}},$$

where the first inequality follows by replacing the s in the logarithm with $1/\Delta_i^2$ and adding the $\Delta_i \times 1/\Delta_i^2$ correction term to compensate for the first Δ_i^{-2} rounds where this fails to hold. Then we use Lemma 8.2 and the monotonicity of $x \mapsto x^{-1-p}\log^+(ax^2)$ for $p \in [0, 1]$, positive a and $x \geq e/\sqrt{a}$. The last inequality follows by naively bounding $1/8 + 4\log 8 + 2\sqrt{\pi\log 8} + 1 \leq 15$. Then

$$\mathbb{E}\left[\sum_{i:\Delta_i > \max\left\{2\Delta, 8\sqrt{k/n}\right\}} \Delta_i T_i(n)\right] \leq \mathbb{E}\left[\sum_{i:\Delta_i > 8\sqrt{k/n}} \Delta_i \kappa_i\right]$$

$$\leq \sum_{i:\Delta_i > 8\sqrt{k/n}}\left(\Delta_i + 15\sqrt{\frac{n}{k}}\right)$$

$$\leq 15\sqrt{nk} + \sum_{i=1}^k \Delta_i.$$

Combining all the results we have $R_n \leq 39\sqrt{kn} + \sum_{i=1}^k \Delta_i$.   □

9.2   Two Problems

MOSS is not the ultimate algorithm. Here we highlight two drawbacks.

Suboptimality Relative to UCB

Although MOSS is nearly asymptotically optimal (Note 1), all versions of MOSS can be arbitrarily worse than UCB in some regimes. This unpleasantness is hidden by both the minimax and asymptotic optimality criteria, which highlights the importance of fully finite-time upper and lower bounds. The counter-example witnessing the failure is quite simple. Let the rewards for all arms be Gaussian with unit variance and $n = k^3$, $\mu_1 = 0$, $\mu_2 = -\sqrt{k/n}$ and $\mu_i = -1$ for all $i > 2$. From Theorem 8.1, we have that

$$R_n^{\text{UCB}} = O(k \log k),$$

while it turns out that MOSS has a regret of

$$R_n^{\text{MOSS}} = \Omega(\sqrt{kn}) = \Omega(k^2).$$

A rigourous proof of this claim is quite delicate, but we encourage readers to try to understand why it holds intuitively.

Instability

There is a hidden cost of pushing too hard to reduce the expected regret, which is that the distribution of the regret is less well-behaved. Consider a two-armed Gaussian bandit with suboptimality gap Δ. The random (pseudo) regret is $\hat{R}_n = \sum_{t=1}^{n} \Delta_{A_t}$, which for a carefully tuned algorithm has a roughly bimodal distribution:

$$\hat{R}_n \approx \begin{cases} n\Delta & \text{with probability } \delta \\ \frac{1}{\Delta} \log\left(\frac{1}{\delta}\right) & \text{otherwise,} \end{cases}$$

where δ is a parameter of the policy that determines the likelihood that the optimal arm is misidentified. Integrating, one has

$$R_n = \mathbb{E}[\hat{R}_n] = O\left(n\Delta\delta + \frac{1}{\Delta} \log\left(\frac{1}{\delta}\right)\right),$$

The choice of δ that minimises the expected regret depends on Δ and is approximately $1/(n\Delta^2)$. With this choice, the regret is

$$R_n = O\left(\frac{1}{\Delta}\left(1 + \log\left(n\Delta^2\right)\right)\right).$$

Of course Δ is not known in advance, but it can be estimated online so that the above bound is actually realisable by an adaptive policy that does not know Δ in advance (Exercise 9.3). Let F be the (informal) event that $\hat{R}_n = \Omega(n\Delta)$. The problem is that when $\delta = 1/(n\Delta^2)$ is chosen to minimise the expected regret, then the second moment due to failure is

$$\mathbb{E}[\mathbb{I}_F \hat{R}_n^2] = \Omega(n).$$

On the other hand, by choosing $\delta = (n\Delta)^{-2}$, the regret increases only slightly to

$$R_n = O\left(\frac{1}{\Delta}\left(\frac{1}{n} + \log\left(n^2\Delta^2\right)\right)\right).$$

The second moment of the regret due to failure, however, is $\mathbb{E}[\mathbb{I}_F \hat{R}_n^2] = O(1)$.

9.3   Notes

1 MOSS is quite close to asymptotically optimal. You can prove that

$$\limsup_{n\to\infty} \frac{R_n}{\log(n)} \le \sum_{i:\Delta_i>0} \frac{4}{\Delta_i}.$$

By modifying the algorithm slightly, it is even possible to replace the four with a two and recover the optimal asymptotic regret. The trick is to increase g slightly and replace the four in the exploration bonus by two. The major task is then to re-prove Lemma 9.3, which is done by replacing the intervals $[2^j, 2^{j+1}]$ with smaller intervals $[\xi^j, \xi^{j+1}]$, where ξ is tuned subsequently to be fractionally larger than one. This procedure is explained in detail by Garivier [2013]. When the reward distributions are actually Gaussian, there is a more elegant technique that avoids peeling altogether (Exercise 9.4).

2 One way to mitigate the issues raised in Section 9.2 is to replace the index used by MOSS with a less aggressive confidence level:

$$\hat{\mu}_i(t-1) + \sqrt{\frac{4}{T_i(t-1)} \log^+\left(\frac{n}{T_i(t-1)}\right)}. \tag{9.2}$$

The resulting algorithm is never worse than UCB, and you will show in Exercise 9.3 that it has a distribution free regret of $O(\sqrt{nk\log(k)})$. An algorithm that does almost the same thing in disguise is called 'improved UCB', which operates in phases and eliminates arms for which the upper confidence bound drops below a lower confidence bound for some arm [Auer and Ortner, 2010]. This algorithm was the topic of Exercise 6.8.

3 Overcoming the failure of MOSS to be instance optimal without sacrificing minimax optimality is possible by using an adaptive confidence level that tunes the amount of optimism to match the instance. One of the authors has proposed two ways to do this, using one of the following indices:

$$\hat{\mu}_i(t-1) + \sqrt{\frac{2(1+\varepsilon)}{T_i(t-1)} \log\left(\frac{n}{t}\right)}, \text{ or} \tag{9.3}$$

$$\hat{\mu}_i(t-1) + \sqrt{\frac{2}{T_i(t-1)} \log\left(\frac{n}{\sum_{j=1}^k \min\{T_i(t-1), \sqrt{T_i(t-1)T_j(t-1)}\}}\right)}.$$

The first of these algorithms is called the 'optimally confident UCB' [Lattimore, 2015b] while the second is AdaUCB [Lattimore, 2018]. Both algorithms are minimax optimal up to constant factors and never worse than UCB. The latter is also asymptotically optimal. If the horizon is unknown, then AdaUCB can be modified by replacing n with t. It remains a challenge to provide a straightforward analysis for these algorithms.

9.4   Bibliographic Remarks

MOSS is due to Audibert and Bubeck [2009], while an anytime modification is by Degenne and Perchet [2016]. The proof that a modified version of MOSS is asymptotically optimal may be found in the article by Ménard and Garivier [2017]. There is also a variant of MOSS that adapts to the variance for rewards bounded in $[0, 1]$ [Mukherjee et al., 2018]. AdaUCB and its friends are by one of the authors [Lattimore, 2015b, 2016b, 2018]. The idea to modify the confidence level has been seen in several places, with the earliest by Lai [1987] and more recently by Honda and Takemura [2010]. Kaufmann [2018] also used a confidence level like in Eq. (9.2) to derive an algorithm based on Bayesian upper confidence bounds.

9.5   Exercises

9.1 (SUBMARTINGALE PROPERTY) Let $X_1, X_2, \ldots, X_n$ be adapted to filtration $\mathbb{F} = (\mathcal{F}_t)_t$ with $\mathbb{E}[X_t \mid \mathcal{F}_{t-1}] = 0$ almost surely. Prove that $M_t = \exp(\lambda \sum_{s=1}^{t} X_s)$ is a $\mathbb{F}$-submartingale for any $\lambda \in \mathbb{R}$.

9.2 (PROBLEM-DEPENDENT BOUND) Let $\Delta_{\min} = \min_{i:\Delta_i > 0} \Delta_i$. Show there exists a universal constant $C > 0$ such that the regret of MOSS is bounded by

$$R_n \leq \frac{Ck}{\Delta_{\min}} \log^+\left(\frac{n\Delta_{\min}^2}{k}\right) + \sum_{i=1}^{k} \Delta_i.$$

9.3 (UCB*) Suppose we modify the index used by MOSS to be

$$\hat{\mu}_i(t-1) + \sqrt{\frac{4}{T_i(t-1)} \log^+\left(\frac{n}{T_i(t-1)}\right)}.$$

(a) Show that for all 1-subgaussian bandits, this new policy suffers regret at most

$$R_n \leq C\left(\sum_{i:\Delta_i > 0} \Delta_i + \frac{1}{\Delta_i} \log^+(n\Delta_i^2)\right),$$

where $C > 0$ is a universal constant.

(b) Under the same conditions as the previous part, show there exists a universal constant $C > 0$ such that

$$R_n \leq C\sqrt{kn \log(k)} + \sum_{i=1}^{k} \Delta_i.$$

(c) Repeat parts (a) and (b) using the index

$$\hat{\mu}_i(t-1) + \sqrt{\frac{4}{T_i(t-1)} \log^+\left(\frac{t}{T_i(t-1)}\right)}.$$

9.4 (GAUSSIAN NOISE AND THE TANGENT APPROXIMATION) Let $g(t) = at + b$ with $b > 0$ and

$$u(x,t) = \frac{1}{\sqrt{2\pi t}} \exp\left(-\frac{x^2}{2t}\right) - \frac{1}{\sqrt{2\pi t}} \exp\left(-2ab - \frac{(x-2b)^2}{2t}\right).$$

(a) Show that $u(x,t) > 0$ for $x \in (-\infty, g(t))$ and $u(x,t) = 0$ for $x = g(t)$.

(b) Show that $u(x,t)$ satisfies the heat equation:

$$\partial_t u(x,t) = \frac{1}{2}\partial_x^2 u(x,t).$$

(c) Let B_t be a standard Brownian motion, which for any fixed t has density with respect to the Lebesgue measure.

$$p(x,t) = \frac{1}{\sqrt{2\pi t}} \exp\left(-\frac{x^2}{2t}\right).$$

Define $\tau = \min\{t : B_t = g(t)\}$ as the first time the Brownian motion hits the boundary. Put on your physicists hat (or work hard) to argue that

$$\mathbb{P}\left(\tau \geq t\right) = \int_{-\infty}^{g(t)} u(x, t)dx.$$

(d) Let $v(t)$ be the density of time τ with respect to the Lebesgue measure so that $\mathbb{P}\left(\tau_g \leq t\right) = \int_0^t v(t)dt$. Show that

$$v(t) = \frac{b}{\sqrt{2\pi t^3}} \exp\left(-\frac{g(t)^2}{2t}\right)$$

(e) In the last part, you established the exact density of the hitting time of a Brownian motion approaching a linear boundary. We now generalise this to nonlinear boundaries, but at the cost that now we only have a bound. Suppose that $f : [0, \infty) \to [0, \infty)$ is concave and differentiable, and let $\lambda : \mathbb{R} \to \mathbb{R}$ be the intersection of the tangent to f at t with the y-axis given by $\lambda(t) = f(t) - tf'(t)$. Let $\tau = \min\{t : B_t = f(t)\}$ and $v(t)$ be the density of τ. Show that for $t > 0$,

$$v(t) \leq \frac{\lambda(t)}{\sqrt{2\pi t^3}} \exp\left(-\frac{f(t)^2}{2t}\right).$$

(f) Suppose that $X_1, X_2, \ldots$ is a sequence of independent standard Gaussian random variables. Show that

$$\mathbb{P}\left(\text{exists } t \leq n : \sum_{s=1}^t X_s \geq f(t)\right) \leq \int_0^n \frac{\lambda(t)}{\sqrt{2\pi t^3}} \exp\left(-\frac{f(t)^2}{2t}\right) dt.$$

(g) Let $h : (0, \infty) \to (1, \infty)$ be a concave increasing function such that $\sqrt{\log(h(a))}/h(a) \leq c/a$ for some constant $c > 0$ and $f(t) = \sqrt{2t \log h(1/t\delta) + t\Delta}$. Show that

$$\mathbb{P}\left(\text{exists } t : \sum_{s=1}^t X_s \geq f(t)\right) \leq \frac{2c\delta}{\sqrt{\pi}\Delta^2}.$$

(h) Show that $h(a) = 1 + (1 + a)\sqrt{\log(1 + a)}$ satisfies the requirements of the previous part with $c = 11/10$.

(i) Use your results to modify MOSS for the case when the rewards are Gaussian. Compare the algorithms empirically.

(j) Prove for your modified algorithm that

$$\limsup_{n \to \infty} \frac{R_n}{\log(n)} \leq \sum_{i:\Delta_i > 0} \frac{2}{\Delta_i}.$$

HINT   The above exercise has several challenging components and assumes prior knowledge of Brownian motion and its interpretation in terms of the heat equation. We recommend the book by Lerche [1986] as a nice reference on hitting times for Brownian motion against concave barriers. The equation you derived in Part (d) is called the **Bachelier–Lévy formula**, and the technique for doing so is the method of images. The use of this theory in bandits was introduced by one of the authors [Lattimore, 2018], which readers might find useful when working through these questions.

9.5 (ASYMPTOTIC OPTIMALITY AND SUBGAUSSIAN NOISE) In the last exercise, you modified MOSS to show asymptotic optimality when the noise is Gaussian. This is also possible for subgaussian noise.

Follow the advice in the notes of this chapter to adapt MOSS so that for all 1-subgaussian bandits, it holds that

$$\limsup_{n \to \infty} \frac{R_n}{\log(n)} \leq \sum_{i:\Delta_i > 0} \frac{2}{\Delta_i},$$

while maintaining the property that $R_n \leq C\sqrt{kn}$ for universal constant $C > 0$.

10 The Upper Confidence Bound Algorithm: Bernoulli Noise (🦘)

In previous chapters we assumed that the noise of the rewards was σ-subgaussian for some known $\sigma > 0$. This has the advantage of simplicity and relative generality, but stronger assumptions are sometimes justified and often lead to stronger results. In this chapter the rewards are assumed to be Bernoulli, which just means that $X_t \in \{0, 1\}$. This is a fundamental setting found in many applications. For example, in click-through prediction, the user either clicks on the link or not. A Bernoulli bandit is characterised by the mean pay-off vector $\mu \in [0, 1]^k$ and the reward observed in round t is $X_t \sim \mathcal{B}(\mu_{A_t})$.

The Bernoulli distribution is $1/2$-subgaussian regardless of its mean (Exercise 5.12). Hence the results of the previous chapters are applicable, and an appropriately tuned UCB enjoys logarithmic regret. The additional knowledge that the rewards are Bernoulli is not being fully exploited by these algorithms, however. The reason is essentially that the variance of a Bernoulli random variable depends on its mean, and when the variance is small, the empirical mean concentrates faster, a fact that should be used to make the confidence intervals smaller.

10.1 Concentration for Sums of Bernoulli Random Variables

The first step when designing a new optimistic algorithm is to construct confidence sets for the unknown parameters. For Bernoulli bandits, this corresponds to analysing the concentration of the empirical mean for sums of Bernoulli random variables. For this, the following definition will prove useful:

DEFINITION 10.1 (Relative entropy between Bernoulli distributions). The **relative entropy** between Bernoulli distributions with parameters $p, q \in [0, 1]$ is

$$d(p, q) = p \log(p/q) + (1 - p) \log((1 - p)/(1 - q)),$$

where singularities are defined by taking limits: $d(0, q) = \log(1/(1 - q))$ and $d(1, q) = \log(1/q)$ for $q \in [0, 1]$ and $d(p, 0) = 0$ if $p = 0$ and ∞ otherwise and $d(p, 1) = 0$ if $p = 1$ and ∞ otherwise.

 More generally, the **relative entropy** or **Kullback–Leibler divergence** is a measure of similarity between distributions. See Chapter 14 for a generic definition, interpretation and discussion.

LEMMA 10.2. *Let $p, q, \varepsilon \in [0, 1]$. The following hold:*

(a) *The functions $d(\cdot, q)$ and $d(p, \cdot)$ are convex and have unique minimisers at q and p, respectively.*

(b) $d(p, q) \geq 2(p - q)^2$ (**Pinsker's inequality**).

(c) *If $p \leq q - \varepsilon \leq q$, then $d(p, q - \varepsilon) \leq d(p, q) - d(q - \varepsilon, q) \leq d(p, q) - 2\varepsilon^2$.*

Proof We assume that $p, q \in (0, 1)$. The corner cases are easily checked separately. Part (a): $d(\cdot, q)$ is the sum of the negative binary entropy function $h(p) = p \log p + (1-p) \log(1-p)$ and a linear function. The second derivative of h is $h''(p) = 1/p + 1/(1 - p)$, which is positive, and hence h is convex. For fixed p the function $d(p, \cdot)$ is the sum of $h(p)$ and convex functions $p \log(1/q)$ and $(1 - p) \log(1/(1 - q))$. Hence $d(p, \cdot)$ is convex. The minimiser property follows because $d(p, q) > 0$ unless $p = q$ in which case $d(p, p) = d(q, q) = 0$. A more general version of (b) is given in Chapter 15. A proof of the simple version here follows by considering the function $g(x) = d(p, p + x) - 2x^2$, which obviously satisfies $g(0) = 0$. The proof is finished by showing that this is the unique minimiser of g over the interval $[-p, 1 - p]$. The details are left to Exercise 10.1. For (c), notice that

$$h(p) = d(p, q - \varepsilon) - d(p, q) = p \log \frac{q}{q - \varepsilon} + (1 - p) \log \frac{1 - q}{1 - q + \varepsilon}.$$

It is easy to see then that h is linear and increasing in its argument. Therefore, since $p \leq q - \varepsilon$,

$$h(p) \leq h(q - \varepsilon) = -d(q - \varepsilon, q),$$

as required for the first inequality of (c). The second inequality follows by using the result in (b). □

The next lemma controls the concentration of the sample mean of a sequence of independent and identically distributed Bernoulli random variables.

LEMMA 10.3 (Chernoff's bound). *Let $X_1, X_2, \ldots, X_n$ be a sequence of independent random variables that are Bernoulli distributed with mean μ, and let $\hat{\mu} = \frac{1}{n} \sum_{t=1}^{n} X_t$ be the sample mean. Then, for $\varepsilon \in [0, 1 - \mu]$, it holds that*

$$\mathbb{P}(\hat{\mu} \geq \mu + \varepsilon) \leq \exp(-nd(\mu + \varepsilon, \mu)) \tag{10.1}$$

and for $\varepsilon \in [0, \mu]$,

$$\mathbb{P}(\hat{\mu} \leq \mu - \varepsilon) \leq \exp(-nd(\mu - \varepsilon, \mu)). \tag{10.2}$$

Proof We will again use the Cramér–Chernoff method. Let $\lambda > 0$ be some constant to be chosen later. Then,

$$\mathbb{P}(\hat{\mu} \geq \mu + \varepsilon) = \mathbb{P}\left(\exp\left(\lambda \sum_{t=1}^{n}(X_t - \mu)\right) \geq \exp(\lambda n \varepsilon)\right)$$

$$\leq \frac{\mathbb{E}[\exp(\lambda \sum_{t=1}^{n}(X_t - \mu))]}{\exp(\lambda n \varepsilon)}$$

$$= (\mu \exp(\lambda(1 - \mu - \varepsilon)) + (1 - \mu)\exp(-\lambda(\mu + \varepsilon)))^n.$$

This expression is minimised by $\lambda = \log \frac{(\mu+\varepsilon)(1-\mu)}{\mu(1-\mu-\varepsilon)}$. Therefore,

$$\mathbb{P}\left(\hat{\mu} \geq \mu + \varepsilon\right)$$

$$\leq \left(\mu \left(\frac{(\mu+\varepsilon)(1-\mu)}{\mu(1-\mu-\varepsilon)}\right)^{1-\mu-\varepsilon} + (1-\mu)\left(\frac{(\mu+\varepsilon)(1-\mu)}{\mu(1-\mu-\varepsilon)}\right)^{-\mu-\varepsilon}\right)^{n}$$

$$= \left(\frac{\mu}{\mu+\varepsilon}\left(\frac{(\mu+\varepsilon)(1-\mu)}{\mu(1-\mu-\varepsilon)}\right)^{1-\mu-\varepsilon}\right)^{n}$$

$$= \exp\left(-nd(\mu+\varepsilon, \mu)\right).$$

The bound on the left tail is proven identically. $\square$

Using Pinsker's inequality, it follows that $\mathbb{P}\left(\hat{\mu} \geq \mu + \varepsilon\right), \mathbb{P}\left(\hat{\mu} \leq \mu - \varepsilon\right) \leq \exp(-2n\varepsilon^2)$, which is the same as what can be obtained from Hoeffding's lemma (see (5.8)). Solving $\exp(-2n\varepsilon^2) = \delta$, we recover the usual $1 - \delta$ confidence upper bound. In fact, this cannot be improved when $\mu \approx 1/2$, but the Chernoff bound is much stronger when μ is close to either zero or one. Can we invert the Chernoff tail bound to get confidence intervals that get tighter automatically as μ (or $\hat{\mu}$) approaches zero or one? The following corollary shows how to do this.

COROLLARY 10.4. *Let $\mu, \hat{\mu}, n$ be as above. Then, for any $a \geq 0$,*

$$\mathbb{P}\left(d(\hat{\mu}, \mu) \geq a, \hat{\mu} \leq \mu\right) \leq \exp(-na), \tag{10.3}$$

and $$\mathbb{P}\left(d(\hat{\mu}, \mu) \geq a, \hat{\mu} \geq \mu\right) \leq \exp(-na). \tag{10.4}$$

Furthermore, defining

$$U(a) = \max\{u \in [0,1] : d(\hat{\mu}, u) \leq a\},$$

and $$L(a) = \min\{u \in [0,1] : d(\hat{\mu}, u) \leq a\}.$$

Then, $\mathbb{P}\left(\mu \geq U(a)\right) \leq \exp(-na)$ and $\mathbb{P}\left(\mu \leq L(a)\right) \leq \exp(-na)$.

Proof First, we prove (10.3). Note that $d(\cdot, \mu)$ is decreasing on $[0, \mu]$, and thus, for $0 \leq a \leq d(0, \mu)$, $\{d(\hat{\mu}, \mu) \geq a, \hat{\mu} \leq \mu\} = \{\hat{\mu} \leq \mu - x, \hat{\mu} \leq \mu\} = \{\hat{\mu} \leq \mu - x\}$, where x is the unique solution to $d(\mu - x, \mu) = a$ on $[0, \mu]$. Hence, by Eq. (10.2) of Lemma 10.3, $\mathbb{P}\left(d(\hat{\mu}, \mu) \geq a, \hat{\mu} \leq \mu\right) \leq \exp(-na)$. When $a \geq d(0, \mu)$, the inequality trivially holds. The proof of (10.4) is entirely analogous and hence is omitted. For the second part of the corollary, fix a and let $U = U(a)$. First, notice that $U \geq \hat{\mu}$ and $d(\hat{\mu}, \cdot)$ is strictly increasing on $[\hat{\mu}, 1]$. Hence, $\{\mu \geq U\} = \{\mu \geq U, \mu \geq \hat{\mu}\} = \{d(\hat{\mu}, \mu) \geq d(\hat{\mu}, U), \mu \geq \hat{\mu}\} = \{d(\hat{\mu}, \mu) \geq a, \mu \geq \hat{\mu}\}$, where the last equality follows by $d(\hat{\mu}, U) = a$, which holds by the definition of U. Taking probabilities and using the first part of the corollary shows that $\mathbb{P}\left(\mu \geq U\right) \leq \exp(-na)$. The statement concerning $L = L(a)$ follows with a similar reasoning. $\square$

Note that for $\delta \in (0,1)$, $U = U(\log(1/\delta)/n)$ and $L = L(\log(1/\delta)/n)$ are upper and lower confidence bounds for μ. Although the relative entropy has no closed-form inverse, the optimisation problem that defines U and L can be solved to a high degree of accuracy

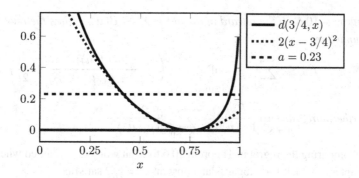

Figure 10.1 Relative entropy and Pinsker's inequality

using Newton's method (the relative entropy d is convex in its second argument). The advantage of this confidence interval relative to the one derived from Hoeffding's bound is now clear. As $\hat{\mu}$ approaches one, the width of the interval $U(a) - \hat{\mu}$ approaches zero, whereas the width of the interval provided by Hoeffding's bound stays at $\sqrt{\log(1/\delta)/(2n)}$. The same holds for $\hat{\mu} - L(a)$ as $\hat{\mu} \to 0$.

EXAMPLE 10.5. Fig. 10.1 shows a plot of $d(3/4, x)$ and the lower bound given by Pinsker's inequality. The approximation degrades as $|x - 3/4|$ grows large, especially for $x > 3/4$. As explained in Corollary 10.4, the graph of $d(\hat{\mu}, \cdot)$ can be used to derive confidence bounds by solving for $d(\hat{\mu}, x) = a = \log(1/\delta)/n$. Assuming $\hat{\mu} = 3/4$ is observed, a confidence level of 90 per cent with $n = 10$, $a \approx 0.23$. The confidence interval can be read out from the figure by finding those values where the horizontal dashed black line intersects the solid blue line. The resulting confidence interval will be highly asymmetric. Note that in this scenario, the lower confidence bounds produced by both Hoeffding's inequality and Chernoff's bound are similar, while the upper bound provided by Hoeffding's bound is vacuous.

10.2 The KL-UCB Algorithm

The difference between KL-UCB and UCB is that Chernoff's bound is used to define the upper confidence bound instead of Lemma 5.5.

1: **Input** k
2: Choose each arm once
3: Subsequently choose

$$A_t = \operatorname{argmax}_i \max \left\{ \tilde{\mu} \in [0,1] : d(\hat{\mu}_i(t-1), \tilde{\mu}) \leq \frac{\log f(t)}{T_i(t-1)} \right\},$$

where $f(t) = 1 + t \log^2(t)$.

Algorithm 8: KL-UCB.

THEOREM 10.6. *If the reward in round t is $X_t \sim \mathcal{B}(\mu_{A_t})$, then the regret of Algorithm 8 is bounded by*

$$R_n \leq \sum_{i:\Delta_i>0} \inf_{\substack{\varepsilon_1,\varepsilon_2>0 \\ \varepsilon_1+\varepsilon_2\in(0,\Delta_i)}} \Delta_i \left(\frac{\log(f(n))}{d(\mu_i+\varepsilon_1,\mu^*-\varepsilon_2)} + \frac{1}{2\varepsilon_1^2} + \frac{2}{\varepsilon_2^2} \right).$$

Furthermore, $\displaystyle \limsup_{n\to\infty} \frac{R_n}{\log(n)} \leq \sum_{i:\Delta_i>0} \frac{\Delta_i}{d(\mu_i,\mu^*)}.$

Comparing the regret in Theorem 10.6 to what would be obtained when using UCB from Chapter 8, which for subgaussian constant $\sigma = 1/2$ satisfies

$$\limsup_{n\to\infty} \frac{R_n}{\log(n)} \leq \sum_{i:\Delta_i>0} \frac{1}{2\Delta_i}.$$

By Pinsker's inequality (part (b) of Lemma 10.2) we see that $d(\mu_i,\mu^*) \geq 2(\mu^*-\mu_i)^2 = 2\Delta_i^2$, which means that the asymptotic regret of KL-UCB is never worse than that of UCB. On the other hand, a Taylor's expansion shows that when μ_i and μ^* are close (the hard case in the asymptotic regime),

$$d(\mu_i,\mu^*) = \frac{\Delta_i^2}{2\mu_i(1-\mu_i)} + o(\Delta_i^2),$$

indicating that the regret of KL-UCB is approximately

$$\limsup_{n\to\infty} \frac{R_n}{\log(n)} \approx \sum_{i:\Delta_i>0} \frac{2\mu_i(1-\mu_i)}{\Delta_i}. \tag{10.5}$$

Notice that $\mu_i(1-\mu_i)$ is the variance of a Bernoulli distribution with mean μ_i. The approximation indicates that KL-UCB will improve on UCB in regimes where μ_i is close to zero or one.

The proof of Theorem 10.6 relies on two lemmas. The first is used to show that the index of the optimal arm is never too far below its true value, while the second shows that the index of any other arm is not often much larger than the same value. These results mirror those given for UCB, but things are complicated by the non-symmetric and hard-to-invert divergence function.

For the next results, we define $\underline{d}(p,q) = d(p,q)\mathbb{I}\{p \leq q\}$.

LEMMA 10.7. *Let $X_1, X_2, \ldots, X_n$ be independent Bernoulli random variables with mean $\mu \in [0,1]$, $\varepsilon > 0$ and*

$$\tau = \min\left\{ t : \max_{1\leq s\leq n} \underline{d}(\hat{\mu}_s, \mu-\varepsilon) - \frac{\log f(t)}{s} \leq 0 \right\}.$$

Then, $\mathbb{E}[\tau] \leq \dfrac{2}{\varepsilon^2}.$

Proof We start with a high-probability bound and then integrate to control the expectation.

$$\mathbb{P}(\tau > t) \leq \mathbb{P}\left(\exists 1 \leq s \leq n : \underline{d}(\hat{\mu}_s, \mu-\varepsilon) > \frac{\log f(t)}{s} \right)$$

$$\leq \sum_{s=1}^{n} \mathbb{P}\left(\underline{d}(\hat{\mu}_s, \mu-\varepsilon) > \frac{\log f(t)}{s} \right)$$

$$= \sum_{s=1}^{n} \mathbb{P} \left(d(\hat{\mu}_s, \mu - \varepsilon) > \frac{\log f(t)}{s}, \hat{\mu}_s < \mu - \varepsilon \right)$$

$$\leq \sum_{s=1}^{n} \mathbb{P} \left(d(\hat{\mu}_s, \mu) > \frac{\log f(t)}{s} + 2\varepsilon^2, \hat{\mu}_s < \mu \right) \qquad \text{((c) of Lemma 10.2)}$$

$$\leq \sum_{s=1}^{n} \exp \left(-s \left(2\varepsilon^2 + \frac{\log f(t)}{s} \right) \right) \qquad \text{(Eq. (10.3) of Corollary 10.4)}$$

$$\leq \frac{1}{f(t)} \sum_{s=1}^{n} \exp \left(-2s\varepsilon^2 \right)$$

$$\leq \frac{1}{2 f(t) \varepsilon^2}.$$

To finish, we integrate the tail,

$$\mathbb{E}[\tau] = \int_0^\infty \mathbb{P} \left(\tau \geq t \right) dt \leq \frac{1}{2\varepsilon^2} \int_0^\infty \frac{dt}{f(t)} \leq \frac{2}{\varepsilon^2}. \qquad \square$$

LEMMA 10.8. *Let $X_1, X_2, \ldots, X_n$ be independent Bernoulli random variables with mean μ. Further, let $\Delta > 0$, $a > 0$ and define*

$$\kappa = \sum_{s=1}^{n} \mathbb{I} \left\{ d(\hat{\mu}_s, \mu + \Delta) \leq \frac{a}{s} \right\}.$$

Then, $\mathbb{E}[\kappa] \leq \inf\limits_{\varepsilon \in (0, \Delta)} \left(\dfrac{a}{d(\mu + \varepsilon, \mu + \Delta)} + \dfrac{1}{2\varepsilon^2} \right).$

Proof Let $\varepsilon \in (0, \Delta)$ and $u = a/d(\mu + \varepsilon, \mu + \Delta)$. Then,

$$\mathbb{E}[\kappa] = \sum_{s=1}^{n} \mathbb{P} \left(d(\hat{\mu}_s, \mu + \Delta) \leq \frac{a}{s} \right)$$

$$\leq \sum_{s=1}^{n} \mathbb{P} \left(\hat{\mu}_s \geq \mu + \varepsilon \text{ or } d(\mu + \varepsilon, \mu + \Delta) \leq \frac{a}{s} \right)$$

$$\qquad \qquad (d(\cdot, \mu + \Delta) \text{ is decreasing on } [0, \mu + \Delta])$$

$$\leq u + \sum_{s=\lceil u \rceil}^{n} \mathbb{P} \left(\hat{\mu}_s \geq \mu + \varepsilon \right)$$

$$\leq u + \sum_{s=1}^{\infty} \exp \left(-sd(\mu + \varepsilon, \mu) \right) \qquad \text{(Lemma 10.3)}$$

$$\leq \frac{a}{d(\mu + \varepsilon, \mu + \Delta)} + \frac{1}{d(\mu + \varepsilon, \mu)}$$

$$\leq \frac{a}{d(\mu + \varepsilon, \mu + \Delta)} + \frac{1}{2\varepsilon^2} \qquad \text{(Pinsker's inequality/Lemma 10.2(b))}$$

as required. $\qquad \square$

Proof of Theorem 10.6 As in other proofs, we assume without loss of generality that $\mu_1 = \mu^*$ and bound $\mathbb{E}[T_i(n)]$ for suboptimal arms i. To this end, fix a suboptimal arm i and let $\varepsilon_1 + \varepsilon_2 \in (0, \Delta_i)$ with both ε_1 and ε_2 positive. Define

$$\tau = \min \left\{ t : \max_{1 \le s \le n} \underline{d}(\hat{\mu}_{1s}, \mu_1 - \varepsilon_2) - \frac{\log f(t)}{s} \le 0 \right\}, \text{ and}$$

$$\kappa = \sum_{s=1}^{n} \mathbb{I} \left\{ d(\hat{\mu}_{is}, \mu_i + \Delta_i - \varepsilon_2) \le \frac{\log f(n)}{s} \right\}.$$

Using a similar argument as in the proof of Theorem 8.1,

$$\mathbb{E}[T_i(n)] = \mathbb{E} \left[\sum_{t=1}^{n} \mathbb{I}\{A_t = i\} \right]$$

$$\le \mathbb{E}[\tau] + \mathbb{E} \left[\sum_{t=\tau+1}^{n} \mathbb{I}\{A_t = i\} \right]$$

$$\le \mathbb{E}[\tau] + \mathbb{E} \left[\sum_{t=1}^{n} \mathbb{I} \left\{ A_t = i \text{ and } d(\hat{\mu}_{i,T_i(t-1)}, \mu_1 - \varepsilon_2) \le \frac{\log f(t)}{T_i(t-1)} \right\} \right]$$

$$\le \mathbb{E}[\tau] + \mathbb{E}[\kappa]$$

$$\le \frac{2}{\varepsilon_2^2} + \frac{f(n)}{d(\mu_i + \varepsilon_1, \mu^* - \varepsilon_2)} + \frac{1}{2\varepsilon_1^2},$$

where the second inequality follows, since by the definition of τ, if $t > \tau$, then the index of the optimal arm is at least as large as $\mu_1 - \varepsilon_2$. The third inequality follows from the definition of κ as in the proof of Theorem 8.1. The final inequality follows from Lemmas 10.7 and 10.8. The first claim of the theorem is completed by substituting the above into the standard regret decomposition

$$R_n = \sum_{i=1}^{k} \Delta_i \mathbb{E}[T_i(n)].$$

The asymptotic claim for you in Exercise 10.2.   □

10.3   Notes

1 The new concentration inequality (Lemma 10.3) holds more generally for any sequence of independent and identically distributed random variables $X_1, X_2, \ldots, X_n$ for which $X_t \in [0, 1]$ almost surely. Therefore all results in this section also hold if the assumption that the noise is Bernoulli is relaxed to the case where it is simply supported in $[0, 1]$ (or other bounded sets by shifting/scaling).

2 Expanding on the previous note, all that is required is a bound on the moment-generating function for random variables X where, $X \in [0, 1]$ almost surely. Garivier and Cappé [2011, Lemma 9] noted that $f(x) = \exp(\lambda x) - x(\exp(\lambda) - 1) - 1$ is negative on $[0, 1]$, and so

$$\mathbb{E}\left[\exp(\lambda X)\right] \le \mathbb{E}\left[X(\exp(\lambda) - 1) + 1\right] = \mu \exp(\lambda) + 1 - \mu,$$

which is precisely the moment-generating function of the Bernoulli distribution with mean μ. Then the remainder of the proof of Lemma 10.3 goes through unchanged. This shows that for any bandit $\nu = (P_i)_i$ with $\text{Supp}(P_i) \in [0, 1]$ for all i the regret of the policy in Algorithm 8 satisfies

$$\limsup_{n \to \infty} \frac{R_n}{\log(n)} \le \sum_{i: \Delta_i > 0} \frac{\Delta_i}{d(\mu_i, \mu^*)}.$$

3 The bounds obtained using the argument in the previous note are not quite tight. Specifically one can show there exists an algorithm such that for all bandits $v = (P_i)_i$ with P_i, the reward distribution of the ith arm supported on $[0, 1]$, then

$$\limsup_{n \to \infty} \frac{R_n}{\log(n)} = \sum_{i : \Delta_i > 0} \frac{\Delta_i}{d_i}, \quad \text{where}$$

$$d_i = \inf\{D(P_i, P) : \mu(P) > \mu^* \text{ and } \mathrm{Supp}(P) \subset [0, 1]\}$$

and $D(P, Q)$ is the relative entropy between measures P_i and P, which we define in Chapter 14. The quantity d_i is never smaller than $d(\mu_i, \mu^*)$. For details on this, see the paper by Honda and Takemura [2010].

4 The approximation in Eq. (10.5) was used to show that the regret for KL-UCB is closely related to the variance of the Bernoulli distribution. It is natural to ask whether or not this result could be derived, at least asymptotically, by appealing to the central limit theorem. The answer is no. First, the quality of the approximation in Eq. (10.5) does not depend on n, so asymptotically it is not true that the Bernoulli bandit behaves like a Gaussian bandit with variances tuned to match. The reason is that as n tends to infinity, the confidence level should be chosen so that the risk of failure also tends to zero. But the central limit theorem does not provide information about the tails with probability mass less than $O(n^{-1/2})$. See Note 1 in Chapter 5.

5 The analysis in this chapter is easily generalised to a wide range of alternative noise models. You will do this for single-parameter exponential families in Exercises 10.4, 10.5 and 34.5.

6 Chernoff credits Lemma 10.3 to his friend Herman Rubin [Chernoff, 2014], but the name seems to have stuck.

10.4 Bibliographic Remarks

Several authors have worked on Bernoulli bandits, and the asymptotics have been well understood since the article by Lai and Robbins [1985]. The earliest version of the algorithm presented in this chapter is due to Lai [1987], who provided asymptotic analysis. The finite-time analysis of KL-UCB was given by two groups simultaneously (and published in the same conference) by Garivier and Cappé [2011] and Maillard et al. [2011] (see also the combined journal article: Cappé et al. 2013). Two alternatives are the DMED [Honda and Takemura, 2010] and IMED [Honda and Takemura, 2015] algorithms. These works go after the problem of understanding the asymptotic regret for the more general situation where the rewards lie in a bounded interval (see Note 3). The latter work covers even the semi-bounded case where the rewards are almost surely upper-bounded. Both algorithms are asymptotically optimal. Ménard and Garivier [2017] combined MOSS and KL-UCB to derive an algorithm that is minimax optimal and asymptotically optimal for single-parameter exponential families. While the subgaussian and Bernoulli examples are very fundamental, there has also been work on more generic set-ups where the unknown reward distribution for each arm is known to lie in some class $\mathcal{F}$. The article by Burnetas and Katehakis [1996] gives the most generic (albeit, asymptotic) results. These generic set-ups remain wide open for further work.

10.5 Exercises

10.1 (PINSKER'S INEQUALITY) Prove Lemma 10.2(b).

HINT   Consider the function $g(x) = d(p, p + x) - 2x^2$ over the $[-p, 1 - p]$ interval. By taking derivatives, show that $g \geq 0$.

10.2 (ASYMPTOTIC OPTIMALITY) Prove the asymptotic claim in Theorem 10.6.

HINT   Choose $\varepsilon_1, \varepsilon_2$ to decrease slowly with n and use the first part of the theorem.

10.3 (CONCENTRATION FOR BOUNDED RANDOM VARIABLES) Let $\mathbb{F} = (\mathcal{F}_t)_t$ be a filtration, $(X_t)_t$ be $[0, 1]$-valued, $\mathbb{F}$-adapted sequence, such that $\mathbb{E}[X_t \mid \mathcal{F}_{t-1}] = \mu_t$ for some $\mu_1, \ldots, \mu_n \in [0, 1]$ non-random numbers. Define $\mu = \frac{1}{n}\sum_{t=1}^n \mu_t$, $\hat{\mu} = \frac{1}{n}\sum_{t=1}^n X_t$. Prove that the conclusion of Lemma 10.3 still holds.

HINT   Read Note 2 at the end of this chapter. Let $g(\cdot, \mu)$ be the cumulant-generating function of the μ-parameter Bernoulli distribution. For $X \sim \mathcal{B}(\mu)$, $\lambda \in \mathbb{R}$, $g(\lambda, \mu) = \log \mathbb{E}[\exp(\lambda X)]$. Show that $g(\lambda, \cdot)$ is concave. Next, use this and the tower rule to show that $\mathbb{E}[\exp(\lambda n(\hat{\mu} - \mu))] \leq g(\lambda, \mu)^n$.

> The bound of the previous exercise is most useful when all μ_t are either all close to zero or they are all close to one. When half of the $\{\mu_t\}$ are close to zero and the other half close to one, then the bound degrades to Hoeffding's bound.

10.4 (KL-UCB FOR EXPONENTIAL FAMILIES) Let $\mathcal{M} = \{P_\theta : \theta \in \Theta\}$ be a regular non-singular exponential family with sufficient statistic $S(x) = x$ and $\mathcal{E} = \{(P_{\theta_i})_{i=1}^k : \theta \in \Theta^k\}$ be the set of bandits with reward distributions in $\mathcal{M}$. Design a policy π such that for all $\nu \in \mathcal{E}$, it holds that

$$\lim_{n\to\infty} \frac{R_n(\pi, \nu)}{\log(n)} \leq \sum_{i:\Delta_i > 0} \frac{\Delta_i}{d_{i,\inf}},$$

where $\mu(\theta) = \int_{\mathbb{R}} x dP_\theta(x)$ is the mean of P_θ and $d_{i,\inf} = \inf\{d(\theta, \phi) : \mu(\phi) > \mu^*, \phi \in \Theta\}$, with $d(\theta, \phi)$ the relative entropy between P_θ and P_ϕ.

HINT   Readers not familiar with exponential families should skip ahead to Section 34.3.1 and then do Exercise 34.5. For the exercise, repeat the proof of Theorem 10.6, adapting as necessary. See also the paper by Cappé et al. [2013].

10.5 (KL-UCB FOR NON-CANONICAL EXPONENTIAL FAMILIES) Repeat the previous exercise, but relax the assumption that $S(x) = x$.

HINT   This is a subtle problem. You should adapt the algorithm so that if there are ties in the upper confidence bounds, then an arm with the largest number of plays is chosen. A solution is available. Korda et al. [2013] analysed Thompson sampling in this setting. Their result only holds when $\theta \mapsto \int_{\mathbb{R}} x p_\theta(x) dh(x)$ is invertible, which does not always hold.

> In the analysis of KL-UCB for canonical exponential families, the asymptotic rate is a good indicator of the finite-time regret in the sense that the $o(\log(n))$ term hidden by the asymptotics has roughly the same leading constant as the dominant term. By contrast, the analysis here indicates that
>
> $$\mathbb{E}[T_i(n)] \approx \frac{\log(n)}{d_{i,\inf}} + \frac{1}{d_{i,\min}},$$
>
> where $d_{i,\min} = d_{i,\min}(0)$. Although the latter term is negligible asymptotically, it may be the dominant term for all reasonable n.

10.6 (COMPARISON TO UCB) In this exercise, you compare KL-UCB and UCB empirically.

(a) Implement Algorithm 8 and Algorithm 6, where the latter algorithm should be tuned for $1/2$-subgaussian bandits so that

$$A_t = \text{argmax}_{i \in [k]}\, \hat{\mu}_i(t-1) + \sqrt{\frac{\log(f(t))}{2T_i(t-1)}}.$$

(b) Let $n = 10000$ and $k = 2$. Plot the expected regret of each algorithm as a function of Δ when $\mu_1 = 1/2$ and $\mu_2 = 1/2 + \Delta$.

(c) Repeat the above experiment with $\mu_1 = 1/10$ and $\mu_1 = 9/10$.

(d) Discuss your results.

Part III

Adversarial Bandits with Finitely Many Arms

Statistician George E. P. Box is famous for writing that 'all models are wrong, but some are useful'. In the stochastic bandit model the reward is sampled from a distribution that depends only on the chosen action. It does not take much thought to realise this model is almost always wrong. At the macroscopic level typically considered in bandit problems, there is not much that is stochastic about the world. And even if there were, it is hard to rule out the existence of other factors influencing the rewards.

The quotation suggests we should not care whether or not the stochastic bandit model is right, only whether it is useful. In science, models are used for predicting the outcomes of future experiments, and their usefulness is measured by the quality of the predictions. But how can this be applied to bandit problems? What predictions can be made based on bandit models? In this respect, we postulate the following:

> The point of bandit models is to facilitate predicting the performance of bandit algorithms on future problem instances that one encounters in their practice.

A model can fail in two fundamentally different ways. It can be too specific, imposing assumptions so detached from reality that a catastrophic mismatch between actual and predicted performance may arise. The second mode of failure occurs when a model is too general, which makes the algorithms designed to do well on the bandit model overly cautious, which can harm performance.

Not all assumptions are equally important. It is a critical assumption in stochastic bandits that the mean reward of individual arms does not change (significantly) over time. On the other hand, the assumption that a single, arm-dependent distribution generates the rewards for a given arm plays a relatively insignificant role. The reader is encouraged to think of cases when the constancy of arm distributions plays no role, and also of cases when it does – furthermore, to decide to what extent the algorithms can tolerate deviations from the assumption that the means of arms stay the same. Stochastic bandits where the means of the arms are changing over time are called **non-stationary** and are the topic of Chapter 31.

If a highly specialised model is actually correct, then the resulting algorithms usually dominate algorithms derived for a more general model. This is a general manifestation of the bias-variance trade-off, well known in supervised learning and statistics. The holy grail is to find algorithms that work 'optimally' across a range of models. The reader should think about examples from the previous chapters that illustrate these points.

The usefulness of the stochastic model depends on the setting. In particular, the designer of the bandit algorithm must carefully evaluate whether stochasticity, stability of the mean and independence are reasonable assumptions. For some applications, the answer will probably be yes, while in others the practitioner may seek something more robust. This latter situation is the topic of the next few chapters.

Adversarial Bandits

The **adversarial bandit** model abandons almost all the assumptions on how the rewards are generated, so much so that the environment is often called the adversary. The adversary has a great deal of power in this model, including the ability to examine the code of the proposed algorithms and choose the rewards accordingly. All that is kept from the previous chapters is that the objective will be framed in terms of how well a policy is able to compete with the best action in hindsight.

At first sight, it seems remarkable that one can say anything at all about such a general model. And yet it turns out that this model is not much harder than the stochastic bandit problem. Why this holds and how to design algorithms that achieve these guarantees will be explained in the following chapters.

To give you a glimmer of hope, imagine playing the following simple bandit game with a friend. The horizon is $n = 1$, and you have two actions. The game proceeds as follows:

1 You tell your friend your strategy for choosing an action.
2 Your friend secretly chooses rewards $x_1 \in \{0, 1\}$ and $x_2 \in \{0, 1\}$.
3 You implement your strategy to select $A \in \{1, 2\}$ and receive reward x_A.
4 The regret is $R = \max\{x_1, x_2\} - x_A$.

Clearly, if your friend chooses $x_1 = x_2$, then your regret is zero no matter what. Now let's suppose you implement the deterministic strategy $A = 1$. Then your friend can choose $x_1 = 0$ and $x_2 = 1$, and your regret is $R = 1$. The trick to improve on this is to randomise. If you tell your friend, 'I will choose $A = 1$ with probability one half', then the best she can do is choose $x_1 = 1$ and $x_2 = 0$ (or reversed), and your expected regret is $R = 1/2$. You are forgiven if you did not settle on this solution yourself because we did not tell you that a strategy may be randomised. With such a short horizon, you cannot do better than this, but for longer games the relative advantage of the adversary decreases, as we shall see soon.

In the next two chapters, we investigate the k-armed adversarial model in detail, providing both algorithms and regret analysis. Like the stochastic model, the adversarial model has many generalisations, which we'll visit in future chapters.

Bibliographic Remarks

The quote by George Box was used several times with different phrasings [Box, 1976, 1979]. The adversarial framework has its roots in game theory, with familiar names like Hannan [1957] and Blackwell [1954] producing some of the early work. The non-statistical approach has enjoyed enormous popularity since the 1990's and has been adopted wholeheartedly by the theoretical computer science community [Vovk, 1990, Littlestone and Warmuth, 1994, and many, many others]. The earliest work on adversarial bandits is by Auer et al. [1995]. There is now a big literature on adversarial bandits, which we will cover in more depth in the chapters that follow. There has been a lot of effort to move away from stochastic assumptions. An important aspect of this is to define a sense of regularity for individual sequences. We refer the reader to some of the classic papers by Martin-Löf [1966] and Levin [1973] and the more recent paper by Ivanenko and Labkovsky [2013].

11 The Exp3 Algorithm

In this chapter we first introduce the formal model of adversarial bandit environments and discuss the relationship to the stochastic bandit model. This is followed by the discussion of importance-weighted estimation, the Exp3 algorithm that uses this technique and the analysis of the regret of Exp3.

11.1 Adversarial Bandit Environments

Let $k > 1$ be the number of arms. A **k-armed adversarial bandit** is an arbitrary sequence of reward vectors $(x_t)_{t=1}^n$, where $x_t \in [0,1]^k$. In each round, the learner chooses a distribution over the actions $P_t \in \mathcal{P}_{k-1}$. Then the action $A_t \in [k]$ is sampled from P_t, and the learner receives reward x_{tA_t}. The interaction protocol is summarised in Fig. 11.2.

A policy in this setting is a function $\pi : ([k] \times [0,1])^* \to \mathcal{P}_{k-1}$ mapping history sequences to distributions over actions (regardless of measurability). The performance of a policy π in environment x is measured by the expected regret, which is the expected loss in revenue of the policy relative to the best fixed action in hindsight.

Figure 11.1 Would you play with this multi-armed bandit?

$$R_n(\pi, x) = \max_{i \in [k]} \sum_{t=1}^n x_{ti} - \mathbb{E}\left[\sum_{t=1}^n x_{tA_t}\right], \tag{11.1}$$

where the expectation is over the randomness of the learner's actions. The arguments π and x are omitted from the regret when they are clear from context.

The only source of randomness in the regret comes from the randomness in the actions of the learner. Of course the interaction with the environment means the action chosen in round t may depend on actions $s < t$ as well as the observed rewards until round t. As we noted, unlike the case of stochastic bandits, here, there is no measurability restriction on the learner's policy π. This is actually by choice, see Note 12 for details.

Adversary secretly chooses rewards $(x_t)_{t=1}^n$ with $x_t \in [0,1]^k$

For rounds $t = 1, 2, \ldots, n$:

    Learner selects distribution $P_t \in \mathcal{P}_{k-1}$ and samples A_t from P_t.

    Learner observes reward $X_t = x_{tA_t}$.

Figure 11.2 Interaction protocol for k-armed adversarial bandits.

The worst-case regret over all environments is

$$R_n^*(\pi) = \sup_{x \in [0,1]^{n \times k}} R_n(\pi, x).$$

The main question is whether or not there exist policies π for which $R_n^*(\pi)$ is sublinear in n. In Exercise 11.2 you will show that for deterministic policies $R_n^*(\pi) \geq n(1 - 1/k)$, which follows by constructing a bandit so that $x_{tA_t} = 0$ for all t and $x_{ti} = 1$ for $i \neq A_t$. Because of this, sublinear worst-case regret is only possible by using a randomised policy.

Readers familiar with game theory will not be surprised by the need for randomisation. The interaction between learner and adversarial bandit can be framed as a two-player zero-sum game between the learner and environment. The moves for the environment are the possible reward sequences, and for the player they are the policies. The pay-off for the environment/learner is the regret and its negation respectively. Since the player goes first, the only way to avoid being exploited is to choose a randomised policy.

While stochastic and adversarial bandits seem quite different, it turns out that the optimal worst-case regret is the same up to constant factors and that lower bounds for adversarial bandits are invariably derived in the same manner as for stochastic bandits (see Part IV). In this chapter, we present a simple algorithm for which the worst-case regret is suboptimal by just a logarithmic factor. First, however, we explore the differences and similarities between stochastic and adversarial environments.

We already noted that deterministic strategies will have linear regret for some adversarial bandit. Since strategies in Part II like UCB and 'Explore-then-Commit' were deterministic, they are not well suited for the adversarial setting. This immediately implies that policies that are good for stochastic bandit can be very suboptimal in the adversarial setting. What about the other direction? Will an adversarial bandit strategy have small expected regret in the stochastic setting? Let π be an adversarial bandit policy and $v = (v_1, \ldots, v_k)$ be a stochastic bandit with $\mathrm{Supp}(v_i) \subseteq [0,1]$ for all i. Next, let X_{ti} be sampled from v_i for each $i \in [k]$ and $t \in [n]$, and assume these random variables are mutually independent. By Jensen's inequality and convexity of the maximum function, we have

$$R_n(\pi, v) = \max_{i \in [k]} \mathbb{E}\left[\sum_{t=1}^n (X_{ti} - X_{tA_t}) \right]$$

$$\leq \mathbb{E}\left[\max_{i \in [k]} \sum_{t=1}^n (X_{ti} - X_{tA_t}) \right]$$

$$= \mathbb{E}\left[R_n(\pi, X) \right] \leq R_n^*(\pi), \tag{11.2}$$

where the regret in the first line is the stochastic regret (using the random table model), and in the last it is the adversarial regret. Therefore the worst-case stochastic regret is upper-bounded by the worst-case adversarial regret. Going the other way, the above inequality also implies that the worst-case regret for adversarial problems is lower-bounded by the worst-case regret on stochastic problems with rewards bounded in $[0, 1]$. In Chapter 15, we prove that the worst-case regret for stochastic Bernoulli bandits is at least $c\sqrt{nk}$, where $c > 0$ is a universal constant (Exercise 15.4). And so for the same universal constant, the minimax regret for adversarial bandits satisfies

$$R_n^* = \inf_\pi \sup_{x \in [0,1]^{n \times k}} R_n(\pi, x) \geq c\sqrt{nk}.$$

There is a little subtlety here. In order to define the expectations in the stochastic regret, the policy should be appropriately measurable. This can be resolved by noting that lower bounds can be proven using Bernoulli bandits. For details, see again Note 12.

11.2 Importance-Weighted Estimators

A key ingredient of all adversarial bandit algorithms is a mechanism for estimating the reward of unplayed arms. Recall that P_t is the conditional distribution of the action played in round t, and so for $i \in [k]$, P_{ti} is the conditional probability

$$P_{ti} = \mathbb{P}(A_t = i \mid A_1, X_1, \ldots, A_{t-1}, X_{t-1}).$$

In what follows, we assume that for all t and i, $P_{ti} > 0$ almost surely. As we shall see later, this will be true for all policies considered in this chapter. The **importance-weighted estimator** of x_{ti} is

$$\hat{X}_{ti} = \frac{\mathbb{I}\{A_t = i\} X_t}{P_{ti}}. \tag{11.3}$$

Let $\mathbb{E}_t[\cdot] = \mathbb{E}[\cdot \mid A_1, X_1, \ldots, A_t, X_t]$ denote the conditional expectation given the history up to time t. The conditional mean of $\hat{X}_{ti}$ satisfies

$$\mathbb{E}_{t-1}[\hat{X}_{ti}] = x_{ti}, \tag{11.4}$$

which means that $\hat{X}_{ti}$ is an unbiased estimate of x_{ti} conditioned on the history observed after $t-1$ rounds. To see why Eq. (11.4) holds, let $A_{ti} = \mathbb{I}\{A_t = i\}$ so that $X_t A_{ti} = x_{ti} A_{ti}$ and

$$\hat{X}_{ti} = \frac{A_{ti}}{P_{ti}} x_{ti}.$$

Now, $\mathbb{E}_{t-1}[A_{ti}] = P_{ti}$, and since P_{ti} is $\sigma(A_1, X_1, \ldots, A_{t-1}, X_{t-1})$-measurable,

$$\mathbb{E}_{t-1}[\hat{X}_{ti}] = \mathbb{E}_{t-1}\left[\frac{A_{ti}}{P_{ti}} x_{ti}\right] = \frac{x_{ti}}{P_{ti}} \mathbb{E}_{t-1}[A_{ti}] = \frac{x_{ti}}{P_{ti}} P_{ti} = x_{ti}.$$

Being unbiased is a good start, but the variance of an estimator is also important. For arbitrary random variable U, the conditional variance $\mathbb{V}_{t-1}[U]$ is the random variable

$$\mathbb{V}_{t-1}[U] = \mathbb{E}_{t-1}\left[(U - \mathbb{E}_{t-1}[U])^2\right].$$

So $\mathbb{V}_{t-1}[\hat{X}_{ti}]$ is a random variable that measures the variance of $\hat{X}_{ti}$ conditioned on the past. Calculating the conditional variance using the definition of $\hat{X}_{ti}$ and Eq. (11.4) shows that

$$\mathbb{V}_{t-1}[\hat{X}_{ti}] = \mathbb{E}_{t-1}[\hat{X}_{ti}^2] - x_{ti}^2 = \mathbb{E}_{t-1}\left[\frac{A_{ti}x_{ti}^2}{P_{ti}^2}\right] - x_{ti}^2 = \frac{x_{ti}^2(1 - P_{ti})}{P_{ti}}. \qquad (11.5)$$

This can be extremely large when P_{ti} is small and x_{ti} is bounded away from zero. In the notes and exercises, we shall see to what extent this can cause trouble. The estimator in (11.3) is the first that comes to mind, but there are alternatives. For example,

$$\hat{X}_{ti} = 1 - \frac{\mathbb{I}\{A_t = i\}}{P_{ti}}(1 - X_t). \qquad (11.6)$$

This estimator is still unbiased. Rewriting the formula in terms of $y_{ti} = 1 - x_{ti}$ and $Y_t = 1 - X_t$ and $\hat{Y}_{ti} = 1 - \hat{X}_{ti}$ leads to

$$\hat{Y}_{ti} = \frac{\mathbb{I}\{A_t = i\}}{P_{ti}} Y_t.$$

This is the same as (11.3) except that Y_t has replaced X_t. The terms y_{ti}, Y_t and $\hat{Y}_{ti}$ should be interpreted as **losses**. Had we started with losses to begin with, then this would have been the estimator that first came to mind. For obvious reasons, the estimator in Eq. (11.6) is called the **loss-based importance-weighted estimator**. The conditional variance of this estimator is essentially the same as Eq. (11.5):

$$\mathbb{V}_t[\hat{X}_{ti}] = \mathbb{V}_t[\hat{Y}_{ti}] = y_{ti}^2 \frac{1 - P_{ti}}{P_{ti}}.$$

The only difference is that the variance now depends on y_{ti}^2 rather than x_{ti}^2. Which is better depends on the rewards for arm i, with smaller rewards suggesting the superiority of the first estimator and larger rewards (or small losses) suggesting the superiority of the second estimator. Can we change the estimator (either one of them) so that it is more accurate for actions whose reward is close to some specific value v? Of course! Just change the estimator so that v is subtracted from the observed reward (or loss), then use the importance-sampling formula, and subsequently add back v. The problem is that the optimal value of v depends on the unknown quantity being estimated. Also note that the dependence of the variance on P_{ti} is the same for both estimators, and since the rewards are bounded, it is this term that usually contributes most significantly. In Exercise 11.5, we ask you to show that all unbiased estimators in this setting are importance-weighted estimators.

Although the two estimators seem quite similar, it should be noted that the first estimator takes values in $[0, \infty)$ while the second takes values in $(-\infty, 1]$. Soon we will see that this difference has a big impact on the usefulness of these estimators when used in the Exp3 algorithm.

11.3 The Exp3 Algorithm

The simplest algorithm for adversarial bandits is called Exp3, which stands for 'exponential-weight algorithm for exploration and exploitation'. The reason for this name will become clear after the explanation of the algorithm. Let $\hat{S}_{ti} = \sum_{s=1}^{t} \hat{X}_{si}$ be the total estimated reward by the end of round t, where $\hat{X}_{si}$ is given in Eq. (11.6). It seems natural to play actions with larger estimated reward with higher probability. While there are many ways to map $\hat{S}_{ti}$ into probabilities, a simple and popular choice is called **exponential weighting**, which for tuning parameter $\eta > 0$ sets

$$P_{ti} = \frac{\exp(\eta \hat{S}_{t-1,i})}{\sum_{j=1}^{k} \exp(\eta \hat{S}_{t-1,j})}. \tag{11.7}$$

The parameter η is called the **learning rate**. When the learning rate is large, P_t concentrates about the arm with the largest estimated reward and the resulting algorithm exploits aggressively. For small learning rates, P_t is more uniform, and the algorithm explores more frequently. Note that as P_t concentrates, the variance of the importance-weighted estimators for poorly performing arms increases dramatically. There are many ways to tune the learning rate, including allowing it to vary with time. In this chapter we restrict our attention to the simplest case by choosing η to depend only on the number of actions k and the horizon n. Since the algorithm depends on η, this means that the horizon must be known in advance, a requirement that can be relaxed (see Note 10).

1: **Input:** n, k, η

2: Set $\hat{S}_{0i} = 0$ for all i

3: **for** $t = 1, \ldots, n$ **do**

4:     Calculate the sampling distribution P_t:

$$P_{ti} = \frac{\exp\left(\eta \hat{S}_{t-1,i}\right)}{\sum_{j=1}^{k} \exp\left(\eta \hat{S}_{t-1,j}\right)}$$

5:     Sample $A_t \sim P_t$ and observe reward X_t

6:     Calculate $\hat{S}_{ti}$:

$$\hat{S}_{ti} = \hat{S}_{t-1,i} + 1 - \frac{\mathbb{I}\{A_t = i\}(1 - X_t)}{P_{ti}}$$

7: **end for**

Algorithm 9: Exp3.

11.4 Regret Analysis

We are now ready to bound the expected regret of Exp3.

THEOREM 11.1. *Let $x \in [0, 1]^{n \times k}$ and π be the policy of Exp3 (Algorithm 9) with learning rate $\eta = \sqrt{\log(k)/(nk)}$. Then,*

$$R_n(\pi, x) \leq 2\sqrt{nk \log(k)}.$$

As we will prove many variants of this result with various tools, here we give a short algebraic proof, saving the development of intuition for later.

Proof For any arm i, define

$$R_{ni} = \sum_{t=1}^{n} x_{ti} - \mathbb{E}\left[\sum_{t=1}^{n} X_t\right],$$

which is the expected regret relative to using action i in all the rounds. The result will follow by bounding R_{ni} for all i, including the optimal arm. For the remainder of the proof, let i be some fixed arm. By the unbiasedness property of the importance-weighted estimator $\hat{X}_{ti}$,

$$\mathbb{E}[\hat{S}_{ni}] = \sum_{t=1}^{n} x_{ti} \quad \text{and also} \quad \mathbb{E}_{t-1}[X_t] = \sum_{i=1}^{k} P_{ti} x_{ti} = \sum_{i=1}^{k} P_{ti} \mathbb{E}_{t-1}[\hat{X}_{ti}]. \quad (11.8)$$

The tower rule says that for any random variable X, $\mathbb{E}[\mathbb{E}_{t-1}[X]] = \mathbb{E}[X]$, which together with the linearity of expectation and Eq. (11.8) means that

$$R_{ni} = \mathbb{E}\left[\hat{S}_{ni}\right] - \mathbb{E}\left[\sum_{t=1}^{n}\sum_{i=1}^{k} P_{ti}\hat{X}_{ti}\right] = \mathbb{E}\left[\hat{S}_{ni} - \hat{S}_n\right], \quad (11.9)$$

where the last equality serves as the definition of $\hat{S}_n = \sum_t \sum_i P_{ti}\hat{X}_{ti}$. To bound the right-hand side of Eq. (11.9), let

$$W_t = \sum_{j=1}^{k} \exp\left(\eta \hat{S}_{tj}\right).$$

By convention an empty sum is zero, which means that $\hat{S}_{0j} = 0$ and $W_0 = k$. Then,

$$\exp(\eta \hat{S}_{ni}) \leq \sum_{j=1}^{k} \exp(\eta \hat{S}_{nj}) = W_n = W_0 \frac{W_1}{W_0} \cdots \frac{W_n}{W_{n-1}} = k \prod_{t=1}^{n} \frac{W_t}{W_{t-1}}. \quad (11.10)$$

The ratio in the product can be rewritten in terms of P_t by

$$\frac{W_t}{W_{t-1}} = \sum_{j=1}^{k} \frac{\exp(\eta \hat{S}_{t-1,j})}{W_{t-1}} \exp(\eta \hat{X}_{tj}) = \sum_{j=1}^{k} P_{tj} \exp(\eta \hat{X}_{tj}). \quad (11.11)$$

We need the following facts:

$$\exp(x) \leq 1 + x + x^2 \text{ for all } x \leq 1 \quad \text{and} \quad 1 + x \leq \exp(x) \text{ for all } x \in \mathbb{R}.$$

Using these two inequalities leads to

$$\frac{W_t}{W_{t-1}} \leq 1 + \eta \sum_{j=1}^{k} P_{tj}\hat{X}_{tj} + \eta^2 \sum_{j=1}^{k} P_{tj}\hat{X}_{tj}^2$$

$$\leq \exp\left(\eta \sum_{j=1}^{k} P_{tj}\hat{X}_{tj} + \eta^2 \sum_{j=1}^{k} P_{tj}\hat{X}_{tj}^2\right). \quad (11.12)$$

Notice that this was only possible because $\hat{X}_{tj}$ is defined by Eq. (11.6), which ensures that $\hat{X}_{tj} \leq 1$ and would not have been true had we used Eq. (11.3). Combining Eq. (11.12) and Eq. (11.10),

$$\exp\left(\eta \hat{S}_{ni}\right) \leq k \exp\left(\eta \hat{S}_n + \eta^2 \sum_{t=1}^{n} \sum_{j=1}^{k} P_{tj} \hat{X}_{tj}^2\right).$$

Taking the logarithm of both sides, dividing by $\eta > 0$ and reordering gives

$$\hat{S}_{ni} - \hat{S}_n \leq \frac{\log(k)}{\eta} + \eta \sum_{t=1}^{n} \sum_{j=1}^{k} P_{tj} \hat{X}_{tj}^2. \tag{11.13}$$

As noted earlier, the expectation of the left-hand side is R_{ni}. The first term on the right-hand side is a constant, which leaves us to bound the expectation of the second term. Letting $y_{tj} = 1 - x_{tj}$ and $Y_t = 1 - X_t$ and expanding the definition of $\hat{X}_{tj}^2$ leads to

$$\mathbb{E}\left[\sum_{j=1}^{k} P_{tj} \hat{X}_{tj}^2\right] = \mathbb{E}\left[\sum_{j=1}^{k} P_{tj}\left(1 - \frac{\mathbb{I}\{A_t = j\} y_{tj}}{P_{tj}}\right)^2\right]$$

$$= \mathbb{E}\left[\sum_{j=1}^{k} P_{tj}\left(1 - 2\frac{\mathbb{I}\{A_t = j\} y_{tj}}{P_{tj}} + \frac{\mathbb{I}\{A_t = j\} y_{tj}^2}{P_{tj}^2}\right)\right]$$

$$= \mathbb{E}\left[1 - 2Y_t + \mathbb{E}_{t-1}\left[\sum_{j=1}^{k} \frac{\mathbb{I}\{A_t = j\} y_{tj}^2}{P_{tj}}\right]\right]$$

$$= \mathbb{E}\left[1 - 2Y_t + \sum_{j=1}^{k} y_{tj}^2\right]$$

$$= \mathbb{E}\left[(1 - Y_t)^2 + \sum_{j \neq A_t} y_{tj}^2\right]$$

$$\leq k.$$

Summing over t, and then substituting into Eq. (11.13), we get

$$R_{ni} \leq \frac{\log(k)}{\eta} + \eta nk = 2\sqrt{nk \log(k)},$$

where the equality follows by substituting $\eta = \sqrt{\log(k)/(nk)}$, which was chosen to optimise this bound. $\qquad\square$

At the heart of the proof are the inequalities:

$$1 + x \leq \exp(x) \text{ for all } x \in \mathbb{R} \qquad \text{and} \qquad \exp(x) \leq 1 + x + x^2 \text{ for } x \leq 1.$$

The former of these inequalities is an ansatz derived from the first-order Taylor expansion of $\exp(x)$ about $x = 0$. The latter, however, is not the second-order Taylor expansion, which

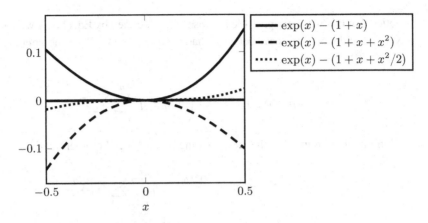

Figure 11.3 Approximations for exp(x) on $[-1/2, 1/2]$.

would be $1 + x + x^2/2$. The problem is that the second-order Taylor series is not an upper bound on $\exp(x)$ for $x \leq 1$, but only for $x \leq 0$:

$$\exp(x) \leq 1 + x + \frac{1}{2}x^2 \text{ for all } x \leq 0. \tag{11.14}$$

But it is nearly an upper bound, and this can be exploited to improve the bound in Theorem 11.1. The mentioned upper and lower bounds on $\exp(x)$ are shown in Fig. 11.3, from which it is quite obvious that the bound in Eq. (11.14) is significantly tighter when $x \leq 0$.

Let us now put Eq. (11.14) to use in proving the following improved version of Theorem 11.1, for which the regret is smaller by a factor of $\sqrt{2}$. The algorithm is unchanged except for a slightly increased learning rate.

THEOREM 11.2. *Let* $x \in [0, 1]^{n \times k}$ *be an adversarial bandit and* π *be the policy of Exp3 with learning rate* $\eta = \sqrt{2\log(k)/(nk)}$. *Then,*

$$R_n(\pi, x) \leq \sqrt{2nk \log(k)}.$$

Proof By construction, $\hat{X}_{tj} \leq 1$. Therefore,

$$\exp\left(\eta \hat{X}_{tj}\right) = \exp(\eta) \exp\left(\eta(\hat{X}_{tj} - 1)\right)$$

$$\leq \exp(\eta) \left\{ 1 + \eta(\hat{X}_{tj} - 1) + \frac{\eta^2}{2}(\hat{X}_{tj} - 1)^2 \right\}.$$

Using the fact that $\sum_j P_{tj} = 1$ and the inequality $1 + x \leq \exp(x)$, we get

$$\frac{W_t}{W_{t-1}} = \sum_{j=1}^{k} P_{tj} \exp(\eta \hat{X}_{tj}) \leq \exp\left(\eta \sum_{j=1}^{k} P_{tj} \hat{X}_{tj} + \frac{\eta^2}{2} \sum_{j=1}^{k} P_{tj}(\hat{X}_{tj} - 1)^2 \right),$$

where the equality is from Eq. (11.11). We see that here we need to bound $\sum_j P_{tj}(\hat{X}_{tj}-1)^2$. Let $\hat{Y}_{tj} = 1 - \hat{X}_{tj}$. Then,

$$P_{tj}(\hat{X}_{tj} - 1)^2 = P_{tj}\hat{Y}_{tj}\hat{Y}_{tj} = \mathbb{I}\{A_t = j\} y_{tj}\hat{Y}_{tj} \leq \hat{Y}_{tj},$$

where the last inequality used $\hat{Y}_{tj} \geq 0$ and $y_{tj} \leq 1$. Thus,

$$\sum_{j=1}^{k} P_{tj}(\hat{X}_{tj} - 1)^2 \leq \sum_{j=1}^{k} \hat{Y}_{tj}.$$

With the same calculations as before, we get

$$\hat{S}_{ni} - \hat{S}_n \leq \frac{\log(k)}{\eta} + \frac{\eta}{2} \sum_{t=1}^{n} \sum_{j=1}^{k} \hat{Y}_{tj}. \tag{11.15}$$

The result is completed by taking expectations of both sides, using $\mathbb{E} \sum_{t,j} \hat{Y}_{tj} = \mathbb{E} \sum_{t,j} \mathbb{E}_{t-1} \hat{Y}_{tj} = \mathbb{E} \sum_{t,j} y_{tj} \leq nk$ and substituting the learning rate. $\qquad \square$

The reader may wonder about the somewhat ad hoc proof. The best we can do for now is to point out a few things about the proof. It is natural to replace the true rewards with the estimated ones. Then, to prove a regret bound in terms of the estimated rewards, an alternative to the proof is to start with the the trivial inequality that states that for any $x = (x_j)$ vector and positive quantity η, the inequality $x_i \leq \frac{1}{\eta} \log \sum_j \exp(\eta x_j)$ holds. Applying this with $x = (\hat{S}_{ni})$ gives

$$\hat{S}_{ni} \leq \frac{1}{\eta} \log(\sum_j \exp(\eta \hat{S}_{nj})) = \frac{1}{\eta} \log(W_n),$$

from where the proof can be continued by introducing the telescoping argument.

11.5 Notes

1 Exp3 is nearly optimal in the sense that its expected regret cannot be improved significantly in the worst case. The distribution of its regret, however, is very far from optimal. Define the **random regret** to be the random variable measuring the actual deficit of the learner relative to the best arm in hindsight:

$$\hat{R}_n = \underbrace{\max_{i \in [k]} \sum_{t=1}^{n} x_{ti} - \sum_{t=1}^{n} X_t}_{\text{in terms of rewards}} = \underbrace{\sum_{t=1}^{n} Y_t - \min_{i \in [k]} \sum_{t=1}^{n} y_{ti}}_{\text{in terms of losses}}.$$

In Exercise 11.6 you will show that for all large enough n and reasonable choices of η, there exists a bandit such that the random regret of Exp3 satisfies $\mathbb{P}(\hat{R}_n \geq n/4) > 1/131$. In the same exercise, you should explain why this does not contradict the upper bound. That Exp3 has such a high variance is a serious limitation, which we address in the next chapter.

2 What happens when the range of the rewards is unbounded? This has been studied by Allenberg et al. [2006], where some (necessarily much weaker) positive results are presented.

3 In the **full information** setting, the learner observes the whole vector $x_t \in [0, 1]^k$ at the end of round t, but the reward is still x_{tA_t}. This setting is also called **prediction with expert advice**. Exponential weighting is still a good idea, but the estimated rewards can now be replaced by the

actual rewards. The resulting algorithm is sometimes called Hedge or the exponential weights algorithm. The proof as written goes through in almost the same way, but one should replace the polynomial upper bound on $\exp(x)$ with Hoeffding's lemma. This analysis gives a regret of $\sqrt{n \log(k)/2}$, which is optimal in an asymptotic sense [Cesa-Bianchi and Lugosi, 2006].

4   We assumed that the adversary chooses the rewards at the start of the game. Such adversaries are called **oblivious**. An adversary is called **reactive** or **non-oblivious** if x_t is allowed to depend on the history $x_1, A_1, \ldots, x_{t-1}, A_{t-1}$. Despite the fact that this is clearly a harder problem, the result we obtained can be generalised to this setting without changing the analysis. It is another question whether the definition of regret makes sense for reactive environments.

5   A more sophisticated algorithm and analysis shaves a factor of $\sqrt{\log(k)}$ from the regret upper bound in Theorem 11.2 [Audibert and Bubeck, 2009, 2010a, Bubeck and Cesa-Bianchi, 2012]. It turns out that this algorithm, just like Exp3, is an instantiation of mirror descent from convex optimisation, which we present in Chapter 28. More details are in Exercise 28.15. Interestingly, this algorithm not only shaves off the extra $\sqrt{\log(k)}$ factor from the regret, but also achieves $O(\log(n))$-regret in the stochastic setting provided that one uses a learning rate of $1/\sqrt{t}$ in round t [Zimmert and Seldin, 2019]. This remarkable result improves in an elegant way on many previous attempts to design algorithms for stochastic and adversarial bandits [Bubeck and Slivkins, 2012, Seldin and Slivkins, 2014, Auer and Chiang, 2016, Seldin and Lugosi, 2017]. There are some complications, however, depending on whether or not the adversary is oblivious. The situation is best summarised by Auer and Chiang [2016], where the authors present upper and lower bounds on what is possible in various scenarios.

6   The initial distribution (the 'prior') P_1 does not have to be uniform. By biasing the prior towards a specific action, the regret can be reduced when the favoured action turns out to be optimal. There is an unavoidable price for this, however, if the optimal arm is not favoured [Lattimore, 2015a].

7   Building on the previous note, suppose the reward in round t is $X_t = f_t(A_1, \ldots, A_t)$ and $f_1, \ldots, f_n$ are a sequence of functions chosen in advance by the adversary with $f_t : [k]^t \to [0, 1]$. Let $\Pi \subset [k]^n$ be a set of action sequences. Then the expected **policy regret** with respect to Π is

$$\max_{a_1, \ldots, a_n \in \Pi} \sum_{t=1}^{n} f_t(a_1, \ldots, a_t) - \mathbb{E}\left[\sum_{t=1}^{n} f_t(A_1, \ldots, A_t) \right].$$

Even if Π only consists of constant sequences, there still does not exist a policy guaranteeing sublinear regret. The reason is simple. Consider the two candidate choices of $f_1, \ldots, f_n$. In the first choice, $f_t(a_1, \ldots, a_t) = \mathbb{I}\{a_1 = 1\}$, and in the second we have $f_t(a_1, \ldots, a_t) = \mathbb{I}\{a_1 = 2\}$. Clearly the learner must suffer linear regret in at least one of these two reactive bandit environments. The problem is that the learner's decision in the first round determines the rewards available in all subsequent rounds, and there is no time for learning. By making additional assumptions, sublinear regret is possible, however – e.g. by assuming the adversary has limited memory [Arora et al., 2012].

8   There is a common misconception that the adversarial framework is a good fit for non-stationary environments. While the framework does not assume the rewards are stationary, the regret concept used in this chapter has stationarity built in. A policy designed for minimising the regret relative to the best action in hindsight is seldom suitable for non-stationary bandits, where the whole point is to adapt to changes in the optimal arm. In such cases a better benchmark is to compete with a sequence of actions. For more on non-stationary bandits, see Chapter 31.

9 The estimators in Eq. (11.3) and Eq. (11.6) both have conditional variance $\mathbb{V}_t[\hat{X}_{ti}] \approx 1/P_{ti}$, which blows up for small P_{ti}. It is instructive to think about whether and how P_{ti} can take on very small values. Consider the loss-based estimator given by (11.6). For this estimator, when P_{tA_t} and X_t are both small, $\hat{X}_{tA_t}$ can take on a large negative value. Through the update formula (11.7), this then translates into P_{t+1,A_t} being squashed aggressively towards zero. A similar issue arises with the reward-based estimator given by (11.3). The difference is that now it will be a 'positive surprise' (P_{tA_t} small, X_t large) that pushes the probabilities towards zero. But note that in this case, $P_{t+1,i}$ is pushed towards zero for all $i \neq A_t$. This means that dangerously small probabilities are expected to be more frequent for the gains estimator Eq. (11.3).

10 Exp3 requires advance knowledge of the horizon. The doubling trick can be used to overcome this issue, but a more elegant solution is to use a decreasing learning rate. The analysis in this chapter can be adapted to this case. More discussion is provided in the notes and exercises of Chapter 28, where we give a more generic solution to this problem (Exercise 28.13).

11 The calculation in Eq. (11.2) is a reduction, showing that algorithms with low regret on finite-armed adversarial bandits also have low regret on stochastic bandits where the reward distributions have appropriately bounded support. Reductions play an important role throughout the bandit literature and we will see many more examples. The reader should be careful not to generalise the idea that adversarial algorithms work well on stochastic problems. The assumptions must be checked (like boundedness of the support), and for different models there can be subtleties. The whole of Chapter 29 is devoted to the linear case.

12 As we mentioned, a policy for k-armed adversarial bandits is defined by any function $\pi : ([k] \times [0,1])^* \to \mathcal{P}_{k-1}$. There is no need to assume that π is measurable because the actions are discrete and the rewards are deterministic. The relations between the stochastic and adversarial regret are only well defined for policies that are probability kernels as defined in Definition 4.7. You might be worried that lower bounds for stochastic bandits only imply lower bounds for measurable adversarial policies. Fortunately, the lower bounds are easily proven for Bernoulli bandits, and in this case the space of reward sequences is finite and measurability is no longer problematic. Later we study adversarial bandits with an infinite action set $\mathcal{A}$, which is equipped with a σ-algebra $\mathcal{G}$. In this case the reward vectors are replaced by functions $(x_t)_{t=1}^n$, where $x_t : \mathcal{A} \to [0,1]$ is $\mathcal{G}$-measurable. Then, the measurability condition on the policy is that for all choices of the adversary and all $B \in \mathfrak{B}(\mathcal{A})$,

$$\pi(B \mid a_1, x_1(a_1), \ldots, a_{t-1}, x_{t-1}(a_{t-1}))$$

must be measurable as a function of $a_1, \ldots, a_{t-1}$. In practice, of course, all the policies you might ever propose would also be measurable as a function of the rewards.

11.6 Bibliographic Remarks

Exponential weighting has been a standard tool in online learning since the papers by Vovk [1990] and Littlestone and Warmuth [1994]. Exp3 and several variations were introduced by Auer et al. [1995], which was also the first paper to study bandits in the adversarial framework. The algorithm and analysis presented here differs slightly because we do not add any additional exploration, while the version of Exp3 in that paper explores uniformly with low probability. The fact that additional exploration is not required was observed by Stoltz [2005].

11.7 Exercises

11.1 (SAMPLING FROM A MULTINOMIAL) In order to implement Exp3, you need a way to sample from the exponential weights distribution. Many programming languages provide a standard way to do this. For example, in Python you can use the Numpy library and `numpy.random.multinomial`. In more basic languages, however, you only have access to a function `rand()` that returns a floating point number 'uniformly' distributed in $[0, 1]$. Describe an algorithm that takes as input a probability vector $p \in \mathcal{P}_{k-1}$ and uses a single call to `rand()` to return $X \in [k]$ with $\mathbb{P}(X = i) = p_i$.

> On most computers, `rand()` will return a pseudo-random number, and since there are only finitely many floating point numbers, the resulting distribution will not really be uniform on $[0, 1]$. Thinking about these issues is a worthy endeavour, and sometimes it really matters. For this exercise you may ignore these issues, however.

11.2 (LINEAR REGRET FOR DETERMINISTIC POLICIES) Show that for any deterministic policy π there exists an environment $x \in [0, 1]^{n \times k}$ such that $R_n(\pi, x) \geq n(1 - 1/k)$. What does your result say about the policies designed in Part II?

11.3 (MAXIMUM AND EXPECTATIONS) Show that the first inequality in (11.2) holds: Moving the maximum inside the expectation increases the value of the expectation.

11.4 (ALTERNATIVE REGRET DEFINITION) Suppose we had defined the regret by

$$R_n^{\text{track}}(\pi, x) = \mathbb{E}\left[\sum_{t=1}^{n} \max_{i \in [k]} x_{ti} - \sum_{t=1}^{n} x_{tA_t}\right].$$

At first sight this definition seems like the right thing because it measures what you actually care about. Unfortunately, however, it gives the adversary too much power. Show that for any policy π (randomised or not), there exists a $x \in [0, 1]^{k \times n}$ such that

$$R_n^{\text{track}}(\pi, x) \geq n\left(1 - \frac{1}{k}\right).$$

11.5 (UNBIASED ESTIMATORS ARE IMPORTANCE WEIGHTED) Let $P \in \mathcal{P}_{k-1}$ be a probability vector with nonzero components and let $A \sim P$. Suppose $\hat{X} : [k] \times \mathbb{R} \to \mathbb{R}$ is a function such that for all $x \in \mathbb{R}^k$,

$$\mathbb{E}[\hat{X}(A, x_A)] = \sum_{i=1}^{k} P_i \hat{X}(i, x_i) = x_1.$$

Show that there exists an $a \in \mathbb{R}^k$ such that $\langle a, P \rangle = 0$ and for all i and z in their respective domains,
$$\hat{X}(i, z) = a_i + \frac{\mathbb{I}\{i = 1\} z}{P_1}.$$

11.6 (VARIANCE OF EXP3) In this exercise, you will show that if $\eta \in [n^{-p}, 1]$ for some $p \in (0, 1)$, then for sufficiently large n, there exists a bandit on which Exp3 has a constant probability of suffering linear regret. We work with losses so that given a bandit $y \in [0, 1]^{n \times k}$, the learner samples A_t from P_t given by

$$P_{ti} = \frac{\exp\left(-\eta \sum_{s=1}^{t-1} \hat{Y}_{si}\right)}{\sum_{j=1}^{k} \exp\left(-\eta \sum_{s=1}^{t-1} \hat{Y}_{sj}\right)},$$

where $\hat{Y}_{ti} = A_{ti} y_{ti}/P_{ti}$. Let $\alpha \in [1/4, 1/2]$ be a constant to be tuned subsequently and define a two-armed adversarial bandit in terms of its losses by

$$y_{t1} = \begin{cases} 0 & \text{if } t \leq n/2 \\ 1 & \text{otherwise} \end{cases} \qquad \text{and} \qquad y_{t2} = \begin{cases} \alpha & \text{if } t \leq n/2 \\ 0 & \text{otherwise.} \end{cases}$$

For simplicity you may assume that n is even.

(a) Define the sequence of real-valued functions $q_1, \ldots, q_n$ on domain $[1/4, 1/2]$ inductively by $q_0(\alpha) = 1/2$ and

$$q_{s+1}(\alpha) = \frac{q_s(\alpha) \exp(-\eta\alpha/q_s(\alpha))}{1 - q_s(\alpha) + q_s(\alpha) \exp(-\eta\alpha/q_s(\alpha))}.$$

Show for $t \leq 1 + n/2$ that $P_{t2} = q_{T_2(t-1)}(\alpha)$, where $T_2(t) = \sum_{s=1}^{t} A_{s2}$.

(b) Show that for sufficiently large n there exists an $\alpha \in [1/4, 1/2]$ and $s \in \mathbb{N}$ such that

$$q_s(\alpha) = \frac{1}{8n} \qquad \text{and} \qquad \sum_{u=0}^{s-1} \frac{1}{q_u(\alpha)} \leq \frac{n}{8}.$$

(c) Prove that $\mathbb{P}(T_2(n/2) \geq s + 1) \geq 1/65$.

(d) Prove that $\mathbb{P}(\hat{R}_n \geq n/4) \geq (1 - n\exp(-\eta n)/2)/65$.

(e) The previous part shows that the regret is linear with constant probability for sufficiently large n. On the other hand, a dubious application of Markov's inequality and Theorem 11.1 shows that

$$\mathbb{P}(\hat{R}_n \geq n/4) \leq \frac{4\mathbb{E}[\hat{R}_n]}{n} = O(n^{-1/2}).$$

Explain the apparent contradiction.

(f) Validate the theoretical results of this exercise in an experimental fashion: Implement Exp3 with the loss sequence suggested to reproduce Fig. 11.4. The learning rate is set to the value computed in Theorem 11.2: $\eta = \sqrt{2\log(k)/(nk)}$. Compare the figure with the theoretical results: Is there an agreement between theory and the empirical results?

11.7 (GUMBEL TRICK) Let $a_1, \ldots, a_k$ be positive real values and $U_1, \ldots, U_k$ be a sequence of independent and identically distributed uniform random variables on $[0, 1]$. Then let $G_i = -\log(-\log(U_i))$, which follows a **standard Gumbel distribution**. Prove that

$$\mathbb{P}\left(\log(a_i) + G_i = \max_{j \in [k]}(\log(a_j) + G_j)\right) = \frac{a_i}{\sum_{j=1}^{k} a_j}.$$

11.8 (EXP3 AS FOLLOW-THE-PERTURBED-LEADER) Let $(Z_{ti})_{ti}$ be a collection of independent and identically distributed random variables. The follow-the-perturbed-leader algorithm chooses

$$A_t = \operatorname{argmax}_{i \in [k]}\left(Z_{ti} - \eta \sum_{s=1}^{t-1} \hat{Y}_{si}\right).$$

Show that if Z_{ti} is a standard Gumbel, then follow-the-perturbed-leader is the same as Exp3.

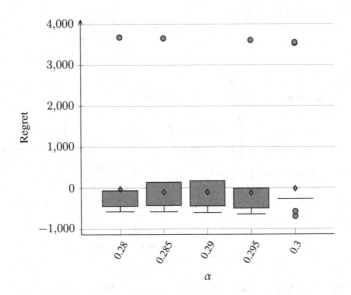

Figure 11.4 Exp3 instability: Box and whisker plot of the distribution of the regret of Exp3 for different values of α over a horizon of $n = 10^4$ with $m = 500$ repetitions for the example of Exercise 11.6. The boxes represent the quartiles of the empirical distribution, the diamond shows the average; the median is equal to the upper quartile (and thus cannot be seen), while the dots show values outside of the "interquartile range".

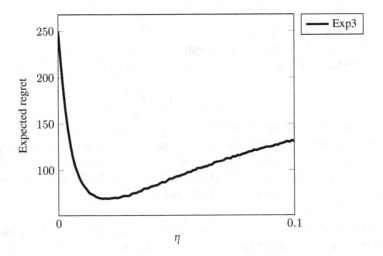

Figure 11.5 Expected regret for Exp3 for different learning rates over $n = 10^5$ rounds on a Bernoulli bandit with means $\mu_1 = 0.5$ and $\mu_2 = 0.55$.

11.9 (Exp3 ON STOCHASTIC BANDITS) In this exercise we compare UCB and Exp3 on stochastic data. Suppose we have a two-armed stochastic Bernoulli bandit with $\mu_1 = 0.5$ and $\mu_2 = \mu_1 + \Delta$ with $\Delta = 0.05$.

(a) Plot the regret of UCB and Exp3 on the same plot as a function of the horizon n using the learning rate from Theorem 11.2.

(b) Now fix the horizon to $n = 10^5$ and plot the regret as a function of the learning rate. Your plot should look like Fig. 11.5.

(c) Investigate how the shape of this graph changes as you change Δ.

(d) Find empirically the choice of η that minimises the worst-case regret over all reasonable choices of Δ, and compare to the value proposed by the theory.

(e) What can you conclude from all this? Tell an interesting story.

HINT   The performance of UCB depends greatly on which version you use. For best results, remember that Bernoulli distributions are $1/2$-subgaussian or use the KL-UCB algorithm from Chapter 10.

12 The Exp3-IX Algorithm

In the last chapter, we proved a sublinear bound on the expected regret of Exp3, but with a disheartening large variance. The objective of this chapter is to modify Exp3 so that the regret stays small in expectation and is simultaneously well concentrated about its mean. Such results are called **high-probability bounds**. By slightly modifying the algorithm, we show that for each $\delta \in (0, 1)$, there exists an algorithm such that with probability at least $1 - \delta$,

$$\hat{R}_n = \max_{a \in \mathcal{A}} \sum_{t=1}^{n} (y_{tA_t} - y_{ta}) = O\left(\sqrt{nk \log\left(\frac{k}{\delta}\right)}\right).$$

The poor behaviour of Exp3 occurs because the variance of the importance-weighted estimators can become very large. In this chapter we modify the reward estimates to control the variance at the price of introducing some bias.

12.1 The Exp3-IX Algorithm

We start by summarising what we know about the behaviour of the random regret of Exp3. Because we want to use the loss-based estimator, it is more convenient to switch to losses, which we do for the remainder of the chapter. Rewriting Eq. (11.15) in terms of losses,

$$\hat{L}_n - \hat{L}_{ni} \le \frac{\log(k)}{\eta} + \frac{\eta}{2} \sum_{j=1}^{k} \hat{L}_{nj}, \tag{12.1}$$

where $\hat{L}_n$ and $\hat{L}_{ni}$ are defined using the loss estimator $\hat{Y}_{tj}$ by

$$\hat{L}_n = \sum_{t=1}^{n} \sum_{j=1}^{k} P_{tj} \hat{Y}_{tj} \quad \text{and} \quad \hat{L}_{ni} = \sum_{t=1}^{n} \hat{Y}_{ti}.$$

Eq. (12.1) holds no matter how the loss estimators are chosen, provided they satisfy $0 \le \hat{Y}_{ti} \le 1/P_{ti}$ for all t and i. Of course, the left-hand side of Eq. (12.1) is not close to the regret unless $\hat{Y}_{ti}$ is a reasonable estimator of the loss y_{ti}.

We also need to define the sum of losses observed by the learner and for each fixed action, which are

$$\tilde{L}_n = \sum_{t=1}^{n} y_{tA_t} \quad \text{and} \quad L_{ni} = \sum_{t=1}^{n} y_{ti}$$

Like in the previous chapter, we need to define the (random) regret with respect to a given arm i as follows:

$$\hat{R}_{ni} = \sum_{t=1}^{n} x_{ti} - \sum_{t=1}^{n} X_t = \tilde{L}_n - L_{ni}. \tag{12.2}$$

By substituting the above definitions into Eq. (12.1) and rearranging, the regret with respect to arm i is bounded by

$$\hat{R}_{ni} = \tilde{L}_n - L_{ni} = (\tilde{L}_n - \hat{L}_n) + (\hat{L}_n - \hat{L}_{ni}) + (\hat{L}_{ni} - L_{ni})$$

$$\leq \frac{\log(k)}{\eta} + (\tilde{L}_n - \hat{L}_n) + (\hat{L}_{ni} - L_{ni}) + \frac{\eta}{2} \sum_{j=1}^{k} \hat{L}_{nj}. \tag{12.3}$$

This means the random regret can be bounded by controlling $\tilde{L}_n - \hat{L}_n$, $\hat{L}_{nj} - L_{nj}$ and $\hat{L}_{nj}$ for each j. As promised we now modify the loss estimate. Let $\gamma > 0$ be a small constant to be chosen later and define the biased estimator

$$\hat{Y}_{ti} = \frac{\mathbb{I}\{A_t = i\} Y_t}{P_{ti} + \gamma}. \tag{12.4}$$

First, note that $\hat{Y}_{ti}$ still satisfies $0 \leq \hat{Y}_{ti} \leq 1/P_{ti}$, so (12.3) is still valid. As γ increases, the predictable variance decreases, but the bias increases. The optimal choice of γ depends on finding the sweet spot, which we will do once the dust has settled in the analysis. When Eq. (12.4) is used in the exponential update in Exp3, the resulting algorithm is called Exp3-IX (Algorithm 10). The suffix 'IX' stands for implicit exploration, a name justified by the following argument. A simple calculation shows that

$$\mathbb{E}_t[\hat{Y}_{ti}] = \frac{P_{ti} y_{ti}}{P_{ti} + \gamma} = y_{ti} - \frac{\gamma y_{ti}}{P_{ti} + \gamma} \leq y_{ti}.$$

Since small losses correspond to large rewards, the estimator is optimistically biased. The effect is a smoothing of P_t so that actions with large losses for which Exp3 would assign negligible probability are still chosen occasionally. In fact, the smaller is P_{ti}, the larger the bias is. As a result, Exp3-IX will explore more than the standard Exp3 algorithm (see Exercise 12.5).

> The reason for calling the exploration implicit is because the algorithm explores more as a consequence of modifying the reward estimates, rather than directly alternating P_t.

1: **Input:** n, k, η, γ
2: Set $\hat{L}_{0i} = 0$ for all i
3: **for** $t = 1, \ldots, n$ **do**
4:     Calculate the sampling distribution P_t:

$$P_{ti} = \frac{\exp\left(-\eta\hat{L}_{t-1,i}\right)}{\sum_{j=1}^{k} \exp\left(-\eta\hat{L}_{t-1,j}\right)}$$

5:     Sample $A_t \sim P_t$ and observe reward X_t
6:     Calculate $\hat{L}_{ti} = \hat{L}_{t-1,i} + \dfrac{\mathbb{I}\{A_t = i\}(1 - X_t)}{P_{ti} + \gamma}$
7: **end for**

Algorithm 10: Exp3-IX.

12.2 Regret Analysis

We now prove the following theorem bounding the random regret of Exp3-IX with high probability.

THEOREM 12.1. *Let $\delta \in (0, 1)$ and define*

$$\eta_1 = \sqrt{\frac{2\log(k+1)}{nk}} \qquad and \qquad \eta_2 = \sqrt{\frac{\log(k) + \log(\frac{k+1}{\delta})}{nk}}.$$

The following statements hold:

1 If Exp3-IX is run with parameters $\eta = \eta_1$ and $\gamma = \eta/2$, then

$$\mathbb{P}\left(\hat{R}_n \geq \sqrt{8nk\log(k+1)} + \sqrt{\frac{nk}{2\log(k+1)}}\log\left(\frac{1}{\delta}\right) + \log\left(\frac{k+1}{\delta}\right)\right) \leq \delta.$$

$$(12.5)$$

2 If Exp3-IX is run with parameters $\eta = \eta_2$ and $\gamma = \eta/2$, then

$$\mathbb{P}\left(\hat{R}_n \geq 2\sqrt{(2\log(k+1) + \log(1/\delta))nk} + \log\left(\frac{k+1}{\delta}\right)\right) \leq \delta. \qquad (12.6)$$

The value of η_1 is independent of δ, which means that using this choice of learning rate leads to a single algorithm with a high-probability bound for all δ. On the other hand, η_2 does depend on δ, so the user must choose a confidence level from the beginning. The advantage is that the bound is improved, but only for the specified confidence level. We will show in Chapter 17 that this trade-off is unavoidable.

The proof follows by bounding each of the terms in Eq. (12.3), which we do via a series of lemmas. The first of these lemmas is a new concentration bound. To state the lemma, we recall two useful notions: Recall that given a filtration $\mathbb{F} = (\mathcal{F}_t)_{t=0}^{n}$, $(Z_t)_{t=1}^{n}$ is $\mathbb{F}$-adapted if for $t \in [n]$, Z_t is $\mathcal{F}_t$-measurable and $(Z_t)_{t=1}^n$ is $\mathbb{F}$-predictable, if for $t \in [n]$, Z_t is $\mathcal{F}_{t-1}$-measurable.

LEMMA 12.2. *Let* $\mathbb{F} = (\mathcal{F}_t)_{t=0}^n$ *be a filtration and for* $i \in [k]$ *let* $(\tilde{Y}_{ti})_t$ *be* $\mathbb{F}$-*adapted such that:*

1 for any $S \subset [k]$ *with* $|S| > 1$, $\mathbb{E}\left[\prod_{i \in S} \tilde{Y}_{ti} \,\middle|\, \mathcal{F}_{t-1}\right] \leq 0$; *and*

2 $\mathbb{E}\left[\tilde{Y}_{ti} \,\middle|\, \mathcal{F}_{t-1}\right] = y_{ti}$ *for all* $t \in [n]$ *and* $i \in [k]$.

Furthermore, let $(\alpha_{ti})_{ti}$ *and* $(\lambda_{ti})_{ti}$ *be real-valued* $\mathbb{F}$-*predictable random sequences such that for all* t, i *it holds that* $0 \leq \alpha_{ti} \tilde{Y}_{ti} \leq 2\lambda_{ti}$. *Then, for all* $\delta \in (0, 1)$,

$$\mathbb{P}\left(\sum_{t=1}^n \sum_{i=1}^k \alpha_{ti}\left(\frac{\tilde{Y}_{ti}}{1 + \lambda_{ti}} - y_{ti}\right) \geq \log\left(\frac{1}{\delta}\right)\right) \leq \delta.$$

The proof relies on the Cramér–Chernoff method and is deferred until the end of the chapter. Condition 1 states that the variables $\{\tilde{Y}_{ti}\}_i$ are negatively correlated, and it helps us save a factor of k. Equipped with this result, we can easily bound the terms $\hat{L}_{ni} - L_{ni}$.

LEMMA 12.3 (Concentration – variance). *Let* $\delta \in (0, 1)$. *With probability at least* $1 - \delta$, *the following inequalities hold simultaneously:*

$$\max_{i \in [k]}\left(\hat{L}_{ni} - L_{ni}\right) \leq \frac{\log(\frac{k+1}{\delta})}{2\gamma} \quad \text{and} \quad \sum_{i=1}^k \left(\hat{L}_{ni} - L_{ni}\right) \leq \frac{\log(\frac{k+1}{\delta})}{2\gamma}. \tag{12.7}$$

Proof Fix $\delta' \in (0, 1)$ to be chosen later and let $A_{ti} = \mathbb{I}\{A_t = i\}$ as before. Then

$$\sum_{i=1}^k (\hat{L}_{ni} - L_{ni}) = \sum_{t=1}^n \sum_{i=1}^k \left(\frac{A_{ti} y_{ti}}{P_{ti} + \gamma} - y_{ti}\right)$$

$$= \frac{1}{2\gamma} \sum_{t=1}^n \sum_{i=1}^k 2\gamma \left(\frac{1}{1 + \frac{\gamma}{P_{ti}}} \frac{A_{ti} y_{ti}}{P_{ti}} - y_{ti}\right).$$

Introduce $\lambda_{ti} = \frac{\gamma}{P_{ti}}$, $\tilde{Y}_{ti} = \frac{A_{ti} y_{ti}}{P_{ti}}$ and $\alpha_{ti} = 2\gamma$. Notice that the conditions of Lemma 12.2 are now satisfied. In particular, for any $S \subset [k]$ with $|S| > 1$, it holds that $\prod_{i \in S} A_{ti} = 0$ and hence $\prod_{i \in S} \tilde{Y}_{ti} = 0$. Therefore,

$$\mathbb{P}\left(\sum_{i=1}^k (\hat{L}_{ni} - L_{ni}) \geq \frac{\log(1/\delta')}{2\gamma}\right) \leq \delta'. \tag{12.8}$$

Similarly, for any fixed i,

$$\mathbb{P}\left(\hat{L}_{ni} - L_{ni} \geq \frac{\log(1/\delta')}{2\gamma}\right) \leq \delta'. \tag{12.9}$$

To see this, use the previous argument with $\alpha_{tj} = \mathbb{I}\{j = i\} 2\gamma$. The result follows by choosing $\delta' = \delta/(k+1)$ and the union bound. $\qquad\square$

LEMMA 12.4 (Bias). $\tilde{L}_n - \hat{L}_n = \gamma \sum_{j=1}^k \hat{L}_{nj}$.

Proof Let $A_{ti} = \mathbb{I}\{A_t = i\}$ as before. Writing $Y_t = \sum_j A_{tj} y_{tj}$, we calculate

$$Y_t - \sum_{j=1}^{k} P_{tj} \hat{Y}_{tj} = \sum_{j=1}^{k} \left(1 - \frac{P_{tj}}{P_{tj} + \gamma}\right) A_{tj} y_{tj} = \gamma \sum_{j=1}^{k} \frac{A_{tj}}{P_{tj} + \gamma} y_{tj} = \gamma \sum_{j=1}^{k} \hat{Y}_{tj}.$$

Therefore $\tilde{L}_n - \hat{L}_n = \gamma \sum_{j=1}^{k} \hat{L}_{nj}$ as required. □

Proof of Theorem 12.1   By Eq. (12.3) and Lemma 12.4, we have

$$\hat{R}_n \leq \frac{\log(k)}{\eta} + (\tilde{L}_n - \hat{L}_n) + \max_{i \in [k]}(\hat{L}_{ni} - L_{ni}) + \frac{\eta}{2} \sum_{j=1}^{k} \hat{L}_{nj}$$

$$= \frac{\log(k)}{\eta} + \max_{i \in [k]}(\hat{L}_{ni} - L_{ni}) + \left(\frac{\eta}{2} + \gamma\right) \sum_{j=1}^{k} \hat{L}_{nj}.$$

Therefore, by Lemma 12.3, with probability at least $1 - \delta$,

$$\hat{R}_n \leq \frac{\log(k)}{\eta} + \frac{\log\left(\frac{k+1}{\delta}\right)}{2\gamma} + \left(\gamma + \frac{\eta}{2}\right) \left(\sum_{j=1}^{k} L_{nj} + \frac{\log\left(\frac{k+1}{\delta}\right)}{2\gamma}\right)$$

$$\leq \frac{\log(k)}{\eta} + \left(\gamma + \frac{\eta}{2}\right) nk + \left(\gamma + \frac{\eta}{2} + 1\right) \frac{\log\left(\frac{k+1}{\delta}\right)}{2\gamma},$$

where the second inequality follows since $L_{nj} \leq n$ for all j. The result follows by substituting the definitions of $\eta \in \{\eta_1, \eta_2\}$ and $\gamma = \eta/2$. □

The attentive reader may be wondering whether proving the new concentration inequality of Lemma 12.2, which looks a bit ad hoc, was really necessary to get the bounds on $\hat{L}_{ni}$ that were stated in the next lemma. After all, we had a number of concentration inequalities available to us that could be applied. As it turns out, one could also use Bernstein inequality to get a result that only loses a factor of two compared to the specialised lemma. The details are in Exercise 12.1. There are two important lessons that are the basis of both proofs. The first is that since $\mathbb{E}[\hat{L}_{ni}] < L_{ni}$ and the gap between these two quantities is large enough in a manner that we make precise in Exercise 12.1, the deviation $\hat{L}_{ni} - L_{ni}$ can be bounded independently of P_{ti}, A_{ti} and y_{ti}. The price is that instead of $\sqrt{\log(1/\delta)}$, the bound scales linearly with the generally larger quantity $\log(1/\delta)$. The factor $1/\gamma$ here is the maximum scale of the individual summands in $\hat{L}_{ni}$. The second lesson is specific to how in bounding $\sum_i \hat{L}_{ni} - L_{ni}$ a union bound over i is avoided: this works because for a fixed time index t, $(A_{ti})_i$ are negatively correlated. Negative dependence/association/correlation are known to be good substitutes for independence, and by exploiting such properties one can often demonstrate better concentration.

12.2.1 Proof of Lemma 12.2

We start with a technical inequality:

LEMMA 12.5. *For any $0 \leq x \leq 2\lambda$ it holds that* $\exp\left(\frac{x}{1+\lambda}\right) \leq 1 + x$.

Note that $1 + x \leq \exp(x)$. What the lemma shows is that by slightly discounting the argument of the exponential function, in a bounded neighbourhood of zero, $1 + x$ can be an upper bound for the resulting function. Or, equivalently, slightly inflating the linear term in $1 + x$, the linear lower bound becomes an upper bound.

Proof of Lemma 12.5   We have

$$\exp\left(\frac{x}{1+\lambda}\right) \leq \exp\left(\frac{x}{1+x/2}\right) \leq 1 + x,$$

where the first inequality is because $\lambda \mapsto \exp(\frac{x}{1+\lambda})$ is decreasing in λ, and the second is because $\frac{2u}{1+u} \leq \log(1 + 2u)$ holds for all $u \geq 0$. This latter inequality can be seen to hold by noting that for $u = 0$, the two sides are equal, while the derivative of the left-hand side is smaller than that of the right-hand side at any $u \geq 0$. ☐

Proof of Lemma 12.2   Fix $t \in [n]$ and let $\mathbb{E}_t[\cdot] = \mathbb{E}[\cdot \mid \mathcal{F}_t]$ denote the conditional expectation with respect to $\mathcal{F}_t$. By Lemma 12.5 and the assumption that $0 \leq \alpha_{ti}\tilde{Y}_{ti} \leq 2\lambda_{ti}$, we have

$$\exp\left(\frac{\alpha_{ti}\tilde{Y}_{ti}}{1 + \lambda_{ti}}\right) \leq 1 + \alpha_{ti}\tilde{Y}_{ti}.$$

Taking the product of these inequalities over i,

$$\mathbb{E}_{t-1}\left[\exp\left(\sum_{i=1}^{k}\frac{\alpha_{ti}\tilde{Y}_{ti}}{1+\lambda_{ti}}\right)\right] \leq \mathbb{E}_{t-1}\left[\prod_{i=1}^{k}(1 + \alpha_{ti}\tilde{Y}_{ti})\right] \leq 1 + \mathbb{E}_{t-1}\left[\sum_{i=1}^{k}\alpha_{ti}\tilde{Y}_{ti}\right]$$

$$= 1 + \sum_{i=1}^{k}\alpha_{ti}y_{ti} \leq \exp\left(\sum_{i=1}^{k}\alpha_{ti}y_{ti}\right), \qquad (12.10)$$

where the second inequality follows from $\prod_{i=1}^{k}(1 + a_i) = \sum_{b \in \{0,1\}^k}\prod_{i=1}^{k}a_i^{b_i}$ and the assumption that for $S \subset [k]$ with $|S| > 1$, $\mathbb{E}_{t-1}[\prod_{i \in S}\tilde{Y}_{ti}] \leq 0$, the third one follows from the assumption that $\mathbb{E}_{t-1}[\tilde{Y}_{ti}] = y_{ti}$, while the last one follows from $1 + x \leq \exp(x)$. Define

$$Z_t = \exp\left(\sum_{i=1}^{k}\alpha_{ti}\left(\frac{\tilde{Y}_{ti}}{1+\lambda_{ti}} - y_{ti}\right)\right)$$

and let $M_t = Z_1 \ldots Z_t$, $t \in [n]$ with $M_0 = 1$. By (12.10), $\mathbb{E}_{t-1}[Z_t] \leq 1$. Therefore

$$\mathbb{E}[M_t] = \mathbb{E}[\mathbb{E}_{t-1}[M_t]] = \mathbb{E}[M_{t-1}\mathbb{E}_{t-1}[Z_t]] \leq \mathbb{E}[M_{t-1}] \leq \cdots \leq \mathbb{E}[M_0] = 1.$$

Setting $t = n$ and combining the above display with Markov's inequality leads to $\mathbb{P}\left(\log(M_n) \geq \log(1/\delta)\right) = \mathbb{P}\left(M_n\delta \geq 1\right) \leq \mathbb{E}[M_n]\delta \leq \delta$. ☐

12.3   Notes

1 An alternative to the somewhat custom-made Lemma 12.2 is to use a Bernstein-type bound that simply bounds the deviation of a martingale from its mean in terms of its quadratic variation. The slight disadvantage of this is that this way we lose a factor of two. If this is not a concern, one may even prefer this approach due to its greater transparency. For details, see Exercise 12.1.

2 An upper bound on the expected regret of Exp3-IX can be obtained by integrating the tail:

$$R_n \le \mathbb{E}[(\hat{R}_n)^+] = \int_0^\infty \mathbb{P}\left((\hat{R}_n)^+ \ge x\right) dx \le \int_0^\infty \mathbb{P}\left(\hat{R}_n \ge x\right) dx,$$

where the first equality follows from Proposition 2.8. The result is completed using either the high-probability bound in Theorem 12.1 and by straightforward integration. We leave the details to the reader in Exercise 12.7.

3 The analysis presented here uses a fixed learning rate that depends on the horizon. Replacing η and γ with $\eta_t = \sqrt{\log(k)/(kt)}$ and $\gamma_t = \eta_t/2$ leads to an anytime algorithm with about the same regret [Kocák et al., 2014, Neu, 2015a].

4 There is another advantage of the modified importance-weighted estimators used by Exp3-IX, which leads to an improved regret in the special case that one of the arms has small losses. Specifically, it is possible to show that

$$R_n = O\left(\sqrt{k \min_{i \in [k]} L_{ni} \log(k)}\right).$$

In the worst case, L_{ni} is linear in n and the usual bound is recovered. But if the optimal arm enjoys low cumulative regret, then the above can be a big improvement over the bounds given in Theorem 12.1. Bounds of this kind are called **first-order bounds**. We refer the interested reader to the papers by Allenberg et al. [2006], Abernethy et al. [2012] and Neu [2015b] and Exercise 28.14.

5 Another situation where one might hope to have a smaller regret is when the rewards/losses for each arm do not deviate too far from their averages. Define the **quadratic variation** by

$$Q_n = \sum_{t=1}^n \|x_t - \mu\|^2, \quad \text{where } \mu = \frac{1}{n}\sum_{t=1}^n x_t.$$

Hazan and Kale [2011] gave an algorithm for which $R_n = O(k^2 \sqrt{Q_n})$, which can be better than the worst-case bound of Exp3 or Exp3-IX when the quadratic variation is very small. The factor of k^2 is suboptimal and can be removed using a careful instantiation of the mirror descent algorithm [Bubeck et al., 2018]. We do not cover this exact algorithm in this book, but the techniques based on mirror descent are presented in Chapter 28.

6 An alternative to the algorithm presented here is to mix the probability distribution computed using exponential weights with the uniform distribution, while biasing the estimates. This leads to the Exp3.P algorithm due to Auer et al. [2002b], who considered the case where δ is given and derived a bound that is similar to Eq. (12.6) of Theorem 12.1. With an appropriate modification of their proof, it is possible to derive a weaker bound similar to Eq. (12.5), where the knowledge of δ is not needed by the algorithm. This has been explored by Beygelzimer et al. [2010] in the context of a related algorithm, which will be considered in Chapter 18. One advantage of this approach is that it generalises to the case where the loss estimators are sometimes negative, a situation that can arise in more complicated settings. For technical details, we advise the reader to work through Exercise 12.3.

12.4 Bibliographic Remarks

The Exp3-IX algorithm is due to Kocák et al. [2014], who also introduced the biased loss estimators. The focus of that paper was to improve algorithms for more complex models with potentially large action sets and side information, though their analysis can still be applied to the model studied in this chapter. The observation that this algorithm also leads to high-probability bounds appeared in a follow-up paper by Neu [2015a]. High-probability bounds for adversarial bandits were first provided by Auer et al. [2002b] and explored in a more generic way by Abernethy and Rakhlin [2009]. The idea to reduce the variance of importance-weighted estimators is not new and seems to have been applied in various forms [Uchibe and Doya, 2004, Wawrzynski and Pacut, 2007, Ionides, 2008, Bottou et al., 2013]. All of these papers are based on truncating the estimators, which makes the resulting estimator less smooth. Surprisingly, the variance-reduction technique used in this chapter seems to be recent [Kocák et al., 2014].

12.5 Exercises

12.1 (BERNSTEIN-TYPE INEQUALITY AND LEMMA 12.3) Using the Berstein-type inequality stated in Exercise 5.15, show the following:

(a) For any $\delta \in (0, 1)$, with probability at least $1 - \delta$, $\hat{L}_{ni} - L_{ni} < \frac{1}{\gamma} \log(1/\delta)$.

(b) For any $\delta \in (0, 1)$, with probability at least $1 - \delta$, $\sum_i \hat{L}_{ni} - \sum_i L_{ni} < \frac{1}{\gamma} \log(1/\delta)$.

12.2 Prove the claims made in Note 3.

HINT   The source for this exercise is theorem 1 of the paper by Neu [2015a]. You can also read ahead and use the techniques from Exercise 28.13.

12.3 (EXP3.P) In this exercise we ask you to analyse the Exp3.P algorithm, which as we mentioned in the notes is another way to obtain high probability bounds. The idea is to modify Exp3 by biasing the estimators and introducing some forced exploration. Let $\hat{Y}_{ti} = A_{ti} y_{ti}/P_{ti} - \beta/P_{ti}$ be a biased version of the loss-based importance-weighted estimator that was used in the previous chapter. Define $\hat{L}_{ti} = \sum_{s=1}^{t} \hat{Y}_{si}$ and consider the policy that samples $A_t \sim P_t$, where

$$P_{ti} = (1 - \gamma)\tilde{P}_{ti} + \frac{\gamma}{k} \qquad \text{with} \qquad \tilde{P}_{ti} = \frac{\exp\left(-\eta \hat{L}_{t-1,i}\right)}{\sum_{j=1}^{k} \exp\left(-\eta \hat{L}_{t-1,j}\right)}.$$

(a) Let $\delta \in (0, 1)$ and $i \in [k]$. Show that with probability $1 - \delta$, the random regret $\hat{R}_{ni}$ against i (cf. (12.2)) satisfies

$$\hat{R}_{ni} < n\gamma + (1 - \gamma)\sum_{t=1}^{n}\sum_{j=1}^{k} \tilde{P}_{tj}(\hat{Y}_{tj} - y_{ti}) + \sum_{t=1}^{n} \frac{\beta}{P_{tA_t}} + \sqrt{\frac{n \log(1/\delta)}{2}}.$$

(b) Show that

$$\sum_{t=1}^{n}\sum_{j=1}^{k} \tilde{P}_{tj}(\hat{Y}_{tj} - y_{ti}) = \sum_{t=1}^{n}\sum_{j=1}^{k} \tilde{P}_{tj}(\hat{Y}_{tj} - \hat{Y}_{ti}) + \sum_{t=1}^{n}(\hat{Y}_{ti} - y_{ti}).$$

(c) Show that

$$\sum_{t=1}^{n}\sum_{j=1}^{k}\tilde{P}_{tj}(\hat{Y}_{tj} - \hat{Y}_{ti}) \le \frac{\log(k)}{\eta} + \eta\sum_{t=1}^{n}\sum_{j=1}^{k}\tilde{P}_{tj}\hat{Y}_{tj}^2.$$

(d) Show that

$$\sum_{t=1}^{n}\sum_{j=1}^{k}\tilde{P}_{tj}\hat{Y}_{tj}^2 \le \frac{nk^2\beta^2}{\gamma} + \sum_{t=1}^{n}\frac{1}{P_{tA_t}}.$$

(e) Suppose that $\gamma = k\eta$ and $\eta = \beta$. Apply the result of Exercise 5.15 to show that for any $\delta \in (0, 1)$, the following hold:

$$\mathbb{P}\left(\sum_{t=1}^{n}\frac{1}{P_{tA_t}} \ge 2nk + \frac{k}{\gamma}\log\left(\frac{1}{\delta}\right)\right) \le \delta.$$

$$\mathbb{P}\left(\sum_{t=1}^{n}\hat{Y}_{ti} - y_{ti} \ge \frac{1}{\beta}\log\left(\frac{1}{\delta}\right)\right) \le \delta.$$

(f) Combining the previous steps, show that there exists a universal constant $C > 0$ such that for any $\delta \in (0, 1)$, for an appropriate choice of η, γ and β, with probability at least $1 - \delta$ it holds that the random regret $\hat{R}_n$ of Exp3.P satisfies

$$\hat{R}_n \le C\sqrt{nk\log(k/\delta)}.$$

(g) In which step did you use the modified estimators?

(h) Show a bound where the algorithm parameters η, γ, β can only depend on n, k, but not on δ.

(i) Compare the bounds with the analogous bounds for Exp3-IX in Theorem 12.1.

12.4 (GENERIC EXP3.P ANALYSIS) This exercise is concerned with a generalisation of the core idea underlying Exp3.P of the previous exercise in that rather than giving explicit expressions for the biased loss estimates, we focus on the key properties required by the analysis of Exp3.P. To reduce clutter, we assume for the remainder that t ranges in $[n]$ and $a \in [k]$. Let $(\Omega, \mathcal{F}, \mathbb{F}, \mathbb{P})$ be a filtered probability space with $\mathbb{F} = (\mathcal{F}_t)_{t=0}^{n}$. Let $(Z_t), (\hat{Z}_t), (\tilde{Z}_t), (\beta_t)$ be sequences of random elements in $\mathbb{R}^k$, where $\tilde{Z}_t = \hat{Z}_t - \beta_t$ and $(Z_t), (\beta_t)$ are $\mathbb{F}$-predictable, whereas $(\hat{Z}_t)$ and therefore also $(\tilde{Z}_t)$ are $\mathbb{F}$-adapted. You should think of $\hat{Z}_t$ as the estimate of Z_t that uses randomisation, and β_t is the bias as in the previous exercise. Given positive constant η, define the probability vector $P_t \in \mathcal{P}_{k-1}$ by

$$P_{ta} = \frac{\exp\left(-\eta\sum_{s=1}^{t-1}\tilde{Z}_{sa}\right)}{\sum_{b=1}^{k}\exp\left(-\eta\sum_{s=1}^{t-1}\tilde{Z}_{sb}\right)}.$$

Let $\mathbb{E}_{t-1}[\cdot] = \mathbb{E}[\cdot \mid \mathcal{F}_{t-1}]$. Assume the following hold for all $a \in [k]$:

(a) $\eta|\hat{Z}_{ta}| \le 1$,   (b) $\eta\beta_{ta} \le 1$,

(c) $\eta\mathbb{E}_{t-1}[\hat{Z}_{ta}^2] \le \beta_{ta}$ almost surely,   (d) $\mathbb{E}_{t-1}[\hat{Z}_{ta}] = Z_{ta}$ almost surely.

Let $A^* = \operatorname{argmin}_{a \in [k]} \sum_{t=1}^{n} Z_{ta}$ and $R_n = \sum_{t=1}^{n}\sum_{a=1}^{k} P_{ta}(Z_{ta} - Z_{tA^*})$.

(a) Show that

$$\sum_{t=1}^{n}\sum_{a=1}^{k} P_{ta}(Z_{ta} - Z_{tA^*})$$

$$= \sum_{t=1}^{n}\sum_{a=1}^{k} P_{ta}(\tilde{Z}_{ta} - \tilde{Z}_{tA^*}) + \sum_{t=1}^{n}\sum_{a=1}^{k} P_{ta}(Z_{ta} - \tilde{Z}_{ta}) + \sum_{t=1}^{n}(\tilde{Z}_{tA^*} - Z_{tA^*}).$$

$$\underbrace{\qquad\qquad\qquad}_{(A)} \qquad \underbrace{\qquad\qquad\qquad}_{(B)} \qquad \underbrace{\qquad\qquad}_{(C)}$$

(b) Show that

$$(A) \le \frac{\log(k)}{\eta} + \eta \sum_{t=1}^{n}\sum_{a=1}^{k} P_{ta}\hat{Z}_{ta}^2 + 3\sum_{t=1}^{n}\sum_{a=1}^{k} P_{ta}\beta_{ta}.$$

(c) Show that with probability at least $1 - \delta$,

$$(B) \le 2\sum_{t=1}^{n}\sum_{a=1}^{k} P_{ta}\beta_{ta} + \frac{\log(1/\delta)}{\eta}.$$

(d) Show that with probability at least $1 - k\delta$,

$$(C) \le \frac{\log(1/\delta)}{\eta}.$$

(e) Conclude that for any $\delta \le 1/(k+1)$, with probability at least $1 - (k+1)\delta$,

$$R_n \le \frac{3\log(1/\delta)}{\eta} + \eta \sum_{t=1}^{n}\sum_{a=1}^{k} P_{ta}\hat{Z}_{ta}^2 + 5\sum_{t=1}^{n}\sum_{a=1}^{k} P_{ta}\beta_{ta}.$$

HINT   This is a long and challenging exercise. You may find it helpful to use the result in Exercise 5.15. The solution is also available.

12.5 (IMPLEMENTATION) Consider the Bernoulli bandit with $k = 5$ arms and $n = 10^4$ with means $\mu_1 = 1/2$ and $\mu_i = 1/2 - \Delta$ for $i > 1$. Plot the regret of Exp3 and Exp3-IX for $\Delta \in [0, 1/2]$. You should get a plot similar to that of Fig. 12.1. Does the result surprise you?

12.6 (IMPLEMENTATION: VARIANCE OF EXP3-IX) Repeat the experiment that led to Fig. 11.4 but with Exp3 swapped to Exp3-IX. Use the confidence parameter independent value of η and γ from

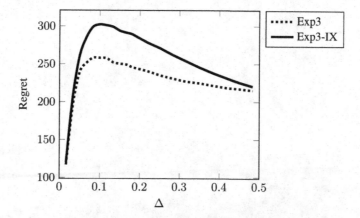

Figure 12.1   Comparison between Exp3 and Exp3-IX on Bernoulli bandit

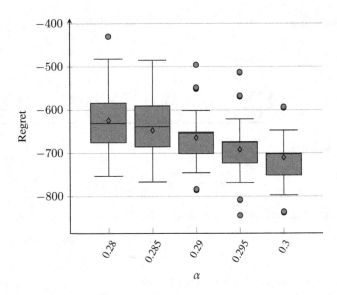

Figure 12.2 Box and whisker plot of the regret of Exp3-IX for the same setting as those used to produce Fig. 11.4. For details of the experimental settings, see the text of Exercise 11.6.

Theorem 12.1. You should get a figure similar to Fig. 12.2. Compare the new and the old figures and summarise your findings, including the outcome of the results of Exercise 12.5.

12.7 (EXPECTED REGRET OF EXP3-IX) In this exercise, you will complete the steps explained in Note 2 to prove a bound on the expected regret of Exp3-IX.

(a) Find a choice of η and universal constant $C > 0$ such that

$$R_n \le C\sqrt{kn \log(k)}.$$

(b) What happens as η grows? Write a bound on the expected regret of Exp3-IX in terms of η and k and n.

Part IV

Lower Bounds for Bandits with Finitely Many Arms

Until now, we have indulged ourselves by presenting algorithms and upper bounds on their regret. As satisfying as this is, the real truth of a problem is usually to be found in the lower bounds. There are several reasons for this:

1 An upper bound does not tell you much about what you could be missing out on. The only way to demonstrate that your algorithm really is (close to) optimal is to prove a lower bound showing that no algorithm can do better.

2 The second reason is that lower bounds are often more informative in the sense that it usually turns out to be easier to get the lower bound right than the upper bound. History shows a list of algorithms with steadily improving guarantees until eventually someone hits upon the idea for which the upper bound matches some known lower bound.

3 Finally, thinking about lower bounds forces you to understand what is hard about the problem. This is so useful that the best place to start when attacking a new problem is usually to try and prove lower bounds. Too often we have not heeded our own advice and started trying to design an algorithm, only to discover later that had we tackled the lower bound first, then the right algorithm would have fallen in our laps with almost no effort at all.

So what is the form of a typical lower bound? In the chapters that follow, we will see roughly two flavours. The first is the worst-case lower bound, which corresponds to a claim of the form

'For any policy you give me, I will give you an instance of a bandit problem v on which the regret is at least L'.

Results of this kind have an adversarial flavour, which makes them suitable for understanding the robustness of a policy. The second type is a lower bound on the regret of an algorithm for specific instances. These bounds have a different form that usually reads like the following:

'If you give me a *reasonable* policy, then its regret on any instance v is at least $L(v)$'.

The statement only holds for some policies – the 'reasonable' ones, whatever that means. But the guarantee is also more refined because bound controls the regret for these policies on every instance by a function that depends on this instance. This kind of bound will allow us to show that the instance-dependent bounds for stochastic bandits of $O(\sum_{i:\Delta_i>0} \Delta_i + \log(n)/\Delta_i)$ are not improvable. The inclusion of the word 'reasonable' is unfortunately necessary. For every bandit instance v there is a policy that just chooses the optimal action in v. Such policies are not reasonable because they have linear regret for bandits with a different optimal arm. There are a number of ways to define 'reasonable' in a way that is simultaneously rigorous and, well, reasonable.

The contents of this part is roughly as follows. First we introduce the definition of worst-case regret and discuss the line of attack for proving lower bounds (Chapter 13). The next chapter takes us on a brief excursion into information theory, where we explain the necessary mathematical tools (Chapter 14). Readers familiar with information theory could skim this chapter. The final three chapters are devoted to applying information theory to prove lower bounds on the regret for both stochastic and adversarial bandits.

13 Lower Bounds: Basic Ideas

The **worst-case regret** of a policy π on a set of stochastic bandit environments $\mathcal{E}$ is

$$R_n(\pi, \mathcal{E}) = \sup_{v \in \mathcal{E}} R_n(\pi, v).$$

Let Π be the set of all policies. The **minimax regret** is

$$R_n^*(\mathcal{E}) = \inf_{\pi \in \Pi} R_n(\pi, \mathcal{E}) = \inf_{\pi \in \Pi} \sup_{v \in \mathcal{E}} R_n(\pi, v).$$

A policy is called **minimax optimal** for $\mathcal{E}$ if $R_n(\pi, \mathcal{E}) = R_n^*(\mathcal{E})$. The value $R_n^*(\mathcal{E})$ is of interest by itself. A small value of $R_n^*(\mathcal{E})$ indicates that the underlying bandit problem is less challenging in the worst-case sense. A core activity in bandit theory is to understand what makes $R_n^*(\mathcal{E})$ large or small, often focusing on its behaviour as a function of the number of rounds n.

> Minimax optimality is not a property of a policy alone. It is a property of a policy together with a set of environments and a horizon.

Finding a minimax policy is generally too computationally expensive to be practical. For this reason, we almost always settle for a policy that is nearly minimax optimal.

One of the main results of this part is a proof of the following theorem, which together with Theorem 9.1 shows that Algorithm 7 from Chapter 9 is minimax optimal up to constant factors for 1-subgaussian bandits with suboptimality gaps in $[0, 1]$.

THEOREM 13.1. *Let $\mathcal{E}^k$ be the set of k-armed Gaussian bandits with unit variance and means $\mu \in [0, 1]^k$. Then there exists a universal constant $c > 0$ such that for all $k > 1$ and $n \geq k$, it holds that $R_n^*(\mathcal{E}^k) \geq c\sqrt{kn}$.*

We will prove this theorem in Chapter 15, but first we give an informal justification.

13.1 Main Ideas Underlying Minimax Lower Bounds

Let $X_1, \ldots, X_n$ be a sequence of independent Gaussian random variables with unknown mean μ and known variance 1. Assume you are told that μ takes on one of two values: $\mu = 0$ or $\mu = \Delta$ for some known $\Delta > 0$. Your task is to guess the value of μ based on your observation of $X_1, \ldots, X_n$. Let $\hat{\mu} = \frac{1}{n} \sum_{i=1}^n X_i$ be the sample mean, which is Gaussian with mean μ and variance $1/n$. While it is not immediately obvious how easy this task is, intuitively we expect the optimal decision is to predict that $\mu = 0$ if $\hat\mu$ is closer to 0 than to Δ, and otherwise to predict $\mu = \Delta$. For large n we expect our prediction will probably be correct. Supposing that $\mu = 0$ (the other case is symmetric), then the prediction will be wrong only if $\hat\mu \geq \Delta/2$. Using the fact that $\hat\mu$ is Gaussian with mean $\mu = 0$ and variance $1/n$, combined with known bounds on the Gaussian tail probabilities (see Eq. (13.4)), leads to

$$\frac{1}{\sqrt{n\Delta^2} + \sqrt{n\Delta^2 + 16}} \sqrt{\frac{8}{\pi}} \exp\left(-\frac{n\Delta^2}{8}\right) \leq \mathbb{P}\left(\hat\mu \geq \frac{\Delta}{2}\right)$$

$$\leq \frac{1}{\sqrt{n\Delta^2} + \sqrt{n\Delta^2 + 32/\pi}} \sqrt{\frac{8}{\pi}} \exp\left(-\frac{n\Delta^2}{8}\right). \quad (13.1)$$

The upper and lower bounds only differ in the constant in the square root of the denominator. One might believe that the decision procedure could be improved, but the symmetry of the problem makes this seem improbable. The formula exhibits the expected behaviour, which is that once n is large relative to $8/\Delta^2$, then the probability that this procedure fails drops exponentially with further increases in n. But the lower bound also shows that if n is small relative to $8/\Delta^2$, then the procedure fails with constant probability.

The problem described is called hypothesis testing, and the ideas underlying the argument above are core to many impossibility results in statistics. The next task is to reduce our bandit problem to hypothesis testing. The high-level idea is to select two bandit problem instances in such a way that the following two conditions hold simultaenously:

1 *Competition*: An action, or, more generally, a sequence of actions that is good for one bandit is not good for the other.
2 *Similarity*: The instances are 'close' enough that the policy interacting with either of the two instances cannot statistically identify the true bandit with reasonable statistical accuracy.

The two requirements are clearly conflicting. The first makes us want to choose instances with means $\mu, \mu' \in [0, 1]^k$ that are far from each other, while the second requirement makes us want to choose them to be close to each other. The lower bound will follow by optimising this trade-off.

Let us start to make things concrete by choosing bandits $v = (P_i)_{i=1}^k$ and $v' = (P_i')_{i=1}^k$, where $P_i = \mathcal{N}(\mu_i, 1)$ and $P_i' = \mathcal{N}(\mu_i', 1)$ are Gaussian and $\mu, \mu' \in [0, 1]^k$. We will also assume that n is larger than k by some suitably large constant factor. In order to prove a lower bound, it suffices to show that for every strategy π, there exists a choice of μ and μ' such that

$$\max\{R_n(\pi, v), R_n(\pi, v')\} \geq c\sqrt{kn},$$

where $c > 0$ is a universal constant. Let $\Delta \in (0, 1/2]$ be a constant to be tuned subsequently and choose $\mu = (\Delta, 0, 0, \ldots, 0)$, which means that the first arm is optimal in instance v and

$$R_n(\pi, v) = (n - \mathbb{E}[T_1(n)])\Delta, \quad (13.2)$$

where the expectation is taken with respect to the induced measure on the sequence of outcomes when π interacts with v. Now we need to choose μ' to satisfy the two requirements above. Since we want v and v' to be hard to distinguish and yet have different optimal actions, we should make μ' as close to μ except in a coordinate where π expects to explore the least. To this end, let

$$i = \operatorname{argmin}_{j>1} \mathbb{E}[T_j(n)]$$

be the suboptimal arm in v that π expects to play least often. From $n = \mathbb{E}[T_1(n)] + \sum_{j>1} \mathbb{E}[T_j(n)] \geq (k-1)\mathbb{E}[T_i(n)]$ we see that

$$\mathbb{E}[T_i(n)] \leq \frac{n}{k-1}$$

must hold. Then, define $\mu' \in \mathbb{R}^k$ by

$$\mu'_j = \begin{cases} \mu_j, & \text{if } j \neq i; \\ 2\Delta, & \text{otherwise.} \end{cases}$$

The regret in this bandit is

$$R_n(\pi, v') = \Delta\mathbb{E}'[T_1(n)] + \sum_{j \notin 1, i} 2\Delta\mathbb{E}'[T_j(n)] \geq \Delta\mathbb{E}'[T_1(n)], \qquad (13.3)$$

where $\mathbb{E}'[\cdot]$ is the expectation operator on the sequence of outcomes when π interacts with v'. So now we have the following situation: the strategy π interacts with either v or v', and when interacting with v, it expects to play arm i at most $n/(k-1)$ times. But the two instances only differ when playing arm i. The time has come to tune Δ. Because the strategy expects to play arm i only about $n/(k-1)$ times, taking inspiration from the previous discussion on distinguishing samples from Gaussian distributions with different means, we will choose

$$\Delta = \sqrt{\frac{1}{\mathbb{E}[T_i(n)]}} \geq \sqrt{\frac{k-1}{n}}.$$

If we are prepared to ignore the fact that $T_i(n)$ is a random variable and take for granted the claims in the first part of the chapter, then with this choice of Δ, the strategy cannot distinguish between instances v and v', and in particular we expect that $\mathbb{E}[T_1(n)] \approx \mathbb{E}'[T_1(n)]$. If $\mathbb{E}[T_1(n)] < n/2$, then by Eq. (13.2) we have

$$R_n(\pi, v) \geq \frac{n}{2}\sqrt{\frac{k-1}{n}} = \frac{1}{2}\sqrt{n(k-1)}.$$

On the other hand, if $\mathbb{E}[T_1(n)] \geq n/2$, then

$$R_n(\pi, v') \geq \Delta\mathbb{E}'[T_1(n)] \approx \Delta\mathbb{E}[T_i(n)] \geq \frac{1}{2}\sqrt{n(k-1)},$$

which completes our heuristic argument that there exists a universal constant $c > 0$ such that

$$R_n^*(\mathcal{E}^k) \geq c\sqrt{nk}.$$

We have been sloppy in many places. The claims in the first part of the chapter have not been proven yet, and $T_i(n)$ is a random variable. Before we can present the rigourous argument, we need a chapter to introduce some ideas from information theory. Readers already familiar with these concepts can skip to Chapter 15 for the proof of Theorem 13.1.

13.2   Notes

1 The worst-case regret has a game-theoretic interpretation. Imagine a game between a protagonist and an antagonist that works as follows: for $k > 1$ and $n \geq k$ the protagonist proposes a bandit policy π. The antagonist looks at the policy and chooses a bandit v from the class of environments considered. The utility for the antagonist is the expected regret, and for the protagonist it is the negation of the expected regret, which makes this a zero-sum game. Both players aim to maximise their pay-offs. The game is completely described by n and $\mathcal{E}$. One characteristic value in a game is its minimax value. As described above, this is a sequential game (the protagonist moves first, then the antagonist). The minimax value of this game from the perspective of the antagonist is exactly $R_n^*(\mathcal{E})$, while for the protagonist, it is $\sup_\pi \inf_v(-R_n(\pi, v)) = -R_n^*(\mathcal{E})$.

2 We mentioned that finding the minimax optimal policy is usually computationally infeasible. In fact it is not clear we should even try. In classical statistics, it often turns out that minimising the worst case leads to a flat risk profile. In the language of bandits, this would mean that the regret is the same for every bandit (where possible). What we usually want in practice is to have low regret against 'easy' bandits and larger regret against 'hard' bandits. The analysis in Part II suggests that easy bandits are those where the suboptimality gaps are large or very small. There is evidence to suggest that the exact minimax optimal strategy may not exploit these easy instances, so in practice one might prefer to find a policy that is nearly minimax optimal and has much smaller regret on easy bandits. We will tackle questions of this nature in Chapter 16.

3 The regret on a class of bandits $\mathcal{E}$ is a multi-objective criterion. Some policies will be good for some instances and bad on others, and there are clear trade-offs. One way to analyse the performance in a multi-objective setting is called **Pareto optimality**. A policy is Pareto optimal if there does not exist another policy that is a strict improvement – more precisely, if there does not exist a π' such that $R_n(\pi', v) \leq R_n(\pi, v)$ for all $v \in \mathcal{E}$ and $R_n(\pi', v) < R_n(\pi, v)$ for at least one instance $v \in \mathcal{E}$.

4 When we say a policy is minimax optimal up to constant factors for finite-armed 1-subgaussian bandits with suboptimality gaps in $[0, 1]$, we mean there exists a $C > 0$ such that

$$\frac{R_n(\pi, \mathcal{E}^k)}{R_n^*(\mathcal{E}^k)} \leq C \text{ for all } k \text{ and } n,$$

where $\mathcal{E}^k$ is the set of k-armed 1-subgaussian bandits with suboptimality gaps in $[0, 1]$. We often say a policy is minimax optimal up to logarithmic factors, by which we mean that

$$\frac{R_n(\pi, \mathcal{E}^k)}{R_n^*(\mathcal{E}^k)} \leq C(n, k) \text{ for all } k \text{ and } n,$$

where $C(n, k)$ is logarithmic in n and k. We hope the reader will forgive us for not always specifying in the text exactly what is meant and promise that statements of theorems will always be precise.

13.3   Bibliographic Remarks

The bound on Gaussian tails used in Eq. (13.1) is derived from §7.1.13 of the reference book by Abramowitz and Stegun [1964], which bounds

$$\frac{\exp(-x^2)}{x + \sqrt{x^2 + 2}} \leq \int_x^\infty \exp(-t^2)dt \leq \frac{\exp(-x^2)}{x + \sqrt{x^2 + 4/\pi}} \qquad \text{for all } x \geq 0. \qquad (13.4)$$

13.4   Exercises

13.1 (MINIMAX RISK FOR HYPOTHESIS TESTING) Let $\mathbb{P}_\mu = \mathcal{N}(\mu, 1)$ be the Gaussian measure on $(\mathbb{R}, \mathfrak{B}(\mathbb{R}))$ with mean $\mu \in \{0, \Delta\}$ and unit variance. Let $X : \mathbb{R} \to \mathbb{R}$ be the identity random variable $(X(\omega) = \omega)$. For decision rule $d : \mathbb{R} \to \{0, \Delta\}$, define the risk

$$R(d) = \max_{\mu \in \{0, \Delta\}} \mathbb{P}_\mu(d(X) \neq \mu),$$

Prove that $R(d)$ is minimised by $d(x) = \operatorname{argmin}_{\tilde{\mu} \in \{0, \mu\}} |X - \tilde{\mu}|$.

13.2 (PARETO OPTIMAL POLICIES) Let $k > 1$ and $\mathcal{E} = \mathcal{E}_\mathcal{N}^k(1)$ be the set of Gaussian bandits with unit variance. Find a Pareto optimal policy for this class.

HINT   Think about simple policies (not necessarily good ones) and use the definition.

14 Foundations of Information Theory (🦘)

To make the arguments in the previous chapter rigourous and generalisable to other settings, we need some tools from information theory and statistics. The most important of these is the **relative entropy**, also known as the **Kullback–Leibler divergence** named for Solomon Kullback and Richard Leibler (KL divergence, for short).

14.1 Entropy and Optimal Coding

Alice wants to communicate with Bob. She wants to tell Bob the outcome of a sequence n of independent random variables sampled from known distribution Q. Alice and Bob agree to communicate using a binary code that is fixed in advance in such a way that the expected message length is minimised. The **entropy** of Q is the expected number of bits necessary per random variable using the optimal code as n tends to infinity. The relative entropy between distributions P and Q is the price in terms of expected message length that Alice and Bob have to pay if they believe the random variables are sampled from Q when in fact they are sampled from P.

Let P be a measure on $[N]$ with σ-algebra $2^{[N]}$ and $X : [N] \to [N]$ be the identity random variable, $X(\omega) = \omega$. Alice observes a realisation of X and wants to communicate the result to Bob using a **binary code** that they agree upon in advance. For example, when $N = 4$, they might agree on the following code: $1 \to 00, 2 \to 01, 3 \to 10, 4 \to 11$. Then if Alice observes a 3, she sends Bob a message containing 10. For our purposes, a code is a function $c : [N] \to \{0,1\}^*$, where $\{0,1\}^*$ is the set of finite sequences of zeros and ones.

Of course c must be injective so that no two numbers (or **symbols**) have the same code. We also require that c be **prefix free**, which means that no code is a prefix of any other. This is justified by supposing that Alice would like to tell Bob about multiple samples. Then Bob needs to know where the message for one symbol starts and ends.

Using a prefix code is not the only way to enforce unique decodability, but all uniquely decodable codes have equivalent prefix codes (see Note 1).

The easiest choice is to use $\lceil \log_2(N) \rceil$ bits no matter the value of X. This simple code is sometimes effective, but is not entirely satisfactory if X is far from uniform. To understand why, suppose that N is extremely large and $P(X = 1) = 0.99$, and the remaining probability mass is uniform over $[N] \setminus \{1\}$. Then it seems preferable to have a short code for one and slightly longer codes for the alternatives. With this in mind, a natural objective is to find a code that minimises the expected code length. That is,

␣	111	L	10101	B	011000
E	010	D	01101	V	1100000
T	1101	C	00001	K	11000011
A	1011	U	00000	X	110000100
O	1001	F	110011	J	1100001011
I	1000	M	110010	Q	11000010101
N	0111	W	110001	Z	11000010100
S	0011	Y	101001		
H	0010	P	101000		
R	0001	G	011001		

$$c^* = \operatorname{argmin}_c \sum_{i=1}^{N} p_i \ell(c(i)), \qquad (14.1)$$

Figure 14.1   A Huffman code for the English alphabet, including space.

where the argmin is taken over valid codes and $\ell(\cdot)$ is a function that returns the length of a code. The optimisation problem in (14.1) can be solved using **Huffman coding**, and the optimal value satisfies

$$H_2(P) \le \sum_{i=1}^{N} p_i \ell(c^*(i)) \le H_2(P) + 1, \qquad (14.2)$$

where $H_2(P)$ is the **entropy** of P,

$$H_2(P) = \sum_{i \in [N]: p_i > 0} p_i \log_2 \left(\frac{1}{p_i} \right).$$

When $p_i = 1/N$ is uniform, the naive idea of using a code of uniform length is recovered, but for non-uniform distributions, the code adapts to assign shorter codes to symbols with larger probability. It is worth pointing out that the sum is only over outcomes that occur with non-zero probability, which is motivated by observing that $\lim_{x \to 0+} x \log(1/x) = 0$ or by thinking of the entropy as an expectation of the log probability with respect to P, and expectations should not change when the value of the random variable is perturbed on a measure zero set.

It turns out that $H_2(P)$ is not just an approximation on the expected length of the Huffman code, but is itself a fundamental quantity. Imagine that Alice wants to transmit a long string of symbols sampled from P. She could use a Huffman code to send Bob each symbol one at a time, but this introduces rounding errors that accumulate as the message length grows. There is another scheme called **arithmetic coding** for which the average number of bits per symbol approaches $H_2(P)$ and the **source coding theorem** says that this is unimprovable.

The definition of entropy using base 2 makes sense from the perspective of sending binary message. Mathematically, however, it is more convenient to define the entropy using the natural logarithm:

$$H(P) = \sum_{i \in [N]: p_i > 0} p_i \log \left(\frac{1}{p_i} \right). \qquad (14.3)$$

This is nothing more than a scaling of the H_2. Measuring information using base 2 logarithms has a unit of **bits**, and for the natural logarithm the unit is **nats**. By slightly abusing terminology, we will also call $H(P)$ the entropy of P.

14.2 Relative Entropy

Suppose that Alice and Bob agree to use a code that is optimal when X is sampled from distribution Q. Unbeknownst to them, however, X is actually sampled from distribution P. The relative entropy between P and Q measures how much longer the messages are expected to be using the optimal code for Q than what would be obtained using the optimal code for P. Letting $p_i = P(X = i)$ and $q_i = Q(X = i)$, assuming Shannon coding, working out the math while dropping $\lceil \cdot \rceil$ leads to the definition of **relative entropy** as

$$
D(P,Q) = \sum_{i \in [N]: p_i > 0} p_i \log\left(\frac{1}{q_i}\right) - \sum_{i \in [N]: p_i > 0} p_i \log\left(\frac{1}{p_i}\right) = \sum_{i \in [N]: p_i > 0} p_i \log\left(\frac{p_i}{q_i}\right)
$$

$$
(14.4)
$$

From the coding interpretation, one conjectures that $D(P,Q) \geq 0$. Indeed, this is easy to verify using Jensen's inequality. Still poking around the definition, what happens when $q_i = 0$ and $p_i = 0$? This means that symbol i is superfluous and the value of $D(P,Q)$ should not be impacted by introducing superfluous symbols. And again, it is not by the definition of the expectations. We also see that the sufficient and necessary condition for $D(P,Q) < \infty$ is that for each i with $q_i = 0$, we also have $p_i = 0$. The condition we discovered is equivalent to saying that P is absolutely continuous with respect to Q. Note that absolute continuity only implies a finite relative entropy when X takes on finitely many values (Exercise 14.2).

This brings us back to defining relative entropy between probability measures P and Q on arbitrary measurable spaces $(\Omega, \mathcal{F})$. When the support of P is uncountable, defining the entropy via communication is hard because infinitely many symbols are needed to describe some outcomes. This seems to be a fundamental difficulty. Luckily, the impasse gets resolved automatically if we only consider relative entropy. While we cannot communicate the outcome, for any finite discretisation of the possible outcomes, the discretised values can be communicated finitely, and all our definitions will work. Formally, a discretisation to $[N]$ is specified by a $\mathcal{F}/2^{[N]}$-measurable map $X : \Omega \to [N]$. Then the entropy of P relative Q can be defined as

$$
D(P,Q) = \sup_{N \in \mathbb{N}^+} \sup_X D(P_X, Q_X),
\tag{14.5}
$$

where P_X is the push-forward of P on $[N]$ defined by $P_X(A) = P(X \in A)$. The inner supremum is over all $\mathcal{F}/2^N$-measurable maps. Informally we take all possible discretisations X (with no limit on the 'fineness' of the discretisation) and define $D(P,Q)$ as the excess information when expecting to see X with $X \sim Q_X$, while in reality $X \sim P_X$. As we shall see soon, this is indeed a reasonable definition.

THEOREM 14.1. *Let $(\Omega, \mathcal{F})$ be a measurable space, and let P and Q be measures on this space. Then,*

$$D(P,Q) = \begin{cases} \int \log\left(\frac{dP}{dQ}(\omega)\right) dP(\omega), & \text{if } P \ll Q; \\ \infty, & \text{otherwise.} \end{cases}$$

Note that the relative entropy between P and Q can still be infinite even when $P \ll Q$. Note also that in the case of discrete measures, the above expression reduces to (14.4). For calculating relative entropies densities one often uses densities: If λ is a common dominating σ-finite measure for P and Q (that is, $P \ll \lambda$ and $Q \ll \lambda$ both hold), then letting $p = \frac{dP}{d\lambda}$ and $q = \frac{dQ}{d\lambda}$, if also $P \ll Q$, the chain rule gives $\frac{dP}{dQ}\frac{dQ}{d\lambda} = \frac{dP}{d\lambda}$, which lets us write

$$D(P,Q) = \int p \log\left(\frac{p}{q}\right) d\lambda. \tag{14.6}$$

This is probably the best-known expression for relative entropy and is often used as a definition. Note that for probability measures, a common dominating σ-finite measure can always be bound. For example, $\lambda = P + Q$ always dominates both P and Q.

Relative entropy is a kind of 'distance' measure between distributions P and Q. In particular, $D(P,Q) = 0$ whenever $P = Q$, and otherwise $D(P,Q) > 0$. However, strictly speaking, the relative entropy is not a distance because it satisfies neither the triangle inequality nor is it symmetric. Nevertheless, it serves the same purpose.

The relative entropy between many standard distributions is often quite easy to compute. For example, the relative entropy between two Gaussians with means $\mu_1, \mu_2 \in \mathbb{R}$ and common variance σ^2 is

$$D(\mathcal{N}(\mu_1, \sigma^2), \mathcal{N}(\mu_2, \sigma^2)) = \frac{(\mu_1 - \mu_2)^2}{2\sigma^2}.$$

The dependence on the difference in means and the variance is consistent with our intuition. If μ_1 is close to μ_2, then the 'difference' between the distributions should be small, but if the variance is very small, then there is little overlap, and the difference is large. The relative entropy between two Bernoulli distributions with means $p, q \in [0, 1]$ is

$$D(\mathcal{B}(p), \mathcal{B}(q)) = p \log\left(\frac{p}{q}\right) + (1-p) \log\left(\frac{1-p}{1-q}\right),$$

where $0 \log(\cdot) = 0$. Due to its frequent appearance at various places, $D(\mathcal{B}(p), \mathcal{B}(q))$ gets the honour of being abbreviated to $d(p, q)$, which we have met before in Definition 10.1.

We are nearing the end of our whirlwind tour of relative entropy. It remains to state the key lemma that connects the relative entropy to the hardness of hypothesis testing.

THEOREM 14.2 (Bretagnolle–Huber inequality). *Let P and Q be probability measures on the same measurable space $(\Omega, \mathcal{F})$, and let $A \in \mathcal{F}$ be an arbitrary event. Then,*

$$P(A) + Q(A^c) \geq \frac{1}{2} \exp\left(-D(P,Q)\right), \tag{14.7}$$

where $A^c = \Omega \setminus A$ is the complement of A.

The proof may be found at the end of the chapter, but first some interpretation and a simple application. Suppose that $D(P, Q)$ is small; then P is close to Q in some sense. Since P is a probability measure, we have $P(A) + P(A^c) = 1$. If Q is close to P, then we might expect that $P(A) + Q(A^c)$ should be large. The purpose of the theorem is to quantify just how large. Note that if P is not absolutely continuous with respect to Q, then $D(P, Q) = \infty$, and the result is vacuous. Also note that the result is symmetric. We could replace $D(P, Q)$ with $D(Q, P)$, which sometimes leads to a stronger result because the relative entropy is not symmetric.

Returning to the hypothesis-testing problem described in the previous chapter, let X be normally distributed with unknown mean $\mu \in \{0, \Delta\}$ and variance $\sigma^2 > 0$. We want to bound the quality of a rule for deciding what is the real mean from a single observation. The decision rule is characterised by a measurable set $A \subseteq \mathbb{R}$ on which the predictor guesses $\mu = \Delta$ (it predicts $\mu = 0$ on the complement of A). Let $P = \mathcal{N}(0, \sigma^2)$ and $Q = \mathcal{N}(\Delta, \sigma^2)$. Then the probability of an error under P is $P(A)$, and the probability of error under Q is $Q(A^c)$. The reader surely knows what to do next. By Theorem 14.2, we have

$$P(A) + Q(A^c) \geq \frac{1}{2} \exp\left(-D(P, Q)\right) = \frac{1}{2} \exp\left(-\frac{\Delta^2}{2\sigma^2}\right).$$

If we assume that the signal-to-noise ratio is small, $\Delta^2/\sigma^2 \leq 1$, then

$$P(A) + Q(A^c) \geq \frac{1}{2} \exp\left(-\frac{1}{2}\right) \geq \frac{3}{10},$$

which implies $\max\{P(A), Q(A^c)\} \geq 3/20$. This means that no matter how we chose our decision rule, we simply do not have enough data to make a decision for which the probability of error on either P or Q is smaller than $3/20$.

Proof of Theorem 14.2   For reals a, b, we abbreviate $\max\{a, b\} = a \vee b$ and $\min\{a, b\} = a \wedge b$. The result is trivial if $D(P, Q) = \infty$. On the other hand, by Theorem 14.1, $D(P, Q) < \infty$ implies that $P \ll Q$. Let $\nu = P + Q$. Then $P, Q \ll \nu$, which by Theorem 2.13 ensures the existence of the Radon–Nikodym derivatives $p = \frac{dP}{d\nu}$ and $q = \frac{dQ}{d\nu}$. By Eq. (14.6), $D(P, Q) = \int p \log\left(\frac{p}{q}\right) d\nu$. For brevity, when writing integrals with respect to ν, in this proof, we will drop $d\nu$. Thus, we will write, for example, $\int p \log(p/q)$ for the above integral. Instead of (14.7), we prove the stronger result that

$$\int p \wedge q \geq \frac{1}{2} \exp(-D(P, Q)). \tag{14.8}$$

This indeed is sufficient since $\int p \wedge q = \int_A p \wedge q + \int_{A^c} p \wedge q \leq \int_A p + \int_{A^c} q = P(A) + Q(A^c)$. We start with an inequality attributed to French mathematician Lucien Le Cam, which lower-bounds the left-hand side of Eq. (14.8). The inequality states that

$$\int p \wedge q \geq \frac{1}{2} \left(\int \sqrt{pq}\right)^2. \tag{14.9}$$

Starting from the right-hand side above, using $pq = (p \wedge q)(p \vee q)$ and Cauchy–Schwarz we get

$$\left(\int \sqrt{pq} \right)^2 = \left(\int \sqrt{(p \wedge q)(p \vee q)} \right)^2 \leq \left(\int p \wedge q \right) \left(\int p \vee q \right).$$

Now, using $p \wedge q + p \vee q = p + q$, the proof is finished by substituting $\int p \vee q = 2 - \int p \wedge q \leq 2$ and dividing both sides by two. It remains to lower-bound the right-hand side of (14.9). For this, we use Jensen's inequality. First, we write $(\cdot)^2$ as $\exp(2 \log(\cdot))$ and then move the log inside the integral:

$$\left(\int \sqrt{pq} \right)^2 = \exp \left(2 \log \int \sqrt{pq} \right) = \exp \left(2 \log \int_{p>0} p \sqrt{\frac{q}{p}} \right)$$

$$\geq \exp \left(2 \int_{p>0} p \frac{1}{2} \log \left(\frac{q}{p} \right) \right) = \exp \left(- \int_{pq>0} p \log \left(\frac{p}{q} \right) \right)$$

$$= \exp \left(- \int p \log \left(\frac{p}{q} \right) \right) = \exp \left(- D(P, Q) \right).$$

In the fourth and the last step, we used that since $P \ll Q$, $q = 0$ implies $p = 0$, and so $p > 0$ implies $q > 0$, and eventually $pq > 0$. The result is completed by chaining the inequalities. $\square$

14.3 Notes

1 A code $c : \mathbb{N}^+ \to \{0, 1\}^*$ is uniquely decodable if $i_1, \ldots, i_n \mapsto c(i_1) \cdots c(i_n)$ is injective, where on the right-hand side the codes are simply concatenated. **Kraft's inequality** states that for any uniquely decodable code c,

$$\sum_{i=1}^{\infty} 2^{-\ell(c(i))} \leq 1. \tag{14.10}$$

Furthermore, for any $(\ell_n)_{n=1}^{\infty}$ satisfying $\sum_{i=1}^{\infty} 2^{-\ell} \leq 1$, there exists a prefix code $c : \mathbb{N}^+ \to \{0, 1\}^*$ such that $\ell(c(i)) = \ell_i$. The second part justifies our restriction to prefix codes rather than uniquely decodable codes in the definition of the entropy.

2 The supremum in the definition given in Eq. (14.5) may often be taken over a smaller set. Precisely, let $(\mathcal{X}, \mathcal{G})$ be a measurable space and suppose that $\mathcal{G} = \sigma(\mathcal{F})$ where $\mathcal{F}$ is a field. Note that a field is defined by the same axioms as a σ-algebra except that being closed under countable unions is replaced by the condition that it be closed under finite unions. Then, for measures P and Q on $(\mathcal{X}, \mathcal{G})$, it holds that

$$D(P, Q) = \sup_f D(P_f, Q_f),$$

where the supremum is over $\mathcal{F}/2^{[n]}$-measurable functions. This result is known as **Dobrushin's theorem**.

3 How tight is Theorem 14.2? We remarked already that $D(P, Q) = 0$ if and only if $P = Q$. But in this case, Theorem 14.2 only gives

$$1 = P(A) + Q(A^c) \geq \frac{1}{2} \exp \left(- D(P, Q) \right) = \frac{1}{2},$$

which does not seem so strong. From where does the weakness arise? The answer is in Eq. (14.9), which can be refined by

$$\left(\int \sqrt{pq}\right)^2 \leq \left(\int p \wedge q\right)\left(\int p \vee q\right) = \left(\int p \wedge q\right)\left(2 - \int p \wedge q\right).$$

By solving the quadratic inequality, we have

$$P(A) + Q(A^c) \geq \int p \wedge q \geq 1 - \sqrt{1 - \left(\int \sqrt{pq}\right)^2}$$

$$\geq 1 - \sqrt{1 - \exp\left(-D(P, Q)\right)}, \tag{14.11}$$

which gives a modest improvement on Theorem 14.2 that becomes more pronounced when $D(P, Q)$ is close to zero, as demonstrated by Fig. 14.2. This stronger bound might be useful for fractionally improving constant factors in lower bounds, but we do not know of any application for which it is really crucial, and the more complicated form makes it cumbersome to use. Part of the reason for this is that the situation where $D(P, Q)$ is small is better dealt with using a different inequality, as explained in the next note.

4 Another inequality from information theory is **Pinsker's inequality,** which states for measures P and Q on the same probability space $(\Omega, \mathcal{F})$ that

$$\delta(P, Q) = \sup_{A \in \mathcal{F}} P(A) - Q(A) \leq \sqrt{\frac{1}{2} D(P, Q)}. \tag{14.12}$$

The quantity on the left-hand side is called the **total variation distance** between P and Q, which is a distance on the space of probability measures on a probability space. From this we can derive for any measurable $A \in \mathcal{F}$ that

$$P(A) + Q(A^c) \geq 1 - \sqrt{\frac{1}{2} D(P, Q)} = 1 - \sqrt{\frac{1}{2} \log\left(\frac{1}{\exp(-D(P, Q))}\right)}. \tag{14.13}$$

Examining Fig. 14.2 shows that this is an improvement on Eq. (14.11) when $D(P, Q)$ is small. However, we also see that in the opposite case, when $D(P, Q)$ is large, Eq. (14.13) is worse than Eq. (14.11), or the inequality in Theorem 14.2.

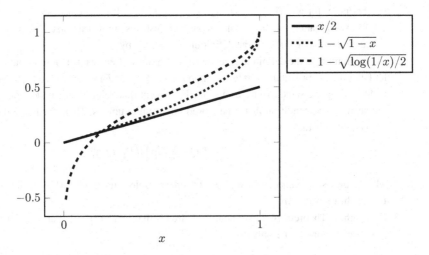

Figure 14.2 Tightening the inequality of Le Cam

5 We saw the total variation distance in Eq. (14.12). There are two other 'distances' that are occasionally useful. These are the **Hellinger distance** and the χ-**squared distance**, which, using the notation in the proof of Theorem 14.2, are defined by

$$h(P,Q) = \sqrt{\int \left(\sqrt{p} - \sqrt{q}\right)^2} = \sqrt{2\left(1 - \int \sqrt{pq}\right)} \tag{14.14}$$

$$\chi^2(P,Q) = \int \frac{(p-q)^2}{q} = \int \frac{p^2}{q} - 1. \tag{14.15}$$

The Hellinger distance is bounded and exists for all probability measures P and Q. A necessary condition for the χ^2-distance to exist is that $P \ll Q$. Like the total variation distance, the Hellinger distance is actually a distance (it is symmetric and satisfies triangle inequality), but the χ^2-'distance' is not. It is possible to show (Tsybakov [2008], chapter 2) that

$$\delta(P,Q)^2 \le h(P,Q)^2 \le D(P,Q) \le \chi^2(P,Q). \tag{14.16}$$

All the inequalities are tight for some choices of P and Q, but the examples do not chain together, as evidenced by Pinsker's inequality, which shows that $\delta(P,Q)^2 \le D(P,Q)/2$ (which is also tight for some P and Q).

6 The entropy for distribution P was defined as $H(P)$ in Eq. (14.3). If X is a random variable, then $H(X)$ is defined to be the entropy of the law of X. This is a convenient notation because it allows one to write $H(f(X))$ and $H(XY)$ and similar expressions.

14.4 Bibliographic Remarks

There are many references for information theory. Most well known (and comprehensive) is the book by Cover and Thomas [2012]. Another famous book is the elementary and enjoyable introduction by MacKay [2003]. The approach we have taken for defining and understanding the relative entropy is inspired by an excellent shorter book by Gray [2011]. Theorem 14.1 connects our definition of relative entropies to densities (the 'classic definition'). It can be found in §5.2 of the aforementioned book. Dobrushin's theorem is due to him [Dobrushin, 1959]. An alternative source is lemma 5.2.2 in the book of Gray [2011]. Theorem 14.2 is due to Bretagnolle and Huber [1979]. We also recommend the book by Tsybakov [2008] as a good source for learning about information theoretic lower bounds in statistical settings.

14.5 Exercises

14.1 Let P be a probability distribution on $\mathbb{N}^+$ and $p_i = P(\{i\})$. Show that for any prefix code $c : \mathbb{N}^+ \to \{0,1\}^*$, it holds that

$$\sum_{i=1}^{\infty} p_i \ell(c(i)) \ge H_2(P).$$

HINT   Use Kraft's inequality from Note 1.

14.2 Find probability measures P and Q on $\mathbb{N}^+$ with $P \ll Q$ and $D(P,Q) = \infty$.

14.3 Prove the inequality in Eq. (14.10) for prefix free codes c.

HINT   Consider an infinite sequence of independent Bernoulli random variables $(X_n)_{n=1}^{\infty}$ where $X_n \sim \mathcal{B}(1/2)$. Viewing X as an infinite binary string, what is the probability that X has a prefix that is a code for some symbol?

14.4 Let $(\Omega, \mathcal{F})$ be a measurable space, and let $P, Q : \mathcal{F} \to [0, 1]$ be probability measures. Let $a < b$ and $X : \Omega \to [a, b]$ be a $\mathcal{F}$-measurable random variable. Prove that

$$\left| \int_{\Omega} X(\omega) dP(\omega) - \int_{\Omega} X(\omega) dQ(\omega) \right| \le (b - a)\delta(P, Q).$$

14.5 (ENTROPY INEQUALITIES) Prove that each of the inequalities in Eq. (14.16) is tight.

14.6 (COUNTING MEASURE ABSOLUTE CONTINUITY AND DERIVATIVES) Let Ω be a countable set and $p : \Omega \to [0, 1]$ be a distribution on Ω so that $\sum_{\omega \in \Omega} p(\omega) = 1$. Let P be the measure associated with p, which means that $P(A) = \sum_{\omega \in A} p(\omega)$. Recall that the counting measure μ is the measure on $(\Omega, 2^{\Omega})$ given by $\mu(A) = |A|$ if A is finite and $\mu(A) = \infty$ otherwise.

(a) Show that P is absolutely continuous with respect to μ.
(b) Show that the Radon–Nykodim $dP/d\mu$ exists and that $dP/d\mu(\omega) = p(\omega)$.

14.7 (RELATIVE ENTROPY FOR GAUSSIAN DISTRIBUTIONS) For each $i \in \{1, 2\}$, let $\mu_i \in \mathbb{R}$, $\sigma_i^2 > 0$ and $P_i = \mathcal{N}(\mu_i, \sigma_i^2)$. Show that

$$D(P_1, P_2) = \frac{1}{2} \left(\log \left(\frac{\sigma_2^2}{\sigma_1^2} \right) + \frac{\sigma_1^2}{\sigma_2^2} - 1 \right) + \frac{(\mu_1 - \mu_2)^2}{2\sigma_2^2}.$$

14.8 Let λ be the Lebesgue measure on $(\mathbb{R}, \mathcal{B}(\mathbb{R}))$. Find

(a) a probability measure $(\mathbb{R}, \mathcal{B}(\mathbb{R}))$ that is not absolutely continuous with respect to λ; and
(b) a probability measure P on $(\mathbb{R}, \mathcal{B}(\mathbb{R}))$ that is absolutely continuous to λ with $D(P, Q) = \infty$ where $Q = \mathcal{N}(0, 1)$ is the standard Gaussian measure.

14.9 (DATA PROCESSING INEQUALITY) Let P and Q be measures on $(\Omega, \mathcal{F})$, and let $\mathcal{G}$ be a sub-σ-algebra of $\mathcal{F}$ and $P_{\mathcal{G}}$ and $Q_{\mathcal{G}}$ be the restrictions of P and Q to $(\Omega, \mathcal{G})$. Show that $D(P_{\mathcal{G}}, Q_{\mathcal{G}}) \le D(P, Q)$.

14.10 Let $(\Omega, \mathcal{F})$ be a measurable space and $P, Q : \mathcal{B}(\mathbb{R}) \times \Omega \to [0, 1]$ be a pair of probability kernels from $(\Omega, \mathcal{F})$ to $(\mathbb{R}, \mathcal{B}(\mathbb{R}))$. Prove that

$$V = \{\omega \in \Omega : D(P(\cdot \,|\, \omega), Q(\cdot \,|\, \omega)) = \infty\} \in \mathcal{F}.$$

HINT   Apply Dobrushin's theorem to the field of finite unions of rational-valued intervals in $\mathbb{R}$.

14.11 (CHAIN RULE) Let P and Q be measures on $(\mathbb{R}^n, \mathcal{B}(\mathbb{R}^n))$, and for $t \in [n]$, let $X_t(x) = x_t$ be the coordinate project from $\mathbb{R}^n \to \mathbb{R}$. Then let P_t and Q_t be regular versions of X_t given $X_1, \ldots, X_{t-1}$ under P and Q, respectively. Show that

$$D(P, Q) = \sum_{t=1}^{n} \mathbb{E}_P \left[D(P_t(\cdot \,|\, X_1, \ldots, X_{t-1}), Q_t(\cdot \,|\, X_1, \ldots, X_{t-1})) \right]. \qquad (14.17)$$

HINT   This is a rather technical exercise. You will likely need to apply a monotone class argument [Kallenberg, 2002, theorem 1.1]. For the definition of a regular version, see [Kallenberg, 2002, theorem 5.3] or Theorem 3.11. Briefly, P_t is a probability kernel from $(\mathbb{R}^{t-1}, \mathcal{B}(\mathbb{R}^{t-1}))$ to $(\mathbb{R}, \mathcal{B}(\mathbb{R}))$

such that $P_t(A \mid x_1, \ldots, x_{t-1}) = P(X_t \in A \mid X_1, \ldots, X_{t-1})$ with P-probability one for all $A \in \mathfrak{B}(\mathbb{R})$.

14.12 (CHAIN RULE (CONT.)) Let P and Q be measures on $(\mathbb{R}^n, \mathfrak{B}(\mathbb{R}^n))$, and for $t \in [n]$, let $X_t(x) = x_t$ be the coordinate project from $\mathbb{R}^n \to \mathbb{R}$. Then let P_t and Q_t be regular versions of X_t given $X_1, \ldots, X_{t-1}$ under P and Q, respectively. Let τ be a stopping time adapted to the filtration generated by $X_1, \ldots, X_n$ with $\tau \in [n]$ almost surely. Show that

$$D(P_{\mid \mathcal{F}_\tau}, Q_{\mid \mathcal{F}_\tau}) = \mathbb{E}_P \left[\sum_{t=1}^{\tau} D(P_t(\cdot \mid X_1, \ldots, X_{t-1}), Q_t(\cdot \mid X_1, \ldots, X_{t-1})) \right].$$

15 Minimax Lower Bounds

After the short excursion into information theory, let us return to the world of k-armed stochastic bandits. In what follows, we fix the horizon $n > 0$ and the number of actions $k > 1$. This chapter has two components. The first is an exact calculation of the relative entropy between measures in the canonical bandit model for a fixed policy and different bandits. In the second component, we prove a minimax lower bound that formalises the intuitive arguments given in Chapter 13.

15.1 Relative Entropy Between Bandits

The following result will be used repeatedly. Some generalisations are provided in the exercises.

LEMMA 15.1 (Divergence decomposition). *Let* $v = (P_1, \ldots, P_k)$ *be the reward distributions associated with one k-armed bandit, and let* $v' = (P'_1, \ldots, P'_k)$ *be the reward distributions associated with another k-armed bandit. Fix some policy π and let* $\mathbb{P}_v = \mathbb{P}_{v\pi}$ *and* $\mathbb{P}_{v'} = \mathbb{P}_{v'\pi}$ *be the probability measures on the canonical bandit model (Section 4.6) induced by the n-round interconnection of π and v (respectively, π and v'). Then,*

$$D(\mathbb{P}_v, \mathbb{P}_{v'}) = \sum_{i=1}^{k} \mathbb{E}_v[T_i(n)]\, D(P_i, P'_i). \tag{15.1}$$

Proof Assume that $D(P_i, P'_i) < \infty$ for all $i \in [k]$. It follows that $P_i \ll P'_i$. Define $\lambda = \sum_{i=1}^{k} P_i + P'_i$, which is the measure defined by $\lambda(A) = \sum_{i=1}^{k} (P_i(A) + P'_i(A))$ for any measurable set A. Theorem 14.1 shows that, as long as $\frac{d\mathbb{P}_v}{d\mathbb{P}_{v'}} < +\infty$,

$$D(\mathbb{P}_v, \mathbb{P}_{v'}) = \mathbb{E}_v\left[\log\left(\frac{d\mathbb{P}_v}{d\mathbb{P}_{v'}}\right)\right].$$

Recalling that ρ is the counting measure over $[k]$, we find that the Radon–Nikodym derivative of $\mathbb{P}_v$ with respect to the product measure $(\rho \times \lambda)^n$ is given in Eq. (4.7) as

$$p_{v\pi}(a_1, x_1, \ldots, a_n, x_n) = \prod_{t=1}^{n} \pi_t(a_t \mid a_1, x_1, \ldots, a_{t-1}, x_{t-1}) p_{a_t}(x_t).$$

The density of $\mathbb{P}_{v'}$ is identical except that p_{a_t} is replaced by p'_{a_t}. Then

$$\log \frac{d\mathbb{P}_v}{d\mathbb{P}_{v'}}(a_1, x_1, \ldots, a_n, x_n) = \sum_{t=1}^{n} \log \frac{p_{a_t}(x_t)}{p'_{a_t}(x_t)},$$

where we used the chain rule for Radon–Nikodym derivatives and the fact that the terms involving the policy cancel. Taking expectations of both sides,

$$\mathbb{E}_v \left[\log \frac{d\mathbb{P}_v}{d\mathbb{P}_{v'}}(A_1, X_1, \ldots, A_n, X_n) \right] = \sum_{t=1}^{n} \mathbb{E}_v \left[\log \frac{p_{A_t}(X_t)}{p'_{A_t}(X_t)} \right],$$

and

$$\mathbb{E}_v \left[\log \frac{p_{A_t}(X_t)}{p'_{A_t}(X_t)} \right] = \mathbb{E}_v \left[\mathbb{E}_v \left[\log \frac{p_{A_t}(X_t)}{p'_{A_t}(X_t)} \middle| A_t \right] \right] = \mathbb{E}_v \left[D(P_{A_t}, P'_{A_t}) \right],$$

where in the second equality we used that under $\mathbb{P}_v(\cdot|A_t)$, the distribution of X_t is $dP_{A_t} = p_{A_t} d\lambda$. Plugging back into the previous display,

$$\mathbb{E}_v \left[\log \frac{d\mathbb{P}_v}{d\mathbb{P}_{v'}}(A_1, X_1, \ldots, A_n, X_n) \right] = \sum_{t=1}^{n} \mathbb{E}_v \left[\log \frac{p_{A_t}(X_t)}{p'_{A_t}(X_t)} \right]$$

$$= \sum_{t=1}^{n} \mathbb{E}_v \left[D(P_{A_t}, P'_{A_t}) \right] = \sum_{i=1}^{k} \mathbb{E}_v \left[\sum_{t=1}^{n} \mathbb{I}\{A_t = i\} D(P_{A_t}, P'_{A_t}) \right]$$

$$= \sum_{i=1}^{k} \mathbb{E}_v \left[T_i(n) \right] D(P_i, P'_i).$$

When the right-hand side of (15.1) is infinite, by our previous calculation, it is not hard to see that the left-hand side will also be infinite. □

We note in passing that the divergence decomposition holds regardless of whether the action set is discrete or not. In its more general form, the sum over the actions must be replaced by an integral with respect to an appropriate non-negative measure, which generalises the expected number of pulls of arms. For details, see Exercise 15.8.

15.2 Minimax Lower Bounds

Recall that $\mathcal{E}_{\mathcal{N}}^k(1)$ is the class of Gaussian bandits with unit variance, which can be parameterised by their mean vector $\mu \in \mathbb{R}^k$. Given $\mu \in \mathbb{R}^k$, let v_μ be the Gaussian bandit for which the ith arm has reward distribution $\mathcal{N}(\mu_i, 1)$.

THEOREM 15.2. *Let $k > 1$ and $n \geq k - 1$. Then, for any policy π, there exists a mean vector $\mu \in [0, 1]^k$ such that*

$$R_n(\pi, v_\mu) \geq \frac{1}{27} \sqrt{(k-1)n}.$$

Since $v_\mu \in \mathcal{E}_{\mathcal{N}}^k(1)$, it follows that the minimax regret for $\mathcal{E}_{\mathcal{N}}^k(1)$ is lower-bounded by the right-hand side of the above display as soon as $n \geq k - 1$:

$$R_n^*(\mathcal{E}_{\mathcal{N}}^k(1)) \geq \frac{1}{27} \sqrt{(k-1)n}.$$

The idea of the proof is illustrated in Fig. 15.1.

Figure 15.1 The idea of the minimax lower bound. Given a policy and one environment, the evil antagonist picks another environment so that the policy will suffer a large regret in at least one environment.

Proof Fix a policy π. Let $\Delta \in [0, 1/2]$ be some constant to be chosen later. As suggested in Chapter 13, we start with a Gaussian bandit with unit variance and mean vector $\mu = (\Delta, 0, 0, \ldots, 0)$. This environment and π give rise to the distribution $\mathbb{P}_{v_\mu,\pi}$ on the canonical bandit model $(\mathcal{H}_n, \mathcal{F}_n)$. For brevity we will use $\mathbb{P}_\mu$ in place of $\mathbb{P}_{v_\mu,\pi}$, and expectations under $\mathbb{P}_\mu$ will be denoted by $\mathbb{E}_\mu$. To choose the second environment, let

$$i = \operatorname{argmin}_{j>1} \mathbb{E}_\mu[T_j(n)].$$

Since $\sum_{j=1}^k \mathbb{E}_\mu[T_j(n)] = n$, it holds that $\mathbb{E}_\mu[T_i(n)] \leq n/(k-1)$. The second bandit is also Gaussian with unit variance and means

$$\mu' = (\Delta, 0, 0, \ldots, 0, 2\Delta, 0, \ldots, 0),$$

where specifically $\mu'_i = 2\Delta$. Therefore, $\mu_j = \mu'_j$ except at index i and the optimal arm in v_μ is the first arm, while in $v_{\mu'}$ arm i is optimal. We abbreviate $\mathbb{P}_{\mu'} = \mathbb{P}_{v_{\mu'},\pi}$. Lemma 4.5 and a simple calculation lead to

$$R_n(\pi, v_\mu) \geq \mathbb{P}_\mu(T_1(n) \leq n/2)\frac{n\Delta}{2} \quad \text{and} \quad R_n(\pi, v_{\mu'}) > \mathbb{P}_{\mu'}(T_1(n) > n/2)\frac{n\Delta}{2}.$$

Then, applying the Bretagnolle–Huber inequality from the previous chapter (Theorem 14.2),

$$R_n(\pi, v_\mu) + R_n(\pi, v_{\mu'}) > \frac{n\Delta}{2}\left(\mathbb{P}_\mu(T_1(n) \leq n/2) + \mathbb{P}_{\mu'}(T_1(n) > n/2)\right)$$

$$\geq \frac{n\Delta}{4}\exp(-\operatorname{D}(\mathbb{P}_\mu, \mathbb{P}_{\mu'})). \tag{15.2}$$

It remains to upper-bound $\operatorname{D}(\mathbb{P}_\mu, \mathbb{P}_{\mu'})$. For this, we use Lemma 15.1 and the definitions of μ and μ' to get

$$\operatorname{D}(\mathbb{P}_\mu, \mathbb{P}_{\mu'}) = \mathbb{E}_\mu[T_i(n)]\operatorname{D}(\mathcal{N}(0, 1), \mathcal{N}(2\Delta, 1)) = \mathbb{E}_\mu[T_i(n)]\frac{(2\Delta)^2}{2} \leq \frac{2n\Delta^2}{k-1}.$$

Plugging this into the previous display, we find that

$$R_n(\pi, \nu_\mu) + R_n(\pi, \nu_{\mu'}) \geq \frac{n\Delta}{4} \exp\left(-\frac{2n\Delta^2}{k-1}\right).$$

The result is completed by choosing $\Delta = \sqrt{(k-1)/4n} \leq 1/2$, where the inequality follows from the assumptions in the theorem statement. The final steps are lower bounding $\exp(-1/2)$ and using $2\max(a,b) \geq a + b$. $\square$

We encourage readers to go through the alternative proof outlined in Exercise 15.2, which takes a slightly different path.

15.3 Notes

1 We used the Gaussian noise model because the KL divergences are so easily calculated in this case, but all that we actually used was that $D(P_i, P_i') = O((\mu_i - \mu_i')^2)$ when the gap between the means $\Delta = \mu_i - \mu_i'$ is small. While this is certainly not true for *all* distributions, it very often is. Why is that? Let $\{P_\mu : \mu \in \mathbb{R}\}$ be some parametric family of distributions on Ω and assume that distribution P_μ has mean μ. Assuming the densities are twice differentiable and that everything is sufficiently nice that integrals and derivatives can be exchanged (as is almost always the case), we can use a Taylor expansion about μ to show that

$$D(P_\mu, P_{\mu+\Delta}) \approx \frac{\partial}{\partial\Delta} D(P_\mu, P_{\mu+\Delta})\Big|_{\Delta=0} \Delta + \frac{1}{2}\frac{\partial^2}{\partial\Delta^2} D(P_\mu, P_{\mu+\Delta})\Big|_{\Delta=0} \Delta^2$$

$$= \frac{\partial}{\partial\Delta} \int_\Omega \log\left(\frac{dP_\mu}{dP_{\mu+\Delta}}\right) dP_\mu \Big|_{\Delta=0} \Delta + \frac{1}{2}I(\mu)\Delta^2$$

$$= -\int_\Omega \frac{\partial}{\partial\Delta} \log\left(\frac{dP_{\mu+\Delta}}{dP_\mu}\right)\Big|_{\Delta=0} dP_\mu \Delta + \frac{1}{2}I(\mu)\Delta^2$$

$$= -\int_\Omega \frac{\partial}{\partial\Delta} \frac{dP_{\mu+\Delta}}{dP_\mu}\Big|_{\Delta=0} dP_\mu \Delta + \frac{1}{2}I(\mu)\Delta^2$$

$$= -\frac{\partial}{\partial\Delta} \int_\Omega \frac{dP_{\mu+\Delta}}{dP_\mu} dP_\mu \Big|_{\Delta=0} \Delta + \frac{1}{2}I(\mu)\Delta^2$$

$$= -\frac{\partial}{\partial\Delta} \int_\Omega dP_{\mu+\Delta}\Big|_{\Delta=0} \Delta + \frac{1}{2}I(\mu)\Delta^2$$

$$= \frac{1}{2}I(\mu)\Delta^2,$$

where $I(\mu)$, introduced in the second line, is called the **Fisher information** of the family $(P_\mu)_\mu$ at μ. Note that if λ is a common dominating measure for $(P_{\mu+\Delta})$ for Δ small, $dP_{\mu+\Delta} = p_{\mu+\Delta}d\lambda$ and we can write

$$I(\mu) = -\int \frac{\partial^2}{\partial\Delta^2} \log p_{\mu+\Delta}\Big|_{\Delta=0} p_\mu d\lambda,$$

which is the form that is usually given in elementary texts. The upshot of all this is that $D(P_\mu, P_{\mu+\Delta})$ for Δ small is indeed quadratic in Δ, with the scaling provided by $I(\mu)$, and as a result the worst-case regret is always $O(\sqrt{nk})$, provided the class of distributions considered is sufficiently rich and not too bizarre.

2 We have now shown a lower bound that is $\Omega(\sqrt{nk})$, while many of the upper bounds were $O(\log(n))$. There is no contradiction because the logarithmic bounds depended on the inverse suboptimality gaps, which may be very large.

3 Our lower bound was only proven for $n \geq k - 1$. In Exercise 15.3, we ask you to show that when $n < k - 1$, there exists a bandit such that

$$R_n \geq \frac{n(2k - n - 1)}{2k} > \frac{n}{2}.$$

4 The method used to prove Theorem 15.2 can be viewed as a generalisation and strengthening of **Le Cam's method** in statistics. Recall that Eq. (15.2) establishes that for any μ and μ',

$$\inf_{\pi} \sup_{\nu} R_n(\pi, \nu) \geq \frac{n\Delta}{8} \exp(-D(\mathbb{P}_\mu, \mathbb{P}_{\mu'})).$$

To explain Le Cam's method, we need a little notation. Let $\mathcal{X}$ be an outcome space, $\mathcal{P}$ a set of measures on $\mathcal{X}$ and $\theta : \mathcal{P} \rightarrow \Theta$, where (Θ, d) is a metric space. An estimator is a function $\hat{\theta} : \mathcal{X}^n \rightarrow \Theta$. Le Cam's method is used for proving minimax lower bounds on the expected error of the estimator, which is

$$\inf_{\hat{\theta}} \sup_{P \in \mathcal{P}} \mathbb{E}_{X_1, \ldots, X_n \sim P^n} \left[d(\hat{\theta}(X_1, \ldots, X_n), \theta(P)) \right]. \tag{15.3}$$

The idea is to choose $P_0, P_1 \in \mathcal{P}$ to maximise $d(\theta(P_0), \theta(P_1)) \exp(-n D(P_0, P_1))$, on the basis that for any $P_0, P_1 \in \mathcal{P}$,

$$Eq. (15.3) \geq \frac{\Delta}{8} \exp(-n D(P_0, P_1)), \tag{15.4}$$

where $\Delta = d(\theta(P_0), \theta(P_1))$. There are two differences compared to the bandit lower bound: *(i)* we deal with the sequential setting, and *(ii)* having chosen P_0 we choose P_1 in a way that depends on the algorithm. This provides a much needed extra boost, without which the method would be unable to capture how the characteristics of $\mathcal{P}$ are reflected in the minimax risk (or regret, in our case).

15.4 Bibliographic Remarks

The first work on lower bounds that we know of was the remarkably precise minimax analysis of two-armed Bernoulli bandits by Vogel [1960]. The Bretagnolle–Huber inequality (Theorem 14.2) was first used for bandits by Bubeck et al. [2013b]. As mentioned in the notes, the use of this inequality for proving lower bounds is known as Le Cam's method in statistics [Le Cam, 1973]. The proof of Theorem 15.2 uses the same ideas as Gerchinovitz and Lattimore [2016], while the alternative proof in Exercise 15.2 is essentially due to Auer et al. [1995], who analysed the more difficult case where the rewards are Bernoulli (see Exercise 15.4). Yu [1997] describes some alternatives to Le Cam's method for the passive, statistical setting. These alternatives can be (and often are) adapted to the sequential setting.

15.5 Exercises

15.1 (LE CAM'S METHOD) Establish the claim in Eq. (15.4).

15.2 (ALTERNATIVE PROOF OF THEOREM 15.2) Here you will prove Theorem 15.2 with a different method. Let $c > 0$ and $\Delta = 2c\sqrt{k/n}$, and for each $i \in \{0, 1, \ldots, k\}$, let $\mu^{(i)} \in \mathbb{R}^k$ satisfy $\mu_j^{(i)} = \mathbb{I}\{i = j\}\Delta$. Further abbreviate the notation in the proof of Theorem 15.2 by letting $\mathbb{E}_i[\cdot] = \mathbb{E}_{\mu^{(i)}}[\cdot]$.

(a) Use Pinsker's inequality (Eq. 14.12) and Lemma 15.1 and the result of Exercise 14.4 to show

$$\mathbb{E}_i[T_i(n)] \leq \mathbb{E}_0[T_i(n)] + n\sqrt{\frac{1}{4}\Delta^2\mathbb{E}_0[T_i(n)]} = \mathbb{E}_0[T_i(n)] + c\sqrt{nk\mathbb{E}_0[T_i(n)]}.$$

(b) Using the previous part, Jensen's inequality and the identity $\sum_{i=1}^{k}\mathbb{E}_0[T_i(n)] = n$, show that

$$\sum_{i=1}^{k}\mathbb{E}_i[T_i(n)] \leq n + c\sum_{i=1}^{k}\sqrt{nk\mathbb{E}_0[T_i(n)]} \leq n + ckn.$$

(c) Let $R_i = R_n(\pi, G_{\mu^{(i)}})$. Find a choice of $c > 0$ for which

$$\sum_{i=1}^{k}R_i = \Delta\sum_{i=1}^{k}(n - \mathbb{E}_i[T_i(n)]) \geq \Delta(nk - n - ckn)$$

$$= 2c\sqrt{\frac{k}{n}}(nk - n - ckn) \geq \frac{nk}{8}\sqrt{\frac{k}{n}}$$

(d) Conclude that there exists an $i \in [k]$ such that

$$R_i \geq \frac{1}{8}\sqrt{kn}.$$

The method used in this exercise is borrowed from Auer et al. [2002b] and is closely related to the lower-bound technique known as Assouad's method in statistics [Yu, 1997].

15.3 (LOWER BOUND FOR SMALL HORIZONS) Let $k > 1$ and $n < k$. Prove that for any policy π there exists a Gaussian bandit with unit variance and means $\mu \in [0, 1]^k$ such that $R_n(\pi, \nu_\mu) \geq n(2k - n - 1)/(2k) > n/2$.

15.4 (LOWER BOUNDS FOR BERNOULLI BANDITS) Recall from Table 4.1 that $\mathcal{E}_B^k$ is the set of k-armed Bernoulli bandits. Show that there exists a universal constant $c > 0$ such that for any $2 \leq k \leq n$, it holds that:

$$R_n^*(\mathcal{E}_B^k) = \inf_{\pi}\sup_{\nu \in \mathcal{E}_B^k}R_n(\pi, \nu) \geq c\sqrt{nk}.$$

HINT   Use the fact that KL divergence is upper bounded by the χ-squared distance (Eq. (14.16)).

15.5 In Chapter 9 we proved that if π is the MOSS policy and $\nu \in \mathcal{E}_{SG}^k(1)$, then

$$R_n(\pi, \nu) \leq C\left(\sqrt{kn} + \sum_{i:\Delta_i > 0}\Delta_i\right),$$

where $C > 0$ is a universal constant. Prove that the dependence on the sum cannot be eliminated.

HINT   You will have to use that $T_i(t)$ is an integer for all t.

15.6 (LOWER BOUND FOR EXPLORE-THEN-COMMIT) Let ETC_{nm} be the explore-then-commit policy with inputs n and m respectively (Algorithm 1). Prove that for all m, there exists a $\mu \in [0, 1]^k$ such that

$$R_n(\mathrm{ETC}_{nm}, \nu_\mu) \geq c \min\left\{n, n^{2/3}k^{1/3}\right\},$$

where $c > 0$ is a universal constant.

15.7 (STOPPING-TIME VERSION OF DIVERGENCE DECOMPOSITION) Consider the setting of Lemma 15.1, and let $\mathcal{F}_t = \sigma(A_1, X_1, \ldots, A_t, X_t)$ and τ be an $(\mathcal{F}_t)$-measurable stopping time. Then, for any random element X that is $\mathcal{F}_\tau$-measurable,

$$D(\mathbb{P}_{\nu X}, \mathbb{P}_{\nu' X}) \leq \sum_{i=1}^{k} \mathbb{E}_\nu[T_i(\tau)] \, D(P_i, P_i'),$$

where $\mathbb{P}_{\nu X}$ and $\mathbb{P}_{\nu' X}$ are the laws X under ν and ν' respectively.

15.8 (DIVERGENCE DECOMPOSITION FOR MORE GENERAL ACTION SPACES) The purpose of this exercise is to show that the divergence decomposition lemma (Lemma 15.1) continues to hold for more general action spaces $(\mathcal{A}, \mathcal{G})$. Starting from the set-up of Section 4.7, let $\mathbb{P}_\nu = \mathbb{P}_{\nu\pi}$ and $\mathbb{P}_{\nu'} = \mathbb{P}_{\nu'\pi}$ be the measures on the canonical bandit model induced by the interconnection of π and ν (respectively, π and ν').

(a) Prove that

$$D(\mathbb{P}_\nu, \mathbb{P}_{\nu'}) = \int_{\mathcal{A}} D(P_a, P_a') \, dG_\nu(a), \tag{15.5}$$

where G_ν is a measure on $(\mathcal{A}, \mathcal{G})$ defined by $G_\nu(B) = \mathbb{E}_\nu[\sum_{t=1}^{n} \mathbb{I}\{A_t \in B\}]$.

(b) Prove that

$$D(\mathbb{P}_\nu, \mathbb{P}_{\nu'}) = \mathbb{E}\left[\sum_{t=1}^{n} D(P_{A_t}, P_{A_t}')\right].$$

HINT   Use an appropriately adjusted form of the chain rule for relative entropy from Exercise 14.11.

16 Instance-Dependent Lower Bounds

In the last chapter, we proved a lower bound on the minimax regret for subgaussian bandits with suboptimality gaps in $[0, 1]$. Such bounds serve as a useful measure of the robustness of a policy, but are often excessively conservative. This chapter is devoted to understanding **instance-dependent** lower bounds, which try to capture the optimal performance of a policy on a specific bandit instance.

Because the regret is a multi-objective criteria, an algorithm designer might try and design algorithms that perform well on one kind of instance or another. An extreme example is the policy that chooses $A_t = 1$ for all t, which suffers zero regret when the first arm is optimal and linear regret otherwise. This is a harsh trade-off, with the price for reducing the regret from logarithmic to zero on just a few instances being linear regret on the remainder. Surprisingly, this is the nature of the game in bandits. One can assign a measure of difficulty to each instance such that policies performing overly well relative to this measure on some instances pay a steep price on others. The situation is illustrated in Fig. 16.1.

In finite time, the situation is a little messy, but if one pushes these ideas to the limit, then for many classes of bandits one can define a precise notion of instance-dependent optimality.

16.1 Asymptotic Bounds

We need to define exactly what is meant by a reasonable policy. If one is only concerned with asymptotics, then a rather conservative definition suffices.

DEFINITION 16.1. A policy π is called **consistent** over a class of bandits $\mathcal{E}$ if for all $v \in \mathcal{E}$ and $p > 0$, it holds that

$$\lim_{n \to \infty} \frac{R_n(\pi, v)}{n^p} = 0. \tag{16.1}$$

The class of consistent policies over $\mathcal{E}$ is denoted by $\Pi_{\text{cons}}(\mathcal{E})$.

Theorem 7.1 shows that UCB is consistent over $\mathcal{E}_{\text{SG}}^k(1)$. The strategy that always chooses the first action is not consistent on any class $\mathcal{E}$ unless the first arm is optimal for every $v \in \mathcal{E}$.

Consistency is an asymptotic notion. A policy could be consistent and yet play $A_t = 1$ for all $t \leq 10^{100}$. For this reason, an assumption of consistency is insufficient to derive non-asymptotic lower bounds. In Section 16.2, we introduce a finite-time version of consistency that allows us to prove finite-time instance-dependent lower bounds.

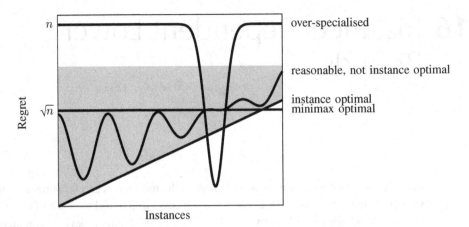

Figure 16.1 On the x-axis, the instances are ordered according to the measure of difficulty, and the y-axis shows the regret (on some scale). In the previous chapter, we proved that no policy can be entirely below the horizontal 'minimax optimal' line. The results in this chapter show that if the regret of a policy is below the 'instance optimal' line at any point, then it must have regret above the shaded region for other instances. For example, the 'overly specified' policy.

Recall that a class $\mathcal{E}$ of stochastic bandits is unstructured if $\mathcal{E} = \mathcal{M}_1 \times \cdots \times \mathcal{M}_k$ with $\mathcal{M}_1, \ldots, \mathcal{M}_k$ sets of distributions. The main theorem of this chapter is a generic lower bound that applies to any unstructured class of stochastic bandits. After the proof, we will see some applications to specific classes. Let $\mathcal{M}$ be a set of distributions with finite means, and let $\mu : \mathcal{M} \to \mathbb{R}$ be the function that maps $P \in \mathcal{M}$ to its mean. Let $\mu^* \in \mathbb{R}$ and $P \in \mathcal{M}$ have $\mu(P) < \mu^*$ and define

$$d_{\text{inf}}(P, \mu^*, \mathcal{M}) = \inf_{P' \in \mathcal{M}} \{D(P, P') : \mu(P') > \mu^*\}.$$

THEOREM 16.2. *Let $\mathcal{E} = \mathcal{M}_1 \times \cdots \times \mathcal{M}_k$ and $\pi \in \Pi_{cons}(\mathcal{E})$ be a consistent policy over $\mathcal{E}$. Then, for all $v = (P_i)_{i=1}^k \in \mathcal{E}$, it holds that*

$$\liminf_{n \to \infty} \frac{R_n}{\log(n)} \geq c^*(v, \mathcal{E}) = \sum_{i : \Delta_i > 0} \frac{\Delta_i}{d_{\text{inf}}(P_i, \mu^*, \mathcal{M}_i)}, \tag{16.2}$$

where Δ_i is the suboptimality gap of the ith arm in v and μ^* is the mean of the optimal arm.

Proof Let μ_i be the mean of the ith arm in v and $d_i = d_{\text{inf}}(P_i, \mu^*, \mathcal{M}_i)$. The result will follow from Lemma 4.5, and by showing that for any suboptimal arm i it holds that

$$\liminf_{n \to \infty} \frac{\mathbb{E}_{v\pi}[T_i(n)]}{\log(n)} \geq \frac{1}{d_i}.$$

Fix a suboptimal arm i, and let $\varepsilon > 0$ be arbitrary and $v' = (P'_j)_{j=1}^k \in \mathcal{E}$ be a bandit with $P'_j = P_j$ for $j \neq i$ and $P'_i \in \mathcal{M}_i$ be such that $D(P_i, P'_i) \leq d_i + \varepsilon$ and $\mu(P'_i) > \mu^*$, which exists by the definition of d_i. Let $\mu' \in \mathbb{R}^k$ be the vector of means of distributions of v'. By Lemma 15.1, we have $D(\mathbb{P}_{v\pi}, \mathbb{P}_{v'\pi}) \leq \mathbb{E}_{v\pi}[T_i(n)](d_i + \varepsilon)$, and by Theorem 14.2, for any event A,

$$\mathbb{P}_{v\pi}(A) + \mathbb{P}_{v'\pi}(A^c) \geq \frac{1}{2}\exp\left(-D(\mathbb{P}_{v\pi}, \mathbb{P}_{v'\pi})\right) \geq \frac{1}{2}\exp\left(-\mathbb{E}_{v\pi}[T_i(n)](d_i + \varepsilon)\right).$$

Now choose $A = \{T_i(n) > n/2\}$, and let $R_n = R_n(\pi, v)$ and $R'_n = R_n(\pi, v')$. Then,

$$R_n + R'_n \geq \frac{n}{2}\left(\mathbb{P}_{v\pi}(A)\Delta_i + \mathbb{P}_{v'\pi}(A^c)(\mu'_i - \mu^*)\right)$$

$$\geq \frac{n}{2}\min\{\Delta_i, \mu'_i - \mu^*\}\left(\mathbb{P}_{v\pi}(A) + \mathbb{P}_{v'\pi}(A^c)\right)$$

$$\geq \frac{n}{4}\min\{\Delta_i, \mu'_i - \mu^*\}\exp\left(-\mathbb{E}_{v\pi}[T_i(n)](d_i + \varepsilon)\right).$$

Rearranging and taking the limit inferior leads to

$$\liminf_{n\to\infty}\frac{\mathbb{E}_{v\pi}[T_i(n)]}{\log(n)} \geq \frac{1}{d_i + \varepsilon}\liminf_{n\to\infty}\frac{\log\left(\frac{n\min\{\Delta_i, \mu'_i - \mu^*\}}{4(R_n + R'_n)}\right)}{\log(n)}$$

$$= \frac{1}{d_i + \varepsilon}\left(1 - \limsup_{n\to\infty}\frac{\log(R_n + R'_n)}{\log(n)}\right) = \frac{1}{d_i + \varepsilon},$$

where the last equality follows from the definition of consistency, which says that for any $p > 0$, there exists a constant C_p such that for sufficiently large n, $R_n + R'_n \leq C_p n^p$, which implies that

$$\limsup_{n\to\infty}\frac{\log(R_n + R'_n)}{\log(n)} \leq \limsup_{n\to\infty}\frac{p\log(n) + \log(C_p)}{\log(n)} = p,$$

which gives the result since $p > 0$ was arbitrary and by taking the limit as ε tends to zero. □

Table 16.1 provides explicit formulas for $d_{\text{inf}}(P, \mu^*, \mathcal{M})$ for common choices of $\mathcal{M}$. The calculation of these quantities are all straightforward (Exercise 16.1). The lower bound and definition of $c^*(v, \mathcal{E})$ are quite fundamental quantities in the sense that for most classes $\mathcal{E}$, there exists a policy π for which

$$\lim_{n\to\infty}\frac{R_n(\pi, v)}{\log(n)} = c^*(v, \mathcal{E}) \qquad \text{for all } v \in \mathcal{E}. \tag{16.3}$$

Table 16.1 Expressions for d_{inf} for different parametric families when the mean of P is less than μ^*.

$\mathcal{M}$	P	$d_{\text{inf}}(P, \mu^*, \mathcal{M})$
$\{\mathcal{N}(\mu, \sigma^2) : \mu \in \mathbb{R}\}$	$\mathcal{N}(\mu, \sigma^2)$	$\dfrac{(\mu - \mu^*)^2}{2\sigma^2}$
$\{\mathcal{N}(\mu, \sigma^2) : \mu \in \mathbb{R}, \sigma^2 \in (0, \infty)\}$	$\mathcal{N}(\mu, \sigma^2)$	$\dfrac{1}{2}\log\left(1 + \dfrac{(\mu - \mu^*)^2}{2\sigma^2}\right)$
$\{\mathcal{B}(\mu) : \mu \in [0, 1]\}$	$\mathcal{B}(\mu)$	$\mu\log\left(\dfrac{\mu}{\mu^*}\right) + (1 - \mu)\log\left(\dfrac{1 - \mu}{1 - \mu^*}\right)$
$\{\mathcal{U}(a, b) : a, b \in \mathbb{R}\}$	$\mathcal{U}(a, b)$	$\log\left(1 + \dfrac{2((a + b)/2 - \mu^*)^2}{b - a}\right)$

This justifies calling a policy **asymptotically optimal** on class $\mathcal{E}$ if Eq. (16.3) holds. For example, UCB from Chapter 8 and KL-UCB from Chapter 10 are asymptotically optimal for $\mathcal{E}_\mathcal{N}^k(1)$ and $\mathcal{E}_\mathcal{B}^k$, respectively.

16.2   Finite-Time Bounds

By making a finite-time analogue of consistency, it is possible to prove a finite-time instance-dependent bound. First, a lemma that summarises what can be obtained by chaining the Bretagnolle–Huber inequality (Theorem 14.2) with the divergence decomposition lemma (Lemma 15.1).

LEMMA 16.3. *Let $v = (P_i)$ and $v' = (P_i')$ be k-armed stochastic bandits that differ only in the distribution of the reward for action $i \in [k]$. Assume that i is suboptimal in v and uniquely optimal in v'. Let $\lambda = \mu_i(v') - \mu_i(v)$. Then, for any policy π,*

$$\mathbb{E}_{v\pi}[T_i(n)] \geq \frac{\log\left(\frac{\min\{\lambda - \Delta_i(v), \Delta_i(v)\}}{4}\right) + \log(n) - \log(R_n(v) + R_n(v'))}{D(P_i, P_i')}. \qquad (16.4)$$

The lemma holds for finite n and any v and can be used to derive finite-time instance-dependent lower bounds for any environment class $\mathcal{E}$ that is rich enough. The following result provides a finite-time instance-dependence bound for Gaussian bandits where the asymptotic notion of consistency is replaced by an assumption that the minimax regret is not too large. This assumption alone is enough to show that no policy that is remotely close to minimax optimal can be much better than UCB on any instance.

THEOREM 16.4. *Let $v \in \mathcal{E}_\mathcal{N}^k$ be a k-armed Gaussian bandit with mean vector $\mu \in \mathbb{R}^k$ and suboptimality gaps $\Delta \in [0, \infty)^k$. Let*

$$\mathcal{E}(v) = \{v' \in \mathcal{E}_\mathcal{N}^k : \mu_i(v') \in [\mu_i, \mu_i + 2\Delta_i]\}.$$

Suppose $C > 0$ and $p \in (0, 1)$ are constants and π is a policy such that $R_n(\pi, v') \leq Cn^p$ for all n and $v' \in \mathcal{E}(v)$. Then, for any $\varepsilon \in (0, 1]$,

$$R_n(\pi, v) \geq \frac{2}{(1 + \varepsilon)^2} \sum_{i : \Delta_i > 0} \left(\frac{(1 - p)\log(n) + \log\left(\frac{\varepsilon \Delta_i}{8C}\right)}{\Delta_i}\right)^+. \qquad (16.5)$$

Proof   Let i be suboptimal in v, and choose $v' \in \mathcal{E}(v)$ such that $\mu_j(v') = \mu_j(v)$ for $j \neq i$ and $\mu_j(v') = \mu_i + \Delta_i(1 + \varepsilon)$. Then, by Lemma 16.3 with $\lambda = \Delta_i(1 + \varepsilon)$,

$$\mathbb{E}_{v\pi}[T_i(n)] \geq \frac{2}{\Delta_i^2(1 + \varepsilon)^2}\left(\log\left(\frac{n}{2Cn^p}\right) + \log\left(\frac{\min\{\lambda - \Delta_i, \Delta_i\}}{4}\right)\right)$$

$$= \frac{2}{\Delta_i^2(1 + \varepsilon)^2}\left((1 - p)\log(n) + \log\left(\frac{\varepsilon \Delta_i}{8C}\right)\right).$$

Plugging this into the basic regret decomposition identity (Lemma 4.5) gives the result.   □

When $p = 1/2$, the leading term in this lower bound is approximately half that of the asymptotic bound. This effect may be real. The class of policies considered is larger than in the asymptotic lower bound, and so there is the possibility that the policy that is best tuned for a given environment achieves a smaller regret.

16.3 Notes

1 We mentioned that for most classes $\mathcal{E}$ there is a policy satisfying Eq. (16.3). Its form is derived from the lower bound, and by making some additional assumptions on the underlying distributions. For details, see the article by Burnetas and Katehakis [1996], which is also the original source of Theorem 16.2.

2 The analysis in this chapter only works for unstructured classes. Without this assumption a policy can potentially learn about the reward from one arm by playing other arms and this greatly reduces the regret. Lower bounds for structured bandits are more delicate and will be covered on a case-by-case basis in subsequent chapters.

3 The classes analysed in Table 16.1 are all parametric, which makes the calculation possible analytically. There has been relatively little analysis in the non-parametric case, but we know of three exceptions for which we simply refer the reader to the appropriate source. The first is the class of distributions with bounded support: $\mathcal{M} = \{P : \mathrm{Supp}(P) \subseteq [0, 1]\}$, which has been analysed exactly [Honda and Takemura, 2010]. The second is the class of distributions with semi-bounded support, $\mathcal{M} = \{P : \mathrm{Supp}(P) \subseteq (-\infty, 1]\}$ [Honda and Takemura, 2015]. The third is the class of distributions with bounded kurtosis, $\mathcal{M} = \{P : \mathrm{Kurt}_{X \sim P}[X] \leq \kappa\}$ [Lattimore, 2017].

16.4 Bibliographic Remarks

Asymptotic optimality via a consistency assumption first appeared in the seminal paper by Lai and Robbins [1985], which was later generalised by Burnetas and Katehakis [1996]. In terms of upper bounds, there now exist policies that are asymptotic optimal for single-parameter exponential families [Cappé et al., 2013]. Until recently, there were no results on asymptotic optimality for multi-parameter classes of reward distributions. There has been some progress on this issue recently for the Gaussian distribution with unknown mean and variance [Cowan et al., 2018] and for the uniform distribution [Cowan and Katehakis, 2015]. There are plenty of open questions related to asymptotically optimal strategies for non-parametric classes of reward distributions. When the reward distributions are discrete and finitely supported, an asymptotically optimal policy is given by Burnetas and Katehakis [1996], though the precise constant is hard to interpret. A relatively complete solution is available for classes with bounded support [Honda and Takemura, 2010]. Already for the semi-bounded case, things are getting murky [Honda and Takemura, 2015]. One of the authors thinks that classes with bounded kurtosis are quite interesting, but here things are only understood up to constant factors [Lattimore, 2017]. An asymptotic variant of Theorem 16.4 is by Salomon et al. [2013]. Finite-time instance-dependent lower bounds have been proposed by several authors, including Kulkarni and Lugosi [2000], for two arms, and Garivier et al. [2019] and Lattimore [2018], for the general case. As noted earlier, neither ETC policies, nor elimination-based algorithms are able to achieve asymptotic optimality: as shown by Garivier et al. [2016b], these algorithms (no matter how they are tuned) must incur an additional multiplicative penalty of a factor of two on the standard Gaussian bandit problems as compared to the optimal asymptotic regret.

16.5 Exercises

16.1 (RELATIVE ENTROPY CALCULATIONS) Verify the calculations in Table 16.1.

16.2 (Rademacher noise) Let $\mathcal{R}(\mu)$ be the shifted Rademacher distribution, which for $\mu \in \mathbb{R}$ and $X \sim \mathcal{R}(\mu)$ is characterised by $\mathbb{P}(X = \mu + 1) = \mathbb{P}(X = \mu - 1) = 1/2$.

(a) Show that $d_{\inf}(\mathcal{R}(\mu), \mu^*, \mathcal{M}) = \infty$ for any $\mu < \mu^*$.

(b) Design a policy π for bandits with shifted Rademacher rewards such that the regret is bounded by

$$R_n(\pi, v) \leq 3 \sum_{i=1}^{k} \Delta_i \qquad \text{for all } n \text{ and } v \in \mathcal{M}^k.$$

(c) The results from parts (a) and (b) seem to contradict the heuristic analysis in Note 1 at the end of Chapter 15. Explain.

16.3 (Asymptotic lower bound for exponential families) Let $\mathcal{M} = \{P_\theta : \theta \in \Theta\}$ be an exponential family with sufficient statistic equal to the identity and $\mathcal{E} = \mathcal{M}^k$ and π be a consistent policy for $\mathcal{E}$. Prove that the asymptotic upper bound on the regret proven in Exercise 10.4 is tight.

16.4 (Unknown subgaussian constant) Let

$$\mathcal{M} = \{P : \text{there exists a } \sigma^2 \geq 0 \text{ such that } P \text{ is } \sigma^2\text{-subgaussian}\}.$$

(a) Find a distribution P such that $P \notin \mathcal{M}$.

(b) Suppose that $P \in \mathcal{M}$ has mean $\mu \in \mathbb{R}$. Prove that $d_{\inf}(P, \mu^*, \mathcal{M}) = 0$ for all $\mu^* > \mu$.

(c) Let $\mathcal{E} = \{(P_i) : P_i \in \mathcal{M} \text{ for all } 1 \leq i \leq k\}$. Prove that if $k > 1$, then for all consistent policies π,

$$\liminf_{n \to \infty} \frac{R_n(\pi, v)}{\log(n)} = \infty \qquad \text{for all } v \in \mathcal{E}.$$

(d) Let $f : \mathbb{N} \to [0, \infty)$ be any increasing function with $\lim_{n \to \infty} f(n)/\log(n) = \infty$. Prove there exists a policy π such that

$$\limsup_{n \to \infty} \frac{R_n(\pi, v)}{f(n)} = 0 \qquad \text{for all } v \in \mathcal{E},$$

where $\mathcal{E}$ is as in the previous part.

(e) Conclude that there exists a consistent policy for $\mathcal{E}$.

16.5 (Minimax lower bound) Use Lemma 16.3 to prove Theorem 15.2, possibly with different constants.

16.6 (Refining the lower-order terms) Let $k = 2$, and for $v \in \mathcal{E}_N^2$ let $\Delta(v) = \max\{\Delta_1(v), \Delta_2(v)\}$. Suppose that π is a policy such that for all $v \in \mathcal{E}_N^2$ with $\Delta(v) \leq 1$, it holds that

$$R_n(\pi, v) \leq \frac{C \log(n)}{\Delta(v)}. \qquad (16.6)$$

(a) Give an example of a policy satisfying Eq. (16.6).

(b) Assume that $i = 2$ is suboptimal for v and that $\alpha \in (0, 1)$ be such that $\mathbb{E}_{v\pi}[T_2(n)] = \frac{1}{2\Delta(v)^2} \log(\alpha)$. Let v' be the alternative environment where $\mu_1(v') = \mu_1(v)$ and $\mu_2(v') = \mu_1(v) + 2\Delta(v)$. Show that

$$\exp(-D(\mathbb{P}_{v\pi}, \mathbb{P}_{v'\pi})) = \frac{1}{\alpha}.$$

(c) Let A be the event that $T_2(n) \geq n/2$. Show that

$$\mathbb{P}_{v\pi}(A) \leq \frac{2C \log(n)}{n\Delta(v)^2} \quad \text{and} \quad \mathbb{P}_{v'\pi}(A) \geq \frac{1}{2\alpha} - \frac{2C \log(n)}{n\Delta(v)^2}.$$

(d) Show that

$$R_n(\pi, v') \geq \frac{n\Delta(v)}{2} \left(\frac{1}{2\alpha} - \frac{2C \log(n)}{n\Delta(v)^2} \right).$$

(e) Show that $\alpha \geq \frac{n\Delta(v)^2}{8C \log(n)}$ and conclude that

$$R_n(\pi, v) \geq \frac{1}{2\Delta(v)} \log \left(\frac{n\Delta(v)^2}{8C \log(n)} \right).$$

(f) Generalise the argument to an arbitrary number of arms.

In Exercise 7.6 you showed that there exists a bandit policy π such that for some universal constant $C > 0$ and for any $v \in \mathcal{E}_{[0,b]}^k$ k-armed bandit with rewards taking values in $[0, b]$, the regret $R_n(\pi, v)$ of π on v after n rounds satisfies

$$R_n(\pi, v) \leq C \sum_{i:\Delta_i>0} \left(\Delta_i + \left(b + \frac{\sigma_i^2}{\Delta_i} \right) \log(n) \right),$$

where $\Delta_i = \Delta_i(v)$ is the action gap of action i and $\sigma_i^2 = \sigma_i^2(v)$ is the variance of the reward of arm i. In particular, this is the inequality shown in Eq. (7.14). The next exercise asks you to show that the appearance of both b and $\frac{\sigma_i^2}{\Delta_i}$ is necessary in this bound.

16.7 (SHARPNESS OF EQ. (7.14)) Let $k > 1$, $b > 0$ and $c > 0$ be arbitrary. Show that there is no policy π for which either

$$\limsup_{n\to\infty} \frac{R_n(\pi, v)}{\log(n)} \leq cb, \qquad \forall v \in \mathcal{E}_{[0,b]}^k \tag{16.7}$$

or

$$\limsup_{n\to\infty} \frac{R_n(\pi, v)}{\log(n)} \leq c \sum_{i:\Delta_i>0} \frac{\sigma_i^2(v)}{\Delta_i(v)}, \qquad \forall v \in \mathcal{E}_{[0,b]}^k \tag{16.8}$$

would hold true.

The intuition underlying this result is the following: Eq. (16.7) cannot hold because this would mean that for some policy, the regret is logarithmic with a constant independent of the gaps, while intuitively, if the variance is constant, the coefficient of the logarithmic regret must increase as the gaps get close. Similarly, Eq. (16.8) cannot hold either because we expect a logarithmic regret with a coefficient proportional to the inverse gap even as the variance gets zero, as the case of Bernoulli bandits shows. This exercise is due to Audibert et al. [2007].

16.8 (LOWER BOUND ON REGRET VARIANCE) Let $k > 1$ and $\mathcal{E} \subset \mathcal{E}_N^k$ be the set of k-armed Gaussian bandits with mean rewards in $[0, 1]$ for all arms. Suppose that π is a policy such that for all $v \in \mathcal{E}$,

$$\limsup_{n\to\infty} \frac{R_n(\pi, v)}{\log(n)} \leq \sum_{i:\Delta_i>0} \frac{2(1 + p)}{\Delta_i}.$$

Prove that

$$\limsup_{n \to \infty} \sup_{v \in \mathcal{E}} \frac{\log(\mathbb{V}[\hat{R}_n(\pi, v)])}{(1 - p) \log(n)} \geq 1,$$

where $\hat{R}_n(\pi, v) = n\mu^*(v) - \sum_{t=1}^{n} \mu_{A_t}(v)$.

17 High-Probability Lower Bounds

The lower bounds proven in the last two chapters were for stochastic bandits. In this chapter, we prove high probability lower bounds for both stochastic and adversarial bandits. Recall that for adversarial bandit $x \in [0, 1]^{n \times k}$, the random regret is

$$\hat{R}_n = \max_{i \in [k]} \sum_{t=1}^{n} x_{ti} - x_{tA_t}$$

and the (expected) regret is $R_n = \mathbb{E}[\hat{R}_n]$. To set expectations, remember that in Chapter 12 we proved two high-probability upper bounds on the regret of Exp3-IX. In the first, we showed there exists a policy π such that for all adversarial bandits $x \in [0, 1]^{n \times k}$ and $\delta \in (0, 1)$, it holds with probability at least $1 - \delta$ that

$$\hat{R}_n = O\left(\sqrt{kn \log(k)} + \sqrt{\frac{kn}{\log(k)}} \log\left(\frac{1}{\delta}\right) \right). \tag{17.1}$$

We also gave a version of the algorithm that depended on $\delta \in (0, 1)$ for which with probability at least $1 - \delta$,

$$\hat{R}_n = O\left(\sqrt{kn \log\left(\frac{k}{\delta}\right)} \right). \tag{17.2}$$

The important difference is the order of quantifiers. In the first, we have a single algorithm and a high-probability guarantee that holds simultaneously for any confidence level. The second algorithm needs the confidence level to be specified in advance. The price for using the generic algorithm appears to be $\sqrt{\log(1/\delta)/\log(k)}$, which is usually quite small but not totally insignificant. We will see that both bounds are tight up to constant factors, which implies that knowing the desired confidence level in advance really does help. One reason why choosing the confidence level in advance is not ideal is that the resulting high-probability bound cannot be integrated to prove a bound in expectation. For algorithms satisfying (17.1), the expected regret can be bounded by

$$R_n \le \int_0^{\infty} \mathbb{P}\left(\hat{R}_n \ge u \right) du = O(\sqrt{kn \log(k)}). \tag{17.3}$$

On the other hand, if the high-probability bound only holds for a single δ, as in (17.2), then it seems hard to do much better than

$$R_n \le n\delta + O\left(\sqrt{kn \log\left(\frac{k}{\delta}\right)} \right),$$

which with the best choice of δ leads to a bound of $O(\sqrt{kn \log(n)})$.

17.1 Stochastic Bandits

For simplicity, we start with the stochastic setting before explaining how to convert the arguments to the adversarial model. There is no randomness in the expected regret, so in order to derive a high-probability bound, we define the **random pseudo-regret** by

$$\bar{R}_n = \sum_{i=1}^{k} T_i(n)\Delta_i,$$

which is a random variable through the pull counts $T_i(n)$.

 For all results in this section, we let $\mathcal{E}^k \subset \mathcal{E}_\mathcal{N}^k$ denote the set of k-armed Gaussian bandits with suboptimality gaps bounded by one. For $\mu \in [0, 1]^d$ we let $\nu_\mu \in \mathcal{E}^k$ be the Gaussian bandit with means μ.

THEOREM 17.1. *Let $n \geq 1$ and $k \geq 2$ and $B > 0$ and π be a policy such that for any $\nu \in \mathcal{E}^k$,*

$$R_n(\pi, \nu) \leq B\sqrt{(k-1)n}. \tag{17.4}$$

Let $\delta \in (0,1)$. Then there exists a bandit ν in $\mathcal{E}^k$ such that

$$\mathbb{P}\left(\bar{R}_n(\pi, \nu) \geq \frac{1}{4}\min\left\{n, \frac{1}{B}\sqrt{(k-1)n}\log\left(\frac{1}{4\delta}\right)\right\}\right) \geq \delta.$$

Proof Let $\Delta \in (0, 1/2]$ be a constant to be tuned subsequently and $\nu = \nu_\mu$ where the mean vector $\mu \in \mathbb{R}^d$ is defined by $\mu_1 = \Delta$ and $\mu_i = 0$ for $i > 1$. Abbreviate $R_n = R_n(\pi, \nu)$ and $\mathbb{P} = \mathbb{P}_{\nu\pi}$ and $\mathbb{E} = \mathbb{E}_{\nu\pi}$. Let $i = \text{argmin}_{i>1}\mathbb{E}[T_i(n)]$. Then, by Lemma 4.5 and the assumption in Eq. (17.4),

$$\mathbb{E}[T_i(n)] \leq \frac{R_n}{\Delta(k-1)} \leq \frac{B}{\Delta}\sqrt{\frac{n}{k-1}}. \tag{17.5}$$

Define alternative bandit $\nu' = \nu_{\mu'}$ where $\mu' \in \mathbb{R}^d$ is equal to μ except $\mu_i' = \mu_i + 2\Delta$. Abbreviate $\mathbb{P}' = \mathbb{P}_{\nu'\pi}$ and $\bar{R}_n = \bar{R}_n(\pi, \nu)$ and $\bar{R}_n' = \bar{R}_n(\pi, \nu')$. By Lemma 4.5, the Bretagnolle–Huber inequality (Theorem 14.2) and the divergence decomposition (Lemma 15.1), we have

$$\mathbb{P}\left(\bar{R}_n \geq \frac{\Delta n}{2}\right) + \mathbb{P}'\left(\bar{R}_n' \geq \frac{\Delta n}{2}\right) \geq \mathbb{P}\left(T_i(n) \geq \frac{n}{2}\right) + \mathbb{P}'\left(T_i(n) < \frac{n}{2}\right)$$

$$\geq \frac{1}{2}\exp\left(-D(\mathbb{P}, \mathbb{P}')\right) \geq \frac{1}{2}\exp\left(-2B\Delta\sqrt{\frac{n}{k-1}}\right) \geq 2\delta,$$

where the last line follows by choosing

$$\Delta = \min\left\{\frac{1}{2}, \frac{1}{2B}\sqrt{\frac{k-1}{n}}\log\left(\frac{1}{4\delta}\right)\right\}.$$

The result follows since $\max\{a, b\} \geq (a + b)/2$. □

COROLLARY 17.2. *Let $n \geq 1$ and $k \geq 2$. Then, for any policy π and $\delta \in (0, 1)$ such that*

$$n\delta \leq \sqrt{n(k-1)\log\left(\frac{1}{4\delta}\right)}, \tag{17.6}$$

there exists a bandit problem $v \in \mathcal{E}^k$ such that

$$\mathbb{P}\left(\bar{R}_n(\pi, v) \geq \frac{1}{4}\min\left\{n, \sqrt{\frac{n(k-1)}{2}\log\left(\frac{1}{4\delta}\right)}\right\}\right) \geq \delta. \tag{17.7}$$

Proof We prove the result by contradiction. Assume that the conclusion does not hold for π and let $\delta \in (0, 1)$ satisfy (17.6). Then, for any bandit problem $v \in \mathcal{E}^k$, the expected regret of π is bounded by

$$R_n(\pi, v) \leq n\delta + \sqrt{\frac{n(k-1)}{2}\log\left(\frac{1}{4\delta}\right)} \leq \sqrt{2n(k-1)\log\left(\frac{1}{4\delta}\right)}.$$

Therefore, π satisfies the conditions of Theorem 17.1 with $B = \sqrt{2\log(1/(4\delta))}$, which implies that there exists some bandit problem $v \in \mathcal{E}^k$ such that (17.7) holds, contradicting our assumption. □

COROLLARY 17.3. *Let $k \geq 2$ and $p \in (0, 1)$ and $B > 0$. Then, there does not exist a policy π such that for all $n \geq 1$, $\delta \in (0, 1)$ and $v \in \mathcal{E}^k$,*

$$\mathbb{P}\left(\bar{R}_n(\pi, v) \geq B\sqrt{(k-1)n}\log^p\left(\frac{1}{\delta}\right)\right) < \delta.$$

Proof We proceed by contradiction. Suppose that such a policy exists. Choosing δ sufficiently small and n sufficiently large ensures that

$$\frac{1}{B}\log\left(\frac{1}{4\delta}\right) \geq B\log^p\left(\frac{1}{\delta}\right) \quad \text{and} \quad \frac{1}{B}\sqrt{n(k-1)}\log\left(\frac{1}{4\delta}\right) \leq n.$$

Now, by assumption, for any $v \in \mathcal{E}^k$ we have

$$R_n(\pi, v) \leq \int_0^\infty \mathbb{P}\left(\bar{R}_n(\pi, v) \geq x\right) dx$$

$$\leq B\sqrt{n(k-1)}\int_0^\infty \exp\left(-x^{1/p}\right) dx \leq B\sqrt{n(k-1)}.$$

Therefore, by the Theorem 17.1, there exists a bandit $v \in \mathcal{E}^k$ such that

$$\mathbb{P}\left(\bar{R}_n(\pi, v) \geq B\sqrt{n(k-1)}\log\left(\frac{1}{\delta}\right)\right)$$

$$\geq \mathbb{P}\left(\bar{R}_n(\pi, v) \geq \frac{1}{4}\min\left\{n, \frac{1}{B}\sqrt{n(k-1)}\log\left(\frac{1}{4\delta}\right)\right\}\right) \geq \delta,$$

which contradicts our assumption and completes the proof. □

We suspect there exists a policy π and universal constant $B > 0$ such that for all $v \in \mathcal{E}^k$,

$$\mathbb{P}\left(\bar{R}_n(\pi, v) \geq B\sqrt{kn}\log\left(\frac{1}{\delta}\right)\right) \leq \delta.$$

17.2 Adversarial Bandits

We now explain how to translate the ideas in the previous section to the adversarial model. Let $\pi = (\pi_t)_{t=1}^n$ be a fixed policy, and recall that for $x \in [0,1]^{n \times k}$, the random regret is

$$\hat{R}_n = \max_{i \in [k]} \sum_{t=1}^n (x_{ti} - x_{tA_t}).$$

Let F_x be the cumulative distribution function of the law of $\hat{R}_n$ when policy π interacts with the adversarial bandit $x \in [0,1]^{n \times k}$.

THEOREM 17.4. *Let $c, C > 0$ be sufficiently small/large universal constants and $k \geq 2$, $n \geq 1$ and $\delta \in (0,1)$ be such that $n \geq Ck\log(1/(2\delta))$. Then there exists a reward sequence $x \in [0,1]^{n \times k}$ such that*

$$1 - F_x\left(c\sqrt{nk\log\left(\frac{1}{2\delta}\right)}\right) \geq \delta.$$

The proof is a bit messy, but is not completely without interest. For the sake of brevity, we explain only the high-level ideas and refer you elsewhere for the gory details. There are two difficulties in translating the arguments in the previous section to the adversarial model. First, in the adversarial model, we need the rewards to be bounded in $[0,1]$. The second difficulty is we now analyse the adversarial regret rather than the random pseudo-regret. Given a measure Q, let $X \in [0,1]^{n \times k}$ and $(A_t)_{t=1}^n$ be a collection of random variables on a probability space $(\Omega, \mathcal{F}, \mathbb{P}_Q)$ such that

(a) $\mathbb{P}_Q(X \in B) = Q(B)$ for all $B \in \mathfrak{B}([0,1]^{n \times k})$; and
(b) $\mathbb{P}_Q(A_t \mid A_1, X_1, \ldots, A_{t-1}, X_{t-1}) = \pi_t(A_t \mid A_1, X_1, \ldots, A_{t-1}, X_{t-1})$ almost surely, where $X_s = X_{tA_s}$.

Then the regret is a random variable $\hat{R}_n : \Omega \to \mathbb{R}$ defined by

$$\hat{R}_n = \max_{i \in [k]} \sum_{t=1}^n (X_{ti} - X_{tA_t}).$$

Suppose we sample $X \in [0,1]^{n \times k}$ from distribution Q on $([0,1]^{n \times k}, \mathfrak{B}([0,1]^k))$.

CLAIM 17.5. *Suppose that $X \sim Q$, where Q is a measure on $[0,1]^{n \times k}$ with the Borel σ-algebra and that $\mathbb{E}_Q[1 - F_X(u)] \geq \delta$. Then there exists an $x \in [0,1]^{n \times k}$ such that $1 - F_x(u) \geq \delta$.*

The next step is to choose Q and argue that $\mathbb{E}_Q[1 - F_X(u)] \geq \delta$ for sufficiently large u. To do this, we need a truncated normal distribution. Defining clipping function

$$\text{clip}_{[0,1]}(x) = \begin{cases} 1 & \text{if } x > 1 \\ 0 & \text{if } x < 0 \\ x & \text{otherwise.} \end{cases}$$

Let σ and Δ be positive constants to be chosen later and $(\eta_t)_{t=1}^n$ a sequence of independent random variables with $\eta_t \sim \mathcal{N}(1/2, \sigma^2)$. For each $i \in [k]$, let Q_i be the distribution of $X \in [0,1]^{n \times k}$, where

$$X_{tj} = \begin{cases} \text{clip}_{[0,1]}(\eta_t + \Delta) & \text{if } j = 1 \\ \text{clip}_{[0,1]}(\eta_t + 2\Delta) & \text{if } j = i \text{ and } i \neq 1 \\ \text{clip}_{[0,1]}(\eta_t) & \text{otherwise.} \end{cases}$$

Notice that under any Q_i for fixed t, the random variables $X_{t1}, \ldots, X_{tk}$ are not independent, but for fixed j, the random variables $X_{1j}, \ldots, X_{nj}$ are independent and identically distributed. Let $\mathbb{P}_{Q_i}$ be the law of $X_1, A_1, \ldots, A_n, X_n$ when policy π interacts with adversarial bandit sampled from $X \sim Q_i$.

CLAIM 17.6. *If $\sigma > 0$ and $\Delta = \sigma\sqrt{\frac{k-1}{2n}\log\left(\frac{1}{8\delta}\right)}$, then there exists an arm i such that*

$$\mathbb{P}_{Q_i}(T_i(n) < n/2) \geq 2\delta.$$

The proof of this claim follows along the same lines as the theorems in the previous section. All that changes is the calculation of the relative entropy. The last step is to relate $T_i(n)$ to the random regret. In the stochastic model, this was straightforward, but for adversarial bandits there is an additional step. Notice that under Q_i, it holds that $X_{ti} - X_{tA_t} \geq 0$ and that if $X_{ti}, X_{tA_t} \in (0,1)$ and $A_t \neq i$, then $X_{ti} - X_{tA_t} \geq \Delta$. From this we conclude that

$$\hat{R}_n \geq \Delta\left(n - T_i(n) - \sum_{t=1}^n \mathbb{I}\{\text{exists } j \in [k] : X_{tj} \in \{0,1\}\}\right). \tag{17.8}$$

The following claim upper-bounds the number of rounds in which clipping occurs with high probability.

CLAIM 17.7. *If $\sigma = 1/10$ and $\Delta < 1/8$ and $n \geq 32\log(1/\delta)$, then*

$$\mathbb{P}_{Q_i}\left(\sum_{t=1}^n \mathbb{I}\{\text{exists } j \in [k] : X_{tj} \in \{0,1\}\} \geq \frac{n}{4}\right) \leq \delta.$$

Combining Claim 17.6 and Claim 17.7 with Eq. (17.8) shows there exists an arm i such that

$$\mathbb{P}_{Q_i}\left(\hat{R}_n \geq \frac{n\Delta}{4}\right) \geq \delta,$$

which by the definition of Δ and Claim 17.5 implies Theorem 17.4.

17.3   Notes

1 The adversarial bandits used in Section 17.2 had the interesting property that the same arm has the best reward in every round (not just the best mean). This cannot be exploited by an algorithm, however, because it only gets a single observation in each round.

2 In Theorem 17.4, we did not make any assumptions on the algorithm. If we had assumed the algorithm enjoyed an expected regret bound of $R_n \leq B\sqrt{kn}$, then we could conclude that for each sufficiently small $\delta \in (0, 1)$ there exists an adversarial bandit such that

$$\mathbb{P}\left(\hat{R}_n \geq \frac{c}{B}\sqrt{kn}\log\left(\frac{1}{2\delta}\right) \right) \geq \delta,$$

which shows that our high-probability upper bounds for Exp3-IX are nearly tight.

17.4   Bibliographic Remarks

The results in this chapter are by Gerchinovitz and Lattimore [2016], who also provide lower bounds on what is achievable when the loss matrix exhibits nice structure such as low variance or similarity between losses of the arms.

17.5   Exercises

17.1 Prove each of the claims in Section 17.2.

Part V

Contextual and Linear Bandits

The algorithms introduced so far work well in stationary environments with only a few actions. Real-world problems are seldom this simple. For example, a bandit algorithm designed for targeted advertising may have thousands of actions. Even more troubling, the algorithm has access to contextual information about the user and the advertisement. Ignoring this information would make the problem highly non-stationary, but algorithms introduced in the previous chapter cannot make use of side information.

Large action sets are usually dealt with by introducing structure that allows the algorithm to generalise from one action to another. For example, advertisements can usually be associated with features describing their topic. Then the reward can be described as a function of the features, usually assumed to be nice in some way (linear or smooth, for example). Contextual information is dealt with in a similar fashion by assuming the mean reward of an action is a function of the context features and action features. As we explain, this leads to a model where the action set is essentially changing in each round.

Of course the world is messy in other ways. Rewards are often delayed, and may be unattributed, or the world may be non-stationary. The first of these issues is discussed briefly in the introduction to Part VII while non-stationarity is the subjection of Chapter 31.

Except for the first chapter, which is generic, the focus of this part will be on the special case that the expected reward of each arm is a linear function of some feature vector in a way that will be made precise in Chapter 19. Along the way, we will discuss many generalisations and give references to the literature. One aspect that will play a far larger role is computation. While finite-armed bandits with few arms present no computation difficulties, when the number of actions is very large or the information structure of the feedback model is not so easily separable, then computation can be a serious challenge.

18 Contextual Bandits

In many bandit problems, the learner has access to additional information that may help predict the quality of the actions. Imagine designing a movie recommendation system where users sequentially request recommendations for which movie to watch next. It would be inadvisable to ignore demographic information about the user making the request, or other contextual history such as previously watched movies or ratings. None of the algorithms presented so far make use of this kind of additional information. Indeed, they optimise a benchmark (the regret) that also disregards such contextual data. Essentially they would try to identify the best single movie in hindsight. In this chapter, we present an augmented framework and regret definition that better models real-world problems where contextual information is available.

 Whenever you design a new benchmark, there are several factors to consider. Competing with a poor benchmark does not make sense, since even an algorithm that perfectly matches the benchmark will perform poorly. At the same time, competing with a better benchmark can be harder from a learning perspective, and this penalty must be offset against the benefits.

The trade-off just described is fundamental to all machine learning problems. In statistical estimation, the analoguous trade-off is known as the **bias-variance trade-off**. We will not attempt to answer the question of how to resolve this trade-off in this chapter because first we need to see how to effectively compete with improved benchmarks. The good news is that many of the techniques developed earlier are easily generalised.

18.1 Contextual Bandits: One Bandit per Context

While contextual bandits can be studied in both the adversarial and stochastic frameworks, in this chapter we focus on the k-armed adversarial model. As usual, the adversary secretly chooses $(x_t)_{t=1}^n$, where $x_t \in [0,1]^k$ with x_{ti} the reward associated with arm i in round t. The adversary also secretly chooses a sequence of contexts $(c_t)_{t=1}^n$, where $c_t \in \mathcal{C}$ with $\mathcal{C}$ a set of possible contexts. In each round, the learner observes c_t, chooses an action A_t and receives reward x_{tA_t}. The interaction protocol is shown in Fig. 18.1.

Adversary secretly chooses rewards $(x_t)_{t=1}^n$ with $x_t \in [0,1]^k$

Adversary secretly chooses contexts $(c_t)_{t=1}^n$ with $c_t \in \mathcal{C}$

For rounds $t = 1, 2, \ldots, n$:

    Learner observes context $c_t \in \mathcal{C}$ where $\mathcal{C}$ is an arbitrary fixed set of contexts.

    Learner selects distribution $P_t \in \mathcal{P}_{k-1}$ and samples A_t from P_t.

    Learner observes reward $X_t = x_{tA_t}$.

Figure 18.1 Interaction protocol for k-armed contextual bandits.

A natural way to define the regret is to compare the rewards collected by the learner with the rewards collected by the best context-dependent policy in hindsight:

$$R_n = \mathbb{E}\left[\sum_{c \in \mathcal{C}} \max_{i \in [k]} \sum_{t \in [n]:c_t=c} (x_{ti} - X_t)\right]. \tag{18.1}$$

If the set of possible contexts is finite, then a simple approach is to use a separate instance of Exp3 for each context. Let

$$R_{nc} = \mathbb{E}\left[\max_{i \in [k]} \sum_{t \in [n]:c_t=c} (x_{ti} - X_t)\right]$$

be the regret due to context $c \in \mathcal{C}$. When using a separate instance of Exp3 for each context, we can use the results of Chapter 11 to bound

$$R_{nc} \leq 2\sqrt{k\sum_{t=1}^n \mathbb{I}\{c_t = c\}\log(k)}, \tag{18.2}$$

where the sum inside the square root counts the number of times context $c \in \mathcal{C}$ is observed. Because this is not known in advance, it is important to use an anytime version of Exp3 for which the above regret bound holds without needing to tune a learning rate that depends on the number of times the context is observed (see Exercise 28.13). Substituting (18.2) into the regret leads to

$$R_n = \sum_{c \in \mathcal{C}} R_{nc} \leq 2\sum_{c \in \mathcal{C}}\sqrt{k\log(k)\sum_{t=1}^n \mathbb{I}\{c_t = c\}}. \tag{18.3}$$

The magnitude of the right-hand side depends on the distribution of observed contexts. On one extreme, there is only one observed context, and the bound is the same as the standard finite-armed bandit problem. The other extreme occurs when all contexts are observed equally often, in which case we have

$$R_n \leq 2\sqrt{nk|\mathcal{C}|\log(k)}. \tag{18.4}$$

Jensen's inequality applied to Eq. (18.3) shows that this really is the worst case (Exercise 18.1).

The regret in Eq. (18.4) is different than the regret studied in Chapter 11. If we ignore the context and run the standard Exp3 algorithm, then we would have

$$\mathbb{E}\left[\sum_{t=1}^{n} X_t\right] \geq \max_{i\in[k]} \sum_{t=1}^{n} x_{ti} - 2\sqrt{kn\log(k)}.$$

Using one version of Exp3 per context leads to

$$\mathbb{E}\left[\sum_{t=1}^{n} X_t\right] \geq \sum_{c\in\mathcal{C}} \max_{i\in[k]} \sum_{t\in[n]:c_t=c} x_{ti} - 2\sqrt{kn|\mathcal{C}|\log(k)}.$$

Which of these bounds is preferable depends on the magnitude of n and how useful the context is. When n is very large, the second bound is more likely to be preferable. On the other hand, the second bound is completely vacuous when $n \leq 4k|\mathcal{C}|\log(k)$.

18.2 Bandits with Expert Advice

When the context set $\mathcal{C}$ is large, using one bandit algorithm per context will almost always be a poor choice because the additional precision is wasted unless the amount of data is enormous. Fortunately, however, it is seldom the case that the context set is both large and unstructured. To illustrate a common situation, we return to the movie recommendation theme, where the actions are movies and the context contains user information such as age, gender and recent movie preferences. In this case, the context space is combinatorially large, but there is a lot of structure inherited from the fact that the space of movies is highly structured and users with similar demographics are more likely to have similar preferences. We start by rewriting Eq. (18.1) in an equivalent form. Let Φ be the set of all functions from $\mathcal{C} \to [k]$. Then,

$$R_n = \mathbb{E}\left[\max_{\phi\in\Phi} \sum_{t=1}^{n} (x_{t\phi(c_t)} - X_t)\right]. \tag{18.5}$$

The discussion above suggests that a slightly smaller set Φ may lead to more reward. In what follows, we describe some of the most common ideas of how to do this.

Partitions
Let $\mathcal{P} \subset 2^{\mathcal{C}}$ be a partition of $\mathcal{C}$, which means that sets (or parts) in $\mathcal{P}$ are disjoint and $\cup_{P\in\mathcal{P}} P = \mathcal{C}$. Then define Φ to be the set of functions from $\mathcal{C}$ to $[k]$ that are constant on each part in $\mathcal{P}$. In this case, we can run a version of Exp3 for each part, which means the regret depends on the number of parts $|\mathcal{P}|$ rather than on the number of contexts.

Similarity Functions
Let $s : \mathcal{C} \times \mathcal{C} \to [0, 1]$ be a function measuring the similarity between pairs of contexts on the $[0, 1]$-scale. Then let Φ be the set of functions $\phi : \mathcal{C} \to [k]$ such that the average dissimilarity

$$\frac{1}{|\mathcal{C}|^2} \sum_{c,d \in \mathcal{C}} (1 - s(c,d)) \mathbb{I}\{\phi(c) \neq \phi(d)\}$$

is below a user-tuned threshold $\theta \in (0,1)$. It is not clear anymore that we can control the regret (18.5) using some simple meta-algorithm on Exp3, but keeping the regret small is still a meaningful objective.

From Supervised Learning to Bandits with Expert Advice

Yet another option is to run your favorite supervised learning method, training on batch data to find a collection of predictors $\phi_1, \ldots, \phi_M : \mathcal{C} \to [k]$. Then we could use a bandit algorithm to compete with the best of these in an online fashion. This has the advantage that the offline training procedure can use the power of batch data and the whole army of supervised learning, without relying on potentially inaccurate evaluation methods that aim to pick the best of the pack. And why pick if one does not need to?

The possibilities are endless, but ultimately we always end up with a set of functions Φ with the goal of competing with the best of them. This suggests we should think more generally about some subset Φ of functions without considering the internal structure of Φ. In fact, once Φ has been chosen, the contexts play very little role. All we need in each round is the output of each function.

18.2.1 Bandits with Expert Advice Framework

The **bandits with expert advice** setting is a k-armed adversarial bandit, but with M experts making recommendations to the learner. At the beginning of each round, the experts announce their predictions about which actions are the most promising. For the sake of generality, the experts report a probability distribution over the actions. The interpretation is that the expert, if the decision were left to them, would choose the action for the round at random from the probability distribution it reported. As discussed before, in an adversarial setting it is natural to consider randomised algorithms, hence one should not be too surprised that the experts are also allowed to randomise. An application to an important practical problem is illustrated in Fig. 18.2.

The predictions of the M experts in round t are represented by a matrix $E^{(t)} \in [0,1]^{M \times k}$, where the mth row $E_m^{(t)}$ is a probability vector over $[m]$ representing the recommendations of expert m in round t. Since $E_m^{(t)}$ is a row vector, for a k-dimensional vector x, the expression $E_m^{(t)} x_t$ is well defined. The learner and the environment interact according to the protocol in Fig. 18.3.

The regret measures the cumulative rewards collected by the learner relative to the best expert in hindsight:

$$R_n = \mathbb{E}\left[\max_{m \in [M]} \sum_{t=1}^{n} E_m^{(t)} x_t - \sum_{t=1}^{n} X_t \right]. \tag{18.6}$$

This framework assumes the experts are oblivious in the sense that their predictions do not depend on the actions of the learner.

Figure 18.2 Prediction with expert advice. The experts, upon seeing a foot give expert advice on what socks should fit it best. If the owner of the foot is happy, the recommendation system earns a cookie!

Adversary secretly chooses rewards $x \in [0, 1]^{n \times k}$

Experts secretly choose predictions $E^{(1)}, \ldots, E^{(n)}$

For rounds $t = 1, 2, \ldots, n$:

    Learner observes predictions of all experts, $E^{(t)} \in [0, 1]^{M \times k}$.

    Learner selects a distribution $P_t \in \mathcal{P}_{k-1}$.

    Action A_t is sampled from P_t and the reward is $X_t = x_{tA_t}$.

Figure 18.3 Interaction protocol for bandits with expert advice.

18.3 Exp4

The number 4 in Exp4 is not just an increased version number, but indicates the four e's in the long name of the algorithm, which is **e**xponential weighting for **e**xploration and **e**xploitation with **e**xperts. The idea of the algorithm is very simple. Since exponential weighting worked so well in the standard bandit problem, we aim to adopt it to the problem at hand. However, since the goal is to compete with the best expert in hindsight, it is not the actions that we will score, but the experts. Exp4 thus maintains a probability distribution Q_t over experts and uses this to come up with the next action in the obvious way, by first choosing an expert M_t at random from Q_t and then following the chosen expert's advice to choose $A_t \sim E_{M_t}^{(t)}$. The reader is invited to check for themself that this is the same as sampling A_t from $P_t = Q_t E^{(t)}$ where Q_t is treated as a row vector. Once the action is chosen, one can use their favorite reward estimation procedure to estimate the rewards for all the actions, which is then used to estimate how much total reward the individual experts would have made so far. The reward estimates are then used to update Q_t using exponential weighting. The pseudocode of Exp4 is given in Algorithm 11.

The algorithm uses $O(M)$ memory and $O(M + k)$ computation per round (when sampling in two steps). Hence it is only practical when both M and k are reasonably small.

1: **Input:** n, k, M, η, γ

2: Set $Q_1 = (1/M, \ldots, 1/M) \in [0,1]^{1 \times M}$ (a row vector)

3: **for** $t = 1, \ldots, n$ **do**

4:    Receive advice $E^{(t)}$

5:    Choose the action $A_t \sim P_t$, where $P_t = Q_t E^{(t)}$

6:    Receive the reward $X_t = x_{tA_t}$

7:    Estimate the action rewards: $\hat{X}_{ti} = 1 - \frac{\mathbb{I}\{A_t = i\}}{P_{ti} + \gamma}(1 - X_t)$

8:    Propagate the rewards to the experts: $\tilde{X}_t = E^{(t)}\hat{X}_t$

9:    Update the distribution Q_t using exponential weighting:

$$Q_{t+1,i} = \frac{\exp(\eta \tilde{X}_{ti})Q_{ti}}{\sum_j \exp(\eta \tilde{X}_{tj})Q_{tj}} \quad \text{for all } i \in [M]$$

10: **end for**

Algorithm 11: Exp4.

18.4   Regret Analysis

We restrict our attention to the case when $\gamma = 0$, which is the original algorithm. The version where $\gamma > 0$ is called Exp4-IX and its analysis is left for Exercise 18.3.

THEOREM 18.1. *Let $\gamma = 0$ and $\eta = \sqrt{2\log(M)/(nk)}$, and denote by R_n the expected regret of Exp4 defined in Algorithm 11 after n rounds. Then,*

$$R_n \leq \sqrt{2nk\log(M)}. \tag{18.7}$$

After translating the notation, the proof of the following lemma can be extracted from the analysis of Exp3 in the proof of Theorem 11.2 (Exercise 18.2).

LEMMA 18.2. *For any $m^* \in [M]$, it holds that*

$$\sum_{t=1}^{n} \tilde{X}_{tm^*} - \sum_{t=1}^{n}\sum_{m=1}^{M} Q_{tm}\tilde{X}_{tm} \leq \frac{\log(M)}{\eta} + \frac{\eta}{2}\sum_{t=1}^{n}\sum_{m=1}^{M} Q_{tm}(1 - \hat{X}_{tm})^2.$$

Proof of Theorem 18.1   Let $\mathcal{F}_t = \sigma(E^{(1)}, A_1, E^{(2)}, A_2, \ldots, A_{t-1}, E^{(t)})$ and abbreviate $\mathbb{E}_t[\cdot] = \mathbb{E}[\cdot \mid \mathcal{F}_t]$. Let m^* be the index of the best-performing expert in hindsight:

$$m^* = \text{argmax}_{m \in [M]} \sum_{t=1}^{n} E_m^{(t)} x_t, \tag{18.8}$$

which is not random by the assumption that the experts are oblivious. Applying Lemma 18.2 shows that

$$\sum_{t=1}^{n} \tilde{X}_{tm^*} - \sum_{t=1}^{n}\sum_{m=1}^{M} Q_{tm}\tilde{X}_{tm} \leq \frac{\log(M)}{\eta} + \frac{\eta}{2}\sum_{t=1}^{M}\sum_{m=1}^{M} Q_{tm}(1 - \tilde{X}_{tm})^2. \tag{18.9}$$

When $\gamma = 0$ the estimator $\hat{X}_{ti}$ is unbiased so that $\mathbb{E}_t[\hat{X}_t] = x_t$ and

$$\mathbb{E}_t[\tilde{X}_t] = \mathbb{E}_t[E^{(t)}\hat{X}_t] = E^{(t)}\mathbb{E}[\hat{X}_t] = E^{(t)}x_t. \tag{18.10}$$

Taking the expectation of both sides of Eq. (18.9) and using the tower rule for conditional expectation and the fact that Q_t is $\mathcal{F}_t$-measurable leads to

$$R_n \leq \frac{\log(M)}{\eta} + \frac{\eta}{2} \sum_{t=1}^{n} \sum_{m=1}^{M} \mathbb{E}\left[Q_{tm}(1 - \tilde{X}_{tm})^2\right]. \tag{18.11}$$

Like in Chapter 11, it is more convenient to work with losses. Let $\hat{Y}_{ti} = 1 - \hat{X}_{ti}$, $y_{ti} = 1 - x_{ti}$ and $\tilde{Y}_{tm} = 1 - \tilde{X}_{tm}$. Note that $\tilde{Y}_t = E^{(t)}\hat{Y}_t$ and recall the notation $A_{ti} = \mathbb{I}\{A_t = i\}$, which means that $\hat{Y}_{ti} = \frac{A_{ti} y_{ti}}{P_{ti}}$ and

$$\mathbb{E}_t[\tilde{Y}_{tm}^2] = \mathbb{E}_t\left[\left(\frac{E^{(t)}_{mA_t} y_{tA_t}}{P_{tA_t}}\right)^2\right] = \sum_{i=1}^{k} \frac{\left(E^{(t)}_{mi} y_{ti}\right)^2}{P_{ti}} \leq \sum_{i=1}^{k} \frac{E^{(t)}_{mi}}{P_{ti}}. \tag{18.12}$$

Therefore, using the definition of P_{ti},

$$\mathbb{E}\left[\sum_{m=1}^{M} Q_{tm}(1 - \tilde{X}_{tm})^2\right] \leq \mathbb{E}\left[\sum_{m=1}^{M} Q_{tm} \sum_{i=1}^{k} \frac{E^{(t)}_{mi}}{P_{ti}}\right]$$

$$= \mathbb{E}\left[\sum_{i=1}^{k} \frac{\sum_{m=1}^{M} Q_{tm} E^{(t)}_{mi}}{P_{ti}}\right] = k.$$

Substituting into Eq. (18.11) leads to

$$R_n \leq \frac{\log(M)}{\eta} + \frac{\eta n k}{2} = \sqrt{2nk \log(M)}. \qquad \square$$

Let us see how this theorem can be applied to the contextual bandit where $\mathcal{C}$ is a finite set and Φ is the set of all functions from $\mathcal{C} \to [k]$. To each of these functions $\phi \in \Phi$, we associate an expert m with $E^{(t)}_{mi} = \mathbb{I}\{\phi(c_t) = i\}$. Then $M = k^{\mathcal{C}}$, and Theorem 18.1 says that

$$R_n \leq \sqrt{2nk|\mathcal{C}| \log(k)},$$

which is the same bound we derived using an independent copy of Exp3 for each context. More generally, if $\mathcal{C}$ is arbitrary (possibly infinite) and Φ is a finite set of functions from $\mathcal{C}$ to $[k]$, then the theorem ensures that

$$R_n \leq \sqrt{2nk \log(|\Phi|)}.$$

These results seem quite promising already, but in fact there is another improvement possible. The intuition is that learning should be easier if the experts have a high degree of agreement. One way to measure this is by

$$E_t^* = \sum_{s=1}^{t} \sum_{i=1}^{k} \max_{m \in [M]} E^{(s)}_{mi}.$$

In Exercise 18.7, you will show that if all experts make identical recommendations, then $E_t^* = t$ and that no matter how the experts behave,

$$E_n^* \leq n \min(k, M). \tag{18.13}$$

In this sense E_n^*/n can be viewed as the effective number of experts, which depends on the degree of disagreement in the expert's recommendations. By modifying the algorithm to use a time varying learning rate, one can prove the following theorem.

THEOREM 18.3. *Assume the same conditions as in Theorem 18.1, except let* $\eta_t = \sqrt{\log(M)/E_t^*}$. *Then there exists a universal constant* $C > 0$ *such that*

$$R_n \leq C\sqrt{E_n^* \log(M)}. \tag{18.14}$$

The proof of Theorem 18.3 is not hard and is left to Exercise 18.4. The bound tells us that Exp4 with the suggested learning rate is able to adapt to degree of disagreement between the experts, which seems like quite an encouraging result. As a further benefit, the learning rate does not depend on the horizon so the algorithm is anytime.

18.5 Notes

1 The most important concept in this chapter is that there are trade-offs when choosing the competitor class. A large class leads to a more meaningful definition of the regret, but also increases the regret. This is similar to what we have observed in stochastic bandits. Tuning an algorithm for a restricted environment class usually allows faster learning, but the resulting algorithms can fail when interacting with an environment that does not belong to the restricted class.

2 The Exp4 algorithm serves as a tremendous building block for other bandit problems by defining your own experts. An example is the application of Exp4 to non-stationary bandits that we explore in Chapter 31, which is one of the rare cases where Exp4 can be computed efficiently with a combinatorially large number of experts. When Exp4 does not have an efficient implementation, it often provides a good starting place to derive regret bounds without worrying about computation (for an example, see Exercise 18.5).

3 The bandits with expert advice framework is clearly more general than contextual bandits. With the terminology of the bandits with expert advice framework, the contextual bandit problem arises when the experts are given by static $\mathcal{C} \to [k]$ maps.

4 A significant challenge is that a naive implementation of Exp4 has running time $O(M + k)$ per round, which can be enormous if either M or k is large. In general there is no solution to this problem, but in some cases the computation can be reduced significantly. One situation where this is possible is when the learner has access to an **optimisation oracle** that for any context/reward sequence returns the expert that would collect the most reward in this sequence (this is equivalent to solving the offline problem Eq. (18.8)). In Chapter 30 we show how to use an offline optimisation oracle to learn efficiently in combinatorial bandit problems. The idea is to solve a randomly perturbed optimisation problem (leading to the so-called follow-the-perturbed-leader class of algorithms) and then show that the randomness in the outputs provides sufficient exploration. However, as we shall see there, these algorithms will have some extra information, which makes estimating the rewards possible.

5 In the stochastic contextual bandit problem, it is assumed that the context/reward pairs form a sequence of independent and identically distributed random variables. Let Φ be a set of functions from $\mathcal{C}$ to $[k]$ and suppose the learner has access to an optimisation oracle capable of finding

$$\operatorname{argmax}_{\phi \in \Phi} \sum_{s=1}^{t} x_{s\phi(c_s)}$$

for any sequence of reward vectors $x_1, \ldots, x_t$ and contexts $c_1, \ldots, c_t$. A simple and efficient algorithm that exploits such an oracle is based on explore-then-commit, which has $O(n^{2/3})$ regret (Exercise 18.8). There is a more sophisticated algorithm that is still polynomial-time and for which the regret is about the same as the result in Theorem 18.1 [Agarwal et al., 2014]. The algorithm computes importance-weighted estimates of the rewards in each round. These are used to estimate the regret of all the experts. Based on this, a distribution over the experts (with a small support) is computed by solving a feasibility problem. The distribution is constrained so that the importance weights will not be too large, while the regret estimates averaged over the chosen distribution will stay small. To reduce the computation cost, this distribution is updated periodically with the length of the interval between the updates exponentially growing. The significance of this result is that it reduces contextual bandits to (cost-sensitive) empirical risk minimisation (ERM), which means that any advance in solving cost-sensitive ERM problems automatically translates to bandits.

6 The development of efficient algorithms for ERM is a major topic in supervised learning. Note that ERM can be NP-hard even in simple cases like linear classification [Shalev-Shwartz and Ben-David, 2014, §8.7].

7 The bound on the regret stated in Theorem 18.3 is data dependent. Note that in adversarial bandits the data and instance are the same thing, while in stochastic bandits the instance determines the probability distributions associated with each arm and the data corresponds to samples from those distributions. In any case a data/instance-dependent bound should usually be preferred if it is tight enough to imply the worst-case optimal bounds.

8 There are many points we have not developed in detail. One is high-probability bounds, which we saw in Chapter 12 and can also be derived here. We also have not mentioned lower bounds. The degree to which the bounds are tight depends on whether or not there is additional structure in the experts. In later chapters we will see examples when the results are essentially tight, but there are also cases when they are not.

9 Theorem 18.3 is the first result where we used a time-varying learning rate. As we shall see in later chapters, time-varying learning rates are a powerful way to make online algorithms adapt to specific characteristics of the problem instance.

18.6 Bibliographic Remarks

For a good account on the history of contextual bandits, see the article by Tewari and Murphy [2017]. The Exp4 algorithm was introduced by Auer et al. [2002b], and Theorem 18.1 essentially matches theorem 7.1 of their paper (the constant in Theorem 18.1 is slightly smaller). McMahan and Streeter [2009] noticed that neither the number of experts nor the size of the action set are what really matters for the regret, but rather the extent to which the experts tend to agree. McMahan and Streeter [2009] also introduced the idea of finding the distribution to be played to be maximally 'similar' to $P_t(i)$ while ensuring sufficient exploration of each of the experts. The idea of explicitly optimising a probability distribution with these objectives in mind is at the heart of several subsequent works [e.g. Agarwal et al., 2014]. While Theorem 18.3 is inspired by this work, the result appears to be new and goes beyond the work of McMahan and Streeter [2009] because it shows that all one needs is to adapt the learning rate based on the degree of agreement amongst the experts. Neu [2015a] proves high-probability bounds for Exp4-IX. You can follow in his footsteps by solving Exercise 18.3. Another way to get high-probability bounds is to generalise Exp3.P, which was done by Beygelzimer et al. [2011]. As we mentioned in Note 5, there exist efficient algorithms for stochastic contextual bandit problems when a suitable optimisation oracle is available [Agarwal et al., 2014]. An earlier attempt to address the problem of reducing contextual bandits to cost-sensitive ERM is by Dudík et al. [2011]. The adversarial case of static experts is considered by Syrgkanis et al. [2016], who prove suboptimal (worse than $\sqrt{n}$) regret bounds under various conditions for follow-the-perturbed-leader for the transductive setting when the contexts are available at the start. The case when the contexts are independent and identically distributed, but the reward is adversarial is studied by Lazaric and Munos [2009] for the finite expert case, while Rakhlin and Sridharan [2016] considers the case when an ERM oracle is available. The paper of Rakhlin and Sridharan [2016] also considers the more realistic case when only an approximation oracle is available for the ERM problem. What is notable about this work is that they demonstrate regret bounds with a moderate blow-up, but without changing the definition of the regret. Kakade et al. [2008] consider contextual bandit problems with adversarial context-loss sequences, where all but one action suffers a loss of one in every round. This can also be seen as an instance of **multi-class classification with bandit feedback** where labels to be predicted are identified with actions and the only feedback received is whether the label predicted was correct, with the goal of making as few mistakes as possible. Since minimising the regret is in general hard in this non-convex setting, just like most of the machine learning literature on classification, Kakade et al. [2008] provide results in the form of mistake bounds for linear classifiers where the baseline is not the number of mistakes of the best linear classifier, but is a convex upper bound on it. The recent book by Shalev-Shwartz and Ben-David [2014] lists some hardness results for ERM. For a more comprehensive treatment of computation in learning theory, the reader can consult the book by Kearns and Vazirani [1994].

18.7 Exercises

18.1 Let $\mathcal{C}$ be a finite context set, and let $c_1, \ldots, c_n \in \mathcal{C}$ be an arbitrary sequence of contexts.

(a) Show that $\sum_{c \in \mathcal{C}} \sqrt{\sum_{t=1}^{n} \mathbb{I}\{c_t = c\}} \le \sqrt{n|\mathcal{C}|}$.

(b) Assume that n is an integer multiple of $|\mathcal{C}|$. Show that the choice that maximises the right-hand side of the previous inequality is the one when each context occurs $n/|\mathcal{C}|$ times.

18.2 Prove Lemma 18.2.

18.3 In this exercise you will prove an analogue of Theorem 12.1 for Exp4-IX. In the contextual setting, the random regret is

$$\hat{R}_n = \max_{m \in [M]} \sum_{t=1}^{n} \left(E_m^{(t)} x_t - X_t \right).$$

Design an algorithm that accepts a parameter $\delta \in (0, 1)$ such that

$$\mathbb{P}\left(\hat{R}_n \ge C \left(\sqrt{nk \log(m)} + \sqrt{\frac{nk}{\log(m)}} \log\left(\frac{1}{\delta}\right) \right) \right) \le \delta.$$

18.4 Prove Theorem 18.3.

HINT   The key idea is to modify the analysis of Exp3 to handle decreasing learning rates. Of course you can do this directly yourself, or you can peek ahead to Chapter 28, and specifically Exercises 28.12 and 28.13.

18.5 Let $x_1, \ldots, x_n$ be a sequence of reward vectors chosen in advance by an adversary with $x_t \in [0, 1]^k$. Furthermore, let $o_1, \ldots, o_n$ be a sequence of observations, also chosen in advance by an adversary with $o_t \in [O]$ for some fixed $O \in \mathbb{N}^+$. Then let $\mathcal{H}$ be the set of functions $\phi : [O]^m \to [k]$ where $m \in \mathbb{N}^+$. In each round the learner observes o_t and should choose an action A_t based on $o_1, A_1, X_1, \ldots, o_{t-1}, A_{t-1}, X_{t-1}, o_t$,   and   the regret is

$$R_n = \max_{\phi \in \mathcal{H}} \sum_{t=1}^{n} x_{t\phi(o_t, o_{t-1}, \ldots, o_{t-m})} - x_{tA_t},$$

where $o_t = 1$ for $t \leq 0$. This means the learner is competing with the best predictor in hindsight that uses only the last m observations. Prove there exists an algorithm such that

$$\mathbb{E}[R_n] \leq \sqrt{2knO^m \log(k)}.$$

18.6 In this problem we consider non-oblivious experts. Consider the following modified regret definition:

$$R_n' = \max_{m \in [M]} \mathbb{E}\left[\sum_{t=1}^{n} E_m^{(t)} x_t - \sum_{t=1}^{n} X_t \right].$$

Show the following:

(a) $R_n' \leq R_n$ regardless of whether the experts are oblivious or not.

(b) Theorem 18.1 remains valid for non-oblivious experts if in Eq. (18.7) we replace R_n with R_n'. In particular, explain how to modify the proof.

(c) Research question: give a non-trivial bound on R_n.

18.7 Prove Eq. (18.13).

18.8 (EXPLORE-THEN-COMMIT) Consider a stochastic contextual bandit environment where $(C_t)_{t=1}^{n}$ is a sequence of contexts sampled from distribution ξ on $\mathcal{C}$ and the rewards are $(X_t)_{t=1}^{n}$, where the conditional law of X_t given C_t and A_t is $P_{C_t A_t}$. The mean reward when choosing action $i \in [k]$ having observed context $c \in \mathcal{C}$ is $\mu(c, i) = \int x \, dP_{ci}(x)$. Let Φ be a subset of functions from $\mathcal{C}$ to $[k]$. The regret is

$$R_n = n \sup_{\phi \in \Phi} \mu(\phi) - \mathbb{E}\left[\sum_{t=1}^{n} X_t \right],$$

where $\mu(\phi) = \int \mu(c, \phi(c)) d\xi(c)$. Consider a variation of explore-then-commit, which explores uniformly at random for the first m rounds. Then define

$$\hat{\mu}(\phi) = \frac{k}{m} \sum_{t=1}^{m} \mathbb{I}\{A_t = \phi(C_t)\} X_t.$$

For rounds $t > m$, the algorithm chooses $A_t = \hat{\phi}^*(C_t)$, where

$$\hat{\phi}^* = \mathrm{argmax}_{\phi \in \Phi} \, \hat{\mu}(\phi) = \mathrm{argmax}_{\phi \in \Phi} \sum_{t=1}^{n} \hat{X}_{t\phi(C_t)},$$

where $\hat{X}_{ti} = k\mathbb{I}\{A_t = \phi(C_t)\} X_t$. When no maximiser exists you may assume that $\hat{\mu}(\hat{\phi}^*) \geq \sup_{\phi \in \Phi} \hat{\mu}(\phi) - \varepsilon$ for any $\varepsilon > 0$ of your choice. Show that when Φ is finite, then for appropriately tuned m the expected regret of this algorithms satisfies

$$R_n = O\left(n^{2/3}(k\log(|\Phi|))^{1/3}\right).$$

> This algorithm is the explore-then-commit version of the epoch-greedy algorithm by Langford and Zhang [2008]. You should not worry too much about these details, but of course $\mathcal{C}$ should be associated with a σ-algebra and the family of distributions $(P_{ca} : c \in \mathcal{C}, a \in [k])$ should be a probability kernel from $\mathcal{C} \times [k]$ to $\mathbb{R}$.

18.9 Consider a stochastic contextual bandit problem with the same set-up as the previous exercise and $k = 2$ arms. As before, let Φ be a set of functions from $\mathcal{C}$ to $[k]$. Design a policy such that

$$R_n = n\max_{\phi \in \Phi} \mu(\phi) - \mathbb{E}\left[\sum_{t=1}^{n} X_t\right] \leq C\sqrt{ndk\log\left(\frac{n}{d}\right)},$$

where $C > 0$ is a universal constant and $d = \mathrm{VC}(\Phi)$ is the VC dimension of Φ.

HINT   Use an initial period of exploration to choose a finite 'representative' subset of Φ, and then run Exp4 on this subset. The result that you need to know in connection to the VC dimension is known as Sauer's lemma, which states that if Φ has VC dimension d, then for any sequence $c = (c_i)_{i=1}^{m} \subset \mathcal{C}$, the cardinality of the set $\Phi_c = \{(\phi(c_1), \dots, \phi(c_m)) : \phi \in \Phi\}$ is at most $(em/d)^d$. You may also find it useful that an i.i.d. sequence $C_1, \dots, C_n$ is 'exchangeable': for any set $A \subset \mathcal{C}^n$ and any $\pi : [n] \to [n]$ bijection, $\mathbb{P}((C_1, \dots, C_n) \in A) = \mathbb{P}((C_{\pi(1)}, \dots, C_{\pi(n)}) \in A)$. This property helps you to argue that the finite subset of Φ obtained by choosing functions from Φ that all disagree on the first m elements on the contexts will be representative of the behaviour of functions in Φ on the rest of the contexts.

> We did not talk about VC dimension in this book. An introduction is given by Shalev-Shwartz and Ben-David [2014], or there is the classic text by Vapnik [1998]. The application to bandits is due to Beygelzimer et al. [2011].

19 Stochastic Linear Bandits

Contextual bandits generalise the finite-armed setting by allowing the learner to make use of side information. This chapter focusses on a specific type of contextual bandit problem in the stochastic set-up where the reward is assumed to have a linear structure that allows for learning to transfer from one context to another. This leads to a useful and rich model that will be the topic of the next few chapters. To begin, we describe the **stochastic linear bandit** problem and start the process of generalising the upper confidence bound algorithm.

19.1 Stochastic Contextual Bandits

The stochastic contextual bandit problem mirrors the adversarial contextual bandit set-up discussed in Chapter 18. At the beginning of round t, the learner observes a context $C_t \in \mathcal{C}$, which may be random or not. Having observed the context, the learner chooses their action $A_t \in [k]$ based on the information available. So far everything is the same as the adversarial setting. The difference comes from the assumption that the reward X_t satisfies

$$X_t = r(C_t, A_t) + \eta_t,$$

where $r : \mathcal{C} \times [k] \to \mathbb{R}$ is called the **reward function** and η_t is the noise, which we will assume is conditionally 1-subgaussian. Precisely, let

$$\mathcal{F}_t = \sigma(C_1, A_1, X_1, \ldots, C_{t-1}, A_{t-1}, X_{t-1}, C_t, A_t)$$

be the σ-field summarising the information available just before X_t is observed. Then, we assume that

$$\mathbb{E}\left[\exp(\lambda \eta_t) \mid \mathcal{F}_t\right] \leq \exp\left(\frac{\lambda^2}{2}\right) \quad \text{almost surely.}$$

The noise could have been chosen to be σ-subgaussian for any known σ^2, but like in earlier chapters, we save ourselves some ink by fixing its value to $\sigma^2 = 1$. Remember from Chapter 5 that subgaussian random variables have zero mean, so the assumption also implies that $\mathbb{E}[\eta_t \mid \mathcal{F}_t] = 0$ and $\mathbb{E}[X_t \mid \mathcal{F}_t] = r(C_t, A_t)$.

If $\mathcal{F} \subset \mathcal{G}$ are σ-algebras, and $\mathbb{E}[\exp(\lambda \eta) \mid \mathcal{G}] \leq \exp(\lambda^2/2)$ almost surely, then by the tower rule, $\mathbb{E}[\exp(\lambda \eta) \mid \mathcal{F}] \leq \exp(\lambda^2/2)$ almost surely. Hence, the condition that η_t is subgaussian with respect to $\mathcal{F}_t$ can be 'relaxed' to the condition that it be subgaussian with respect to any σ-algebra containing $\mathcal{F}_t$.

If r was given, then the action in round t with the largest expected return is $A_t^* \in$ $\operatorname{argmax}_{a \in [k]} r(C_t, a)$. Notice that this action is now a random variable because it depends on the context C_t. The loss due to the lack of knowledge of r makes the learner incur the (expected) regret

$$R_n = \mathbb{E}\left[\sum_{t=1}^n \max_{a \in [k]} r(C_t, a) - \sum_{t=1}^n X_t\right].$$

Like in the adversarial setting, there is one big caveat in this definition of the regret. Since we did not make any restrictions on how the contexts are chosen, it could be that choosing a low-rewarding action in the first round might change the contexts observed in subsequent rounds. Then the learner could potentially achieve an even higher cumulative reward by choosing a 'suboptimal' arm initially. As a consequence, this definition of the regret is most meaningful when the actions of the learner do not (greatly) affect subsequent contexts.

One way to eventually learn an optimal policy is to estimate $r(c, a)$ for each $(c, a) \in C \times [k]$ pair. As in the adversarial setting, this is ineffective when the number of context-action pairs is large. In particular, the worst-case regret over all possible contextual problems with M contexts and mean reward in $[0, 1]$ is at least $\Omega(\sqrt{nMk})$. While this may not look bad, M is often astronomical (for example, 2^{100}). The argument that gives rise to the mentioned lower bound relies on designing a problem where knowledge of $r(c, \cdot)$ for context c provides no useful information about $r(c', \cdot)$ for some different context c'. Fortunately, in most interesting applications, the set of contexts is highly structured, which is often captured by the fact that $r(\cdot, \cdot)$ changes 'smoothly' as a function of its arguments.

A simple, yet interesting assumption to capture further information about the dependence of rewards on context is to assume that the learner has access to a map $\psi : C \times [k] \to \mathbb{R}^d$, and for an unknown parameter vector $\theta_* \in \mathbb{R}^d$, it holds that

$$r(c, a) = \langle \theta_*, \psi(c, a) \rangle, \qquad \text{for all } (c, a) \in C \times [k]. \tag{19.1}$$

The map ψ is called a **feature map**, which is the standard nomenclature in machine learning. The idea of feature maps is best illustrated with an example. Suppose the context denotes the visitor of a website selling books, the actions are books to recommend and the reward is the revenue on a book sold. The features could indicate the interests of the visitors as well as the domain and topic of the book. If the visitors and books are assigned to finitely many categories, indicator variables of all possible combinations of these categories could be used to create the feature map. Of course, many other possibilities exist. For example, you can train a neural network (deep or not) on historical data to predict the revenue and use the nonlinear map that we obtained by removing the last layer of the neural network. The subspace Ψ spanned by the **feature vectors** $\{\psi(c, a)\}_{c,a}$ in $\mathbb{R}^d$ is called the **feature space**.

If $\|\cdot\|$ is a norm on $\mathbb{R}^d$ then, an assumption on $\|\theta_*\|$ implies **smoothness** of r. In particular, from Hölder's inequality,

$$|r(c, a) - r(c', a')| \le \|\theta_*\| \|\psi(c, a) - \psi(c', a')\|_*,$$

where $\|\cdot\|_*$ denotes the dual of $\|\cdot\|$. Restrictions on $\|\theta_*\|$ have a similar effect to assuming that the dimensionality d is finite. In fact, one may push this to the extreme and allow d to be infinite, an approach that can buy tremendous flexibility and makes the linearity assumption less limiting.

19.2 Stochastic Linear Bandits

Stochastic linear bandits arise from realising that under Eq. (19.1), all that matters is the feature vector that results from choosing a given action and not the 'identity' of the action itself. This justifies studying the following simplified model: in round t, the learner is given the decision set $\mathcal{A}_t \subset \mathbb{R}^d$, from which it chooses an action $A_t \in \mathcal{A}_t$ and receives reward

$$X_t = \langle \theta_*, A_t \rangle + \eta_t,$$

where η_t is 1-subgaussian given $\mathcal{A}_1, A_1, X_1, \ldots, \mathcal{A}_{t-1}, A_{t-1}, X_{t-1}, \mathcal{A}_t$ and A_t. The random (pseudo-)regret and regret are defined by

$$\hat{R}_n = \sum_{t=1}^{n} \max_{a \in \mathcal{A}_t} \langle \theta_*, a - A_t \rangle,$$

$$R_n = \mathbb{E}\left[\hat{R}_n\right] = \mathbb{E}\left[\sum_{t=1}^{n} \max_{a \in \mathcal{A}_t} \langle \theta_*, a \rangle - \sum_{t=1}^{n} X_t\right],$$

respectively. Different choices of $\mathcal{A}_t$ lead to different settings, some of which we have seen before. For example, if $(e_i)_i$ are the unit vectors and $\mathcal{A}_t = \{e_1, \ldots, e_d\}$, then the resulting stochastic linear bandit problem reduces to the finite-armed setting. On the other hand, if $\mathcal{A}_t = \{\psi(C_t, i) : i \in [k]\}$, then we have a **contextual linear bandit**. Yet another possibility is a **combinatorial action set** $\mathcal{A}_t \subseteq \{0, 1\}^d$. Many combinatorial problems (such as matching, least-cost problems in directed graphs and choosing spanning trees) can be written as linear optimisation problems over some combinatorial set $\mathcal{A}$ obtained from considering incidence vectors often associated with some graph. Some of these topics will be covered later in Chapter 30.

As we have seen in earlier chapters, the UCB algorithm is an attractive approach for finite-action stochastic bandits. Its best variants are nearly minimax optimal, instance optimal and exactly optimal asymptotically. With these merits in mind, it seems quite natural to try and generalise the idea to the linear setting.

The generalisation is based on the view that UCB implements the 'optimism in the face of uncertainty' principle, which is to act in each round as if the environment is as nice as plausibly possible. In finite-action stochastic bandits, this means choosing the action with the largest upper confidence bound. In the case of linear bandits, the idea remains the same, but the form of the confidence bound is more complicated because rewards received yield information about more than just the arm played.

The first step is to construct a confidence set $\mathcal{C}_t \subset \mathbb{R}^d$ based on $(A_1, X_1, \ldots, A_{t-1}, X_{t-1})$ that contains the unknown parameter vector θ_* with high probability. Leaving the details of how the confidence set is constructed aside for a moment, and assuming that the confidence set indeed contains θ_*, for any given action $a \in \mathbb{R}^d$, let

$$\text{UCB}_t(a) = \max_{\theta \in \mathcal{C}_t} \langle \theta, a \rangle \tag{19.2}$$

be an upper bound on the mean pay-off $\langle \theta_*, a \rangle$ of a. The UCB algorithm that uses the confidence set C_t at time t then selects

$$A_t = \text{argmax}_{a \in A_t} \text{UCB}_t(a). \tag{19.3}$$

UCB applied to linear bandits is known by various names, including LinRel (**lin**ear **re**inforcement **l**earning), LinUCB and OFUL (**o**ptimism in the **f**ace of **u**ncertainty for **l**inear bandits). We will not be very dogmatic of this name and call algorithms with the above construct instances of LinUCB.

The main question is how to choose the confidence set $C_t \subset \mathbb{R}^d$. As usual, there are conflicting desirable properties:

(a) C_t should contain θ_* with high probability.
(b) C_t should be as small as possible.

At first sight it is not at all obvious what C_t should look like. After all, it is a subset of $\mathbb{R}^d$, not just an interval like the confidence intervals about the empirical estimate of the mean reward for a single action that we saw in the previous chapters. While we specify the analytic form of a possible construction for C_t here, there are some details in choosing some of the parameters in this construction. As they are both delicate and important, we dedicate the next chapter to discussing them.

Following the idea for UCB, we need an analogue for the empirical estimate of the unknown quantity, which in this case is θ_*. There are several principles one might use for deriving such an estimate. For now we use the **regularised least-squares estimator**, which is

$$\hat{\theta}_t = \text{argmin}_{\theta \in \mathbb{R}^d} \left(\sum_{s=1}^{t} (X_s - \langle \theta, A_s \rangle)^2 + \lambda \|\theta\|_2^2 \right), \tag{19.4}$$

where $\lambda \geq 0$ is called the **penalty factor**. Choosing $\lambda > 0$ helps because it ensures that the loss function has a unique minimiser even when $A_1, \ldots, A_t$ do not span $\mathbb{R}^d$, which simplifies the math. The solution to Eq. (19.4) is obtained easily by differentiation and is

$$\hat{\theta}_t = V_t^{-1} \sum_{s=1}^{t} A_s X_s, \tag{19.5}$$

where $(V_t)_t$ are $d \times d$ matrices given by

$$V_0 = \lambda I \quad \text{and} \quad V_t = V_0 + \sum_{s=1}^{t} A_s A_s^\top. \tag{19.6}$$

So $\hat{\theta}_t$ is an estimate of θ_*, which makes it natural to choose C_t to be centered at $\hat{\theta}_{t-1}$. For what follows, we will simply assume that the confidence set C_t is closed and satisfies

$$C_t \subseteq \mathcal{E}_t = \left\{ \theta \in \mathbb{R}^d : \|\theta - \hat{\theta}_{t-1}\|_{V_{t-1}}^2 \leq \beta_t \right\}, \tag{19.7}$$

where $(\beta_t)_t$ is an increasing sequence of constants with $\beta_1 \geq 1$. The set $\mathcal{E}_t$ is an ellipsoid centred at $\hat{\theta}_{t-1}$ and with principle axis being the eigenvectors of V_t with corresponding lengths being the reciprocal of the eigenvalues. Notice that as t grows, the matrix V_t has increasing eigenvalues, which means the volume of the ellipse is also shrinking (at least, provided β_t does not grow too fast). As noted beforehand, the next chapter will be devoted to show that $C_t = \mathcal{E}_t$ is a natural choice for carefully chosen β_t. In the rest of this chapter, we simply examine the consequence of using a confidence set satisfying Eq. (19.7) and assume all the desirable properties.

 The impatient reader who is puzzled of the form $\mathcal{E}_t$ may briefly think of the case when $\eta_s \sim \mathcal{N}(0, \sigma^2)$, $A_1, \ldots, A_{t-1}$ are deterministic and span $\mathbb{R}^d$ so that we can take $\lambda = 0$. In this case, one easily computes that with $V = V_{t-1}$, $Z = V^{1/2}(\hat{\theta}_{t-1} - \theta_*) \sim \mathcal{N}(0, I)$, or that $\|Z\|^2$ is the sum of d, independent standard normal random variables, and thus it follows the χ^2-distribution (with d degrees of freedom), from which one can find the appropriate value of β_{t-1}. As we shall see, the expression one can get from this calculation, will, more or less, be still correct in the general case.

19.3 Regret Analysis

We prove a regret bound for LinUCB under the assumption that the confidence intervals indeed contain the true parameter with high probability and boundedness conditions on the action set and rewards.

ASSUMPTION 19.1. The following hold:

(a) $1 \leq \beta_1 \leq \beta_2 \leq \ldots \beta_n$.
(b) $\max_{t \in [n]} \sup_{a,b \in A_t} \langle \theta_*, a - b \rangle \leq 1$.
(c) $\|a\|_2 \leq L$ for all $a \in \bigcup_{t=1}^n A_t$.
(d) There exists a $\delta \in (0, 1)$ such that with probability $1 - \delta$, for all $t \in [n]$, $\theta_* \in C_t$ where C_t satisfies Eq. (19.7).

THEOREM 19.2. *Under the conditions of Assumption 19.1 with probability $1 - \delta$, the regret of LinUCB satisfies*

$$\hat{R}_n \leq \sqrt{8n\beta_n \log\left(\frac{\det V_n}{\det V_0}\right)} \leq \sqrt{8dn\beta_n \log\left(\frac{d\lambda + nL^2}{d\lambda}\right)}.$$

Theorem 20.5 in the next chapter shows that β_n may be chosen to be

$$\sqrt{\beta_n} = \sqrt{\lambda} m_2 + \sqrt{2 \log\left(\frac{1}{\delta}\right) + d \log\left(\frac{d\lambda + nL^2}{d\lambda}\right)}, \tag{19.8}$$

where m_2 is an upper bound on $\|\theta_*\|_2$. By choosing $\delta = 1/n$, we obtain the following corollary bounding the expected regret.

COROLLARY 19.3. *Under the conditions of Assumption 19.1, the expected regret of LinUCB with $\delta = 1/n$ is bounded by*

$$R_n \leq Cd\sqrt{n} \log(nL),$$

where $C > 0$ is a suitably large universal constant.

The proof of Theorem 19.2 depends on the following lemma, often called the elliptical potential lemma.

LEMMA 19.4. *Let $V_0 \in \mathbb{R}^{d \times d}$ be positive definite and $a_1, \ldots, a_n \in \mathbb{R}^d$ be a sequence of vectors with $\|a_t\|_2 \leq L < \infty$ for all $t \in [n]$, $V_t = V_0 + \sum_{s \leq t} a_s a_s^\top$. Then,*

$$\sum_{t=1}^{n} \left(1 \wedge \|a_t\|_{V_{t-1}^{-1}}^2 \right) \leq 2 \log \left(\frac{\det V_n}{\det V_0} \right) \leq 2d \log \left(\frac{\operatorname{trace} V_0 + nL^2}{d \det(V_0)^{1/d}} \right).$$

Proof Using that for any $u \geq 0$, $u \wedge 1 \leq 2 \ln(1 + u)$, we get

$$\sum_{t=1}^{n} \left(1 \wedge \|a_t\|_{V_{t-1}^{-1}}^2 \right) \leq 2 \sum_{t} \log \left(1 + \|a_t\|_{V_{t-1}^{-1}}^2 \right).$$

We now argue that this last expression is $\log \left(\frac{\det V_n}{\det V_0} \right)$. For $t \geq 1$, we have

$$V_t = V_{t-1} + a_t a_t^\top = V_{t-1}^{1/2} (I + V_{t-1}^{-1/2} a_t a_t^\top V_{t-1}^{-1/2}) V_{t-1}^{1/2}.$$

Now, since the determinant is a multiplicative map,

$$\det(V_t) = \det(V_{t-1}) \det \left(I + V_{t-1}^{-1/2} a_t a_t^\top V_{t-1}^{-1/2} \right) = \det(V_{t-1}) \left(1 + \|a_t\|_{V_{t-1}^{-1}}^2 \right),$$

where the second equality follows because the matrix $I + yy^\top$ has eigenvalues $1 + \|y\|_2^2$ and 1 as well as the fact that the determinant of a matrix is the product of its eigenvalues. Putting things together, we see that

$$\det(V_n) = \det(V_0) \prod_{t=1}^{n} \left(1 + \|a_t\|_{V_{t-1}^{-1}}^2 \right), \tag{19.9}$$

which is equivalent to the first inequality that we wanted to prove. To get the second inequality, note that by the inequality of arithmetic and geometric means,

$$\det(V_n) = \prod_{i=1}^{d} \lambda_i \leq \left(\frac{1}{d} \operatorname{trace} V_n \right)^d \leq \left(\frac{\operatorname{trace} V_0 + nL^2}{d} \right)^d,$$

where $\lambda_1, \ldots, \lambda_d$ are the eigenvalues of V_n. $\square$

Proof of Theorem 19.2   By part (d) of Assumption 19.1, it suffices to prove the bound on the event that $\theta_* \in \mathcal{C}_t$ for all rounds $t \in [n]$. Let $A_t^* = \operatorname{argmax}_{a \in \mathcal{A}_t} \langle \theta_*, a \rangle$ be an optimal action for round t and r_t be the instantaneous regret in round t defined by

$$r_t = \langle \theta_*, A_t^* - A_t \rangle.$$

Let $\tilde{\theta}_t \in \mathcal{C}_t$ be the parameter in the confidence set for which $\langle \tilde{\theta}_t, A_t \rangle = \operatorname{UCB}_t(A_t)$. Then, using the fact that $\theta_* \in \mathcal{C}_t$ and the definition of the algorithm leads to

$$\langle \theta_*, A_t^* \rangle \leq \operatorname{UCB}_t(A_t^*) \leq \operatorname{UCB}_t(A_t) = \langle \tilde{\theta}_t, A_t \rangle.$$

Using Cauchy–Schwarz inequality and the assumption that $\theta_* \in C_t$ and facts that $\tilde{\theta}_t \in C_t$ and $C_t \subseteq \mathcal{E}_t$ leads to

$$r_t = \langle \theta_*, A_t^* - A_t \rangle \leq \langle \tilde{\theta}_t - \theta_*, A_t \rangle \leq \|A_t\|_{V_{t-1}^{-1}} \|\tilde{\theta}_t - \theta_*\|_{V_{t-1}}$$

$$\leq 2\|A_t\|_{V_{t-1}^{-1}} \sqrt{\beta_t}. \tag{19.10}$$

By part (b) we also have $r_t \leq 2$, which, combined with $\beta_n \geq \max\{1, \beta_t\}$, yields

$$r_t \leq 2 \wedge 2\sqrt{\beta_t}\|A_t\|_{V_{t-1}^{-1}} \leq 2\sqrt{\beta_n}\left(1 \wedge \|A_t\|_{V_{t-1}^{-1}}\right).$$

Then, by Cauchy–Schwarz inequality,

$$\hat{R}_n = \sum_{t=1}^{n} r_t \leq \sqrt{n \sum_{t=1}^{n} r_t^2} \leq 2\sqrt{n\beta_n \sum_{t=1}^{n}\left(1 \wedge \|A_t\|_{V_{t-1}^{-1}}^2\right)}. \tag{19.11}$$

The result is completed using Lemma 19.4, which depends on part (c) of Assumption 19.1. □

19.3.1 Computation

An obvious question is whether or not the optimisation problem in Eq. (19.3) can be solved efficiently. First note that the computation of A_t can also be written as

$$(A_t, \tilde{\theta}_t) = \operatorname{argmax}_{(a,\theta) \in \mathcal{A}_t \times C_t} \langle \theta, a \rangle. \tag{19.12}$$

This is a bilinear optimisation problem over the set $\mathcal{A}_t \times C_t$. In general, not much can be said about the computational efficiency of solving this problem. There are two notable special cases, however.

(a) Suppose that $a(\theta) = \operatorname{argmax}_{a \in \mathcal{A}_t} \langle \theta, a \rangle$ can be computed efficiently for any θ and that $C_t = \operatorname{co}(\phi_1, \ldots, \phi_m)$ is the convex hull of a finite set. Then A_t can be computed by finding $a(\phi_1), \ldots, a(\phi_m)$ and choosing $A_t = a(\phi_i)$, where i maximises $\langle \phi_i, a(\phi_i) \rangle$.

(b) Assume that $C_t = \mathcal{E}_t$ is the ellipsoid given in Eq. (19.7) and $\mathcal{A}_t$ is a small finite set. Then the action A_t from Eq. (19.12) can be found using

$$A_t = \operatorname{argmax}_{a \in \mathcal{A}_t} \langle \hat{\theta}_{t-1}, a \rangle + \sqrt{\beta_t}\|a\|_{V_{t-1}^{-1}}, \tag{19.13}$$

which may be solved by simply iterating over the arms and calculating the term inside the argmax. Further implementation issues are explored in Exercise 19.8.

19.4 Notes

1 It was mentioned that ψ may map its arguments to an infinite dimensional space. There are several issues that arise in this setting. The first is whether or not the algorithm can be computed efficiently. This is usually tackled via the **kernel trick**, which assumes the existence of an efficiently computable **kernel function** $\kappa : (C \times [k]) \times (C \times [k]) \to \mathbb{R}$ such that

$$\langle \psi(c, a), \psi(c', a') \rangle = \kappa((c, a), (c', a')).$$

The trick is to rewrite all computations in terms of the kernel function so that $\psi(c, a)$ is neither computed, nor stored. The second issue is that the claim made in Theorem 19.2 depends on the dimension d and becomes vacuous when d is large or infinite. This dependence arises from Lemma 19.4. It is possible to modify this result by replacing d with a data-dependent quantity that measures the 'effective dimension' of the image of the data under ϕ. The final challenge is to define an appropriate confidence set. See the bibliographic remarks for further details and references.

2 The bound given in Theorem 19.2 is essentially a worst-case style of bound, with little dependence on the parameter θ_* or the geometry of the action set. Instance-dependent bounds for linear bandits are still an open topic of research, and the asymptotics are only understood in the special case where the action set is finite and unchanging (Chapter 25).

3 Theorem 20.5 in the next chapter shows that $(\beta_t)_{t=1}^n$ as defined in Eq. (19.8) can be replaced with a data-dependent quantity that is strictly smaller:

$$\beta_t^{1/2} = m_2\sqrt{\lambda} + \sqrt{2\log\left(\frac{1}{\delta}\right) + \log\left(\frac{\det(V_{t-1})}{\lambda^d}\right)}. \tag{19.14}$$

Empirically this choice is never worse than the value suggested in Eq. (19.8) and sometimes better, typically by a modest amount.

4 The application of Cauchy–Schwarz in Eq. (19.11) often loses a logarithm, as it does, for example, when $r_t = \sqrt{1/t}$. Recently, however, a lower bound for contextual linear bandits has been derived by constructing a sequence for which this Cauchy–Schwarz is tight, as well as Lemma 19.4 [Li et al., 2019b].

5 In the worst case, the bound in Theorem 19.2 is tight up to logarithmic factors. More details are in Chapter 24, which is devoted to lower bounds for stochastic linear bandits. The environments for which the lower bound nearly matches the upper bound have action sets that are either infinite or exponentially large in the dimension. When $|\mathcal{A}_t| \le k$ for all rounds t, there are algorithms for which the regret is

$$R_n = O\left(\sqrt{dn\log^3(nk)}\right).$$

The special case where the action set does not change with time is treated in Chapter 22, where references to the literature are also provided.

6 The calculation in Eq. (19.13) shows that LinUCB has more than just a passing resemblance to the UCB algorithm introduced in Chapter 7. The term $\langle\hat{\theta}_{t-1}, a\rangle$ may be interpreted as an empirical estimate of the reward from choosing action a, and $\sqrt{\beta_t}\|a\|_{V_{t-1}^{-1}}$ is a bonus term that ensures sufficient exploration. If the penalty term vanishes ($\lambda = 0$) and $\mathcal{A}_t = \{e_1, \ldots, e_d\}$ for all $t \in [n]$, then $\hat{\theta}_i$ becomes the empirical mean of action e_i, and the matrix V_t is diagonal, with its ith diagonal entry being the number of times action e_i is used up to and including round t. Then the bonus term has order

$$\sqrt{\beta_t}\|e_i\|_{V_{t-1}^{-1}} = \sqrt{\frac{\beta_t}{T_i(t-1)}},$$

where $T_i(t-1)$ is the number of times action e_i has been chosen before the tth round. So UCB for finite-armed bandits is recovered by choosing $\beta_t = 2\log(\cdot)$, where the term inside the logarithm can be chosen in a variety of ways as discussed in earlier chapters. Notice now that the simple analysis given in this chapter leads to a regret bound of $O(\sqrt{dn\log(\cdot)})$, which is quite close to the highly specialised analysis given in Chapters 7 to 9. Note however that the dimension-free choice of β_t does not satisfy Eq. (19.7), but this happens to be unnecessary for the proof of Theorem 19.2 to go through.

7 An extension of considerably interest of the linear model is the **generalised linear model** where the reward is

$$X_t = \mu(\langle \theta_*, A_t \rangle) + \eta_t, \tag{19.15}$$

where $\mu^{-1} : \mathbb{R} \to \mathbb{R}$ is called the **link function**. A common choice is the sigmoid function: $\mu(x) = 1/(1+\exp(-x))$ Bandits with rewards from a generalised linear model have been studied by Filippi et al. [2010], who prove a bound with a similar form as Theorem 19.2. Unfortunately, however, the bound depends in a slightly unpleasant manner on the form of the link function, and it seems there may be significant room for improvement. You will analyse and algorithm for generalised linear bandits in Exercise 19.6.

8 Beyond optimism, there are at least three other principles for constructing algorithms for stochastic linear bandits. The first is Thompson sampling, which is a randomised Bayesian algorithm discussed at length in Chapter 36. The second is a class of algorithms designed to achieve asymptotic optimality in the special cases where the action set is fixed, or sampled i.i.d. from a fixed distribution with finite support. These algorithms are fall into the class of 'optimisation-based' algorithms that estimate the unknown parameter and then solve an optimisation problem to determine an optimal allocation over the actions [Lattimore and Szepesvári, 2017, Ok et al., 2018, Combes et al., 2017, Hao et al., 2020]. A downside of optimisation-based approaches is that so far the results have a very asymptotic nature and the algorithms are not very practical. These ideas are discussed a little more in Chapter 25, where we prove asymptotic lower bounds for linear bandits. The third design principle is called information-directed sampling, which has a Bayesian version [Russo and Van Roy, 2014a] and frequentist analogue [Kirschner and Krause, 2018]. In rough terms, these algorithms choose a distribution over actions that minimises the ratio of a squared expected instantaneous regret and the information gain about the optimal action, which in the frequentist version is replaced by a potential function that mimics the information gain.

19.5 Bibliographic Remarks

Stochastic linear bandits were introduced by Abe and Long [1999]. The first paper to consider algorithms based on the optimism principle for linear bandits is by Auer [2002], who considered the case when the number of actions is finite. The core ideas of the analysis of optimistic algorithms (and more) is already present in this paper. An algorithm based on confidence ellipsoids is described in the papers by Dani et al. [2008], Rusmevichientong and Tsitsiklis [2010] and Abbasi-Yadkori et al. [2011]. The regret analysis presented here, and the discussion of the computational questions, is largely based on the former of these works, which also stresses that an expected regret of $\tilde{O}(d\sqrt{n})$ can be achieved regardless of the shape of the decision sets $\mathcal{A}_t$ as long as the means are guaranteed to lie in a bounded interval. Rusmevichientong and Tsitsiklis [2010] consider both optimistic and explore-then-commit strategies, which they call 'phased exploration and greedy exploitation' (PEGE). They focus on the case where $\mathcal{A}_t$ is the unit ball or some other compact set with a smooth boundary and show that PEGE is optimal up to logarithmic factors. The observation that explore-then-commit works for the unit ball (and other action sets with a smooth boundary) was independently made by Abbasi-Yadkori et al. [2009], further expanded in [Abbasi-Yadkori, 2009a]. Generalised linear models are credited to Nelder and Wedderburn [1972]. We mentioned already that LinUCB was generalised to this model by Filippi et al. [2010]. A more computationally efficient algorithm has recently been proposed by Jun et al. [2017]. Nonlinear structured bandits where the pay-off function belongs to a known set have also been studied [Anantharam et al., 1987, Russo and Van Roy, 2013, Lattimore and Munos, 2014]. Kernelised versions of UCB have been given by Srinivas et al. [2010], Abbasi-Yadkori [2012] and Valko et al. [2013b]. We mentioned early in the chapter that making assumptions on the norm θ_* is related to smoothness of the reward function with smoother functions leading to stronger guarantees. For an example of where this is done, see the paper on 'spectral bandits' by Valko et al. [2014] and Exercise 19.7.

19.6   Exercises

19.1 (LEAST-SQUARES SOLUTION) Prove that the solution given in Eq. (19.5) is indeed the minimiser of Eq. (19.4).

19.2 (ACTION SELECTION WITH ELLIPSOIDAL CONFIDENCE SETS) Show that the action selection in LinUCB can indeed be done as shown in Eq. (19.13) when $\mathcal{C}_t = \mathcal{E}_t$ is an ellipsoid given in Eq. (19.7).

19.3 (ELLIPTICAL POTENTIALS: YOU CANNOT HAVE MORE THAN $O(d)$ BIG INTERVALS) Let $V_0 = \lambda I$ and $a_1, \ldots, a_n \in \mathbb{R}^d$ be a sequence of vectors with $\|a_t\|_2 \leq L$ for all $t \in [n]$. Then let $V_t = V_0 + \sum_{s=1}^{t} a_s a_s^\top$ and show that the number of times $\|a_t\|_{V_{t-1}^{-1}} \geq 1$ is at most

$$\frac{3d}{\log(2)} \log\left(1 + \frac{L^2}{\lambda \log(2)}\right).$$

The proof of Theorem 19.2 depended on part (b) of Assumption 19.1, which asserts that the mean rewards are bounded by one. Suppose we replace this assumption with the relaxation that there exists a $B > 0$ such that

$$\max_{t \in [n]} \sup_{a, b \in \mathcal{A}_t} \langle \theta_*, a - b \rangle \leq B.$$

Then, Exercise 19.3 allows you to bound the number of rounds when $\|x_t\|_{V_{t-1}^{-1}} \geq 1$, and in these rounds the naive bound of $r_t \leq B$ is used. For the remaining rounds, the analysis of Theorem 19.2 goes through unaltered. As a consequence we see that the dependence on B is an additive constant term that does not grow with the horizon.

19.4 (COMPUTATION COST SAVINGS WITH FIXED LARGE ACTION SET) When the action set $\mathcal{A}_t = \mathcal{A}$ is fixed and $|\mathcal{A}| = k$, the total computation cost of LinUCB after n rounds is $O(kd^2n)$ in n rounds if the advice on implementation of Exercise 19.8 is used. This can be reduced to $O(k\log(n) + d^2n)$ with almost no increase of the regret, a significant reduction when $k \gg d^2$. For this, LinUCB should be modified to work in phases, where in a given fixed it uses the same action computed in the usual way at the beginning of the phase. A phase ends when $\log \det V_t(\lambda)$ increases by $\log(1 + \varepsilon)$.

(a) Prove that if $0 \prec B \preceq A$ then $\sup_{x \neq 0} \frac{\|x\|_A^2}{\|x\|_B^2} \leq \frac{\det A}{\det B}$.

(b) Let Assumption 19.1 hold. Let $\hat{R}_n(\beta_n)$ be the regret bound of LinUCB stated Theorem 19.2. Show that with probability $1 - \delta$ the random pseudo-regret $\hat{R}_n$ of the phased version of LinUCB, as described above, satisfies $\hat{R}_n \leq \hat{R}_n((1 + \varepsilon)\beta_n)$.

19.5 (LIPSCHITZ REWARD FUNCTIONS) Consider the k-armed stochastic contextual setting of Section 19.1, and assume that $\mathcal{C} = [0, 1]$ and that the reward functions $r(\cdot, i) : \mathcal{C} \to [0, 1]$ are L-

Lipschitz:

$$|r(x, i) - r(y, i)| \leq L|x - y| \quad \text{for all } x, y \in [0, 1], i \in [k].$$

(a) Construct an algorithm whose regret R_n after n rounds is $O((Lk \log k)^{1/3} n^{2/3})$.

(b) Show that the minimax optimal regret is of the order $\Omega((Lk)^{1/3} n^{2/3})$.

(c) Generalise the result to the case when $\mathcal{C} = [0, 1]^d$ and in the definition of Lipschitzness we use the Euclidean norm. Show the dependence on the dimension in the lower and upper bounds. Discuss the influence of the choice of the norm.

HINT   Consider discretising $\mathcal{C}$. Alternatively, use Exp4.

This exercise is inspired by the work of Perchet and Rigollet [2013], who focus on improving the regret bound by adaptive discretisation when a certain margin condition holds. There are many variations of the problem of the previous exercise. For starters, the domain of contexts could be more general: one may consider higher-order smoothness, continuous action and context spaces. What is the role of the context distribution? In some applications, the context distribution can be estimated for free, in which case you might assume the context distribution is known. How to take a known context distribution into account? To whet your appetite, if the context distribution is concentrated on a handful of contexts, the discretisation should respect which contexts the distribution is concentrated on. Instead of discretisation, one may also consider function approximation. An interesting approach that goes beyond discretisation is by Combes et al. [2017] (see also Magureanu et al. 2014). The approach in these papers is to derive an asymptotic, instance-dependent lower bound, which is then used to guide the algorithm (much like the track-and-stop algorithm in Section 33.2). An open problem is to design algorithms that are simultaneously near minimax optimal and asymptotically optimal. As described in Part II, this problem is now settled for finite-armed stochastic bandits, the only case where we can say this in the whole literature of bandits.

19.6 (GENERALISED LINEAR BANDITS) In this exercise you will design and analyse an algorithm for the generalised linear bandit problem mentioned in Note 7. Let Θ be a convex compact subset of $\mathbb{R}^d$ and assume that $\theta_* \in \Theta$. The only difference relative to the standard model is that the reward is

$$X_t = \mu(\langle \theta_*, A_t \rangle) + \eta_t,$$

where $\mu : \mathbb{R} \to \mathbb{R}$ is a continuously differentiable function such that

$$c_1 = \min \left(1, \min_{a \in \cup_{t=1}^n \mathcal{A}_t} \min_{\theta \in \Theta} \mu'(\langle \theta, a \rangle) \right) > 0 \quad \text{and}$$

$$c_2 = \max \left(1, \max_{a \in \cup_{t=1}^n \mathcal{A}_t} \max_{\theta \in \Theta} \mu'(\langle \theta, a \rangle) \right) < \infty.$$

That $c_1 > 0$ is assumed implies that μ is increasing on the relevant area of its domain. Like in the standard model, for each $t \geq 1$, η_t is 1-subgaussian given $A_1, X_1, \ldots, A_{t-1}, X_{t-1}, A_t$, and you may as well assume that rewards and feature vectors are bounded:

$$\max_{a, b \in \cup_{t=1}^n \mathcal{A}_t} \mu(\langle \theta_*, a \rangle) - \mu(\langle \theta_*, b \rangle) \leq 1 \quad \text{and} \quad \max_{a \in \cup_{t=1}^n \mathcal{A}_t} \|a\|_2 \leq L \quad \text{and} \quad \|\theta_*\|_2 \leq m_2.$$

Recall that λ is the regularisation parameter in the definition of V_t (see Eq. (19.6)) and let

$$g_t(\theta) = \lambda\theta + \sum_{s=1}^{t} \mu(\langle\theta, A_s\rangle)A_s, \qquad L_t(\theta) = \left\| g_t(\theta) - \sum_{s=1}^{t} X_s A_s \right\|_{V_t^{-1}}.$$

(a) Let β_t be as in Eq. (19.8) and define a confidence set C_t by

$$C_t = \left\{ \theta \in \Theta : L_{t-1}(\theta) \leq \beta_{t-1}^{1/2} \right\}.$$

Show that $\theta_* \in C_t$ for all t with probability at least $1 - \delta$.

(b) Prove that for all $\theta, \theta' \in \Theta$, $c_1\|\theta - \theta'\|_{V_t} \leq \|g_t(\theta) - g_t(\theta')\|_{V_t^{-1}}$.

(c) Consider the algorithm that chooses

$$A_t = \operatorname{argmax}_{a \in A_t} \max_{\theta \in C_t} \mu(\langle\theta, a\rangle).$$

Prove that on the event that $\theta_* \in C_t$, for $A_t^* = \operatorname{argmax}_{a \in A_t} \mu(\langle\theta_*, a\rangle)$,

$$r_t = \mu(\langle\theta_*, A_t^*\rangle) - \mu(\langle\theta_*, A_t\rangle) \leq \frac{2c_2\beta_{t-1}^{1/2}}{c_1} \|A_t\|_{V_{t-1}^{-1}}.$$

(d) Prove that with probability at least $1 - \delta$, the random regret $\hat{R}_n = \sum_{t=1}^{n} r_t$ is bounded by

$$\hat{R}_n \leq \frac{c_2}{c_1} \sqrt{8nd\beta_n \log\left(1 + \frac{nL^2}{d}\right)}.$$

HINT   For (a), you should peek into the future and use Theorem 20.4. The mean value theorem will help with Part (b).

19.7 (SPECTRAL BANDITS) The regret of LinUCB can be improved considerably if an appropriate norm of θ_* is known to be small. In this exercise you will investigate this phenomenon. Suppose that V_0 is positive definite with eigenvalues $\lambda_1, \ldots, \lambda_d$, respective eigenvectors $v_1, \ldots, v_d$, and $V_t = V_0 + \sum_{s=1}^{t} A_s A_s^\top$. All other quantities are left unchanged, but the alternative value of V_0 means that $\hat{\theta}_t$ is heavily regularised in the direction of each v_i for which λ_i is large. Without loss of generality, assume that $(\lambda_i)_{i=1}^{d}$ is increasing and let $\lambda = \lambda_1$ be the smallest eigenvalue. Define the 'effective dimension' by

$$d_{\text{eff}} = \max\left\{ i \in [d] : (i-1)\lambda_i \leq \frac{n}{\log(1 + nL^2/\lambda)} \right\} \in [d].$$

(a) Prove that $\log\left(\frac{\det(V_t)}{\det(V_0)}\right) \leq 2d_{\text{eff}} \log\left(1 + \frac{nL^2}{\lambda}\right)$.

(b) Let $m > 0$ be a user-defined constant and

$$\beta_t^{1/2} = m + \sqrt{2\log\left(\frac{1}{\delta}\right) + \log\left(\frac{\det(V_t)}{\det(V_0)}\right)}$$

and let $C_t = \{\theta : \|\theta - \hat{\theta}_{t-1}\|_{V_{t-1}}^2 \leq \beta_{t-1}\}$. Assume that $\|\theta_*\|_{V_0} \leq m$ and prove that $\theta_* \in C_t$ for all t with probability at least $1 - \delta$.

(c) Prove that if $\|\theta_*\|_{V_0} \leq m$, then with probability at least $1 - \delta$, the random regret of LinUCB in this setting is bounded by

$$\hat{R}_n \leq \sqrt{8\beta_n d_{\text{eff}} \log\left(1 + \frac{nL^2}{\lambda}\right)}.$$

(d) Show that with an appropriate choice of δ,

$$\mathbb{E}[\hat{R}_n] = O\left(d_{\text{eff}}\sqrt{n}\log(nL^2)\right),\tag{19.16}$$

where the last equality suppresses dependence on m and $\lambda = \lambda_1$.

(e) The result of the previous display explains the definition of the 'effective dimension' d_{eff}. When $V_0 = I$, which gives rise to uniform regularisation, Corollary 19.3 states that for $\|\theta_*\| \le m$, $\mathbb{E}[\hat{R}_n] = O(d\sqrt{n}\log(nL^2))$. Given Eq. (19.16), for a fixed n, d_{eff} can be thought of as replacing the dimension d when V_0 is chosen as any positive definite matrix with $V_0 \succeq \lambda I$. It follows then that when $d_{\text{eff}} \le d$, the upper bound for non-uniform regularisation will be smaller. Given this, explain the potential pros and cons of non-uniform regularisation. What happens when $\|\theta_*\|_{V_0} \le m$ fails to hold? Show a bound on the degradation of the expected regret as a function of $\max(0, \|\theta_*\|_{V_0} - m)$.

HINT   For Part (b), you should peek into the next chapter and modify Theorem 20.5.

Valko et al. [2014] had a particular application in mind when designing the algorithm in Exercise 19.7. Consider a large graph with k vertices and similarity matrix between the vertices $W \in [0,\infty)^{k\times k}$. The **graph Laplacian** is the matrix $\mathcal{L} = D - W$, where D is diagonal with $D_{ii} = \sum_{j=1}^{k} W_{ij}$. Let $\mu \in [0,1]^k$ be an unknown reward function and consider a bandit algorithm with k actions corresponding to the vertices of the graph. Without further assumptions, this is a finite-armed bandit, which for large k is hopeless without further assumptions. Valko et al. [2014] assume the rewards for well-connected vertices are similar – a kind of smoothness. Let $\mathcal{L} = Q^\top \Lambda Q$ be the spectral decomposition of $\mathcal{L}$ and $\theta = Q^\top \mu$. Then,

$$\frac{1}{2}\sum_{i,j\in[k]} W_{ij}(\mu_i - \mu_j)^2 = \|\theta\|_\Lambda^2.$$

The left-hand side measures the variability of μ, weighted by connectivity of the graph. Hence, assuming that $\|\theta\|_\Lambda$ is small corresponds to assuming that μ changes only a little between well-connected vertices. Valko et al. [2014] then let $V_0 = \Lambda + \lambda I$ and analyse/implement the algorithm described in Exercise 19.7. A more detailed exposition is by Valko [2016].

19.8 (IMPLEMENTATION) If the action set is the same in every round, then the assumptions are satisfied for the various versions of UCB discussed in Chapters 7 to 9. How does LinUCB compare to UCB? Implement the version of LinUCB using the value of β_t given in Eq. (19.8) and/or Eq. (19.14) and compare it the version of UCB given in Algorithm 6. In particular:

(a) Compare LinUCB with UCB on the 2-armed bandit with $n = 1000$ where the reward distributions are Gaussian with unit variance and mean $\mu = (0, -\Delta)$ where $\Delta \in [0, 1]$, which for LinUCB corresponds to using $\mathcal{A}_t = \{e_1, e_2\}$ with $d = 2$.

(b) Now compare LinUCB with UCB on k-armed stochastic linear bandits where the $d = 5$ and $\mathcal{A}_t = \mathcal{A}$ is composed of k unit vectors sampled from the uniform distribution on the sphere (sample these vectors once). The unknown parameter θ should also lie on the unit sphere and the noise should be standard Gaussian. Plot the expected regret as a function of k ranging from 2 to 1000 with a horizon of $n = 5000$.

(c) What conclusions can you draw from the experimental results you obtained?

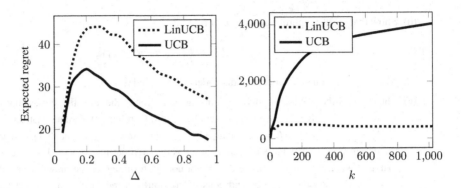

Figure 19.1 The plot on the left compares the regret of UCB (Algorithm 6) and LinUCB on a Gaussian bandit with $k = 2$, $n = 1000$ and varying suboptimality gaps Δ. The plot on the right compares the same algorithms on a linear bandit with actions uniformly distributed on the sphere and with $d = 5$ and $n = 5000$. The parameter θ is also uniformly generated on the sphere.

(d) Show how one can use the **Sherman-Morrison formula** to implement LinUCB using $O(kd^2)$ computation cost per round.

For parts (a) and (b) you should produce something comparable to Fig. 19.1.

20 Confidence Bounds for Least Squares Estimators

In the last chapter, we derived a regret bound for a version of the upper confidence bound algorithm that depended on a particular kind of confidence set. The purpose of this chapter is to justify these choices.

Suppose a bandit algorithm has chosen actions $A_1, \ldots, A_t \in \mathbb{R}^d$ and received the rewards $X_1, \ldots, X_t$ with $X_s = \langle \theta_*, A_s \rangle + \eta_s$ where η_s is zero-mean noise. Recall from the previous chapter that the penalised least-squares estimate of θ_* is the minimiser of

$$L_t(\theta) = \sum_{s=1}^{t} (X_s - \langle \theta, A_s \rangle)^2 + \lambda \|\theta\|_2^2,$$

where $\lambda \geq 0$ is the penalty factor. This is minimised by

$$\hat{\theta}_t = V_t(\lambda)^{-1} \sum_{s=1}^{t} X_s A_s \quad \text{with } V_t(\lambda) = \lambda I + \sum_{s=1}^{t} A_s A_s^\top. \tag{20.1}$$

It is convenient for the remainder to abbreviate $V_t = V_t(0)$. Designing confidence sets for θ_* when $A_1, \ldots, A_t$ have been chosen by a bandit algorithm is a surprisingly delicate matter. The difficulty stems from the fact that the actions are neither fixed nor independent but are intricately correlated via the rewards. We spend the first section of this chapter building intuition by making some simplifying assumptions. Eager readers may skip directly to Section 20.1. For the rest of this section, we assume the following:

1 *No regularisation:* $\lambda = 0$ and V_t is invertible.

2 *Independent subgaussian noise:* $(\eta_s)_s$ are independent and 1-subgaussian.

3 *Fixed design:* $A_1, \ldots, A_t$ are deterministically chosen without the knowledge of $X_1, \ldots, X_t$.

None of these assumptions is plausible in the bandit setting, but the simplification eases the analysis and provides insight.

> The assumption that $\lambda = 0$ means that in this section, $\hat{\theta}_t$ is just the ordinary least squares estimator of θ. The requirement that V_t be non-singular means that $(A_s)_{s=1}^t$ must span $\mathbb{R}^d$, and so t must be at least d.

Comparing θ_* and $\hat{\theta}_t$ in the direction $x \in \mathbb{R}^d$, we have

$$\langle \hat{\theta}_t - \theta_*, x \rangle = \left\langle x, V_t^{-1} \sum_{s=1}^{t} A_s X_s - \theta_* \right\rangle = \left\langle x, V_t^{-1} \sum_{s=1}^{t} A_s \left(A_s^\top \theta_* + \eta_s \right) - \theta_* \right\rangle$$

$$= \left\langle x, V_t^{-1} \sum_{s=1}^{t} A_s \eta_s \right\rangle = \sum_{s=1}^{t} \langle x, V_t^{-1} A_s \rangle \eta_s.$$

Since $(\eta_s)_s$ are independent and 1-subgaussian, by Lemma 5.4 and Theorem 5.3,

$$\mathbb{P} \left(\langle x, \hat{\theta}_t - \theta_* \rangle \geq \sqrt{2 \sum_{s=1}^{t} \langle x, V_t^{-1} A_s \rangle^2 \log \left(\frac{1}{\delta} \right)} \right) \leq \delta.$$

A little linear algebra shows that $\sum_{s=1}^{t} \langle x, V_t^{-1} A_s \rangle^2 = \|x\|_{V_t^{-1}}^2$ and so

$$\mathbb{P} \left(\langle \hat{\theta}_t - \theta_*, x \rangle \geq \sqrt{2 \|x\|_{V_t^{-1}}^2 \log \left(\frac{1}{\delta} \right)} \right) \leq \delta. \tag{20.2}$$

If we only care about confidence bounds for one or a few vectors x, we could stop here. For large action sets (with more than $\Omega(2^d)$ actions), one approach is to convert this bound to a bound on $\|\hat{\theta}_t - \theta_*\|_{V_t}$. To begin this process, notice that

$$\|\hat{\theta}_t - \theta_*\|_{V_t} = \langle \hat{\theta}_t - \theta_*, V_t^{1/2} X \rangle, \text{ where } X = \frac{V_t^{1/2} (\hat{\theta}_t - \theta_*)}{\|\hat{\theta}_t - \theta_*\|_{V_t}}.$$

The problem is that X is random, while we have only proven (20.2) for deterministic x. The standard way of addressing problems like this is to use a **covering argument**. First we identify a finite set $\mathcal{C}_\varepsilon \subset \mathbb{R}^d$ such that whatever value X takes, there exists some $x \in \mathcal{C}_\varepsilon$ that is ε-close to X. Then a union bound and a triangle inequality allows one to finish. By its definition, we have $\|X\|_2^2 = X^\top X = 1$, which means that $X \in S^{d-1} = \{x \in \mathbb{R}^d : \|x\|_2 = 1\}$. Using that $X \in S^{d-1}$, we see it suffices to cover S^{d-1}. The following lemma provides the necessary guarantees on the size of the covering set.

LEMMA 20.1. *There exists a set $\mathcal{C}_\varepsilon \subset \mathbb{R}^d$ with $|\mathcal{C}_\varepsilon| \leq (3/\varepsilon)^d$ such that for all $x \in S^{d-1}$ there exists a $y \in \mathcal{C}_\varepsilon$ with $\|x - y\|_2 \leq \varepsilon$.*

The proof of this lemma requires a bit work, but nothing really deep is needed. This work is deferred to Exercises 20.3 and 20.4. Let $\mathcal{C}_\varepsilon$ be the covering set given by the lemma, and define event

$$E = \left\{ \text{exists } x \in \mathcal{C}_\varepsilon : \left\langle V_t^{1/2} x, \hat{\theta}_t - \theta_* \right\rangle \geq \sqrt{2 \log \left(\frac{|\mathcal{C}_\varepsilon|}{\delta} \right)} \right\}.$$

Using the fact that $\|V_t^{1/2}x\|_{V_t^{-1}} = \|x\|_2 = 1$, and a union bound combined with Eq. (20.2) shows that $P(E) \leq \delta$. When E does not occur, Cauchy–Schwarz shows that

$$\|\hat{\theta}_t - \theta_*\|_{V_t} = \max_{x \in S^{d-1}} \left\langle V_t^{1/2}x, \hat{\theta}_t - \theta_* \right\rangle$$

$$= \max_{x \in S^{d-1}} \min_{y \in C_\varepsilon} \left[\left\langle V_t^{1/2}(x - y), \hat{\theta}_t - \theta_* \right\rangle + \left\langle V_t^{1/2}y, \hat{\theta}_t - \theta_* \right\rangle \right]$$

$$< \max_{x \in S^{d-1}} \min_{y \in C_\varepsilon} \left[\|\hat{\theta}_t - \theta_*\|_{V_t} \|x - y\|_2 + \sqrt{2 \log\left(\frac{|C_\varepsilon|}{\delta} \right)} \right]$$

$$\leq \varepsilon \|\hat{\theta}_t - \theta_*\|_{V_t} + \sqrt{2 \log\left(\frac{|C_\varepsilon|}{\delta} \right)}.$$

Rearranging yields

$$\|\hat{\theta}_t - \theta_*\|_{V_t} < \frac{1}{1 - \varepsilon} \sqrt{2 \log\left(\frac{|C_\varepsilon|}{\delta} \right)}.$$

Now there is a tension in the choice of $\varepsilon > 0$. The term in the denominator suggests that ε should be small, but by Lemma 20.1 the cardinality of C_ε grows rapidly as ε tends to zero. By lazily choosing $\varepsilon = 1/2$,

$$\mathbb{P}\left(\|\hat{\theta}_t - \theta_*\|_{V_t} \geq 2\sqrt{2\left(d \log(6) + \log\left(\frac{1}{\delta} \right) \right)} \right) \leq \delta. \tag{20.3}$$

Except for constants and other minor differences, this turns out to be about as good as you can get. Unfortunately, however, this analysis only works because V_t was assumed to be deterministic. When the actions are chosen by a bandit algorithm, this assumption does not hold, and the ideas need to be modified.

20.1 Martingales and the Method of Mixtures

We now remove the limiting assumptions in the previous section. Of course some conditions are still required. For the remainder of this section the following is assumed:

1 There exists a $\theta_* \in \mathbb{R}^d$ such that $X_t = \langle \theta_*, A_t \rangle + \eta_t$ for all $t \geq 1$.
2 The noise is conditionally 1-subgaussian:

$$\text{for all } \alpha \in \mathbb{R} \text{ and } t \geq 1, \qquad \mathbb{E}\left[\exp(\alpha \eta_t) \,|\, \mathcal{F}_{t-1} \right] \leq \exp\left(\frac{\alpha^2}{2} \right) \quad \text{a.s.,} \tag{20.4}$$

where $\mathcal{F}_{t-1}$ is such that $A_1, X_1, \ldots, A_{t-1}, X_{t-1}, A_t$ are $\mathcal{F}_{t-1}$-measurable.
3 In addition, we assume that $\lambda > 0$.

The inclusion of A_t in the definition of $\mathcal{F}_{t-1}$ allows the noise to depend on past choices, including the most recent action. This is often essential, as the case of Bernoulli rewards shows. We have now dropped the assumption that $(A_t)_{t=1}^{\infty}$ are fixed in advance.

The assumption that $\lambda > 0$ ensures that $V_t(\lambda)$ is invertible and allows us to relax the requirement that the actions span $\mathbb{R}^d$. Notice also that in this section, we allow the interaction sequence to be infinitely long.

Since we want exponentially decaying tail probabilities, one is tempted to try the Cramér–Chernoff method:

$$\mathbb{P}\left(\|\hat{\theta}_t - \theta_*\|_{V_t(\lambda)}^2 \geq u^2\right) \leq \inf_{\alpha > 0} \mathbb{E}\left[\exp\left(\alpha\|\hat{\theta}_t - \theta_*\|_{V_t(\lambda)}^2 - \alpha u^2\right)\right].$$

Sadly, we do not know how to bound this expectation. Can we still somehow use the Cramér–Chernoff method? We take inspiration from looking at the special case of $\lambda = 0$ one last time, assuming that $V_t = \sum_{s=1}^t A_s A_s^\top$ is invertible. Let

$$S_t = \sum_{s=1}^t \eta_s A_s.$$

Recall that $\hat{\theta}_t = V_t^{-1} \sum_{s=1}^t X_s A_s = \theta_* + V_t^{-1} S_t$. Hence,

$$\frac{1}{2}\|\hat{\theta}_t - \theta_*\|_{V_t}^2 = \frac{1}{2}\|S_t\|_{V_t^{-1}}^2 = \max_{x \in \mathbb{R}^d}\left(\langle x, S_t\rangle - \frac{1}{2}\|x\|_{V_t}^2\right).$$

The point of the second equality is to separate the martingale $(S_t)_t$ from V_t at the price of the introduction of a maximum. This second equality is a special case of (Fenchel) duality. As we shall see later in Chapter 26, for sufficiently nice convex functions f one can show that with an appropriate function f^*, for any $x \in \mathbb{R}^d$ from the domain of f, $f(x) = \sup_{u \in \mathbb{R}^d}\langle u, x\rangle - f^*(u)$. The advantage of this is that for any fixed u, x appears in a linear fashion.

The next lemma shows that the exponential of the term inside the maximum is a super-martingale even when $\lambda > 0$.

LEMMA 20.2. *For all $x \in \mathbb{R}^d$ the process $M_t(x) = \exp(\langle x, S_t\rangle - \frac{1}{2}\|x\|_{V_t(\lambda)}^2)$ is an $\mathbb{F}$-adapted non-negative supermartingale with $M_0(x) \leq 1$.*

Proof of Lemma 20.2 That $M_t(x)$ is $\mathcal{F}_t$-measurable for all t and that it is nonnegative are immediate from the definition. We need to show that $\mathbb{E}[M_t(x) \,|\, \mathcal{F}_{t-1}] \leq M_{t-1}(x)$ almost surely. The fact that (η_t) is conditionally 1-subgaussian means that

$$\mathbb{E}\left[\exp\left(\eta_t \langle x, A_t\rangle\right) \,|\, \mathcal{F}_{t-1}\right] \leq \exp\left(\frac{\langle x, A_t\rangle^2}{2}\right) = \exp\left(\frac{\|x\|_{A_t A_t^\top}^2}{2}\right) \quad \text{a.s.}$$

Hence

$$\mathbb{E}[M_t(x) \mid \mathcal{F}_{t-1}] = \mathbb{E}\left[\exp\left(\langle x, S_t\rangle - \frac{1}{2}\|x\|_{V_t}^2\right) \bigg| \mathcal{F}_{t-1}\right]$$

$$= M_{t-1}(x)\mathbb{E}\left[\exp\left(\eta_t\langle x, A_t\rangle - \frac{1}{2}\|x\|_{A_t A_t^\top}^2\right) \bigg| \mathcal{F}_{t-1}\right]$$

$$\leq M_{t-1}(x) \quad \text{a.s.}$$

Finally, note that $M_0(x) \leq 1$ is immediate.   □

For simplicity, consider now again the case when $\lambda = 0$. Combining the lemma and the linearisation idea almost works. The Cramér–Chernoff method leads to

$$\mathbb{P}\left(\frac{1}{2}\|\hat{\theta}_t - \theta_*\|_{V_t}^2 \geq \log(1/\delta)\right) = \mathbb{P}\left(\exp\left(\max_{x\in\mathbb{R}^d}\left(\langle x, S_t\rangle - \frac{1}{2}\|x\|_{V_t}^2\right)\right) \geq 1/\delta\right)$$

$$\leq \delta\mathbb{E}\left[\exp\left(\max_{x\in\mathbb{R}^d}\left(\langle x, S_t\rangle - \frac{1}{2}\|x\|_{V_t}^2\right)\right)\right]$$

$$= \delta\mathbb{E}\left[\max_{x\in\mathbb{R}^d} M_t(x)\right]. \tag{20.5}$$

Lemma 20.2 shows that $\mathbb{E}[M_t(x)] \leq 1$. This seems quite promising, but the presence of the maximum is a setback because $\mathbb{E}[\max_{x\in\mathbb{R}^d} M_t(x)] \geq \max_{x\in\mathbb{R}^d} \mathbb{E}[M_t(x)]$, which is the wrong direction to be used above. This means we cannot directly use the lemma to bound Eq. (20.5). There are two ways to proceed. The first is to use a covering argument over possible near-maximisers of x, which eventually works. A more elegant way is to take inspiration from Eq. (20.5) and use Laplace's method for approximating integrals of well-behaved exponentials, as we now explain.

20.1.1 Laplace's Method (✦)

We briefly review Laplace's method for one-dimensional functions. Assume that $f : [a, b] \to \mathbb{R}$ is twice differentiable and has a unique maximum at $x_0 \in (a, b)$ with $-q = f''(x_0) < 0$. Laplace's method for approximating $f(x_0)$ is to compute the integral

$$I_s = \int_a^b \exp(sf(x))dx$$

for some large value of $s > 0$. From a Taylor expansion, we may write

$$f(x) = f(x_0) - \frac{q}{2}(x - x_0)^2 + R(x),$$

where $R(x) = o((x - x_0)^2)$. Under appropriate technical assumptions,

$$I_s \sim \exp(sf(x_0)) \int_a^b \exp\left(-\frac{sq(x - x_0)^2}{2}\right) dx \qquad \text{as } s \to \infty.$$

Furthermore, as s gets large,

$$\int_a^b \exp\left(-\frac{sq(x - x_0)^2}{2}\right) dx \sim \int_{-\infty}^\infty \exp\left(-\frac{sq(x - x_0)^2}{2}\right) dx = \sqrt{\frac{2\pi}{sq}}$$

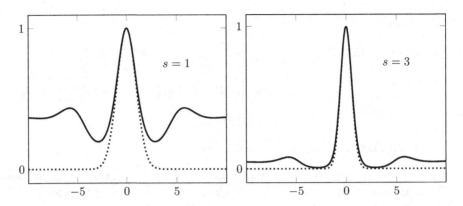

Figure 20.1 The plots depict Laplace's approximation with $f(x) = \cos(x)\exp(-x^2/20)$, which is maximised at $x_0 = 0$ and has $q = -f''(x_0) = 11/10$. The solid line is a plot of $\exp(sf(x))/\exp(sf(x_0))$, and the dotted line is $\exp(-sq(x - x_0)^2)$.

and hence

$$I_s \sim \exp(sf(x_0))\sqrt{\frac{2\pi}{sq}}.$$

It should also be clear that the fact that we integrate with respect to the Lebesgue measure does not matter much. We could have integrated with respect to any other measure as long as that measure puts a positive mass on the neighbourhood of the maximiser. The method is illustrated in Fig. 20.1. The take-home message is that if we integrate the exponential of a function that has a pronounced maximum, then we can expect that the integral will be close to the exponential function of the maximum.

20.1.2 Method of Mixtures

Laplace's approximation suggests that

$$\max_x M_t(x) \approx \int_{\mathbb{R}^d} M_t(x)dh(x), \tag{20.6}$$

where h is some measure on $\mathbb{R}^d$ chosen so that the integral can be calculated in closed form. This is not a requirement of the method, but it does make the argument shorter. The main benefit of replacing the maximum with an integral is that we obtain the following lemma, which you will prove in Exercise 20.5.

LEMMA 20.3. *Let h be a probability measure on $\mathbb{R}^d$; then, $\bar{M}_t = \int_{\mathbb{R}^d} M_t(x)dh(x)$ is an $\mathbb{F}$-adapted non-negative supermartingale with $\bar{M}_0 = 1$.*

The following theorem is the key result from which the confidence set will be derived.

THEOREM 20.4. *For all $\lambda > 0$ and $\delta \in (0,1)$,*

$$\mathbb{P}\left(exists\ t \in \mathbb{N} : \|S_t\|_{V_t(\lambda)^{-1}}^2 \geq 2\log\left(\frac{1}{\delta}\right) + \log\left(\frac{\det(V_t(\lambda))}{\lambda^d}\right)\right) \leq \delta.$$

The proof will be given momentarily. First, though, the implications.

THEOREM 20.5. *Let $\delta \in (0, 1)$. Then, with probability at least $1 - \delta$, it holds that for all $t \in \mathbb{N}$,*

$$\|\hat{\theta}_t - \theta_*\|_{V_t(\lambda)} < \sqrt{\lambda}\|\theta_*\|_2 + \sqrt{2\log\left(\frac{1}{\delta}\right) + \log\left(\frac{\det V_t(\lambda)}{\lambda^d}\right)}.$$

Furthermore, if $\|\theta_*\|_2 \le m_2$, then $\mathbb{P}\left(exists\ t \in \mathbb{N}^+ : \theta_* \notin C_t\right) \le \delta$ with

$$C_t = \left\{\theta \in \mathbb{R}^d : \|\hat{\theta}_{t-1} - \theta\|_{V_{t-1}(\lambda)} < m_2\sqrt{\lambda} + \sqrt{2\log\left(\frac{1}{\delta}\right) + \log\left(\frac{\det V_{t-1}(\lambda)}{\lambda^d}\right)}\right\}.$$

Proof   We only have to compare $\|S_t\|_{V_t(\lambda)^{-1}}$ and $\|\hat{\theta}_t - \theta_*\|_{V_t(\lambda)}$:

$$\begin{aligned}
\|\hat{\theta}_t - \theta_*\|_{V_t(\lambda)} &= \|V_t(\lambda)^{-1}S_t + (V_t(\lambda)^{-1}V_t - I)\theta_*\|_{V_t(\lambda)} \\
&\le \|S_t\|_{V_t(\lambda)^{-1}} + (\theta_*^\top(V_t(\lambda)^{-1}V_t - I)V_t(\lambda)(V_t(\lambda)^{-1}V_t - I)\theta_*)^{1/2} \\
&= \|S_t\|_{V_t(\lambda)^{-1}} + \lambda^{1/2}(\theta_*^\top(I - V_t(\lambda)^{-1}V_t)\theta_*)^{1/2} \\
&\le \|S_t\|_{V_t(\lambda)^{-1}} + \lambda^{1/2}\|\theta_*\|,
\end{aligned}$$

and the result follows from Theorem 20.4.   ◻

Proof of Theorem 20.4   Let $H = \lambda I \in \mathbb{R}^{d \times d}$ and $h = \mathcal{N}(0, H^{-1})$ and

$$\begin{aligned}
\bar{M}_t &= \int_{\mathbb{R}^d} M_t(x)dh(x) \\
&= \frac{1}{\sqrt{(2\pi)^d \det(H^{-1})}} \int_{\mathbb{R}^d} \exp\left(\langle x, S_t\rangle - \frac{1}{2}\|x\|_{V_t}^2 - \frac{1}{2}\|x\|_H^2\right) dx.
\end{aligned}$$

By Lemma 20.3, $\bar{M}_t$ is a non-negative supermartingale, and thus the maximal inequality (Theorem 3.9) shows that

$$\mathbb{P}\left(\sup_{t\in\mathbb{N}}\log(\bar{M}_t) \ge \log\left(\frac{1}{\delta}\right)\right) = \mathbb{P}\left(\sup_{t\in\mathbb{N}}\bar{M}_t \ge \frac{1}{\delta}\right) \le \delta. \tag{20.7}$$

Now we turn to studying $\bar{M}_t$. Completing the square in the definition of $\bar{M}_t$ we get

$$\langle x, S_t\rangle - \frac{1}{2}\|x\|_{V_t}^2 - \frac{1}{2}\|x\|_H^2 = \frac{1}{2}\|S_t\|_{(H+V_t)^{-1}}^2 - \frac{1}{2}\|x - (H + V_t)^{-1}S_t\|_{H+V_t}^2.$$

The first term $\|S_t\|_{(H+V_t)^{-1}}^2$ does not depend on x and can be moved outside the integral, which leaves a quadratic 'Gaussian' term that may be integrated exactly and results in

$$\bar{M}_t = \left(\frac{\det(H)}{\det(H + V_t)}\right)^{1/2} \exp\left(\frac{1}{2}\|S_t\|_{(H+V_t)^{-1}}^2\right). \tag{20.8}$$

The result follows by substituting this expression into Eq. (20.7) and rearranging.   ◻

20.2   Notes

1 Recall from the previous chapter that when $\|A_t\|_2 \le L$ is assumed, then

$$\frac{\det V_t(\lambda)}{\lambda^d} \le \left(\text{trace}\left(\frac{V_t(\lambda)}{\lambda d}\right)\right)^d \le \left(1 + \frac{nL^2}{\lambda d}\right)^d. \tag{20.9}$$

In general, the log determinant form should be preferred when confidence intervals are used as part of an algorithm, but the right-hand side has a concrete form that can be useful when stating regret bounds.

2 Plugging the bounds of the previous note into Theorem 20.5 and choosing $\lambda = 1$ gives the confidence set

$$C_t = \left\{ \theta \in \mathbb{R}^d : \|\hat{\theta}_{t-1} - \theta\|_{V_{t-1}(1)} < m_2 + \sqrt{2 \log\left(\frac{1}{\delta}\right) + d \log\left(1 + \frac{nL^2}{d}\right)} \right\}.$$

The dependence of the radius on n, d and δ, up to constants and a $\sqrt{\log(n)}$ factor, is the same as what we got in the fixed design case (cf. Eq. (20.3)), which suggests that Theorem 20.5 can be quite tight. By considering the case when each basis vector $\{e_1, \ldots, e_d\}$ is played m times, then $D = \|\hat{\theta}_t - \theta\|_{V_t}^2$ is distributed like a chi-squared distribution with d degrees of freedom. From this, we see that the first term under the square root with the coefficient two is stemming from variance of the noise, while the term that involved $d \log(n)$ is the bias (the expected value of D). In particular, this shows that the $\sqrt{d}$ factor cannot be avoided.

3 If either of the above confidence sets is used (either the one from the theorem, or that from Eq. (20.3)) to derive confidence bounds for the prediction error $\langle \hat{\theta}_t - \theta, x \rangle$ at some *fixed* $x \in \mathbb{R}^d$, we get a confidence width that scales with $\sqrt{d}$ (e.g., Eq. (19.13)), unlike the confidence width in Eq. (20.2), which is independent of d. It follows that if one is interested in high-probability bounds for the mean at a fixed input x, one should avoid going through a confidence set for the whole parameter vector. What this leaves open is whether a bound like in Eq. (20.2) is possible at a fixed input x, but with a sequential design. In Exercise 20.2 you will answer this question in the negative. First note that when the actions are chosen using a fixed design, integrating Eq. (20.2) shows that $\mathbb{E}[\langle \hat{\theta}_t - \theta_*, x \rangle^2 / \|x\|_{V_t^{-1}}^2] = O(1)$. In the exercise, you will show that there exists a sequential design such that

$$\mathbb{E}\left[\langle \hat{\theta}_t - \theta_*, x \rangle^2 / \|x\|_{V_t^{-1}}^2 \right] = \Omega(d),$$

showing that for some sequential designs the factor $\sqrt{d}$ is necessary. It remains an interesting open question to design confidence bounds for sequential design for fixed x that adapts to the amount of dependence in the design.

4 Supermartingales arise naturally in proofs relying on the Cramér–Chernoff method. Just one example is the proof of Lemma 12.2. One could rewrite most of the proofs involving sums of random variables relying on the Cramér–Chernoff method in a way that it would become clear that the proof hinges on the supermartingale property of an appropriate sequence.

20.3   Bibliographic Remarks

Bounds like those given in Theorem 20.5 are called self-normalised bounds [de la Peña et al., 2008]. The method of mixtures goes back to the work by Robbins and Siegmund [1970]. In practice, the improvement provided by the method of mixtures relative to the covering arguments is quite large. A historical account of martingale methods in sequential analysis is by Lai [2009]. A simple proof of Lemma 20.1 appears as lemma 2.5 in the book by van de Geer [2000]. Calculating covering numbers (or related packing numbers) is a whole field by itself, with open questions even in the most obvious examples. The main reference is by Rogers [1964], which by now is a little old, but still interesting.

20.4 Exercises

20.1 (LOWER BOUNDS FOR FIXED DESIGN) Let $n = md$ for integer m and $A_1, \ldots, A_n$ be a fixed design where each basis vector in $\{e_1, \ldots, e_d\}$ is played exactly m times. Then let $(\eta_t)_{t=1}^n$ be a sequence of independent standard Gaussian random variables and $X_t = \langle \theta_*, A_t \rangle + \eta_t$. Finally, let $\hat{\theta}_n$ be the ordinary least squares estimator of $\theta_* \in \mathbb{R}^d$. Show that

$$\mathbb{E}\left[\|\hat{\theta}_n - \theta_*\|_{V_n}^2\right] = d.$$

This exercise shows that the d-dependence in Eq. (20.3) is unavoidable in general for a self-normalised bound, even in the fixed design setting.

20.2 (LOWER BOUNDS FOR SEQUENTIAL DESIGN) Let $n \geq 2d$ and $(\eta_t)_{t=1}^n$ be a sequence of independent standard Gaussian random variables. Find a sequence of random vectors $(A_t)_{t=1}^n$, with $A_t \in \mathbb{R}^d$ such that $V_n = \sum_{t=1}^n A_t A_t^\top$ is invertible almost surely and A_t is $\sigma(A_1, \eta_1, \ldots, A_{t-1}, \eta_{t-1})$-measurable for all t and

$$\mathbb{E}\left[\langle \hat{\theta}_n, \mathbf{1}\rangle^2 / \|\mathbf{1}\|_{V_n^{-1}}^2\right] \geq cd,$$

where $c > 0$ is a universal constant and $S_n = \sum_{t=1}^n \eta_t A_t$ and $\hat{\theta}_n = V_n^{-1} S_n$.

HINT Choose $A_1, \ldots, A_d$ to be the standard basis vectors. Subsequently choose selected basis vectors adaptively to push the estimate of $\langle \hat{\theta}_n, \mathbf{1}\rangle$ away from zero.

For Exercise 20.4, where we ask you to prove Lemma 20.1, a few standard definitions will be useful.

DEFINITION 20.6 (Covering and packing). Let $\mathcal{A} \subset \mathbb{R}^d$. A subset $\mathcal{C} \subset \mathcal{A}$ is said to be an ε-**cover** of $\mathcal{A}$ if $\mathcal{A} \subset \cup_{x \in \mathcal{C}} B(x, \varepsilon)$, where $B(x, \varepsilon) = \{y \in \mathbb{R}^d : \|x - y\| \leq \varepsilon\}$ is the ε ball centered at x. An ε-**packing** of $\mathcal{A}$ is a subset $\mathcal{P} \subset \mathcal{A}$ such that for any $x, y \in \mathcal{P}$, $\|x - y\| > \varepsilon$ (note the strict inequality). The ε-**covering number** of $\mathcal{A}$ is $N(\mathcal{A}, \varepsilon) = \min\{|\mathcal{C}| : \mathcal{C}$ is an ε-covering of $\mathcal{A}\}$, while the ε-**packing number** of $\mathcal{A}$ is $M(\mathcal{A}, \varepsilon) = \max\{|\mathcal{P}| : \mathcal{P}$ is an ε-packing of $\mathcal{A}\}$, where we allow for both the covering and packing numbers to take on the value of $+\infty$.

The definitions can be repeated for pseudo-metric spaces. Let X be a set and $d : X \times X \to [0, \infty)$ be a function that is symmetric, satisfies the triangle inequality and for which $d(x, x) = 0$ for all $x \in X$. Note that $d(x, y) = 0$ is allowed for distinct x and y, so d need not be a metric. The basic results concerning covering and packing stated in the next exercise remain valid with this more general definition. In applications we often need the logarithm of the covering and packing numbers, which are called the **metric entropy** of X at scale ε. As we shall see, these are often close no matter whether we consider packing or covering.

20.3 (COVERINGS AND PACKINGS) Let $\mathcal{A} \subset \mathbb{R}^d$, B be the unit ball of $\mathbb{R}^d$ and $\mathrm{vol}(\cdot)$ the usual volume (measure under the Lebesgue measure). For brevity let $N(\varepsilon) = N(\mathcal{A}, \varepsilon)$ and $M(\varepsilon) = M(\mathcal{A}, \varepsilon)$. Show that the following hold:

(a) $\varepsilon \to N(\varepsilon)$ is increasing as $\varepsilon \geq 0$ is decreasing.

(b) $M(2\varepsilon) \leq N(\varepsilon) \leq M(\varepsilon)$.

(c) We have

$$\left(\frac{1}{\varepsilon}\right)^d \frac{\text{vol}(\mathcal{A})}{\text{vol}(B)} \leq N(\varepsilon) \leq M(\varepsilon) \leq \frac{\text{vol}(\mathcal{A} + \frac{\varepsilon}{2}B)}{\text{vol}(\frac{\varepsilon}{2}B)} \stackrel{(*)}{\leq} \frac{\text{vol}(\frac{3}{2}\mathcal{A})}{\text{vol}(\frac{\varepsilon}{2}B)} \leq \left(\frac{3}{\varepsilon}\right)^d \frac{\text{vol}(\mathcal{A})}{\text{vol}(B)},$$

where (*) holds under the assumption that $\varepsilon B \subset \mathcal{A}$ and that $\mathcal{A}$ is convex and for $U, V \subset \mathbb{R}^d$, $c \in \mathbb{R}$, $U + V = \{u + v : u \in U, v \in V\}$ and $cU = \{cu : u \in U\}$;

(d) Fix $\varepsilon > 0$. Then $N(\varepsilon) < +\infty$ if and only if $\mathcal{A}$ is bounded. The same holds for $M(\varepsilon)$.

20.4 Use the results of the previous exercise to prove Lemma 20.1.

20.5 Prove Lemma 20.3.

HINT   Use the 'sections' lemma [Kallenberg, 2002, Lemma 1.26] to established that $\bar{M}_t$ is $\mathcal{F}_t$-measurable.

20.6 (HOEFFDING–AZUMA) Let $X_1, \ldots, X_n$ be a sequence of random variables adapted to a filtration $\mathbb{F} = (\mathcal{F}_t)_t$. Suppose that $|X_t| \in [a_t, b_t]$ almost surely for arbitrary fixed sequences (a_t) and (b_t) with $a_t \leq b_t$ for all $t \in [n]$. Show that for any $\varepsilon > 0$,

$$\mathbb{P}\left(\sum_{t=1}^{n}(X_t - \mathbb{E}[X_t \mid \mathcal{F}_{t-1}]) \geq \varepsilon\right) \leq \exp\left(-\frac{2n^2\varepsilon^2}{\sum_{t=1}^{n}(b_t - a_t)^2}\right).$$

HINT   It may help to recall Hoeffding's lemma from Note 4 in Chapter 5, which states that for a random variable $X \in [a, b]$, the moment-generating function satisfies

$$M_X(\lambda) \leq \exp(\lambda^2(b - a)^2/8).$$

20.7 (EXTENSION OF HOEFFDING–AZUMA) The following simple extension of Hoeffding–Azuma is often useful. Let $n \in \mathbb{N}^+$ and (a_t) and (b_t) be fixed sequences with $a_t \leq b_t$ for all $t \in [n]$. Let $X_1, \ldots, X_n$ be a sequence of random variables adapted to a filtration $\mathbb{F} = (\mathcal{F}_t)_t$ and A be an event. Assume that $\mathbb{P}(\text{exists } t \in [n] : A \text{ and } X_t \notin [a_t, b_t]) = 0$ and $\varepsilon > 0$, and show that

(a) $\mathbb{P}\left(A \cap \sum_{t=1}^{n}(X_t - \mathbb{E}[X_t \mid \mathcal{F}_{t-1}]) \geq \varepsilon\right) \leq \exp\left(-\frac{2n^2\varepsilon^2}{\sum_{t=1}^{n}(b_t - a_t)^2}\right).$

(b) $\mathbb{P}\left(\sum_{t=1}^{n}(X_t - \mathbb{E}[X_t \mid \mathcal{F}_{t-1}]) \geq \varepsilon\right) \leq \mathbb{P}(A^c) + \exp\left(-\frac{2n^2\varepsilon^2}{\sum_{t=1}^{n}(b_t - a_t)^2}\right).$

The utility of this result comes from the fact that very often the range of some adapted sequence is itself random and could be arbitrarily large with low probability (when A does not hold). A reference for the above result is the survey by McDiarmid [1998].

20.8 Let $\delta \in (0, 1)$ and $\mathbb{F} = (\mathcal{F}_t)_{t=1}^{\infty}$ be a filtration and $(X_t)_{t=1}^{\infty}$ be $\mathbb{F}$-adapted such that

for all $\lambda \in \mathbb{R}$, $\mathbb{E}[\exp(\lambda X_t) \mid \mathcal{F}_{t-1}] \leq \exp(\lambda^2\sigma^2/2)$ a.s.

Let $S_n = \sum_{t=1}^{n} X_t$. Show that

$$\mathbb{P}\left(\text{exists } t : |S_t| \geq \sqrt{2\sigma^2(t+1)\log\left(\frac{\sqrt{t\sigma^2+1}}{\delta}\right)}\right) \leq \delta.$$

20.9 (LAW OF THE ITERATED LOGARITHM AND METHOD OF MIXTURES) This exercise uses the same notation as Exercise 20.8. Let f be a probability density function supported on $[0, \infty)$ and

$$M_n = \int_0^\infty f(\lambda)\exp\left(\lambda S_n - \frac{\lambda^2 n}{2}\right)d\lambda.$$

(a) Show that $\operatorname{argmax}_{\lambda \in \mathbb{R}} \lambda S_n - \lambda^2 n/2 = S_n/n$.

(b) Suppose that $f(\lambda)$ is decreasing for $\lambda > 0$. Show that for any $\varepsilon > 0$ and $\Lambda_n = S_n/n$, that,

$$M_n \geq \varepsilon \Lambda_n f(\Lambda_n(1+\varepsilon))\exp\left(\frac{(1-\varepsilon^2)S^2}{2n}\right)$$

(c) Use the previous result to show that for any $\delta \in (0, 1)$,

$$\mathbb{P}\left(\text{exists } n : S_n \geq \inf_{\varepsilon > 0}\sqrt{\frac{2n}{(1-\varepsilon^2)}\left(\log\left(\frac{1}{\delta}\right) + \log\left(\frac{1}{\varepsilon\Lambda_n f(\Lambda_n(1+\varepsilon))}\right)\right)}\right) \leq \delta.$$

(d) Find an f such that $\int_0^\infty f(\lambda)d\lambda = 1$ and $f(\lambda) \geq 0$ for all $\lambda \in \mathbb{R}$ and

$$\log\left(\frac{1}{\lambda f(\lambda)}\right) = (1 + o(1))\log\log\left(\frac{1}{\lambda}\right)$$

as $\lambda \to 0$.

(e) Use the previous results to show that

$$\mathbb{P}\left(\limsup_{n\to\infty}\frac{S_n}{\sqrt{2n\log\log(n)}} \leq 1\right) = 1.$$

The last part of the previous exercises is one-half of the statement of the law of iterated logarithm, which states that

$$\limsup_{n\to\infty}\frac{S_n}{\sqrt{2n\log\log(n)}} = 1 \quad \text{almost surely.}$$

In other words, the magnitude of the largest fluctuations of the partial sum $(S_n)_n$ is almost surely of the order $\sqrt{2n\log\log n}$ as $n \to \infty$.

20.10 Let $\mathbb{F} = (\mathcal{F}_t)_{t=0}^n$ be a filtration and $X_1, X_2, \ldots, X_n$ be a sequence of $\mathbb{F}$-adapted random variables with $X_t \in \{-1, 0, 1\}$ and $\mu_t = \mathbb{E}[X_t \mid \mathcal{F}_{t-1}, X_t \neq 0]$, which we define to be zero whenever $\mathbb{P}(X_t \neq 0 \mid \mathcal{F}_{t-1}) = 0$. Then, with $S_t = \sum_{s=1}^t (X_s - \mu_s|X_s|)$ and $N_t = \sum_{s=1}^t |X_s|$,

$$\mathbb{P}\left(\text{exists } t \leq n : |S_t| \geq \sqrt{2N_t \log\left(\frac{c\sqrt{N_t}}{\delta}\right)} \text{ and } N_t > 0\right) \leq \delta,$$

where $c > 0$ is a universal constant.

This result appeared in a paper by the authors and others with the constant $c = 4\sqrt{2/\pi}/\operatorname{erf}(\sqrt{2}) \approx 3.43$ [Lattimore et al., 2018].

20.11 (SEQUENTIAL LIKELIHOOD RATIOS AND CONFIDENCE SETS) Let $(\Theta, \mathcal{G})$ be a measurable space and $(P_\theta : \theta \in \Theta)$ be a probability kernel from $(\Theta, \mathcal{G})$ to $(\mathbb{R}, \mathfrak{B}(\mathbb{R}))$. Assume there exists a common measure μ such that $P_\theta \ll \mu$ for all $\theta \in \Theta$, and let $\{p_\theta : \theta \in \Theta\}$ be a family of densities with $p_\theta = dP_\theta/d\mu$. You may assume that $p_\theta(x)$ is jointly measurable in θ and x. Such a choice is guaranteed to exist, as we explain in Note 8 at the end of Chapter 34. Fix $\theta_* \in \Theta$ and let $(X_t)_{t=1}^\infty$ be a sequence of independent random variables with law P_{θ_*}. Let $\hat{\theta}_t \in \Theta$ be $\sigma(X_1, \ldots, X_t)$-measurable. For $\theta \in \Theta$, define $L_t(\theta) = \sum_{s=1}^t \log(p_{\hat{\theta}_{s-1}}(X_s)/p_\theta(X_s))$.

(a) Show that $\mathbb{P}\left(\sup_{t\geq1} L_t(\theta_*) \geq \log(1/\delta)\right) \leq \delta$ for any $\delta \in (0,1)$.
(b) Show that $\Theta_t = \{\theta : L_t(\theta) < \log(1/\delta)\}$ is a sequence of confidence sets such that $\mathbb{P}\left(\text{exists } t \in \mathbb{N} \text{ such that } \theta_* \notin \Theta_t\right) \leq \delta$.
(c) Let $\Theta = \mathbb{R}$ and $\mathcal{G} = \mathfrak{B}(\mathbb{R})$ and $P_\theta = \mathcal{N}(0, \theta)$ and μ be the Lebesgue measure. Then let $\hat{\theta}_t = 0$ for $t = 0$ and $\frac{1}{t}\sum_{s=1}^t X_s$ otherwise. Write an expression for $\mathcal{C}_t$, and investigate how it compares to the usual confidence intervals for Gaussian random variables.

HINT   Use Cramér–Chernoff method and observe that $(\exp(L_t(\theta_*)))_{t=1}^\infty$ is a martingale.

The quantities $p_{\theta'}(X_s)/p_\theta(X_s)$ are called **likelihood ratios**. That the product of likelihood ratios forms a martingale is a cornerstone result of classical parametric statistics. The sequential form that appears in the above exercise is based on lemma 2 of Lai and Robbins [1985], who cite Robbins and Siegmund [1972] as the original source.

21 Optimal Design for Least Squares Estimators

In the preceding chapter, we showed how to construct confidence intervals for least squares estimators when the design is chosen sequentially. We now study the problem of choosing actions for which the resulting confidence sets are small. This plays an important role in the analysis of stochastic linear bandits with finitely many arms (Chapter 22) and adversarial linear bandits (Part VI).

21.1 The Kiefer–Wolfowitz Theorem

Let $\eta_1, \ldots, \eta_n$ be a sequence of independent 1-subgaussian random variables and $a_1, \ldots, a_n \in \mathbb{R}^d$ be a fixed sequence with $\text{span}(a_1, \ldots, a_n) = \mathbb{R}^d$ and $X_1, \ldots, X_n$ be given by $X_t = \langle \theta_*, a_t \rangle + \eta_t$ for some $\theta_* \in \mathbb{R}^d$. The least squares estimator of θ_* is $\hat{\theta} = V^{-1} \sum_{t=1}^{n} a_t X_t$ with $V = \sum_{t=1}^{n} a_t a_t^\top$.

> The least squares estimator used here is not regularised. This eases the calculations, and the lack of regularisation will not harm us in future applications.

Eq. (20.2) from Chapter 20 shows that for any $a \in \mathbb{R}^d$ and $\delta \in (0, 1)$,

$$\mathbb{P}\left(\langle \hat{\theta} - \theta_*, a \rangle \geq \sqrt{2 \|a\|_{V^{-1}}^2 \log\left(\frac{1}{\delta}\right)} \right) \leq \delta. \tag{21.1}$$

For our purposes, both $a_1, \ldots, a_n$ and a will be actions from some (possibly infinite) set $\mathcal{A} \subset \mathbb{R}^d$ and the question of interest is finding the shortest sequence of exploratory actions $a_1, \ldots, a_n$ such that the confidence bound in the previous display is smaller than some threshold for all $a \in \mathcal{A}$. To solve this exactly is likely an intractable exercise in integer programming. Finding an accurate approximation turns out to be efficient for a broad class of action sets, however. Let $\pi : \mathcal{A} \to [0, 1]$ be a distribution on $\mathcal{A}$ so that $\sum_{a \in \mathcal{A}} \pi(a) = 1$ and $V(\pi) \in \mathbb{R}^{d \times d}$ and $g(\pi) \in \mathbb{R}$ be given by

$$V(\pi) = \sum_{a \in \mathcal{A}} \pi(a) a a^\top, \qquad g(\pi) = \max_{a \in \mathcal{A}} \|a\|_{V(\pi)^{-1}}^2. \tag{21.2}$$

In the subfield of statistics called optimal experimental design, the distribution π is called a **design**, and the problem of finding a design that minimises g is called the **G-optimal design problem**. So how to use this? Suppose that π is a design and $a \in \text{Supp}(\pi)$ and

$$n_a = \left\lceil \frac{\pi(a)g(\pi)}{\varepsilon^2} \log\left(\frac{1}{\delta}\right) \right\rceil. \tag{21.3}$$

Then, choosing each action $a \in \text{Supp}(\pi)$ exactly n_a times ensures that

$$V = \sum_{a \in \text{Supp}(\pi)} n_a a a^\top \geq \frac{g(\pi)}{\varepsilon^2} \log\left(\frac{1}{\delta}\right) V(\pi),$$

which by Eq. (21.1) means that for any $a \in \mathcal{A}$, with probability $1 - \delta$,

$$\langle \hat\theta - \theta_*, a \rangle \leq \sqrt{2\|a\|_{V^{-1}}^2 \log\left(\frac{1}{\delta}\right)} \leq \varepsilon.$$

By Eq. (21.3), the total number of actions required to ensure a confidence width of no more than ε is bounded by

$$n = \sum_{a \in \text{Supp}(\pi)} n_a = \sum_{a \in \text{Supp}(\pi)} \left\lceil \frac{\pi(a)g(\pi)}{\varepsilon^2} \log\left(\frac{1}{\delta}\right) \right\rceil \leq |\text{Supp}(\pi)| + \frac{g(\pi)}{\varepsilon^2} \log\left(\frac{1}{\delta}\right).$$

The set $\text{Supp}(\pi)$ is sometimes called the **core set**. The following theorem characterises the size of the core set and the minimum of g.

THEOREM 21.1 (Kiefer–Wolfowitz). *Assume that $\mathcal{A} \subset \mathbb{R}^d$ is compact and $\text{span}(\mathcal{A}) = \mathbb{R}^d$. The following are equivalent:*

(a) π^* *is a minimiser of g.*
(b) π^* *is a maximiser of $f(\pi) = \log \det V(\pi)$.*
(c) $g(\pi^*) = d$.

Furthermore, there exists a minimiser π^* of g such that $|\text{Supp}(\pi^*)| \leq d(d+1)/2$.

A design that maximises f is known as a **D-optimal design**, and thus the theorem establishes the equivalence of G-optimal and D-optimal designs.

Proof We give the proof for finite $\mathcal{A}$. The general case follows by passing to the limit (Exercise 21.3). When it is convenient, distributions π on $\mathcal{A}$ are treated as vectors in $\mathbb{R}^{|\mathcal{A}|}$. You will show in Exercises 21.1 and 21.2 that f is concave and that

$$(\nabla f(\pi))_a = \|a\|_{V(\pi)^{-1}}^2. \tag{21.4}$$

Also notice that

$$\sum_{a \in \mathcal{A}} \pi(a)\|a\|_{V(\pi)^{-1}}^2 = \text{trace}\left(\sum_a \pi(a)aa^\top V(\pi)^{-1}\right) = \text{trace}(I) = d. \tag{21.5}$$

(b)$\Rightarrow$(a): Suppose that π^* is a maximiser of f. By the first-order optimality criterion (see Section 26.5), for any π distribution on $\mathcal{A}$,

$$0 \geq \langle \nabla f(\pi^*), \pi - \pi^* \rangle$$
$$= \sum_{a \in \mathcal{A}} \pi(a)\|a\|_{V(\pi^*)^{-1}}^2 - \sum_{a \in \mathcal{A}} \pi^*(a)\|a\|_{V(\pi^*)^{-1}}^2$$
$$= \sum_{a \in \mathcal{A}} \pi(a)\|a\|_{V(\pi^*)^{-1}}^2 - d.$$

For an arbitrary $a \in \mathcal{A}$, choosing π to be the Dirac at $a \in \mathcal{A}$ proves that $\|a\|^2_{V(\pi^*)^{-1}} \leq d$. Hence $g(\pi^*) \leq d$. Since $g(\pi) \geq d$ for all π by Eq. (21.5), it follows that π^* is a minimiser of g and that $\min_\pi g(\pi) = d$. (c) $\Longrightarrow$ (b): Suppose that $g(\pi^*) = d$. Then, for any π,

$$\langle \nabla f(\pi^*), \pi - \pi^* \rangle = \sum_{a \in \mathcal{A}} \pi(a)\|a\|_{V(\pi^*)^{-1}} - d \leq 0.$$

And it follows that π^* is a maximiser of f by the first-order optimality conditions and the concavity of f. That (a) $\Longrightarrow$ (c) is now trivial. To prove the second part of the theorem, let π^* be a minimiser of g, which by the previous part is a maximiser of f. Let $S = \text{Supp}(\pi^*)$, and suppose that $|S| > d(d+1)/2$. Since the dimension of the subspace of $d \times d$ symmetric matrices is $d(d+1)/2$, there must be a non-zero function $v : \mathcal{A} \to \mathbb{R}$ with $\text{Supp}(v) \subseteq S$ such that

$$\sum_{a \in S} v(a)aa^\top = 0. \tag{21.6}$$

Notice that for any $a \in S$, the first-order optimality conditions ensure that $\|a\|^2_{V(\pi^*)^{-1}} = d$ (Exercise 21.5). Hence

$$d \sum_{a \in S} v(a) = \sum_{a \in S} v(a)\|a\|^2_{V(\pi^*)^{-1}} = 0,$$

where the last equality follows from Eq. (21.6). Let $\pi(t) = \pi^* + tv$ and let $\tau = \max\{t > 0 : \pi(t) \in \mathcal{P}_\mathcal{A}\}$, which exists since $v \neq 0$ and $\sum_{a \in S} v(a) = 0$ and $\text{Supp}(v) \subseteq S$. By Eq. (21.6), $V(\pi(t)) = V(\pi^*)$, and hence $f(\pi(\tau)) = f(\pi^*)$, which means that $\pi(\tau)$ also maximises f. The claim follows by checking that $|\text{Supp}(\pi(T))| < |\text{Supp}(\pi^*)|$ and then using induction. $\qquad\square$

Geometric Interpretation

There is a geometric interpretation of the D-optimal design problem. Let π be a D-optimal design for $\mathcal{A}$ and $V = \sum_{a \in \mathcal{A}} \pi(a)aa^\top$ and

$$\mathcal{E} = \{x \in \mathbb{R}^d : \|x\|^2_{V^{-1}} \leq d\},$$

which is a centered ellipsoid. By Theorem 21.1, it holds that $\mathcal{A} \subset \mathcal{E}$ with the core set lying on the boundary (see Fig. 21.1). As you might guess from the figure, the ellipsoid $\mathcal{E}$ is the minimum volume centered ellipsoid containing $\mathcal{A}$. This is known to be unique and the optimisation problem that characterises it is in fact the dual of the log determinant problem that determines the D-optimal design.

21.2 Notes

1 The letter 'd' in D-optimal design comes from the determinant in the objective. The 'g' in G-optimal design stands for 'globally optimal'. The names were coined by Kiefer and Wolfowitz, though both problems appeared in the literature before them.

2 In applications we seldom need an exact solution to the design problem. Finding a distribution π such that $g(\pi) \leq (1 + \varepsilon)g(\pi^*)$ will increase the regret of our algorithms by a factor of just $(1 + \varepsilon)^{1/2}$.

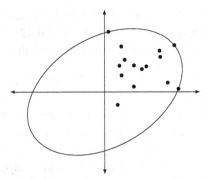

Figure 21.1 The minimum volume centered ellipsoid containing a point cloud. The points on the boundary are the core set. The ellipse is $\mathcal{E} = \{x : \|x\|^2_{V(\pi)^{-1}} = d\}$, where π is an optimal design.

3 The computation of an optimal design for finite action sets is a convex problem for which there are numerous efficient approximation algorithms. The Frank–Wolfe algorithm is one such algorithm, which can be used to find a near-optimal solution for modestly sized problems. The algorithm starts with an initial π_0 and updates according to

$$\pi_{k+1}(a) = (1 - \gamma_k)\pi_k(a) + \gamma_k \mathbb{I}\{a_k = a\}, \qquad (21.7)$$

where $a_k = \operatorname{argmax}_{a \in \mathcal{A}} \|a\|^2_{V(\pi_k)^{-1}}$ and the step size is chosen to optimise f along the line connecting π_k and δ_{a_k}.

$$\gamma_k = \operatorname{argmax}_{\gamma \in [0,1]} f((1 - \gamma)\pi_k + \gamma \delta_{a_k}) = \frac{\frac{1}{d}\|a_k\|^2_{V(\pi_k)^{-1}} - 1}{\|a_k\|^2_{V(\pi_k)^{-1}} - 1}. \qquad (21.8)$$

If π_0 is chosen to be the uniform distribution over $\mathcal{A}$, then the number of iterations before $g(\pi_k) \le (1+\varepsilon)g(\pi^*)$ is at most $O(d \log \log |\mathcal{A}| + d/\varepsilon)$. For a slightly more sophisticated choice of initialisation the dependence on $|\mathcal{A}|$ can be eliminated entirely. More importantly, this other initialisation has a core set of size $O(d)$ and running the algorithm in Eq. (21.7) for just $O(d \log \log d)$ iterations is guaranteed to produce a design with $g(\pi) \le 2g(\pi^*)$ and a core set of size $O(d \log \log d)$.

4 If the action set is infinite, then approximately optimal designs can sometimes still be found efficiently. Unfortunately the algorithms in the infinite case tend to be much 'heavier' and less practical.

5 The smallest ellipsoid containing some set $\mathcal{K} \subset \mathbb{R}^d$ is called the **minimum volume enclosing ellipsoid** (MVEE) of $\mathcal{K}$. As remarked, the D-optimal design problem is equivalent to finding an MVEE of $\mathcal{A}$ with the added constraint that the ellipsoid must be centred – or equivalently, finding the MVEE of the symmetrised set $\mathcal{A} \cup \{-a : a \in \mathcal{A}\}$. The MVEE of a convex set is also called John's ellipsoid, which has many applications in optimisation and beyond.

6 In Exercise 21.6, you will generalise Kiefer–Wolfowitz theorem to sets that do not span $\mathbb{R}^d$. When $\mathcal{A}$ is compact and $\dim(\operatorname{span}(\mathcal{A})) = m \in [d]$, then there exists a distribution π^* supported on at most $m(m+1)/2$ points of $\mathcal{A}$ and for which $g(\pi^*) = m = \inf_\pi g(\pi)$.

21.3 Bibliographic Remarks

The Kiefer–Wolfowitz theorem is due to Kiefer and Wolfowitz [1960]. The algorithm in Note 3 is due to Fedorov [1972]. A similar variant was also proposed by Wynn [1970], and the name Wynn's method is sometimes used. The algorithm is a specialisation of Frank–Wolfe's algorithm, which was originally intended for quadratic programming [Frank and Wolfe, 1956]. Todd [2016] wrote a nice book about minimum volume ellipsoids and related algorithms, where you can also find many more references and improvements to the basic algorithms. Chapter 3 of his book also includes discussion of alternative initialisations and convergence rates for various algorithms. The duality between D-optimal design and the MVEE problem was shown by Silvey and Sibson [1972]. Although the connection between minimum volume ellipsoids and experimental design is well known, previous applications of these results to bandits used John's theorem without appropriate symmetrisation, which made the resulting arguments more cumbersome. For more details on finding approximately optimal designs for infinite sets, see the article by Hazan et al. [2016], references there-in and the book by Grötschel et al. [2012].

21.4 Exercises

21.1 (DERIVATIVE OF LOG DETERMINANT) Prove the correctness of the derivative in Eq. (21.4).

HINT   For square matrix A let $\mathrm{adj}(A)$ be the transpose of the cofactor matrix of A. Use the facts that the inverse of a matrix A is $A^{-1} = \mathrm{adj}(A)^{\top} / \det(A)$ and that if $A : \mathbb{R} \to \mathbb{R}^{d \times d}$, then

$$\frac{d}{dt} \det(A(t)) = \mathrm{trace}\left(\mathrm{adj}(A) \frac{d}{dt} A(t) \right).$$

21.2 (CONCAVITY OF LOG DETERMINANT) Prove that $H \mapsto \log \det(H)$ is concave where H is a symmetric, positive definite matrix.

HINT   Consider $t \mapsto \log \det(H + tZ)$ for Z symmetric, and show that this is a concave function.

21.3 (KIEFER–WOLFOWITZ FOR COMPACT SETS) Generalise the proof of Theorem 21.1 to compact action sets.

21.4 Prove the second inequality in Eq. (21.8).

21.5 Let π^* be a G-optimal design and $a \in \mathrm{Supp}(\pi^*)$. Prove that $\|a\|^2_{V(\pi^*)^{-1}} = d$.

21.6 Prove that if $\mathcal{A}$ is compact and $\dim(\mathrm{span}(\mathcal{A})) = m \in [d]$, then there exists a distribution π^* over $\mathcal{A}$ supported on at most $m(m+1)/2$ points and for which $g(\pi^*) = m$.

21.7 (IMPLEMENTATION) Write a program that accepts as parameters a finite set $\mathcal{A} \subset \mathbb{R}^d$ and returns a design $\pi : \mathcal{A} \to [0, 1]$ such that $g(\pi) \leq d + \varepsilon$ for some given $\varepsilon > 0$. How robust is your algorithm? Experiment with different choices of $\mathcal{A}$ and d, and report your results.

HINT   The easiest pure way to do this is to implement the Frank–Wolfe algorithm described in Note 3. All quantities can be updated incrementally using rank-one update formulas, and this will lead to a significant speedup. You might like to read the third chapter of the book by Todd [2016] and experiment with the proposed variants.

22 Stochastic Linear Bandits with Finitely Many Arms

The optimal design problem from the previous chapter has immediate applications to stochastic linear bandits. In Chapter 19, we developed a linear version of the upper confidence bound algorithm that achieves a regret of $R_n = O(d\sqrt{n}\log(n))$. The only required assumptions were that the sequence of available action sets were bounded. In this short chapter, we consider a more restricted setting where:

1. the set of actions available in round t is $\mathcal{A} \subset \mathbb{R}^d$ and $|\mathcal{A}| = k$ for some natural number k;
2. the reward is $X_t = \langle \theta_*, A_t \rangle + \eta_t$ where η_t is conditionally 1-subgaussian:

$$\mathbb{E}[\exp(\lambda \eta_t)|A_1, \eta_1, \ldots, A_{t-1}] \leq \exp(\lambda^2/2) \quad \text{almost surely for all } \lambda \in \mathbb{R}; \text{ and}$$

3. the suboptimality gaps satisfy $\Delta_a = \max_{b \in \mathcal{A}} \langle \theta_*, b - a \rangle \leq 1$ for all $a \in \mathcal{A}$.

The key difference relative to Chapter 19 is that now the set of actions is finite and does not change with time. Under these conditions, it becomes possible to design a policy such that

$$R_n = O\left(\sqrt{dn\log(nk)}\right).$$

For moderately sized k, this bound improves the regret by a factor of $d^{1/2}$, which in some regimes is large enough to be worth the effort. The policy is an instance of phase-based elimination algorithms. As usual, at the end of a phase, arms that are likely to be suboptimal with a gap exceeding the current target are eliminated. In fact, this elimination is the only way the data collected in a phase is being used. In particular, the actions to be played during a phase are chosen based entirely on the data from previous phases: the data collected in the present phase do not influence which actions are played. This decoupling allows us to make use of the tighter confidence bounds available in the fixed design setting, as discussed in the previous chapter. The choice of policy within each phase uses the solution to an optimal design problem to minimise the number of required samples to eliminate arms that are far from optimal.

THEOREM 22.1. *With probability at least $1 - \delta$, the regret of Algorithm 12 satisfies*

$$R_n \leq C\sqrt{nd\log\left(\frac{k\log(n)}{\delta}\right)},$$

where $C > 0$ is a universal constant. If $\delta = O(1/n)$, then $\mathbb{E}[R_n] \leq C\sqrt{nd\log(kn)}$ for an appropriately chosen universal constant $C > 0$.

Input $\mathcal{A} \subset \mathbb{R}^d$ and δ

Step 0 Set $\ell = 1$ and let $\mathcal{A}_1 = \mathcal{A}$

Step 1 Let $t_\ell = t$ be the current timestep and find G-optimal design $\pi_\ell \in \mathcal{P}(\mathcal{A}_\ell)$ with $\mathrm{Supp}(\pi_\ell) \leq d(d+1)/2$ that maximises

$$\log \det V(\pi_\ell) \text{ subject to } \sum_{a \in \mathcal{A}_\ell} \pi_\ell(a) = 1$$

Step 2 Let $\varepsilon_\ell = 2^{-\ell}$ and

$$T_\ell(a) = \left\lceil \frac{2d\pi_\ell(a)}{\varepsilon_\ell^2} \log\left(\frac{k\ell(\ell+1)}{\delta}\right) \right\rceil \text{ and } T_\ell = \sum_{a \in \mathcal{A}_\ell} T_\ell(a)$$

Step 3 Choose each action $a \in \mathcal{A}_\ell$ exactly $T_\ell(a)$ times

Step 4 Calculate the empirical estimate:

$$\hat{\theta}_\ell = V_\ell^{-1} \sum_{t=t_\ell}^{t_\ell + T_\ell} A_t X_t \quad \text{with} \quad V_\ell = \sum_{a \in \mathcal{A}_\ell} T_\ell(a) a a^\mathsf{T}$$

Step 5 Eliminate low rewarding arms:

$$\mathcal{A}_{\ell+1} = \left\{ a \in \mathcal{A}_\ell : \max_{b \in \mathcal{A}_\ell} \langle \hat{\theta}_\ell, b - a \rangle \leq 2\varepsilon_\ell \right\}.$$

Step 6 $\ell \leftarrow \ell + 1$ and **Goto Step 1**

Algorithm 12: Phased elimination with G-optimal exploration.

The proof of this theorem follows relatively directly from the high-probability correctness of the confidence intervals used to eliminate low-rewarding arms. We leave the details to the reader in Exercise 22.1.

22.1 Notes

1 The assumption that the action set does not change is crucial for Algorithm 12. Several complicated algorithms have been proposed and analysed for the case where $\mathcal{A}_t$ is allowed to change from round to round under the assumption that $|\mathcal{A}_t| \leq k$ for all rounds. For these algorithms, it has been proven that

$$R_n = O\left(\sqrt{nd \log^3(nk)}\right). \tag{22.1}$$

When k is small, these results improve on the bound for LinUCB in Chapter 19 by a factor of up to $\sqrt{d}$.

2 Algorithm 12 can be adapted to the case where k is infinite by using confidence intervals derived in Chapter 20. Once the dust has settled, you should find the regret is

$$R_n = O\left(d\sqrt{n \log(n)}\right).$$

3 One advantage of Algorithm 12 is that it behaves well even when the linear model is misspecified. Suppose the reward is $X_t = \langle \theta, A_t \rangle + \eta_t + f(A_t)$, where η_t is noise as usual and $f : \mathcal{A} \to \mathbb{R}$ is some function with $\|f\|_\infty \leq \varepsilon$. Then the regret of Algorithm 12 can be shown to be

$$R_n = O\left(\sqrt{dn\log(nk)} + n\varepsilon\sqrt{d}\log(n)\right).$$

The linear dependence on the horizon should be expected when k is large. The presence of $\sqrt{d}$ in the second term is unfortunate, but unavoidable in many regimes as discussed by Lattimore and Szepesvári [2019b].

22.2 Bibliographic Remarks

The algorithms achieving Eq. (22.1) for changing action sets are SupLinRel [Auer, 2002] and SupLinUCB [Chu et al., 2011]. Both introduce phases to decouple the dependence of the design on the outcomes. Unfortunately the analysis of these algorithms is long and technical, which prohibited us from presenting the ideas here. These algorithms are also not the most practical relative to LinUCB (Chapter 19) or Thompson sampling (Chapter 36). Of course this does not diminish the theoretical breakthrough. Phased elimination algorithms have appeared in many places, but the most similar to the algorithm presented here is the work on spectral bandits by Valko et al. [2014] (and we have also met them briefly in earlier chapters on finite-armed bandits). None of the works just mentioned used the Kiefer–Wolfowitz theorem. This idea is apparently new, but it is based on the literature on adversarial linear bandits where John's ellipsoid has been used to define exploration policies [Bubeck et al., 2012]. For more details on adversarial linear bandits, read on to Part VI.

Ghosh et al. [2017] address misspecified (stochastic) linear bandits with a fixed action set. In misspecified linear bandits, the reward is nearly a linear function of the feature vectors associated with the actions. Ghosh et al. [2017] demonstrate that in the favourable case when one can cheaply test linearity, an algorithm that first runs a test and then switches to either a linear bandit or a finite-armed bandit based on the outcome will achieve $(\sqrt{k} \wedge d)\sqrt{n}$ regret up to log factors. We will return to misspecified linear bandits a few more times in the book.

22.3 Exercises

22.1 In this exercise, you will prove Theorem 22.1.

(a) Use Theorem 21.1 to show that the length of the ℓth phase is bounded by

$$T_\ell \leq \frac{2d}{\varepsilon_\ell^2} \log\left(\frac{k\ell(\ell+1)}{\delta}\right) + \frac{d(d+1)}{2}.$$

(b) Let $a^* \in \operatorname{argmax}_{a \in \mathcal{A}} \langle \theta_*, a \rangle$ be the optimal arm and use Theorem 21.1 to show that

$$\mathbb{P}\left(\text{exists phase } \ell \text{ such that } a^* \notin \mathcal{A}_\ell\right) \leq \frac{\delta}{k}.$$

(c) For action a define $\ell_a = \min\{\ell : 2\varepsilon_\ell < \Delta_a\}$ to be the first phase where the suboptimality gap of arm a is smaller than $2\varepsilon_\ell$. Show that

$$\mathbb{P}\left(a \in \mathcal{A}_{\ell_a}\right) \leq \frac{\delta}{k}.$$

(d) Show that with probability at least $1 - \delta$ the regret is bounded by

$$R_n \leq C \sqrt{dn \log \left(\frac{k \log(n)}{\delta} \right)},$$

where $C > 0$ is a universal constant.

(e) Show that this implies Theorem 22.1 for the given choice of δ.

22.2 (MISSPECIFIED LINEAR BANDITS) Assume the reward satisfies $X_t = \langle \theta, A_t \rangle + \eta_t + f(A_t)$, where η_t is 1-subgaussian noise as usual and $f : \mathcal{A} \to \mathbb{R}$ is some function with $\|f\|_\infty \leq \varepsilon$, show that the expected regret of Algorithm 12 with the choice $\delta = 1/n$ is

$$R_n = O\left(\sqrt{dn \log(nk)} + n\varepsilon\sqrt{d}\log(n) \right).$$

23 Stochastic Linear Bandits with Sparsity

In Chapter 19 we showed the linear variant of UCB has regret bounded by

$$R_n = O(d\sqrt{n}\log(n)),$$

which for fixed finite action sets can be improved to

$$R_n = O(\sqrt{dn\log(nk)}).$$

For moderately sized action sets, these approaches lead to a big improvement over what could be obtained by using the policies that do not make use of the linear structure.

The situation is still not perfect, though. In typical applications, the features are chosen by the user of the system, and one can easily imagine there are many candidate features and limited information about which will be most useful. This presents the user with a challenging trade-off. If they include many features, then d will be large, and the algorithm may be slow to learn. But if a useful feature is omitted, then the linear model will almost certainly be quite wrong. Ideally, one should be able to add features without suffering much additional regret if the added feature does not contribute in a significant way. This can be captured by the notion of sparsity, which is the central theme of this chapter.

23.1 Sparse Linear Stochastic Bandits

Like in the standard stochastic linear bandit setting, at the beginning of round t, the learner receives a decision set $\mathcal{A}_t \subset \mathbb{R}^d$. They then choose an action $A_t \in \mathcal{A}_t$ and receive a reward

$$X_t = \langle \theta_*, A_t \rangle + \eta_t, \tag{23.1}$$

where $(\eta_t)_t$ is zero-mean noise and $\theta_* \in \mathbb{R}^d$ is an unknown vector. The only difference in the sparse setting is that the parameter vector θ_* is assumed to have many zero entries. For $\theta \in \mathbb{R}^d$ let

$$\|\theta\|_0 = \sum_{i=1}^{d} \mathbb{I}\{\theta_i \neq 0\},$$

which is sometimes called the zero-'norm' (quotations because it is not really a norm; see Exercise 23.1).

ASSUMPTION 23.1. The following hold:

(a) *(Sparse parameter)* There exist known constants m_0 and m_2 such that $\|\theta_*\|_0 \leq m_0$ and $\|\theta_*\|_2 \leq m_2$.

(b) *(Bounded mean rewards)* $\langle \theta_*, a \rangle \leq 1$ for all $a \in \mathcal{A}_t$ and all rounds t.

(c) *(Subgaussian noise)* The noise is conditionally 1-subgaussian:

$$\text{for all } \lambda \in \mathbb{R}, \qquad \mathbb{E}[\exp(\lambda \eta_t) \mid \mathcal{F}_{t-1}] \leq \exp(\lambda^2/2) \text{ a.s.,}$$

where $\mathcal{F}_t = \sigma(A_1, X_1, \ldots, A_t, X_t, A_{t+1})$.

Much ink has been spilled on what can be said about the speed of learning in linear models like (23.1) when $(A_t)_t$ are passively generated and the parameter vector is known to be sparse. Most results are phrased about recovering θ_*, but there also exist a few results that quantify the error when predicting X_t. The ideal outcome would be that the learning speed depends mostly on m_0, with only a mild dependence on d. Almost all the results come under the assumption that the covariance matrix of the actions $(A_t)_t$ is well conditioned.

> The **condition number** of a positive definite matrix A is the ratio of its largest and smallest eigenvalues. A matrix is **well conditioned** if it has a small condition number.

The details are a bit more complicated than just the conditioning, but the main point is that the usual assumptions imposed on the covariance matrix of the actions for passive learning are never satisfied when the actions are chosen by a good bandit policy. The reason is simple. Bandit algorithms want to choose the optimal action as often as possible, which means the covariance matrix will have an eigenvector that points (approximately) towards the optimal action with a large corresponding eigenvalue. We need some approach that does not rely on such strong assumptions.

23.2 Elimination on the Hypercube

As a warm-up, consider the case where the action set is the d-dimensional hypercube: $\mathcal{A}_t = \mathcal{A} = [-1, 1]^d$. To reduce clutter, we denote the true parameter vector by $\theta = \theta_*$. The hypercube is notable as an action set because it enjoys perfect separability. For each dimension $i \in [d]$, the value of $A_{ti} \in [-1, 1]$ can be chosen independently of A_{tj} for $j \neq i$. Because of this, the optimal action is $a^* = \text{sign}(\theta)$, where

$$\text{sign}(\theta)_i = \text{sign}(\theta_i) = \begin{cases} 1, & \text{if } \theta_i > 0; \\ 0, & \text{if } \theta_i = 0; \\ -1, & \text{if } \theta_i < 0. \end{cases}$$

So learning the optimal action amounts to learning the sign of θ_i for each dimension. A disadvantage of this structure is that in the worst case the sign of each θ_i must be learned independently, which in Chapter 24 we show leads to a worst-case regret of $R_n = \Omega(d\sqrt{n})$. On the positive side, the seperability means that θ_i can be estimated in each dimension independently while paying absolutely no price for this experimentation when $\theta_i = 0$. It turns out that this allows us to design a policy for which $R_n = O(\|\theta\|_0\sqrt{n})$, even without knowing the value of $\|\theta\|_0$.

Let $\mathcal{G}_t = \sigma(A_1, X_1, \ldots, A_t, X_t)$ be the σ-algebra containing information up to time $t - 1$ (this differs from $\mathcal{F}_t$, which also includes information about the action chosen). Now suppose that $(A_{ti})_{i=1}^d$ are chosen to be conditionally independent given $\mathcal{G}_{t-1}$, and further assume for some specific $i \in [d]$ that A_{ti} is sampled from a Rademacher distribution so that $\mathbb{P}(A_{ti} = 1 \mid \mathcal{G}_{t-1}) = \mathbb{P}(A_{ti} = -1 \mid \mathcal{G}_{t-1}) = 1/2$. Then

$$\mathbb{E}[A_{ti}X_t \mid \mathcal{G}_{t-1}] = \mathbb{E}\left[A_{ti}\left(\sum_{j=1}^d A_{tj}\theta_j + \eta_t \right) \Big| \mathcal{G}_{t-1} \right]$$

$$= \theta_i \mathbb{E}[A_{ti}^2 \mid \mathcal{G}_{t-1}] + \sum_{j \neq i} \theta_j \mathbb{E}[A_{tj}A_{ti} \mid \mathcal{G}_{t-1}] + \mathbb{E}[A_{ti}\eta_t \mid \mathcal{G}_{t-1}]$$

$$= \theta_i,$$

where the first equality is the definition of $X_t = \langle \theta, A_t \rangle + \eta_t$, the second by linearity of expectation and the third by the conditional independence of $(A_{ti})_i$ and the fact that $\mathbb{E}[A_{ti} \mid \mathcal{G}_{t-1}] = 0$ and $\mathbb{E}[A_{ti}^2 \mid \mathcal{G}_{t-1}] = 1$. This looks quite promising, but we should also check the variance. Using our assumptions that (η_t) is conditionally 1-subgaussian and that $\langle \theta, a \rangle \leq 1$ for all actions a, we have

$$\mathbb{V}[A_{ti}X_t \mid \mathcal{G}_{t-1}] = \mathbb{E}[A_{ti}^2 X_t^2 \mid \mathcal{G}_{t-1}] - \theta_i^2 = \mathbb{E}[(\langle \theta, A_t \rangle + \eta_t)^2 \mid \mathcal{G}_{t-1}] - \theta_i^2 \leq 2. \tag{23.2}$$

And now we have cause for celebration. The value of θ_i can be estimated by choosing A_{ti} to be a Rademacher random variable independent of the choices in other dimensions. All the policy does is treat all dimensions independently. For a particular dimension (say i), it explores by choosing $A_{ti} \in \{-1, 1\}$ uniformly at random until its estimate is sufficiently accurate to commit to either $A_{ti} = 1$ or $A_{ti} = -1$ for all future rounds. How long this takes depends on $|\theta_i|$, but note that if $|\theta_i|$ is small, then the price of exploring is also limited. The policy that results from this idea is called selective explore-then-commit (Algorithm 13, SETC).

THEOREM 23.2. *There exists a universal constants $C, C' > 0$ such that the regret of SETC satisfies*

$$R_n \leq 3\|\theta\|_1 + C \sum_{i:\theta_i \neq 0} \frac{\log(n)}{|\theta_i|} \quad \text{and} \quad R_n \leq 3\|\theta\|_1 + C'\|\theta\|_0 \sqrt{n \log(n)}.$$

By appealing to the central limit theorem and the variance calculation in Eq. (23.2), we should be hopeful that the confidence intervals used by the algorithm are sufficiently large to contain the true θ_i with high probability, but this still needs to be proven.

LEMMA 23.3. *Define $\tau_i = n \wedge \max\{t : E_{ti} = 1\}$, and let $F_i = \mathbb{I}\{\theta_i \notin C_{\tau_i+1,i}\}$ be the event that θ_i is not in the confidence interval constructed at time τ_i. Then $\mathbb{P}(F_i) \leq 1/n$.*

The proof of Lemma 23.3 is left until after the proof of Theorem 23.2.

1: **Input** n and d

2: Set $E_{1i} = 1$ and $C_{1i} = \mathbb{R}$ for all $i \in [d]$

3: **for** $t = 1, \ldots, n$ **do**

4:     For each $i \in [d]$ sample $B_{ti} \sim$ RADEMACHER

5:     Choose action:

$$(\forall i) \quad A_{ti} = \begin{cases} B_{ti} & \text{if } 0 \in C_{ti} \\ 1 & \text{if } C_{ti} \subset (0, \infty] \\ -1 & \text{if } C_{ti} \subset [-\infty, 0). \end{cases}$$

6:     Play A_t and observe X_t

7:     Construct empirical estimators:

$$(\forall i) \quad T_i(t) = \sum_{s=1}^{t} E_{si} \qquad \hat{\theta}_{ti} = \frac{\sum_{s=1}^{t} E_{si} A_{si} X_s}{T_i(t)}$$

8:     Construct confidence intervals:

$$(\forall i) \quad W_{ti} = 2\sqrt{\left(\frac{1}{T_i(t)} + \frac{1}{T_i(t)^2}\right) \log\left(n\sqrt{2T_i(t) + 1}\right)}$$

$$(\forall i) \quad C_{t+1,i} = \left[\hat{\theta}_{ti} - W_{ti}, \hat{\theta}_{ti} + W_{ti}\right]$$

9:     Update exploration parameters:

$$(\forall i) \quad E_{t+1,i} = \begin{cases} 0 & \text{if } 0 \notin C_{t+1,i} \text{ or } E_{ti} = 0 \\ 1 & \text{otherwise.} \end{cases}$$

10: **end for**

Algorithm 13: Selective explore-then-commit.

Proof of Theorem 23.2   Recalling the definition of the regret and using the fact that the optimal action is $a^* = \text{sign}(\theta)$, we have the following regret decomposition:

$$R_n = \max_{a \in \mathcal{A}} \langle \theta, a \rangle - \mathbb{E}\left[\sum_{t=1}^{n} \langle \theta, A_t \rangle\right] = \sum_{i=1}^{d} \underbrace{\left(n|\theta_i| - \mathbb{E}\left[\sum_{t=1}^{n} A_{ti}\theta_i\right]\right)}_{R_{ni}}. \tag{23.3}$$

Clearly, if $\theta_i = 0$, then $R_{ni} = 0$. And so it suffices to bound R_{ni} for each i with $|\theta_i| > 0$. Suppose that $|\theta_i| > 0$ for some i and the failure event F_i given in Lemma 23.3 does not occur. Then $\theta_i \in C_{\tau_i+1,t}$, and by the definition of the algorithm, $A_{ti} = \text{sign}(\theta_i)$ for all $t \geq \tau_i$. Therefore,

$$R_{ni} = n|\theta_i| - \mathbb{E}\left[\sum_{t=1}^{n} A_{ti}\theta_i\right] = \mathbb{E}\left[\sum_{t=1}^{n} |\theta_i|(1 - A_{ti}\text{sign}(\theta_i))\right]$$

$$\leq 2n|\theta_i|\mathbb{P}(F_i) + |\theta_i|\mathbb{E}\left[\mathbb{I}\{F_i^c\}\tau_i\right]. \tag{23.4}$$

Since τ_i is the first round t when $0 \notin C_{t+1,i}$ it follows that if F_i does not occur, then $\theta_i \in C_{\tau_i,i}$ and $0 \in C_{\tau_i,i}$. Thus the width of the confidence interval $C_{\tau_i,i}$ must be at least $|\theta_i|$, and so

$$2W_{\tau_i-1,i} = 4\sqrt{\left(\frac{1}{\tau_i - 1} + \frac{1}{(\tau_i - 1)^2}\right) \log\left(n\sqrt{2\tau_i - 1}\right)} \geq |\theta_i|,$$

which after rearranging shows for some universal constant $C > 0$ that

$$\mathbb{I}\{F_i^c\}(\tau_i - 1) \leq 1 + \frac{C\log(n)}{\theta_i^2}.$$

Combining this result with Eq. (23.4) leads to

$$R_{ni} \leq 2n|\theta_i|\mathbb{P}(F_i) + |\theta_i| + \frac{C\log(n)}{|\theta_i|}.$$

Using Lemma 23.3 to bound $\mathbb{P}(F_i)$ and substituting into the decomposition Eq. (23.3) completes the proof of the first part. The second part is left as a treat for you (Exercise 23.2). $\square$

Proof of Lemma 23.3   Let $S_{ti} = \sum_{j \neq i} A_{tj}\theta_j$ and $Z_{ti} = A_{ti}\eta_t + A_{ti}S_{ti}$. For $t \leq \tau_i$,

$$\hat{\theta}_{ti} - \theta_i = \frac{1}{t}\sum_{s=1}^{t} Z_{si}.$$

The next step is to show that Z_{ti} is conditionally $\sqrt{2}$-subgaussian for $t \leq \tau_i$:

$$\mathbb{E}\left[\exp(\lambda Z_{ti}) \mid \mathcal{G}_{t-1}\right] = \mathbb{E}\left[\mathbb{E}\left[\exp(\lambda Z_{ti}) \mid \mathcal{F}_{t-1}\right] \mid \mathcal{G}_{t-1}\right]$$

$$= \mathbb{E}\left[\exp(\lambda A_{ti}S_{ti})\mathbb{E}\left[\exp(\lambda A_{ti}\eta_t) \mid \mathcal{F}_{t-1}\right] \mid \mathcal{G}_{t-1}\right]$$

$$\leq \mathbb{E}\left[\exp(\lambda A_{ti}S_{ti})\exp\left(\frac{\lambda^2}{2}\right) \mid \mathcal{G}_{t-1}\right]$$

$$= \exp\left(\frac{\lambda^2}{2}\right)\mathbb{E}\left[\mathbb{E}\left[\exp(\lambda A_{ti}S_{ti}) \mid \mathcal{G}_{t-1}, S_{ti}\right] \mid \mathcal{G}_{t-1}\right]$$

$$\leq \exp\left(\frac{\lambda^2}{2}\right)\mathbb{E}\left[\exp\left(\frac{\lambda^2 S_{ti}^2}{2}\right) \mid \mathcal{G}_{t-1}\right]$$

$$\leq \exp(\lambda^2).$$

The first inequality used the fact that η_t is conditionally 1-subgaussian. The second-to-last inequality follows because A_{ti} is conditionally Rademacher for $t \leq \tau_i$, which is 1-subgaussian by Hoeffding's lemma (5.11). The final inequality follows because $S_{ti} \leq \|A_t\|_\infty \|\theta\|_1 \leq 1$. The result follows by applying the concentration bound from Exercise 20.8. $\square$

23.3 Online to Confidence Set Conversion

A new plan is needed to relax the assumption that the action set is a hypercube. The idea is to modify the ellipsoidal confidence set used in Chapter 19 to have a smaller radius. We will see that modifying the algorithm in Chapter 19 to use the smaller confidence intervals improves the regret to $R_n = O(\sqrt{dpn}\log(n))$.

Without assumptions on the action set, one cannot hope to have a regret smaller than $O(\sqrt{dn})$. To see this, recall that d-armed bandits can be represented as linear bandits with $\mathcal{A}_t = \{e_1, \ldots, e_d\}$. For these problems, Theorem 15.2 shows that for any policy there exists a d-armed bandit for which $R_n = \Omega(\sqrt{dn})$. Checking the proof reveals that when adapted to the linear setting the parameter vector is 2-sparse.

The construction that follows makes use of a kind of duality between online prediction and confidence sets. While we will only apply the idea to the sparse linear case, the approach is generic.

The prediction problem considered is **online linear prediction** under the squared loss. This is also known as **online linear regression**. The learner interacts with an environment in a sequential manner where in each round $t \in \mathbb{N}^+$:

1. The environment chooses $X_t \in \mathbb{R}$ and $A_t \in \mathbb{R}^d$ in an arbitrary fashion.
2. The value of A_t is revealed to the learner (but not X_t).
3. The learner produces a real-valued prediction $\hat{X}_t \in \mathbb{R}$ in some way.
4. The environment reveals X_t to the learner and the loss is $(X_t - \hat{X}_t)^2$.

The regret of the learner relative to a linear predictor that uses the weights $\theta \in \mathbb{R}^d$ is

$$\rho_n(\theta) = \sum_{t=1}^{n}(X_t - \hat{X}_t)^2 - \sum_{t=1}^{n}(X_t - \langle\theta, A_t\rangle)^2. \tag{23.5}$$

We say that the learner enjoys a regret guarantee B_n relative to $\Theta \subseteq \mathbb{R}^d$ if for any strategy of the environment,

$$\sup_{\theta\in\Theta} \rho_n(\theta) \le B_n. \tag{23.6}$$

The online learning literature has a number of powerful techniques for this learning problem. Later we will give a specific result for the sparse case when $\Theta = \{x : \|x\|_0 \le m_0\}$, but first we show how to use such a learning algorithm to construct a confidence set. Take any learner for online linear regression, and assume the environment generates X_t in a stochastic manner like in linear bandits:

$$X_t = \langle\theta_*, A_t\rangle + \eta_t. \tag{23.7}$$

Combining Eqs. (23.5) to (23.7) with elementary algebra,

$$Q_t = \sum_{t=1}^{n}(\hat{X}_t - \langle\theta_*, A_t\rangle)^2 = \rho_n(\theta_*) + 2\sum_{t=1}^{n}\eta_t(\hat{X}_t - \langle\theta_*, A_t\rangle)$$

$$\le B_n + 2\sum_{t=1}^{n}\eta_t(\hat{X}_t - \langle\theta_*, A_t\rangle), \tag{23.8}$$

where the first equality serves as the definition of Q_t. Let us now take stock for a moment. If we could somehow remove the dependence on the noise η_t in the right-hand side, then we could define a confidence set consisting of all θ that satisfy the equation. Of course the noise has zero mean and is conditionally independent of its multiplier, so the expectation of this term is zero. The fluctuations can be controlled with high probability using a little concentration analysis. Let

$$Z_t = \sum_{s=1}^{t} \eta_s(\hat{X}_s - \langle \theta_*, A_s \rangle).$$

Since $\hat{X}_t$ is chosen based on information available at the beginning of the round, $\hat{X}_t$ is $\mathcal{F}_{t-1}$-measurable, and so

for all $\lambda \in \mathbb{R}$, $\qquad \mathbb{E}[\exp(\lambda(Z_t - Z_{t-1})) \,|\, \mathcal{F}_{t-1}] \leq \exp(\lambda^2 \sigma_t^2/2)$,

where $\sigma_t^2 = (\hat{X}_t - \langle \theta_*, A_t \rangle)^2$. The uniform self-normalised tail bound (Theorem 20.4) with $\lambda = 1$ implies that,

$$\mathbb{P}\left(\text{exists } t \geq 0 \text{ such that } |Z_t| \geq \sqrt{(1 + Q_t)\log\left(\frac{1 + Q_t}{\delta^2}\right)}\right) \leq \delta.$$

Provided this low-probability event does not occur, then from Eq. (23.8) we have

$$Q_t \leq B_t + 2\sqrt{(1 + Q_t)\log\left(\frac{1 + Q_t}{\delta^2}\right)}. \tag{23.9}$$

While both sides depend on Q_t, the left-hand side grows linearly, while the right-hand side grows sublinearly in Q_t. This means that the largest value of Q_t that satisfies the above inequality is finite. A tedious calculation then shows this value must be less than

$$\beta_t(\delta) = 1 + 2B_t + 32\log\left(\frac{\sqrt{8} + \sqrt{1 + B_t}}{\delta}\right). \tag{23.10}$$

By piecing together the parts, we conclude that with probability at least $1 - \delta$ the following holds for all t:

$$Q_t = \sum_{s=1}^{t}(\hat{X}_s - \langle \theta_*, A_s \rangle)^2 \leq \beta_t(\delta).$$

We could define $\mathcal{C}_{t+1}$ to be the set of all θ such that the above holds with θ_* replaced by θ, but there is one additionally subtlety, which is that the resulting confidence interval may be unbounded (think about the case that $\sum_{s=1}^{t} A_s A_s^\top$ is not invertible). In Chapter 19 we overcame this problem by regularising the least squares estimator. Since we have assumed that $\|\theta_*\|_2 \leq m_2$, the previous display implies that

$$\|\theta_*\|_2^2 + \sum_{s=1}^{t}(\hat{X}_s - \langle \theta_*, A_s \rangle)^2 \leq m_2^2 + \beta_t(\delta).$$

All together, we have the following theorem:

THEOREM 23.4. *Let* $\delta \in (0,1)$ *and assume that* $\theta_* \in \Theta$ *and* $\sup_{\theta \in \Theta} \rho_t(\theta) \leq B_t$. *If*

$$C_{t+1} = \left\{ \theta \in \mathbb{R}^d : \|\theta\|_2^2 + \sum_{s=1}^{t} (\hat{X}_s - \langle \theta, A_s \rangle)^2 \leq m_2^2 + \beta_t(\delta) \right\},$$

then $\mathbb{P}$ *(exists* $t \in \mathbb{N}$ *such that* $\theta_* \notin C_{t+1}) \leq \delta$.

The confidence set in Theorem 23.4 is not in the most convenient form. By defining $V_t = I + \sum_{s=1}^{t} A_s A_s^\top$ and $S_t = \sum_{s=1}^{t} A_s \hat{X}_s$ and $\hat{\theta}_t = V_t^{-1} S_t$ and performing an algebraic calculation that we leave to the reader (see Exercise 23.5), one can see that

$$\|\theta\|_2^2 + \sum_{s=1}^{t} (\hat{X}_s - \langle \theta, A_s \rangle)^2 = \|\theta - \hat{\theta}_t\|_{V_t}^2 + \sum_{s=1}^{t} (\hat{X}_s - \langle \hat{\theta}_t, A_s \rangle)^2 + \|\hat{\theta}_t\|_2^2. \quad (23.11)$$

Using this, the confidence set can be rewritten in the familiar form of an ellipsoid:

$$C_{t+1} = \left\{ \theta \in \mathbb{R}^d : \|\theta - \hat{\theta}_t\|_{V_t}^2 \leq m_2^2 + \beta_t(\delta) - \|\hat{\theta}_t\|_2^2 - \sum_{s=1}^{t} (\hat{X}_s^2 - \langle \hat{\theta}_t, A_s \rangle)^2 \right\}.$$

1: **Input** Online linear predictor and regret bound B_t, confidence parameter $\delta \in (0,1)$
2: **for** $t = 1, \ldots, n$ **do**
3:     Receive action set $\mathcal{A}_t$
4:     Computer confidence set:

$$C_t = \left\{ \theta \in \mathbb{R}^d : \|\theta\|_2^2 + \sum_{s=1}^{t-1} (\hat{X}_s - \langle \theta, A_s \rangle)^2 \leq m_2^2 + \beta_t(\delta) \right\}$$

5:     Calculate optimistic action

$$A_t = \mathrm{argmax}_{a \in \mathcal{A}_t} \max_{\theta \in C_t} \langle \theta, a \rangle$$

6:     Feed A_t to the online linear predictor and obtain prediction $\hat{X}_t$
7:     Play A_t and receive reward X_t
8:     Feed X_t to online linear predictor as feedback
9: **end for**

Algorithm 14: Online linear predictor UCB (OLR-UCB).

It is not obvious that C_{t+1} is not empty because the radius could be negative. Theorem 23.4 shows, however, that with high probability $\theta_* \in C_{t+1}$. At last we have established all the conditions required for Theorem 19.2, which implies the following theorem bounding the regret of Algorithm 14:

THEOREM 23.5. *With probability at least* $1 - \delta$ *the pseudo-regret of OLR-UCB satisfies*

$$\hat{R}_n \leq \sqrt{8dn \left(m_2^2 + \beta_{n-1}(\delta) \right) \log \left(1 + \frac{n}{d} \right)}.$$

23.4   Sparse Online Linear Prediction

THEOREM 23.6. *There exists a strategy π for the learner such that for any $\theta \in \mathbb{R}^d$, the regret $\rho_n(\theta)$ of π against any strategic environment such that $\max_{t \in [n]} \|A_t\|_2 \leq L$ and $\max_{t \in [n]} |X_t| \leq X$ satisfies*

$$\rho_n(\theta) \leq cX^2\|\theta\|_0 \left\{ \log(e + n^{1/2}L) + C_n \log\left(1 + \frac{\|\theta\|_1}{\|\theta\|_0}\right) \right\} + (1 + X^2)C_n,$$

where $c > 0$ is some universal constant and $C_n = 2 + \log_2 \log(e + n^{1/2}L)$.

Note that $C_n = O(\log \log(n))$, so by dropping the dependence on X and L, we have

$$\sup_{\theta : \|\theta\|_0 \leq m_0, \|\theta\|_2 \leq L} \rho_n(\theta) = O(m_0 \log(n)).$$

As a final catch, the rewards (X_t) in sparse linear bandits with subgaussian noise are not necessarily bounded. However, the subgaussian property implies that with probability $1 - \delta$, $|\eta_t| \leq \log(2/\delta)$. By choosing $\delta = 1/n^2$ and Assumption 23.1, we have

$$\mathbb{P}\left(\max_{t \in [n]} |X_t| \geq 1 + \log\left(2n^2\right)\right) \leq \frac{1}{n}.$$

Putting all the pieces together shows that the expected regret of OLR-UCB when using the predictor provided by Theorem 23.6 and when $\|\theta\|_0 \leq m_0$ satisfies

$$R_n = O\left(\sqrt{dnm_0} \log(n)^2\right).$$

23.5   Notes

1 The strategy achieving the bound in Theorem 23.6 is not computationally efficient. In fact we do not know of any polynomial time algorithm with logarithmic regret for this problem. The consequence is that Algorithm 14 does not yet have an efficient implementation.

2 While we focused on the sparse case, the results and techniques apply to other settings. For example, we can also get alternative confidence sets from results in online learning even for the standard non-sparse case. Or one may consider additional or different structural assumptions on θ.

3 When the online linear regression results are applied, it is important to use the tightest possible, data-dependent regret bounds B_n. In online learning most regret bounds start as tight, data-dependent bounds, which are then loosened to get further insight into the structure of problems. For our application, naturally one should use the tightest available regret bounds (or modify the existing proofs to get tighter data-dependent bounds). The gains from using data-dependent bounds can be significant.

4 The confidence set used by Algorithm 14 depends on the sparsity parameter m_0, which must be known in advance. No algorithm can enjoy a regret of $O(\sqrt{\|\theta_*\|_0 dn})$ for all $\|\theta_*\|_0$ simultaneously (see Chapter 24).

5 The bound in Theorem 23.5 still depends on the ambient dimension. In general this is unavoidable, as we show in Theorem 24.3. For this reason it recently became popular to study the contextual setting with changing actions and make assumptions on the distribution of the contexts so that techniques from high-dimensional statistics can be brought to bear. These approaches are still in

their infancy and deciding on the right assumptions is a challenge. The reader is referred to the recent papers by Kim and Paik [2019] and Bastani and Bayati [2020].

23.6 Bibliographical Remarks

The selective explore-then-commit algorithm is due to the authors [Lattimore et al., 2015]. The construction for the sparse case is from another paper co-authored by one of the authors [Abbasi-Yadkori et al., 2012]. The online linear predictor that competes with sparse parameter vectors and its analysis summarised in Theorem 23.6 is due to Gerchinovitz [2013, theorem 10]. A recent paper by Rakhlin and Sridharan [2017] also discusses the relationship between online learning regret bounds and self-normalised tail bounds of the type given here. Interestingly, what they show is that the relationship goes in both directions: tail inequalities imply regret bounds, and regret bounds imply tail inequalities. We are told by Francesco Orabona that confidence set constructions similar to those in Section 23.3 have been used earlier in a series of papers by Claudio Gentile and friends [Dekel et al., 2010, 2012, Crammer and Gentile, 2013, Gentile and Orabona, 2012, 2014]. Carpentier and Munos [2012] consider a special case where the action set is the unit sphere and the noise is vector valued so that the reward is $X_t = \langle A_t, \theta + \eta_t \rangle$. They prove bounds that essentially depend on the sparsity of θ and $\mathbb{E}[\|\eta_t\|_2^2]$. Our setting is recovered by choosing η_t to be a vector of independent standard Gaussian random variables, but in this case the bounds recovered by the proposed algorithm are suboptimal.

23.7 Exercises

23.1 (THE ZERO-'NORM') A norm on $\mathbb{R}^d$ is a function $\|\cdot\| : \mathbb{R}^d \to \mathbb{R}$ such that for all $a \in \mathbb{R}$ and $x, y \in \mathbb{R}^d$, it holds that: (a) $\|x\| = 0$ if and only if $x = 0$ and (b) $\|ax\| = |a|\|x\|$ and (c) $\|x + y\| \le \|x\| + \|y\|$ and (d) $\|x\| \ge 0$. Show that $\|\cdot\|_0$ given by $\|x\|_0 = \sum_{i=1}^d \mathbb{I}\{x_i \ne 0\}$ is not a norm.

23.2 (MINIMAX BOUND FOR SETC) Prove the second part of Theorem 23.2.

23.3 (ANYTIME ALGORITHM) Algorithm 13 is not anytime (it requires advance knowledge of the horizon). Design a modified version that does not require this knowledge and prove a comparable regret bound to what was given in Theorem 23.2.

HINT   One way is to use the doubling trick, but a more careful approach will lead to a more practical algorithm.

23.4 Complete the calculation to derive Eq. (23.10) from Eq. (23.9).

23.5 Prove the equality in Eq. (23.11).

24 Minimax Lower Bounds for Stochastic Linear Bandits

Lower bounds for linear bandits turn out to be more nuanced than those for the classical finite-armed bandit. The difference is that for linear bandits the shape of the action set plays a role in the form of the regret, not just the distribution of the noise. This should not come as a big surprise because the stochastic finite-armed bandit problem can be modeled as a linear bandit with actions being the standard basis vectors, $\mathcal{A} = \{e_1, \ldots, e_k\}$. In this case the actions are orthogonal, which means that samples from one action do not give information about the rewards for other actions. Other action sets such as the unit ball ($\mathcal{A} = B_2^d = \{x \in \mathbb{R}^d : \|x\|_2 \leq 1\}$) do not share this property. For example, if $d = 2$ and $\mathcal{A} = B_2^d$ and an algorithm chooses actions $e_1 = (1, 0)$ and $e_2 = (0, 1)$ many times, then it can deduce the reward it would obtain from choosing any other action.

All results of this chapter have a worst-case flavour showing what is (not) achievable in general, or under a sparsity constraint, or if the realisable assumption is not satisfied. The analysis uses the information-theoretic tools introduced in Part IV combined with careful choices of action sets. The hard part is guessing what is the worst case, which is followed by simply turning the crank on the usual machinery.

In all lower bounds, we use a simple model with Gaussian noise. For action $A_t \in \mathcal{A} \subseteq \mathbb{R}^d$ the reward is $X_t = \mu(A_t) + \eta_t$ where $\eta_t \sim \mathcal{N}(0, 1)$ is a sequence of independent standard Gaussian noise and $\mu : \mathcal{A} \to \mathbb{R}$ is the mean reward. We will usually assume there exists a $\theta \in \mathbb{R}^d$ such that $\mu(a) = \langle a, \theta \rangle$. We write $\mathbb{P}_\mu$ to indicate the measure on outcomes induced by the interaction of the fixed policy and the Gaussian bandit paramterised by μ. Because we are now proving lower bounds, it becomes necessary to be explicit about the dependence of the regret on $\mathcal{A}$ and μ or θ. The regret of a policy is:

$$R_n(\mathcal{A}, \mu) = n \max_{a \in \mathcal{A}} \mu(a) - \mathbb{E}_\mu \left[\sum_{t=1}^n X_t \right],$$

where the expectation is taken with respect to $\mathbb{P}_\mu$. Except in Section 24.4, we assume the reward function is linear, which means there exists a $\theta \in \mathbb{R}^d$ such that $\mu(a) = \langle a, \theta \rangle$. In these cases, we write $R_n(\mathcal{A}, \theta)$ and $\mathbb{E}_\theta$ and $\mathbb{P}_\theta$. Recall the notation used for finite-armed bandits by defining $T_x(t) = \sum_{s=1}^t \mathbb{I}\{A_s = x\}$.

24.1 Hypercube

The first lower bound is for the hypercube action set and shows that the upper bounds in Chapter 19 cannot be improved in general.

THEOREM 24.1. *Let $\mathcal{A} = [-1,1]^d$ and $\Theta = \{-n^{-1/2}, n^{-1/2}\}^d$. Then, for any policy, there exists a vector $\theta \in \Theta$ such that:*

$$R_n(\mathcal{A}, \theta) \geq \frac{\exp(-2)}{8} d\sqrt{n}.$$

Proof By the relative entropy identities in Exercise 15.8.(b) and Exercise 14.7, we have for $\theta, \theta' \in \Theta$ that

$$D(\mathbb{P}_\theta, \mathbb{P}_{\theta'}) = \mathbb{E}_\theta \left[\sum_{t=1}^n D(\mathcal{N}(\langle A_t, \theta\rangle, 1), \mathcal{N}(\langle A_t, \theta'\rangle, 1)) \right]$$

$$= \frac{1}{2} \sum_{t=1}^n \mathbb{E}_\theta \left[\langle A_t, \theta - \theta'\rangle^2 \right]. \tag{24.1}$$

For $i \in [d]$ and $\theta \in \Theta$, define

$$p_{\theta i} = \mathbb{P}_\theta \left(\sum_{t=1}^n \mathbb{I} \{\mathrm{sign}(A_{ti}) \neq \mathrm{sign}(\theta_i)\} \geq n/2 \right).$$

Now let $i \in [d]$ and $\theta \in \Theta$ be fixed, and let $\theta'_j = \theta_j$ for $j \neq i$ and $\theta'_i = -\theta_i$. Then, by the Bretagnolle–Huber inequality (Theorem 14.2) and Eq. (24.1),

$$p_{\theta i} + p_{\theta' i} \geq \frac{1}{2} \exp\left(-\frac{1}{2} \sum_{t=1}^n \mathbb{E}_\theta[\langle A_t, \theta - \theta'\rangle^2] \right) \geq \frac{1}{2} \exp(-2). \tag{24.2}$$

Applying an 'averaging hammer' over all $\theta \in \Theta$, which satisfies $|\Theta| = 2^d$, we get

$$\sum_{\theta \in \Theta} \frac{1}{|\Theta|} \sum_{i=1}^d p_{\theta i} = \frac{1}{|\Theta|} \sum_{i=1}^d \sum_{\theta \in \Theta} p_{\theta i} \geq \frac{d}{4} \exp(-2).$$

This implies that there exists a $\theta \in \Theta$ such that $\sum_{i=1}^d p_{\theta i} \geq d\exp(-2)/4$. By the definition of $p_{\theta i}$, the regret for this choice of θ is at least

$$R_n(\mathcal{A}, \theta) = \mathbb{E}_\theta \left[\sum_{t=1}^n \sum_{i=1}^d (\mathrm{sign}(\theta_i) - A_{ti})\theta_i \right]$$

$$\geq \sqrt{\frac{1}{n}} \sum_{i=1}^d \mathbb{E}_\theta \left[\sum_{t=1}^n \mathbb{I} \{\mathrm{sign}(A_{ti}) \neq \mathrm{sign}(\theta_i)\} \right]$$

$$\geq \frac{\sqrt{n}}{2} \sum_{i=1}^d \mathbb{P}_\theta \left(\sum_{t=1}^n \mathbb{I} \{\mathrm{sign}(A_{ti}) \neq \mathrm{sign}(\theta_i)\} \geq n/2 \right)$$

$$= \frac{\sqrt{n}}{2} \sum_{i=1}^d p_{\theta i} \geq \frac{\exp(-2)}{8} d\sqrt{n},$$

where the first line follows since the optimal action satisfies $a_i^* = \mathrm{sign}(\theta_i)$ for $i \in [d]$, the first inequality follows from a simple case-based analysis showing that $(\mathrm{sign}(\theta_i) - A_{ti})\theta_i \geq |\theta_i|\mathbb{I} \{\mathrm{sign}(A_{ti}) \neq \mathrm{sign}(\theta_i)\}$, the second inequality is Markov's inequality (see Lemma 5.1), and the last inequality follows from the choice of θ. □

Except for logarithmic factors, this shows that the algorithm of Chapter 19 is near optimal for this action set. The same proof works when $\mathcal{A} = \{-1, 1\}^d$ is restricted to the corners of the hypercube, which is a finite-armed linear bandit. In Chapter 22, we gave a policy with regret $R_n = O(\sqrt{nd \log(nk)})$, where $k = |\mathcal{A}|$. There is no contradiction because the action set in the above proof has $k = |\mathcal{A}| = 2^d$ elements.

24.2 Unit Ball

Lower-bounding the minimax regret when the action set is the unit ball presents an additional challenge relative to the hypercube. The product structure of the hypercube means that the actions of the learner in one dimension do not constraint their choices in other dimensions. For the unit ball, this is not true, and this complicates the analysis. Nevertheless, a small modification of the technique allows us to prove a similar bound.

THEOREM 24.2. *Assume $d \leq 2n$ and let $\mathcal{A} = \{x \in \mathbb{R}^d : \|x\|_2 \leq 1\}$. Then there exists a parameter vector $\theta \in \mathbb{R}^d$ with $\|\theta\|_2^2 = d^2/(48n)$ such that $R_n(\mathcal{A}, \theta) \geq d\sqrt{n}/(16\sqrt{3})$.*

Proof Let $\Delta = \frac{1}{4\sqrt{3}}\sqrt{d/n}$ and $\theta \in \{\pm\Delta\}^d$ and for $i \in [d]$, define $\tau_i = n \wedge \min\{t : \sum_{s=1}^{t} A_{si}^2 \geq n/d\}$. Then,

$$R_n(\mathcal{A}, \theta) = \Delta\mathbb{E}_\theta \left[\sum_{t=1}^{n} \sum_{i=1}^{d} \left(\frac{1}{\sqrt{d}} - A_{ti} \operatorname{sign}(\theta_i) \right) \right]$$

$$\geq \frac{\Delta\sqrt{d}}{2} \mathbb{E}_\theta \left[\sum_{t=1}^{n} \sum_{i=1}^{d} \left(\frac{1}{\sqrt{d}} - A_{ti} \operatorname{sign}(\theta_i) \right)^2 \right]$$

$$\geq \frac{\Delta\sqrt{d}}{2} \sum_{i=1}^{d} \mathbb{E}_\theta \left[\sum_{t=1}^{\tau_i} \left(\frac{1}{\sqrt{d}} - A_{ti} \operatorname{sign}(\theta_i) \right)^2 \right],$$

where the first inequality uses that $\|A_t\|_2^2 \leq 1$. Fix $i \in [d]$. For $x \in \{\pm 1\}$, define $U_i(x) = \sum_{t=1}^{\tau_i} (1/\sqrt{d} - A_{ti}x)^2$ and let $\theta' \in \{\pm\Delta\}^d$ be another parameter vector such that $\theta_j = \theta_j'$ for $j \neq i$ and $\theta_i' = -\theta_i$. Assume without loss of generality that $\theta_i > 0$. Let $\mathbb{P}$ and $\mathbb{P}'$ be the laws of $U_i(1)$ with respect to the bandit/learner interaction measure induced by θ and θ', respectively. Then,

$$\mathbb{E}_\theta[U_i(1)] \geq \mathbb{E}_{\theta'}[U_i(1)] - \left(\frac{4n}{d} + 2 \right) \sqrt{\frac{1}{2} \operatorname{D}(\mathbb{P}, \mathbb{P}')}$$

$$\geq \mathbb{E}_{\theta'}[U_i(1)] - \frac{\Delta}{2} \left(\frac{4n}{d} + 2 \right) \sqrt{\mathbb{E}\left[\sum_{t=1}^{\tau_i} A_{ti}^2 \right]} \quad (24.3)$$

$$\geq \mathbb{E}_{\theta'}[U_i(1)] - \frac{\Delta}{2} \left(\frac{4n}{d} + 2 \right) \sqrt{\frac{n}{d} + 1} \quad (24.4)$$

$$\geq \mathbb{E}_{\theta'}[U_i(1)] - \frac{4\sqrt{3}\Delta n}{d} \sqrt{\frac{n}{d}}, \quad (24.5)$$

where in the first inequality we used Pinsker's inequality (Eq. (14.12)), the result in Exercise 14.4, the bound

$$U_i(1) = \sum_{t=1}^{\tau_i}(1/\sqrt{d} - A_{ti})^2 \le 2\sum_{t=1}^{\tau_i}\frac{1}{d} + 2\sum_{t=1}^{\tau_i}A_{ti}^2 \le \frac{4n}{d} + 2,$$

and the assumption that $d \le 2n$. The inequality in Eq. (24.3) follows from the chain rule for the relative entropy up to a stopping time (Exercise 15.7). Eq. (24.4) is true by the definition of τ_i and Eq. (24.5) by the assumption that $d \le 2n$. Then,

$$\mathbb{E}_\theta[U_i(1)] + \mathbb{E}_{\theta'}[U_i(-1)] \ge \mathbb{E}_{\theta'}[U_i(1) + U_i(-1)] - \frac{4\sqrt{3}n\Delta}{d}\sqrt{\frac{n}{d}}$$

$$= 2\mathbb{E}_{\theta'}\left[\frac{\tau_i}{d} + \sum_{t=1}^{\tau_i}A_{ti}^2\right] - \frac{4\sqrt{3}n\Delta}{d}\sqrt{\frac{n}{d}} \ge \frac{2n}{d} - \frac{4\sqrt{3}n\Delta}{d}\sqrt{\frac{n}{d}} = \frac{n}{d}.$$

The proof is completed using the randomisation hammer:

$$\sum_{\theta \in \{\pm\Delta\}^d} R_n(\mathcal{A}, \theta) \ge \frac{\Delta\sqrt{d}}{2}\sum_{i=1}^d \sum_{\theta \in \{\pm\Delta\}^d} \mathbb{E}_\theta[U_i(\text{sign}(\theta_i))]$$

$$= \frac{\Delta\sqrt{d}}{2}\sum_{i=1}^d \sum_{\theta_{-i}\in\{\pm\Delta\}^{d-1}} \sum_{\theta_i\in\{\pm\Delta\}} \mathbb{E}_\theta[U_i(\text{sign}(\theta_i))]$$

$$\ge \frac{\Delta\sqrt{d}}{2}\sum_{i=1}^d \sum_{\theta_{-i}\in\{\pm\Delta\}^{d-1}} \frac{n}{d} = 2^{d-2}n\Delta\sqrt{d}.$$

Hence there exists a $\theta \in \{\pm\Delta\}^d$ such that $R_n(\mathcal{A}, \theta) \ge \dfrac{n\Delta\sqrt{d}}{4} = \dfrac{d\sqrt{n}}{16\sqrt{3}}.$ □

The same proof works when $\mathcal{A} = \{x \in \mathbb{R}^d : \|x\|_2 = 1\}$ is the unit sphere. In fact, given a set $X \subset \mathbb{R}^d$. A minimax lower bound that holds for $\mathcal{A} = \text{co}(X)$ continues to hold when $\mathcal{A} = X$.

24.3 Sparse Parameter Vectors

In Chapter 23 we gave an algorithm with $R_n = \tilde{O}(\sqrt{dpn})$ where $p \ge \|\theta\|_0$ is a known bound on the sparsity of the unknown parameter. Except for logarithmic terms this bound cannot be improved. An extreme case is when $p = 1$, which essentially reduces to the finite-armed bandit problem where the minimax regret has order $\sqrt{dn}$ (see Chapter 15). For this reason we cannot expect too much from sparsity and in particular the worst-case bound will depend polynomially on the ambient dimension d.

Constructing a lower bound for $p > 1$ is relatively straightforward. For simplicity we assume that $d = pk$ for some integer $k > 1$. A sparse linear bandit can mimic the learner playing p finite-armed bandits simultaneously, each with k arms. Rather than observing the reward for each bandit, however, the learner only observes the sum of the rewards and the noise is added at the end. This is sometimes called the **multi-task bandit** problem.

THEOREM 24.3. *Assume $pd \leq n$ and that $d = pk$ for some integer $k \geq 2$. Let $\mathcal{A} = \{e_i \in \mathbb{R}^k : i \in [k]\}^p \subset \mathbb{R}^d$. Then, for any policy there exists a parameter vector $\theta \in \mathbb{R}^d$ with $\|\theta\|_0 = p$ and $\|\theta\|_\infty \leq \sqrt{d/(pn)}$ such that $R_n(\mathcal{A}, \theta) \geq \frac{1}{8}\sqrt{pdn}$.*

Proof Let $\Delta > 0$ and $\Theta = \{\Delta e_i : i \in [k]\} \subset \mathbb{R}^k$. Given $\theta \in \Theta^p \subset \mathbb{R}^d$ and $i \in [p]$, let $\theta^{(i)} \in \mathbb{R}^k$ be defined by $\theta_k^{(i)} = \theta_{(i-1)p+k}$, which means that

$$\theta^\top = [\theta^{(1)\top}, \theta^{(2)\top}, \dots, \theta^{(p)\top}].$$

Next define matrix $V \in \mathbb{R}^{p \times d}$ to be a block-diagonal matrix with $1 \times k$ blocks, each containing the row vector $(1, 2, \dots, k)$. For example, when $p = 3$, we have

$$V = \begin{bmatrix} 1 & \cdots & k & 0 & \cdots & 0 & 0 & \cdots & 0 \\ 0 & \cdots & 0 & 1 & \cdots & k & 0 & \cdots & 0 \\ 0 & \cdots & 0 & 0 & \cdots & 0 & 1 & \cdots & k \end{bmatrix}.$$

Let $B_t = V A_t \in [k]^p$ represent the vector of 'base' actions chosen by the learner in each of the p bandits in round t. The optimal action in the ith bandit is

$$b_i^*(\theta) = \text{argmax}_{b \in [k]} \, \theta_b^{(i)}.$$

The regret can be decomposed into the regrets in the p 'base bandit' problems (a form of separability, again):

$$R_n(\theta) = \sum_{i=1}^p \Delta \, \mathbb{E}_\theta \underbrace{\left[\sum_{t=1}^n \mathbb{I}\{B_{ti} \neq b_i^*\} \right]}_{R_{ni}(\theta)}.$$

For $i \in [p]$, we abbreviate $\theta^{(-i)} = (\theta^{(1)}, \dots, \theta^{(i-1)}, \theta^{(i+1)}, \dots, \theta^{(p)})$. Then,

$$\frac{1}{|\Theta|^p} \sum_{\theta \in \Theta^p} R_n(\theta) = \frac{1}{|\Theta|^p} \sum_{i=1}^p \sum_{\theta \in \Theta^p} R_{ni}(\theta)$$

$$= \sum_{i=1}^p \frac{1}{|\Theta|^{p-1}} \sum_{\theta^{(-i)} \in \Theta^{p-1}} \frac{1}{|\Theta|} \sum_{\theta^{(i)} \in \Theta} R_{ni}(\theta)$$

$$\geq \frac{1}{8} \sum_{i=1}^p \frac{1}{|\Theta|^{p-1}} \sum_{\theta^{(-i)} \in \Theta^{p-1}} \sqrt{kn} \qquad (24.6)$$

$$= \frac{1}{8} p \sqrt{kn} = \frac{1}{8} \sqrt{dpn}.$$

Here, in the second equality, we use the convention that θ denotes the vector obtained by 'inserting' $\theta^{(i)}$ into $\theta^{(-i)}$ at the ith 'block'. Other than this, the only tricky step is the inequality, which follows by choosing $\Delta \approx \sqrt{k/n}$ and repeating the argument outlined in Exercise 15.2. We leave it to the reader to check the details (Exercise 24.1). $\square$

24.4 Misspecified Models

An important generalisation of the linear model is the **misspecified** case, where the mean rewards are not assumed to follow a linear model exactly. Suppose that $\mathcal{A} \subset \mathbb{R}^d$ is a finite set with $|\mathcal{A}| = k$ and that $X_t = \eta_t + \mu(A_t)$, where $\mu : \mathcal{A} \to \mathbb{R}$ is an unknown function. Let $\theta \in \mathbb{R}^d$ be the parameter vector for which $\sup_{a \in \mathcal{A}} |\langle \theta, a \rangle - \mu(a)|$ is as small as possible:

$$\theta = \operatorname{argmin}_{\alpha \in \mathbb{R}^d} \sup_{a \in \mathcal{A}} |\langle \alpha, a \rangle - \mu(a)|.$$

Then let $\varepsilon = \sup_{a \in \mathcal{A}} |\langle \theta, a \rangle - \mu(a)|$ be the maximum error. It would be very pleasant to have an algorithm such that

$$R_n(\mathcal{A}, \mu) = n \max_{a \in \mathcal{A}} \mu(a) - \mathbb{E}\left[\sum_{t=1}^{n} \mu(A_t)\right] = \tilde{O}(\min\{d\sqrt{n} + \varepsilon n, \sqrt{kn}\}). \quad (24.7)$$

Unfortunately, it turns out that results of this kind are not achievable. To show this, we will prove a generic bound for the classical finite-armed bandit problem and afterwards show how this implies the impossibility of an adaptive bound like the above.

THEOREM 24.4. *Let* $\mathcal{A} = [k]$, *and for* $\mu \in [0,1]^k$ *the reward is* $X_t = \mu_{A_t} + \eta_t$ *and the regret is*

$$R_n(\mu) = n \max_{i \in \mathcal{A}} \mu_i - \mathbb{E}_\mu\left[\sum_{t=1}^{n} \mu_{A_t}\right].$$

Define $\Theta, \Theta' \subset \mathbb{R}^k$ *by*

$$\Theta = \left\{\mu \in [0,1]^k : \mu_i = 0 \text{ for } i > 1\right\} \qquad \Theta' = \left\{\mu \in [0,1]^k\right\}.$$

If $V \in \mathbb{R}$ *is such that* $2(k-1) \leq V \leq \sqrt{n(k-1)\exp(-2)/8}$ *and* $\sup_{\mu \in \Theta} R_n(\mu) \leq V$, *then*

$$\sup_{\mu' \in \Theta'} R_n(\mu') \geq \frac{n(k-1)}{8V} \exp(-2).$$

Proof Recall that $T_i(n) = \sum_{t=1}^{n} \mathbb{I}\{A_t = i\}$ is the number of times arm i is played after all n rounds. Let $\mu \in \Theta$ be given by $\mu_1 = \Delta = (k-1)/V \leq 1/2$. The regret is then decomposed as:

$$R_n(\mu) = \Delta \sum_{i=2}^{k} \mathbb{E}_\mu[T_i(n)] \leq V.$$

Rearranging shows that $\sum_{i=2}^{k} \mathbb{E}_\mu[T_i(n)] \leq \frac{V}{\Delta}$, and so by the pigeonhole principle there exists an $i > 1$ such that

$$\mathbb{E}_\mu[T_i(n)] \leq \frac{V}{(k-1)\Delta} = \frac{1}{\Delta^2}.$$

Then, define $\mu' \in \Theta'$ by

$$
\mu'_j = \begin{cases}
\Delta & \text{if } j = 1 \\
2\Delta & \text{if } j = i \\
0 & \text{otherwise.}
\end{cases}
$$

Next, by Theorem 14.2 and Lemma 15.1, for any event A, we have

$$
\mathbb{P}_\mu(A) + \mathbb{P}_{\mu'}(A^c) \geq \frac{1}{2} \exp\left(D(\mathbb{P}_\mu, \mathbb{P}_{\mu'})\right) = \frac{1}{2} \exp\left(-2\Delta^2 \mathbb{E}[T_i(n)]\right) \geq \frac{1}{2} \exp\left(-2\right).
$$

By choosing $A = \{T_1(n) \leq n/2\}$ we have

$$
R_n(\mu) + R_n(\mu') \geq \frac{n\Delta}{4} \exp(-2) = \frac{n(k-1)}{4V} \exp(-2).
$$

Therefore, by the assumption that $R_n(\mu) \leq V \leq \sqrt{n(k-1)\exp(-2)/8}$ we have

$$
R_n(\mu') \geq \frac{n(k-1)}{8V} \exp(-2). \qquad \square
$$

As promised, we now relate this to the misspecified linear bandits. Suppose that $d = 1$ (an absurd case) and that there are k arms $\mathcal{A} = \{a_1, a_2, \ldots, a_k\} \subset \mathbb{R}^1$, where $a_1 = (1)$ and $a_i = (0)$ for $i > 1$. Clearly, if $\theta > 0$ and $\mu(a_i) = \langle a_i, \theta \rangle$, then the problem can be modelled as a finite-armed bandit with means $\mu \in \Theta \subset [0,1]^k$. In the general case, we just have a finite-armed bandit with $\mu \in \Theta'$. If in the first case we have $R_n(\mathcal{A}, \mu) = O(\sqrt{n})$, then the theorem shows for large enough n that

$$
\sup_{\mu \in \Theta'} R_n(\mathcal{A}, \mu) = \Omega(k\sqrt{n}).
$$

It follows that Eq. (24.7) is a pipe dream. To our knowledge, it is still an open question of what is possible on this front. We speculate that for $k \geq d^2$, there is a policy for which

$$
R_n(\mathcal{A}, \theta) = \tilde{O}\left(\min\left\{d\sqrt{n} + \varepsilon n\sqrt{d}, \frac{k}{d}\sqrt{n}\right\}\right).
$$

24.5   Notes

1 The worst-case bound demonstrates the near optimality of the OFUL algorithm for a specific action set. It is an open question to characterise the optimal regret for a wide range of action sets. We will return to these issues in the next part of the book, where we discuss adversarial linear bandits.

2 We return to misspecified bandits in the notes and exercises of Chapter 29, where algorithms from the adversarial linear bandit framework are applied to this problem in special cases. In many applications, the number of actions is so large that $R_n = \tilde{O}(d\sqrt{n} + \varepsilon n\sqrt{d})$ should be considered acceptable. There exist algorithms achieving this bound, which for large k is essentially not improvable in the worst case [Lattimore and Szepesvári, 2019b]. For small k, recent work by Foster and Rakhlin [2020] shows that one can achieve $R_n = \tilde{O}(\sqrt{dkn} + \varepsilon n\sqrt{k})$.

24.6   Bibliographic Remarks

Worst-case lower bounds for stochastic bandits have appeared in a variety of places, all with roughly the same bound, but for different action sets. Our very simple proof for the hypercube is new, but takes inspiration from the paper by Shamir [2015]. Rusmevichientong and Tsitsiklis [2010] proved that $R_n = \Omega(d\sqrt{n})$ when $\mathcal{A}$ is the unit sphere. Our proof for the unit ball strengthens their result marginally and is much simpler. As far as we know, the first lower bound of $\Omega(d\sqrt{n})$ was given by Dani et al. [2008] for an action set equal to the product of two-dimensional disks. The results for the misspecified case are inspired by the work of one of the authors on the Pareto-regret frontier for bandits, which characterises what trade-offs are available when it is desirable to have a regret that is unusually small relative to some specific arms [Lattimore, 2015a].

24.7   Exercises

24.1 Complete the missing steps to prove the inequality in Eq. (24.6).

25 Asymptotic Lower Bounds for Stochastic Linear Bandits

The lower bounds in the previous chapter were derived by analysing the worst case for specific action sets and/or constraints on the unknown parameter. In this chapter, we focus on the asymptotics and aim to understand the influence of the action set on the regret. We start with a lower bound, and argue that the lower bound can be achieved. We finish by arguing that the optimistic algorithms (and Thompson sampling) will perform arbitrarily worse than what can be achieved by non-optimistic algorithms.

25.1 An Asymptotic Lower Bound for Fixed Action Sets

We assume that $\mathcal{A} \subset \mathbb{R}^d$ is finite with $|\mathcal{A}| = k$ and that the reward is $X_t = \langle A_t, \theta \rangle + \eta_t$, where $\theta \in \mathbb{R}^d$ and $(\eta_t)_{t=1}^{\infty}$ is a sequence of independent standard Gaussian random variables. Of course the regret of a policy in this setting is

$$R_n(\mathcal{A}, \theta) = \mathbb{E}_\theta \left[\sum_{t=1}^{n} \Delta_{A_t} \right], \qquad \Delta_a = \max_{a' \in \mathcal{A}} \langle a' - a, \theta \rangle,$$

where the dependence on the policy is omitted for readability and $\mathbb{E}_\theta[\cdot]$ is the expectation with respect to the measure on outcomes induced by the interaction of the policy and the linear bandit determined by θ. Like the asymptotic lower bounds in the classical finite-armed case (Chapter 16), the results of this chapter are proven only for consistent policies. Recall that a policy is consistent in some class of bandits $\mathcal{E}$ if the regret is sub-polynomial for any bandit in that class. Here this means that

$$R_n(\mathcal{A}, \theta) = o(n^p) \qquad \text{for all } p > 0 \text{ and } \theta \in \mathbb{R}^d. \tag{25.1}$$

The main objective of the chapter is to prove the following theorem on the behaviour of any consistent policy and discuss the implications.

THEOREM 25.1. *Assume that $\mathcal{A} \subset \mathbb{R}^d$ is finite and spans $\mathbb{R}^d$, and suppose a policy is consistent (satisfies Eq. 25.1). Let $\theta \in \mathbb{R}^d$ be any parameter such that there is a unique optimal action, and let $\bar{G}_n = \mathbb{E}_\theta \left[\sum_{t=1}^n A_t A_t^\top \right]$. Then $\liminf_{n \to \infty} \lambda_{\min}(\bar{G}_n)/\log(n) > 0$. Furthermore, for any $a \in \mathcal{A}$, it holds that*

$$\limsup_{n \to \infty} \log(n) \|a\|_{\bar{G}_n^{-1}}^2 \le \frac{\Delta_a^2}{2}.$$

The reader should recognise $\|a\|_{\bar{G}_n^{-1}}^2$ as the key term in the width of the confidence interval for the least squares estimator (Chapter 20). This is quite intuitive. The theorem is saying that any consistent algorithm must prove statistically that all suboptimal arms are indeed suboptimal by making the size of the confidence interval smaller than the suboptimality gap. Before the proof of this result, we give a corollary that characterises the asymptotic regret that must be endured by any consistent policy.

COROLLARY 25.2. *Let $\mathcal{A} \subset \mathbb{R}^d$ be a finite set that spans $\mathbb{R}^d$ and $\theta \in \mathbb{R}^d$ be such that there is a unique optimal action. Then, for any consistent policy,*

$$\liminf_{n \to \infty} \frac{R_n(\mathcal{A}, \theta)}{\log(n)} \geq c(\mathcal{A}, \theta),$$

where $c(\mathcal{A}, \theta)$ is defined as

$$c(\mathcal{A}, \theta) = \inf_{\alpha \in [0, \infty)^{\mathcal{A}}} \sum_{a \in \mathcal{A}} \alpha(a) \Delta_a$$

$$\text{subject to } \|a\|_{H_\alpha^{-1}}^2 \leq \frac{\Delta_a^2}{2} \text{ for all } a \in \mathcal{A} \text{ with } \Delta_a > 0,$$

with $H_\alpha = \sum_{a \in \mathcal{A}} \alpha(a) a a^\top$.

The lower bound is complemented by a matching upper bound that we will not prove.

THEOREM 25.3. *Let $\mathcal{A} \subset \mathbb{R}^d$ be a finite set that spans $\mathbb{R}^d$. Then there exists a policy such that*

$$\limsup_{n \to \infty} \frac{R_n(\mathcal{A}, \theta)}{\log(n)} \leq c(\mathcal{A}, \theta),$$

where $c(\mathcal{A}, \theta)$ is defined as in Corollary 25.2.

Proof of Theorem 25.1 The proof of the first part is simply omitted (see the reference below for details). It follows along similar lines to what follows, essentially that if G_n is not sufficiently large in every direction, then some alternative parameter is not sufficiently identifiable. Let $a^* = \operatorname{argmax}_{a \in \mathcal{A}} \langle a, \theta \rangle$ be the optimal action, which we assumed to be unique. Let $\theta' \in \mathbb{R}^d$ be an alternative parameter to be chosen subsequently, and let $\mathbb{P}$ and $\mathbb{P}'$ be the measures on the sequence of outcomes $A_1, X_1, \ldots, A_n, X_n$ induced by the interaction between the policy and the bandit determined by θ and θ' respectively. Let $\mathbb{E}[\cdot]$ and $\mathbb{E}'[\cdot]$ be the expectation operators of $\mathbb{P}$ and $\mathbb{P}'$, respectively. By Theorem 14.2 and Lemma 15.1, for any event E,

$$\mathbb{P}(E) + \mathbb{P}'(E^c) \geq \frac{1}{2} \exp\left(- D(\mathbb{P}, \mathbb{P}')\right)$$

$$= \frac{1}{2} \exp\left(-\frac{1}{2} \mathbb{E}\left[\sum_{t=1}^n \langle A_t, \theta - \theta' \rangle^2\right]\right) = \frac{1}{2} \exp\left(-\frac{1}{2} \|\theta - \theta'\|_{\bar{G}_n}^2\right).$$

$$(25.2)$$

A simple re-arrangement shows that

$$\frac{1}{2} \|\theta - \theta'\|_{\bar{G}_n}^2 \geq \log\left(\frac{1}{2\mathbb{P}(E) + 2\mathbb{P}'(E^c)}\right).$$

Now we follow the usual plan of choosing θ' to be close to θ, but so that the optimal action in the bandit determined by θ' is not a^*. Let $\Delta_{\min} = \min\{\Delta_a : a \in \mathcal{A}, \Delta_a > 0\}$ and

$\varepsilon \in (0, \Delta_{\min})$ and H be a positive definite matrix to be chosen later such that $\|a - a^*\|_H^2 > 0$. Then define

$$\theta' = \theta + \frac{\Delta_a + \varepsilon}{\|a - a^*\|_H^2} H(a - a^*),$$

which is chosen so that

$$\langle a - a^*, \theta' \rangle = \langle a - a^*, \theta \rangle + \Delta_a + \varepsilon = \varepsilon.$$

This means that a^* is ε-suboptimal for bandit θ'. We abbreviate $R_n = R_n(\mathcal{A}, \theta)$ and $R'_n = R_n(\mathcal{A}, \theta')$. Then

$$R_n = \mathbb{E}\left[\sum_{a \in \mathcal{A}} T_a(n)\Delta_a\right] \geq \frac{n\Delta_{\min}}{2}\mathbb{P}\left(T_{a^*}(n) < n/2\right) \geq \frac{n\varepsilon}{2}\mathbb{P}\left(T_{a^*}(n) < n/2\right),$$

where $T_a(n) = \sum_{t=1}^n \mathbb{I}\{A_t = a\}$. Similarly, a^* is ε-suboptimal in bandit θ' so that

$$R'_n \geq \frac{n\varepsilon}{2}\mathbb{P}'\left(T_{a^*}(n) \geq n/2\right).$$

Therefore,

$$\mathbb{P}\left(T_{a^*}(n) < n/2\right) + \mathbb{P}'\left(T_{a^*}(n) \geq n/2\right) \leq \frac{2}{n\varepsilon}(R_n + R'_n). \tag{25.3}$$

Note that this holds for any choice of H with $\|a - a^*\|_H > 0$. The logical next step is to select H (which determines θ') to make (25.2) as large as possible. The main difficulty is that this depends on n, so instead we aim to choose an H so the quantity is large enough infinitely often. We start by just re-arranging things:

$$\frac{1}{2}\|\theta - \theta'\|_{\bar{G}_n}^2 = \frac{(\Delta_a + \varepsilon)^2}{2} \cdot \frac{\|a - a^*\|_{H\bar{G}_n H}^2}{\|a - a^*\|_H^4} = \frac{(\Delta_a + \varepsilon)^2}{2\|a - a^*\|_{\bar{G}_n^{-1}}^2}\rho_n(H),$$

where we introduced

$$\rho_n(H) = \frac{\|a - a^*\|_{\bar{G}_n^{-1}}^2 \|a - a^*\|_{H\bar{G}_n H}^2}{\|a - a^*\|_H^4}.$$

Therefore, by choosing E to be the event that $T_{a^*}(n) < n/2$ and using (25.3) and (25.2), we have

$$\frac{(\Delta_a + \varepsilon)^2}{2\|a - a^*\|_{\bar{G}_n^{-1}}^2}\rho_n(H) \geq \log\left(\frac{n\varepsilon}{4R_n + 4R'_n}\right),$$

which after re-arrangement leads to

$$\frac{(\Delta_a + \varepsilon)^2}{2\log(n)\|a - a^*\|_{\bar{G}_n^{-1}}^2}\rho_n(H) \geq 1 - \frac{\log((4R_n + 4R'_n)/\varepsilon)}{\log(n)}.$$

The definition of consistency means that R_n and R'_n are both sub-polynomial, which implies that the second term in the previous expression tends to zero for large n and so by sending ε to zero,

$$\liminf_{n \to \infty} \frac{\rho_n(H)}{\log(n)\|a - a^*\|_{\bar{G}_n^{-1}}^2} \geq \frac{2}{\Delta_a^2}. \tag{25.4}$$

We complete the result using proof by contradiction. Suppose that

$$\limsup_{n \to \infty} \log(n)\|a - a^*\|_{\bar{G}_n^{-1}}^2 > \frac{\Delta_a^2}{2}. \tag{25.5}$$

Then there exists an $\varepsilon > 0$ and infinite set $S \subseteq \mathbb{N}$ such that

$$\log(n)\|a - a^*\|_{\bar{G}_n^{-1}}^2 \geq \frac{(\Delta_a + \varepsilon)^2}{2} \qquad \text{for all } n \in S.$$

Hence, by (25.4), $\liminf_{n \in S} \rho_n(H) > 1$. We now choose H to be a cluster point of the sequence $(\bar{G}_n^{-1}/\|\bar{G}_n^{-1}\|)_{n \in S}$ where $\|\bar{G}_n^{-1}\|$ is the spectral norm of the matrix $\bar{G}_n^{-1}$. Such a point must exist, since matrices in this sequence have unit spectral norm by definition and the set of such matrices is compact. We let $S' \subseteq S$ be a subset so that $\bar{G}_n^{-1}/\|\bar{G}_n^{-1}\|$ converges to H on $n \in S'$. We now check that $\|a - a^*\|_H > 0$:

$$\|a - a^*\|_H^2 = \lim_{n \in S'} \frac{\|a - a^*\|_{\bar{G}_n^{-1}}^2}{\|\bar{G}_n^{-1}\|} > 0,$$

where the last inequality follows from the assumption in (25.5) and the first part of the theorem. Therefore,

$$1 < \liminf_{n \in S} \rho_n(H) \leq \liminf_{n \in S'} \frac{\|a - a^*\|_{\bar{G}_n^{-1}}^2 \|a - a^*\|_{H\bar{G}_n H}^2}{\|a - a^*\|_H^4} = 1,$$

which is a contradiction, and hence (25.5) does not hold. Thus,

$$\limsup_{n \to \infty} \log(n)\|a - a^*\|_{\bar{G}_n^{-1}}^2 \leq \frac{\Delta_a^2}{2}. \qquad \square$$

We leave the proof of the corollary as an exercise for the reader. Essentially, though, any consistent algorithm must choose its actions so that in expectation

$$\|a - a^*\|_{\bar{G}_n^{-1}}^2 \leq (1 + o(1)) \frac{\Delta_a^2}{2\log(n)}.$$

Now, since a^* will be chosen linearly, often it is easily shown for suboptimal a that $\lim_{n \to \infty} \|a - a^*\|_{\bar{G}_n^{-1}}/\|a\|_{\bar{G}_n^{-1}} \to 1$. This leads to the required constraint on the actions of the algorithm, and the optimisation problem in the corollary is derived by minimising the regret subject to this constraint.

25.2 Clouds Looming for Optimism

The theorem and its corollary have disturbing implications for policies based on the principle of optimism in the face of uncertainty, which is that they
can never be asymptotically optimal. The reason is
that these policies do not choose actions for which
they have collected enough statistics to prove they
are suboptimal, but in the linear setting it can be
worth playing these actions when they are very informative about other actions for which the statistics
are not yet so clear. As we shall see, a problematic
example appears in the simplest case where there
is information sharing between the arms. Namely,
when the dimension is $d = 2$, and there are $k = 3$ arms.

Let $\mathcal{A} = \{a_1, a_2, a_3\}$, where $a_1 = e_1$ and $a_2 = e_2$ and $a_3 = (1 - \varepsilon, \gamma\varepsilon)$ with $\gamma \geq 1$
and $\varepsilon > 0$ is small. Let $\theta = (1, 0)$ so that the optimal action is $a^* = a_1$ and $\Delta_{a_2} = 1$
and $\Delta_{a_3} = \varepsilon$. If ε is very small, then a_1 and a_3 point in nearly the same direction, and so
choosing only these arms does not provide sufficient information to quickly learn which of
a_1 or a_3 is optimal. On the other hand, a_2 and $a_1 - a_3$ point in very different directions,
which means that choosing a_2 allows a learning agent to quickly identify that a_1 is in fact
optimal. We now show how the theorem and corollary demonstrate this. First we calculate
the optimal solution to the optimisation problem in Corollary 25.2. Recall we are trying to
minimise

$$\sum_{a \in \mathcal{A}} \alpha(a)\Delta_a \qquad \text{subject to } \|a\|^2_{H(\alpha)^{-1}} \leq \frac{\Delta_a^2}{2} \text{ for all } a \in \mathcal{A} \text{ with } \Delta_a > 0,$$

where $H(\alpha) = \sum_{a \in \mathcal{A}} \alpha(a) aa^\top$. Clearly we should choose $\alpha(a_1)$ arbitrarily large, then a
computation shows that

$$\lim_{\alpha(a_1) \to \infty} H(\alpha)^{-1} = \begin{bmatrix} 0 & 0 \\ 0 & \frac{1}{\alpha(a_3)\varepsilon^2\gamma^2 + \alpha(a_2)} \end{bmatrix}.$$

The constraints mean that

$$\frac{1}{\alpha(a_3)\varepsilon^2\gamma^2 + \alpha(a_2)} = \lim_{\alpha(a_1) \to \infty} \|a_2\|^2_{H(\alpha)^{-1}} \leq \frac{1}{2}$$

$$\frac{\gamma^2\varepsilon^2}{\alpha(a_3)\varepsilon^2\gamma^2 + \alpha(a_2)} = \lim_{\alpha(a_1) \to \infty} \|a_3\|^2_{H(\alpha)^{-1}} \leq \frac{\varepsilon^2}{2}.$$

Provided that $\gamma \geq 1$, this reduces to the constraint that

$$\alpha(a_3)\varepsilon^2 + \alpha(a_2) \geq 2\gamma^2.$$

Since we are minimising $\alpha(a_2) + \varepsilon\alpha(a_3)$ we can easily see that $\alpha(a_2) = 2\gamma^2$ and $\alpha(a_3) = 0$
provided that $2\gamma^2 \leq 2/\varepsilon$. Therefore, if ε is chosen sufficiently small relative to γ, then the
optimal rate of the regret is $c(\mathcal{A}, \theta) = 2\gamma^2$, and so by Theorem 25.3 there exists a policy
such that

$$\limsup_{n\to\infty} \frac{R_n(\mathcal{A}, \theta)}{\log(n)} = 2\gamma^2.$$

Now we argue that for γ sufficiently large and ε arbitrarily small that the regret for any consistent optimistic algorithm is at least

$$\limsup_{n\to\infty} \frac{R_n(\mathcal{A}, \theta)}{\log(n)} = \Omega(1/\varepsilon),$$

which can be arbitrarily worse than the optimal rate! So why is this so? Recall that optimistic algorithms choose

$$A_t = \mathrm{argmax}_{a\in\mathcal{A}} \max_{\tilde{\theta}\in\mathcal{C}_t} \left\langle a, \tilde{\theta} \right\rangle,$$

where $\mathcal{C}_t \subset \mathbb{R}^d$ is a confidence set that we assume contains the true θ with high probability. So far this does not greatly restrict the class of algorithms that we might call optimistic. We now assume that there exists a constant $c > 0$ such that

$$\mathcal{C}_t \subseteq \left\{ \tilde{\theta} : \|\hat{\theta}_t - \tilde{\theta}\|_{V_t} \le c\sqrt{\log(n)} \right\},$$

where $V_t = \sum_{s=1}^{t} A_s A_s^\top$. So now we ask how often we can expect the optimistic algorithm to choose action $a_2 = e_2$ in the example described above. Since we have assumed $\theta \in \mathcal{C}_t$ with high probability, we have that

$$\max_{\tilde{\theta}\in\mathcal{C}_t} \langle a_1, \tilde{\theta} \rangle \ge 1.$$

On the other hand, if $T_{a_2}(t-1) > 4c^2 \log(n)$, then

$$\max_{\tilde{\theta}\in\mathcal{C}_t} \langle a_2, \tilde{\theta} \rangle = \max_{\tilde{\theta}\in\mathcal{C}_t} \langle a_2, \tilde{\theta} - \theta \rangle \le 2c\sqrt{\|a_2\|_{V_t^{-1}} \log(n)} \le 2c\sqrt{\frac{\log(n)}{T_{a_2}(t-1)}} < 1,$$

which means that a_2 will not be chosen more than $1 + 4c^2 \log(n)$ times. So if $\gamma = \Omega(c^2)$, then the optimistic algorithm will not choose a_2 sufficiently often and a simple computation shows it must choose a_3 at least $\Omega(\log(n)/\varepsilon^2)$ times and suffers regret of $\Omega(\log(n)/\varepsilon)$. The key take away from this is that optimistic algorithms do not choose actions that are statistically suboptimal, but for linear bandits it can be optimal to choose these actions more often to gain information about other actions.

> This conclusion generalises to structured bandit problems where choosing one action allows you to gain information about the rewards of other actions. In such models the optimism principle often provides basic guarantees, but may fail to optimally exploit the structure of the problem.

25.3 Notes

1 All algorithms known to match the lower bound in Theorem 25.3 are based on (or inspired by) solving the optimisation problem that defines $c(\mathcal{A}, \theta)$ with estimated value θ. Unfortunately, these

algorithms are not especially practical in finite time. As far as we know, none are simultaneously near-optimal in a minimax sense. Constructing a practical asymptotically optimal algorithm for linear bandits is a fascinating open problem.

2 In Chapter 36 we will introduce the randomised Bayesian algorithm called Thompson sampling algorithm for finite-armed and linear bandits. While Thompson sampling is often empirically superior to UCB, it does not overcome the issues described here.

25.4 Bibliographic Remarks

The theorems of this chapter are by the authors: Lattimore and Szepesvári [2017]. The example in Section 25.2 first appeared in a paper by Soare et al. [2014], which deals with the problem of best-arm identification for linear bandits (for an introduction to best-arm identification, see Chapter 33). The optimisation-based algorithms that match the lower bound are by Lattimore and Szepesvári [2017], Ok et al. [2018], Combes et al. [2017] and Hao et al. [2020], with the latter handling also the contextual case with finitely many contexts.

25.5 Exercises

25.1 Prove Corollary 25.2.

25.2 Prove the first part of Theorem 25.1.

25.3 Give examples of action sets $\mathcal{A}$, parameter vectors $\theta \in \mathbb{R}^d$ and vectors $a \in \mathbb{R}^d$ such that:

(a) $c(\mathcal{A} \cup \{a\}, \theta) > c(\mathcal{A}, \theta)$; and
(b) $c(\mathcal{A} \cup \{a\}, \theta) < c(\mathcal{A}, \theta)$.

Part VI

Adversarial Linear Bandits

The adversarial linear bandit is superficially a generalisation of the stochastic linear bandit where the unknown parameter vector is chosen by an adversary. There are many similarities between the two topics. Indeed, the techniques in this part combine the ideas of optimal design presented in Chapter 22 with the exponential weighting algorithm of Chapter 11. The intuitions gained by studying stochastic bandits should not be taken too seriously, however. There are subtle differences between the model of adversarial bandits introduced here and the stochastic linear bandits examined in previous chapters. These differences will be discussed at length in Chapter 29. The adversarial version of the linear bandits turns out to be remarkably rich, both because of the complex information structure and because of the challenging computational issues.

The part is split into four chapters, the first of which is an introduction to the necessary tools from convex analysis and optimisation. In the first chapter on bandits, we show how to combine the core ideas of the Exp3 policy of Chapter 11 with the optimal experimental design for least-squares estimators in Chapter 21. When the number of actions is large (or infinite), the approach based on Exp3 is hard to make efficient. These shortcomings are addressed in the next chapter, where we introduce the mirror descent and follow-the-regularised leader algorithms for bandits and show how they can be used to design efficient algorithms. We conclude the part with a discussion on the relationship between adversarial and stochastic linear bandits, which is more subtle than the situation with finite-armed bandits.

26 Foundations of Convex Analysis (🦘)

Our coverage of convex analysis is necessarily extremely brief. We introduce only what is necessary and refer the reader to standard texts for the proofs.

26.1 Convex Sets and Functions

A set $A \subseteq \mathbb{R}^d$ is convex if for any $x, y \in A$ it holds that $\alpha x + (1 - \alpha)y \in A$ for all $\alpha \in (0, 1)$. The **convex hull** of a collection of points $x_1, x_2, \ldots, x_n \in \mathbb{R}^d$ is the smallest convex set containing the points, which also happens to satisfy

$$\mathrm{co}(x_1, x_2, \ldots, x_n) = \left\{ x \in \mathbb{R}^d : x = \sum_{i=1}^{n} p_i x_i \text{ for some } p \in \mathcal{P}_{n-1} \right\}.$$

The convex hull $\mathrm{co}(A)$ is also defined for an arbitrary set $A \subset \mathbb{R}^d$ and is still the smallest convex set that contains A (see (c) in Figure 26.1). For the rest of the section, we let $A \subseteq \mathbb{R}^d$ be convex. Let $\bar{R} = \mathbb{R} \cup \{-\infty, \infty\}$ be the extended real number system and define operations involving infinities in the natural way (see notes).

DEFINITION 26.1. An extended real-valued function $f : \mathbb{R}^d \to \bar{\mathbb{R}}$ is **convex** if its **epigraph** $E_f = \{(x, y) \in \mathbb{R}^d \times \mathbb{R} : y \geq f(x)\} \subset \mathbb{R}^{d+1}$ is a convex set.

The term 'epi' originates in greek and it means upon or over: The epigraph of a function is the set of points that sit on the top of the function's graph.

The **domain** of an extended real-valued function on $\mathbb{R}^d$ is $\mathrm{dom}(f) = \{x \in \mathbb{R}^d : f(x) < \infty\}$. For $S \subset \mathbb{R}^d$, a function $f : S \to \bar{\mathbb{R}}$ is identified with the function $\bar{f} : \mathbb{R}^d \to \bar{\mathbb{R}}$, which coincides with f on S and is defined to take the value ∞ outside of S. It follows that if $f : S \to \mathbb{R}$, then $\mathrm{dom}(f) = S$. A convex function is **proper** if its range does not include $-\infty$ and its domain is nonempty.

 For the rest of the chapter, we will write 'let f be a convex' to mean that $f : \mathbb{R}^d \to \bar{\mathbb{R}}$ is a proper convex function.

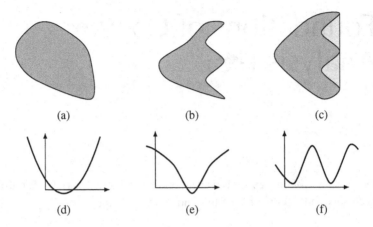

Figure 26.1   (a) is a convex set. (b) is a non-convex set. (c) is the convex hull of a non-convex set. (d) is a convex function. (e) is non-convex, but all local minimums are global. (f) is not convex.

Permitting convex functions to take values of $-\infty$ is a convenient standard because certain operations on proper convex functions result in improper ones (infimal convolution, for example). These technicalities will never bother us in this book, however.

A consequence of the definition is that for convex f, we have

$$f(\alpha x + (1 - \alpha)y) \le \alpha f(x) + (1 - \alpha)f(y)$$
$$\text{for all } \alpha \in (0, 1) \text{ and } x, y \in \operatorname{dom}(f). \tag{26.1}$$

In fact, the inequality holds for all $x, y \in \mathbb{R}^d$.

Some authors use Eq. (26.1) as the definition of a convex function along with a specification that the domain is convex: If $A \subseteq \mathbb{R}^d$ is convex, then $f : A \to \mathbb{R}$ is convex if it satisfies Eq. (26.1), with $f(x) = \infty$ assumed for $x \notin A$.

The reader is invited to prove that all convex functions are continuous on the interior of their domain (Exercise 26.1).

A function is **strictly convex** if the inequality in Eq. (26.1) is always strict. The **Fenchel dual** of a function f is $f^*(u) = \sup_x \langle x, u \rangle - f(x)$, which is convex because the maximum of convex functions is convex. The Fenchel dual has many nice properties. Most important for us is that for sufficiently nice functions, ∇f^* is the inverse of ∇f (Theorem 26.6). Another useful property is that when f is a proper convex function and its epigraph is closed, then $f = f^{**}$, where f^{**} denotes the **bidual** of f: $f^{**} = (f^*)^*$. The Fenchel dual is also called the convex conjugate. If $f : \mathbb{R}^d \to \bar{\mathbb{R}}$ is twice differentiable on the interior of its domain, then convexity of f is equivalent to its Hessian having non-negative eigenvalues for all $x \in \operatorname{int}(\operatorname{dom}(f))$. The field of optimisation is obsessed with convex functions because all local minimums are global (see Fig. 26.1). This means that minimising a convex function is usually possible (efficiently) using some variation of gradient descent. A function $f : \mathbb{R}^d \to \bar{\mathbb{R}}$ is **concave** if $-f$ is convex.

26.2 Jensen's Inequality

One of the most important results for convex functions is Jensen's inequality:

THEOREM 26.2 (Jensen's inequality). *Let $f : \mathbb{R}^d \to \bar{\mathbb{R}}$ be a measurable convex function and X be an $\mathbb{R}^d$-valued random element on some probability space such that $\mathbb{E}[X]$ exists and $X \in \mathrm{dom}(f)$ holds almost surely. Then $\mathbb{E}[f(X)] \geq f(\mathbb{E}[X])$.*

If we allowed Lebesgue integrals to take on the value of ∞, the condition that X is almost surely an element of the domain of f could be removed and the result would still be true. Indeed, in this case we would immediately conclude that $\mathbb{E}[f(X)] = \infty$ and Jensen's inequality would trivially hold.

The basic inequality of (26.1) is trivially a special case of Jensen's inequality. Jensen's inequality is so central to convexity that it can actually be used as the definition (a function if convex if and only if it satisfies Jensen's inequality). The proof of Jensen's using Definition 26.1 in full generality is left to the reader (Exercise 26.2). However, we cannot resist to include here a simple 'graphical proof' that works in the simple case when X is supported on $x_1, \ldots, x_n$ and $\mathbb{P}(X = x_k) = p_k$. Then, letting $\bar{x} = \sum_{k=1}^{n} p_k x_k$, one can

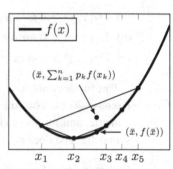

notice that the point $(\bar{x}, \sum_k p_k x_k)$ lies in the convex hull of $\{(x_k, f(x_k))_k\}$, which is a convex subset of the epigraph $E_f \subset \mathbb{R}^{d+1}$. The result follows because $(\bar{x}, f(\bar{x}))$ is on the boundary of E_f as shown in the figure. The direction of Jensen's inequality is reversed if 'convex' is replaced by 'concave'.

26.3 Bregman Divergence

Let $f : \mathbb{R}^d \to \mathbb{R}$ be convex and $x, y \in \mathbb{R}^d$ with $y \in \mathrm{dom}(f)$. The **Bregman divergence** at y induced by f is defined by

$$D_f(x, y) = f(x) - f(y) - \nabla_{x-y} f(y),$$

where $\nabla_v f(y) = \lim_{h \to 0}(f(y + hv) - f(y))/h \in \mathbb{R} \cup \{-\infty, \infty\}$ is the directional derivative of f at y in direction v. The directional derivative is always well defined for convex functions, but can be positive/negative infinity. When f is differentiable at y, then $\nabla_v f(y) = \langle v, \nabla f(y) \rangle$ and thus $D_f(x, y) = f(x) - f(y) - \langle x - y, \nabla f(y) \rangle$, which is the more usual definition. For the geometric intuition see Fig. 26.2. Let $\mathrm{dom}(\nabla f)$ denote the set of points in the domain of f where f is differentiable.

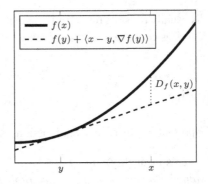

Figure 26.2 The Bregman divergence $D_f(x, y)$ is the difference between $f(x)$ and the Taylor series approximation of f at y. When f is convex the, linear approximation is a lower bound on the function and the Bregman divergence is positive.

THEOREM 26.3. *The following hold:*

(a) $D_f(x, y) \geq 0$ *for all $y \in \mathrm{dom}(f)$.*

(b) $D_f(x, x) = 0$ *for all $x \in \mathrm{dom}(f)$.*

(c) $D_f(x, y)$ *is convex as a function of x for any $y \in \mathrm{dom}(\nabla f)$.*

Part (c) does not hold in general when f is not differentiable at y, as you will show in Exercise 26.14. The square root of the Bregman divergence shares many properties with a metric, and for some choices of f, it actually is a metric. In general, however, it is not symmetric and does not satisfy the triangle inequality.

EXAMPLE 26.4. Let $f(x) = \frac{1}{2}\|x\|_2^2$. Then $\nabla f(x) = x$ and

$$D_f(x, y) = \frac{1}{2}\|x\|_2^2 - \frac{1}{2}\|y\|_2^2 - \langle x - y, y \rangle = \frac{1}{2}\|x - y\|_2^2.$$

EXAMPLE 26.5. Let $A = [0, \infty)^d$, $\mathrm{dom}(f) = A$ and for $x \in A$, $f(x) = \sum_{i=1}^d (x_i \log(x_i) - x_i)$, where $0 \log(0) = 0$. Then, for $y \in (0, \infty)^d$, $\nabla f(y) = \log(y)$ and

$$D_f(x, y) = \sum_{i=1}^d (x_i \log(x_i) - x_i) - \sum_{i=1}^d (y_i \log y_i - y_i) - \sum_{i=1}^d \log(y_i)(x_i - y_i)$$

$$= \sum_{i=1}^d x_i \log\left(\frac{x_i}{y_i}\right) + \sum_{i=1}^d (y_i - x_i).$$

Notice that if $x, y \in \mathcal{P}_{d-1}$ are in the unit simplex, then $D_f(x, y)$ is the relative entropy between probability vectors x and y. The function f is called the **unnormalised negentropy**, which will feature heavily in many of the chapters that follow. When $y \not> 0$, the Bregman divergence is infinite if there exists an i such that $y_i = 0$ and $x_i > 0$. Otherwise, $D_f(x, y) = \sum_{i:x_i>0} x_i \log(x_i/y_i) + \sum_{i=1}^d (y_i - x_i)$.

26.4 Legendre Functions

In this section we use various topological notions such as the interior, closed set and boundary. The definitions of these terms are given in the notes. Let f be a convex function and $A = \mathrm{dom}(f)$ and $C = \mathrm{int}(A)$. Then f is **Legendre** if

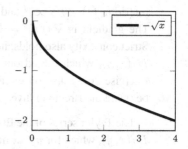

(a) C is non-empty;
(b) f is differentiable and strictly convex on C; and
(c) $\lim_{n\to\infty} \|\nabla f(x_n)\|_2 = \infty$ for any sequence $(x_n)_n$ with $x_n \in C$ for all n and $\lim_{n\to\infty} x_n = x$ and some $x \in \partial C$.

Figure 26.3 $f(x) = -\sqrt{x}$: the archetypical Legendre function

The intuition is that the set $\{(x, f(x)) : x \in \mathrm{dom}(A)\}$ is a 'dish' with ever-steepening edges towards the boundary of the domain. Legendre functions have some very convenient properties:

THEOREM 26.6. *Let $f : \mathbb{R}^d \to \bar{\mathbb{R}}$ be a Legendre function. Then,*

(a) ∇f *is a bijection between* $\mathrm{int}(\mathrm{dom}(f))$ *and* $\mathrm{int}(\mathrm{dom}(f^*))$ *with the inverse* $(\nabla f)^{-1} = \nabla f^*$;
(b) $D_f(x, y) = D_{f^*}(\nabla f(y), \nabla f(x))$ *for all* $x, y \in \mathrm{int}(\mathrm{dom}(f))$; *and*
(c) *the Fenchel conjugate f^* is Legendre.*

The next result formalises the 'dish' intuition by showing the directional derivative along any straight path from a point in the interior to the boundary blows up. You should supply the proof of the following results in Exercise 26.6.

PROPOSITION 26.7. *Let f be Legendre and $x \in \mathrm{int}(\mathrm{dom}(f))$ and $y \in \partial \mathrm{int}(\mathrm{dom}(f))$, then* $\lim_{\alpha \to 1} \langle y - x, \nabla f((1 - \alpha)x + \alpha y) \rangle = \infty$.

COROLLARY 26.8. *If f is Legendre and $x^* \in \mathrm{argmin}_{x \in \mathrm{dom}(f)} f(x)$, then $x^* \in \mathrm{int}(\mathrm{dom}(f))$.*

EXAMPLE 26.9. Let f be the Legendre function given by $f(x) = \frac{1}{2}\|x\|_2^2$, which has domain $\mathrm{dom}(f) = \mathbb{R}^d$. Then, $f^*(x) = f(x)$ and ∇f and ∇f^* are the identity functions.

EXAMPLE 26.10. Let $f(x) = -2\sum_{i=1}^d \sqrt{x_i}$ when $x_i \geq 0$ for all i and ∞ otherwise, which has $\mathrm{dom}(f) = [0, \infty)^d$ and $\mathrm{int}(\mathrm{dom}(f)) = (0, \infty)^d$. The gradient is $\nabla f(x) = -1/\sqrt{x}$, which blows up (in norm) on any sequence (x_n) approaching $\partial \mathrm{int}(\mathrm{dom}(f)) = \{x \in [0, \infty)^d : x_i = 0 \text{ for some } i \in [d]\}$. Here, $\sqrt{x}$ stands for the vector $(\sqrt{x_i})_i$. In what follows we will often use the underlying convention of extending univariate functions to vector by applying them componentwise. Note that $\|\nabla f(x)\| \to 0$ as $\|x\| \to \infty$: '∞' is not part of the boundary of $\mathrm{dom}(f)$. Strict convexity is also obvious so f is Legendre. In Exercise 26.8, we ask you to calculate the Bregman divergences with respect to f and f^* and verify the results of Theorem 26.6.

EXAMPLE 26.11. Let $f(x) = \sum_i x_i \log(x_i) - x_i$ be the unnormalised negentropy, which we met in Example 26.5. Similarly to the previous example, $\mathrm{dom}(f) = [0, \infty)^d$, $\mathrm{int}(\mathrm{dom}(f)) = (0, \infty)^d$ and $\partial\,\mathrm{int}(\mathrm{dom}(f)) = \{x \in [0, \infty)^d : x_i = 0 \text{ for some } i \in [d]\}$. The gradient is $\nabla f(x) = \log(x)$, and thus $\|\nabla f(x)\| \to \infty$ as $x \to \partial\,\mathrm{int}(\mathrm{dom}(f))$. Strict convexity also holds, hence f is Legendre. You already met the Bregman divergence $D_f(x, y)$, which turned out to be the relative entropy when x, y belong to the simplex. Exercise 26.9 asks you to calculate the dual of f (can you guess what this function will be?) and the Bregman divergence induced by f^* and to verify Theorem 26.6.

The Taylor series of the Bregman divergence is often a useful approximation. Let $g(y) = D_f(x, y)$, which for $y = x$ has $\nabla g(y) = 0$ and $\nabla^2 g(y) = \nabla^2 f(x)$. A second-order Taylor expansion suggests that

$$D_f(x, y) = g(y) \approx g(x) + \langle y - x, \nabla g(x)\rangle + \frac{1}{2}\|y - x\|_{\nabla^2 f(x)}^2 = \frac{1}{2}\|y - x\|_{\nabla^2 f(x)}^2.$$

This approximation can be very poor if x and y are far apart. Even when x and y are close, the lower-order terms are occasionally problematic, but nevertheless the approximation can guide intuition. The next theorem, which is based on Taylor's theorem and measurable selections, gives an exact result (Exercise 26.15).

THEOREM 26.12. *If f is convex and twice differentiable in $A = \mathrm{int}(\mathrm{dom}(f))$ and $x, y \in A$, then there exists an $\alpha \in [0, 1]$ and $z = \alpha x + (1 - \alpha)y$ such that*

$$D_f(x, y) = \frac{1}{2}\|x - y\|_{\nabla^2 f(z)}^2.$$

Suppose furthermore that $\nabla^2 f$ is continuous on $\mathrm{int}(\mathrm{dom}(f))$; then there exists a measurable function $g : \mathrm{int}(\mathrm{dom}(f)) \times \mathrm{int}(\mathrm{dom}(f)) \to \mathrm{int}(\mathrm{dom}(f))$ such that for all $x, y \in \mathrm{int}(\mathrm{dom}(f))$,

$$D_f(x, y) = \frac{1}{2}\|x - y\|_{\nabla^2 f(g(x,y))}^2.$$

The next result will be useful.

THEOREM 26.13. *Let $\eta > 0$ and f be Legendre and twice differentiable in $A = \mathrm{int}(\mathrm{dom}(f))$, $x, y \in A$, and let $z \in [x, y]$ be the point such that $D_f(x, y) = \frac{1}{2}\|x - y\|_{\nabla^2 f(z)}^2$. Then, for all $u \in \mathbb{R}^d$,*

$$\langle x - y, u\rangle - \frac{D_f(x, y)}{\eta} \leq \frac{\eta}{2}\|u\|_{(\nabla^2 f(z))^{-1}}^2.$$

Although the Bregman divergence is not symmetric, the right-hand side does not depend on the order of x and y in the Bregman divergence except that $z \in [x, y]$ may be different.

Proof Strict convexity of f ensures that $H = \nabla^2 f(z)$ is invertible. Applying Cauchy–Schwarz,

$$\langle x - y, u\rangle \leq \|x - y\|_H \|u\|_{H^{-1}} = \|u\|_{H^{-1}}\sqrt{2D_f(x, y)}.$$

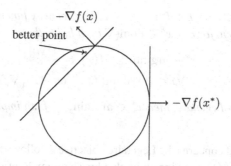

Figure 26.4 Illustration of first-order optimality conditions. The point at the top is not a minimiser because the hyperplane with normal as gradient does not support the convex set. The point at the right is a minimiser.

Therefore,

$$\langle x - y, u \rangle - \frac{D_f(x,y)}{\eta} \le \|u\|_{H^{-1}} \sqrt{2D_f(x,y)} - \frac{D_f(x,y)}{\eta} \le \frac{\eta}{2} \|u\|_{H^{-1}}^2,$$

where the last step follows from the ever useful $\max_{x \in \mathbb{R}} ax - bx^2 = a^2/(4b)$ which holds for any $b > 0$ and $a \in \mathbb{R}$. $\qquad\square$

26.5 Optimisation

The **first-order optimality condition** states that if $x \in \mathbb{R}^d$ is the minimiser of a differentiable function $f : \mathbb{R}^d \to \mathbb{R}$, then $\nabla f(x) = 0$. One of the things we like about convex functions is that when f is convex, the first-order optimality condition is both necessary and sufficient. In particular, if $\nabla f(x) = 0$ for some $x \in \mathbb{R}^d$ then x is a minimiser of f. The first-order optimality condition can also be generalised to constrained minima: if $f : \mathbb{R}^d \to \mathbb{R}$ is convex and differentiable and $A \subseteq \mathbb{R}^d$ is a non-empty convex set, then

$$x^* \in \operatorname{argmin}_{x \in A} f(x) \Leftrightarrow \forall x \in A : \langle x - x^*, \nabla f(x^*) \rangle \ge 0. \qquad (26.2)$$

The necessity of the condition on the right-hand side is easy to understand by a geometric reasoning. If $\nabla f(x^*) = 0$, then the said condition trivially holds. If $\nabla f(x^*) \ne 0$, the hyperplane H_{x^*} whose normal is $\nabla f(x^*)$ and goes through x^* must be a **supporting hyperplane** of A at x^*, with $-\nabla f(x^*)$ being the outer normal of A at x^* otherwise x^* could be moved by a small amount while staying inside A and improving the value of f. Since A is convex, it thus lies entirely on the side of H_{x^*} that $\nabla f(x^*)$ points into. This is clearly equivalent to (26.2). The sufficiency of the condition also follows from this geometric viewpoint as the reader may verify from the figure.

The above statement continues to hold with a small modification even when f is not differentiable everywhere. In particular, in this case the equivalence (26.2) holds for any $x^* \in \operatorname{dom}(\nabla f)$ with the modification that on the right side of the equivalence, A should be replaced by $A \cap \operatorname{dom}(f)$:

PROPOSITION 26.14. *Let* $f : \mathbb{R}^d \to \bar{\mathbb{R}}$ *be a convex function and* $A \subset \mathbb{R}^d$ *a non-empty convex set. Then, for any* $x^* \in \mathrm{dom}(\nabla f)$, *it holds that*

$$x^* \in \mathrm{argmin}_{x \in A} f(x) \Longleftrightarrow$$
$$\forall x \in A \cap \mathrm{dom}(f): \quad \langle x - x^*, \nabla f(x^*) \rangle \geq 0. \tag{26.3}$$

Further, if f *is Legendre, then* $x^* \in \mathrm{argmin}_{x \in A} f(x)$ *implies* $x^* \in \mathrm{dom}(\nabla f)$ *and hence also* (26.3).

The part that concerns the Legendre objective f follows by noting that by Corollary 26.8, $x^* \in \mathrm{int}(\mathrm{dom}(f))$ combined with that by Theorem 26.6(a), $\mathrm{int}(\mathrm{dom}(f)) = \mathrm{dom}(\nabla f)$.

26.6 Projections

If $A \subset \mathbb{R}^d$ and $x \in \mathbb{R}^d$, then the Euclidean projection of x on A is $\Pi_A(x) = \mathrm{argmin}_{y \in A} \|x - y\|_2^2$. One can also project with respect to a Bregman divergence induced by convex function f. Let $\Pi_{A,f}$ be defined by

$$\Pi_{A,f}(x) = \mathrm{argmin}_{y \in A} D_f(y, x).$$

An important property of the projection is that minimising a Legendre function f on a convex set A is (usually) equivalent to finding the unconstrained minimum on the domain of f and then projecting that point on to A.

THEOREM 26.15. *Let* $f : \mathbb{R}^d \to \bar{\mathbb{R}}$ *be Legendre,* $A \subset \mathbb{R}^d$ *a non-empty, closed convex set with* $A \cap \mathrm{dom}(f)$ *non-empty and assume that* $\tilde{y} = \mathrm{argmin}_{z \in \mathbb{R}^d} f(z)$ *exists. Then the following hold:*

(a) $y = \mathrm{argmin}_{z \in A} f(z)$ *exists and is unique;*
(b) $y = \mathrm{argmin}_{z \in A} D_f(z, \tilde{y})$.

The assumption that $\tilde{y}$ exists is necessary. For example $f(x) = -\sqrt{x}$ for $x \geq 0$ and $f(x) = \infty$ for $x < 0$ is Legendre with domain $\mathrm{dom}(f) = [0, \infty)$, but f does not have a minimum on its domain.

26.7 Notes

1 The 'infinity arithmetic' on the extended real line is as follows:

$$\alpha + \infty = \infty \qquad \text{for } \alpha \in (-\infty, \infty]$$
$$\alpha - \infty = -\infty \qquad \text{for } \alpha \in [-\infty, \infty)$$
$$\alpha \cdot \infty = \infty \text{ and } \alpha \cdot (-\infty) = -\infty \qquad \text{for } \alpha > 0$$
$$\alpha \cdot \infty = -\infty \text{ and } \alpha \cdot (-\infty) = \infty \qquad \text{for } \alpha < 0$$
$$0 \cdot \infty = 0 \cdot (-\infty) = 0.$$

Like $\alpha/0$, the value of $\infty - \infty$ is not defined. We also have $\alpha \leq \infty$ for all α and $\alpha \geq -\infty$ for all α.

2 There are many ways to define the topological notions used in this chapter. The most elegant is also the most abstract, but there is no space for that here. Instead we give the classical definitions that are specific to $\mathbb{R}^d$ and subsets. Let A be a subset of $\mathbb{R}^d$. A point $x \in A$ is an **interior point** if there exists an $\varepsilon > 0$ such that $B_\varepsilon(x) = \{y : \|x - y\|_2 \leq \varepsilon\} \subset A$. The **interior** of A is $\text{int}(A) = \{x \in A : x \text{ is an interior point}\}$. The set A is **open** if $\text{int}(A) = A$ and **closed** if its complement $A^c = \mathbb{R}^d \setminus A$ is open. The **boundary** of A is denoted by ∂A and is the set of points in $x \in \mathbb{R}^d$ such that for all $\varepsilon > 0$ the set $B_\varepsilon(x)$ contains points from A and A^c. Note that points in the boundary need not be in A. Some examples: $\partial[0, \infty) = \{0\} = \partial(0, \infty)$ and $\partial \mathbb{R}^n = \emptyset$.

26.8 Bibliographic Remarks

The main source for these notes is the excellent book by Rockafellar [2015]. The basic definitions are in part I. The Fenchel dual is analysed in part III while Legendre functions are found in part V. Convex optimisation is a huge topic. The standard text is by Boyd and Vandenberghe [2004].

26.9 Exercises

26.1 Let $f : \mathbb{R}^d \to \mathbb{R}$ be convex. Prove that f is continuous on $\text{int}(\text{dom}(f))$.

26.2 Prove Jensen's inequality (Theorem 26.2). Precisely, let $X \in \mathbb{R}^d$ be a random variable for which $\mathbb{E}[X]$ exists and $f : \mathbb{R}^d \to \bar{R}$ a measurable convex function. Prove that $\mathbb{E}[f(x)] \geq f(\mathbb{E}[X])$.

HINT   Let $x_0 = \mathbb{E}[X] \in \mathbb{R}^d$ and define a linear function $g : \mathbb{R}^d \to \mathbb{R}$ such that $g(x_0) = f(x_0)$ and $g(x) \leq f(x)$ for all $x \in \mathbb{R}^d$. To guarantee the existence of g, you may use the **supporting hyperplane theorem**, which states that if $S \subset \mathbb{R}^m$ is a convex set and $s \in \partial S$, then there exists a supporting hyperplane containing s.

26.3 Let $f : \mathbb{R}^d \to \mathbb{R} \cup \{-\infty, \infty\}$.

(a) Prove that $f^{**}(x) \leq f(x)$.

(b) Assume that f is convex and differentiable on $\text{int}(\text{dom}(f))$. Show that $f^{**}(x) = f(x)$ for $x \in \text{int}(\text{dom}(f))$.

 As mentioned in the text, the assumption that f is differentiable can be relaxed to an assumption that the epigraph of f is closed, in which case the result holds over the whole domain. The proof is not hard, but you will need to use the sub-differential rather than the gradient, and the boundary must be treated with care.

26.4 For each of the real-valued functions below, decide whether or not it is Legendre on the given domain:

(a) $f(x) = x^2$ on $[-1, 1]$.

(b) $f(x) = -\sqrt{x}$ on $[0, \infty)$.

(c) $f(x) = \log(1/x)$ on $[0, \infty)$ with $f(0) = \infty$.

(d) $f(x) = x \log(x)$ on $[0, \infty)$ with $f(0) = 0$.

(e) $f(x) = |x|$ on $\mathbb{R}$.

(f) $f(x) = \max\{|x|, x^2\}$ on $\mathbb{R}$.

26.5 Prove Theorem 26.3.

26.6 Prove Proposition 26.7 and Corollary 26.8.

26.7 Prove Proposition 26.14.

26.8 Let f be the convex function given in Example 26.10.

(a) For $x, y \in \text{dom}(f)$, find $D_f(x, y)$.

(b) Compute $f^*(u)$ and $\nabla f^*(u)$.

(c) Find $\text{dom}(\nabla f^*)$.

(d) Show that for $u, v \in (-\infty, 0]^d$,

$$D_{f^*}(u, v) = -\sum_{i=1}^{d} \frac{(u_i - v_i)^2}{u_i v_i^2}.$$

(e) Verify the claims in Theorem 26.6.

26.9 Let $f : \mathbb{R}^d \to \bar{\mathbb{R}}$ be the unnormalised negentropy function from Example 26.11. We have seen in Example 26.5 that $D_f(x, y) = \sum_i (x_i \log(x_i/y_i) + y_i - x_i)$.

(a) Compute $f^*(u)$ and $\nabla f^*(u)$.

(b) Find $\text{dom}(\nabla f^*)$.

(c) Show that for $u, v \in \mathbb{R}^d$,

$$D_{f^*}(u, v) = \sum_{i=1}^{d} \exp(v_i)(v_i - u_i) + \exp(u_i) - \exp(v_i).$$

(d) Verify the claims in Theorem 26.6.

26.10 Let f be Legendre. Show that $\tilde{f}$ given by $\tilde{f}(x) = f(x) + \langle x, u \rangle$ is also Legendre for any $u \in \mathbb{R}^d$.

26.11 Let f be the unnormalised negentropy function from Example 26.5.

(a) Prove that f is Legendre.

(b) Given $y \in [0, \infty)^d$, prove that $\text{argmin}_{x \in \mathcal{P}_{d-1}} D_f(x, y) = y/\|y\|_1$.

26.12 Let $\alpha \in [0, 1/d]$ and $\mathcal{A} = \mathcal{P}_{d-1} \cap [\alpha, 1]^d$ and f be the unnormalised negentropy function. Let $y \in [0, \infty)^d$ and $x = \text{argmin}_{x \in \mathcal{A}} D_f(x, y)$ and assume that $y_1 \leq y_2 \leq \cdots \leq y_d$. Let m be the smallest value such that

$$y_m(1 - (m - 1)\alpha) \geq \alpha \sum_{j=m}^{d} y_j.$$

Show that

$$x_i = \begin{cases} \alpha & \text{if } i < m \\ (1 - (m - 1)\alpha)y_i / \sum_{j=m}^{d} y_j & \text{otherwise.} \end{cases}$$

26.13 (GENERALISED PYTHAGOREAN IDENTITY) Let $A \subset \mathbb{R}^d$ be convex and closed and $f : \mathbb{R}^d \to \bar{\mathbb{R}}$ be a convex function with $A \cap \mathrm{dom}(f)$ non-empty.

(a) Suppose that $x \in A$ and $y \in \mathbb{R}^d$ and $z = \Pi_{A,f}(y)$ and f is differentiable at y. Prove that

$$D_f(x, y) \geq D_f(x, z) + D_f(z, y).$$

(b) Prove that the condition that f be differentiable at y cannot be relaxed.

26.14 Prove Theorem 26.3 and show that Part (c) does not hold in general when f is not differentiable at y.

26.15 Prove Theorem 26.12

HINT   For the first part, simply apply Taylor's theorem. For the second part, you will probably need to use a measurable selection theorem. For example, the theorem by Kuratowski and Ryll-Nardzewski, which appears as theorem 6.9.4 in the second volume of the book by Bogachev [2007].

27 Exp3 for Adversarial Linear Bandits

The model for adversarial linear bandits is as follows. The learner is given an action set $\mathcal{A} \subset \mathbb{R}^d$ and the number of rounds n. As usual in the adversarial setting, it is convenient to switch to losses. An instance of the adversarial problem is a sequence of loss vectors $y_1, \ldots, y_n$ taking values in $\mathbb{R}^d$. In each round $t \in [n]$, the learner selects a possibly random action $A_t \in \mathcal{A}$ and observes a loss $Y_t = \langle A_t, y_t \rangle$. The learner does not observe the loss vector y_t. The regret of the learner after n rounds is

$$R_n = \mathbb{E}\left[\sum_{t=1}^n Y_t\right] - \min_{a \in \mathcal{A}} \sum_{t=1}^n \langle a, y_t \rangle.$$

Clearly, the finite-armed adversarial bandits discussed in Chapter 11 is a special case of adversarial linear bandits corresponding to the choice $\mathcal{A} = \{e_1, \ldots, e_d\}$, where $e_1, \ldots, e_d$ are the unit vectors of the d-dimensional standard Euclidean basis.

For this chapter, we assume that

(a) for all $t \in [n]$ the loss satisfies $y_t \in \mathcal{L} = \{x \in \mathbb{R}^d : \sup_{a \in \mathcal{A}} |\langle a, x \rangle| \leq 1\}$; and
(b) the action set $\mathcal{A}$ spans $\mathbb{R}^d$.

The latter assumption is for convenience only and may be relaxed with a little care (Exercise 27.7).

27.1 Exponential Weights for Linear Bandits

We adapt the exponential-weighting algorithm of Chapter 11. Like in that setting, we need a way to estimate the individual losses for each action, but now we make use of the linear structure to share information between the arms and decrease the variance of our estimators. For now we assume that $\mathcal{A}$ is finite, which we relax in Section 27.3. Let $t \in [n]$ be the index of the current round. Assuming the loss estimate for action $a \in \mathcal{A}$ in round $s \in [n]$ is $\hat{Y}_s(a)$, then the probability distribution proposed by exponential weights is given by the probability mass function $\tilde{P}_t : \mathcal{A} \to [0, 1]$ given by

$$\tilde{P}_t(a) \propto \exp\left(-\eta \sum_{s=1}^{t-1} \hat{Y}_s(a)\right),$$

where $\eta > 0$ is the learning rate. To control the variance of the loss estimates, it will be useful to mix this distribution with an exploration distribution π ($\pi : \mathcal{A} \to [0,1]$ and $\sum_{a \in \mathcal{A}} \pi(a) = 1$). The mixture distribution is

$$P_t(a) = (1 - \gamma)\tilde{P}_t(a) + \gamma\pi(a),$$

where γ is a constant mixing factor to be chosen later. The algorithm then simply samples its action A_t from P_t:

$$A_t \sim P_t.$$

Recall that $Y_t = \langle A_t, y_t \rangle$ is the observed loss after taking action A_t. We need a way to estimate $y_t(a) \doteq \langle a, y_t \rangle$. The idea is to use least squares to estimate y_t with $\hat{Y}_t = R_t A_t Y_t$, where $R_t \in \mathbb{R}^{d \times d}$ is selected so that $\hat{Y}_t$ is an unbiased estimate of y_t given the history. Then the loss for a given action is estimated by $\hat{Y}_t(a) = \langle a, \hat{Y}_t \rangle$. To find the choice of R_t that makes $\hat{Y}_t$ unbiased, let $\mathbb{E}_t[\cdot] = \mathbb{E}[\cdot|P_t]$ and calculate

$$\mathbb{E}_t[\hat{Y}_t] = R_t \mathbb{E}_t[A_t A_t^\top]y_t = R_t \underbrace{\left(\sum_{a \in \mathcal{A}} P_t(a)aa^\top\right)}_{Q_t} y_t.$$

Using $R_t = Q_t^{-1}$ leads to $\mathbb{E}_t[\hat{Y}_t] = y_t$ as desired. Of course Q_t should be non-singular, which will follow by choosing π so that

$$Q(\pi) = \sum_{a \in \mathcal{A}} \pi(a)aa^\top$$

is non-singular. The complete algorithm is summarised in Algorithm 15.

1: **Input** Finite action set $\mathcal{A} \subset \mathbb{R}^d$, learning rate η, exploration distribution π, exploration parameter γ

2: **for** $t = 1, 2, \ldots, n$ **do**

3:      Compute sampling distribution:

$$P_t(a) = \gamma\pi(a) + (1 - \gamma)\frac{\exp\left(-\eta\sum_{s=1}^{t-1}\hat{Y}_s(a)\right)}{\sum_{a' \in \mathcal{A}}\exp\left(-\eta\sum_{s=1}^{t-1}\hat{Y}_s(a')\right)}.$$

4:      Sample action $A_t \sim P_t$

5:      Observe loss $Y_t = \langle A_t, y_t \rangle$ and compute loss estimates:

$$\hat{Y}_t = Q_t^{-1}A_t Y_t \quad \text{and} \quad \hat{Y}_t(a) = \langle a, \hat{Y}_t \rangle.$$

6: **end for**

Algorithm 15: Exp3 for linear bandits.

27.2   Regret Analysis

THEOREM 27.1. *Assume that $\mathcal{A}$ is non-empty and let $k = |\mathcal{A}|$. For any exploration distribution π, for some parameters η and γ, for all $(y_t)_t$ with $y_t \in \mathcal{L}$, the regret of Algorithm 15 satisfies*

$$R_n \leq 2\sqrt{(2g(\pi) + d)n \log(k)}, \tag{27.1}$$

where $g(\pi) = \max_{a \in \mathcal{A}} \|a\|^2_{Q^{-1}(\pi)}$. Furthermore, there exists an exploration distribution π and parameters η and γ such that $g(\pi) \leq d$, and hence $R_n \leq 2\sqrt{3dn \log(k)}$.

The utility of (27.1) is that at times, calculating the distribution that minimises $g(\pi)$ or sampling from it may be difficult, in which case, one may employ a distribution that trades off computation with the regret.

Proof   Assume that the learning rate η is chosen so that for each round t the loss estimates satisfy

$$\eta \hat{Y}_t(a) \geq -1, \qquad \forall a \in \mathcal{A}. \tag{27.2}$$

Then, by adopting the proof of Theorem 11.1 (see Exercise 27.1), the regret is bounded by

$$R_n \leq \frac{\log k}{\eta} + 2\gamma n + \eta \sum_{t=1}^{n} \mathbb{E}\left[\sum_{a \in \mathcal{A}} P_t(a) \hat{Y}_t^2(a)\right]. \tag{27.3}$$

Note that we cannot use the proof that leads to the tighter constant (η getting replaced by $\eta/2$ in the second term above) because we would loose too much in other parts of the proof by guaranteeing that the loss estimates are bounded by one (see below). To get a regret bound, it remains to set γ and η so that (27.2) is satisfied and to bound $\mathbb{E}\left[\sum_a P_t(a) \hat{Y}_t^2(a)\right]$. We start with the latter. Let $M_t = \sum_a P_t(a) \hat{Y}_t^2(a)$. By the definition of the loss estimate,

$$\hat{Y}_t^2(a) = (a^\top Q_t^{-1} A_t Y_t)^2 = Y_t^2 A_t^\top Q_t^{-1} aa^\top Q_t^{-1} A_t,$$

which means that $M_t = \sum_a P_t(a) \hat{Y}_t^2(a) = Y_t^2 A_t^\top Q_t^{-1} A_t \leq A_t^\top Q_t^{-1} A_t = \text{trace}(A_t A_t^\top Q_t^{-1})$, and by the linearity of trace,

$$\mathbb{E}[M_t \mid P_t] \leq \text{trace}\left(\sum_{a \in \mathcal{A}} P_t(a) aa^\top Q_t^{-1}\right) = d.$$

It remains to choose γ and η. Strengthen (27.2) to $|\eta \hat{Y}_t(a)| \leq 1$ and note that since $|Y_t| \leq 1$,

$$|\eta \hat{Y}_t(a)| = |\eta a^\top Q_t^{-1} A_t Y_t| \leq \eta |a^\top Q_t^{-1} A_t|.$$

Recall that $Q(\pi) = \sum_{a \in \mathcal{A}} \pi(a) aa^\top$. Clearly $Q_t \succeq \gamma Q(\pi)$, and hence $Q_t^{-1} \preceq Q(\pi)^{-1}/\gamma$ by Exercise 27.4. Using this and the Cauchy–Schwarz inequality shows that

$$|a^\top Q_t^{-1} A_t| \leq \|a\|_{Q_t^{-1}} \|A_t\|_{Q_t^{-1}} \leq \max_{v \in \mathcal{A}} v^\top Q_t^{-1} v \leq \frac{1}{\gamma} \max_{v \in \mathcal{A}} v^\top Q^{-1}(\pi) v = \frac{g(\pi)}{\gamma},$$

which implies that

$$|\eta \hat{Y}_t(a)| \leq \frac{\eta}{\gamma} g(\pi). \tag{27.4}$$

Choosing $\gamma = \eta g(\pi)$ guarantees $|\eta \hat{Y}_t(a)| \leq 1$. Plugging this choice into (27.3), we get

$$R_n \leq \frac{\log k}{\eta} + \eta n(2g(\pi) + d) = 2\sqrt{(2g(\pi) + d)n \log(k)},$$

where the last equality is derived by choosing $\eta = \sqrt{\frac{\log(k)}{(2g(\pi)+d)n}}$ finishing the proof of (27.1).

For the second half, recall that by the Kiefer–Wolfowitz theorem (Theorem 21.1 and Exercise 21.6), there exists a sampling distribution π such that $g(\pi) \leq d$. Plugging this value into (27.1), finishes the proof. □

27.3 Continuous Exponential Weights

The dependence on $\log(k)$ in the regret guarantee provided by Theorem 27.1 is objectionable when the number of arms is extremely large or infinite. One approach is to find a finite subset $\mathcal{C} \subseteq \mathcal{A}$ for which

$$\sup_{a \in \mathcal{A}} \min_{b \in \mathcal{C}} \sup_{y \in \mathcal{L}} |\langle a - b, y \rangle| \leq 1/n.$$

A standard calculation shows (Exercise 27.6) shows that $\mathcal{C}$ can always be chosen so that $\log |\mathcal{C}| \leq d \log(6dn)$. Then it is easy to check that Exp3 on $\mathcal{C}$ suffers regret relative to the best action in $\mathcal{A}$ of at most $R_n = O(d\sqrt{n \log(nd)})$. The problem with this approach is that $\mathcal{C}$ is exponentially large in d, which makes this algorithm intractable in most situations. When $\mathcal{A}$ is convex, a more computationally tractable approach is to use the **continuous exponential weights** algorithm.

 For this section, we assume that $\mathcal{A}$ is convex and has positive Lebesgue measure. The latter condition can be relaxed with some care (Exercise 27.10).

Let π be a probability measure supported on $\mathcal{A}$. The continuous exponential weights policy samples A_t from $P_t = (1 - \gamma)\tilde{P}_t + \gamma\pi$, where $\tilde{P}_t$ is a measure supported on $\mathcal{A}$ defined by

$$\tilde{P}_t(B) = \frac{\int_B \exp\left(-\eta \sum_{s=1}^{t-1} \hat{Y}_s(a)\right) da}{\int_{\mathcal{A}} \exp\left(-\eta \sum_{s=1}^{t-1} \hat{Y}_s(a)\right) da}. \tag{27.5}$$

We will shortly see that the analysis in the previous section can be copied almost verbatim to prove a regret bound for this strategy. But what has been bought here? Rather than sampling from a discrete distribution on a large number of arms, we now have to sample from a probability measure on a convex set. Sampling from arbitrary probability measures is itself a challenging problem, but under certain conditions there are polynomial time algorithms for this problem. The factors that play the biggest role in the feasibility of sampling from a measure are *(a)* the form of the measure or its density and *(b)* how the convex set is represented. As it happens, the measure defined in the last display is **log-concave**, which means that the logarithm of the density, with respect to the Lebesgue measure on $\mathcal{A}$, is a concave function.

THEOREM 27.2. *Let $p(a) \propto \mathbb{I}_{\mathcal{A}}(a) \exp(-f(a))$ be a density with respect to the Lebesgue measure on $\mathcal{A}$ such that $f : \mathcal{A} \to \mathbb{R}$ is a convex function. Then there exists a polynomial-time algorithm for sampling from p, provided one can compute the following efficiently:*

1 *(First-order information): $\nabla f(a)$ where $a \in \mathcal{A}$.*
2 *(Euclidean projections): $\operatorname{argmin}_{x \in \mathcal{A}} \|x - y\|_2$ where $y \in \mathbb{R}^d$.*

The probability distribution defined by Eq. (27.5) satisfies the first condition. Efficiently computing a projection on to a convex set is a more delicate issue. A general criterion that makes this efficient is access to a **separation oracle**, which is a computational procedure ϕ that accepts a point $x \in \mathbb{R}^d$ as input and responds $\phi(x) = \text{TRUE}$ if $x \in \mathcal{A}$ and otherwise $\phi(x) = u$, where $\langle y, u \rangle > \langle x, u \rangle$ for all $y \in \mathcal{A}$ (see Fig. 27.1).
   Define $\log_+(x) = \max(0, \log(x))$.

THEOREM 27.3. *Assume that $\mathcal{A}$ is compact, convex and has volume $\mathrm{vol}(\mathcal{A}) = \int_{\mathcal{A}} da > 0$. Then an appropriately tuned instantiation of the continuous exponential weights algorithm with Kiefer–Wolfowitz exploration has regret bounded by*

$$R_n \leq 2d\sqrt{3n(1 + \log_+(2n/d))}.$$

The proof of Theorem 27.3 relies on the following proposition, which we leave as an exercise (Exercise 27.11).

PROPOSITION 27.4. *Let $\mathcal{K} \subset \mathbb{R}^d$ be a compact convex set with $\mathrm{vol}(\mathcal{K}) > 0$, $u \in \mathbb{R}^d$ and let $x^* = \operatorname{argmin}_{x \in \mathcal{K}} \langle x, u \rangle$. Then,*

$$\log \left(\frac{\mathrm{vol}(\mathcal{K})}{\int_{\mathcal{K}} \exp\left(-\langle x - x^*, u \rangle\right) dx} \right) \leq d \left(1 + \log_+ \left(\frac{\sup_{x,y \in \mathcal{K}} \langle x - y, u \rangle}{d} \right) \right).$$

 The left-hand side in the above display is the logarithmic Laplace transform of the uniform measure on $\mathcal{K} - \{x^*\}$ evaluated at u.

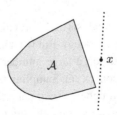

Figure 27.1   Separation oracle returns the normal of a hyperplane that separates x from $\mathcal{A}$ whenever $x \notin \mathcal{A}$. When $x \in \mathcal{A}$, the separation oracle returns TRUE.

Proof of Theorem 27.3   As before, choosing $\gamma = d\eta$ ensures that $|\eta\langle a, \hat{Y}_t\rangle| \leq 1$ for all $a \in \mathcal{A}$ (see the proof of Theorem 27.1). The standard argument (Exercise 27.9) shows that

$$R_n \leq \frac{1}{\eta}\mathbb{E}\left[\log\left(\frac{\text{vol}(\mathcal{A})}{\int_{\mathcal{A}}\exp\left(-\eta\sum_{t=1}^{n}(\hat{Y}_t(a) - \hat{Y}_t(a^*))\right)da}\right)\right] + 3\eta dn. \tag{27.6}$$

Using again that $\eta|\langle a, \hat{Y}_t\rangle| \leq 1$ and Proposition 27.4 with $u = \eta\sum_{t=1}^{n}\hat{Y}_t$ shows that

$$R_n \leq \frac{d(1 + \log_+(n/d))}{\eta} + 3\eta dn \leq 2d\sqrt{3n(1 + \log_+(2n/d))}. \qquad \square$$

27.4 Notes

1 A naive implementation of Algorithm 15 has computation complexity $O(kd + d^3)$ per round. There is also the one-off cost of computing the exploration distribution, the complexity of which was discussed in Chapter 21. The real problem is that k can be extremely large. This is especially true when the action set is combinatorial. For example, when $\mathcal{A} = \{a \in \mathbb{R}^d : a_i = \pm 1\}$ is the corners of the hypercube $|\mathcal{A}| = 2^d$, which is much too large unless the dimension is small. Such problems call for a different approach that we present in the next chapter and in Chapter 30.

2 It is not important to find exactly the optimal exploration distribution. All that is needed is a bound on Eq. (27.4), which for the exploration distribution based on the Kiefer–Wolfowitz theorem is just d. However, unlike in the finite case, exploration is crucial and cannot be removed (Exercise 27.8).

3 The $O(\sqrt{n})$ dependence of the regret on the horizon is not improvable, but the linear dependence on the dimension is suboptimal for certain action sets and optimal for others. An example where improvement is possible occurs when $\mathcal{A}$ is the unit ball, which is analysed in the next chapter.

4 A slight modification of the set-up allows the action set to change in each round, but where actions have identities. Suppose that $k \in \{1, 2, \ldots\}$ and $\mathcal{A}_t = \{a_1(t), \ldots, a_k(t)\}$ and the adversary chooses losses so that $\max_{a \in \mathcal{A}_t} |\langle a, y_t\rangle| \leq 1$ for all t. Then a straightforward adaptation of Algorithm 15 and Theorem 27.1 leads to an algorithm for which

$$R_n = \max_{i \in [k]}\mathbb{E}\left[\sum_{t=1}^{n}\langle A_t - a_i(t), y_t\rangle\right] \leq 2\sqrt{3dn\log(k)}.$$

The definition of the regret still compares the learner to the best single action in hindsight, which makes it less meaningful than the definition of the regret in Chapter 19 for stochastic linear bandits with changing action sets. These differences are discussed in more detail in Chapter 29. See also Exercise 27.5.

27.5 Bibliographic Remarks

The results in Sections 27.1 and 27.2 follow the article by Bubeck et al. [2012], with minor modifications to make the argument more pedagogical. The main difference is that they used John's ellipsoid over the action set for exploration, which is only the right thing when John's ellipsoid is also a central ellipsoid. Here we use Kiefer–Wolfowitz, which is equivalent to finding the minimum volume central ellipsoid containing the action set. Theorem 27.2, which guarantees the existence of a polynomial time sampling algorithm for convex sets with gradient information and projections is by Bubeck et al. [2015b]. We warn the reader that these algorithms are not very practical, especially if theoretically justified parameters are used. The study of sampling from convex bodies is quite fascinating. There is an overview by Lovász and Vempala [2007], though it is a little old. The continuous exponential weights algorithm is perhaps attributable to Cover [1991] in the special setting of online learning called universal portfolio optimisation. The first application to linear bandits is by Hazan et al. [2016]. Their algorithm and analysis are more complicated because they seek to improve the computation properties by replacing the exploration distribution based on Kiefer–Wolfowitz with an adaptive randomised exploration basis that can be computed in polynomial time under weaker assumptions. Continuous exponential weights for linear bandits using the core set of John's ellipsoid for exploration (rather than Kiefer–Wolfowitz) was recently analysed by van der Hoeven et al. [2018]. Another path towards an efficient $O(d\sqrt{n\log(\cdot)})$ policy for convex action sets is to use the tools from online optimisation. We explain some of these ideas in more detail in the next chapter, but the reader is referred to the paper by Bubeck and Eldan [2015].

27.6   Exercises

27.1 ('MIXED' EXP3 ANALYSIS) Prove Eq. (27.3).

27.2 (DEPENDENCE ON THE RANGE OF LOSSES) Suppose that instead of assuming $y_t \in \mathcal{L}$, we assume that $y_t \in \{y \in \mathbb{R}^d : \sup_{a \in \mathcal{A}} |\langle a, y \rangle| \leq b\}$ for some known $b > 0$. Modify the algorithm to accommodate this change, and explain how the regret guarantee changes.

27.3 (DEPENDENCE ON THE RANGE OF LOSSES (II)) Now suppose that $a < b$ are known and $y_t \in \{y \in \mathbb{R}^d : \langle a, y \rangle \in [a, b]$ for all $a \in \mathcal{A}\}$. How can you adapt the algorithm now, and what is its regret?

27.4 (INVERSION REVERSES LOEWNER ORDERS) Let $A, B \in \mathbb{R}^{d \times d}$ and suppose that $A \succeq B$ and B is invertible. Show that $A^{-1} \preceq B^{-1}$.

27.5 (CHANGING ACTION SETS) Provide the necessary corrections to Algorithm 15 and its analysis to prove the result claimed in Note 4.

HINT   You will need to choose a new exploration distribution in every round. Otherwise everything is more or less the same.

27.6 (COVERING NUMBERS FOR CONVEX SETS) For $\mathcal{K} \subset \mathbb{R}^d$ let $\|x\|_{\mathcal{K}} = \sup_{y \in \mathcal{K}} |\langle x, y \rangle|$. Let $\mathcal{A} \subset \mathbb{R}^d$ and $\mathcal{L} = \{y : \|y\|_{\mathcal{A}} \leq 1\}$. Let $N(\mathcal{A}, \varepsilon)$ be the size of the smallest subset $\mathcal{C} \subseteq \mathcal{A}$ such that $\min_{x' \in \mathcal{C}} \|x - x'\|_{\mathcal{L}} \leq \varepsilon$ for all $x \in \mathcal{A}$. Show the following:

(a) When $\mathcal{A} = \{x \in \mathbb{R}^d : \|x\|_{V^{-1}} \leq 1\}$, we have $N(\mathcal{A}, \varepsilon) \leq (3/\varepsilon)^d$.

(b) When $\mathcal{A}$ is convex, bounded and $\mathrm{span}(\mathcal{A}) = \mathbb{R}^d$ we have $N(\mathcal{A}, \varepsilon) \leq (3d/\varepsilon)^d$.

(c) For any bounded $\mathcal{A} \subset \mathbb{R}^d$ we have $N(\mathcal{A}, \varepsilon) \leq (6d/\varepsilon)^d$.

HINT   For the first part, find a linear map from $\mathcal{A}$ to the Euclidean ball and use the fact that the Euclidean ball can be covered with a set of size $(3/\varepsilon)^d$. For the second part use the fact that for any symmetric, convex and compact set $\mathcal{K}$ there exists an ellipsoid $\mathcal{E} = \{x : \|x\|_V \leq 1\}$ such that $\mathcal{E} \subseteq \mathcal{K} \subseteq d\mathcal{E}$.

27.7 (LOW RANK ACTION SETS (I)) In the definition of the algorithm and the proof of Theorem 27.1, we assumed that $\mathcal{A}$ spans $\mathbb{R}^d$ and that it has positive Lebesgue measure. Show that this assumption may be relaxed by carefully adapting the algorithm and analysis.

27.8 (NECESSITY OF EXPLORATION) We saw in Chapter 11 that the exponential weights algorithm achieved near-optimal regret without mixing additional exploration. Show that exploration is crucial here. More precisely, construct a finite action set $\mathcal{A}$ and reward sequence $y_t \in \mathcal{L}$ such that the regret of Algorithm 15 with $\gamma = 0$ becomes very poor (even with η optimally tuned) relative to the optimal choice.

27.9 (CONTINUOUS EXPONENTIAL WEIGHTS) Complete the missing steps in the proof of Theorem 27.3.

27.10 (LOW RANK ACTION SETS (II)) In the definition of the algorithm and the proof of Theorem 27.3, we assumed that $\mathcal{A}$ spans $\mathbb{R}^d$ and that it has positive Lebesgue measure. Show that this assumption may be relaxed by carefully adapting the algorithm and analysis.

27.11 (VOLUME BOUNDS) Prove Proposition 27.4.

28 Follow-the-regularised-Leader and Mirror Descent

In the last chapter, we showed that if $\mathcal{A} \subset \mathbb{R}^d$ has k elements, then the regret of Exp3 with a careful exploration distribution has regret

$$R_n = O(\sqrt{dn \log(k)}).$$

We also showed the continuous version of this algorithm has regret at most

$$R_n = O(d\sqrt{n \log(n)}).$$

Although this algorithm can often be made to run in polynomial time, the degree tends to be high and the implementation complicated, making the algorithm impractical. In many cases this can be improved, both in terms of the regret and computation. In this chapter we demonstrate this in the case when $\mathcal{A}$ is the unit ball by showing that for this case there is an efficient, low-complexity algorithm for which the regret is $R_n = O(\sqrt{dn \log(n)})$. More importantly, however, we introduce a pair of related algorithms called **follow-the-regularised-leader** and **mirror descent**, which are powerful tools for the design and analysis of bandit algorithms. In fact, the exponential weights algorithm turns out to be a special case.

28.1 Online Linear Optimisation

Mirror descent originated in the convex optimisation literature. The idea has since been adapted to online learning and specifically to **online linear optimisation**. Online linear optimisation is the full information version of the adversarial linear bandit, where at the end of each round the learner observes the full vector y_t. Let $\mathcal{A} \subset \mathbb{R}^d$ be a convex set and $\mathcal{L} \subset \mathbb{R}^d$ be an arbitrary set called the **loss space**. Let $y_1, \ldots, y_n$ be a sequence

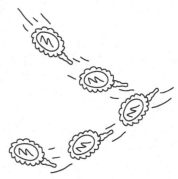

Figure 28.1   Mirror descent is a modern art, as well as science

of loss vectors with $y_t \in \mathcal{L}$ for $t \in [n]$. In each round the learner chooses $a_t \in \mathcal{A}$ and subsequently observes the vector y_t. The regret relative to a fixed comparator $a \in \mathcal{A}$ is

$$R_n(a) = \sum_{t=1}^{n} \langle a_t - a, y_t \rangle,$$

and the regret is $R_n = \max_{a \in \mathcal{A}} R_n(a)$. We emphasise that the only difference relative to the adversarial linear bandit is that now y_t is observed rather than $\langle a_t, y_t \rangle$. Actions are not capitalised in this section because the algorithms presented here do not randomise.

Mirror descent

The basic version of mirror descent has two extra parameters beyond n and $\mathcal{A}$. A learning rate $\eta > 0$ and a convex function $F : \mathbb{R}^d \to \bar{\mathbb{R}}$ with domain $\mathcal{D} = \mathrm{dom}(F)$. Usually F will be Legendre. The function F is called a **potential function** or **regulariser**. In the first round, mirror descent predicts

$$a_1 = \mathrm{argmin}_{a \in \mathcal{A}} F(a). \tag{28.1}$$

Subsequently it predicts

$$a_{t+1} = \mathrm{argmin}_{a \in \mathcal{A}} \left(\eta \langle a, y_t \rangle + D_F(a, a_t) \right), \tag{28.2}$$

where $D_F(a, a_t)$ is the F-induced Bregman divergence between a and a_t. Implicit in the definition is that $a_1, a_2, \ldots$ are well-defined. The reader is invited to construct examples when this is not the case (Exercise 28.2). A simple case when $(a_t)_{t=1}^n$ are guaranteed are well-defined is when $\mathcal{A}$ is compact and F is Legendre.

Follow-the-Regularised-Leader

Like mirror descent, follow-the-regularised-leader depends on a convex potential F with domain $\mathcal{D} = \mathrm{dom}(F)$ and predicts $a_1 = \mathrm{argmin}_{a \in \mathcal{A}} F(a)$. In subsequent rounds $t \in [n]$, the predictions are

$$a_{t+1} = \mathrm{argmin}_{a \in \mathcal{A}} \left(\eta \sum_{s=1}^{t} \langle a, y_s \rangle + F(a) \right). \tag{28.3}$$

The intuition is that the algorithm chooses a_{t+1} to be the action that performed best in hindsight with respect to the regularised loss. Again, the definition of follow-the-regularised-leader implicitly assumes that $(a_t)_{t=1}^n$ are well-defined. As for mirror descent, the regularisation serves to stabilise the algorithm, which turns out to be a key property of good algorithms for online linear prediction.

> **Follow-the-leader** chooses the action that appears best in hindsight, $a_{t+1} = \mathrm{argmin}_{a \in \mathcal{A}} \sum_{s=1}^{t} \langle a, y_s \rangle$. In general this algorithm is not well suited for online linear optimisation because the absence of regularisation makes it unstable (Exercise 28.4).

Equivalence of Mirror Descent and Follow-the-Regularised-Leader

At first sight these algorithms do not look that similar. To clarify matters, let us suppose that F is Legendre with domain $\mathcal{D} \subseteq \mathcal{A}$. In this setting, mirror descent and follow-the-regularised-leader are identical. To see this, let

$$\Phi_t(a) = \eta \langle a, y_t \rangle + D_F(a, a_t) = \eta \langle a, y_t \rangle + F(a) - F(a_t) - \langle a - a_t, \nabla F(a_t) \rangle.$$

Now mirror descent chooses a_{t+1} to minimise Φ_t. The reader should check that the assumption that F is Legendre on domain $\mathcal{D} \subseteq \mathcal{A}$ implies that the minimiser occurs in the interior of $\mathcal{D} \subseteq \mathcal{A}$ and that $\nabla \Phi_t(a_{t+1}) = 0$ (see Exercise 28.1). This means that $\eta y_t = \nabla F(a_t) - \nabla F(a_{t+1})$, and so

$$\nabla F(a_{t+1}) = -\eta y_t + \nabla F(a_t) = \nabla F(a_1) - \eta \sum_{s=1}^{t} y_s = -\eta \sum_{s=1}^{t} y_s,$$

where the last equality is true because a_1 is chosen as the minimiser of F in $\mathcal{A} \cap \mathcal{D} = \mathcal{D}$, and again the fact that F is Legendre ensures this minimum occurs at an interior point where the gradient vanishes. Follow the regularised leader chooses a_{t+1} to minimise $\Phi'_t(a) = \eta \sum_{s=1}^{t} \langle a, y_s \rangle + F(a)$. The same argument shows that $\nabla \Phi'_t(a_{t+1}) = 0$, which means that

$$\nabla F(a_{t+1}) = -\eta \sum_{s=1}^{t} y_s.$$

The last two displays and the fact that the gradient for Legendre functions is invertible shows that mirror descent and follow-the-regularised-leader are the same in this setting.

> The equivalence between these algorithms is far from universal. First of all, it does not generally hold when F is not Legendre or its domain is larger than $\mathcal{A}$. Second, in many applications of these algorithms, the learning rate or potential change with time, and in either case the algorithms will typically produce different action sequences. For example, if a learning rate η_t is used rather than η in the definition of Φ_t, then mirror descent chooses $\nabla F(a_{t+1}) = -\sum_{s=1}^{t} \eta_s y_s$, while follow-the-regularised-leader chooses $\nabla F(a_{t+1}) = -\eta_t \sum_{s=1}^{t} y_s$. We return to this issue in the notes and exercises.

EXAMPLE 28.1. Let $\mathcal{A} = \mathbb{R}^d$ and $F(a) = \frac{1}{2}\|a\|_2^2$. Then $\nabla F(a) = a$ and $D(a, a_t) = \frac{1}{2}\|a - a_t\|_2^2$. Clearly F is Legendre and $\mathcal{D} = \mathcal{A}$, so mirror descent and follow-the-regularised-leader are the same. By simple calculus we see that

$$a_{t+1} = \text{argmin}_{a \in \mathbb{R}^d} \, \eta \langle a, y_t \rangle + \frac{1}{2}\|a - a_t\|_2^2 = a_t - \eta y_t,$$

which may be familiar as **online gradient descent** with linear losses. For the extension to nonlinear convex loss functions, see Note 12.

EXAMPLE 28.2. Let $\mathcal{A}$ be a compact convex subset of $\mathbb{R}^d$ and $F(a) = \frac{1}{2}\|a\|_2^2$. Then mirror descent chooses

$$a_{t+1} = \text{argmin}_{a \in \mathcal{A}} \, \eta \langle a, y_t \rangle + \frac{1}{2}\|a - a_t\|_2^2 = \Pi(a_t - \eta y_t), \qquad (28.4)$$

where $\Pi(a)$ is the Euclidean projection of a on to $\mathcal{A}$. This algorithm is usually called online projected gradient descent. On the other hand, for follow-the-regularised-leader we have

$$a_{t+1} = \text{argmin}_{a \in \mathcal{A}} \, \eta \sum_{s=1}^{t} \langle a, y_s \rangle + \frac{1}{2}\|a - a_t\|_2^2 = \Pi\left(-\eta \sum_{s=1}^{t} y_s\right),$$

which may be a different choice than that of mirror descent.

EXAMPLE 28.3. The exponential weights algorithm that appeared in various forms on numerous occasions in earlier chapters is a special case of mirror descent corresponding to choosing the constraint set $\mathcal{A}$ as the simplex in $\mathbb{R}^d$ and choosing F to be the unnormalised negentropy function of Example 26.5. In this case follow-the-regularised-leader chooses

$$a_{t+1} = \operatorname{argmin}_{a \in \mathcal{A}} \eta \sum_{s=1}^{t} \langle a, y_s \rangle + \sum_{i=1}^{d} a_i \log(a_i) - a_i.$$

You will show in Exercise 28.8 that

$$a_{t+1,i} = \frac{\exp\left(-\eta \sum_{s=1}^{t} y_{si}\right)}{\sum_{j=1}^{d} \exp\left(-\eta \sum_{s=1}^{t} y_{sj}\right)}. \tag{28.5}$$

28.1.1 A Two-Step Process for Implementation

Solving the optimisation problem in Eq. (28.2) is often made easier by using Theorem 26.15 from Chapter 26. Assume F is Legendre and $\mathcal{A}$ is compact and non-empty, and suppose that

$$\nabla F(a) - \eta y \in \operatorname{int}(\operatorname{dom}(F^*)) \text{ for all } a \in \mathcal{A} \cap \mathcal{D} \text{ and } y \in \mathcal{L}. \tag{28.6}$$

Then the solution to Eq. (28.2) can be found using the following two-step procedure:

$$\tilde{a}_{t+1} = \operatorname{argmin}_{a \in \mathcal{D}} \eta \langle a, y_t \rangle + D_F(a, a_t) \quad \text{and} \tag{28.7}$$
$$a_{t+1} = \operatorname{argmin}_{a \in \mathcal{A}} D_F(a, \tilde{a}_{t+1}). \tag{28.8}$$

Eq. (28.6) means the first optimisation problem can be evaluated explicitly as the solution to

$$\eta y_t + \nabla F(\tilde{a}_{t+1}) - \nabla F(a_t) = 0. \tag{28.9}$$

Since F is Legendre, Theorem 26.6 shows that ∇F is a bijection between $\operatorname{int}(\operatorname{dom}(F))$ and $\operatorname{int}(\operatorname{dom}(F^*))$, which means that $\tilde{a}_{t+1} = (\nabla F)^{-1}(\nabla F(a_t) - \eta y_t)$. The optimisation problem in Eq. (28.8) is usually harder to calculate analytically, but there are important exceptions, as we shall see.

All potentials and losses that appear in positive results in this book guarantee that mirror descent (and also follow-the-regularised-leader) are well defined, and that condition in Eq. (28.6) holds.

The two-step implementation of mirror descent also explains its name. The update in round t can be seen as transforming the action $a_t \in \mathcal{A}$ into the 'mirror' (dual) space using ∇F, where it is combined with the most recent (scaled) loss ηy_t. Then ∇F^{-1} is used to transform the updated vector back to the original (primal) space. The function ∇F is called the mirror map.

The same idea works for follow-the-regularised-leader. Assuming F is Legendre, $\mathcal{A}$ is compact and nonempty and $-\eta \sum_{s=1}^{t} y_s \in \text{int}(\text{dom}(F^*))$, then for follow-the-regularised-leader

$$a_{t+1} = \Pi_{\mathcal{A},F}\left(\nabla F^{-1}\left(-\eta \sum_{s=1}^{t} y_s\right)\right),$$

where $\Pi_{\mathcal{A},F}$ is the projection on to $\mathcal{A}$ with respect to D_F as described in Section 26.6.

Some of the differences between follow-the-regularised-leader and mirror descent are illustrated in Fig. 28.2, which shows how the algorithms differ once projections start to occur.

28.2 Regret Analysis

Although mirror descent and follow-the-regularised-leader are not the same, the bounds presented here are identical. The theorem for mirror descent has two parts, the first of which is a little stronger than the second. To minimise clutter, we abbreviate D_F by D.

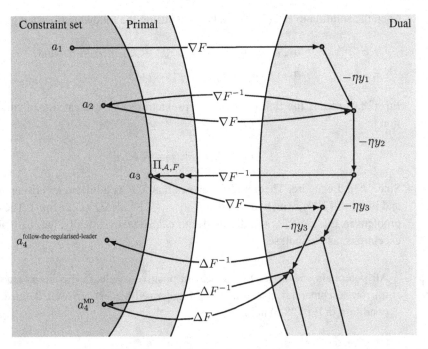

Figure 28.2 Illustration of follow-the-regularised-leader and mirror descent. The constraint set is $\mathcal{A}$, and the function $\Pi_{\mathcal{A},F}$ is the projection on to $\mathcal{A}$ with respect to the Bregman divergence induced by Legendre function F. Follow-the-regularised-leader accumulates the scaled losses in the dual space, mapping back to the primal using the inverse map ∇F^{-1}. Mirror descent computes the next iterate by $a_{t+1} = \Pi_{\mathcal{A},F}(\nabla F^{-1}(\nabla F(a_t) - \eta y_t))$. The algorithms generally behave differently in the presence of projections. In the figure, the algorithms behave the same until the fourth iterate, after which the projection that appeared in the computation of the third iterate breaks the equivalence.

THEOREM 28.4 (Mirror descent regret bound). *Let $\eta > 0$ and F be Legendre with domain D and $A \subset \mathbb{R}^d$ be a non-empty convex set with $\text{int}(\text{dom}(F)) \cap A \neq \emptyset$. Let $a_1, \ldots, a_{n+1}$ be the actions chosen by mirror descent, which are assumed to be well-defined. Then, for any $a \in A$, the regret of mirror descent is bounded by*

$$R_n(a) \leq \frac{F(a) - F(a_1)}{\eta} + \sum_{t=1}^{n} \langle a_t - a_{t+1}, y_t \rangle - \frac{1}{\eta} \sum_{t=1}^{n} D(a_{t+1}, a_t).$$

Furthermore, suppose that Eq. (28.6) holds and $\tilde{a}_2, \tilde{a}_3, \ldots, \tilde{a}_{n+1}$ are given by Eq. (28.7). Then,

$$R_n(a) \leq \frac{1}{\eta} \left(F(a) - F(a_1) + \sum_{t=1}^{n} D(a_t, \tilde{a}_{t+1}) \right).$$

Proof Fix $a \in A$. The result trivially holds when $a \notin D$. Hence, we assume that $a \in D$. For the first part of the claim, we split the inner product:

$$\langle a_t - a, y_t \rangle = \langle a_t - a_{t+1}, y_t \rangle + \langle a_{t+1} - a, y_t \rangle.$$

In Exercise 28.1, you will show that $a_t \in \text{int}(\text{dom}(F))$, and hence the Bregman divergence $D(b, a_t) = F(b) - F(a_t) - \langle b - a_t, \nabla F(a_t) \rangle$ for any $b \in \text{dom}(F)$. By definition, $a_{t+1} = \text{argmin}_{b \in A} \, \eta \langle b, y_t \rangle + D(b, a_t)$. Hence, the first-order optimality conditions for a_{t+1} (Proposition 26.14) show that

$$\langle a - a_{t+1}, \eta y_t + \nabla F(a_{t+1}) - \nabla F(a_t) \rangle \geq 0.$$

Reordering and using the definition of the Bregman divergence,

$$\langle a_{t+1} - a, y_t \rangle \leq \frac{1}{\eta} \langle a - a_{t+1}, \nabla F(a_{t+1}) - \nabla F(a_t) \rangle$$

$$= \frac{1}{\eta} \left(D(a, a_t) - D(a, a_{t+1}) - D(a_{t+1}, a_t) \right).$$

Using this, along with the definition of the regret,

$$R_n = \sum_{t=1}^{n} \langle a_t - a, y_t \rangle$$

$$\leq \sum_{t=1}^{n} \langle a_t - a_{t+1}, y_t \rangle + \frac{1}{\eta} \sum_{t=1}^{n} \left(D(a, a_t) - D(a, a_{t+1}) - D(a_{t+1}, a_t) \right)$$

$$= \sum_{t=1}^{n} \langle a_t - a_{t+1}, y_t \rangle + \frac{1}{\eta} \left(D(a, a_1) - D(a, a_{n+1}) - \sum_{t=1}^{n} D(a_{t+1}, a_t) \right)$$

$$\leq \sum_{t=1}^{n} \langle a_t - a_{t+1}, y_t \rangle + \frac{F(a) - F(a_1)}{\eta} - \frac{1}{\eta} \sum_{t=1}^{n} D(a_{t+1}, a_t), \qquad (28.10)$$

where the final inequality follows from the fact that $D(a, a_{n+1}) \geq 0$ and $D(a, a_1) \leq F(a) - F(a_1)$, the latter of which is true by the first-order optimality conditions for $a_1 = \text{argmin}_{b \in A} F(b)$. To see the second part, note that

$$\langle a_t - a_{t+1}, y_t \rangle = \frac{1}{\eta} \langle a_t - a_{t+1}, \nabla F(a_t) - \nabla F(\tilde{a}_{t+1}) \rangle$$

$$= \frac{1}{\eta} \left(D(a_{t+1}, a_t) + D(a_t, \tilde{a}_{t+1}) - D(a_{t+1}, \tilde{a}_{t+1}) \right)$$

$$\leq \frac{1}{\eta} \left(D(a_{t+1}, a_t) + D(a_t, \tilde{a}_{t+1}) \right).$$

The result follows by substituting this into Eq. (28.10). □

The assumption that a_1 minimises the potential was only used to bound $D(a, a_1) \leq F(a) - F(a_1)$. For a different initialisation, the following bound still holds:

$$R_n(a) \leq \frac{1}{\eta} \left(D(a, a_1) + \sum_{t=1}^{n} D(a_t, \tilde{a}_{t+1}) \right). \qquad (28.11)$$

As we shall see in Chapter 31, this is useful when using mirror descent to analyse non-stationary bandits.

The first part of Theorem 28.4 also holds for follow-the-regularised-leader as stated in the next result, the proof of which is left for Exercise 28.5.

THEOREM 28.5 (Follow-the-regularised-leader regret bound). *Let $\eta > 0$, F be convex with domain $\mathcal{D}$, $\mathcal{A} \subseteq \mathbb{R}^d$ be a non-empty convex set. Assume that $a_1, \ldots, a_{n+1}$ chosen by follow-the-regularised-leader are well defined. Then, for any $a \in \mathcal{A}$, the regret of follow-the-regularised-leader is bounded by*

$$R_n(a) \leq \frac{F(a) - F(a_1)}{\eta} + \sum_{t=1}^{n} \langle a_t - a_{t+1}, y_t \rangle - \frac{1}{\eta} \sum_{t=1}^{n} D(a_{t+1}, a_t).$$

We now give two applications of the regret bound of Theorem 28.4 for mirror descent. The same results would hold for the same problems for FTRL just in this case we would need to use Theorem 28.5. Let $\operatorname{diam}_F(\mathcal{A}) = \max_{a,b \in \mathcal{A}} F(a) - F(b)$ be the diameter of $\mathcal{A}$ with respect to F.

PROPOSITION 28.6 (Regret on the unit-ball). *Let $\mathcal{A} = B_2^d = \{a \in \mathbb{R}^d : \|a\|_2 \leq 1\}$ be the standard unit ball and assume $y_t \in B_2^d$ for all t. Then mirror descent with potential $F(a) = \frac{1}{2}\|a\|_2^2$ and $\eta = \sqrt{1/n}$ is well defined and its regret satisfies $R_n \leq \sqrt{n}$.*

Proof That mirror descent is well defined follows by a direct calculation (cf. Example 28.1). By Eq. (28.9), we have $\tilde{a}_{t+1} = a_t - \eta y_t$ so

$$D(a_t, \tilde{a}_{t+1}) = \frac{1}{2}\|\tilde{a}_{t+1} - a_t\|_2^2 = \frac{\eta^2}{2}\|y_t\|_2^2.$$

Therefore, since $\operatorname{diam}_F(\mathcal{A}) = 1/2$ and $\|y_t\|_2 \leq 1$ for all t,

$$R_n \leq \frac{\operatorname{diam}_F(\mathcal{A})}{\eta} + \frac{\eta}{2} \sum_{t=1}^{n} \|y_t\|_2^2 \leq \frac{1}{2\eta} + \frac{\eta n}{2} = \sqrt{n}. \qquad \square$$

PROPOSITION 28.7 (Regret on the simplex). *Let $\mathcal{A} = \mathcal{P}_{d-1}$ be the probability simplex and $y_t \in \mathcal{L} = [0,1]^d$ for all t. Then mirror descent with the unnormalised negentropy potential and $\eta = \sqrt{2\log(d)/n}$ is well defined and its regret satisfies $R_n \le \sqrt{2n\log(d)}$.*

Proof That mirror descent is well-defined follows because the simplex is compact. The Bregman divergence with respect to the unnormalised negentropy potential for $a, b \in \mathcal{A}$ is $D(a,b) = \sum_{i=1}^{d} a_i \log(a_i/b_i)$. Therefore,

$$R_n(a) \le \frac{F(a) - F(a_1)}{\eta} + \sum_{t=1}^{n} \langle a_t - a_{t+1}, y_t \rangle - \frac{1}{\eta} \sum_{t=1}^{n} D(a_{t+1}, a_t)$$

$$\le \frac{\log(d)}{\eta} + \sum_{t=1}^{n} \|a_t - a_{t+1}\|_1 \|y_t\|_\infty - \frac{1}{\eta} \sum_{t=1}^{n} \frac{1}{2} \|a_t - a_{t+1}\|_1^2$$

$$\le \frac{\log(d)}{\eta} + \frac{\eta}{2} \sum_{t=1}^{n} \|y_t\|_\infty^2 \le \frac{\log(d)}{\eta} + \frac{\eta n}{2} = \sqrt{2n\log(d)},$$

where the first inequality follows from Theorem 28.4, the second from Pinsker's inequality and the facts that $\mathrm{diam}_F(\mathcal{A}) = \log(d)$. In the third inequality, we used 'optimise to bound'. In particular, we used that for any $a \in \mathbb{R}$ and $b > 0$, $\max_{x \in \mathbb{R}} ax - bx^2/2 = a^2/(2b)$. The last inequality follows from the assumption that $\|y_t\|_\infty \le 1$. $\qquad\square$

The last few steps in the above proof are so routine that we summarise their use in a corollary, the proof of which we leave to the reader (Exercise 28.6).

COROLLARY 28.8. *Let F be a Legendre potential and $\|\cdot\|_t$ be a norm on $\mathbb{R}^d$ for each $t \in [n]$ such that $D_F(a_{t+1}, a_t) \ge \frac{1}{2} \|a_{t+1} - a_t\|_t^2$. Then the regret of mirror descent or follow-the-regularised-leader satisfies*

$$R_n \le \frac{\mathrm{diam}_F(\mathcal{A})}{\eta} + \frac{\eta}{2} \sum_{t=1}^{n} \|y_t\|_{t*}^2,$$

where $\|y\|_{t*} = \max_{x: \|x\|_t \le 1} \langle x, y \rangle$ is the dual norm of $\|\cdot\|_t$.

It often happens that the easiest way to bound the regret of mirror descent is to find a norm that satisfies the conditions of Corollary 28.8. Often, Theorem 26.13 provides a good approach.

EXAMPLE 28.9. To illustrate a suboptimal application of mirror descent, suppose we had chosen $F(a) = \frac{1}{2}\|a\|_2^2$ in the setting of Proposition 28.7. Then $D_F(a_{t+1}, a_t) = \frac{1}{2}\|a_{t+1} - a_t\|_2^2$ suggests choosing $\|\cdot\|_t$ to be the standard Euclidean norm. Since $\mathrm{diam}_F(\mathcal{A}) = 1/2$ and $\|\cdot\|_{2*} = \|\cdot\|_2$, applying Corollary 28.8 shows that

$$R_n \le \frac{1}{2\eta} + \frac{\eta}{2} \sum_{t=1}^{n} \|y_t\|_2^2.$$

But now we see that $\|y_t\|_2^2$ can be as large as d, and tuning η would lead to a rate of $O(\sqrt{nd})$ rather than $O(\sqrt{n\log(d)})$.

Both Theorems 28.4 and 28.5 were presented for the oblivious case where $(y_t)_{t=1}^n$ are chosen in advance. This assumption was not used, however, and in fact the bounds continue to hold when y_t is chosen strategically as a function of $a_1, y_1, \ldots, y_{t-1}, a_t$. This is analogous to how the basic regret bound for exponential weights continues to hold in the face of strategic losses. But be cautioned, this result does not carry immediately to the application of mirror descent to bandits, as discussed at the end in Note 9.

28.3 Application to Linear Bandits

We now show how mirror descent and follow-the-regularised-leader can be used to construct algorithms for adversarial linear bandit problems. Like in the previous chapter, the adversary chooses a sequence of vectors $y_1, \ldots, y_n$ with $y_t \in \mathcal{L} \subset \mathbb{R}^d$. In each round the learner chooses $A_t \in \mathcal{A} \subset \mathbb{R}^d$ and observes $\langle A_t, y_t \rangle$. The regret relative to action $a \in \mathcal{A}$ is

$$R_n(a) = \mathbb{E}\left[\sum_{t=1}^n \langle A_t - a, y_t \rangle\right].$$

The regret is $R_n = \max_{a \in \mathcal{A}} R_n(a)$. The application of mirror descent and follow-the-regularised-leader to linear bandits is straightforward. The only difficulty is that the learner does not observe y_t but instead $\langle A_t, y_t \rangle$. The solution is to replace y_t with an estimator, which is typically some kind of importance-weighted estimator as in the previous chapter. Because estimation of y_t is only possible using randomisation, the algorithm cannot play the suggested action of mirror descent, but instead plays a distribution over actions with the same mean as the proposed action. This is often necessary anyway, when $\mathcal{A}$ is not convex. Since the losses are linear, the expected additional regret by playing according to the distribution vanishes. The algorithm is summarised in Algorithm 16. We have switched to capital letters because the actions are now randomised.

THEOREM 28.10 (Regret of Mirror-Descent and FTRL with bandit feedback). *Suppose that Algorithm 16 is run with Legendre potential F, convex action set $\mathcal{A} \subset \mathbb{R}^d$ and learning rate $\eta > 0$ such that the loss estimators are unbiased: $\mathbb{E}[\hat{Y}_t \mid \bar{A}_t] = y_t$ for all $t \in [n]$. Then the regret for either variant of Algorithm 16, provided that they are well defined, is bounded by*

$$R_n(a) \le \mathbb{E}\left[\frac{F(a) - F(\bar{A}_1)}{\eta} + \sum_{t=1}^n \langle \bar{A}_t - \bar{A}_{t+1}, \hat{Y}_t \rangle - \frac{1}{\eta}\sum_{t=1}^n D(\bar{A}_{t+1}, \bar{A}_t)\right].$$

Furthermore, letting

$$\tilde{A}_{t+1} = \operatorname{argmin}_{a \in \operatorname{dom}(F)} \eta\langle a, \hat{Y}_t \rangle + D_F(a, \bar{A}_t)$$

and assuming that $-\eta\hat{Y}_t + \nabla F(a) \in \nabla F(\operatorname{dom}(F))$ for all $a \in \mathcal{A}$ almost surely, the regret of the mirror descent variation satisfies

$$R_n \le \frac{\operatorname{diam}_F(\mathcal{A})}{\eta} + \frac{1}{\eta}\sum_{t=1}^n \mathbb{E}\left[D(\bar{A}_t, \tilde{A}_{t+1})\right].$$

Proof Using the definition of the algorithm and the assumption that $\hat{Y}_t$ is unbiased given $\bar{A}_t$ and that P_t has mean $\bar{A}_t$ leads to

$$\mathbb{E}\left[\langle A_t, y_t\rangle\right] = \mathbb{E}\left[\langle \bar{A}_t, y_t\rangle\right] = \mathbb{E}\left[\mathbb{E}\left[\langle \bar{A}_t, y_t\rangle \mid \bar{A}_t\right]\right] = \mathbb{E}\left[\mathbb{E}\left[\langle \bar{A}_t, \hat{Y}_t\rangle \mid \bar{A}_t\right]\right],$$

where the last equality used the linearity of expectations. Hence,

$$R_n(a) = \mathbb{E}\left[\sum_{t=1}^{n}\langle A_t, y_t\rangle - \langle a, y_t\rangle\right] = \mathbb{E}\left[\sum_{t=1}^{n}\langle \bar{A}_t - a, \hat{Y}_t\rangle\right],$$

which is the expected random regret of mirror descent or follow-the-regularised-leader on the recursively constructed sequence $\hat{Y}_t$. The result follows from Theorem 28.4 or Theorem 28.5 and the note at the end of the last section that says these theorems continue to hold even for recursively constructed loss sequences. ☐

1: **Input** Legendre potential F, action set $\mathcal{A}$ and learning rate $\eta > 0$
2: Choose $\bar{A}_1 = \mathrm{argmin}_{a \in \mathcal{A} \cap \mathrm{dom}(F)} F(a)$
3: **for** $t = 1, \ldots, n$ **do**
4:     Choose measure P_t on $\mathcal{A}$ with mean $\bar{A}_t$
5:     Sample action A_t from P_t and observe $\langle A_t, y_t\rangle$
6:     Compute estimate $\hat{Y}_t$ of the loss vector y_t
7:     Update:

$$\bar{A}_{t+1} = \mathrm{argmin}_{a \in \mathcal{A} \cap \mathrm{dom}(F)}\ \eta\langle a, \hat{Y}_t\rangle + D_F(a, \bar{A}_t) \qquad\qquad \text{(Mirror descent)}$$

$$\bar{A}_{t+1} = \mathrm{argmin}_{a \in \mathcal{A} \cap \mathrm{dom}(F)}\ \eta\sum_{s=1}^{t}\langle a, \hat{Y}_s\rangle + F(a) \quad \text{(follow-the-regularised-leader)}$$

8: **end for**

Algorithm 16: Online stochastic mirror descent/follow-the-regularised-leader.

28.4 Linear Bandits on the Unit Ball

To illustrate the power of these methods, we return to adversarial linear bandits and the special case where the action set is the unit ball. In the previous chapter, we showed that continuous exponential weights on the unit ball with Kiefer-Wolfowitz exploration has a regret of

$$R_n = O(d\sqrt{n \log(n)}).$$

Surprisingly, follow-the-regularised-leader with a carefully chosen potential improves on this bound by a factor of $\sqrt{d}$.

For the remainder of this section, let $\|\cdot\| = \|\cdot\|_2$ be the standard Euclidean norm and $\mathcal{A} = B_2^d$ be the standard unit ball. In order to instantiate follow-the-regularised-leader we need a potential, a sampling rule, an unbiased estimator and a learning rate. Note that the only source of randomness is the randomisation in the algorithm. Hence, let

$\mathbb{E}_t[\cdot] = \mathbb{E}[\cdot \mid A_1, \dots, A_{t-1}]$. We start with the sampling rule and estimator. Recall that in round t we need to choose a distribution on $\mathcal{A}$ with mean $\bar{A}_t$ and sufficient variability that the variance of the estimator is not too large. Given the past, let E_t and U_t be independent, where $E_t \in \{0,1\}$ is such that $\mathbb{E}_t[E_t] = 1 - \|\bar{A}_t\|$ and U_t is uniformly distributed on $\{\pm e_1, \dots, \pm e_d\}$. The algorithm chooses

$$A_t = E_t U_t + \frac{(1 - E_t)\bar{A}_t}{\|\bar{A}_t\|}.$$

In other words, $E_t = 1$ indicates that the algorithm explores, which happens with probability $1 - \|\bar{A}_t\|$. Clearly, $\mathbb{E}_t[A_t] = \bar{A}_t$. (The sampling distribution P_t is just the law of A_t given the past, which remains implicit.) For the estimator we use a variant of the importance-weighted estimator from the last chapter:

$$\hat{Y}_t = \frac{d\, E_t\, A_t \langle A_t, y_t \rangle}{1 - \|\bar{A}_t\|}. \tag{28.12}$$

The reader can check for themselves that this estimator is unbiased. Next, we inspect the contents of our magician's hat and select the potential

$$F(a) = -\log\left(1 - \|a\|\right) - \|a\|.$$

There is one more modification. Rather than instantiating follow-the-regularised-leader with action set $\mathcal{A}$, we use $\tilde{\mathcal{A}} = \{x \in \mathbb{R}^d : \|x\|_2 \leq r\}$, where $r < 1$ is a radius to be tuned subsequently. The reason for this modification is to control the variance of the estimator in Eq. (28.12), which blows up as $\bar{A}_t$ gets close to the boundary. You will show in Exercise 28.7 that

$$\bar{A}_t = \Pi\left(\frac{-\eta \hat{L}_{t-1}}{1 + \eta \|\hat{L}_{t-1}\|}\right) \qquad \text{with} \qquad \hat{L}_{t-1} = \sum_{s=1}^{t-1} \hat{Y}_s, \tag{28.13}$$

where $\Pi(x)$ is the projection operator on to $\tilde{\mathcal{A}}$ with respect to $\|\cdot\|_2$.

1: **Input** Learning rate $\eta > 0$
2: **for** $t = 1, \dots, n$ **do**
3:     Compute

$$\bar{A}_t = \Pi\left(\frac{-\eta \hat{L}_{t-1}}{1 + \eta \|\hat{L}_{t-1}\|}\right) \qquad \text{with} \qquad \hat{L}_{t-1} = \sum_{s=1}^{t-1} \hat{Y}_s$$

4:     Sample $E_t \in \{0,1\}$ from Binomial with bias $1 - \|\bar{A}_t\|$ and U_t uniformly on $\{e_1, \dots, e_d\}$
5:     Play action $A_t = E_t U_t + \frac{(1-E_t)\bar{A}_t}{\|\bar{A}_t\|}$
6:     Observe $\langle A_t, y_t \rangle$ and estimate loss vector $\hat{Y}_t = \frac{d\, E_t\, A_t \langle A_t, y_t \rangle}{1 - \|\bar{A}_t\|}$
7: **end for**

Algorithm 17: Follow-the-regularised-leader for linear bandits on the unit ball

THEOREM 28.11. *Assume that $(y_t)_{t=1}^n$ are a sequence of losses such that $\|y_t\|_2 \le 1$ for all t. Suppose that Algorithm 16 is run using the sampling rule, estimator and potential as described above, shrunken action set $\tilde{A}$ with $r = 1 - 2\eta d$ where the learning rate is $\eta = \sqrt{\log(n)/(3dn)}$. Then, the algorithm is well defined and its regret satisfies $R_n \le 2\sqrt{3nd\log(n)}$.*

You might notice that in some regimes this is smaller than the lower bound for stochastic linear bandits (Theorem 24.2). There is no contradiction because the adversarial and stochastic linear bandit models are actually quite different. More details are in Chapter 29.

Proof That the algorithm is well defined follows because $\tilde{A}$ is compact. Let $a^* = \text{argmin}_{a \in A} \sum_{t=1}^n \langle a, y_t \rangle$ be the optimal action. Then

$$R_n = \mathbb{E}\left[\sum_{t=1}^n \langle A_t - ra^*, y_t \rangle\right] + \sum_{t=1}^n \langle ra^* - a^*, y_t \rangle \le R_n(ra^*) + (1-r)n,$$

where the inequality follows from the definition of A and Cauchy–Schwarz. By Theorems 26.13 and 28.10,

$$R_n(ra^*) \le \frac{\text{diam}_F(\tilde{A})}{\eta} + \frac{\eta}{2}\mathbb{E}\left[\sum_{t=1}^n \|\hat{Y}_t\|^2_{(\nabla^2 F(Z_t))^{-1}}\right],$$

where $Z_t \in [\tilde{A}_t, \tilde{A}_{t+1}]$ lies on the chord connecting $\tilde{A}_t$ and $\tilde{A}_{t+1}$. The algorithm is stable in the sense that no matter how the losses are chosen, $\tilde{A}_{t+1}$ cannot be too far from $\tilde{A}_t$. This also means that Z_t is close to $\tilde{A}_t$. By definition, $\eta\|\hat{Y}_t\| \le \eta d/(1-r) = 1/2$. Combining this with Eq. (28.13) shows that

$$\frac{1-\|Z_t\|}{1-\|\tilde{A}_t\|} \le \sup_{\alpha \in [0,1]} \frac{1 - \|\alpha\tilde{A}_t + (1-\alpha)\tilde{A}_{t+1}\|}{1 - \|\tilde{A}_t\|} = \max\left\{1, \frac{1-\|\tilde{A}_{t+1}\|}{1-\|\tilde{A}_t\|}\right\}$$

$$\le \max\left\{1, \frac{1+\eta\|\hat{L}_{t-1}\|}{1+\eta\|\hat{L}_t\|}\right\} \le \max\left\{1, \frac{1+\eta\|\hat{L}_{t-1}\|}{1/2 + \eta\|\hat{L}_{t-1}\|}\right\} \le 2.$$

Here, the second inequality is proved by noting that if the maximum is not one, $\|\tilde{A}_{t+1}\| < \|\tilde{A}_t\|$. The next step is to find the Hessian of F, which is

$$\nabla^2 F(a) = \frac{I}{1-\|a\|} + \frac{aa^\top}{\|a\|(1-\|a\|)^2} \succeq \frac{I}{1-\|a\|}.$$

Therefore, $(\nabla^2 F(a))^{-1} \le (1 - \|a\|)I$, and so

$$\mathbb{E}\left[\|\hat{Y}_t\|^2_{(\nabla^2 F(Z_t))^{-1}}\right] \le \mathbb{E}\left[(1-\|Z_t\|)\|\hat{Y}_t\|^2\right] = d^2\mathbb{E}\left[\frac{(1-\|Z_t\|)E_t\langle U_t, y_t\rangle^2}{(1-\|\tilde{A}_t\|)^2}\right] \le 2d.$$

The diameter satisfies $\mathrm{diam}_F(\tilde{A}) \le \log(1/(1-r))$, and hence

$$R_n \le (1-r)n + \frac{1}{\eta} \log\left(\frac{1}{1-r}\right) + \eta nd$$

$$= \frac{1}{\eta} \log\left(\frac{1}{2\eta d}\right) + 3\eta nd$$

$$\le 2\sqrt{3nd\log(n)},$$

where the last two relations follow from the choices of r and η, respectively. $\square$

> We could have used mirror descent rather than follow-the-regularised-leader with a slightly more complicated proof and the same bound except for constants. Using continuous exponential weights and the analysis in Section 27.3 would yield a bound that is a factor of $\sqrt{d}$ worse than the above, and we believe that this cannot be improved.

28.5 Notes

1 Our assumptions on the potential and action set in the analysis of mirror descent (Theorem 28.4) can be relaxed significantly. What is important is that F is convex and the directional derivative $v \mapsto \nabla_v F(x)$ is linear for all values for which it exists. Our assumptions are chosen to ensure that $a_t \in \mathrm{int}(\mathrm{dom}(F))$, which for Legendre F means that $\nabla F(a_t)$ exists, and hence $\nabla_v F(a_t) = \langle v, \nabla F(a_t) \rangle$ is linear. A comprehensive examination of various generalisations is given by Joulani et al. [2017]. For follow-the-regularised-leader, convexity of F suffices, as you will show using directional derivatives in Exercise 28.5.

2 Finding a_{t+1} for both mirror descent and follow-the-regularised-leader requires solving a convex optimisation problem. Provided the dimension is not too large and the action set and potential are reasonably nice, there exist practical approximation algorithms for this problem. The two-step process described in Eqs. (28.7) and (28.8) is sometimes an easier way to go. Usually (28.7) can be solved analytically, while (28.8) can be quite expensive. In some important special cases, however, the projection step can be written in closed form or efficiently approximated.

3 We saw that follow-the-regularised-leader with a carefully chosen potential function achieves $O(\sqrt{dn\log(n)})$ regret on the ℓ_2-ball. On the ℓ_∞ ball (hypercube), the optimal regret is $O(d\sqrt{n})$. Interestingly, as n tends to infinity the optimal dependence on the dimension for $\mathcal{A} = B_p^d = \{x \in \mathbb{R}^d : \|x\|_p \le 1\}$ with $p \ge 1$ is either d or $\sqrt{d}$ with a complete classification given by Bubeck et al. [2018].

4 Adversarial linear bandits with $\mathcal{A} = \mathcal{P}_{k-1}$ are essentially equivalent to k-armed adversarial bandits. There exists a potential such that the resulting algorithm satisfies $R_n = O(\sqrt{kn})$, which matches the lower bound up to constant factors and shaves a factor of $\sqrt{\log k}$ from the upper bounds presented in Chapters 11 and 12. For more details, see Exercise 28.15.

5 Most of the bounds proven for adversarial bandits have a worst-case flavour. The tools in this chapter can often be applied to prove adaptive bounds. In Exercise 28.14, you will analyse a simple algorithm for k-armed adversarial bandits for which

$$R_n = O\left(\sqrt{k\left(1 + \min_{a \in [k]} \sum_{t=1}^{n} y_{ta}\right) \log\left(\frac{n}{k}\right)}\right).$$

Bounds of this kind are called **first-order bounds** [Allenberg et al., 2006, Abernethy et al., 2012, Neu, 2015b, Wei and Luo, 2018]. The $\log(n/k)$ term can be improved to $\log(k)$ using a more sophisticated algorithm/analysis.

6 Both mirror descent and follow-the-regularised-leader depend on the potential function. Currently there is no characterisation of exactly what this potential should be or how to find it. At least in the full information setting, there are quite general universality results showing that if a certain regret is achievable by some algorithm, then that same regret is nearly achievable by mirror descent with some potential [Srebro et al., 2011]. In practice this result is not useful for constructing new potential functions, however. There have been some attempts to develop 'universal' potential functions that exhibit nice behaviour for any action sets [Bubeck et al., 2015b, and others]. These can be useful, but as yet we do not know precisely what properties are crucial, especially in the bandit case.

7 When the horizon is unknown, the learning rate cannot be tuned ahead of time. One option is to apply the doubling trick. A more elegant solution is to use a decreasing schedule of learning rates. This requires an adaptation of the proofs of Theorems 28.4 and 28.5, which we outline in Exercises 28.11 and 28.12. This is one situation where mirror descent and follow-the-regularised-leader are not the same and where the latter algorithm is usually to be preferred.

8 In much of the literature the potential is chosen in such a way that mirror descent and follow-the-regularised-leader are the same algorithm. For historical reasons, the name mirror descent is more commonly used in the bandit community. Unfortunately 'mirror descent' is often used, sometimes with qualifiers, when the algorithm being analysed is actually follow-the-regularised-leader. This is confusing and makes it hard to identify for which algorithm the results actually hold. Naming aside, we encourage the reader to keep both algorithms in mind, since the analysis of one or the other can sometimes be slightly easier.

9 Mirror descent and follow-the-regularised-leader are used as modules for converting loss sequences to distributions. Since these losses depend on past actions, it is crucial that both algorithm are well-behaved in the full-information setting when the losses are chosen non-obliviously. This does not translate to the bandit setting for a subtle reason. Let $\hat{R}_n(a) = \sum_{t=1}^{n} \langle A_t - a, y_t \rangle$ be the random regret so that

$$R_n = \mathbb{E}\left[\max_{a \in \mathcal{A}} \hat{R}_n(a)\right] = \mathbb{E}\left[\sum_{t=1}^{n} \langle A_t, y_t \rangle - \min_{a \in \mathcal{A}} \sum_{t=1}^{n} \langle a, y_t \rangle\right].$$

The second sum is constant when the losses are oblivious, which means the maximum can be brought outside the expectation, which is not true if the loss vectors are non-oblivious. It is still possible to bound the expected loss relative to a fixed comparator a so that

$$R_n(a) = \mathbb{E}\left[\sum_{t=1}^{n} \langle A_t - a, y_t \rangle\right] \le B,$$

where B is whatever bound obtained from the analysis presented above. Using $\max_a \hat{R}_n(a) \le \max_a \hat{R}_n(a) - R_n(a) + \max_a R_n(a)$ shows that

$$R_n = \mathbb{E}\left[\max_{a \in \mathcal{A}} \hat{R}_n(a)\right] \le B + \mathbb{E}\left[\max_{a \in \mathcal{A}} \hat{R}_n(a) - R_n(a)\right].$$

The second term on the right-hand side can be bounded using tools from empirical process theory, but the resulting bound is $O(\sqrt{n})$ only if $\mathbb{V}[\hat{R}_n(a)] = O(n)$. In general, however, the variance can be much larger (for an example, see Exercise 11.6). We emphasise again that the non-oblivious regret is a strange measure because it does not capture the reactive nature of the environment. The details of the application of empirical process theory is beyond the scope of this book. For an introduction to that topic, we recommend the books by van der Vaart and Wellner [1996], van de Geer [2000], Boucheron et al. [2013] and Dudley [2014].

10 The price of bandit information on the unit ball is an extra $\sqrt{d\log(n)}$ (compare Proposition 28.6 and Theorem 28.11). Except for log factors, this is also true for the simplex (Proposition 28.7 and Note 4). One might wonder if the difference is always about $\sqrt{d}$, but this is not true. The price of bandit information can be as high as $\Theta(d)$. Overall the dimension dependence in the regret in terms of the action set is still not well understood except for special cases.

11 The poor behaviour of follow-the-leader in the full information setting depends on (a) the environment being adversarial rather than stochastic and (b) the action set having sharp corners. When either of these factors is missing, follow-the-leader is a reasonable choice [Huang et al., 2017b]. Note that with bandit feedback, the failure is primarily due to a lack of exploration (Exercises 4.11 and 4.12).

12 A generalisation of online linear optimisation is **online convex optimisation**, where the adversary secretly chooses a sequence of convex functions $f_1, \ldots, f_n$. In each round the learner chooses $a_t \in \mathcal{A}$ and observes the entire function f_t. As usual, the regret is relative to $a \in \mathcal{A}$ is

$$R_n(a) = \sum_{t=1}^{n} f_t(a_t) - f_t(a).$$

One way to tackle this problem is to **linearise** the loss functions. Let $y_t = \nabla f_t(a_t)$. Then, by convexity of the loss functions,

$$R_n(a) \leq \sum_{t=1}^{n} \langle a_t - a, y_t \rangle,$$

which shows that an algorithm for online linear optimisation can be used to analyse the more general case. Now look again at Example 28.1 and notice that online mirror descent with a quadratic potential and linearised losses is really the same gradient descent we know and love. Online convex optimisation is a rich topic by itself. We refer the interested reader to the books by Shalev-Shwartz [2012] and Hazan [2016].

13 There is a nice application of online linear optimisation to minimax theorems. Let X and Y be arbitrary sets. For any function $f : X \times Y \to \mathbb{R}$,

$$\inf_{x \in X} \sup_{y \in Y} f(x,y) \geq \sup_{y \in Y} \inf_{x \in X} f(x,y).$$

Under certain conditions, the inequality becomes an equality. Theorems guaranteeing this are called minimax theorems. The following result by Sion [1958] is one of the more generic variants. The statement uses notions of quasi-convexity and semi-continuity, which are defined in the next note.

THEOREM 28.12 (Sion's minimax theorem). *Suppose that X and Y are convex subsets of linear topological spaces with at least one of X or Y compact. Let $f : X \times Y \to \mathbb{R}$ be a function such that $f(\cdot, y)$ is lower semi-continuous and quasi-convex for all $y \in Y$ and $f(x, \cdot)$ is upper semi-continuous and quasi-concave for all $x \in X$. Then*

$$\inf_{x \in X} \sup_{y \in Y} f(x,y) = \sup_{y \in Y} \inf_{x \in X} f(x,y).$$

There is a short topological proof of this theorem [Komiya, 1988]. You will use the tools of online linear optimisation to analyse two special cases in Exercise 28.16. When X and Y are probability simplexes and f is linear, the resulting theorem is von Neumann's minimax theorem [von Neumann, 1928]. The minimax theorems form a bridge between minimax adversarial regret and Bayesian regret, which we discuss in Chapters 34 and 36.

14 Let X be a subset of a linear topological space and $f : X \to \mathbb{R}$. The function f is **quasi-convex** if $f^{-1}((-\infty, a))$ is convex for all $a \in \mathbb{R}$ and **quasi-concave** if $-f$ is quasi-convex. f is **upper semi-continuous** if for all $x \in X$ and $\varepsilon > 0$ there exists a neighborhood U of x such that $f(y) \le f(x) + \varepsilon$ for all $y \in U$. It is **lower semi-continuous** if for all $x \in X$ and $\varepsilon > 0$ there exists a neighborhood U of x such that $f(y) \ge f(x) - \varepsilon$ for all $y \in U$.

28.6 Bibliographic Remarks

The results in this chapter come from a wide variety of sources. The online convex optimisation framework was popularised by Zinkevich [2003]. The framework has been briefly considered by Warmuth and Jagota [1997], then reintroduced by Gordon [1999] (without noticing the earlier work of Warmuth and Jagota). While the framework was introduced relatively recently, the core ideas have been worked out earlier in the special case of linear prediction with nonlinear losses (the book of Cesa-Bianchi and Lugosi [2006] can be used as a reference to this literature). Mirror descent was first developed by Nemirovsky [1979] and Nemirovsky and Yudin [1983] for classical optimisation. In statistical learning, follow-the-regularised-leader is known as **regularised risk minimisation** and has a long history. In the context of online learning, Gordon [1999] considered follow-the-regularised-leader and called it 'generalised gradient descent'. The name seems to originate from the work of Shalev-Shwartz [2007] and Shalev-Shwartz and Singer [2007]. An implicit form of regularisation is to add a perturbation of the losses, leading to the 'follow-the-perturbed-leader' algorithm [Hannan, 1957, Kalai and Vempala, 2002], which is further explored in the context of combinatorial bandit problems in Chapter 30 (and see also Exercise 11.7). Readers interested in an overview of online learning will like the short books by Shalev-Shwartz [2012] and Hazan [2016], while the book by Cesa-Bianchi and Lugosi [2006] has a little more depth (but is also older). As far as we know, the first explicit application of mirror descent to bandits was by Abernethy et al. [2008]. Since then the idea has been used extensively, with some examples by Audibert et al. [2013], Abernethy et al. [2015], Bubeck et al. [2018] and Wei and Luo [2018]. Mirror descent has been adapted in a generic way to prove high-probability bounds by Abernethy and Rakhlin [2009]. The reader can find (slightly) different proofs of some mirror descent results in the book by Bubeck and Cesa-Bianchi [2012]. The results for the unit ball are from a paper by Bubeck et al. [2012], but we have reworked the proof to be more in line with the rest of the book. Mirror descent can be generalised to Banach spaces. For details, see the article by Sridharan and Tewari [2010].

28.7 Exercises

28.1 Let $F : \mathbb{R}^d \to \mathbb{R} \cup \{\infty\}$ be Legendre with domain $\mathcal{D} \subseteq \mathbb{R}^d$ and $\mathcal{A} \subseteq \mathbb{R}^d$ be convex, and for $b \in \text{int}(\mathcal{D})$ and $y \in \mathbb{R}^d$ let $\Phi(a) = \langle a, y \rangle + D_F(a, b)$. Suppose that $c \in \text{argmin}_{a \in \mathcal{A}} \Phi(a)$ exists and $\mathcal{A} \cap \text{int}(\mathcal{D}) \ne \emptyset$. Show that $c \in \text{int}(\mathcal{D})$

28.2 (ILL-DEFINED ACTIONS) Given an example of a non-empty bounded convex action set $\mathcal{A}$, convex potential F and sequences of losses $(y_t)_{t=1}^n$ where the choices of mirror descent and/or follow-the-regularised-leader either:

(a) exist but are not unique;
(b) do not exist at all.

Prove that if F is Legendre and $\mathcal{A}$ is non-empty and compact, then $(a_t)_{t=1}^n$ exist and are unique for both mirror descent and follow-the-regularised-leader.

28.3 Prove the correctness of the two-step procedure described in Section 28.1.1.

28.4 (LINEAR REGRET FOR FOLLOW-THE-LEADER) Let $\mathcal{A} = [-1, 1]$, and let $y_1 = 1/2$ and $y_s = 1$ for odd $s > 1$ and $y_s = -1$ for even $s > 1$.

(a) Recall that follow-the-leader (without regularisation) chooses $a_t = \operatorname{argmin}_a \sum_{s=1}^{t-1} \langle a, y_s \rangle$. Show that this algorithm suffers linear regret on the above sequence.
(b) Implement follow-the-regularised-leader or mirror descent on this problem with quadratic potential $F(a) = a^2$ and plot a_t as a function of time.

28.5 (REGRET FOR FOLLOW-THE-REGULARISED-LEADER) Prove Theorem 28.5.

28.6 (REGRET IN TERMS OF LOCAL DUAL NORMS) Prove Corollary 28.8.

28.7 (FOLLOW-THE-REGULARISED-LEADER FOR THE UNIT BALL) Prove the equality in Eq. (28.13).

28.8 (EXPONENTIAL WEIGHTS AS MIRROR DESCENT) Prove the equality in Eq. (28.5).

28.9 (EXP3 AS MIRROR DESCENT) Let $\mathcal{A} = \mathcal{P}_{k-1}$ be the simplex, F the unnormalised negentropy potential and $\eta > 0$. Let $P_1 = \operatorname{argmin}_{p \in \mathcal{A}} F(p)$, and for $t > 1$,

$$P_{t+1} = \operatorname{argmin}_{p \in \mathcal{A}} \eta \langle p, \hat{Y}_t \rangle + D_F(p, P_t),$$

where $\hat{Y}_{ti} = \mathbb{I}\{A_t = i\} y_{ti} / P_{ti}$ and A_t is sampled from P_t.

(a) Show that the resulting algorithm is exactly Exp3 from Chapter 11.
(b) What happens if you replace mirror descent by follow-the-regularised-leader,

$$P_{t+1} = \operatorname{argmin}_{p \in \mathcal{A}} \sum_{s=1}^t \langle p, \hat{Y}_s \rangle + F(p) \qquad ?$$

28.10 (EXP3 AS MIRROR DESCENT (II)) Here you will show that the tools in this chapter not only lead to the same algorithm, but also the same bounds.

(a) Let $\tilde{P}_{t+1} = \operatorname{argmin}_{p \in [0, \infty)^k} \eta \langle p, \hat{Y}_t \rangle + D_F(p, P_t)$. Show both relations in the following display:

$$D_F(P_t, \tilde{P}_{t+1}) = \sum_{i=1}^k P_{ti} \left(\exp(-\eta \hat{Y}_{ti}) - 1 + \eta \hat{Y}_{ti} \right) \le \frac{\eta^2}{2} \sum_{i=1}^k P_{ti} \hat{Y}_{ti}^2.$$

(b) Show that $\dfrac{1}{\eta} \mathbb{E}\left[\sum_{t=1}^n D_F(P_t, \tilde{P}_{t+1}) \right] \le \dfrac{\eta n k}{2}.$

(c) Show that $\operatorname{diam}_F(\mathcal{P}_{k-1}) = \log(k)$.

(d) Conclude that for appropriately tuned $\eta > 0$, the regret of Exp3 satisfies,

$$R_n \leq \sqrt{2nk\log(k)}.$$

HINT   Use Theorem 26.6(b).

28.11 (MIRROR DESCENT AND CHANGING LEARNING RATES) Let $\mathcal{A}$ be a convex set and $y_1, \ldots, y_n \in \mathcal{L} \subseteq \mathbb{R}^d$. Let F be Legendre with domain $\mathcal{D}$ with $\mathcal{A} \cap \text{int}(\mathcal{D})$ non-empty and assume that Eq. (28.6) holds. Let $\eta_0, \eta_1, \ldots, \eta_n > 0$, $a_1, a_2, \ldots, a_{n+1} \in \mathcal{A}$ and $\tilde{a}_2, \ldots, \tilde{a}_{n+1}$ be sequences so that $\eta_0 = \infty$, $a_1 = \text{argmin}_{a\in\mathcal{A}} F(a)$ and

$$\tilde{a}_{t+1} = \text{argmin}_{a\in\mathcal{D}} \eta_t \langle a, y_t \rangle + D_F(a, a_t),$$
$$a_{t+1} = \text{argmin}_{a\in\mathcal{A}\cap\mathcal{D}} D_F(a, \tilde{a}_{t+1}).$$

Show that for all $a \in \mathcal{A}$,

(a) $R_n(a) = \sum_{t=1}^{n} \langle a_t - a, y_t \rangle \leq \sum_{t=1}^{n} \frac{D_F(a_t, \tilde{a}_{t+1})}{\eta_t} + \sum_{t=1}^{n} \frac{D_F(a, a_t) - D_F(a, \tilde{a}_{t+1})}{\eta_t}$; and

(b) $R_n(a) \leq \sum_{t=1}^{n} \frac{D_F(a_t, \tilde{a}_{t+1})}{\eta_t} + \sum_{t=1}^{n} D_F(a, a_t) \left(\frac{1}{\eta_t} - \frac{1}{\eta_{t-1}} \right).$

The statement allows the time-varying learning rate sequence $(\eta_t)_t$ to be constructed in any way. This flexibility can be useful when designing adaptive algorithms. A sequence of learning rates $(\eta_t)_t$ is said to be **non-anticipating** if for each t, η_t depends on data available at the end of round t.

28.12 (FOLLOW-THE-REGULARISED-LEADER AND CHANGING POTENTIALS) Like in the previous exercise, let $\mathcal{A}$ be non-empty and convex and $y_1, \ldots, y_n \in \mathcal{L} \subseteq \mathbb{R}^d$. Let $F_1, \ldots, F_n, F_{n+1}$ be a sequence of convex functions and $\Phi_t(a) = F_t(a) + \sum_{s=1}^{t-1}\langle a, y_s \rangle$ and $a_t = \text{argmin}_{a\in\mathcal{A}} \Phi_t(a)$, which you may assume are well defined.

(a) Show that

$$R_n(a) \leq \sum_{t=1}^{n} \left(\langle a_t - a_{t+1}, y_t \rangle - D_{F_t}(a_{t+1}, a_t) \right)$$

$$+ F_{n+1}(a) - F_1(a_1) + \sum_{t=1}^{n} \left(F_t(a_{t+1}) - F_{t+1}(a_{t+1}) \right).$$

(b) Show that if $F_t = F/\eta_t$ and $(\eta_t)_{t=1}^{n+1}$ is decreasing with $\eta_n = \eta_{n+1}$, then

$$R_n(a) \leq \frac{F(a) - \min_{b\in\mathcal{A}} F(b)}{\eta_n} + \sum_{t=1}^{n} \left(\langle a_t - a_{t+1}, y_t \rangle - \frac{D_F(a_{t+1}, a_t)}{\eta_t} \right).$$

Again, the statement applies to any sequence of Legendre functions, including those that are constructed based on the past.

28.13 (ANYTIME VERSION OF EXP3) Consider the k-armed adversarial bandit problem described in Chapter 11, where the adversary chooses $(y_t)_{t=1}^n$ with $y_t \in [0, 1]^k$. Let $P_t \in \mathcal{P}_{k-1}$ be defined by

$$P_{ti} = \frac{\exp\left(-\eta_t \sum_{s=1}^{t-1} \hat{Y}_{si}\right)}{\sum_{j=1}^{k} \exp\left(-\eta_t \sum_{s=1}^{t-1} \hat{Y}_{sj}\right)},$$

where $(\eta_t)_{t=1}^{\infty}$ is an infinite sequence of learning rates and $\hat{Y}_{ti} = \mathbb{I}\{A_t = i\} y_{ti}/P_{ti}$ and A_t is sampled from P_t.

(a) Let $\mathcal{A} = \mathcal{P}_{k-1}$ be the simplex, F be the unnormalised negentropy potential, $F_t(p) = F(p)/\eta_t$ and $\Phi_t(p) = F(p)/\eta_t + \sum_{s=1}^{t-1}\langle p, \hat{Y}_s \rangle$. Show that P_t is the choice of follow-the-regularised-leader with potentials $(F_t)_{t=1}^{n}$ and losses $(\hat{Y}_t)_{t=1}^{n}$.

(b) Assume that $(\eta_t)_{t=1}^{n}$ are decreasing and then use Exercise 28.12 to show that

$$R_n \leq \frac{\log(k)}{\eta_n} + \mathbb{E}\left[\sum_{t=1}^{n}\langle P_t - P_{t+1}, \hat{Y}_t \rangle - \frac{D_F(P_{t+1}, P_t)}{\eta_t}\right].$$

(c) Use Theorem 26.13 in combination with the facts that $\hat{Y}_{ti} \geq 0$ for all i and $\hat{Y}_{ti} = 0$ unless $A_t = i$ to show that

$$\langle P_t - P_{t+1}, \hat{Y}_t \rangle - \frac{D_F(P_{t+1}, P_t)}{\eta_t} \leq \frac{\eta_t}{2P_{tA_t}}.$$

(d) Prove that $R_n \leq \frac{\log(k)}{\eta_n} + \frac{k}{2}\sum_{t=1}^{n}\eta_t$.

(e) Choose $(\eta_t)_{t=1}^{\infty}$ so that $R_n \leq 2\sqrt{nk\log(k)}$ for all $n \geq 1$.

28.14 (THE LOG BARRIER AND FIRST-ORDER BOUNDS) Your mission in this exercise is to prove first-order bounds for finite-armed bandits as studied in Chapter 11. The notation is the same as the previous exercise. Let $(y_t)_{t=1}^{n}$ be a sequence of loss vectors with $y_t \in [0, 1]^k$ for all t and $F(a) = -\sum_{i=1}^{k}\log(a_i)$. Consider the instance of follow-the-regularised-leader for bandits that samples A_t from P_t defined by

$$P_t = \text{argmin}_{p \in \mathcal{P}_{k-1}} \eta_t \sum_{s=1}^{t-1}\langle p, \hat{Y}_s \rangle + F(p).$$

(a) Show a particular, non-anticipating choice of the learning rates $(\eta_t)_{t=1}^{n}$ so that

$$R_n \leq k + 2\sqrt{k\left(1 + \mathbb{E}\left[\sum_{t=1}^{n-1} y_{tA_t}^2\right]\right)\log\left(\frac{n \vee k}{k}\right)}. \tag{28.14}$$

(b) Prove that any algorithm satisfying Eq. (28.14) also satisfies

$$R_n \leq k + k\log\left(\frac{n \vee k}{k}\right) + C\sqrt{k\left(1 + \min_{a \in [k]}\sum_{t=1}^{n} y_{ta}\right)\log\left(\frac{n \vee k}{k}\right)},$$

where C is a suitably large universal constant.

HINT For choosing the learning rate, you might take inspiration from Theorem 18.3.

The algorithm in this exercise is a simplified variant of the algorithm analysed by Wei and Luo [2018].

28.15 (MINIMAX REGRET FOR FINITE-ARMED ADVERSARIAL BANDITS) Let $(y_t)_{t=1}^n$ be a sequence of loss vectors with $y_t \in [0,1]^k$ for all t and $F(a) = -2\sum_{i=1}^k \sqrt{a_i}$. Consider the instance of follow-the-regularised-leader for k-armed adversarial bandits that samples $A_t \in [k]$ from P_t defined by

$$P_t = \operatorname{argmin}_{p \in \mathcal{P}_{k-1}} \eta \sum_{s=1}^{t-1} \langle p, \hat{Y}_s \rangle + F(p),$$

where $\hat{Y}_{si} = \mathbb{I}\{A_s = i\} y_{si}/P_{si}$ is the importance-weighted estimator of y_{si} and $\eta > 0$ is the learning rate.

(a) Show that

$$P_{ti} = \left(\lambda + \sum_{s=1}^{t-1} \hat{Y}_{si} \right)^{-2},$$

where $\lambda \in \mathbb{R}$ is the largest value such that $P_{ti} \in \mathcal{P}_{k-1}$.

(b) Show that $P_{t+1,A_t} \leq P_{tA_t}$ for all $t \in [n-1]$.

(c) Show that $\nabla^2 F(x) = \frac{1}{2} \operatorname{diag}(x^{-3/2})$.

(d) Show that $\operatorname{diam}_F(\mathcal{A}) \leq 2\sqrt{k}$.

(e) Prove that the regret of this algorithm is bounded by $R_n \leq \sqrt{8kn}$.

(f) What happens if you use mirror descent instead of follow-the-regularised-leader. Are the resulting algorithms the same? And if not, what can you prove for mirror descent?

(g) Explain how you would implement this algorithm.

(h) Prove that if the learning rate is chosen in a time-dependent way to be $\eta_t = 1/\sqrt{t}$, then the resulting instantiation of follow-the-regularised-leader satisfies $R_n = O(\sqrt{nk})$ for adversarial bandits and $R_n = O(\sum_{i:\Delta_i > 0} \log(n)/\Delta_i)$ for stochastic bandits with losses in $[0,1]$.

The algorithm in the above exercise is called the **implicitly normalised forecaster** (INF) and was introduced by Audibert and Bubeck [2009]. The last part of the exercise is very difficult. For 'hints', see the articles by Zimmert and Seldin [2019] and Zimmert et al. [2019].

28.16 (MINIMAX THEOREM) In this exercise you will prove simplified versions of Sion's minimax theorem.

(a) Use the tools from online linear optimisation to prove Sion's minimax theorem when $X = \mathcal{P}_{k-1}$ and $Y = \mathcal{P}_{j-1}$ and $f(x,y) = x^\top G y$ for some $G \in \mathbb{R}^{k \times j}$.

(b) Generalise your result to the case when X and Y are non-empty, convex, compact subsets of $\mathbb{R}^d$ and $f : X \times Y \to \mathbb{R}$ is convex/concave and has bounded gradients.

HINT   Consider a repeated simultaneous game where the first player chooses $(x_t)_{t=1}^\infty$ and the second player chooses $(y_t)_{t=1}^\infty$. The loss in round t to the first player is $f(x_t, y_t)$, and the loss to the second player is $-f(x_t, y_t)$. See what happens to the average iterates $\bar{x}_n = \frac{1}{n}\sum_{t=1}^n x_t$ and $\bar{y}_n = \frac{1}{n}\sum_{t=1}^n y_t$ when (x_t) and (y_t) are chosen by (appropriate) regret-minimising algorithms. For the second part, see Note 12. Also observe that there is nothing fundamental about X and Y both having dimension d.

28.17 (COUNTEREXAMPLE TO SION WITHOUT COMPACTNESS) Find examples of X, Y and f that satisfy the conditions of Sion's theorem except that neither X nor Y are compact and where the statement does not hold. Can you choose f to be bounded?

29 The Relation between Adversarial and Stochastic Linear Bandits

The purpose of this chapter is to highlight some of the differences and connections between adversarial and stochastic linear bandits. As it turns out, the connection between these are not as straightforward as for finite-armed bandits. We focus on three topics:

(a) For fixed action sets, there is a reduction from stochastic linear bandits to adversarial linear bandits. This does not come entirely for free. The action set needs to be augmented for things to work (Section 29.2).

(b) The adversarial and stochastic settings make different assumptions about the variability of the losses/rewards. This will explain the apparently contradictory result that the upper bound for adversarial bandits on the unit ball is $O(\sqrt{dn \log(n)})$ (Theorem 28.11), while the lower bound for stochastic bandits also for the unit ball is $\Omega(d\sqrt{n})$ (Theorem 24.2).

(c) When the action set is changing, the notion of regret in the adversarial setting must be carefully chosen, and for the 'right' choice, we do not yet have effective algorithms (Section 29.4).

We start with a unified view of the two settings.

29.1 Unified View

To make the notation consistent, we present the stochastic and adversarial linear bandit frameworks again using losses for both. Let $A \subset \mathbb{R}^d$ be the action set. In each round, the learner chooses $A_t \in A$ and receives the loss Y_t, where

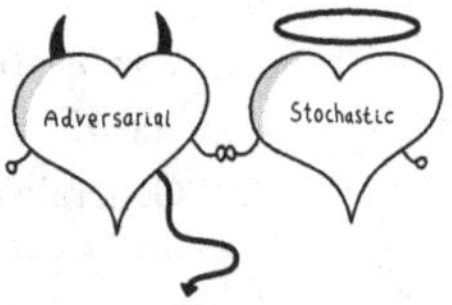

$$Y_t = \langle A_t, \theta \rangle + \eta_t, \qquad \text{(Stochastic setting)} \qquad (29.1)$$
$$Y_t = \langle A_t, \theta_t \rangle, \qquad \text{(Adversarial setting)} \qquad (29.2)$$

Figure 29.1 A tricky relationship

and $(\eta_t)_{t=1}^n$ is a sequence of independent and identically distributed 1-subgaussian random variables and $(\theta_t)_{t=1}^n$ is a sequence of loss vectors chosen by the adversary. As noted earlier, the assumptions on the noise can be relaxed significantly. For example, if $\mathcal{F}_t = \sigma(A_1, Y_1, \ldots, A_t, Y_t, A_{t+1})$, then the results of the previous chapters hold as soon as η_t is 1-subgaussian conditioned on $\mathcal{F}_{t-1}$. The expected regret for the two cases are defined as follows:

$$R_n = \sum_{t=1}^{n} \mathbb{E}\left[\langle A_t, \theta \rangle\right] - n \inf_{a \in \mathcal{A}} \langle a, \theta \rangle, \qquad \text{(Stochastic setting)}$$

$$R_n = \sum_{t=1}^{n} \mathbb{E}\left[\langle A_t, \theta_t \rangle\right] - n \inf_{a \in \mathcal{A}} \langle a, \bar{\theta}_n \rangle. \qquad \text{(Adversarial setting)}$$

In the last display, $\bar{\theta}_n = \frac{1}{n}\sum_{t=1}^{n} \theta_t$ is the average of the loss vectors chosen by the adversary.

29.2 Reducing Stochastic Linear Bandits to Adversarial Linear Bandits

To formalise the intuition that adversarial environments are harder than stochastic environments, one may try to find a **reduction** where learning in the stochastic setting is reduced to learning in the adversarial setting. Here, reducing problem E ('**easy**') to problem H ('**hard**') just means that we can use algorithms designed for problem H to solve instances of problem E. In order to do this, we need to transform instances of problem E into instances of problem H and translate back the actions of algorithms designed for H to actions for problem E. To get a regret bound for problem E from a regret bound for problem H, one needs to ensure that the losses translate properly between the problem classes.

Of course, based on our previous discussion, we know that if there is a reduction from stochastic linear bandits to adversarial linear bandits, then somehow the adversarial problem must change so that no contradiction is created in the curious case of the unit ball. To be able to use an adversarial algorithm in the stochastic environment, we need to specify a sequence $(\theta_t)_t$ so that the adversarial feedback matches the stochastic one. Comparing Eq. (29.1) and Eq. (29.2), we can see that the crux of the problem is incorporating the noise η_t into θ_t while satisfying the other requirements. One simple way of doing this is by introducing an extra dimension for the adversarial problem.

In particular, suppose that the stochastic problem is d-dimensional so that $\mathcal{A} \subset \mathbb{R}^d$. For the sake of simplicity, assume furthermore that the noise and parameter vector satisfy $|\langle a, \theta \rangle + \eta_t| \le 1$ almost surely for all $a \in \mathcal{A}$ and that $a_* = \operatorname{argmin}_{a \in \mathcal{A}} \langle a, \theta \rangle$ exists. Then define $\mathcal{A}_{\text{aug}} = \{(a, 1) : a \in \mathcal{A}\} \subset \mathbb{R}^{d+1}$ and let the adversary choose $\theta_t = (\theta, \eta_t) \in \mathbb{R}^{d+1}$. Here, we slightly abuse notation: for $x \in \mathbb{R}^d$ and $y \in \mathbb{R}$, we use (x, y) to denote the $d+1$ dimensional vector whose first d components are those of x and whose last component is y. The reduction is now straightforward: for $t = 1, 2, \ldots$, do the following:

1 Initialise adversarial bandit policy with action set $\mathcal{A}_{\text{aug}}$.
2 Collect action $A'_t = (A_t, 1)$ from the policy.
3 Play A_t and observe loss Y_t.
4 Feed Y_t to the adversarial bandit policy, increment t and repeat from step 2.

Suppose the adversarial policy guarantees a bound B_n on the expected regret:

$$R'_n = \mathbb{E}\left[\sum_{t=1}^{n} \langle A'_t, \theta_t \rangle - \inf_{a' \in \mathcal{A}_{\text{aug}}} \sum_{t=1}^{n} \langle a', \theta_t \rangle\right] \le B_n.$$

Let $a'_* = (a_*, 1)$. Note that for any $a' = (a, 1) \in \mathcal{A}_{\text{aug}}$, $\langle A_t, \theta \rangle - \langle a, \theta \rangle = \langle A'_t, \theta_t \rangle - \langle a', \theta_t \rangle$ and thus adversarial regret, and eventually B_n, will upper bound the stochastic regret:

$$\mathbb{E}\left[\sum_{t=1}^{n} \langle A_t, \theta \rangle - n\langle a_*, \theta \rangle\right] = \mathbb{E}\left[\sum_{t=1}^{n} \langle A'_t, \theta_t \rangle - n\langle a'_*, \bar{\theta}_n \rangle\right] \leq R'_n \leq B_n.$$

Therefore, the expected regret in the stochastic bandit is also at most B_n. We have to emphasise that this reduction changes the geometry of the decision sets for both the learner and the adversary. For example, if $\mathcal{A} = B_2^d$ is the unit ball, then neither $\mathcal{A}_{\text{aug}}$ nor

$$\left\{ y \in \mathbb{R}^d : \sup_{a \in \mathcal{A}_{\text{aug}}} |\langle a, y \rangle| \leq 1 \right\}$$

are unit balls. It does not seem like this should make much difference, but at least in the case of the ball, from our $\Omega(d\sqrt{n})$ lower bound on the regret for the stochastic case, we see that the changed geometry must make the adversary more powerful. This reinforces the importance of the geometry of the action set, which we have already seen in the previous chapter.

While the reduction shows one way to use adversarial algorithms in stochastic environments, the story seems to be unfinished. When facing a linear bandit problem with some action set $\mathcal{A}$, the user is forced to decide whether or not the environment is stochastic. Strangely enough, for stochastic environments the recommendation is to run your favorite adversarial linear bandit algorithm on the augmented action set. What if the environment may or may not be stochastic? One can still run the adversarial linear bandit algorithm on the original action set. This usually works, but the algorithm may need to be tuned differently (Exercises 29.2 and 29.3).

29.3 Stochastic Linear Bandits with Parameter Noise

The real reason for all these discrepancies is that the adversarial linear bandit model is better viewed as relaxation of another class of stochastic linear bandits. Rather than assuming the noise is added after taking an inner product, assume that $(\theta_t)_{t=1}^n$ is a sequence of vectors sampled independently from a fixed distribution ν on $\mathbb{R}^d$. The resulting model is called a **stochastic linear bandit with parameter noise**. This new problem can be trivially reduced to adversarial bandits when $\text{Supp}(\nu)$ is bounded (Exercise 29.1). In particular, there is no need to change the action set.

 Combining the stochastic linear bandits with parameter noise model with the techniques in Chapter 24 is the standard method for proving lower bounds for adversarial linear bandits.

Parameter noise environments form a subset of all possible stochastic environments. To see this, let $\theta = \int x\nu(dx)$ be the mean parameter vector under ν. Then the loss in round t is

$$\langle A_t, \theta_t \rangle = \langle A_t, \theta \rangle + \langle A_t, \theta_t - \theta \rangle.$$

Let $\mathbb{E}_t[\cdot] = \mathbb{E}[\cdot \mid \mathcal{F}_{t-1}]$. By our assumption that ν has mean θ, the second term vanishes in expectation, $\mathbb{E}_t[\langle A_t, \theta_t - \theta \rangle] = 0$. This implies that we can make a connection to the 'vanilla' stochastic setting by letting $\tilde{\eta}_t = \langle A_t, \theta_t - \theta \rangle$. Now consider the conditional variance of $\tilde{\eta}_t$:

$$\mathbb{V}_t[\tilde{\eta}_t] = \mathbb{E}_t[\langle A_t, \theta_t - \theta \rangle^2] = A_t^\top \mathbb{E}_t[(\theta_t - \theta)(\theta_t - \theta)^\top] A_t = A_t^\top \Sigma A_t, \qquad (29.3)$$

where Σ is the covariance matrix of multivariate distribution ν. Eq. (29.3) implies that the variance of the noise $\tilde{\eta}_t$ now depends on the choice of action and in particular the noise variance scales with the length of A_t. This can make parameter noise problems easier. For example, if ν is a Gaussian with identity covariance, then $\mathbb{V}_t[\tilde{\eta}_t] = \|A_t\|_2^2$ so that long actions have more noise than short actions. By contrast, in the usual stochastic linear bandit, the variance of the noise is unrelated to the length of the action. In particular, even the noise accompanying short actions can be large. This makes quite a bit of difference in cases when the action set has both short and long actions. In the standard stochastic model, shorter actions have the disadvantage of having a worse **signal-to-noise ratio**, which an adversary can exploit.

This calculation also provides the reason for the different guarantees for the unit ball. For stochastic linear bandits with 1-subgaussian noise the regret is $\tilde{O}(d\sqrt{n})$, while in the last chapter we showed that for adversarial linear bandits, the regret is $\tilde{O}(\sqrt{dn})$. This discrepancy is explained by the variance of the noise. Suppose that ν is supported on the unit sphere. Then the eigenvalues of its covariance matrix sum to one and if the learner chooses A_t from the uniform probability measure μ on the sphere, then

$$\mathbb{E}[\mathbb{V}_t[\tilde{\eta}_t]] = \int a^\top \Sigma a \, d\mu(a) = 1/d.$$

By contrast, in the standard stochastic model with 1-subgaussian noise, the predictable variation of the noise is just 1. If the adversary were allowed to choose its loss vectors from the sphere of radius $\sqrt{d}$, then the expected predictable variation would be 1, matching the standard stochastic case, and the regret would scale linearly in d, which also matches the vanilla stochastic case. This example further emphasises the importance of the assumptions that restrict the choices of the adversary.

> The best way to think about the standard adversarial linear model is that it generalises the stochastic linear bandit with parameter noise. Linear bandits with parameter noise are sometimes easier than the standard model because parameter noise limits the adversary's control of the signal-to-noise ratio experienced by the learner.

29.4 Contextual Linear Bandits

In practical applications the action set is usually changing from round to round. Although it is possible to prove bounds for adversarial linear bandits with changing action sets, the notion of regret makes the results less meaningful than what one obtains in the stochastic setting. Suppose that $(\mathcal{A}_t)_{t=1}^n$ are a sequence of action sets. In the stochastic setting, the actions $(A_t)_t$ selected by the LinUCB algorithm satisfy

$$\mathbb{E}\left[\sum_{t=1}^{n}\langle A_t - a_t^*, \theta\rangle\right] = \tilde{O}(d\sqrt{n}),$$

where $a_t^* = \operatorname{argmax}_{a\in\mathcal{A}_t}\langle a, \theta\rangle$ is the optimal action in round t. This definition of the regret measures the right thing: the action a_t^* really is the optimal action in round t. The analogous result for adversarial bandits would be a bound on

$$R_n(\Theta) = \max_{\theta\in\Theta}\mathbb{E}\left[\sum_{t=1}^{n}\langle A_t - a_t(\theta), y_t\rangle\right], \tag{29.4}$$

where Θ is a subset of $\mathbb{R}^d$ and $a_t(\theta) = \operatorname{argmax}_{a\in\mathcal{A}_t}\langle a, \theta\rangle$. Unfortunately, however, we do not currently know how to design algorithms for which this regret is small. For finite Θ, the techniques of Chapter 27 are easily adapted to prove a bound of $O(\sqrt{dn\log|\Theta|})$, but this algorithm is *(a)* not computationally efficient for large $|\Theta|$, and *(b)* choosing Θ as an ε-covering of a continuous set does not guarantee a bound against the larger set. Providing a meaningful bound on Eq. (29.4) when Θ is a continuous set like $\{\theta : \|\theta\|_2 \leq 1\}$ is a fascinating challenge. The reader may recall that the result in Exercise 27.5 provides a bound for adversarial linear bandits with changing action sets. However, in this problem the actions have 'identities', and the regret is measured with respect to the best action in hindsight, which is a markedly different objective than the one in Eq. (29.4).

29.5   Notes

1 For the reduction in Section 29.2, we assumed that $|Y_t| \leq 1$ almost surely. This is not true for many classical noise models like the Gaussian. One way to overcome this annoyance is to apply the adversarial analysis on the event that $|Y_t| \leq C$ for some constant $C > 0$ that is sufficiently large that the probability that this event occurs is high. For example, if η_t is a standard Gaussian and $\sup_{a\in\mathcal{A}}|\langle a, \theta\rangle| \leq 1$, then C may be chosen to be $1 + \sqrt{4\log(n)}$, and the failure event that there exists a t such that $|\langle A_t, \theta\rangle + \eta_t| \geq C$ has probability at most $1/n$ by Theorem 5.3 and a union bound.

2 The mirror descent analysis of adversarial linear bandits also works for stochastic bandits. Recall that mirror descent samples A_t from a distribution with a conditional mean of $\bar{A}_t$, and suppose that $\hat{\theta}_t$ is a conditionally unbiased estimator of θ. Then the regret for a stochastic linear bandit with optimal action a^* can be rewritten as

$$R_n = \mathbb{E}\left[\sum_{t=1}^{n}\langle A_t - a^*, \theta\rangle\right] = \mathbb{E}\left[\sum_{t=1}^{n}\langle \bar{A}_t - a^*, \theta\rangle\right] = \mathbb{E}\left[\sum_{t=1}^{n}\langle \bar{A}_t - a^*, \hat{\theta}_t\rangle\right],$$

which is in the standard format necessary for the analysis of mirror descent/follow-the-regularised-leader. In the stochastic setting, the covariance of the least squares estimator $\hat{\theta}_t$ will not be the same as in the adversarial setting, however, which leads to different results. When $\hat{\theta}_t$ is biased, the bias term can be incorporated into the above formula and then bounded separately.

3 Consider a stochastic bandit with $\mathcal{A} = B_2^d$ the unit ball and $Y_t = \langle A_t, \theta\rangle + \eta_t$ where $|Y_t| \leq 1$ almost surely and $\|\theta\|_2 \leq 1$. Adapting the analysis of the algorithm in Section 28.4 leads to a bound of $R_n = O(d\sqrt{n\log(n)})$. Essentially the only change is the variance calculation, which increases by roughly a factor of d. The details of this calculation are left to you in Exercise 29.2. When $\mathcal{A}$ is finite, the analysis of Exp3 with Kiefer–Wolfowitz exploration (Theorem 27.1) leads to

an algorithm for which $R_n = O(\sqrt{dn\log(k)})$. For convex $\mathcal{A}$, you can use continuous exponential weights (Section 27.3).

4 You might wonder whether or not an adversarial bandit algorithm is well behaved for stochastic bandits where the model is almost linear (the misspecified linear bandit). Suppose the loss is nearly linear in the sense that

$$Y_t = \ell(A_t) + \eta_t,$$

where $\ell(A_t) = \langle A_t, \theta \rangle + \varepsilon(A_t)$ and $\varepsilon : \mathcal{A} \to \mathbb{R}$ is some function with small supremum norm. Because $\varepsilon(A_t)$ depends on the chosen action, it is not possible to write $Y_t = \langle A_t, \theta_t \rangle$ for θ_t independent of A_t. When $\mathcal{A} = B_2^d$ is the unit ball, you will show in Exercise 29.4 that an appropriately tuned instantiation of follow-the-regularised-leader satisfies $R_n = O(d\sqrt{n\log(n)} + \varepsilon n\sqrt{d})$, where $\varepsilon = \sup_{a \in \mathcal{A}} \varepsilon(a)$. This improves by logarithmic factors on the more generic algorithm in Chapter 22.

29.6 Bibliographic Remarks

Linear bandits on the sphere with parameter noise have been studied by Carpentier and Munos [2012]. However they consider the case where the action set is the *sphere* and the components of the noise are independent so that the reward is $X_t = \langle A_t, \theta + \eta_t \rangle$ where the coordinates of $\eta_t \in \mathbb{R}^d$ are independent with unit variance. In this case, the predictable variation is $\mathbb{V}[X_t \mid A_t] = \sum_{i=1}^d A_{ti}^2 = 1$ for all actions A_t and the parameter noise is equivalent to the standard model. We are not aware of any systematic studies of parameter noise in the stochastic setting. With only a few exceptions, the impact on the regret of the action set and adversary's choices is not well understood beyond the case where $\mathcal{A}$ is an ℓ_p-ball, which has been mentioned in the previous section. A variety of lower bounds illustrating the complications are given by Shamir [2015]. Perhaps the most informative is the observation that obtaining $O(\sqrt{dn})$ regret is not possible when $\mathcal{A} = \{a + x : \|x\|_2 \le 1\}$ is a shifted unit ball with $a = (2, 0, \ldots, 0)$, which also follows from our reduction in Section 29.2.

29.7 Exercises

29.1 (REDUCTIONS) Let $\mathcal{A} \subset \mathcal{R}^d$ be an action set and $\mathcal{L} = \{y \in \mathbb{R}^d : \sup_{a \in \mathcal{A}} |\langle a, y \rangle| \le 1\}$. Take an adversarial linear bandit algorithm that enjoys a worst-case guarantee B_n on its n-round expected regret R_n when the adversary is restricted to playing $\theta_t \in \mathcal{L}$. Show that if this algorithm is used in a stochastic linear bandit problem with parameter noise where $\theta_t \sim \nu$ and $\text{Supp}(\nu) \subseteq \mathcal{L}$, then the expected regret R_n' is still bounded by B_n.

29.2 (FOLLOW-THE-REGULARISED-LEADER FOR STOCHASTIC BANDITS (I)) Consider a stochastic linear bandit with $\mathcal{A} = B_2^d$ and loss $Y_t = \langle A_t, \theta \rangle + \eta_t$ where $(\eta_t)_{t=1}^n$ are independent with zero mean and $Y_t \in [-1, 1]$ almost surely. Adapt the proof of Theorem 28.11 to show that with appropriate tuning the algorithm in Section 28.4 satisfies $R_n \le Cd\sqrt{n\log(n)}$ for universal constant $C > 0$.

HINT Repeat the analysis in the proof of Theorem 28.11, update the learning rate and check the bounds on the norm of the estimators.

29.3 (FOLLOW-THE-REGULARISED-LEADER FOR STOCHASTIC BANDITS (II)) Repeat the previous exercise using exponential weights or continuous exponential weights with Kiefer–Wolfowitz exploration where

(a) $\mathcal{A}$ is finite; and
(b) $\mathcal{A}$ is convex.

29.4 (MISSPECIFIED LINEAR BANDITS) Let $\mathcal{A} \subset \mathbb{R}^d$ and $(\eta_t)_{t=1}^n$ be a sequence of independent zero-mean random variables and assume the loss is

$$Y_t = \ell(A_t) + \eta_t,$$

where $\ell(A_t) = \langle A_t, \theta \rangle + \varepsilon(A_t)$ and $\varepsilon = \sup_{a \in \mathcal{A}} \varepsilon(a)$ and $|Y_t| \leq 1$ almost surely.

(a) Suppose that $\mathcal{A} = B_2^d$. Show that the expected regret of an appropriately tuned version of the algorithm in Section 28.4 satisfies

$$R_n \leq C(d\sqrt{n \log(n)} + \varepsilon n\sqrt{d}),$$

where $C > 0$ is a universal constant.
(b) Do you think the result from Part (a) can be improved?
(c) Suppose that $\mathcal{A}$ is finite. What goes wrong in the analysis of exponential weights with Kiefer–Wolfowitz exploration (Algorithm 15)?

Part VII

Other Topics

In the penultimate part, we collect a few topics to which we could not dedicate a whole part. When deciding what to include, we balanced our subjective views on what is important, pedagogical and sufficiently well understood for a book. Of course we have played favourites with our choices and hope the reader can forgive us for the omissions. We spend the rest of this intro outlining some of the omitted topics.

Continuous-Armed Bandits

There is a small literature on bandits where the number of actions is infinitely large. We covered the linear case in earlier chapters, but the linear assumption can be relaxed significantly. Let $\mathcal{A}$ be an arbitrary set and $\mathcal{F}$ a set of functions from $\mathcal{A} \to \mathbb{R}$. The learner is given access to the action set $\mathcal{A}$ and function class $\mathcal{F}$. In each round, the learner chooses an action $A_t \in \mathcal{A}$ and receives reward $X_t = f(A_t) + \eta_t$, where η_t is noise and $f \in \mathcal{F}$ is fixed, but unknown. Of course this set-up is general enough to model all of the stochastic bandits so far, but is perhaps too general to say much. One interesting relaxation is the case where $\mathcal{A}$ is a metric space and $\mathcal{F}$ is the set of Lipschitz functions. We refer the reader to papers by Kleinberg [2005], Auer et al. [2007], Kleinberg et al. [2008], Bubeck et al. [2011], Slivkins [2014], Magureanu et al. [2014] and Combes et al. [2017], as well as the book of Slivkins [2019].

Infinite-Armed Bandits

Consider a bandit problem where in each round the learner can choose to play an arm from an existing pool of Bernoulli arms or to add another Bernoulli arm to the pool with mean sampled from a uniform distribution. The regret in this setting is defined as

$$R_n = n - \mathbb{E}\left[\sum_{t=1}^{n} X_t\right].$$

This problem is studied by Berry et al. [1997], who show that $R_n = \Theta(n^{1/2})$ is the optimal regret. There are now a number of strengthening and generalisations of this work [Wang et al., 2009, Bonald and Proutiere, 2013, Carpentier and Valko, 2015, for example], which sadly must be omitted from this book. The notable difficulty is generalising the algorithms and analysis to the case where reservoir distribution from which the new arms are sampled is unknown and/or does not exhibit a nice structure.

Duelling Bandits

In the duelling bandit problem, the learner chooses two arms in each round A_{t1}, A_{t2}. Rather than observing a reward for each arm, the learner observes the winner of a 'duel' between the two arms. Let k be the number of arms and $P \in [0,1]^{k \times k}$ be a matrix where P_{ij} is the probability that arm i beats arm j in a duel. It is natural to assume that $P_{ij} = 1 - P_{ji}$. A common, but slightly less justifiable, assumption is the existence of a total ordering on the arms such that if $i \succ j$, then $P_{ij} > 1/2$. There are at least two notions of regret. Let i^* be the optimal arm so that $i^* \succ j$ for all $j \neq i^*$. Then the strong and weak regret are defined by

$$\text{Strong regret} = \mathbb{E}\left[\sum_{t=1}^{n}\left(P_{i^*,A_{t1}} + P_{i^*,A_{t2}} - 1\right)\right],$$

$$\text{Weak regret} = \mathbb{E}\left[\sum_{t=1}^{n}\min\left\{P_{i^*,A_{t1}} - 1/2, P_{i^*,A_{t2}} - 1/2\right\}\right].$$

Both definitions measure the number of times arms with low probability of winning a duel against the optimal arm is played. The former definition only vanishes when $A_{t1} = A_{t2} = i^*$, while the latter is zero as soon as $i^* \in \{A_{t1}, A_{t2}\}$. The duelling bandit problem was introduced by Yue et al. [2009] and has seen quite a lot of interest since then [Yue and Joachims, 2009, 2011, Ailon et al., 2014, Zoghi et al., 2014, Dudík et al., 2015, Jamieson et al., 2015, Komiyama et al., 2015a, Zoghi et al., 2015, Wu and Liu, 2016, Zimmert and Seldin, 2019].

Convex Bandits
Let $\mathcal{A} \subset \mathbb{R}^d$ be a convex set. The convex bandit problem comes in both stochastic and adversarial varieties. In both cases, the learner chooses A_t from $\mathcal{A}$. In the stochastic case, the learner receives a reward $X_t = f(A_t) + \eta_t$ where f is an unknown convex function and η_t is noise. In the adversarial setting, the adversary chooses a sequence of convex functions $f_1, \ldots, f_n$ and the learner receives reward $X_t = f_t(A_t)$. This turned out to be a major challenge over the last decade with most approaches leading to suboptimal regret in terms of the horizon. The best bounds in the stochastic case are by Agarwal et al. [2011], while in the adversarial case there has been a lot of recent progress [Bubeck et al., 2015a, Bubeck and Eldan, 2016, Bubeck et al., 2017]. In both cases the dependence of the regret on the horizon is $O(\sqrt{n})$, which is optimal in the worst case. Many open question remain, such as the optimal dependence on the dimension, or the related problem of designing practical low-regret algorithms. The interested reader may consult Shamir [2013] and Hu et al. [2016] for some of the open problems.

Budgeted Bandits
In many problems, choosing an action costs some resources. In the bandits-with-knapsacks problem, the learner starts with a fixed budget $B \in [0, \infty)^d$ over d resource types. Like in the standard K-armed stochastic bandit, the learner chooses $A_t \in [K]$ and receives a reward X_t sampled from a distribution depending on A_t. The twist is that the game does not end after a fixed number of rounds. Instead, in each round, the environment samples a cost vector $C_t \in [0, 1]^d$ from a distribution that depends on A_t. The game ends in the first round τ for which there exists an $i \in [d]$ such that $\sum_{t=1}^{\tau} C_{ti} > B_i$. This line of work was started by Badanidiyuru et al. [2013] and has been extended in many directions by Agrawal and Devanur [2014], Tran-Thanh et al. [2012], Ashwinkumar et al. [2014], Xia et al. [2015], Agrawal and Devanur [2016], Tran-Thanh et al. [2010] and Hanawal et al. [2015]. A somewhat related idea is the conservative bandit problem where the goal is to minimise regret subject to the constraint that the learner must not be much worse than some known baseline. The constraint limits the amount of exploration and makes the regret guarantees slightly worse [Sui et al., 2015, Wu et al., 2016, Kazerouni et al., 2017].

Learning with Delays

In many practical applications, the feedback to the learner is not immediate. The time between clicking on a link and buying a product could be minutes, days, weeks or longer. Similarly, the response to a drug does not come immediately. In most cases, the learner does not have the choice to wait before making the next decision. Buyers and patients just keep coming. Perhaps the first paper for online learning with delays is by Weinberger and Ordentlich [2002], who consider the full information setting. Recently this has become a hot topic, and there has been a lot of follow-up work extending the results in various directions [Joulani et al., 2013, Desautels et al., 2014, Cesa-Bianchi et al., 2016, Vernade et al., 2017, 2018, Pike-Burke et al., 2018, and others]. Learning with delays is an interesting example where the adversarial and stochastic models lead to quite different outcomes. In general the increase in regret due to rewards being delayed by at most τ rounds is a multiplicative $\sqrt{\tau}$ factor for adversarial models and an additive term only for stochastic models.

Graph Feedback

There is growing interest in feedback models that lie between the full information and bandit settings. One way to do this is to let G be a directed graph with K vertices. The adversary chooses a sequence of loss vectors in $[0, 1]^K$ as usual. In each round, the learner chooses a vertex and observes the loss corresponding to that vertex and its neighbours. The full information and bandit settings are recovered by choosing the graph to be fully connected or have no edges respectively, but of course there are many interesting regimes in between. There are many variants on this basic problem. For example, G might change in each round or be undirected. Or perhaps the graph is changing, and the learner only observes it after choosing an action. The reader can explore this topic by reading the articles by Mannor and Shamir [2011], Alon et al. [2013], Kocák et al. [2014] and Alon et al. [2015] or the short book by Valko [2016].

30 Combinatorial Bandits

A combinatorial bandit is a linear bandit with an action set that is a subset of the d-dimensional binary hypercube: $\mathcal{A} \subset \{0,1\}^d$. Elements of $\mathcal{A}$ are thus d-dimensional, binary-valued vectors. Each component may be on or off, but some combinations are not allowed – hence the combinatorial structure. Combinatorial bandit problems arise in many applications, some of which are detailed shortly.

The setting is studied in both the adversarial and stochastic models. We focus on the former in this chapter and discuss the latter in the notes. In the adversarial setting, as usual, the environment chooses a sequence of loss vectors $y_1, \ldots, y_n$ with $y_t \in \mathbb{R}^d$, and the regret of the learner is

$$R_n = \max_{a \in \mathcal{A}} \mathbb{E}\left[\sum_{t=1}^{n} \langle A_t - a, y_t \rangle\right],$$

where as usual A_t is the action chosen by the learner in round t.

Unsurprisingly, the algorithms and analysis from Chapters 27 and 28 are applicable in this setting. The main challenge is controlling the computation complexity of the resulting algorithms. As we will soon argue, except in special cases, it is natural to be hopeful when there exists an optimisation oracle that computes the map $y \mapsto \operatorname{argmin}_{a \in \mathcal{A}} \langle a, y \rangle$ is efficient. The most important result of this chapter gives a strategy based on **follow-the-perturbed-leader** that makes a single call to such an optimisation oracle in every round for a suitable chosen vector $\tilde{L}_t \in \mathbb{R}^d$ (a perturbed estimate of the cumulative loss vector). This is done in the **semi-bandit** setting, an in-between setting where the learner receives **semi-bandit feedback**, which is the vector $(A_{t1}y_{t1}, \ldots, A_{td}y_{td})$. Since $A_{ti} \in \{0,1\}$, this is equivalent to observing y_{ti} for all i for which $A_{ti} = 1$.

The rest of this chapter is organised as follows: the next section describes some additional useful notation. There follows a section that describes selected applications. In Section 30.3 we describe an application of Exp3 to the case when the learner receives only bandit feedback and explain the computational challenges that arise due to the combinatorial nature of the problem. Section 30.4 explains how online stochastic mirror descent can be applied to the semi-bandit setting, which still fails to give an efficient algorithm. Finally, the follow-the-perturbed-leader algorithm is introduced and analysed in Section 30.5.

30.1 Notation and Assumptions

In the applications, a key quantity associated with combinatorial action sets is the largest number of elements m that can be simultaneously 'on' in any given action:

$$\mathcal{A} \subseteq \{a \in \{0, 1\}^d : \|a\|_1 \leq m\}.$$

In Chapters 27 and 28, we assumed that $y_t \in \{y : \sup_{a \in \mathcal{A}} |\langle a, y \rangle| \leq 1\}$. This restriction is not consistent with the applications we have in mind, so instead we assume that $y_t \in [0, 1]^d$, which by the definition of $\mathcal{A}$ ensures that $|\langle A_t, y_t \rangle| \leq m$ for all t. In the standard bandit model, the learner observes $\langle A_t, y_t \rangle$ in each round.

30.2 Applications

Shortest-Path Problems

Let $G = (V, E)$ be a fixed graph with a finite set of vertices V and edges $E \subseteq V \times V$, with $|E| = d$. The online shortest-path problem is a game over n rounds between an adversary and a learner. Given fixed vertices $u, v \in V$, the learner's objective in each round is to find the shortest path between u and v. At the beginning of the game, the adversary chooses a sequence of vectors $y_1, \ldots, y_n$, with $y_t \in [0, 1]^d$ and y_{ti} representing the length of the ith edge in E in round t. In each round, the learner chooses a path between u and v. The regret of the learner is the difference between the distance they travelled and the distance of the optimal path in hindsight. A path is represented by a vector $a \in \{0, 1\}^d$ where $a_i = 1$ if the ith edge is part of the path. Let $\mathcal{A}$ be the set of paths connecting vertices u and v, then the length of path a in round t is $\langle a, y_t \rangle$. In this problem, m is the length of the longest path. Fig. 30.1 illustrates a typical example.

Ranking

Suppose a company has d ads and m locations in which to display them. In each round t, the learner should choose the m ads to display, which is represented by a vector $A_t \in \{0, 1\}^d$ with $\|A_t\|_1 = m$. As before, the adversary chooses $y_t \in [0, 1]^d$ that measures the quality of each placement and the learner suffers loss $\langle A_t, y_t \rangle$. This problem could also be called

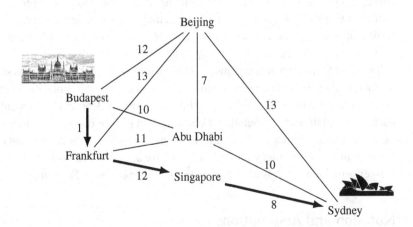

Figure 30.1 Shortest-path problem between Budapest and Sydney. The learner chooses the path Budapest–Frankfurt–Singapore–Sydney. In the bandit setting, they observe total travel time (21 hours), while in the semi-bandit they observe the length of each flight on the route they took (1 hour, 12 hours, 8 hours).

'selection' because the order of the items play no role. Problems where the order plays a direct role are analysed in Chapter 32.

Multitask Bandits

Consider playing m multi-armed bandits simultaneously, each with k arms. If the losses for each bandit problem are observed, then it is easy to apply Exp3 or Exp3-IX to each bandit independently. But now suppose the learner only observes the sum of the losses. This problem is represented as a combinatorial bandit by letting $d = mk$ and

$$\mathcal{A} = \left\{ a \in \{0, 1\}^d : \sum_{i=1}^{k} a_{i+kj} = 1 \text{ for all } 0 \le j < m \right\}.$$

In words, the d coordinates are partitioned into m parts and the learner needs to select exactly one coordinate ("primitive action") from each part. The resulting problem is called the **multi-task bandit** problem: This problem is like making m independent choices in parallel in m bandit problems blindly and then receiving an aggregated feedback for all the m choices made. This scenario can arise in practice when a company is making multiple independent interventions, but the quality of the interventions are only observed via a single change in revenue.

30.3 Bandit Feedback

The easiest approach is to apply the version of Exp3 for linear bandits described in Chapter 27. The only difference is that now $|\langle A_t, y_t \rangle|$ can be as large as m, which increases the regret by a factor of m. We leave the proof of the following theorem to the reader (Exercise 30.1).

THEOREM 30.1. *Consider the setting of Section 30.1. If Algorithm 15 is run on action set $\mathcal{A}$ with appropriately chosen learning rate, then*

$$R_n \le 2m\sqrt{3dn \log |\mathcal{A}|} \le m^{3/2} \sqrt{12dn \log \left(\frac{ed}{m} \right)}.$$

There are two issues with this approach, both computational. First, the action set is typically so large that finding the core set of the central minimum volume enclosing ellipsoid that determines the Kiefer–Wolfowitz exploration distribution of Algorithm 15 is hopeless. Second, efficiently sampling from the resulting exponential weights distribution may not be possible. There is no silver bullet for these issues. The combinatorial bandit can model a repeated version of the travelling salesman problem, which is hard even to approximate. Since an online learning algorithm with $O(n^p)$ regret with $p < 1$ can be used to approximate the optimal solution, it follows that no such algorithm can be computationally efficient. There are, however, special cases where efficient algorithms exist, and we give some pointers to the relevant literature on this at the end of the chapter. One modification that greatly eases computation is to replace the optimal Kiefer–Wolfowitz exploration distribution with a distribution that can be computed and sampled from in an efficient manner, as noted after Theorem 27.1.

30.4 Semi-bandit Feedback and Mirror Descent

In the semi-bandit setting, the learner observes the loss associated with all non-zero coordinates of the chosen action. The additional information is exploited by noting that y_t can now be estimated in each coordinate. Let

$$\hat{Y}_{ti} = \frac{A_{ti} y_{ti}}{\bar{A}_{ti}}, \tag{30.1}$$

where $\bar{A}_{ti} = \mathbb{E}[A_{ti} \mid \mathcal{F}_{t-1}]$ with $\mathcal{F}_t = \sigma(A_1, \dots, A_t)$. An easy calculation shows that $\mathbb{E}[\hat{Y}_t \mid \mathcal{F}_{t-1}] = y_t$, so this estimate is still unbiased. Unsurprisingly we will again use online stochastic mirror descent, which is summarised for this setting in Algorithm 18.

1: **Input** $\mathcal{A}, \eta, F$
2: $\bar{A}_1 = \mathrm{argmin}_{a \in \mathrm{co}(\mathcal{A})} F(a)$
3: **for** $t = 1, \dots, n$ **do**
4:     Choose distribution P_t on $\mathcal{A}$ such that $\sum_{a \in \mathcal{A}} P_t(a) a = \bar{A}_t$
5:     Sample $A_t \sim P_t$ and observe $A_{t1} y_{t1}, \dots, A_{td} y_{td}$
6:     Compute $\hat{Y}_{ti} = A_{ti} y_{ti} / \bar{A}_{ti}$ for all $i \in [d]$
7:     Update $\bar{A}_{t+1} = \mathrm{argmin}_{a \in \mathrm{co}(\mathcal{A})} \eta \langle a, \hat{Y}_t \rangle + D_F(a, \bar{A}_t)$
8: **end for**

Algorithm 18: Online stochastic mirror descent for semi-bandits.

THEOREM 30.2. *Consider the setting of Section 30.1. Let $F : \mathbb{R}^d \to \mathbb{R}$ be the unnormalised negentropy potential:*

$$F(a) = \sum_{i=1}^{d} (a_i \log(a_i) - a_i)$$

for $a \in [0, \infty)^d$ and $F(a) = \infty$ otherwise. Then, Algorithm 18 is well defined and, provided $\eta = \sqrt{2m(1 + \log(d/m))/(nd)}$, its regret R_n satisfies

$$R_n \leq \sqrt{2nmd(1 + \log(d/m))}.$$

Proof Since $\mathcal{A}$ is a finite set, the algorithm is well defined. In particular, $\bar{A}_t > 0$ exists and is unique for all $t \in [n]$. By Theorem 28.10,

$$R_n \leq \frac{\mathrm{diam}_F(\mathrm{co}(\mathcal{A}))}{\eta} + \mathbb{E}\left[\sum_{t=1}^{n} \langle \bar{A}_t - \bar{A}_{t+1}, \hat{Y}_t \rangle - \frac{1}{\eta} D_F(\bar{A}_{t+1}, \bar{A}_t)\right]. \tag{30.2}$$

The diameter is easily bounded by noting that F is negative in $\mathrm{co}(\mathcal{A})$ and using Jensen's inequality:

$$\mathrm{diam}_F(\mathrm{co}(\mathcal{A})) \leq \sup_{a \in \mathrm{co}(\mathcal{A})} \sum_{i=1}^{d} \left(a_i + a_i \log\left(\frac{1}{a_i}\right)\right) \leq m(1 + \log(d/m)).$$

For the second term in Eq. (30.2), let $\hat{Y}'_{ti} = \hat{Y}_{ti}\mathbb{I}\{\bar{A}_{t+1,i} \le \bar{A}_{ti}\}$. Since $\hat{Y}_t$ is positive,

$$\langle \bar{A}_t - \bar{A}_{t+1}, \hat{Y}_t \rangle - \frac{1}{\eta}D_F(\bar{A}_{t+1}, \bar{A}_t) \le \langle \bar{A}_t - \bar{A}_{t+1}, \hat{Y}'_t \rangle - \frac{1}{\eta}D_F(\bar{A}_{t+1}, \bar{A}_t)$$

$$\le \frac{\eta}{2}\|\hat{Y}'_t\|^2_{\nabla^2 F(Z_t)^{-1}} \le \frac{\eta}{2}\sum_{i=1}^d \frac{A_{ti}}{\bar{A}_{ti}},$$

where Z_t is provided by Theorem 26.12 and lies on the chord $[\bar{A}_t, \bar{A}_{t+1}]$. The final inequality follows because $\nabla^2 F(z) = \text{diag}(1/z)$ and using the definition of $\hat{Y}'_t$, which ensures that the worst case occurs when $Z_t = \bar{A}_t$. Summing and taking the expectation:

$$\mathbb{E}\left[\sum_{t=1}^n \langle \bar{A}_t - \bar{A}_{t+1}, \hat{Y}_t \rangle - \frac{1}{\eta}D_F(\bar{A}_{t+1}, \bar{A}_t)\right] \le \frac{\eta}{2}\mathbb{E}\left[\sum_{t=1}^n\sum_{i=1}^d \frac{A_{ti}}{\bar{A}_{ti}}\right] = \frac{\eta nd}{2}.$$

Putting together the pieces shows that

$$R_n \le \frac{m(1 + \log(d/m))}{\eta} + \frac{\eta nd}{2} = \sqrt{2nmd(1 + \log(d/m))}. \qquad \square$$

Algorithm 18 plays mirror descent on the convex hull of the actions, which has dimension $d - 1$. In principle it would be possible to do the same thing on the set of distributions over actions, which has dimension $|\mathcal{A}| - 1$. Repeating the analysis leads to a suboptimal regret of $O(m\sqrt{dn\log(d/m)})$. We encourage the reader to go through this calculation to see where things go wrong.

Like in Section 30.3, the main problem is computation. In each round the algorithm needs to find a distribution P_t over $\mathcal{A}$ such that $\sum_{a\in\mathcal{A}} P_t(a) = \bar{A}_t$. Feasibility follows from the definition of $\text{co}(\mathcal{A})$, while Carathéodory's theorem proves the support of P_t never needs to be larger than $d + 1$. Since $\mathcal{A}$ is finite, we can write the problem of finding P_t in terms of linear constraints, but naively the computation complexity is polynomial in $k = |\mathcal{A}|$, which is exponential in m. The algorithm also needs to compute $\bar{A}_{t+1}$ from $\bar{A}_t$ and $\hat{Y}_t$. This is a convex optimisation problem, but the computation complexity depends on the representation of $\mathcal{A}$ and may be intractable. See Note 6 for a few more details on this.

30.5 Follow-the-Perturbed-Leader

In this section, we help ourselves to find a computationally efficient algorithm by adding the assumption that for all $y \in [0, \infty)^d$, the optimisation problem of finding

$$a^* = \text{argmin}_{a\in\mathcal{A}}\langle a, y \rangle \tag{30.3}$$

admits a computationally efficient algorithm. This assumption feels close to the minimum one could get away with in the sense that if the offline problem in Eq. (30.3) is hard to approximate, then any algorithm with low regret must also be inefficient. A marginally more reasonable assumption is that Eq. (30.3) can be approximated efficiently. For simplicity we assume exact solutions, however.

If the algorithm observed the losses in every round, adding a random vector to the sum of previous losses and then finding the action that minimises the total randomly perturbed loss leads to what is known as the **follow-the-perturbed-leader** (FTPL) algorithm. As discussed before, the random perturbation is necessary to achieve sublinear regret. In semi-bandit setting which is considered here, the full loss vector is unobserved and hence needs to be estimated. Letting $\hat{L}_{t-1} = \sum_{s=1}^{t-1} \hat{Y}_s$ be the cumulative loss estimates before round t, FTPL chooses

$$A_t = \operatorname{argmin}_{a \in \mathcal{A}} \langle a, \eta \hat{L}_{t-1} - Z_t \rangle, \tag{30.4}$$

where $\eta > 0$ is the learning rate and $Z_t \in \mathbb{R}^d$ is sampled from a carefully chosen distribution Q. The random perturbations is chosen to both guard against worst-case, and to induce necessary exploration. Notice that if η is small, then the effect of Z_t is larger and the algorithm can be expected to explore more, which is consistent with the learning rate used in mirror descent or exponential weighting studied in previous chapters.

Before defining the loss estimations and perturbation distribution, we make a connection between FTPL and mirror descent. Given Legendre potential F with $\operatorname{dom}(\nabla F) = \operatorname{int}(\operatorname{co}(\mathcal{A}))$, online stochastic mirror descent chooses $\bar{A}_t$ so that

$$\bar{A}_t = \operatorname{argmin}_{a \in \operatorname{co}(\mathcal{A})} \langle a, \eta \hat{Y}_{t-1} \rangle + D_F(a, \bar{A}_{t-1}).$$

Taking derivatives and using the fact that $\operatorname{dom}(\nabla F) = \operatorname{int}(\operatorname{co}(\mathcal{A}))$, we have

$$\nabla F(\bar{A}_t) = \nabla F(\bar{A}_{t-1}) - \eta \hat{Y}_{t-1} = -\eta \hat{L}_{t-1}.$$

By duality (Theorem 26.6), this implies that $\bar{A}_t = \nabla F^*(-\eta \hat{L}_{t-1})$. On the other hand, examining Eq. (30.4), we see that for FTPL,

$$\bar{A}_t = \mathbb{E}[A_t \mid \mathcal{F}_{t-1}] = \mathbb{E}\left[\operatorname{argmin}_{a \in \mathcal{A}} \langle a, \eta \hat{L}_{t-1} - Z_t \rangle \mid \mathcal{F}_{t-1}\right],$$

where $\mathcal{F}_t = \sigma(Z_1, \ldots, Z_t)$. Thus, in order to view FTPL as an instance of mirror descent, it suffices to find a Legendre potential F with $\operatorname{dom}(\nabla F) = \operatorname{int}(\operatorname{co}(\mathcal{A}))$ and

$$\nabla F^*(-\eta \hat{L}_{t-1}) = \mathbb{E}\left[\operatorname{argmin}_{a \in \mathcal{A}} \langle a, \eta \hat{L}_{t-1} - Z_t \rangle \mid \mathcal{F}_{t-1}\right]$$

$$= \mathbb{E}\left[\operatorname{argmax}_{a \in \mathcal{A}} \langle a, Z_t - \eta \hat{L}_{t-1} \rangle \mid \mathcal{F}_{t-1}\right].$$

Since $\hat{L}_{t-1}$ is more or less uncontrolled, the latter condition is most easily satisfied by requiring that for any $x \in \mathbb{R}^d$, $\nabla F^*(x) = \int_{\mathbb{R}^d} \operatorname{argmax}_{a \in \operatorname{co}(\mathcal{A})} \langle a, x + z \rangle \, dQ(z)$. To remove clutter in the notation, define

$$a(x) = \operatorname{argmax}_{a \in \mathcal{A}} \langle a, x \rangle,$$

where $a(x)$ is chosen to be an arbitrary maximiser if multiple maximisers exist. Readers with some familiarity with convex analysis will remember that if a convex set $\mathcal{A}$ has a smooth boundary, then the **support function** of $\mathcal{A}$,

$$\phi(x) = \max_{a \in \mathcal{A}} \langle a, x \rangle,$$

satisfies $\nabla\phi(x) = a(x)$. For combinatorial bandits, $\mathcal{A}$ is not smooth, but if Q is absolutely continuous with respect to the Lebesgue measure, then you will show in Exercise 30.5 that

$$\nabla \int_{\mathbb{R}^d} \phi(x + z) \, dQ(z) = \int_{\mathbb{R}^d} a(x + z) \, dQ(z) \quad \text{for all } x \in \mathbb{R}^d.$$

The key to this argument is that the derivative of ϕ exists almost everywhere and is equal to $a(x)$. All this shows is that FTPL can be interpreted as mirror descent with potential F defined in terms of its Fenchel dual,

$$F^*(x) = \int_{\mathbb{R}^d} \phi(x + z) \, dQ(z). \tag{30.5}$$

Of course we have not shown that F is Legendre or that $\text{int}(\text{dom}(F)) = \text{int}(\text{co}(\mathcal{A}))$, both of which you will do in Exercise 30.6 under appropriate conditions on Q.

There are more reasons for making this connection than mere curiosity. The classical analysis of FTPL involves at least one 'leap of faith' in the analysis. In contrast, the analysis via the mirror descent interpretation is more mechanical. Recall that mirror descent depends on choosing a potential, an exploration distribution and an estimator. We now make the choice of these explicit. The exploration distribution is a distribution P_t on $\mathcal{A}$ such that

$$\bar{A}_t = \sum_{a \in \mathcal{A}} P_t(a)a,$$

which in our case is implicitly defined by the distribution of Z_t:

$$P_t(a) = \mathbb{P}(a(Z_t - \eta\hat{L}_{t-1}) = a \mid \mathcal{F}_{t-1}).$$

It remains to choose the loss estimator. A natural choice would be the same as Eq. (30.1), which is $\hat{Y}_{ti} = A_{ti}y_{ti}/P_{ti}$ with $P_{ti} = \mathbb{P}(A_{ti} = 1 \mid \mathcal{F}_{t-1}) = \bar{A}_{ti}$. The problem is that P_{ti} does not generally have a closed-form solution. And while P_{ti} can be estimated by sampling, the number of samples required for sufficient accuracy can be quite large. The next idea is to replace $1/P_{ti}$ in the importance-weighted estimator with a random variable with conditional expectation equal to $1/P_{ti}$. This is based on the following well-known result:

LEMMA 30.3. *Let $U \in \{1, 2, \ldots\}$ be geometrically distributed with parameter $\theta \in [0, 1]$ so that $\mathbb{P}(U = j) = (1 - \theta)^{j-1}\theta$. Then $\mathbb{E}[U] = 1/\theta$.*

You can sample from a geometric distribution with parameter θ by counting the number of flips of a biased coin with bias θ until the first head. That is, if $(X_t)_{t=1}^{\infty}$ is an independent sequence of Bernoulli random variables with bias θ, then $U = \min\{t \geq 1 : X_t = 1\}$ is geometrically distributed with parameter θ.

Define a sequence of d-dimensional random vectors $K_1, \ldots, K_n$, where $(K_{ti})_{i=1}^d$ is a sequence of geometric random variables that are conditionally independent given $\mathcal{F}_t$ so that the conditional law of K_{ti} given $\mathcal{F}_t$ is Geometric(P_{ti}) and where we now redefine $\mathcal{F}_t = \sigma(Z_1, K_1, \ldots, Z_{t-1}, K_{t-1}, Z_t)$. The estimator of y_{ti} can now be defined by

$$\hat{Y}_{ti} = \min(\beta, K_{ti})A_{ti}y_{ti},$$

1: **Input** $\mathcal{A}, n, \eta, \beta, Q$
2: $\hat{L}_0 = \mathbf{0} \in \mathbb{R}^d$
3: **for** $t = 1, \ldots, n$ **do**
4:     Sample $Z_t \sim Q$
5:     Compute $A_t = \operatorname{argmax}_{a \in \mathcal{A}} \langle a, Z_t - \eta \hat{L}_{t-1} \rangle$
6:     Observe $A_{t1} y_{t1}, \ldots, A_{td} y_{td}$
7:     For each $i \in [d]$ sample $K_{ti} \sim \text{Geometric}(P_{ti})$
8:     For each $i \in [d]$ compute $\hat{Y}_{ti} = \min(\beta, K_{ti}) A_{ti} y_{ti}$
9:     $\hat{L}_t = \hat{L}_{t-1} + \hat{Y}_t$
10: **end for**

Algorithm 19: Follow-the-perturbed-leader for semi-bandits.

where β is a positive integer to be chosen subsequently. Note that

$$\mathbb{E}[K_{ti} A_{ti} y_{ti} \mid \mathcal{F}_{t-1}] = y_{ti}.$$

The truncation parameter β is needed to ensure that $\hat{Y}_{ti}$ is never too large. We have now provided all the pieces to define a version of FTPL that is a special case of mirror descent. The algorithm is summarised in Algorithm 19.

THEOREM 30.4. *Consider the setting of Section 30.1. Let Q have density with respect to the Lebesgue measure of $q(z) = 2^{-d} \exp(-\|z\|_1)$, and choose the parameters η, β as follows:*

$$\eta = \sqrt{\frac{2(1 + \log(d))}{(1 + e^2) dnm}}, \qquad\qquad \beta = \left\lceil \frac{1}{\eta m} \right\rceil.$$

Then the algorithm Algorithm 19 is well defined and provided that $\eta m \geq 1$ its regret is bounded by $R_n \leq m \sqrt{2(1 + e^2) n d(1 + \log(d))}$.

Proof First, note that A_t is almost surely uniquely defined and so is $\bar{A}_t = \mathbb{E}[A_t \mid \mathcal{F}_{t-1}]$. Therefore, by isolating the bias in the loss estimators, and thanks to Exercise 30.6, we can apply Theorem 28.4 to get that

$$R_n(a) = \mathbb{E}\left[\sum_{t=1}^{n} \langle A_t - a, y_t \rangle\right] = \mathbb{E}\left[\sum_{t=1}^{n} \langle \bar{A}_t - a, y_t \rangle\right]$$

$$= \mathbb{E}\left[\sum_{t=1}^{n} \langle \bar{A}_t - a, \hat{Y}_t \rangle\right] + \mathbb{E}\left[\sum_{t=1}^{n} \langle \bar{A}_t - a, y_t - \hat{Y}_t \rangle\right]$$

$$\leq \frac{\operatorname{diam}_F(\mathcal{A})}{\eta} + \mathbb{E}\left[\frac{1}{\eta} \sum_{t=1}^{n} D_F(\bar{A}_t, \bar{A}_{t+1})\right] + \mathbb{E}\left[\sum_{t=1}^{n} \langle \bar{A}_t - a, y_t - \hat{Y}_t \rangle\right]. \quad (30.6)$$

Of the three terms, the diameter is most easily bounded. For $Z \sim Q$,

$$F(a) = \sup_{x \in \mathbb{R}^d} (\langle a, x \rangle - F^*(x)) = \sup_{x \in \mathbb{R}^d} (\langle a, x \rangle - \mathbb{E}[\max_{b \in \mathcal{A}} \langle b, x + Z \rangle]) \quad (30.7)$$

$$\geq -\mathbb{E}[\max_{b \in \mathcal{A}} \langle b, Z \rangle] \geq -m \mathbb{E}[\|Z\|_\infty] = -m \sum_{i=1}^{d} \frac{1}{d} \geq -m(1 + \log(d)),$$

where the first inequality follows by choosing $x = 0$ and the second follows from Hölder's inequality and that $\|a\|_1 \le m$ for any $a \in \mathcal{A}$. The last equality is non-trivial and is explained in Exercise 30.4. By the convexity of the maximum function and the fact that Z is centered, we also have from Eq. (30.7) that $F(a) \le 0$, which means that

$$\operatorname{diam}_F(\mathcal{A}) = \max_{a,b \in \mathcal{A}} F(a) - F(b) \le m(1 + \log(d)). \tag{30.8}$$

The next step is to bound the Bregman divergence induced by F. We will shortly show that the Hessian $\nabla^2 F^*(x)$ of F^* exists, so by Part (b) of Theorem 26.6 and Taylor's theorem, there exists an $\alpha \in [0, 1]$ and $\xi = -\eta \hat{L}_{t-1} - \alpha \eta \hat{Y}_t$ such that

$$D_F(\bar{A}_t, \bar{A}_{t+1}) = D_{F^*}(\nabla F(\bar{A}_{t+1}), \nabla F(\bar{A}_t))$$

$$= D_{F^*}(-\eta \hat{L}_{t-1} - \eta \hat{Y}_t, -\eta \hat{L}_{t-1}) = \frac{\eta^2}{2} \|\hat{Y}_t\|^2_{\nabla^2 F^*(\xi)}, \tag{30.9}$$

where the last equality follows from Taylor's theorem (see Theorem 26.12). To calculate the Hessian, we use a change of variable to avoid applying the gradient to the non-differentiable argmax:

$$\nabla^2 F^*(x) = \nabla(\nabla F^*(x)) = \nabla \mathbb{E}\left[a(x + Z)\right] = \nabla \int_{\mathbb{R}^d} a(x + z)q(z)dz$$

$$= \nabla \int_{\mathbb{R}^d} a(u)q(u - x)du = \int_{\mathbb{R}^d} a(u)(\nabla q(u - x))^\top du$$

$$= \int_{\mathbb{R}^d} a(u) \operatorname{sign}(u - x)^\top q(u - x)du = \int_{\mathbb{R}^d} a(x + z) \operatorname{sign}(z)^\top q(z)dz.$$

Using the definition of ξ and the fact that $a(x)$ is non-negative,

$$\nabla^2 F^*(\xi)_{ij} = \int_{\mathbb{R}^d} a(\xi + z)_i \operatorname{sign}(z)_j q(z)dz \tag{30.10}$$

$$\le \int_{\mathbb{R}^d} a(\xi + z)_i q(z)dz$$

$$= \int_{\mathbb{R}^d} a(z - \eta \hat{L}_{t-1} - \alpha \eta \hat{Y}_t)_i q(z)dz$$

$$= \int_{\mathbb{R}^d} a(u - \eta \hat{L}_{t-1})_i q(u + \alpha \eta \hat{Y}_t)du$$

$$\le \exp\left(\|\alpha \eta \hat{Y}_t\|_1\right) \int_{\mathbb{R}^d} a(u - \eta \hat{L}_{t-1})_i q(u)du$$

$$\le e^2 P_{ti}, \tag{30.11}$$

where the last inequality follows since $\alpha \in [0, 1]$ and $\hat{Y}_{ti} \le \beta = \lceil 1/(m\eta) \rceil$, $\eta m \ge 1$ and $\hat{Y}_t$ has at most m non-zero entries. Continuing on from Eq. (30.9), we have

$$\frac{\eta^2}{2} \|\hat{Y}_t\|^2_{\nabla^2 F^*(\xi)} \le \frac{e^2 \eta^2}{2} \sum_{i=1}^{d} P_{ti} \hat{Y}_{ti} \sum_{j=1}^{d} \hat{Y}_{tj} \le \frac{e^2 \eta^2}{2} \sum_{i=1}^{d} \sum_{j=1}^{d} P_{ti} K_{ti} A_{ti} K_{tj} A_{tj}.$$

Chaining together the parts and taking the expectation shows that

$$\mathbb{E}[D_F(\bar{A}_t, \bar{A}_{t+1})] \le \frac{e^2\eta}{2}\mathbb{E}\left[\sum_{i=1}^{d}\sum_{j=1}^{d} P_{ti}K_{ti}A_{ti}K_{tj}A_{tj}\right]$$

$$= \frac{e^2\eta^2}{2}\mathbb{E}\left[\sum_{i=1}^{d}\sum_{j=1}^{d}\frac{A_{ti}A_{tj}}{P_{tj}}\right] \le \frac{e^2 m d\eta^2}{2}.$$

The last step is to control the bias term. For this, first note that since $A_{ti}y_{ti} \in \{0, 1\}$,

$$\mathbb{E}[\hat{Y}_{ti}\,|\,\mathcal{F}_t] = \mathbb{E}[\min(\beta, K_{ti})A_{ti}y_{ti}\,|\,\mathcal{F}_t] = A_{ti}y_{ti}\mathbb{E}[\min(\beta, K_{ti})\,|\,\mathcal{F}_t]$$

$$= y_{ti}\frac{A_{ti}}{P_{ti}}(1 - (1 - P_{ti})^\beta),$$

where the last equality follows from the definition of K_{ti} using a direct calculation. Thus, $\mathbb{E}[\hat{Y}_{ti}\,|\,\mathcal{F}_{t-1}] = (1 - (1 - P_{ti})^\beta)y_{ti}$ and

$$\mathbb{E}\left[\sum_{t=1}^{n}\langle \bar{A}_t - a, y_t - \hat{Y}_t\rangle\right] \le \mathbb{E}\left[\sum_{t=1}^{n}\langle \bar{A}_t, y_t - \hat{Y}_t\rangle\right]$$

$$= \mathbb{E}\left[\sum_{t=1}^{n}\sum_{i=1}^{d} y_{ti}P_{ti}(1 - P_{ti})^\beta\right] \le \frac{dn}{2\beta} = \frac{dnm\eta}{2},$$

where the last inequality follows from using that for $x \in [0, 1]$, $s > 0$, $x(1-x)^s \le xe^{-sx} \le 1/s$. Putting together all the pieces into Eq. (30.6) leads to

$$R_n \le \frac{m(1 + \log(d))}{\eta} + \frac{e^2 dnm\eta}{2} + \frac{dnm\eta}{2} \le m\sqrt{2(1 + e^2)nd(1 + \log(d))}. \qquad \square$$

30.6 Notes

1 For a long time, it was speculated that the dependence of the regret on $m^{3/2}$ in Theorem 30.1 (bandit feedback) might be improvable to m. Very recently, however, the lower bound was increased to show the upper bound is tight [Cohen et al., 2017]. For semi-bandits the worst-case lower bound is $\Omega(\sqrt{dnm})$ (Exercise 30.8), which holds for large enough n and $m \le d/2$ and is matched up to constant factors by online stochastic mirror descent with a different potential (Exercise 30.7).

2 The implementation of FTPL shown in Algorithm 19 needs to sample K_{ti} for each i with $A_{ti} = 1$. The conditional expected running time for this is A_{ti}/P_{ti}, which has expectation 1. It follows that the expected running time over the whole n rounds is $O(nd)$ calls to the oracle linear optimisation algorithm. It can happen that the algorithm is unlucky and chooses $A_{ti} = 1$ for some i with P_{ti} quite small and then sampling K_{ti} could be time-consuming. Note, however, that only $\min(K_{ti}, \beta)$ is actually used by the algorithm, and hence the sampling procedure can be truncated at β. This minor modification ensures the algorithm needs at most $O(\beta nd)$ calls to the oracle in the worst case.

3 While FTPL is excellent in the face of semi-bandit information, we do not know of a general result for the bandit model. The main challenge is controlling the variance of the least squares estimator without explicitly inducing exploration using a sophisticated exploration distribution like what is provided by Kiefer–Wolfowitz.

4 Combinatorial bandits can also be studied in a stochastic setting. There are several ways to do this. The first mirrors our assumptions for stochastic linear bandits in Chapter 19, where the loss (more commonly reward) is defined by

$$X_t = \langle A_t, \theta \rangle + \eta_t, \tag{30.12}$$

where $\theta \in \mathbb{R}^d$ is fixed and unknown and η_t is the noise on which statistical assumptions are made (for example, conditionally 1-subgaussian). There are at least two alternatives. Suppose that $\theta_1, \ldots, \theta_n$ are sampled independently from some multivariate distribution, and define the reward by

$$X_t = \langle A_t, \theta_t \rangle. \tag{30.13}$$

This latter version has 'parameter noise' (cf. Chapter 29) and is more closely related to the adversarial set-up studied in this chapter. Finally, one can assume additionally that the distribution of θ_t is a product distribution so that $(\theta_{1i})_{i=1}^d$ are also independent.

5 For some action sets, the off-diagonal elements of the Hessian in Eq. (30.10) are negative, which improves the dependence on m to $\sqrt{m}$. An example where this occurs is when $\mathcal{A} = \{a \in \{0,1\}^d : \|a\|_1 = m\}$. Let $i \neq j$, and suppose that $z, \xi \in \mathbb{R}^d$ and $z_j \geq 0$. Then you can check that $a(z + \xi)_i \leq a(z - 2z_j e_j + \xi)_i$, and so

$$\nabla^2 F^*(\xi)_{ij} = \int_{\mathbb{R}^d} a(z + \xi)_i \operatorname{sign}(z)_j q(z) dz$$
$$= \int_{\mathbb{R}^{d-1}} \int_0^\infty (a(z + \xi)_i - a(z - 2z_j e_j + \xi)_i) q(z) dz_j dz_{-j}$$
$$\leq 0,$$

where dz_{-j} is shorthand for $dz_1 dz_2, \ldots dz_{j-1} dz_{j+1}, \ldots, dz_d$. You are asked to complete all the details in Exercise 30.9. This result unfortunately does not hold for every action set (Exercise 30.10).

6 In order to implement mirror descent or follow-the-regularised-leader with bandit or semi-bandit information, one needs to solve two optimisation problems: (a) a convex optimisation problem of the form $\operatorname{argmin}_{a \in \operatorname{co}(\mathcal{A})} F(a)$ for some convex F and (b) a linear optimisation problem to find a distribution P over $\mathcal{A}$ with mean $\bar{a}$ where $\bar{a} \in \operatorname{co}(\mathcal{A})$. More or less sufficient is an efficient membership oracle for $\operatorname{co}(\mathcal{A})$ and evaluation oracle for F [Grötschel et al., 2012, Lee et al., 2018]. Also necessary for bandits is to identify an exploration distribution, which we discuss in the notes and bibliographic remarks of Chapter 27. This is not required for semi-bandits, however, at least with the negentropy potential used in by Algorithm 18.

30.7 Bibliographic Remarks

The online combinatorial bandit was introduced by Cesa-Bianchi and Lugosi [2012], where you will also find the most comprehensive list of known applications for which efficient algorithms exist. The regret bound for Exp3 given in Theorem 30.1 for the bandit case is due to Bubeck and Cesa-Bianchi [2012] (with a slightly different argument). While computational issues remain in the bandit problem, there has been some progress in certain settings. Combes et al. [2015b] propose playing mirror descent on the convex hull of the action set without fancy exploration, which leads to near-optimal bounds for well-behaved action sets. One could also use continuous exponential weights from Chapter 27. These methods lead to computationally efficient algorithms for some action sets, but this must be checked on a case-by-case basis. The full information setting has been studied quite extensively [Koolen et al., 2010, and references from/to]. FTPL was first proposed (in the full information context) by Hannan [1957], rediscovered by Kalai and Vempala [2002, 2005] and generalised by Hutter and Poland [2005]. Poland [2005] and Kujala and Elomaa [2005] independently applied FTPL to finite-armed adversarial bandits and showed near-optimal regret for this case. Poland [2005] also proposed to use Monte Carlo simulation to estimate the probability of choosing each arm needed in the construction of reward estimates. Kujala and Elomaa [2007] extended the result to non-oblivious adversaries. For combinatorial settings, suboptimal rates have been shown by Awerbuch and Kleinberg [2004], McMahan and Blum [2004] and Dani and Hayes [2006]. Semi-bandits seem to have been introduced in the context of shortest-path problems by György et al. [2007]. The general set-up and algorithmic analysis of FTPL presented follows the work by Neu [2015a], who also introduced the idea to estimate the inverse probabilities via a geometric random variable. Our analysis based on mirror descent is novel. The analysis follows ideas of Abernethy et al. [2014], who present the core ideas in the prediction with expert advice setting, Cohen and Hazan [2015], who consider the combinatorial full information case, and Abernethy et al. [2015], who study finite-armed bandits. The literature on stochastic combinatorial semibandits is also quite large with algorithms and analysis in the frequentist [Gai et al., 2012, Combes et al., 2015b, Kveton et al., 2015b] and Bayesian settings [Wen et al., 2015, Russo and Van Roy, 2016]. These works focus on the case where the reward is given by Eq. (30.13) and the components of θ_t are independent. When the reward is given by Eq. (30.12), one can use the tools for stochastic linear bandits developed in Part V. Some work also pushes beyond the assumption that the rewards are linear [Chen et al., 2013, Lin et al., 2015, Chen et al., 2016a,b, Wang and Chen, 2018]. The focus in these works is on understanding what are the minimal structural assumptions on the reward function and action spaces for which learning in combinatorially large action spaces is still feasible statistically/computationally. Last of all, we mentioned that travelling salesman is computationally hard to approximate, which you can read about in the paper by Papadimitriou and Vempala [2006], and references there-in.

30.8 Exercises

30.1 (MIRROR DESCENT FOR COMBINATORIAL BANDITS) Prove Theorem 30:1.

HINT For the second inequality, you may find it useful to know that for $0 \leq m \leq n$, defining $\Phi_m(n) = \sum_{i=0}^{m} \binom{n}{i}$, it holds that $(m/n)^m \Phi_m(n) \leq e^m$.

30.2 (EFFICIENT COMPUTATION ON m-SETS) Provide an efficient implementation of Algorithm 18 for the m-set: $\mathcal{A} = \{a \in \{0, 1\}^d : \|a\|_1 = m\}$.

30.3 (EFFICIENT COMPUTATION ON SHORTEST-PATH PROBLEMS) Playing mirror descent on $\mathrm{co}(\mathcal{A})$ leads to a good bound for bandit or semi-bandit problems, but sometimes playing Exp3 over $\mathcal{A}$ is more efficient, even when $\mathcal{A}$ is exponentially large. Design and analyse a variant of Exp3 for the online shortest-path problem with semi-bandit feedback described in Section 30.2. Your challenge is to ensure the following:

(a) a regret of $R_n = O(\sqrt{n})$, with dependence on d and m omitted; and

(b) polynomial computation complexity in n and d.

HINT   This is not the easiest exercise. Start by reading the paper by Takimoto and Warmuth [2003], then follow up with that of György et al. [2007].

30.4 (EXPECTED SUPREMUM NORM OF LAPLACE) Let Z be sampled from measure on $\mathbb{R}^d$ with density $f(z) = 2^{-d} \exp(-\|z\|_1)$. The purpose of this exercise is to show that

$$\mathbb{E}[\|Z\|_\infty] = \sum_{i=1}^d \frac{1}{i}. \tag{30.14}$$

(a) Let $X_1, \ldots, X_d$ be independent standard exponentials. Show that $\|Z\|_\infty$ and $\max\{X_1, \ldots, X_d\}$ have the same law.

(b) Let $M_j = \max_{i \leq j} X_i$. Prove for $j \geq 2$ that

$$\mathbb{E}[M_j] = \mathbb{E}[M_{j-1}] + \mathbb{E}[\exp(-M_{j-1})].$$

(c) Prove by induction or otherwise that for all $a, j \in \{1, 2, \ldots\}$,

$$\mathbb{E}[\exp(-aM_j)] = \frac{a!}{\prod_{b=1}^a (j + b)}.$$

(d) Prove the claim in Eq. (30.14).

30.5 (GRADIENT OF EXPECTED SUPPORT FUNCTION) Let $\mathcal{A} \subset \mathbb{R}^d$ be a compact set and $\phi(x) = \max_{a \in \mathcal{A}} \langle a, x \rangle$ its support function. Let Q be a measure on $\mathbb{R}^d$ that is absolutely continuous with respect to the Lebesgue measure, and let $Z \sim Q$. Show that

$$\nabla \mathbb{E}[\phi(x + Z)] = \mathbb{E}\left[\operatorname{argmax}_{a \in \mathcal{A}} \langle a, x + Z \rangle\right].$$

HINT   Recall that the support function ϕ of a non-empty compact set is a proper convex function. Then, note that for any proper convex function $f : \mathbb{R}^d \to \mathbb{R} \cup \{\infty\}$, the set $\mathbb{R}^d \setminus \operatorname{dom}(\nabla f)$ has Lebesgue measure zero [Rockafellar, 2015, Theorem 25.5]. Next, by Danskin's theorem, the directional derivative of ϕ in the direction $v \in \mathbb{R}^d$ is given by $\nabla_v \phi(x) = \max_{a \in A(x)} \langle a, v \rangle$, where $A(x)$ is the set of maximisers of $a \mapsto \langle a, x \rangle$ over $\mathcal{A}$ [Bertsekas, 2015, Proposition 5.4.8 in Appendix B]. Finally, it is worth remembering the following result: let f be an extended real-valued function with $x \in \mathbb{R}^d$ in the interior of its domain. Then, for some $g \in \mathbb{R}^d$, $\nabla_v f(x) = \langle g, v \rangle$ holds true for all $v \in \mathbb{R}^d$ if and only if $\nabla f(x)$ exists and is equal to g.

30.6 A function $f : \mathbb{R}^d \to \bar{R}$ is **closed** if its epigraph is a closed set. Let F^* be the function defined in Section 30.5 and F be the proper convex closed function and whose Fenchel dual is F^*.

(a) Show that the function F is well defined (F^* is the Fenchel dual of a proper convex closed function, and there is only a single such function).

(b) For the remainder of the exercise, let Q be absolutely continuous with respect to the Lebesgue measure with an everywhere positive density, and let $\mathcal{A}$ be the convex hull of finitely many points in $\mathbb{R}^d$ whose span is $\mathbb{R}^d$. Show that the function F is Legendre.

(c) Show that $\operatorname{int}(\operatorname{dom}(F)) = \operatorname{int}(\operatorname{co}(\mathcal{A}))$.

HINT   For Part (a), it may be worth recalling that the **bidual** (the dual of the dual) of a proper convex closed function f is itself: $f = f^{**}(= (f^*)^*)$. Furthermore, the Fenchel dual of a proper function is always a proper convex closed function.

30.7 (MINIMAX BOUND FOR COMBINATORIAL SEMI-BANDITS) Adapt the analysis in Exercise 28.15 to derive an algorithm for combinatorial bandits with semi-bandit feedback for which the regret is $R_n \leq C\sqrt{mdn}$ for universal constant $C > 0$.

30.8 (LOWER BOUND FOR COMBINATORIAL SEMI-BANDITS) Let $m \geq 1$ and $d = km$ for some $k > 1$. Prove that for any algorithm there exists a combinatorial semi-bandit such that $R_n \geq c \min\{nm, \sqrt{mdn}\}$ where $c > 0$ is a universal constant.

HINT   The most obvious choice is $\mathcal{A} = \{a \in \{0,1\}^d : \|a\|_1 = m\}$, which are sometimes called m-sets. A lower bound does hold for this action set [Lattimore et al., 2018]. However, an easier path is to impose a little additional structure such as multi-task bandits.

30.9 (FOLLOW-THE-PERTURBED-LEADER FOR m-SETS) Use the ideas in Note 5 to prove that FTPL has $R_n = \tilde{O}(\sqrt{mnd})$ regret when $\mathcal{A} = \{a \in \{0,1\}^d : \|a\|_1 = m\}$.

HINT   After proving the off-diagonal elements of the Hessian are negative, you will also need to tune the learning rate. We do not know of a source for this result, but the full information case was studied by Cohen and Hazan [2015].

30.10 Construct an action set and $i \neq j$ and $z \in \mathbb{R}^d$ with $z_j > 0$ such that $a(z)_i \geq a(z - 2z_j e_j)_i$.

HINT   Consider the shortest-path problem defined by the graph below.

Choose losses for the edges z, and think about what happens when the loss associated with edge j decreases.

31 Non-stationary Bandits

The competitor class used in the standard definition of the regret is not appropriate when the underlying environment is changing. In this chapter we increase the power of the competitor class to 'track' changing environments and derive algorithms for which the regret relative to this enlarged class is not too large. While the results are specified to bandits with finitely many arms (both stochastic and adversarial), many of the ideas generalise to other models such as linear bandits. This chapter also illustrates the flexibility of the tools presented in the earlier chapters, which are applied here almost without modification. We hope (and expect) that this will also be true for other models you might study.

Figure 31.1 This bandit is definitely not stationary!

31.1 Adversarial Bandits

In contrast to stochastic bandits, the adversarial bandit model presented in Chapter 11 does not prevent the environment from changing over time. The problem is that bounds on the regret can become vacuous when the losses appear non-stationary. To illustrate an extreme situation, suppose you face a two-armed adversarial bandit with losses $y_{t1} = \mathbb{I}\{t \leq n/2\}$ and $y_{t2} = \mathbb{I}\{t > n/2\}$. If we run Exp3 on this problem, then Theorem 11.2 guarantees that

$$R_n = \mathbb{E}\left[\sum_{t=1}^{n} y_{tA_t}\right] - \min_{i \in \{1,2\}} \sum_{t=1}^{n} y_{ti} \leq \sqrt{2nk \log(k)}.$$

Since $\min_{i \in \{1,2\}} \sum_{t=1}^{n} y_{ti} = n/2$, by rearranging we see that

$$\mathbb{E}\left[\sum_{t=1}^{n} y_{tA_t}\right] \leq \frac{n}{2} + \sqrt{2nk \log(k)}.$$

To put this in perspective, a policy that plays each arm with probability half in every round would have $\mathbb{E}[\sum_{t=1}^{n} y_{tA_t}] = n/2$. In other words, the regret guarantee is practically meaningless.

What should we expect for this problem? The sequence of losses is so regular that we might hope that a clever policy will mostly play the second arm in the first $n/2$ rounds and then switch to playing mostly the first arm in the second $n/2$ rounds. Then the cumulative loss would be close to zero and the regret would be negative. Rather than aiming to guarantee negative regret, we redefine the regret by enlarging the competitor class as a way to ensure meaningful results. Let $\Gamma_{nm} \subset [k]^n$ be the set of action sequences of length n with at most $m - 1$ changes:

$$\Gamma_{nm} = \left\{ (a_t) \in [k]^n : \sum_{t=1}^{n-1} \mathbb{I}\{a_t \neq a_{t+1}\} \leq m - 1 \right\}.$$

Then define the **non-stationary regret** with $m - 1$ change points by

$$R_{nm} = \mathbb{E}\left[\sum_{t=1}^n y_{tA_t} \right] - \min_{a \in \Gamma_{nm}} \mathbb{E}\left[\sum_{t=1}^n y_{ta_t} \right].$$

The non-stationary regret is sometimes called the **tracking regret** because a learner that makes it small must 'track' the best arm as it changes. Notice that R_{n1} coincides with the usual definition of the regret. Furthermore, on the sequence described at the beginning of the section, we see that

$$R_{n2} = \mathbb{E}\left[\sum_{t=1}^n y_{tA_t} \right],$$

which means a policy can only enjoy sublinear non-stationary regret if it detects the change point quickly. The obvious question is whether or not such a policy exists and how its regret depends on m.

Exp4 for Non-stationary Bandits
One idea is to use the Exp4 policy from Chapter 18 with a large set of experts, one for each $a \in \Gamma_{nm}$. Theorem 18.1 shows that Exp4 with these experts suffers regret of at most

$$R_{nm} \leq \sqrt{2nk \log |\Gamma_{nm}|}. \tag{31.1}$$

Naively bounding $\log |\Gamma_{nm}|$ (Exercise 31.1) and ignoring constant factors shows that

$$R_{nm} = O\left(\sqrt{nmk \log\left(\frac{kn}{m}\right)} \right). \tag{31.2}$$

To see that you cannot do much better than this, imagine interacting with m adversarial bandit environments sequentially, each with horizon n/m. No matter what policy you propose, there exist choices of bandits such that the expected regret suffered against each bandit is at least $\Omega(\sqrt{nk/m})$. After summing over the m instances, we see that the worst-case regret is at least

$$R_{nm} = \Omega\left(\sqrt{nmk} \right),$$

which matches the upper bound except for logarithmic factors. Notice how this lower bound applies to policies that know the location of the changes, so it is not true that things are significantly harder in the absence of this knowledge. There is one big caveat with all these calculations. The running time of a naive implementation of Exp4 is linear in the number of experts, which even for modestly sized m is very large indeed.

Online Stochastic Mirror Descent

The computational issues faced by Exp4 are most easily overcome using the tools from online convex optimisation developed in Chapter 28. The idea is to use online stochastic mirror descent and the unnormalised negentropy potential. Without further modification, this would be Exp3, which you will show does not work for non-stationary bandits (Exercise 31.3). The trick is to restrict the action set to the clipped simplex $\mathcal{A} = \mathcal{P}_{k-1} \cap [\alpha, 1]^k$ where $\alpha \in [0, 1/k]$ is a constant to be tuned subsequently. The clipping ensures the algorithm does not commit too hard to any single arm. The rationale is that a strong commitment could prevent the discovery of change points.

Let $F : [0, \infty)^k \to \mathbb{R}$ be the unnormalised negentropy potential and $P_1 \in \mathcal{A}$ be the uniform probability vector. In each round t, the learner samples $A_t \sim P_t$ and updates its sampling distribution using

$$P_{t+1} = \mathrm{argmin}_{p \in \mathcal{A}} \, \eta \langle p, \hat{Y}_t \rangle + D_F(p, P_t), \tag{31.3}$$

where $\eta > 0$ is the learning rate and $\hat{Y}_{ti} = \mathbb{I}\{A_t = i\} \, y_{ti}/P_{ti}$ is the importance-weighted estimator of the loss of action i for round t. The solution to the optimisation problem of Eq. (31.3) can be computed efficiently using the two-step process:

$$\tilde{P}_{t+1} = \mathrm{argmin}_{p \in [0, \infty)^k} \, \eta \langle p, \hat{Y}_t \rangle + D_F(p, P_t),$$

$$P_{t+1} = \mathrm{argmin}_{p \in \mathcal{A}} \, D_F(p, \tilde{P}_{t+1}).$$

The first of these sub-problems can be evaluated analytically, yielding $\tilde{P}_{t+1,i} = P_{ti} \exp(-\eta \hat{Y}_{ti})$. The second can be solved efficiently using the result in Exercise 26.12. The algorithm enjoys the following guarantee on its regret:

THEOREM 31.1. *The expected regret of the policy sampling $A_t \sim P_t$ with P_t defined in Eq. (31.3) is bounded by*

$$R_{nm} \leq \alpha n (k-1) + \frac{m \log(1/\alpha)}{\eta} + \frac{\eta n k}{2}.$$

Proof Let $a^* \in \mathrm{argmin}_{a \in \Gamma_{nm}} \sum_{t=1}^n y_{ta_t}$ be an optimal sequence of actions in hindsight constrained to Γ_{nm}. Then let $1 = t_1 < t_2 < \cdots < t_m < t_{m+1} = n+1$ so that a_t^* is constant on each interval $\{t_i, \ldots, t_{i+1} - 1\}$. We abuse notation by writing $a_i^* = a_{t_i}^*$. Then the regret decomposes into

$$R_{nm} = \mathbb{E}\left[\sum_{t=1}^n (y_{tA_t} - y_{ta_t^*}) \right] = \mathbb{E}\left[\sum_{i=1}^m \sum_{t=t_i}^{t_{i+1}-1} (y_{tA_t} - y_{ta_i^*}) \right]$$

$$= \sum_{i=1}^m \mathbb{E}\left[\mathbb{E}\left[\sum_{t=t_i}^{t_{i+1}-1} (y_{tA_t} - y_{ta_i^*}) \,\bigg|\, P_{t_i} \right] \right].$$

The next step is to apply Eq. (28.11) and the solution to Exercise 28.10 to bound the inner expectation, giving

$$\mathbb{E}\left[\sum_{t=t_i}^{t_{i+1}-1} (y_{tA_t} - y_{ta_i^*}) \,\bigg|\, P_{t_i} \right] = \mathbb{E}\left[\sum_{t=t_i}^{t_{i+1}-1} \langle P_t - e_{a_i^*}, y_t \rangle \,\bigg|\, P_{t_i} \right]$$

$$\leq \alpha(t_{i+1} - t_i)(k-1) + \mathbb{E}\left[\max_{p \in \mathcal{A}} \sum_{t=t_i}^{t_{i+1}-1} \langle P_t - p, y_t \rangle \,\bigg|\, P_{t_i} \right]$$

$$= \alpha(t_{i+1} - t_i)(k - 1) + \mathbb{E}\left[\max_{p \in \mathcal{A}} \sum_{t=t_i}^{t_{i+1}-1} \langle P_t - p, \hat{Y}_t \rangle \,\middle|\, P_{t_i}\right]$$

$$\leq \alpha(t_{i+1} - t_i)(k - 1) + \mathbb{E}\left[\max_{p \in \mathcal{A}} \frac{D(p, P_{t_i})}{\eta} + \frac{\eta k(t_{i+1} - t_i)}{2} \,\middle|\, P_{t_i}\right].$$

By assumption, $P_{t_i} \in \mathcal{A}$ and so $P_{t_{ij}} \geq \alpha$ for all j and $D(p, P_{t_i}) \leq \log(1/\alpha)$. Combining this observation with the previous two displays shows that

$$R_{nm} \leq n\alpha(k - 1) + \frac{m \log(1/\alpha)}{\eta} + \frac{\eta n k}{2}. \qquad \square$$

The learning rate and clipping parameters are approximately optimised by

$$\eta = \sqrt{2m \log(1/\alpha)/(nk)} \qquad \text{and} \qquad \alpha = \sqrt{m/(nk)},$$

which leads to a regret of $R_{nm} \leq \sqrt{mnk \log(nk/m)} + \sqrt{mnk}$. In typical applications, the value of m is not known. In this case one can choose $\eta = \sqrt{\log(1/\alpha)/nk}$ and $\alpha = \sqrt{1/nk}$, and the regret increases by a factor of $O(\sqrt{m})$.

31.2 Stochastic Bandits

To keep things simple, we will assume the rewards are Gaussian and that for each arm i there is a function $\mu_i : [n] \to \mathbb{R}$, and the reward is

$$X_t = \mu_{A_t}(t) + \eta_t,$$

where $(\eta_t)_{t=1}^n$ is a sequence of independent standard Gaussian random variables. The optimal arm in round t has mean $\mu^*(t) = \max_{i \in [k]} \mu_i(t)$ and the regret is

$$R_n(\mu) = \sum_{t=1}^n \mu^*(t) - \mathbb{E}\left[\sum_{t=1}^n \mu_{A_t}(t)\right].$$

The amount of non-stationarity is modelled by placing restrictions on the functions $\mu_i : [n] \to \mathbb{R}$. To be consistent with the previous section, we assume the mean vector changes at most $m - 1$ times, which amounts to saying that

$$\sum_{t=1}^{n-1} \max_{i \in [k]} \mathbb{I}\{\mu_i(t) \neq \mu_i(t + 1)\} \leq m - 1.$$

If the locations of the change points were known then, thanks to the concavity of log, running a new copy of UCB on each interval would lead to a bound of

$$R_n(\mu) = O\left(m + \frac{mk}{\Delta_{\min}} \log\left(\frac{n}{m}\right)\right), \qquad (31.4)$$

where $\Delta_{\min}$ is the smallest suboptimality gap over all m blocks and $n \geq m$. This is a non-vacuous bound for n large. Inspired by the results of the last section that showed that the bound achieved by an omniscient policy that knows when the changes occur can be achieved by a policy that does not, one then wonders whether the same holds concerning the bound in Eq. (31.4). As it turns out, the answer in this case is no.

THEOREM 31.2. *Let $k = 2$, and fix $\Delta \in (0, 1)$ and a policy π. Let μ be so that $\mu_i(t) = \mu_i$ is constant for both arms and $\Delta = \mu_1 - \mu_2 > 0$. If the expected regret $R_n(\mu)$ of policy π on bandit μ satisfies $R_n(\mu) = o(n)$, then for all sufficiently large n, there exists a non-stationary bandit μ' with at most two change points and $\min_{t \in [n]} |\mu_1'(t) - \mu_2'(t)| \geq \Delta$ such that $R_n(\mu') \geq n/(22R_n(\mu))$.*

The theorem implies that if a policy enjoys $R_n(\mu) = o(n^{1/2})$ for any non-trivial (stationary) bandit, then its minimax regret is at least $\omega(n^{1/2})$ on some non-stationary bandit. In particular, if $R_n(\mu) = O(\log(n))$, then its worst-case regret against non-stationary bandits with at most two changes is at least $\Omega(n/\log(n))$. This dashes our hopes for a policy that outperforms Exp4 in a stochastic setting with switches, even in an asymptotic sense. The reason for the negative result is that any algorithm anticipating the possibility of an abrupt change must frequently explore all suboptimal arms to check that no change has occurred.

There are algorithms designed for non-stationary bandits in the stochastic setting with abrupt change points as described above. Those that come with theoretical guarantees are based on forgetting or discounting data so that decisions of the algorithm depend almost entirely on recent data. In the notes, we discuss these approaches along with alternative models for non-stationarity. For now, the advantage of the stochastic setting seems to be that in the stochastic setting there are algorithms that do not need to know the number of changes, while, as noted beforehand, such algorithms are not yet known (or maybe not possible) in the nonstochastic setting.

Proof of Theorem 31.2 Let $(S_j)_{j=1}^L$ be a uniform partition of $[n]$ into successive intervals. Let $\mathbb{P}$ and $\mathbb{E}[\cdot]$ denote the probabilities and expectations with respect to the bandit determined by μ and $\mathbb{P}'$ with respect to alternative non-stationary bandit μ' to be defined shortly. By the pigeonhole principle, there exists a $j \in [L]$ such that

$$\mathbb{E}\left[\sum_{t \in S_j} \mathbb{I}\{A_t = 2\}\right] \leq \frac{\mathbb{E}[T_2(n)]}{L}. \tag{31.5}$$

Define an alternative non-stationary bandit with $\mu'(t) = \mu$ except for $t \in S_j$ when we let $\mu_2'(t) = \mu_2 + \varepsilon$, where $\varepsilon = \sqrt{2L/\mathbb{E}[T_2(n)]}$ while $\mu_1'(t) = \mu_1$. Then, by Theorem 14.2 and Lemma 15.1,

$$\mathbb{P}\left(\sum_{t \in S_j} \mathbb{I}\{A_t = 2\} \geq \frac{|S_j|}{2}\right) + \mathbb{P}'\left(\sum_{t \in S_j} \mathbb{I}\{A_t = 2\} < \frac{|S_j|}{2}\right) \geq \frac{1}{2}\exp\left(-D(\mathbb{P}, \mathbb{P}')\right)$$

$$\geq \frac{1}{2}\exp\left(-\frac{\mathbb{E}[T_2(n)]\varepsilon^2}{2L}\right) = \frac{1}{2e}.$$

By Markov's inequality and Eq. (31.5),

$$\mathbb{P}\left(\sum_{t \in S_j} \mathbb{I}\{A_t = 2\} \geq \frac{|S_j|}{2}\right) \leq \frac{2}{|S_j|}\mathbb{E}\left[\sum_{t \in S_j} \mathbb{I}\{A_t = 2\}\right] \leq \frac{2\mathbb{E}[T_2(n)]}{L|S_j|} \leq \frac{1}{\Delta^2|S_j|},$$

where the last inequality follows by choosing $L = \lceil 2\Delta^2 \mathbb{E}[T_2(n)] \rceil$ and assuming n is large enough that $L \leq n$. Then $\varepsilon \geq 2\Delta$ so that μ' satisfies the assumptions of the theorem. Therefore,

$$R_n(\mu') \geq \left(\frac{1}{2e} - \frac{1}{\Delta^2|S_j|}\right) \frac{\varepsilon|S_j|}{4} \geq \left(\frac{1}{2e} - \frac{1}{\Delta^2|S_j|}\right) \frac{|S_j|\Delta}{2} \geq \left\lfloor \frac{n}{L} \right\rfloor \frac{1}{4e\Delta} - \frac{1}{2\Delta}.$$

Then, using $R_n(\mu) = \Delta\mathbb{E}[T_2(n)]$, the definition of L and the assumption that $R_n(\mu) = o(n)$, it follows that for sufficiently large n,

$$R_n(\mu') \geq \frac{n}{22R_n(\mu)}.$$

where the constant is chosen so that $1/22 < 1/(8e)$.   □

31.3   Notes

1 Environments that appear non-stationary can often be made stationary by adding context. For example, when bandit algorithms are used for on-line advertising, gym membership advertisements are received more positively in January than July. A bandit algorithm that is oblivious to the time of year will perceive this environment as non-stationary. You could tackle this problem by using one of the algorithms in this chapter. Or you could use a contextual bandit algorithm and include the time of year in the context. The reader is encouraged to consider whether or not adding contextual information might be preferable to using an algorithm designed for non-stationary bandits.

2 The negative results for stochastic non-stationary bandits do not mean that trying to improve on the adversarial bandit algorithms is completely hopeless. First of all, the adversarial bandit algorithms are not well suited for exploiting distributional assumptions on the noise, which makes things irritating when the losses/rewards are Gaussian (which are unbounded) or Bernoulli (which have small variance near the boundaries). There have been several algorithms designed specifically for stochastic non-stationary bandits. When the reward distributions are permitted to change abruptly, as in the last section, then the two main algorithms are based on the idea of 'forgetting' rewards observed in the distant past. One way to do this is with **discounting**. Let $\gamma \in (0,1)$ be the **discount factor**, and define

$$\hat{\mu}_i^\gamma(t) = \sum_{s=1}^t \gamma^{t-s}\mathbb{I}\{A_s = i\}X_s \qquad\qquad T_i^\gamma(t) = \sum_{s=1}^t \gamma^{t-s}\mathbb{I}\{A_s = i\}.$$

Then, for appropriately tuned constant α, the discounted UCB policy chooses each arm once and subsequently

$$A_t = \operatorname{argmax}_{i \in [k]} \left(\hat{\mu}_i^\gamma(t-1) + \sqrt{\frac{\alpha}{T_i^\gamma(t-1)}\log\left(\sum_{i=1}^k T_i^\gamma(t-1)\right)} \right).$$

The idea is to 'discount' rewards that occurred far in the past, which makes the algorithm most influenced by recent events. A similar algorithm called sliding-window UCB uses a similar approach, but rather than discounting past rewards with a geometric discount function, it simply discards them altogether. Let $\tau \in \mathbb{N}^+$ be a constant, and define

$$\hat{\mu}_i^\tau(t) = \sum_{s=t-\tau+1}^t \mathbb{I}\{A_s = i\}X_s \qquad\qquad T_i^\tau(t) = \sum_{s=t-\tau+1}^t \mathbb{I}\{A_s = i\}.$$

Then sliding-window UCB chooses

$$A_t = \operatorname{argmax}_{i \in [k]} \left(\hat{\mu}_i^\tau(t-1) + \sqrt{\frac{\alpha}{T_i^\tau(t-1)}\log(t \wedge \tau)} \right).$$

Regrettably, however, these algorithms suffer from a tuning problem. There is no choice of γ and τ for which the algorithms enjoy $R_n = O(\sqrt{n \log(n)})$ in a minimax sense. On the positive side, there is empirical evidence to support the use of these algorithms when the stochastic assumption holds. Recently, more complicated algorithms were proposed that can adapt to the number of switches in a stochastic environment and match the regret of an optimally tuned adversarial algorithm [Auer et al., 2019, Chen et al., 2019].

3 An alternative way to model non-stationarity in stochastic bandits is to assume the mean pay-offs of the arms are slowly drifting. One way to do this is to assume that $\mu_i(t)$ follows a reflected Brownian motion in some interval. It is not hard to see that the regret is necessary linear in this case because the best arm changes in any round with constant probability. The objective in this case is to understand the magnitude of the linear regret in terms of the size of the interval or volatility of the Brownian motion.

4 Yet another idea is to allow the means to change in an arbitrary way, but restrict the amount of total variation. Let $\mu_t = (\mu_1(t), \ldots, \mu_k(t))$ and

$$V_n = \sum_{t=1}^{n-1} \|\mu_t - \mu_{t+1}\|_\infty$$

be the cumulative change in mean rewards measured in terms of the supremum norm. Then, for each $V \in [1/k, n/k]$, there exists a policy such that for all bandits with $V_n \leq V$, it holds that

$$R_n \leq C(V k \log(k))^{1/3} n^{2/3}. \tag{31.6}$$

This bound is nearly tight in a minimax sense. The lower bound is obtained by partitioning $[n]$ into m parts, where in each part all arms have equal means except for the optimal arm, which is better by $\Delta = c\sqrt{mk/n}$ for universal constant $c \in \mathbb{R}$. The usual argument shows that the total regret is $\Omega(\sqrt{kmn})$, while $V_n \leq 2cm^{3/2}\sqrt{k/n}$. Tuning m so that $V_n \leq V$ completes the proof. Recent work shows that it is possible to achieve Eq. (31.6) without knowing V. That is, there exists an algorithm that is able to adapt to V. In fact, the algorithm mentioned in Note 2, which is able to adapt to the number of switches, can accomplish this.

31.4 Bibliographic Remarks

Non-stationary bandits have quite a long history. The celebrated Gittins index is based on a model where each arm is associated with a Markov chain that evolves when played, the reward depends on the state, and the state of the chosen Markov chain is observed after it evolves [Gittins, 1979, Gittins et al., 2011]. The classical approaches, as discussed in Chapter 35, address this problem in the Bayesian framework, and the objective is primarily to design efficient algorithms rather than understanding the frequentist regret. Even more related is the **restless bandit**, which is the same as Gittins's set-up except the Markov chain for every arm evolves in every round, while the learner still only observes the state and reward for the action they chose. As a result, the learner needs to reason about the evolution of all the Markov chains, which makes this problem rather challenging. Restless bandits were introduced by Whittle [1988] in the Bayesian framework, where most of the results are not especially positive. There has been some interest in a frequentist analysis, but the challenging nature of the problem makes it difficult to design efficient algorithms with meaningful regret guarantees [Ortner et al., 2012]. Certainly there is potential for more work in this area.

The ideas in Section 31.1 are mostly generalisations of algorithms designed for the full information setting, notably the fixed share algorithm [Herbster and Warmuth, 1998]. The first algorithm designed for the adversarial non-stationary bandit is Exp3.S by Auer et al. [2002b]. This algorithm can be interpreted as an efficient version of Exp4, where experts correspond to sequences of actions that have the permitted number of changes and where the initialisation is carefully chosen so that the computation needed to run Exp4 is made tractable [György et al., 2019]. See also the analysis of fixed share in the book by Cesa-Bianchi and Lugosi [2006]. The Exp3.P policy was originally developed in order to prove high-probability bounds for finite-armed adversarial bandits [Auer et al., 2002b], but Audibert and Bubeck [2010b] proved that with appropriate tuning it also enjoys the same bounds as Exp3.S. Presumably this also holds for Exp3-IX. Mirror descent has been used to prove tracking bounds in the full information setting by Herbster and Warmuth [2001]. A more recent reference is by György and Szepesvári [2016], which makes the justification for clipping explicit. The latter paper considers the linear prediction setting and provides bounds on the regret that scale with the complexity of the sequence of losses as measured by the cumulative change of consecutive loss vectors. The advantage of this is that the complexity measure can distinguish between abrupt and gradual changes. This is similar to the approach of Besbes et al. [2014]. The lower bound for stochastic non-stationary bandits is by Garivier and Moulines [2011], though our proof differs in minor ways. We mentioned that there is a line of work on stochastic non-stationary bandits where the rewards are slowly drifting. The approach based on Brownian motion is due to Slivkins and Upfal [2008], while the variant described in Note 4 is by Besbes et al. [2014], who also gave the lower bound described there. The idea of discounted UCB was introduced without analysis by Kocsis and Szepesvári [2006]. The analysis of this algorithm and also of sliding-window UCB algorithm is by Garivier and Moulines [2011]. The sliding-window algorithm has been extended to linear bandits [Cheung et al., 2019] and learning in Markov decision processes [Gajane et al., 2018]. Contextual bandits have also been studied in the non-stationary setting [Luo et al., 2018, Chen et al., 2019]. We are not aware of an algorithm for the adversarial setting with $R_n = O(\sqrt{mkn \log(n)})$ when the number of switches is unknown. Auer et al. [2018] prove a bound of $R_n = O(\sqrt{mkn} \log(n))$ in the stochastic setting when $k = 2$. The idea underlying this work has been extended to the k-armed case [Auer et al., 2019], as well as to the contextual case [Chen et al., 2019], the latter of which also shows that adapting to the total shift of distributions described in Note 4 is possible. The key novelty in these algorithms is adding explicit exploration whose durations are multi-scale, which is made possible by extra randomisation.

31.5   Exercises

31.1 (EXP4 FOR NON-STATIONARY BANDITS) Let $n, m, k \in \mathbb{N}^+$. Prove (31.2). In particular, specify first what the experts predict in each round and how Theorem 18.1 gives rise to (31.1) and how (31.2) follows from (31.1).

HINT   For the second part, you may find it useful to show the following well-known inequality: for $0 \le m \le n$, defining $\Phi_m(n) = \sum_{i=0}^{m} \binom{n}{i}$, it holds that $(m/n)^m \Phi_m(n) \le e^m$.

31.2 (LOWER BOUND FOR ADVERSARIAL NON-STATIONARY BANDITS) Let $n, m, k \in \mathbb{N}^+$ be such that $n \ge mk$. Prove that for any policy π there exists an adversarial bandit (y_{ti}) such that

$$R_{nm} \ge c\sqrt{nmk},$$

where $c > 0$ is a universal constant.

31.3 (UNSUITABILITY OF EXP3 FOR NON-STATIONARY BANDITS) Prove for all sufficiently large n that Exp3 from Chapter 11 has $R_{n2} \geq cn$ for some universal constant $c > 0$.

31.4 (EMPIRICAL COMPARISON) Let $k = 2$ and $n = 1000$, and define adversarial bandit in terms of losses with $y_{t1} = \mathbb{I}\{t < n/2\}$ and $y_{t2} = \mathbb{I}\{t \geq n/2\}$. Plot the expected regret of Exp3, Exp3-IX and the variant of online stochastic mirror descent proposed in this chapter. Experiment with a number of learning rates for each algorithm.

32 Ranking

Ranking is the process of producing an ordered shortlist of m items from a larger collection of ℓ items. These tasks come in several flavours. Sometimes the user supplies a query, and the system responds with a shortlist of items. In other applications the shortlist is produced without an explicit query. For example, a streaming service might provide a list of recommended movies when you sign in. Our focus here is on the second type of problem.

We examine a sequential version of the ranking problem where the learner selects a ranking, receives feedback about its quality and repeats the process over n rounds. The feedback will be in the form of 'clicks' from the user, which comes from the view that

Figure 32.1 A classic ranking problem: which hats to put where on the stand? Higher and towards the front attracts more attention.

ranking is a common application in on-line recommendation systems and the user selects the items they like by clicking on them. The objective of the learner is to maximise the expected number of clicks.

Ranking is a huge topic, and our approach is necessarily quite narrow. In fact there is still a long way to go before we have a genuinely practical algorithm for large-scale online ranking problems. As usual, we summarise alternative ideas in the notes.

Stochastic Ranking

A **permutation** on $[\ell]$ is an invertible function $\sigma : [\ell] \to [\ell]$. Let $\mathcal{A}$ be the set of all permutations on $[\ell]$. In each round t the learner chooses an action $A_t \in \mathcal{A}$, which should be interpreted as meaning the learner places item $A_t(k)$ in the kth position. Equivalently, $A_t^{-1}(i)$ is the position of the ith item. Since the shortlist has length m, the order of $A_t(m + 1), \ldots, A_t(\ell)$ is not important and is included only for notational convenience. After choosing their action, the learner observes $C_{ti} \in \{0, 1\}$ for each $i \in [\ell]$, where $C_{ti} = 1$ if the user clicked on the ith item. Note that the user may click on multiple items. We will assume a stochastic model where the probability that the user clicks on position k in round t only depends on A_t and is given by $v(A_t, k)$, with $v : \mathcal{A} \times [\ell] \to [0, 1]$ an unknown function. The regret over n rounds is

$$R_n = n \max_{a \in \mathcal{A}} \sum_{k=1}^{\ell} v(a, k) - \mathbb{E}\left[\sum_{t=1}^{n} \sum_{i=1}^{\ell} C_{ti}\right].$$

A naive way to minimise the regret would be to create a finite-armed bandit where each arm corresponds to a ranking of the items and then apply your favourite algorithm from Part II. The problem is that these algorithms treat the arms as independent and cannot exploit any structure in the ranking. This is almost always unacceptable because the number of ways to rank m items from a collection of size ℓ is $\ell! / (\ell - m)!$. Ranking illustrates one of the most fundamental dilemmas in machine learning: choosing a model. A rich model leads to low misspecification error, but takes longer to fit. A coarse model can suffer from large misspecification error. In the context of ranking, a model corresponds to assumptions on the function v.

32.1 Click Models

The only way to avoid the curse of dimensionality is to make assumptions. A natural way to do this for ranking is to assume that the probability of clicking on an item depends on *(a)* the underlying quality of that item and *(b)* the location of that item in the chosen ranking. A formal definition of how this is done is called a **click model**. Deciding which model to use depends on the particulars of the problem at hand, such as how the list is presented to the user and whether or not clicking on an item diverts them to a different page. This issue has been studied by the data retrieval community, and there is now a large literature devoted to the pros and cons of different choices. We limit ourselves to describing the popular choices and give pointers to the literature at the end of the chapter.

Document-Based Model

The **document-based model** is one of the simplest click models, which assumes the probability of clicking on a shortlisted item is equal to its **attractiveness**. Formally, for each item $i \in [\ell]$, let $\alpha(i) \in [0, 1]$ be the attractiveness of item i. The document-based model assumes that

$$v(a, k) = \alpha(a(k)) \mathbb{I}\{k \le m\}.$$

The unknown quantity in this model is the attractiveness function, which has just ℓ parameters.

Position-Based Model

The document-based model might occasionally be justified, but in most cases the position of an item in the ranking also affects the likelihood of a click. A natural extension that accounts for this behaviour is called the **position-based model**, which assumes that

$$v(a, k) = \alpha(a(k)) \chi(k),$$

where $\chi : [\ell] \rightarrow [0, 1]$ is a function that measures the quality of position k. Since the user cannot click on items that are not shown, we assume that $\chi(k) = 0$ for $k > m$. This model is richer than the document-based model, which is recovered by choosing $\chi(k) = \mathbb{I}\{k \leq m\}$. The number of parameters in the position-based models is $m + \ell$.

Cascade Model

The position-based model is not suitable for applications where clicking on an item takes the user to a different page. In the **cascade model**, it is assumed that the learner scans the shortlisted items in order and only clicks on the first item they find attractive. Define $\chi : \mathcal{A} \times [\ell] \rightarrow [0, 1]$ by

$$\chi(a, k) = \begin{cases} 1 & \text{if } k = 1 \\ 0 & \text{if } k > m \\ \prod_{k'=1}^{k-1} (1 - \alpha(a(k'))) & \text{otherwise,} \end{cases}$$

which is the probability that the user has not clicked on the first $k - 1$ items. Then the cascade model assumes that

$$v(a, k) = \alpha(a(k))\chi(a, k). \tag{32.1}$$

The first term in the factorisation is the attractiveness function, which measures the probability that the user is attracted to the ith item. The second term can be interpreted as the probability that the user examines that item. This interpretation is also valid in the position-based model. It is important to emphasise that $v(a, k)$ is the probability of clicking on the kth position when taking action $a \in \mathcal{A}$. This does not mean that $C_{t1}, \ldots, C_{t\ell}$ are independent. The assumptions only restricts the marginal distribution of each C_{ti}, which is sufficient for our purposes. Nevertheless, in the cascade model, it would be standard to assume that $C_{tA_t(k)} = 0$ if there exists an $k' < k$ such that $C_{tA_t(k')} = 1$, and otherwise

$$\mathbb{P}(C_{tA_t(k)} = 1 \mid A_t, C_{tA_t(1)} = 0, \ldots, C_{tA_t(k-1)} = 0) = \mathbb{I}\{k \leq m\} \alpha(A_t(k)).$$

Like the document-based model, the cascade model has ℓ parameters.

Generic Model

We now introduce a model that generalises the last three. Previous models essentially assumed that the probability of a click factorises into an attractiveness probability and an examination probability. We deviate from this norm by making assumptions directly on the function v. Given $\alpha : [\ell] \rightarrow [0, 1]$, an action a is called α-optimal if the shortlisted items are the m most attractive sorted by attractiveness: $\alpha(a(k)) = \max_{k' \geq k} \alpha(a(k'))$ for all $k \in [m]$.

ASSUMPTION 32.1. There exists an attractiveness function $\alpha : [\ell] \rightarrow [0, 1]$ such that the following four conditions are satisfied. Let $a \in \mathcal{A}$ and $i, j, k \in [\ell]$ be such that $\alpha(i) \geq \alpha(j)$, and let σ be the permutation that exchanges i and j.

(a) $v(a, k) = 0$ for all $k > m$.
(b) $\sum_{k=1}^{m} v(a^*, k) = \max_{a \in \mathcal{A}} \sum_{k=1}^{m} v(a, k)$ for all α-optimal actions a^*.

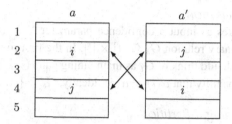

Figure 32.2   Part (c) of Assumption 32.1 says that the probability of clicking in the second position on the left list is larger than the probability of clicking on the second position on the right list by a factor of $\alpha(i)/\alpha(j)$. For the fourth position, the probability is larger for the right list than the left by the same factor.

(c) For all i and j with $\alpha(i) \geq \alpha(j)$,

$$v(a, a^{-1}(i)) \geq \frac{\alpha(i)}{\alpha(j)} v(\sigma \circ a, a^{-1}(i)),$$

where σ is the permutation on $[\ell]$ that exchanges i and j.

(d) If a is an action such that $\alpha(a(k)) = \alpha(a^*(k))$ for some α-optimal action a^*, then
$v(a, k) \geq v(a^*, k)$.

These assumptions may appear quite mysterious. At some level they are chosen to make the proof go through, while simultaneously generalising the document-based, position-based and cascade models (32.1). The choices are not entirely without basis or intuition, however. Part (a) asserts that the user does not click on items that are not placed in the shortlist. Part (b) says that α-optimal actions maximise the expected number of clicks. Note that there are multiple optimal rankings if α is not injective. Part (c) is a little more restrictive and is illustrated in Fig. 32.2. One way to justify this is to assume that $v(a, k) = \alpha(a(k))\chi(a, k)$, where $\chi(a, k)$ is viewed as the probability that the user examines position k. It seems reasonable to assume that the probability the user examines position k should only depend on the first $k - 1$ items. Hence $v(a, 2) = \alpha(i)\chi(a, 2) = \alpha(i)\chi(a', 2) = \alpha(i)/\alpha(j)v(a', 2)$. In order the make the argument for the fourth position, we need to assume that placing less attractive items in the early slots increases the probability that the user examines later positions (searching for a good result). This is true for the position-based and cascade models, but is perhaps the most easily criticised assumption. Part (d) says that the probability that a user clicks on a position with a correctly placed item is at least as large as the probability that the user clicks on that position in an optimal ranking. The justification is that the items $a(1), \ldots, a(k - 1)$ cannot be more attractive than $a^*(1), \ldots, a^*(k - 1)$, which should increase the likelihood that the user makes it the kth position.

The generic model has many parameters, but we will see that the learner does not need to learn all of them in order to suffer small regret. The advantage of this model relative to the previous ones is that it offers more flexibility, and yet it is not so flexible that learning is impossible.

32.2   Policy

We now explain the policy for learning to rank when v is unknown, but satisfies Assumption 32.1. After the description is an illustration that may prove helpful.

Step 0: Initialisation

The policy takes as input a confidence parameter $\delta \in (0, 1)$ and ℓ and m. The policy maintains a binary relation $G_t \subseteq [\ell] \times [\ell]$. In the first round $t = 1$ the relation is empty: $G_1 = \emptyset$. You should think of G_t as maintaining pairs (i, j) for which the policy has proven with high probability that $\alpha(i) < \alpha(j)$. Ideally, $G_t \subseteq \{(i, j) \in [\ell] \times [\ell] : \alpha(i) < \alpha(j)\}$.

Step 1: Defining a Partition

In each round t, the learner computes a partition of the actions based on a topological sort according to relation G_t. Given $A \subset [\ell]$, define $\min_{G_t}(A)$ to be the set of minimum elements of A according to relation G_t:

$$\min_{G_t}(A) = \{i \in A : (i, j) \notin G_t \text{ for all } j \in G_t\}.$$

Then let $\mathcal{P}_{t1}, \mathcal{P}_{t2}, \ldots$ be the partition of $[\ell]$ defined inductively by

$$\mathcal{P}_{td} = \min_{G_t}\left([\ell] \setminus \bigcup_{c=1}^{d-1} \mathcal{P}_{tc}\right).$$

Finally, let $M_t = \max\{d : \mathcal{P}_{td} \neq \emptyset\}$. The reader should check that if G_t does not have cycles, then M_t is well defined and finite and that $\mathcal{P}_{t1}, \ldots, \mathcal{P}_{tM_t}$ is indeed a partition of $[\ell]$ (Exercise 32.5). The event that G_t contains cycles is a failure event. In order for the policy to be well defined, we assume it chooses some arbitrary fixed action in this case.

Step 2: Choosing an Action

Let $\mathcal{I}_{t1}, \ldots, \mathcal{I}_{tM_t}$ be a partition of $[\ell]$ defined inductively by

$$\mathcal{I}_{td} = [|\cup_{c \leq d} \mathcal{P}_{tc}|] \setminus [|\cup_{c < d} \mathcal{P}_{tc}|].$$

Next let $\Sigma_t \subseteq A$ be the set of actions σ such that $\sigma(\mathcal{I}_{td}) = \mathcal{P}_{td}$ for all $d \in [M_t]$. The algorithm chooses A_t uniformly at random from Σ_t. Intuitively the policy first shuffles the items in $\mathcal{P}_{t1}$ and uses these as the first $|\mathcal{P}_{t1}|$ entries in the ranking. Then $\mathcal{P}_{t2}$ is shuffled, and the items are appended to the ranking. This process is repeated until the ranking is complete. For an item $i \in [\ell]$, we denote by D_{ti} the unique index d such that $i \in \mathcal{P}_{td}$.

Step 3: Updating the Relation

For any pair of items $i, j \in [\ell]$, define $S_{tij} = \sum_{s=1}^{t} U_{sij}$ and $N_{tij} = \sum_{s=1}^{t} |U_{sij}|$, where

$$U_{tij} = \mathbb{I}\{D_{ti} = D_{tj}\}(C_{ti} - C_{tj}).$$

All this means is that S_{tij} tracks the difference between the number of clicks on items i and j over rounds when they share a partition. As a final step, the relation G_{t+1} is given by

$$G_{t+1} = G_t \cup \left\{(j, i) : S_{tij} \geq \sqrt{2N_{tij} \log\left(\frac{c\sqrt{N_{tij}}}{\delta}\right)}\right\},$$

where $c \approx 3.43$ is the universal constant given in Exercise 20.10. In the analysis we will show that if $\alpha(i) \geq \alpha(j)$, then with high probability S_{tji} is never large enough for G_{t+1} to include (i, j). In this sense, with high probability, G_t is consistent with the order on $[\ell]$ induced by sorting in decreasing order with respect to $\alpha(\cdot)$. Note that G_t is generally not a partial order because it need not be transitive.

Illustration

Suppose $\ell = 5$ and $m = 4$, and in round t the relation is $G_t = \{(3,1),(5,2),(5,3)\}$, which is represented in the graph below, where an arrow from j to i indicates that $(j,i) \in G_t$.

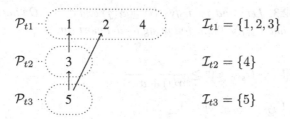

$$\mathcal{I}_{t1} = \{1,2,3\}$$
$$\mathcal{I}_{t2} = \{4\}$$
$$\mathcal{I}_{t3} = \{5\}$$

This means that in round t the first three positions in the ranking will contain items from $\mathcal{P}_{t1} = \{1,2,4\}$ but with random order. The fourth position will be item 3, and item 5 is not shown to the user.

Part (a) of Assumption 32.1 means that items in position $k > m$ are never clicked. As a consequence, the algorithm never needs to actually compute the partitions $\mathcal{P}_{td}$ for which $\min \mathcal{I}_{td} > m$ because items in these partitions are never shortlisted.

32.3 Regret Analysis

THEOREM 32.2. *Let v satisfy Assumption 32.1, and assume that $\alpha(1) > \alpha(2) > \cdots > \alpha(\ell)$. Let $\Delta_{ij} = \alpha(i) - \alpha(j)$ and $\delta \in (0,1)$. Then the regret of TopRank is bounded by*

$$R_n \leq \delta nm\ell^2 + \sum_{j=1}^{\ell} \sum_{i=1}^{\min\{m,j-1\}} \left(1 + \frac{6(\alpha(i) + \alpha(j)) \log\left(\frac{c\sqrt{n}}{\delta}\right)}{\Delta_{ij}} \right).$$

Furthermore, $R_n \leq \delta nm\ell^2 + m\ell + \sqrt{4m^3\ell n \log\left(\frac{c\sqrt{n}}{\delta}\right)}$.

By choosing $\delta = n^{-1}$ the theorem shows that the expected regret is at most

$$R_n = O\left(\sum_{j=1}^{\ell} \sum_{i=1}^{\min\{m,j-1\}} \frac{\alpha(i) \log(n)}{\Delta_{ij}} \right) \quad \text{and} \quad R_n = O\left(\sqrt{m^3\ell n \log(n)} \right).$$

The algorithm does not make use of any assumed ordering on $\alpha(\cdot)$, so the assumption is only used to allow for a simple expression for the regret. The core idea of the proof is to show that *(a)* if the algorithm is suffering regret as a consequence of misplacing an item, then it is gaining information so that G_t will get larger and, *(b)* once G_t is sufficiently rich, the algorithm is playing optimally. Let $\mathcal{F}_t = \sigma(A_1, C_1, \ldots, A_t, C_t)$ and $\mathbb{P}_t(\cdot) = \mathbb{P}(\cdot \mid \mathcal{F}_t)$ and $\mathbb{E}_t[\cdot] = \mathbb{E}[\cdot \mid \mathcal{F}_t]$. For each $t \in [n]$, let F_t be the failure event that there exists $i \neq j \in [\ell]$ and $s < t$ such that $N_{sij} > 0$ and

$$\left| S_{sij} - \sum_{u=1}^{s} \mathbb{E}_{u-1}\left[U_{uij} \mid U_{uij} \neq 0\right] |U_{uij}| \right| \geq \sqrt{2N_{sij}\log(c\sqrt{N_{sij}}/\delta)}.$$

LEMMA 32.3. *Let i and j satisfy $\alpha(i) \geq \alpha(j)$ and $d \geq 1$. On the event that $i, j \in \mathcal{P}_{sd}$ and $d \in [M_s]$ and $U_{sij} \neq 0$, the following hold almost surely:*

(a) $\mathbb{E}_{s-1}[U_{sij} \mid U_{sij} \neq 0] \geq \dfrac{\Delta_{ij}}{\alpha(i) + \alpha(j)}.$

(b) $\mathbb{E}_{s-1}[U_{sji} \mid U_{sji} \neq 0] \leq 0.$

Proof For the remainder of the proof, we focus on the event that $i, j \in \mathcal{P}_{sd}$ and $d \in [M_s]$ and $U_{sij} \neq 0$. We also discard the measure zero subset of this event where $\mathbb{P}_{s-1}(U_{sij} \neq 0) = 0$. From now on, we omit the 'almost surely' qualification on conditional expectations. Under these circumstances, the definition of conditional expectation shows that

$$
\begin{aligned}
\mathbb{E}_{s-1}[U_{sij} \mid U_{sij} \neq 0] &= \frac{\mathbb{P}_{s-1}(C_{si} = 1, C_{sj} = 0) - \mathbb{P}_{s-1}(C_{si} = 0, C_{sj} = 1)}{\mathbb{P}_{s-1}(C_{si} \neq C_{sj})} \\
&= \frac{\mathbb{P}_{s-1}(C_{si} = 1) - \mathbb{P}_{s-1}(C_{sj} = 1)}{\mathbb{P}_{s-1}(C_{si} \neq C_{sj})} \\
&\geq \frac{\mathbb{P}_{s-1}(C_{si} = 1) - \mathbb{P}_{s-1}(C_{sj} = 1)}{\mathbb{P}_{s-1}(C_{si} = 1) + \mathbb{P}_{s-1}(C_{sj} = 1)} \\
&= \frac{\mathbb{E}_{s-1}[v(A_s, A_s^{-1}(i)) - v(A_s, A_s^{-1}(j))]}{\mathbb{E}_{s-1}[v(A_s, A_s^{-1}(i)) + v(A_s, A_s^{-1}(j))]},
\end{aligned}
\tag{32.2}
$$

where in the second equality we added and subtracted $\mathbb{P}_{s-1}(C_{si} = 1, C_{sj} = 1)$. By the design of TopRank, the items in $\mathcal{P}_{td}$ are placed into slots $\mathcal{I}_{td}$ uniformly at random. Let σ be the permutation that exchanges the positions of items i and j. Then using Part (c) of Assumption 32.1,

$$
\begin{aligned}
\mathbb{E}_{s-1}[v(A_s, A_s^{-1}(i))] &= \sum_{a \in \mathcal{A}} \mathbb{P}_{s-1}(A_s = a)v(a, a^{-1}(i)) \\
&\geq \frac{\alpha(i)}{\alpha(j)} \sum_{a \in \mathcal{A}} \mathbb{P}_{s-1}(A_s = a)v(\sigma \circ a, a^{-1}(i)) \\
&= \frac{\alpha(i)}{\alpha(j)} \sum_{a \in \mathcal{A}} \mathbb{P}_{s-1}(A_s = \sigma \circ a)v(\sigma \circ a, (\sigma \circ a)^{-1}(j)) \\
&= \frac{\alpha(i)}{\alpha(j)} \mathbb{E}_{s-1}[v(A_s, A_s^{-1}(j))],
\end{aligned}
$$

where the second equality follows from the fact that $a^{-1}(i) = (\sigma \circ a)^{-1}(j)$ and the definition of the algorithm ensuring that $\mathbb{P}_{s-1}(A_s = a) = \mathbb{P}_{s-1}(A_s = \sigma \circ a)$. The last equality follows from the fact that σ is a bijection. Using this and continuing the calculation in Eq. (32.2) shows that

$$Eq.(32.2) = \frac{\mathbb{E}_{s-1}\big[v(A_s, A_s^{-1}(i)) - v(A_s, A_s^{-1}(j))\big]}{\mathbb{E}_{s-1}\big[v(A_s, A_s^{-1}(i)) + v(A_s, A_s^{-1}(j))\big]}$$

$$= 1 - \frac{2}{1 + \mathbb{E}_{s-1}\big[v(A_s, A_s^{-1}(i))\big] / \mathbb{E}_{s-1}\big[v(A_s, A_s^{-1}(j))\big]}$$

$$\geq 1 - \frac{2}{1 + \alpha(i)/\alpha(j)}$$

$$= \frac{\alpha(i) - \alpha(j)}{\alpha(i) + \alpha(j)} = \frac{\Delta_{ij}}{\alpha(i) + \alpha(j)}.$$

The second part follows from the first since $U_{sji} = -U_{sij}$. $\qquad\square$

The next lemma shows that the failure event occurs with low probability.

LEMMA 32.4. *It holds that* $\mathbb{P}(F_n) \leq \delta\ell^2$.

Proof The proof follows immediately from Lemma 32.3, the definition of F_n, the union bound over all pairs of actions, and a modification of the Azuma–Hoeffding inequality in Exercise 20.10. $\qquad\square$

LEMMA 32.5. *On the event* F_t^c, *it holds that* $(i, j) \notin G_t$ *for all* $i < j$.

Proof Let $i < j$ so that $\alpha(i) \geq \alpha(j)$. On the event F_t^c, either $N_{sji} = 0$ or

$$S_{sji} - \sum_{u=1}^{s} \mathbb{E}_{u-1}[U_{uji} \,|\, U_{uji} \neq 0]|U_{uji}| < \sqrt{2N_{sji}\log\left(\frac{c}{\delta}\sqrt{N_{sji}}\right)} \qquad \text{for all } s < t.$$

When i and j are in different blocks in round $u < t$, then $U_{uji} = 0$ by definition. On the other hand, when i and j are in the same block, $\mathbb{E}_{u-1}[U_{uji} \,|\, U_{uji} \neq 0] \leq 0$ almost surely by Lemma 32.3. Based on these observations,

$$S_{sji} < \sqrt{2N_{sji}\log\left(\frac{c}{\delta}\sqrt{N_{sji}}\right)} \qquad \text{for all } s < t,$$

which by the design of TopRank implies that $(i, j) \notin G_t$. $\qquad\square$

LEMMA 32.6. *Let* $I_{td}^* = \min \mathcal{P}_{td}$ *be the most attractive item in* $\mathcal{P}_{td}$. *Then, on event* F_t^c, *holds that* $I_{td}^* \leq 1 + \sum_{c<d}|\mathcal{P}_{td}|$ *for all* $d \in [M_t]$.

Proof Let $i^* = \min \cup_{c \geq d} \mathcal{P}_{tc}$. Then $i^* \leq 1 + \sum_{c<d}|\mathcal{P}_{td}|$ holds trivially for $\mathcal{P}_{t1}, \ldots, \mathcal{P}_{tM_t}$ and $d \in [M_t]$. Now consider two cases. Suppose that $i^* \in \mathcal{P}_{td}$. Th it must be true that $i^* = I_{td}^*$, and our claim holds. On the other hand, suppose that $i^* \in$ for some $c > d$. Then by Lemma 32.5 and the design of the partition, there must ex sequence of items $i_d, \ldots, i_c$ in blocks $\mathcal{P}_{td}, \ldots, \mathcal{P}_{tc}$ such that $i_d < \cdots < i_c = i^*$. Fron definition of I_{td}^*, $I_{td}^* \leq i_d < i^*$. This concludes our proof.

LEMMA 32.7. *On the event* F_n^c *and for all* $i < j$, *it holds that*

$$S_{nij} \leq 1 + \frac{6(\alpha(i) + \alpha(j))}{\Delta_{ij}} \log\left(\frac{c\sqrt{n}}{\delta}\right).$$

Proof The result is trivial when $N_{nij} = 0$. Assume from now on that $N_{nij} > 0$. By the definition of the algorithm, arms i and j are not in the same block once S_{tij} grows too large relative to N_{tij}, which means that

$$S_{nij} \leq 1 + \sqrt{2N_{nij} \log \left(\frac{c}{\delta} \sqrt{N_{nij}} \right)}.$$

On the event F_n^c and part (a) of Lemma 32.3, it also follows that

$$S_{nij} \geq \frac{\Delta_{ij} N_{nij}}{\alpha(i) + \alpha(j)} - \sqrt{2N_{nij} \log \left(\frac{c}{\delta} \sqrt{N_{nij}} \right)}.$$

Combining the previous two displays shows that

$$\frac{\Delta_{ij} N_{nij}}{\alpha(i) + \alpha(j)} - \sqrt{2N_{nij} \log \left(\frac{c}{\delta} \sqrt{N_{nij}} \right)} \leq S_{nij} \leq 1 + \sqrt{2N_{nij} \log \left(\frac{c}{\delta} \sqrt{N_{nij}} \right)}$$

$$\leq (1 + \sqrt{2}) \sqrt{N_{nij} \log \left(\frac{c}{\delta} \sqrt{N_{nij}} \right)}. \tag{32.3}$$

Using the fact that $N_{nij} \leq n$ and rearranging the terms in the previous display shows that

$$N_{nij} \leq \frac{(1 + 2\sqrt{2})^2 (\alpha(i) + \alpha(j))^2}{\Delta_{ij}^2} \log \left(\frac{c\sqrt{n}}{\delta} \right).$$

The result is completed by substituting this into Eq. (32.3). □

Proof of Theorem 32.2 The first step in the proof is an upper bound on the expected number of clicks in the optimal list a^*. Fix time t, block $\mathcal{P}_{td}$ and recall that $I_{td}^* = \min \mathcal{P}_{td}$ is the most attractive item in $\mathcal{P}_{td}$. Let $k = A_t^{-1}(I_{td}^*)$ be the position of item I_{td}^* and σ be the permutation that exchanges items k and I_{td}^*. By Lemma 32.6, on the event F_t^c, we have $I_{td}^* \leq k$. From Parts (c) and (d) of Assumption 32.1, we have $v(A_t, k) \geq v(\sigma \circ A_t, k) \geq v(a^*, k)$. Hence, on the event F_t^c, the expected number of clicks on I_{td}^* is bounded from below by those on items in a^*,

$$\mathbb{E}_{t-1} \left[C_{tI_{td}^*} \right] = \sum_{k \in \mathcal{I}_{td}} \mathbb{P}_{t-1}(A_t^{-1}(I_{td}^*) = k) \mathbb{E}_{t-1}[v(A_t, k) \mid A_t^{-1}(I_{td}^*) = k]$$

$$= \frac{1}{|\mathcal{I}_{td}|} \sum_{k \in \mathcal{I}_{td}} \mathbb{E}_{t-1}[v(A_t, k) \mid A_t^{-1}(I_{td}^*) = k] \geq \frac{1}{|\mathcal{I}_{td}|} \sum_{k \in \mathcal{I}_{td}} v(a^*, k),$$

also used the fact that TopRank randomises within each block to guarantee that $(I_{td}^*) = k) = 1/|\mathcal{I}_{td}|$ for any $k \in \mathcal{I}_{td}$. Using this and the design of TopRank,

$$\sum_{k=1}^{m} v(a^*, k) = \sum_{d=1}^{M_t} \sum_{k \in \mathcal{I}_{td}} v(a^*, k) \leq \sum_{d=1}^{M_t} |\mathcal{I}_{td}| \mathbb{E}_{t-1} \left[C_{tI_{td}^*} \right].$$

Therefore, under event F_t^c, the conditional expected regret in round t is bounded by

$$\sum_{k=1}^{m} v(a^*, k) - \mathbb{E}_{t-1}\left[\sum_{j=1}^{\ell} C_{tj}\right] \leq \mathbb{E}_{t-1}\left[\sum_{d=1}^{M_t} |\mathcal{P}_{td}| C_{tI_{td}^*} - \sum_{j=1}^{\ell} C_{tj}\right]$$

$$= \mathbb{E}_{t-1}\left[\sum_{d=1}^{M_t} \sum_{j\in\mathcal{P}_{td}} (C_{tI_{td}^*} - C_{tj})\right]$$

$$= \sum_{d=1}^{M_t} \sum_{j\in\mathcal{P}_{td}} \mathbb{E}_{t-1}[U_{tI_{td}^*j}]$$

$$\leq \sum_{j=1}^{\ell} \sum_{i=1}^{\min\{m,j-1\}} \mathbb{E}_{t-1}[U_{tij}]. \qquad (32.4)$$

The last inequality follows by noting that $\mathbb{E}_{t-1}[U_{tI_{td}^*j}] \leq \sum_{i=1}^{\min\{m,j-1\}} \mathbb{E}_{t-1}[U_{tij}]$. To see this, use part (a) of Lemma 32.3 to show that $\mathbb{E}_{t-1}[U_{tij}] \geq 0$ for $i < j$ and Lemma 32.6 to show that when $I_{td}^* > m$, then neither I_{td}^* nor j are not shown to the user in round t so that $U_{tI_{td}^*j} = 0$. Substituting the bound in Eq. (32.4) into the regret leads to

$$R_n \leq nm\mathbb{P}(F_n) + \sum_{j=1}^{\ell} \sum_{i=1}^{\min\{m,j-1\}} \mathbb{E}\left[\mathbb{I}\{F_n^c\} S_{nij}\right], \qquad (32.5)$$

where we used the fact that the maximum number of clicks over n rounds is nm. The proof of the first part is completed by using Lemma 32.4 to bound the first term and Lemma 32.7 to bound the second. The problem-independent bound follows from Eq. (32.5) and by stopping early in the proof of Lemma 32.7 (Exercise 32.6). $\qquad \square$

32.4 Notes

1 At no point in the analysis did we use the fact that v is fixed over time. Suppose that $v_1, \ldots, v_n$ are a sequence of click-probability functions that all satisfy Assumption 32.1 with the same attractiveness function. The regret in this setting is

$$R_n = \sum_{t=1}^{n} \sum_{k=1}^{m} v_t(a^*, k) - \mathbb{E}\left[\sum_{t=1}^{n} \sum_{i=1}^{\ell} C_{ti}\right].$$

Then the bounds in Theorem 32.2 still hold without changing the algorithm.

2 The cascade model is usually formalised in the following more restrictive fashion. Let $\{Z_{ti} : i \in [\ell], t \in [n]\}$ be a collection of independent Bernoulli random variables with $\mathbb{P}(Z_{ti} = 1) = \alpha(i)$. Then define M_t as the first item i in the shortlist with $Z_{ti} = 1$:

$$M_t = \min\{k \in [m] : Z_{tA_t(k)} = 1\},$$

where the minimum of an empty set is ∞. Finally let $C_{ti} = 1$ if and only if $M_t \leq m$ and $A_t(M_t) = i$. This set-up satisfies Eq. (32.1), but the independence assumption makes it possible to estimate α without randomisation. Notice that in any round t with $M_t \leq m$, all items i with $A_t^{-1}(i) < M_t$ must have been unattractive ($Z_{ti} = 0$), while the clicked item must be attractive

($Z_{ti} = 1$). This fact can be used in combination with standard concentration analysis to estimate the attractiveness. The optimistic policy sorts the ℓ items in decreasing order by their upper confidence bounds and shortlists the first m. When the confidence bounds are derived from Hoeffding's inequality , this policy is called CascadeUCB, while the policy that uses Chernoff's lemma is called CascadeKL-UCB. The computational cost of the latter policy is marginally higher than the former, but the improvement is also quite significant because in practice most items have barely positive attractiveness.

3 The linear dependence of the regret on ℓ is unpleasant when the number of items is large, which is the case in many practical problems. Like for finite-armed bandits, one can introduce a linear structure on the items by assuming that $\alpha(i) = \langle \theta, \phi_i \rangle$ where $\theta \in \mathbb{R}^d$ is an unknown parameter vector and $(\phi_i)_{i=1}^{\ell}$ are known feature vectors. This has been investigated in the cascade model by Zong et al. [2016] and with a model resembling that of this chapter by Li et al. [2019a].

4 There is an adversarial variant of the cascade model. In the **ranked bandit model** an adversary secretly chooses a sequence of sets $S_1, \ldots, S_n$, with $S_t \subseteq [\ell]$. In each round t the learner chooses $A_t \in \mathcal{A}$ and receives a reward $X_t(A_t)$, where $X_t : \mathcal{A} \to [0, 1]$ is given by $X_t(a) = \mathbb{I}\{S_t \cap \{a(1), \ldots, a(k)\} \neq \emptyset\}$. The feedback is the position of the clicked action, which is $M_t = \min\{k \in [m] : A_t(k) \in S_t\}$. The regret is

$$R_n = \sum_{t=1}^{n} (X_t(a_*) - X_t(A_t)),$$

where a_* is the optimal ranking in hindsight:

$$a_* = \mathrm{argmin}_{a \in \mathcal{A}} \sum_{t=1}^{n} X_t(a). \tag{32.6}$$

Notice that this is the same as the cascade model when $S_t = \{i : Z_{ti} = 1\}$.

5 A challenge in the ranked bandit model is that solving the offline problem (Eq. 32.6) for known $S_1, \ldots, S_n$ is NP-hard. How can one learn when finding an optimal solution to the offline problem is hard? First, hardness only matters if $|\mathcal{A}|$ is large. When ℓ and m are not too large, then exhaustive search is quite feasible. If this is not an option, one may use an approximation algorithm. It turns out that in a certain sense, the best one can do is to use a greedy algorithm, We omit the details, but the highlight is that there exist efficient algorithms such that

$$\mathbb{E}\left[\sum_{t=1}^{n} X_t(A_t)\right] \geq \left(1 - \frac{1}{e}\right) \max_{a \in \mathcal{A}} \sum_{t=1}^{n} X_t(a) - O\left(m\sqrt{n\ell \log(\ell)}\right).$$

See the article by Radlinski et al. [2008] for more details.

6 By modifying the reward function, one can also define an adversarial variant of the document-based model. As in the previous note, the adversary secretly chooses $S_1, \ldots, S_n$ as subsets of $[\ell]$, but now the reward is

$$X_t(a) = |S_t \cap \{a(1), \ldots, a(k)\}|.$$

The feedback is the positions of the clicked items, $S_t \cap \{a(1), \ldots, a(k)\}$. For this model, there are no computation issues. In fact, the problem can be analysed using a reduction to combinatorial semi-bandits, which we ask you to investigate in Exercise 32.3.

7 The position-based model can also be modelled in the adversarial setting by letting $S_{tk} \subset [\ell]$ for each $t \in [n]$ and $k \in [m]$. Then, defining the reward by

$$X_t(a) = \sum_{k=1}^{m} \mathbb{I}\{A_t(k) \in S_{tk}\}.$$

Again, the feedback is the positions of the clicked items, $\{k \in [m] : A_t(k) \in S_{tk}\}$. This model can also be tackled using algorithms for combinatorial semi-bandits (Exercise 32.4).

32.5 Bibliographic Remarks

The policy and analysis presented in this chapter is by the authors and others [Lattimore et al., 2018]. The most related work is by Zoghi et al. [2017], who assumed a factorisation of the click probabilities $v(a, k) = \alpha(a(k))\chi(a, k)$ and then made assumptions on χ. The assumptions made here are slightly less restrictive, and the bounds are simultaneously stronger. Some experimental results comparing these algorithms are given by Lattimore et al. [2018]. For more information on click models, we recommend the survey paper by Chuklin et al. [2015] and the article by Craswell et al. [2008]. Cascading bandits were first studied by Kveton et al. [2015a], who proposed algorithms based on UCB and KL-UCB and prove finite-time instance-dependence upper bounds and asymptotic lower bounds that match in specific regimes. Around the same time, Combes et al. [2015a] proposed a different algorithm for the same model that is also asymptotically optimal. The optimal regret has a complicated form and is not given explicitly in all generality. We remarked in the notes that the linear dependence on ℓ is problematic for large ℓ. To overcome this problem, Zong et al. [2016] introduce a linear variant where the attractiveness of an item is assumed to be an inner product between an unknown parameter and a known feature vector. A slightly generalised version of this set-up was simultaneously studied by Li et al. [2016], who allowed the features associated with each item to change from round to round. The position-based model is studied by Lagree et al. [2016], who suggest several algorithms and provide logarithmic regret analysis for some of them. Asymptotic lower bounds are also given that match the upper bounds in some regimes. Katariya et al. [2016] study the **dependent click model** introduced by Guo et al. [2009]. This differs from the models proposed in this chapter because the reward is not assumed to be the number of clicks and is actually unobserved. We leave the reader to explore this interesting model on their own. The adversarial variant of the ranking problem mentioned in the notes is due to Radlinski et al. [2008]. Another related problem is the rank-1 bandit problem, where the learner chooses one of ℓ items to place in one of m positions, with all other positions left empty. This model has been investigated by Katariya et al. [2017a,b], who assume the position-based model. The cascade feedback model is also used in a combinatorial setting by Kveton et al. [2015c], but this paper does not have a direct application to ranking. A more in-depth discussion on ranking can be found in the recent book on bandits in information retrieval by Glowacka [2019], which discusses a number of practical considerations, like the cold-start problem.

32.6 Exercises

32.1 (CLICK MODELS AND ASSUMPTIONS) Show that the document-based, position-based and cascade models all satisfy Assumption 32.1.

32.2 (DIVERSITY) Most ranking algorithms are based on assigning an attractiveness value to each item and shortlisting the m most attractive items. Radlinski et al. [2008] criticise this approach in their paper as follows:

"The theoretical model that justifies ranking documents in this way is the probabilistic ranking principle [Robertson, 1977]. It suggests that documents should be ranked by their probability of relevance to the query. However, the optimality of such a ranking relies on the assumption that there are no statistical dependencies between the probabilities of relevance among documents – an assumption that is clearly violated in practice. For example, if one document about jaguar cars is not relevant to a user who issues the query jaguar, other car pages become less likely to be relevant. Furthermore, empirical studies have shown that given a fixed query, the same document can have different relevance to different users [Teevan et al., 2007]. This undermines the assumption that each document has a single relevance score that can be provided as training data to the learning algorithm. Finally, as users are usually satisfied with finding a small number of, or even just one, relevant document, the usefulness and relevance of a document does depend on other documents ranked higher."

The optimality criterion Radlinski et al. [2008] had in mind is to present at least one item that the user is attracted to. Do you find this argument convincing? Why or why not?

The probabilistic ranking principle was put forward by Maron and Kuhns [1960]. The paper by Robertson [1977] identifies some sufficient conditions under which the principle is valid and also discusses its limitations.

32.3 (ADVERSARIAL RANKING AS A SEMI-BANDIT (I)) Frame the adversarial variant of the document-based model in Note 6 as a combinatorial semi-bandit and use the results in Chapter 30 to prove a bound on the regret of

$$R_n \leq \sqrt{2m\ell n(1 + \log(\ell))}.$$

32.4 (ADVERSARIAL RANKING AS A SEMI-BANDIT (II)) Adapt your solution to the previous exercise to the position-based model in Note 7, and prove a bound on the regret of

$$R_n \leq m\sqrt{2\ell n(1 + \log(\ell))}.$$

32.5 (CYCLES IN PARTIAL ORDER) Prove that if G_t does not contain cycles, then M_t defined in Section 32.2 is well defined and that $\mathcal{P}_{t1}, \ldots, \mathcal{P}_{tM_t}$ is a partition of $[\ell]$.

32.6 (WORST-CASE BOUND FOR TOPRANK) Prove the second part of Theorem 32.2.

33 Pure Exploration

All the policies proposed in this book so far were designed to maximise the cumulative reward. As a consequence, the policies must carefully balance exploration against exploitation. But what happens if there is no price to be paid for exploring? Imagine, for example, that a researcher has k configurations of a new drug and a budget to experiment on n mice. The researcher wants to find the most promising drug configuration for subsequent human trials, but is not concerned with the outcomes for the mice. Problems of this nature are called **pure exploration** problems. Although there are similarities to the cumulative regret setting, there are also differences. This chapter outlines a variety of pure exploration problems and describes the basic algorithmic ideas.

Figure 33.1 The mouse never benefits from the experiment.

33.1 Simple Regret

Let v be a k-armed stochastic bandit and $\pi = (\pi_t)_{t=1}^{n+1}$ be a policy. One way to measure the performance of a policy in the pure exploration setting is the **simple regret**,

$$R_n^{\text{SIMPLE}}(\pi, v) = \mathbb{E}_{v\pi}\left[\Delta_{A_{n+1}}(v)\right].$$

The action chosen in round $n + 1$ has a special role. In the example with the mice, it represents the configuration recommended for further investigation at the end of the trial. We start by analysing the **uniform exploration** (UE) policy, which explores deterministically for the first n rounds and recommends the empirically best arm in round $n + 1$. The pseudocode is provided in Algorithm 20.

1: **for** $t = 1, \ldots, n$ **do**
2:     Choose $A_t = 1 + (t \bmod k)$
3: **end for**
4: Choose $A_{n+1} = \operatorname{argmax}_{i \in [k]} \hat{\mu}_i(n)$

Algorithm 20: Uniform exploration.

THEOREM 33.1. *Let π be the policy of Algorithm 20 and $v \in \mathcal{E}_{SG}^k(1)$ be a 1-subgaussian bandit. Then, for all $n \geq k$,*

$$R_n^{\text{simple}}(\pi, v) \leq \min_{\Delta \geq 0} \left(\Delta + \sum_{i:\Delta_i(v) > \Delta} \Delta_i(v) \exp\left(-\frac{\lfloor n/k \rfloor \Delta_i(v)^2}{4} \right) \right).$$

Proof Let $\Delta_i = \Delta_i(v)$ and $\mathbb{P} = \mathbb{P}_{v\pi}$. Assume without loss of generality that $\Delta_1 = 0$, and let i be a suboptimal arm with $\Delta_i > \Delta$. Observe that $A_{n+1} = i$ implies that $\hat{\mu}_i(n) \geq \hat{\mu}_1(n)$. Now $T_i(n) \geq \lfloor n/k \rfloor$ is not random, so by Theorem 5.3 and Lemma 5.4,

$$\mathbb{P}\left(\hat{\mu}_i(n) \geq \hat{\mu}_1(n) \right) = \mathbb{P}\left(\hat{\mu}_i(n) - \hat{\mu}_1(n) \geq 0 \right) \leq \exp\left(-\frac{\lfloor n/k \rfloor \Delta_i^2}{4} \right). \tag{33.1}$$

The definition of the simple regret yields

$$R_n^{\text{SIMPLE}}(\pi, v) = \sum_{i=1}^{k} \Delta_i \mathbb{P}\left(A_{n+1} = i \right) \leq \Delta + \sum_{i:\Delta_i > \Delta} \Delta_i \mathbb{P}\left(A_{n+1} = i \right).$$

The proof is completed by substituting Eq. (33.1) and taking the minimum over all $\Delta \geq 0$. $\qquad\square$

The theorem highlights some important differences between the simple regret and the cumulative regret. If v is fixed and n tends to infinity, then the simple regret converges to zero exponentially fast. On the other hand, if n is fixed and v is allowed to vary, then we are in a worst-case regime. Theorem 33.1 can be used to derive a bound in this case by choosing $\Delta = 2\sqrt{\log(k)/\lfloor n/k \rfloor}$, which after a short algebraic calculation shows that for $n \geq k$ there exists a universal constant $C > 0$ such that

$$R_n^{\text{SIMPLE}}(\text{UE}, v) \leq C\sqrt{\frac{k \log(k)}{n}} \qquad \text{for all } v \in \mathcal{E}_{SG}^k(1). \tag{33.2}$$

In Exercise 33.1 we ask you to use the techniques of Chapter 15 to prove that for all policies there exists a bandit $v \in \mathcal{E}_{\mathcal{N}}^k(1)$ such that $R_n^{\text{SIMPLE}}(\pi, v) \geq C\sqrt{k/n}$ for some universal constant $C > 0$. It turns out the logarithmic dependence on k in Eq. (33.2) is tight for uniform exploration (Exercise 33.2), but there exists another policy for which the simple regret matches the aforementioned lower bound up to constant factors. There are several ways to do this, but the most straightforward is via a reduction from algorithms designed for minimising cumulative regret.

PROPOSITION 33.2. *Let $\pi = (\pi_t)_{t=1}^n$ be a policy, and define*

$$\pi_{n+1}(i \mid a_1, x_1, \ldots, a_n, x_n) = \frac{1}{n} \sum_{t=1}^{n} \mathbb{I}\{a_t = i\}.$$

Then the simple regret of $(\pi_t)_{t=1}^{n+1}$ satisfies

$$R_n^{\text{simple}}((\pi_t)_{t=1}^{n+1}, v) = \frac{R_n(\pi, v)}{n},$$

where $R_n(\pi, v)$ is the cumulative regret of policy $\pi = (\pi_t)_{t=1}^n$ on bandit v.

Proof By the regret decomposition identity (4.5),

$$R_n(\pi, v) = n\mathbb{E}\left[\sum_{i=1}^{k} \Delta_i \frac{T_i(n)}{n}\right] = n\mathbb{E}\left[\Delta_{A_{n+1}}\right] = nR_n^{\text{SIMPLE}}((\pi_t)_{t=1}^{n+1}, v),$$

where the first equality follows from the definition of the cumulative regret, the third from the definition of π_{n+1} and the last from the definition of the simple regret. $\qquad\square$

COROLLARY 33.3. *For all n there exists a policy π such that for all $v \in \mathcal{E}_{SG}^k(1)$ with $\Delta(v) \in [0,1]^k$ it holds that $R_n^{\text{simple}}(\pi, v) \leq C\sqrt{k/n}$, where C is a universal constant.*

Proof Combine the previous result with Theorem 9.1. $\qquad\square$

Proposition 33.2 raises our hopes that policies designed for minimising the cumulative regret might also have well-behaved simple regret. Unfortunately this is only true in the intermediate regimes where the best arm is hard to identify. Policies with small cumulative regret spend most of their time playing the optimal arm and play suboptimal arms just barely enough to ensure they are not optimal. In pure exploration this leads to a highly suboptimal policy for which the simple regret is asymptotically polynomial, while we know from Theorem 33.1 that the simple regret should decrease exponentially fast. More details and pointers to the literature are given in Note 2 at the end of the chapter.

33.2 Best-Arm Identification with a Fixed Confidence

Best-arm identification is a variant of pure exploration where the learner is rewarded only for identifying an exactly optimal arm. There are two variants of best-arm identification. In this section we consider the **fixed confidence** setting when the learner is given a confidence level $\delta \in (0, 1)$ and should use as few samples as possible to output an arm that is optimal with probability at least $1 - \delta$. In the other variant the learner has to make a decision after n rounds and the goal is to minimise the probability of selecting a suboptimal arm. We treat this alternative in the next section.

In the fixed confidence setting, the learner chooses a policy $\pi = (\pi_t)_{t=1}^{\infty}$ as normal. The number of rounds is not fixed in advance, however, the learner chooses a stopping time τ adapted to filtration $\mathbb{F} = (\mathcal{F}_t)_{t=0}^{\infty}$ with $\mathcal{F}_t = \sigma(A_1, X_1, \ldots, A_t, X_t)$. The learner also chooses a $\mathcal{F}_\tau$-measurable random variable ψ taking values in $[k]$. The stopping time represents the time when the learner halts and $\psi \in [k]$ is the recommended action, which by the measurability assumption only depends on $(A_1, X_1, \ldots, A_\tau, X_\tau)$. Note that in line with our definition of stopping times (see Definition 3.6), it is possible that $\tau = \infty$, which just means the learner cannot ever make up their mind to stop. This behaviour of a learner, of course, will not be encouraged! The function ψ is called the **selection rule**.

DEFINITION 33.4. A triple (π, τ, ψ) is **sound** at confidence level $\delta \in (0, 1)$ for environment class $\mathcal{E}$ if for all $v \in \mathcal{E}$,

$$\mathbb{P}_{v\pi}\left(\tau < \infty \text{ and } \Delta_\psi(v) > 0\right) \leq \delta. \tag{33.3}$$

The objective in fixed confidence best-arm identification is to find a sound learner for which $\mathbb{E}_{v\pi}[\tau]$ is minimised over environments $v \in \mathcal{E}$. Since this is a multi-objective criteria, there is a priori no reason to believe that a single optimal learner should exist. Conveniently, however, the condition that the learner must satisfy Eq. (33.3) plays the role of the consistency assumption in the asymptotic lower bounds in Chapter 16, which allows for a sense of instance-dependent asymptotic optimality. The situation in finite time is more complicated, as we discuss in Note 7.

> If $\mathcal{E}$ is sufficiently rich and ν has multiple optimal arms, then no sound learner can stop in finite time with positive probability. The reason is that there is no way to reject the hypothesis that one optimal arm is fractionally better than another. You will investigate this in Exercise 33.10. Also note that in our definition, $\mathbb{I}\{\tau = t\}$ is a deterministic function of $A_1, X_1, \ldots, A_t, X_t$. None of the results that follow would change if you allowed τ or ψ to also depend on some exogenous source of randomness.

33.2.1 Lower Bound

We start with the lower bound, which serves as a target for the upper bound to follow. Let $\mathcal{E}$ be an arbitrary set of k-armed stochastic bandit environments, and for $\nu \in \mathcal{E}$ define

$$i^*(\nu) = \operatorname{argmax}_{i \in [k]} \mu_i(\nu) \quad \text{and} \quad \mathcal{E}_{\text{alt}}(\nu) = \{\nu' \in \mathcal{E} : i^*(\nu') \cap i^*(\nu) = \emptyset\},$$

which is the set of bandits in $\mathcal{E}$ with different optimal arms than ν.

THEOREM 33.5. *Assume that (π, τ, ψ) is sound for $\mathcal{E}$ at confidence level $\delta \in (0, 1)$, and let $\nu \in \mathcal{E}$. Then $\mathbb{E}_{\nu\pi}[\tau] \geq c^*(\nu) \log\left(\frac{4}{\delta}\right)$, where*

$$c^*(\nu)^{-1} = \sup_{\alpha \in \mathcal{P}_{k-1}} \left(\inf_{\nu' \in \mathcal{E}_{\text{alt}}(\nu)} \left(\sum_{i=1}^{k} \alpha_i \, \mathrm{D}(\nu_i, \nu_i') \right) \right) \tag{33.4}$$

with $c^*(\nu) = \infty$ when $c^*(\nu)^{-1} = 0$.

Proof The result is trivial when $\mathbb{E}_{\nu\pi}[\tau] = \infty$. For the remainder, assume that $\mathbb{E}_{\nu\pi}[\tau] < \infty$, which implies that $\mathbb{P}_{\nu\pi}(\tau = \infty) = 0$. Next, let $\nu' \in \mathcal{E}_{\text{alt}}(\nu)$ and define event $E = \{\tau < \infty \text{ and } \psi \notin i^*(\nu')\} \in \mathcal{F}_\tau$. Then,

$$2\delta \geq \mathbb{P}_{\nu\pi}(\tau < \infty \text{ and } \psi \notin i^*(\nu)) + \mathbb{P}_{\nu'\pi}(\tau < \infty \text{ and } \psi \notin i^*(\nu'))$$
$$\geq \mathbb{P}_{\nu\pi}(E^c) + \mathbb{P}_{\nu'\pi}(E)$$
$$\geq \frac{1}{2} \exp\left(-\sum_{i=1}^{k} \mathbb{E}_{\nu\pi}\left[T_i(\tau)\right] \mathrm{D}(\nu_i, \nu_i') \right), \tag{33.5}$$

where the first inequality follows from the definition of soundness and the last from the Bretagnolle–Huber inequality (Theorem 14.2) and the stopping time version of Lemma 15.1 (see Exercise 15.7). The second inequality holds because $\mathbb{P}_{\nu\pi}(\tau = \infty) = 0$ and $i^*(\nu) \cap i^*(\nu') = \emptyset$ and

$$E^c = \{\tau = \infty\} \cup \{\tau < \infty \text{ and } \psi \in i^*(\nu')\}$$
$$\subseteq \{\tau = \infty\} \cup \{\tau < \infty \text{ and } \psi \notin i^*(\nu)\}.$$

Rearranging Eq. (33.5) shows that

$$\sum_{i=1}^{k} \mathbb{E}_{\nu\pi}[T_i(\tau)] \, D(\nu_i, \nu_i') \geq \log\left(\frac{4}{\delta}\right),\tag{33.6}$$

which implies that $\mathbb{E}_{\nu\pi}[\tau] > 0$. Using this, the definition of $c^*(\nu)$ and Eq. (33.6),

$$\frac{\mathbb{E}_{\nu\pi}[\tau]}{c^*(\nu)} = \mathbb{E}_{\nu\pi}[\tau] \sup_{\alpha \in \mathcal{P}_{k-1}} \inf_{\nu' \in \mathcal{E}_{\text{alt}}(\nu)} \sum_{i=1}^{k} \alpha_i \, D(\nu_i, \nu_i')$$

$$\geq \mathbb{E}_{\nu\pi}[\tau] \inf_{\nu' \in \mathcal{E}_{\text{alt}}(\nu)} \sum_{i=1}^{k} \frac{\mathbb{E}_{\nu\pi}[T_i(\tau)]}{\mathbb{E}_{\nu\pi}[\tau]} D(\nu_i, \nu_i')\tag{33.7}$$

$$= \inf_{\nu' \in \mathcal{E}_{\text{alt}}(\nu)} \sum_{i=1}^{k} \mathbb{E}_{\nu\pi}[T_i(\tau)] \, D(\nu_i, \nu_i')$$

$$\geq \log\left(\frac{4}{\delta}\right),$$

where the last inequality follows from Eq. (33.6). Rearranging completes the proof. Note, in the special case that $c^*(\nu)^{-1} = 0$, the assumption that $\mathbb{E}_{\nu\pi}[\tau] < \infty$ would lead to a contradiction. □

Theorem 33.5 does not depend on $\mathcal{E}$ being unstructured. The assumption that the bandits are finite armed could also be relaxed with appropriate measureability assumptions.

In a moment, we will prove that the bound in Theorem 33.5 is asymptotically optimal as $\delta \to 0$ when $\mathcal{E} = \mathcal{E}_\mathcal{N}^k(1)$, a result that holds more generally for Bernoulli bandits or when the distributions come from an exponential family. Before this, we devote a little time to understanding the constant $c^*(\nu)$. Suppose that $\alpha^*(\nu) \in \mathcal{P}_{k-1}$ satisfies

$$c^*(\nu)^{-1} = \inf_{\nu' \in \mathcal{E}_{\text{alt}}(\nu)} \sum_{i=1}^{k} \alpha_i^*(\nu) \, D(\nu_i, \nu_i').$$

A few observations about this optimisation problem:

(a) The value of $\alpha^*(\nu)$ is unique when $\mathcal{E} = \mathcal{E}_\mathcal{N}^k(1)$ and $\nu \in \mathcal{E}$ has a unique optimal arm. Uniqueness continues to hold when $\mathcal{E}$ is unstructured with distributions from an exponential family.
(b) The inequality in Eq. (33.7) is tightest when $\mathbb{E}_{\nu\pi}[T_i(\tau)]/\mathbb{E}_{\nu\pi}[\tau] = \alpha_i^*(\nu)$, which shows a policy can only match the lower bound by playing arm i exactly in proportion to $\alpha_i^*(\nu)$ in the limit as δ tends to zero.
(c) When $\mathcal{E} = \mathcal{E}_\mathcal{N}^2(1)$ and $\nu \in \mathcal{E}$ has a unique optimal arm, then

$$c^*(\nu)^{-1} = \frac{1}{2} \sup_{\alpha \in [0,1]} \inf_{\nu' \in \mathcal{E}_{\text{alt}}(\nu)} \left\{ \alpha(\mu_1(\nu) - \mu_1(\nu'))^2 + (1-\alpha)(\mu_2(\nu) - \mu_2(\nu'))^2 \right\}$$

$$= \frac{1}{2} \sup_{\alpha \in [0,1]} \alpha(1-\alpha)(\mu_1(\nu) - \mu_2(\nu))^2 = \frac{1}{8}(\mu_1(\nu) - \mu_2(\nu))^2.$$

In this case we observe that $\alpha_1^*(\nu) = \alpha_2^*(\nu) = 1/2$.

(d) Suppose that $\sigma^2 \in (0, \infty)^k$ is fixed and $\mathcal{E} = \{(\mathcal{N}(\mu_i, \sigma_i^2)_{i=1}^k : \mu \in \mathbb{R}^k\}$. You are asked in Exercise 33.4 to verify that when $k = 2$,

$$c^*(\nu) = \frac{2(\sigma_1 + \sigma_2)^2}{\Delta_2^2}. \tag{33.8}$$

which unsurprisingly shows the problem becomes harder as the variance of either of the arms increases. In Exercise 33.4, you will show when $k \geq 2$, it holds that

$$\frac{2\sigma_{i^*}^2}{\Delta_{\min}^2} + \sum_{i \neq i^*} \frac{2\sigma_i^2}{\Delta_i^2} \leq c^*(\nu) \leq \frac{2\sigma_{i^*}^2}{\Delta_{\min}^2} + \sum_{i \neq i^*} \frac{2\sigma_i^2}{\Delta_i^2} + 2\sqrt{\frac{2\sigma_{i^*}^2}{\Delta_{\min}^2} \sum_{i \neq i^*} \frac{2\sigma_i^2}{\Delta_i^2}},$$

where $\Delta_{\min} = \min_{i \neq i^*} \Delta_i$ is the smallest suboptimality gap. This bound faithfully captures the intuition that each suboptimal arm must be played sufficiently often to be distinguished from the optimal arm, while the optimal arm must be observed sufficiently many times so that it can be distinguished from the second best arm. For $k = 2$, this bound is smaller than the value of $c^*(\nu)$, as shown in (33.8), showing that there is room for improvement in this case.

33.2.2 Policy, Stopping/Selection Rule and Upper Bounds

The bound in Theorem 33.5 is asymptotically tight for many environment classes. For simplicity, we focus on the Gaussian case.

> For this section, we assume that $\mathcal{E} = \mathcal{E}_{\mathcal{N}}^k(1)$ is the set of k-armed Gaussian bandits with unit variance.

We need to construct a triple (π, τ, ψ) that is sound for $\mathcal{E}$ and for which $\mathbb{E}_{\nu\pi}[\tau]$ matches the lower bound in Theorem 33.5 as $\delta \to 0$. Both are derived using the insights provided by the lower bound. The policy should choose action i in proportion to $\alpha_i^*(\nu)$, which must be estimated from data. The stopping rule is motivated by noting that Eq. (33.6) implies that a sound stopping rule must satisfy

$$\sum_{i=1}^k \mathbb{E}_{\nu\pi}[T_i(\tau)] \, \mathrm{D}(\nu_i, \nu_i') \geq \log\left(\frac{4}{\delta}\right) \qquad \text{for all } \nu' \in \mathcal{E}_{\mathrm{alt}}(\nu).$$

If the inequality is tight, then we might guess that a reasonable stopping rule as the first round t when

$$\inf_{\nu' \in \mathcal{E}_{\mathrm{alt}}(\nu)} \sum_{i=1}^k T_i(t) \, \mathrm{D}(\nu_i, \nu_i') \gtrsim \log\left(\frac{1}{\delta}\right).$$

There are two problems: *(a)* ν is unknown, so the expression cannot be evaluated, and *(b)* we have replaced the expected number of pulls with the actual number of pulls. Still, let us persevere. To deal with the first problem, we can try replacing ν by the Gaussian bandit environment with mean vector $\hat{\mu}(t)$, which we denote by $\hat{\nu}(t)$. Then let

---

1: **Input** δ and $\beta_t(\delta)$
2: Choose each arm once and set $t = k$
3: **while** $Z_t < \beta_t(\delta)$ **do**
4:     **if** $\text{argmin}_{i \in [k]} T_i(t) \leq \sqrt{t}$ **then**
5:         Choose $A_{t+1} = \text{argmin}_{i \in [k]} T_i(t)$
6:     **else**
7:         Choose $A_{t+1} = \text{argmax}_{i \in [k]} (t\hat{a}_i^*(t) - T_i(t))$
8:     **end if**
9:     Observe reward X_{t+1}, update statistics and increment t
10: **end while**
11: **return** $\psi = i^*(\hat{v}(t))$, $\tau = t$

Algorithm 21: Track-and-stop.

$$Z_t = \inf_{v' \in \mathcal{E}_{\text{alt}}(\hat{v}(t))} \sum_{i=1}^{k} T_i(t) \, \text{D}(\hat{v}_i(t), v_i') = \frac{1}{2} \inf_{\mu' \in \mathcal{E}_{\text{alt}}(\hat{\mu}(t))} \sum_{i=1}^{k} T_i(t)(\hat{\mu}_i(t) - \mu_i(v'))^2.$$

We will show there exists a choice of $\beta_t(\delta) \approx \log(t/\delta)$ such that if $\tau = \min\{t : Z_t > \beta_t(\delta)\}$, then the empirically optimal arm at time τ is the best arm with probability at least $1 - \delta$. The next step is to craft a policy for which the expectation of τ matches the lower bound asymptotically. As we remarked earlier, if the policy is to match the lower bound, it should play arm i approximately in proportion to $\alpha_i^*(v)$. This suggests estimating $\alpha^*(v)$ by $\hat{a}(t) = \alpha^*(\hat{v}(t))$ and then playing the arm for which $t\hat{a}_i(t) - T_i(t)$ is maximised. If $\hat{a}(t)$ is inaccurate, then perhaps the samples collected will not allow the algorithm to improve its estimates. To overcome this last challenge, the policy includes enough forced exploration to ensure that eventually $\hat{a}(t)$ converges to $\alpha^*(v)$ with high probability. Combining all these ideas leads to the track-and-stop policy (Algorithm 21).

THEOREM 33.6. *Let (π, τ, ψ) be the policy, stopping time and selection rule of track-and-stop (Algorithm 21). There exists a choice of $\beta_t(\delta)$ such that track-and-stop is sound and for all $v \in \mathcal{E}$ with $|i^*(v)| = 1$ it holds that*

$$\lim_{\delta \to 0} \frac{\mathbb{E}_{v\pi}[\tau]}{\log(1/\delta)} = c^*(v).$$

Note that only π does not depend on δ inside the limit statement of the theorem, but the stopping time does. The following lemma guarantees the soundness of (π, τ, ψ).

LEMMA 33.7. *Let $f : [k, \infty) \to \mathbb{R}$ be given by $f(x) = \exp(k - x)(x/k)^k$ and $\beta_t(\delta) = k \log(t^2 + t) + f^{-1}(\delta)$. Then, for $\tau = \min\{t : Z_t \geq \beta_t(\delta)\}$, it holds that $\mathbb{P}(i^*(\hat{v}(\tau)) \neq i^*(v)) \leq \delta$.*

The inverse $f^{-1}(\delta)$ is well defined because f is strictly decreasing on $[k, \infty)$ with $f(k) = 1$ and $\lim_{x \to \infty} f(x) = 0$. In fact, the inverse has a closed-form solution in terms of the Lambert W function. By staring at the form of f one can check that $\lim_{\delta \to 0} f^{-1}(\delta)/\log(1/\delta) = 1$ or equivalently that $f^{-1}(\delta) = (1 + o(1))\log(1/\delta)$.

Proof of Lemma 33.7 Notice that $|i^*(\hat{v}(t))| > 1$ implies that $Z_t = 0$. Hence $|i^*(\hat{v}(\tau))| = 1$ for $\tau < \infty$, and the selection rule is well defined. Abbreviate $\mu = \mu(v)$ and $\Delta = \Delta(v)$, and assume without loss of generality that $\Delta_1 = 0$. By the definition of τ and Z_t,

$$\{v \in \mathcal{E}_{\text{alt}}(\hat{v}(\tau))\} \subseteq \left\{\frac{1}{2}\sum_{i=1}^{k} T_i(\tau)(\hat{\mu}_i(\tau) - \mu_i)^2 \geq \beta_\tau(\delta)\right\}.$$

Using the definition of $\mathcal{E}_{\text{alt}}(\hat{v}(\tau))$ yields

$$\mathbb{P}(1 \notin i^*(\hat{v}(\tau))) = \mathbb{P}(v \in \mathcal{E}_{\text{alt}}(\hat{v}(\tau))) \leq \mathbb{P}\left(\frac{1}{2}\sum_{i=1}^{k} T_i(\tau)(\hat{\mu}_i(\tau) - \mu_i)^2 \geq \beta_\tau(\delta)\right).$$

Then apply Lemma 33.8 and Proposition 33.9 from Section 33.2.3. $\quad\square$

A candidate for $\beta_t(\delta)$ can be extracted from the proof and satisfies $\beta_t(\delta) \approx 2k\log t + \log(1/\delta)$. This can be improved to approximately $k\log\log(t) + \log(1/\delta)$ by using a law of the iterated logarithm bound instead of Lemma 33.8. Below, we sketch the proof of Theorem 33.6. A more complete outline is given in Exercise 33.6.

Proof sketch of Theorem 33.6 Lemma 33.7 shows that (π, τ) are sound. It remains to control the expectation of the stopping time. The intuition is straightforward. As more samples are collected, we expect that $\hat{a}(t) \approx a^*(v)$ and $\hat{\mu} \approx \mu$ and

$$Z_t = \inf_{\tilde{v} \in \mathcal{E}_{\text{alt}}(\hat{v}(t))} \sum_{i=1}^{k} \frac{T_i(t)(\hat{\mu}_i(t) - \mu_i(\tilde{v}))^2}{2}$$

$$\approx t \inf_{\tilde{v} \in \mathcal{E}_{\text{alt}}(v)} \sum_{i=1}^{k} \frac{a_i^*(v)(\mu_i(v) - \mu_i(\tilde{v}))^2}{2}$$

$$= \frac{t}{c^*(v)}.$$

Provided the approximation is reasonably accurate, the algorithm should halt once

$$\frac{t}{c^*(v)} \geq \beta_t(\delta) = (1 + o(1))\log(1/\delta),$$

which occurs once $t \geq (1 + o(1))c^*(v)\log(1/\delta)$. $\quad\square$

33.2.3 Concentration

The first concentration theorem follows from Corollary 5.5 and a union bound.

LEMMA 33.8. *Let $(X_t)_{t=1}^{\infty}$ be a sequence of independent Gaussian random variables with mean μ and unit variance. Let $\hat{\mu}_n = \frac{1}{n}\sum_{t=1}^{n} X_t$. Then*

$$\mathbb{P}\left(\text{exists } n \in \mathbb{N}^+ : \frac{n}{2}(\hat{\mu}_n - \mu)^2 \geq \log(1/\delta) + \log(n(n+1))\right) \leq \delta.$$

As we remarked earlier, the $\log(n(n+1))$ term can be improved to approximately $\log\log(n)$. You can do this using peeling (Chapter 9) or the method of mixtures (Exercise 20.9). Since (X_t) are Gaussian, you can also use the tangent approximation and the Bachélier–Levy formula (Exercise 9.4).

PROPOSITION 33.9. *Let $g : \mathbb{N} \to \mathbb{R}$ be increasing, and for each $i \in [k]$, let $S_{i1}, S_{i2}, \ldots$ be an infinite sequence of random variables such that for all $\delta \in (0,1)$,*

$$\mathbb{P}\left(\text{exists } s \in \mathbb{N} : S_{is} \geq g(s) + \log(1/\delta)\right) \leq \delta.$$

Then, provided that $(S_i)_{i=1}^k$ are independent and $x \geq 0$,

$$\mathbb{P}\left(\text{exists } s \in \mathbb{N}^k : \sum_{i=1}^k S_{is_i} \geq kg\left(\sum_{i=1}^k s_i\right) + x\right) \leq \left(\frac{x}{k}\right)^k \exp(k - x).$$

Proof For $i \in [k]$, let $W_i = \max\{w \in [0,1] : S_{is} < g(s) + \log(1/w)$ for all $s \in \mathbb{N}\}$, where we define $\log(1/0) = \infty$. Note that W_i are well defined. Then, for any $s \in \mathbb{N}^k$,

$$\sum_{i=1}^k S_{is_i} \leq \sum_{i=1}^k g(s_i) + \sum_{i=1}^k \log(1/W_i) \leq kg\left(\sum_{i=1}^k s_i\right) + \sum_{i=1}^k \log(1/W_i).$$

By assumption, $(W_i)_{i=1}^k$ are independent and satisfy $\mathbb{P}(W_i \leq x) \leq x$ for all $x \in [0,1]$. The proof is completed using the result of Exercise 5.16. □

33.3 Best-Arm Identification with a Budget

In the fixed-budget variant of best-arm identification, the learner is given the horizon n and should choose a policy $\pi = (\pi_t)_{t=1}^{n+1}$ with the objective of minimising the probability that A_{n+1} is suboptimal. The constraint on the horizon rather than the confidence level makes this setting a bit more nuanced than the fixed confidence setting, and the results are not as clean.

A naive option is to use the uniform exploration policy, but as discussed in Section 33.1, this approach leads to poor results when the suboptimality gaps are not similar to each other. To overcome this problem, the sequential halving algorithm divides the budget into $L = \lceil \log_2(k) \rceil$ phases. In the first phase, the algorithm chooses each arm equally often. The bottom half of the arms are then eliminated, and the process is repeated.

THEOREM 33.10. *If $v \in \mathcal{E}_{SG}^k(1)$ has mean vector $\mu = \mu(v)$ and $\mu_1 \geq \cdots \geq \mu_k$ and π is sequential halving, then*

$$\mathbb{P}_{v\pi}(\Delta_{A_{n+1}} > 0) \leq 3\log_2(k) \exp\left(-\frac{n}{16H_2(\mu)\log_2(k)}\right),$$

where $H_2(\mu) = \max_{i:\Delta_i>0} \frac{i}{\Delta_i^2}$.

1: **Input** n and k
2: Set $L = \lceil \log_2(k) \rceil$ and $\mathcal{A}_1 = [k]$.
3: **for** $\ell = 1, \ldots, L$ **do**
4:      Let $T_\ell = \left\lfloor \frac{n}{L|\mathcal{A}_\ell|} \right\rfloor$.
5:      Choose each arm in $\mathcal{A}_\ell$ exactly T_ℓ times
6:      For each $i \in \mathcal{A}_\ell$ compute $\hat{\mu}_i^\ell$ as the empirical mean of arm i based on the last T_ℓ samples
7:      Let $\mathcal{A}_{\ell+1}$ contain the top $\lceil |\mathcal{A}_\ell|/2 \rceil$ arms in $\mathcal{A}_\ell$
8: **end for**
9: **return** A_{n+1} as the arm in $\mathcal{A}_{L+1}$

Algorithm 22: Sequential halving.

The assumption on the ordering of the means is only needed for the clean definition of H_2, which would otherwise be defined by permuting the arms. The algorithm is completely symmetric. In Exercise 33.8 we guide you through the proof of Theorem 33.10.

The quantity $H_2(\mu)$ looks a bit unusual, but arises naturally in the analysis. It is related to a more familiar quantity as follows. Define $H_1(\mu) = \sum_{i=1}^{k} \min\{1/\Delta_i^2, 1/\Delta_{\min}^2\}$. Then

$$H_2(\mu) \leq H_1(\mu) \leq (1 + \log(k))H_2(\mu). \tag{33.9}$$

Furthermore, both inequalities are essentially tight (Exercise 33.7). Let's see how the bound in Theorem 33.10 compares to uniform exploration, which is the same as Algorithm 20. Like in the proof of Theorem 33.1, the probability that uniform exploration selects a suboptimal arm is easily controlled using Theorem 5.3 and Lemma 5.4:

$$\mathbb{P}_{\nu,\mathrm{UE}}(\Delta_{A_{n+1}} > 0) \leq \sum_{i:\Delta_i>0} \mathbb{P}\left(\hat{\mu}_i(n) \geq \hat{\mu}_1(n)\right) \leq \sum_{i:\Delta_i>0} \exp\left(-\frac{\lfloor n/k \rfloor \Delta_i^2}{4}\right).$$

Suppose that $\Delta = \Delta_2 = \Delta_k$ so that all suboptimal arms have the same suboptimality gap. Then $H_2 = k/\Delta^2$ and terms in the exponent for sequential halving and uniform exploration are $\Theta(n\Delta^2/(k \log k))$ and $\Theta(n\Delta^2/k)$, respectively, which means that uniform exploration is actually moderately better than sequential halving, at least if n is sufficiently large. On the other hand, if $\Delta_2 = \Delta$ is small, but $\Delta_i = 1$ for all $i > 2$, then $H_2 = \Theta(1/\Delta^2)$ and the exponents are $\Theta(n\Delta^2)$ and $\Theta(n\Delta^2/k)$ respectively and sequential halving is significantly better. The reason for the disparity is the non-adaptivity of uniform exploration, which wastes many samples on arms $i > 2$. Although there are not asymptotically matching upper and lower bounds in the fixed budget setting, the bound of sequential halving is known to be roughly optimal.

33.4 Notes

1 The problems studied in this chapter belong to the literature on **stochastic optimisation**, where the simple regret is called the **expected suboptimality**. There are many variants of pure exploration. In the example at the start of the chapter, a medical researcher may be interested in getting the most reliable information about differences between treatments. This falls into the class of pure

information-seeking problems, the subject of optimal experimental design from statistics, which we have met earlier.

2   We mentioned that algorithms with logarithmic cumulative regret are not well suited for pure exploration. Suppose π has asymptotically optimal cumulative regret on $\mathcal{E} = \mathcal{E}_N^k$, which means that $\lim_{n \to \infty} \mathbb{E}_{v\pi}[T_i(n)]/\log(n) = 2/\Delta_i(v)$ for all $v \in \mathcal{E}$. You will show in Exercise 33.5 that for any $\varepsilon > 0$, there exists a $v \in \mathcal{E}$ with a unique optimal arm such that

$$\liminf_{n \to \infty} \frac{-\log\left(\mathbb{P}_{v\pi}(A_{n+1} \notin i^*(v))\right)}{\log(n)} \leq 1 + \varepsilon.$$

This shows that using an asymptotically optimal policy for cumulative regret minimisation leads to a best-arm identification policy for which the probability of selecting a suboptimal arm decays only polynomially with n. This result holds no matter how A_{n+1} is selected.

3   A related observation is that the empirical estimates of the means after running an algorithm designed for minimising the cumulative regret tend to be negatively biased. This occurs because these algorithms play arms until their empirical means are sufficiently small.

4   Although there is no exploration/exploitation dilemma in the pure exploration setting, there is still an 'exploration dilemma' in the sense that the optimal exploration policy depends on an unknown quantity. This means the policy must balance (to some extent) the number of samples dedicated to learning how to explore relative to those actually exploring.

5   Best-arm identification is a popular topic that lends itself to simple analysis and algorithms. The focus on the correct identification of an optimal arm makes us question the practicality of the setting, however. In reality, any suboptimal arm is acceptable provided its suboptimality gap is small enough relative to the budget, which is more faithfully captured by the simple regret criterion. Of course the simple regret may be bounded naively by $R_n^{\text{SIMPLE}} \leq \max_i \Delta_i \mathbb{P}\left(\Delta_{A_{n+1}} > 0\right)$, which is tight in some circumstances and loose in others.

6   An equivalent form of the bound shown in Theorem 33.5 is

$$\mathbb{E}_{v\pi}[\tau] \geq \min\left\{\sum_{i=1}^k \alpha_i : \alpha_1, \ldots, \alpha_k \geq 0, \inf_{v \in \mathcal{E}_{\text{alt}}(v)} \sum_{i=1}^k \alpha_i D(v_i, v_i') \geq \log(4/\delta)\right\}.$$

This form follows immediately from Eq. (33.6) by noting that $\mathbb{E}_{v\pi}[\tau] = \sum_i \mathbb{E}_{v\pi}[T_i(\tau)]$. The version given in the theorem is preferred because it is a closed form expression. Exercise 33.3 asks you to explore the relation between the two forms.

7   The forced exploration in the track-and-stop algorithm is sufficient for asymptotic optimality. We are uneasy about the fact that the proof would work for any threshold Ct^p with $p \in (0, 1)$. There is nothing fundamental about $\sqrt{t}$. We do not currently know of a principled way to tune the amount of forced exploration or if there is better algorithm design for best-arm identification. Ideally one should provided finite-time upper bounds that match the finite-time lower bound provided by Theorem 33.5. The extent to which this is possible appears to be an open question.

8   The choice of $\beta_t(\delta)$ significantly influences the practical performance of track-and-stop. We believe the analysis given here is mostly tight except that the naive concentration bound given in Lemma 33.8 can be improved using a finite-time version of the law of the iterated logarithm (see Exercise 20.9, for example).

9   Perhaps the most practical set-up in pure exploration has not yet received any attention, which is upper and lower instance-dependent bounds on the simple regret. Even better would be to have an understanding of the distribution of $\Delta_{A_{n+1}}$.

33.5   Bibliographical Remarks

In the machine learning literature, pure exploration for bandits seems to have been first studied by Even-Dar et al. [2002], Mannor and Tsitsiklis [2004] and Even-Dar et al. [2006] in the 'Probability Approximately Correct' setting, where the objective is to find an ε-optimal arm with high probability with as few samples as possible. After a dry spell, the field was restarted by Bubeck et al. [2009] and Audibert and Bubeck [2010b]. The asymptotically optimal algorithm for the fixed confidence setting of Section 33.2 was introduced by Garivier and Kaufmann [2016], who also provide results for exponential families as well as in-depth intuition and historical background. Degenne and Koolen [2019] and Degenne et al. [2019] have injected some new ideas into the basic principles of track-and-stop by incorporating a kind of optimism and solving the optimisation problem incrementally using online learning, which leads to theoretical and practical improvements. A similar problem is studied in a Bayesian setting by Russo [2016], who focuses on designing algorithms for which the posterior probability of choosing a suboptimal arm converges to zero exponentially fast with an optimal rate. Even more recently, Qin et al. [2017] designed a policy that is optimal in both the frequentist and Bayesian settings. The stopping rule used by Garivier and Kaufmann [2016] is inspired by similar rules by Chernoff [1959]. The sequential halving algorithm is by Karnin et al. [2013], and the best summary of lower bounds is by Carpentier and Locatelli [2016]. Besides this there have been many other approaches, with a summary by Jamieson and Nowak [2014]. The negative result discussed in Note 2 is due to Bubeck et al. [2009]. Pure exploration has recently become a hot topic and is expanding beyond the finite-armed case. For example, to linear bandits [Soare et al., 2014] and continuous-armed bandits [Valko et al., 2013a], tree search [Garivier et al., 2016a, Huang et al., 2017a] and combinatorial bandits [Chen et al., 2014, Huang et al., 2018].

The continuous-armed case is also known as **zeroth-order** (or derivative-free) **stochastic optimisation** and is studied under various assumptions on the unknown reward function, usually assuming that $\mathcal{A} \subset \mathbb{R}^d$. Because of the obvious connection to optimisation, this literature usually considers losses, or cost, rather than reward, and the reward function is then called the objective function. A big part of this literature poses only weak assumptions, such as smoothness, on the objective function. Note that in the continuous-armed case, regret minimisation may only be marginally more difficult than minimising the simple regret because even the instance-dependent simple regret can decay at a slow, polynomial rate. While the literature is vast, most of it is focused on heuristic methods without rigorous finite-time analysis. Methods developed for this case maintain an approximation to the unknown objective and often use branch-and-bound techniques to focus the search for the optimal value. For a taster of the algorithmic ideas, see [Conn et al., 2009, Rios and Sahinidis, 2013]. When the search for the optimum is organised cleverly, the methods can adapt to 'local smoothness' and enjoy various optimality guarantees [Valko et al., 2013a]. A huge portion of this literature considers the easier problem of finding a local minimiser, or just a stationary point. Another large portion of this literature is concerned with the case when the objective function is convex. Chapter 9 of the classic book by Nemirovsky and Yudin [1983] describes two complementary approaches (a geometric, and an analytic) and sketches their analysis. For the class of strongly convex and smooth functions, it is known that the minimax simple regret is $\Theta(\sqrt{d^2/n})$ [Shamir, 2013]. The main outstanding challenge is to understand the dependence of simple regret on the dimension beyond the strongly convex and smooth case. Hu et al. [2016] prove a lower bound of $\Omega(n^{-1/3})$ on the simple-regret for algorithms that construct gradient estimates by injecting random noise (as is done by Katkovnik and Kulchitsky [1972], Nemirovsky and Yudin [1983] and others), which, together with the $O(n^{-1/2})$ upper bound by Nemirovsky and Yudin [1983] (see also Agarwal et al. 2013, Liang et al. 2014), establishes the inferiority of this approach in the $n \gg d$ regime. Interestingly, empirical evidence favours these gradient-based techniques in comparison to the 'optimal algorithms'. Thus, much room remains to improve our understanding of this problem. This setting is to be contrasted to the one when unbiased noisy estimates of the gradient are available where methods such as mirror descent (see Chapter 28) give optimal rates. This is a much better understood problem with matching lower and upper bounds available on the minimax simple regret for various settings (for example, Chapter 5 of Nemirovsky and Yudin [1983], or Rakhlin et al. [2012]).

Variants of the pure exploration problem are studied in a branch of statistics called **ranking and selection**. The earliest literature on ranking and selection goes back to at least the 1950s. A relatively recent paper that gives a glimpse into a small corner of this literature is by Chan and Lai [2006]. The reason we cite this paper is because it is particularly relevant for this chapter. Using our terminology, Chan and Lai consider the PAC setting in the parametric setting when the distributions underlying the arms belong to some known exponential family of distributions. A procedure that is similar to the track-and-stop procedure considered here is shown to be both sound and asymptotically optimal as the confidence parameter approaches one. We also like the short and readable review of the literature up to the 1980s from the perspective of simulation optimisation by Goldsman [1983].

A related setting studied mostly in the operations research community is **ordinal optimisation**. In its simplest form, ordinal optimisation is concerned with finding an arm amongst the αk arms with the highest pay-offs. Ho et al. [1992], who defined this problem in the stochastic simulation optimisation literature, emphasised that the probability of failing to find one of the 'good arms' decays exponentially with the number of observations n per arm, in contrast to the slow $n^{-1/2}$ decay of the error of estimating the value of the best arm, which this literature calls the problem of **cardinal optimisation**. Given the results in this chapter, this should not be too surprising. A nice twist in this literature is that the error probability does not need to depend on k (see Exercise 33.9). The price, of course, is that the simple regret is in general uncontrolled. In a way, ordinal optimisation is a natural generalisation of best-arm identification. As such, it also leads to algorithmic choices that are not the best fit when the actual goal is to keep the simple regret small. Based on a Bayesian reasoning, a heuristic expression for the asymptotically optimal allocation of samples for the Gaussian best-arm identification problem is given by Chen et al. [2000]. They call the problem of finding an optimal allocation the 'optimal computing budget allocation' (OCBA) problem. Their work can be viewed as the precursor to the results in Section 33.2. Glynn and Juneja [2015] gives further pointers to this literature, while connecting it to the bandit literature.

Best-arm identification has also been considered in the adversarial setting [Jamieson and Talwalkar, 2016, Li et al., 2018, Abbasi-Yadkori et al., 2018]. Another related setting is called the **max-armed bandit problem**, where the objective is to obtain the largest possible single reward over n rounds [Cicirello and Smith, 2005, Streeter and Smith, 2006a,b, Carpentier and Valko, 2014, Achab et al., 2017].

33.6 Exercises

33.1 (SIMPLE REGRET LOWER BOUND) Show there exists a universal constant $C > 0$ such that for all $n \geq k > 1$ and all policies π, there exists a $v \in \mathcal{E}_N^k$ such that $R_n^{\text{SIMPLE}}(\pi, v) \geq C\sqrt{k/n}$.

33.2 (SUBOPTIMALITY OF UNIFORM EXPLORATION) Show there exists a universal constant $C > 0$ such that for all $n \geq k > 1$, there exists a $v \in \mathcal{E}_N^k$ such that $R_n^{\text{SIMPLE}}(\text{UE}, v) \geq C\sqrt{k \log(k)/n}$.

33.3 Let $L > 0$ and $D \subset [0, \infty)^k \setminus \{0\}$ be non-empty. Show that

$$\inf\left\{\|\alpha\|_1 \,:\, \alpha \in [0, \infty)^k, \inf_{d \in D} \langle \alpha, d \rangle \geq L\right\} = \left(\sup_{\alpha \in \mathcal{P}_{k-1}} \inf_{d \in D} \langle \alpha, d \rangle\right)^{-1} L.$$

33.4 (BEST-ARM IDENTIFICATION FOR GAUSSIAN BANDITS) Let $\sigma_1^2, \ldots, \sigma_k^2$ be fixed and $\mathcal{E} = \{(\mathcal{N}(\mu_i, \sigma_i^2))_{i=1}^k : \mu \in \mathbb{R}^k\}$ be the set of Gaussian bandits with given variances. Let $v \in \mathcal{E}$ be a bandit with $\mu_1(v) > \mu_i(v)$ for all $i > 1$. Abbreviate $\mu = \mu(v)$ and $\Delta = \Delta(v)$.

(a) For any $\alpha \in [0, \infty)^k$ show that

$$\inf_{\tilde{v} \in \mathcal{E}_{\text{alt}}(v)} \sum_{i=1}^k \alpha_i \, D(v_i, \tilde{v}_i) = \frac{1}{2} \min_{i > 1} \frac{\alpha_1 \alpha_i \Delta_i^2}{\alpha_1 \sigma_i^2 + \alpha_i \sigma_1^2}.$$

(b) Show that if $k = 2$, then $c^*(v) = 2(\sigma_1 + \sigma_2)^2 / \Delta_2^2$.

(c) Show that $c^*(v) \geq \dfrac{2\sigma_1^2}{\Delta_{\min}} + \displaystyle\sum_{i=2}^k \frac{2\sigma_i^2}{\Delta_i^2}$.

(d) Show that

$$c^*(v) \leq \frac{2\sigma_1^2}{\Delta_{\min}} + \sum_{i=2}^k \frac{2\sigma_i^2}{\Delta_i^2} + 2\sqrt{\frac{2\sigma_1^2}{\Delta_{\min}^2} \sum_{i=2}^k \frac{2\sigma_i^2}{\Delta_i^2}}. \tag{33.10}$$

(e) Show that if $\sigma_i^2 / \Delta_i^2 = \sigma_1^2 / \Delta_{\min}^2$ for all i, then equality holds in Eq. (33.10).

33.5 (SUBOPTIMALITY OF CUMULATIVE REGRET ALGORITHMS FOR BEST-ARM IDENTIFICATION) Suppose π is an asymptotically optimal bandit policy in $\mathcal{E} = \mathcal{E}_\mathcal{N}^k$ in the sense that

$$\lim_{n \to \infty} \frac{R_n(\pi, v)}{\log(n)} = \sum_{i:\Delta_i(v) > 0} \frac{2}{\Delta_i(v)} \quad \text{for all } v \in \mathcal{E}.$$

(a) For any $\varepsilon > 0$, prove there exists a $v \in \mathcal{E}$ with a unique optimal arm such that

$$\liminf_{n \to \infty} \frac{-\log(\mathbb{P}_{v\pi}(\Delta_{A_{n+1}} > 0))}{\log(n)} \leq 1 + \varepsilon.$$

(b) Can you prove the same result with lim inf replaced by lim sup?

(c) What happens if the assumption that π is asymptotically optimal is replaced with the assumption that there exists a universal constant $C > 0$ such that

$$R_n(\pi, v) \leq C \sum_{i:\Delta_i(v) > 0} \left(\Delta_i(v) + \frac{\log(n)}{\Delta_i(v)}\right).$$

33.6 (ANALYSIS OF TRACK-AND-STOP) In this exercise, you will complete the proof of Theorem 33.6. Assume that v has a unique optimal arm. Make $\mathcal{E}$ a metric space via the metric $d(v_1, v_2) = \|\mu(v_1) - \mu(v_2)\|_\infty$. Let $\varepsilon > 0$ be a small constant, and define random times

$$\tau_v(\varepsilon) = 1 + \max\{t : d(\hat{v}_t, v) \geq \varepsilon\}$$
$$\tau_a(\varepsilon) = 1 + \max\{t : \|a^*(v) - a^*(\hat{v}_t)\|_\infty \geq \varepsilon\}$$
$$\tau_T(\varepsilon) = 1 + \max\{t : \|T(t)/t - a_i^*(v)\|_\infty \geq \varepsilon\}.$$

Note, these are not stopping times. Do the following:

(a) Show that $\alpha^*(\nu)$ is unique.

(b) Show α^* is continuous at ν.

(c) Prove that $\mathbb{E}[\tau_\nu(\varepsilon)] < \infty$ for all $\varepsilon > 0$.

(d) Prove that $\mathbb{E}[\tau_a(\varepsilon)] < \infty$ for all $\varepsilon > 0$.

(e) Prove that $\mathbb{E}[\tau_T(\varepsilon)] < \infty$ for all $\varepsilon > 0$.

(f) Prove that $\lim_{\delta \to 0} \mathbb{E}[\tau]/\log(1/\delta) \leq c^*(\nu)$.

33.7 (COMPLEXITY MEASURE COMPARISON) Prove the following:

(a) Let $L = 1 + \sum_{i=3}^{k} \frac{1}{i}$ and show that $H_2(\mu) \leq H_1(\mu) \leq LH_2(\mu)$. Combine this with the fact that $L \leq 1 + \log(k)$ to prove that Eq. (33.9) holds.

(b) Find μ and μ' such that $H_2(\mu) = H_1(\mu)$ and $H_1(\mu') = LH_2(\mu')$. Conclude the inequalities in Eq. (33.9) are tight.

33.8 (ANALYSIS OF SEQUENTIAL HALVING) The purpose of this exercise is to prove Theorem 33.10. Assume without loss of generality that $\mu = \mu(\nu)$ satisfies $\mu_1 \geq \mu_2 \geq \ldots \geq \mu_k$. Given a set $A \subset [k]$, let

$$\mathrm{TopM}(A, m) = \left\{ i \in [k] : \sum_{j \leq i} \mathbb{I}\{j \in A\} \leq m \right\}$$

be the top m arms in A. To make life easier, you may also assume that k is a power of two so that $|\mathcal{A}_\ell| = k2^{1-\ell}$ and $T_\ell = n2^{\ell-1}/\log_2(k)$.

(a) Prove that $|\mathcal{A}_{L+1}| = 1$.

(b) Let i be a suboptimal arm in $\mathcal{A}_\ell$, and suppose that $1 \in \mathcal{A}_\ell$. Show that

$$\mathbb{P}\left(\hat{\mu}_1^\ell \leq \hat{\mu}_i^\ell \,\middle|\, i \in \mathcal{A}_\ell, 1 \in \mathcal{A}_\ell \right) \leq \exp\left(-\frac{T_\ell \Delta_i^2}{4} \right).$$

(c) Let $\mathcal{A}_\ell' = \mathcal{A}_\ell \setminus \mathrm{TopM}(\mathcal{A}_\ell, \lceil |\mathcal{A}_\ell|/4 \rceil)$ be the bottom three-quarters of the arms in round ℓ. Show that if the optimal arm is eliminated after the ℓth phase, then

$$N_\ell = \sum_{i \in \mathcal{A}_\ell'} \mathbb{I}\left\{ \hat{\mu}_i^\ell \geq \hat{\mu}_1^\ell \right\} \geq \frac{1}{3}|\mathcal{A}_\ell'|.$$

(d) Let $i_\ell = \min \mathcal{A}_\ell'$ and show that

$$\mathbb{E}[N_\ell \,|\, \mathcal{A}_\ell] \leq |\mathcal{A}_\ell'| \max_{i \in \mathcal{A}_\ell'} \exp\left(-\frac{\Delta_i^2 n 2^{\ell-1}}{4 \log_2(k)} \right) \leq |\mathcal{A}_\ell'| \exp\left(-\frac{n \Delta_{i_\ell}^2}{16 i_\ell \log_2(k)} \right).$$

(e) Combine the previous two parts with Markov's inequality to show that

$$\mathbb{P}\left(1 \notin \mathcal{A}_{\ell+1} \,|\, 1 \in \mathcal{A}_\ell \right) \leq 3 \exp\left(-\frac{T \Delta_{i_\ell}^2}{16 \log_2(k) i_\ell} \right).$$

(f) Join the dots to prove Theorem 33.10.

33.9 Let P be a distribution over the measurable set $\mathcal{X}$, $\mu : \mathcal{X} \to [0, 1]$ be measurable, $\alpha, \delta \in (0, 1)$, and define $\mu_\alpha^* = \inf\{y : \mathbb{P}(\mu(X) < y) \geq 1 - \alpha\}$. Show that if $n \geq \log(1/\delta)/\log(1/(1 - \alpha))$, then for $X_1, \ldots, X_n \sim P$ independent, with probability $1 - \delta$, it holds that $\max_{i \in [n]} \mu(X_i) \geq \mu_\alpha^*$.

33.10 (MULTIPLE OPTIMAL ARMS AND SOUNDNESS) Throughout this exercise, let $k > 1$.

(a) Let $\mathcal{E} = \mathcal{E}^k_\mathcal{N}(1)$. Prove that for any sound pair (π, τ) and $v \in \mathcal{E}$ with $|i^*(v)| > 1$, it holds that
$\mathbb{P}_{v\pi}(\tau = \infty) = 1$.

(b) Repeat the previous part with $\mathcal{E} = \mathcal{E}^k_\mathcal{B}$.

(c) Describe an unstructured class of k-armed stochastic bandits $\mathcal{E}$ and $v \in \mathcal{E}$ with $|i^*(v)| > 1$ and sound pair (π, τ) for which $\mathbb{P}_{v\pi}(\tau = \infty) = 0$.

33.11 (PROBABLY APPROXIMATELY CORRECT ALGORITHMS) This exercise is about designing (ε, δ)-PAC algorithms.

(a) For each $\varepsilon > 0$ and $\delta \in (0, 1)$ and number of arms $k > 1$, design a policy π and stopping time τ such that for all $v \in \mathcal{E}$,

$$\mathbb{P}_{v\pi}(\Delta_{A_\tau} \geq \varepsilon) \leq \delta \qquad \text{and} \qquad \mathbb{E}_{v\pi}[\tau] \leq \frac{Ck}{\varepsilon^2} \log\left(\frac{k}{\delta}\right),$$

for universal constant $C > 0$.

(b) It turns out the logarithmic dependence on k can be eliminated. Design a policy π and stopping time τ such that for all $v \in \mathcal{E}$,

$$\mathbb{P}_{v\pi}(\Delta_{A_\tau} \geq \varepsilon) \leq \delta \qquad \text{and} \qquad \mathbb{E}_{v\pi}[\tau] \leq \frac{Ck}{\varepsilon^2} \log\left(\frac{1}{\delta}\right).$$

(c) Prove a lower bound showing that the bound in part (b) is tight up to constant factors in the worst case.

HINT   Part (b) of the above exercise is a challenging problem. The simplest approach is to use an elimination algorithm that operates in phases where at the end of each phase, the bottom half of the arms (in terms of their empirical estimates) are eliminated. For details, see the paper by Even-Dar et al. [2002].

34 Foundations of Bayesian Learning

Bayesian methods have been used for bandits from the beginning of the field and dominated research from 1950 until 1980. This chapter introduces the Bayesian viewpoint and develops the technical tools necessary for applications in bandits. Readers who are already familiar with the measure-theoretic Bayesian analysis can skim Sections 34.4 and 34.6 for the notation used in subsequent chapters.

34.1 Statistical Decision Theory and Bayesian Learning

The fundamental challenge in learning problems is that the true environment is unknown and policies that are optimal in one environment are usually not optimal in another. This forces the user to make trade-offs, balancing performance between environments. We have already discussed this in the context of finite-armed bandits in Part IV. Here we take a step back and consider a more general set-up.

Let $\mathcal{E}$ be a set of environments and Π a set of policies. These could be bandit environments/policies, but for now an abstract view is sufficient. A loss function is a mapping $\ell : \mathcal{E} \times \Pi \to \mathbb{R}$ with $\ell(v, \pi)$ representing the loss suffered by policy π in environment v. Of course you should choose a policy that makes the loss small, but most choices are incomparable because the loss depends on the environment. Fig. 34.1 illustrates a typical situation with four policies. Some policies can be eliminated from consideration because they are **dominated**, which means they suffer at least as much loss as some other policy on all environments and more loss on at least one. A policy that is not dominated is called **admissible** or **Pareto optimal**. Choosing between admissible policies is non-trivial. One canonical choice of admissible policy (assuming it exists) is a minimax optimal policy $\pi \in \operatorname{argmin}_{\pi'} \sup_v \ell(v, \pi')$. Minimax optimal policies enjoy robustness, but the price may be quite large on average. Would you choose the minimax optimal policy in the example in Fig. 34.1?

In the Bayesian viewpoint, the uncertainty in the environment is captured by choosing a **prior** probability measure on $\mathcal{E}$ that reflects the user's belief about the environment the learner will face. Having committed to a prior, the **Bayesian optimal policy** simply minimises the expected loss with respect to the prior. When $\mathcal{E}$ is countable, a measure corresponds to a probability vector $q \in \mathcal{P}(\mathcal{E})$, and the Bayesian optimal policy with respect to q is an element of

$$\operatorname{argmax}_\pi \sum_{v \in \mathcal{E}} q(v) \ell(v, \pi).$$

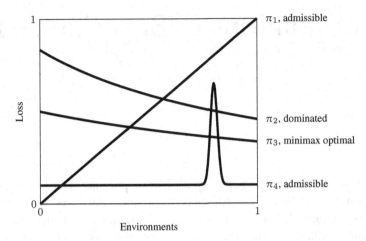

Figure 34.1 Loss as a function of the environment for four different polices $\pi_1, :::, \pi_4$, when $\mathcal{E} = [0, 1]$. Which policy would you choose?

The Bayesian viewpoint is hard to criticise when the user really does know the underlying likelihood of each environment and the user is risk-neutral. Even when the distribution is not known exactly, however, sensible priors often yield provably sensible outcomes, regardless of whether one is interested in the average loss across the environments, or the worst-case loss, or some other metric.

> A distinction is often made between the Bayesian and frequentist viewpoints, which naturally leads to heated discussions on the merits of one viewpoint relative to another. This debate does not interest us greatly. We prefer to think about the pros and cons of problem definitions and solution methods, regardless of the label on them. Bayesian approaches to bandits have their strengths and weaknesses, and we hope to do them a modicum of justice here.

34.2 Bayesian Learning and the Posterior Distribution

The last section explained the 'forward view', where a policy is chosen in advance that minimises the expected loss. The Bayesian can also act sequentially by updating their beliefs (the prior) as data is observed to obtain a new distribution on the set of environments (more generally, the set of hypotheses). The new distribution is called the **posterior**. This is simple and well defined when the environment set is countable, but quickly gets technical for larger spaces. We start gently with a finite case and then explain the measure-theoretic machinery needed to rigourously treat the general case.

Suppose you are given a bag containing two marbles. A trustworthy source tells you the bag contains either *(a)* two white marbles (ww) or *(b)* a white marble and a black marble (wb). You are allowed to choose a marble from the bag (without looking) and observe its colour, which we abbreviate by 'observe white' (ow) or 'observe black' (ob). The question is how to update your 'beliefs' about the contents of the bag having observed one of the marbles. The Bayesian way to tackle this problem starts by choosing a probability distribution on the space of hypotheses, which, incidentally, is also called the prior. This distribution usually reflects one's beliefs about which hypotheses are more probable. In the lack of extra knowledge, for the sake of symmetry, it seems reasonable to choose $\mathbb{P}(\text{ww}) = 1/2$ and $\mathbb{P}(\text{wb}) = 1/2$. The next step is to think about the likelihood of the possible outcomes under each hypothesis. Assuming that the marble is selected blindly (without peeking into the bag) and the marbles in the bag are well shuffled, these are

$$\mathbb{P}(\text{ow} \mid \text{ww}) = 1 \quad \text{and} \quad \mathbb{P}(\text{ow} \mid \text{wb}) = 1/2.$$

The conditioning here indicates that we are including the hypotheses as part of the probability space, which is a distinguishing feature of the Bayesian approach. With this formulation we can apply Bayes' law (Eq. (2.2)) to show that

$$\mathbb{P}(\text{ww} \mid \text{ow}) = \frac{\mathbb{P}(\text{ow} \mid \text{ww})\mathbb{P}(\text{ww})}{\mathbb{P}(\text{ow})} = \frac{\mathbb{P}(\text{ow} \mid \text{ww})\mathbb{P}(\text{ww})}{\mathbb{P}(\text{ow} \mid \text{ww})\mathbb{P}(\text{ww}) + \mathbb{P}(\text{ow} \mid \text{wb})\mathbb{P}(\text{wb})}$$

$$= \frac{1 \times \frac{1}{2}}{1 \times \frac{1}{2} + \frac{1}{2} \times \frac{1}{2}} = \frac{2}{3}.$$

Of course $\mathbb{P}(\text{wb} \mid \text{ow}) = 1 - \mathbb{P}(\text{ww} \mid \text{ow}) = 1/3$. Thus, while in the lack of observations, 'a priori', both hypotheses are equally likely, having observed a white marble, the probability that the bag originally contained two white marbles (and thus the bag has a white marble remaining in it) jumps to $2/3$. An alternative calculation shows that $\mathbb{P}(\text{ww} \mid \text{ob}) = 0$, which makes sense because choosing a black marble rules out the hypothesis that the bag contains two white marbles. The conditional distribution $\mathbb{P}(\cdot \mid \text{ow})$ over the hypotheses is called the **posterior** distribution and represents the Bayesian's belief in each hypothesis after observing a white marble.

34.2.1 A Rigorous Treatment of Posterior Distributions

A more sophisticated approach is necessary when the hypothesis and/or outcome spaces are not discrete. In introductory texts, the underlying details are often (quite reasonably) swept under the rug for the sake of clarity. Besides the desire for generality, there are two reasons not to do this. First, having spent the effort developing the necessary tools in Chapter 2, it would seem a waste not to use them now. And second, the subtle issues that arise highlight some real consequences of the differences between the Bayesian and frequentist viewpoints. As we shall see, there is a real gap between these viewpoints.

Let Θ be a set called the **hypothesis space** and $\mathcal{G}$ be a σ-algebra on Θ. While Θ is often a subset of a Euclidean space, we do not make this assumption. A **prior** is a probability measure Q on $(\Theta, \mathcal{G})$. Next, let $(\mathcal{U}, \mathcal{H})$ be a measurable space and $P = (P_\theta : \theta \in \Theta)$ be a probability kernel from $(\Theta, \mathcal{G})$ to $(\mathcal{U}, \mathcal{H})$. We call P the **model**. Let $\Omega = \Theta \times \mathcal{U}$ and $\mathcal{F} = \mathcal{G} \otimes \mathcal{H}$. The prior and the model combine to yield a probability $\mathbb{P} = Q \otimes P$ on $(\Omega, \mathcal{F})$. The prior is now the marginal distribution of the joint probability measure: $Q(A) = \mathbb{P}(A \times \mathcal{U})$. Suppose a random element X on Ω describes what is observed. Then, generalizing the previous example with the marbles, the posterior should somehow be the marginal of the joint probability measure conditioned X. To make this more precise, let $(\mathcal{X}, \mathcal{J})$ be a measurable space and $X : \Omega \to \mathcal{X}$ a $\mathcal{F}/\mathcal{J}$-measurable map. The posterior having observed that $X = x$ should be a measure $Q(\,\cdot\,|\,x)$ on $(\Theta, \mathcal{G})$.

 We abuse notation by letting $\theta : \Omega \to \Theta$ denote the $\mathcal{F}/\mathcal{G}$-measurable random element given by the projection: $\theta((\phi, u)) = \phi$. This allows θ being used as part of the probability expressions below.

Without much thought, we might try and apply Bayes' law (Eq. (2.2)) to claim that the posterior distribution having observed $X(\omega) = x$ should be a measure on $(\Theta, \mathcal{G})$ given by

$$Q(A \,|\, x) = \mathbb{P}(\theta \in A \,|\, X = x) = \frac{\mathbb{P}(X = x \,|\, \theta \in A)\,\mathbb{P}(\theta \in A)}{\mathbb{P}(X = x)}. \qquad (34.1)$$

The problem with the 'definition' in (34.1) is that $\mathbb{P}(X = x)$ can have measure zero, and then $\mathbb{P}(\theta \in A \,|\, X = x)$ is not defined. This is not an esoteric problem. Consider the problem when θ is randomly chosen from $\Theta = \mathbb{R}$ and its distribution is $Q = \mathcal{N}(0, 1)$, the parameter θ is observed in Gaussian noise with a variance of one: $\mathcal{U} = \mathbb{R}$, $P_\theta = \mathcal{N}(\theta, 1)$ for all $\theta \in \mathbb{R}$ and $X(\phi, u) = u$ for all $(\phi, u) \in \Theta \times \mathcal{U}$. Even in this very simple example, we have $\mathbb{P}(X = x) = 0$ for all $x \in \mathbb{R}$. Having read Chapter 2, the next attempt might be to define $Q(A \,|\, X)$ as a $\sigma(X)$-measurable random variable defined using conditional expectations: for $A \in \mathcal{G}$,

$$Q(A \,|\, x) = \mathbb{E}[\mathbb{I}\{\theta \in A\} \,|\, X](x),$$

where we remind the reader that $\mathbb{E}[\mathbb{I}\{\theta \in A\} \,|\, X]$ is a $\sigma(X)$-measurable random variable that is uniquely defined except for a set of measure zero and also that the notation on the right-hand side is explained in Fig. 2.4 in Chapter 2. For most applications of probability theory, the choice of conditional expectation does not matter. However, as we shortly illustrate with an example, this is not true here. A related annoying issue is that $Q(\,\cdot\,|\,x)$ as defined above need not be a measure. By assuming that $(\Theta, \mathcal{G})$ is a Borel space, this issue can be overcome by using a regular version (Theorem 3.11), a result that we restate here using the present notation.

THEOREM 34.1. *If $(\Theta, \mathcal{G})$ is a Borel space, then there exists a probability kernel $Q : \mathcal{X} \times \mathcal{G} \to [0, 1]$ such that $Q(A \,|\, X) = \mathbb{P}(\theta \in A \,|\, X)$ simultaneously for all $A \in \mathcal{G}$ outside of some $\mathbb{P}$-null set. Furthermore, for any two probability kernels Q, Q' satisfying this condition, $Q(\,\cdot\,|\,x) = Q'(\,\cdot\,|\,x)$ for all x in some set of $\mathbb{P}_X$-probability one.*

The Posterior Density

Theorem 34.1 provides weak conditions under which a posterior exists but does not suggest a useful way of finding it. In many practical situations, the posterior can be calculated using densities. Given $\theta \in \Theta$ let p_θ be the Radon–Nikodym derivative of P_θ with respect to some measure μ and let $q(\theta)$ be the Radon–Nikodym derivative of Q with respect to another measure ν. Provided all terms are appropriately measurable and non-zero, then

$$q(\theta \,|\, x) = \frac{p_\theta(x) q(\theta)}{\int_\Theta p_\theta(x) q(\theta) d\nu(\theta)} \qquad (34.2)$$

is the Radon–Nikodym derivative of $Q(\cdot\,|\,x)$ with respect to ν, also known as the posterior density of Q. In other words, for any $A \in \mathcal{G}$, it holds that $Q(A\,|\,x) = \int_A q(\theta\,|\,x)dv(\theta)$. This corresponds to the usual manipulation of densities when μ and ν are the Lebesgue measures.

The reader may wonder about why all the fuss about the existence of $Q(\cdot\,|\,x)$ in the previous section if we can get its density with a simple formula like (34.2). In other words, why not flip around things and define $Q(\cdot\,|\,x)$ via (34.2)? The crux of the problem is that oftentimes it is hard to come up with an appropriate dominating measure μ, and in general the denominator in the right-hand side of (34.2) could be zero from some particular value of x. But when we can identify an appropriate measure μ and the denominators are non-zero, the above formula can indeed be used as the definition of $Q(\cdot\,|\,x)$ (Exercise 34.4).

The Non-uniqueness Issue Frequentists Face

A minor annoyance when using Bayesian methods as part of a frequentist argument is that the posterior need not be unique.

EXAMPLE 34.2. Consider the situation when the hypothesis set is the $[0,1]$ interval, the prior is the uniform distribution, and the observation is equal to the hypothesis sampled. Formally, $\Theta = [0,1]$ and the prior Q is the uniform measure on $(\Theta, \mathcal{B}(\Theta))$, $P_\theta = \delta_\theta$ is the Dirac measure on $[0,1]$ at θ, and $X : [0,1] \to [0,1]$ is the identity: $X(x) = x$ for all $x \in [0,1]$. Let $C \subset [0,1]$ be an *arbitrary* countable set and μ be an *arbitrary* probability measure on $([0,1], \mathcal{B}(\mathbb{R}))$. It is not hard to see that the probability kernel

$$Q(A\,|\,x) = \begin{cases} \delta_x(A), & \text{if } x \notin C; \\ \mu(A), & \text{if } x \in C \end{cases}$$

satisfies the conditions of Theorem 34.1 and is thus one of the many versions of the posterior, regardless of the choice of C and μ!

A true Bayesian is unconcerned. If θ is sampled from the prior Q, then the event $\{X \in C\}$ has measure zero, and there is little cause to worry about events that happen with probability zero. But for a frequentist using Bayesian techniques for inference, this actually matters. If θ is not sampled from Q, then nothing prevents the situation that $\theta \in C$ and the non-uniqueness of the posterior is an issue (Exercise 34.12). Probability theory does not provide a way around this issue.

> It follows that one must be careful to specify the version of the posterior being used when using Bayesian techniques for inference in a frequentist setting because in the frequentist viewpoint, θ is not part of the probability space and results are proven for P_θ for arbitrary fixed $\theta \in \Theta$. By contrast, the all-in Bayesians include θ in the probability space and thus will not worry about events with negligible prior probability, and for them any version of the posterior will do.

Although it is important to be aware of the non-uniqueness of the posterior, practically speaking it is hard to go wrong. In typical applications, there is a 'canonical' choice. For example, in the Gaussian prior and model case studied below, it feels right to choose the posterior to be Gaussian. More generally, preferring posteriors with continuous densities with respect to the Lebesgue measure is generally a parsimonious choice.

34.3 Conjugate Pairs, Conjugate Priors and the Exponential Family

One of the strengths of the Bayesian approach is the ability to incorporate explicitly specified prior beliefs. This is philosophically attractive and can be enormously beneficial when the user has well-grounded prior knowledge about the problem. When it comes to Bayesian algorithms, however, this advantage is belied a little by the competing necessity of choosing a prior for which the posterior can be efficiently computed or sampled from. The ease of computing (or sampling from) the posterior depends on the interplay between the prior and the model. Given the importance of computation, it is hardly surprising that researchers have worked hard to find models and priors that behave well together. A prior and model are called a **conjugate pair** if the posterior has the same parametric form as the prior. In this case, the prior is called a **conjugate prior** to the model.

Gaussian Model/Gaussian Prior
Suppose that $(\Theta, \mathcal{G}) = (\Omega, \mathcal{F}) = (\mathbb{R}, \mathfrak{B}(\mathbb{R}))$ and $X : \Omega \to \Omega$ is the identity and P_θ is Gaussian with mean θ and known **signal variance** σ_S^2. If the prior Q is Gaussian with mean μ_P and **prior variance** σ_P^2, then the posterior distribution having observed $X = x$ can be chosen to be

$$Q(\cdot \,|\, x) = \mathcal{N}\left(\frac{\mu_P/\sigma_P^2 + x/\sigma_S^2}{1/\sigma_P^2 + 1/\sigma_S^2}, \left(\frac{1}{\sigma_S^2} + \frac{1}{\sigma_P^2} \right)^{-1} \right).$$

The proof is left to the reader in Exercise 34.1.

 Following convention, from now on we sweep under the rug that this posterior is one of many choices, which is justified because all posteriors must agree almost everywhere.

The limiting regimes as the prior/signal variance tend to zero or infinity are quite illuminating. For example, as $\sigma_P^2 \to 0$ the posterior tends to a Gaussian $\mathcal{N}(\mu_P, \sigma_P^2)$, which is equal to the prior and indicates that no learning occurs. This is consistent with intuition. If the prior variance is zero, then the statistician is already certain of the mean, and no amount of data can change their belief. On the other hand, as σ_P^2 tends to infinity, we see the mean of the posterior has no dependence on the prior mean, which means that all prior knowledge is washed away with just one sample. You should think about what happens when $\sigma_S^2 \to \{0, \infty\}$.

Notice how the model has fixed σ_S^2, suggesting that the model variance is known. The Bayesian can also incorporate their uncertainty over the variance. In this case, the model parameters are $\Theta = \mathbb{R} \times [0, \infty)$ and $P_\theta = \mathcal{N}(\theta_1, \theta_2)$. But is there a conjugate prior in this case? Already things are getting complicated, so we will simply let you know that the family of Gaussian-inverse-gamma distributions is conjugate.

Bernoulli Model/Beta Prior

Suppose that $\Theta = [0, 1]$ and $P_\theta = \mathcal{B}(\theta)$ is Bernoulli with parameter θ. In this case, it turns out that the family of beta distributions is conjugate, which for parameters $\theta = (\alpha, \beta) \in (0, \infty)^2$ is given in terms of its probability density function with respect to the Lebesgue measure:

$$p_{\alpha,\beta}(x) = x^{\alpha-1}(1-x)^{\beta-1}\frac{\Gamma(\alpha+\beta)}{\Gamma(\alpha)\Gamma(\beta)}, \tag{34.3}$$

where $\Gamma(x)$ is the Gamma function. Then the posterior having observed $X = x \in \{0, 1\}$ is also a beta distribution with parameters $(\alpha + x, \beta + 1 - x)$. Unlike in the Gaussian case, the posterior for the Bernoulli model and beta prior is unique (Exercise 34.2).

34.3.1 Exponential Families

Both the Gaussian and Bernoulli families are examples of a more general family. Let h be a measure on $(\mathbb{R}, \mathcal{B}(\mathbb{R}))$ and $S, \eta : \mathbb{R} \to \mathbb{R}$ be two 'suitable' functions, where S is called the **sufficient statistic**. Together, h, η and S define a measure P_θ on $(\mathbb{R}, \mathcal{B}(\mathbb{R}))$ for each $\theta \in \Theta \subseteq \mathbb{R}$ in terms of its density with respect to h:

$$\frac{dP_\theta}{dh}(x) = \exp\left(\eta(\theta)S(x) - A(\theta)\right),$$

where $A(\theta) = \log \int_\mathbb{R} \exp(\eta(\theta)S(x))dh(x)$ is the **log-partition** function and $\Theta = \text{dom}(A) = \{\theta : A(\theta) < \infty\}$ is the domain of A. Integrating the density shows that for any $B \in \mathcal{B}(\mathbb{R})$ and $\theta \in \Theta$,

$$P_\theta(B) = \int_B \frac{dP_\theta}{dh}(x)\, dh(x) = \int_B \exp\left(\eta(\theta)S(x) - A(\theta)\right)\, dh(x).$$

The collection $(P_\theta : \theta \in \Theta)$ is called a **single-parameter exponential family**. An exponential family is **regular** if Θ is non-empty and open. It is **non-singular** if $A''(\theta) > 0$ for all $\theta \in \Theta$.

EXAMPLE 34.3. Let $\sigma^2 > 0$ and $h = \mathcal{N}(0, \sigma^2)$ and $\eta(\theta) = \frac{\theta}{\sigma}$ and $S(x) = \frac{x}{\sigma}$. An easy calculation shows that $A(\theta) = \theta^2/(2\sigma^2)$, which has domain $\Theta = \mathbb{R}$ and $P_\theta = \mathcal{N}(\theta, \sigma^2)$.

EXAMPLE 34.4. Let $h = \delta_0 + \delta_1$ be the sum of Dirac measures and $S(x) = x$ and $\eta(\theta) = \theta$. Then $A(\theta) = \log(1 + \exp(\theta))$ and $\Theta = \mathbb{R}$ and $P_\theta = \mathcal{B}(\sigma(\theta))$, where $\sigma(\theta) = \exp(\theta)/(1 + \exp(\theta))$ is the logistic function.

EXAMPLE 34.5. The same family can be parameterised in many different ways. Let $h = \delta_0 + \delta_1$, $S(x) = x$ and $\eta(\theta) = \log(\theta/(1-\theta))$. Then $A(\theta) = -\log(1-\theta)$ and $\Theta = (0, 1)$ and $P_\theta = \mathcal{B}(\theta)$.

Exponential families have many nice properties, some of which you will prove in Exercise 34.5. Of most interest to us here is the existence of conjugate priors. Suppose that $(P_\theta : \theta \in \Theta)$ is a single-parameter exponential family determined by h, η and S, where $S(x) = x$ is the identity map. Let $x_0, n_0 \in \mathbb{R}$, and define prior measure Q on $(\Theta, \mathcal{B}(\Theta))$ in terms of its density $q = dQ/d\lambda$ with λ the Lebesgue measure:

$$q(\theta) = \frac{\exp\left(n_0 x_0 \eta(\theta) - n_0 A(\theta)\right)}{\int_\Theta \exp\left(n_0 x_0 \eta(\theta) - n_0 A(\theta)\right) d\theta},\tag{34.4}$$

where we assume that the integral in the denominator exists and is positive. Suppose we observe $X = x$. Then a choice of posterior has density with respect to the Lebesgue measure given by

$$q(\theta\,|\,x) = \frac{\exp\left(\eta(\theta)(x + n_0 x_0) - (1 + n_0)A(\theta)\right)}{\int_\Theta \exp\left(\eta(\theta)(x + n_0 x_0) - (1 + n_0)A(\theta)\right) d\lambda(\theta)}.$$

What this means is that after observing the value x, the posterior takes the form of the prior except that the parameters (x_0, n_0) associated with the prior get updated to $((n_0 x_0 + x)/(n_0 + 1), n_0 + 1)$. The posterior is both easy to represent and maintain. To see how exponential families recover previous examples, consider the Bernoulli case of Example 34.5. Since

$$\exp(n_0 x_0 \eta(\theta) - n_0 A(\theta)) = \left(\frac{\theta}{1 - \theta}\right)^{n_0 x_0} (1 - \theta)^{n_0} = \theta^{n_0 x_0}(1 - \theta)^{n_0(1 - x_0)},$$

we see that the prior from (34.4) is a beta distribution with parameters $\alpha = 1 + n_0 x_0$ and $\beta = 1 + n_0(1 - x_0)$, as can be seen from (34.3). As expected, the posterior update also works as described earlier.

There are important parametric families with conjugate priors that are not exponential families. One example is the uniform family $(\mathcal{U}(a,b) : a < b)$, which is conjugate to the Pareto family.

34.3.2 Sequences of Random Variables and the Markov Chain View

Let $P^n = (P_\theta^n : \theta \in \Theta)$ be a probability kernel from $(\Theta, \mathcal{G})$ to $(\mathcal{X}^n, \mathcal{H}^{\otimes n})$ and Q a prior on $(\Theta, \mathcal{G})$. Then, let θ and $X_1, \ldots, X_n$ be random elements on some probability space $(\Omega, \mathcal{F}, \mathbb{P})$, where $\theta \in \Theta$ and $X_t \in \mathcal{X}$ such that

(a) the law of θ is $\mathbb{P}_\theta = Q$; and
(b) $\mathbb{P}(X_1, \ldots, X_n \in B\,|\,\theta) = P_\theta(B)$ almost surely for all $B \in \mathcal{H}^{\otimes n}$.

By definition, the posterior after observing $(X_s)_{s=1}^t$ is a probability kernel Q_t from $(\mathcal{X}^t, \mathcal{H}^{\otimes t})$ to $(\Theta, \mathcal{G})$ such that for any $B \in \mathcal{G}$,

$$\mathbb{E}[\mathbb{I}\{\theta \in B\}\,|\,X_1, \ldots, X_t] = Q_t(B\,|\,X_1, \ldots, X_t) \quad \text{almost surely.}$$

Then, by the tower rule, the conditional distribution of X_{t+1} given $(X_s)_{s=1}^t$ almost surely satisfies

$$\mathbb{P}(X_{t+1} \in B\,|\,X_1, \ldots, X_t) = \int_\Theta P_\theta(X_{t+1} \in B\,|\,X_1, \ldots, X_t)Q_t(d\theta\,|\,X_1, \ldots, X_t).\tag{34.5}$$

This identity says that the conditional distribution of X_{t+1} can be written in terms of the model and posterior. In the fundamental setting where $P_\theta^n = P_\theta \otimes \cdots \otimes P_\theta$ is a product probability measure, then Eq. (34.5) reduces to

$$\mathbb{P}(X_{t+1} \in B \mid X_1, \ldots, X_t) = \int_\Theta P_\theta(B) Q_t(d\theta \mid X_1, \ldots, X_t),$$

which shows that in this case the posterior summarises all the useful information in $(X_s)_{s=1}^t$ for predicting future data. By introducing a little measure-theoretic machinery and making suitable regularity assumptions, it is possible to show that the sequence $Q_1, \ldots, Q_n$ is a time-inhomogeneous Markov chain. In many cases, the posterior has a simple form, as you can see in the next two examples.

EXAMPLE 34.6. Suppose $\Theta = [0, 1]$ and $\mathcal{G} = \mathfrak{B}([0, 1])$ and $Q = \text{Beta}(\alpha, \beta)$ and $P_\theta = \mathcal{B}(\theta)$ is Bernoulli. Then the posterior after t observations is $Q_t = \text{Beta}(\alpha + S_t, \beta + t - S_t)$, where $S_t = \sum_{s=1}^t X_s$. Furthermore, $\mathbb{E}[X_{t+1} \mid X_1, \ldots, X_t] = \mathbb{E}_{Q_t}[X_{t+1}] = (\alpha + S_t)/(\alpha + \beta + t)$, and hence

$$\mathbb{P}(S_{t+1} = S_t + 1 \mid S_t) = \frac{\alpha + S_t}{\alpha + \beta + t},$$

$$\mathbb{P}(S_{t+1} = S_t \mid S_t) = \frac{\beta + t - S_t}{\alpha + \beta + t}.$$

So the posterior after t observations is a Beta distribution depending on S_t and $S_1, S_2, \ldots, S_n$ follows a Markov chain evolving according to the above display.

EXAMPLE 34.7. Let $(\Theta, \mathcal{G}) = (\mathbb{R}, \mathfrak{B}(\mathbb{R}))$ and $Q = \mathcal{N}(\mu, \sigma^2)$ and $P_\theta = \mathcal{N}(\theta, 1)$. Then, using the same notation as above the posterior is almost surely $Q_t = \mathcal{N}(\mu_t, \sigma_t^2)$, where

$$\mu_t = \frac{\mu/\sigma^2 + S_t}{1/\sigma^2 + t} \quad \text{and} \quad \sigma_t^2 = \left(\frac{1}{\sigma^2} + t\right)^{-1}.$$

Then $S_1, S_2, \ldots, S_n$ is a Markov chain with the conditional distribution of S_{t+1} given S_t a Gaussian with mean $S_t + \mu_t$ and variance $1 + \sigma_t^2$.

34.4 The Bayesian Bandit Environment

The Bayesian bandit model is the same as the frequentist version introduced in Chapter 4, except that at the beginning of the game, an environment is sampled from the prior. Of course, the chosen environment is not revealed to the learner, but its presence forces us to change our conditions on the rewards because the rewards are dependent on each other through the chosen environment. For simplicity, we treat only the finite, k-armed case, but the more general set-up is handled in the same was as in Chapter 4.

A **k-armed Bayesian bandit environment** is a tuple $(\mathcal{E}, \mathcal{G}, Q, P)$, where $(\mathcal{E}, \mathcal{G})$ is a measurable space and Q is a probability measure on $(\mathcal{E}, \mathcal{G})$ called the prior. The last element $P = (P_{vi} : v \in \mathcal{E}, i \in [k])$ is a probability kernel from $\mathcal{E} \times [k]$ to $(\mathbb{R}, \mathfrak{B}(\mathbb{R}))$, where P_{vi} is the reward distribution associated with the ith arm in bandit v. A Bayesian bandit environment and policy $\pi = (\pi_t)_{t=1}^n$ interact to produce a collection of random variables, $v \in \mathcal{E}$, $(A_t)_{t=1}^n$ and $(X_t)_{t=1}^n$ with $A_t \in [k]$ and $X_t \in \mathbb{R}$ that satisfy

(a) $\mathbb{P}(v \in \cdot) = Q(\cdot)$;

(b) the conditional distribution of action A_t given $v, A_1, X_1, \ldots, A_{t-1}, X_{t-1}$ is $\pi_t(\cdot \mid A_1, X_1, \ldots, A_{t-1}, X_{t-1})$ almost surely; and

(c) the conditional distribution of the reward X_t given $v, A_1, X_1, \ldots, A_t$ is P_{vA_t} almost surely.

The existence of a probability space carrying random elements satisfying these conditions is guaranteed by the Ionescu–Tulcea theorem (Theorem 3.3, Exercise 34.9). The corresponding probability measure will be denoted by $\mathbb{P}_{QP\pi}$.

> Most of the structure of a Bayesian bandit environment is in P, which determines the reward distribution for each arm i in bandits $v \in \mathcal{E}$.

EXAMPLE 34.8. A k-armed Bayesian Bernoulli bandit environment could be defined by letting $\mathcal{E} = [0,1]^k$, $\mathcal{G} = \mathfrak{B}(\mathcal{E})$ and $P_{vi} = \mathcal{B}(v_i)$. A natural prior in this case would be a product of $\text{Beta}(\alpha, \beta)$ distributions:

$$Q(A) = \int_A \prod_{i=1}^{k} q_i(x_i) dx,$$

where $q_i(x) = x^{\alpha-1}(1-x)^{\beta-1}\Gamma(\alpha+\beta)/(\Gamma(\alpha)\Gamma(\beta))$.

34.5 Posterior Distributions in Bandits

Let $(\mathcal{E}, \mathcal{G}, Q, P)$ be a k-armed Bayesian bandit environment. Assuming that $(\mathcal{E}, \mathcal{G})$ is a Borel space, Theorem 34.1 guarantees the existence of the posterior: a probability kernel $Q(\cdot \mid \cdot)$ from the space of histories to $(\mathcal{E}, \mathcal{G})$ so that

$$Q(A \mid a_1, x_1, \ldots, a_t, x_t)$$

is a regular version of $\mathbb{E}[\mathbb{I}_A(v) \mid A_1, X_1, \ldots, A_t, X_t]$. For explicit calculations, it is worth adding some some extra structure: assume there exists a σ-finite measure λ on $(\mathbb{R}, \mathfrak{B}(\mathbb{R}))$ such that $P_{vi} \ll \lambda$ for all $i \in [k]$ and $v \in \mathcal{E}$. Recall from Chapter 15 that the Radon–Nikodym derivative of $\mathbb{P}_{v\pi}$ with respect to $(\rho \times \lambda)^n$ is

$$p_{v\pi}(a_1, x_1, \ldots, a_n, x_n) = \prod_{t=1}^{n} \pi_t(a_t \mid a_1, x_1, \ldots, a_{t-1}x_{t-1})p_{va_t}(x_t), \qquad (34.6)$$

where p_{va} is the density of P_{va} with respect to λ. Then the posterior after t rounds is given by

$$Q(B \mid a_1, x_1, \ldots, a_t, x_t) = \frac{\int_B p_{v\pi}(a_1, x_1, \ldots, a_t, x_t) dQ(v)}{\int_{\mathcal{E}} p_{v\pi}(a_1, x_1, \ldots, a_t, x_t) dQ(v)}$$

$$= \frac{\int_B \prod_{s=1}^{t} p_{va_s}(x_s) dQ(v)}{\int_{\mathcal{E}} \prod_{s=1}^{t} p_{va_s}(x_s) dQ(v)}, \qquad (34.7)$$

where the second equality follows from Eq. (34.6). The posterior is not defined when the denominator is zero, which only occurs with probability zero (Exercise 34.11). Note that the Radon–Nikodym derivatives $p_{va}(x)$ are only unique up to sets of P_{va}-measure zero, and so the 'choice' of posterior has been converted to a choice of the Radon–Nikodym derivatives, which, in all practical situations is straightforward. Observe also that Eq. (34.7) is only well defined if $p_{va_s}(\cdot)$ is $\mathcal{G}$-measurable as a function of v. Fortunately this is always possible (see Note 8).

EXAMPLE 34.9. The posterior for the Bayesian bandit in Example 34.8 in terms of its density with respect to the Lebesgue measure is

$$q(\theta \mid \underbrace{a_1, x_1, \ldots, a_t, x_t}_{h_t}) \propto \prod_{i=1}^{k} \theta_i^{\alpha + s_i(h_t) - 1}(1 - \theta_i)^{\beta + t_i(h_t) - s_i(h_t) - 1},$$

where $s_i(h_t) = \sum_{u=1}^{t} x_u \mathbb{I}\{a_u = i\}$ and $t_i(h_t) = \sum_{u=1}^{t} \mathbb{I}\{a_u = i\}$. This means the posterior is also the product of Beta distributions, each updated according to the observations from the relevant arm.

34.6   Bayesian Regret

Recall that the regret of policy π in k-armed bandit environment v over n rounds is

$$R_n(\pi, v) = n\mu^* - \mathbb{E}\left[\sum_{t=1}^{n} X_t\right], \tag{34.8}$$

where $\mu^* = \max_{i \in [k]} \mu_i$ and μ_i is the mean of P_{vi}. Given a k-armed Bayesian bandit environment $(\mathcal{E}, \mathcal{G}, Q, P)$ and a policy π, the **Bayesian regret** is

$$\mathrm{BR}_n(\pi, Q) = \int_{\mathcal{E}} R_n(\pi, v) dQ(v).$$

The dependence on $\mathcal{E}, \mathcal{G}$ and P is omitted on the grounds that these are always self-evident from the context. The Bayesian optimal regret is $\mathrm{BR}_n^*(Q) = \inf_\pi \mathrm{BR}_n(\pi, Q)$, and the optimal (regret-minimizing) policy is

$$\pi^* = \mathrm{argmin}_\pi \, \mathrm{BR}_n(\pi, Q). \tag{34.9}$$

Note that the regret-minimising policy is the same as the reward-maximising policy $\pi^* = \mathrm{argmax}_\pi \mathbb{E}_{\mathbb{P}_{QP\pi}}[\sum_{t=1}^{n} X_t]$, which is known as the **Bayesian optimal policy** under prior Q. In all generality, there is no guarantee that the (Bayes) optimal policy exists, but the non-negativity of the Bayesian regret ensures that for any $\varepsilon > 0$, there exists a policy π with $\mathrm{BR}_n(\pi, Q) \leq \mathrm{BR}_n^*(Q) + \varepsilon$.

The fact that the expected regret $R_n(\pi, v)$ is non-negative for all v and π means that the Bayesian regret is always non-negative. Perhaps less obviously, the Bayesian regret of the Bayesian optimal policy can be strictly greater than zero (Exercise 34.8).

34.7   Notes

1 In Chapter 4, we defined the environment class $\mathcal{E}$ as a set of tuples of probability distributions over the reals. In a Bayesian bandit environment $(\mathcal{E}, \mathcal{G}, Q, P)$ the set $\mathcal{E}$ is arbitrary and the reward distributions are given by the probability kernel P. The probability kernel and the change of notation is needed because we are now integrating the regret over $\mathcal{E}$, which may not be measurable without additional conditions.

2 The Bayesian regret of an algorithm is less informative than the frequentist regret. By this we mean that a bound on $\mathrm{BR}_n(\pi, Q)$ does not generally imply a meaningful bound on $R_n(\pi, \nu)$, while if $R_n(\pi, \nu) \leq f(\nu)$ for a measurable function f, then $\mathrm{BR}_n(\pi, Q) \leq \mathbb{E}[f(\nu)]$. This is not an argument against using a Bayesian algorithm but rather an argument for the need to analyse the frequentist regret of Bayesian algorithms.

3 The relationship between admissibility, Bayesian optimality and minimax optimality is one of the main topics of statistical decision theory, which intersects heavily with game theory. In many classical statistical settings, all Bayesian optimal policies are admissible (Exercise 34.14), and all admissible policies are either Bayesian optimal for some prior or the limit point of a sequence of Bayesian optimal policies (Exercise 34.13). Be warned, however, that there are counterexamples. A nice book with many examples is by Berger [1985]. In Exercise 34.15, you will prove that all admissible policies for stochastic Bernoulli bandits are Bayesian optimal for some prior.

4 While admissibility and related notions of optimality are helpful in being clear about the goals of algorithm design, we must recognise that these concepts are too binary for most purposes. One problem with the classic decision theory literature is that it puts too much emphasis on these narrow concepts. Who would argue that a policy that is dominated, but just barely, is worth nothing? Especially since the optimal policy is often intractable. Meaningful ways of defining slightly worse usually consider a bigger picture when a policy design approach (**policy schema**) is evaluated across many problem classes. In the Bayesian setting, one may for example consider all k-armed stochastic Bayesian bandits with (say) bounded rewards and consider policy schema that work no matter what the environment is. An example of a policy schema is Thompson sampling, since it can be instantiated for any of the environments. One may ask whether such a policy schema is near Bayesian (or minimax) optimal across all of the considered environments. In fact, most bandit algorithm design is better viewed as designing policy schema.

5 Many algorithms/statistical methods have Bayesian interpretations. One example is ridge regression, which we saw in Chapter 20. Using the notation of that chapter, the estimator given in Eq. (20.1) is the mean of the Bayesian posterior when the model is Gaussian with known variance and the prior on the unknown parameter is a Gaussian with zero mean and covariance I/λ. Another example is the exponential weighting algorithm for prediction with expert advice. Consider a sequence $y_1, \ldots, y_n \in [d]$ and suppose there are set $\mathcal{M}$ of k experts making predictions about y_t. We write $\mu(\cdot \,|\, y_1, \ldots, y_{t-1}) \in \mathcal{P}_{d-1}$ for the distribution of y_t predicted by expert $\mu \in \mathcal{M}$. In each round the learner observes the predictions $\mu(\cdot \,|\, y_1, \ldots, y_{t-1})$ for all experts $\mu \in \mathcal{M}$ and should make a prediction $\xi(\cdot \,|\, y_1, \ldots, y_{t-1}) \in \mathcal{P}_{d-1}$. Notice that defining $\mu(y_1, \ldots, y_n) = \prod_{t=1}^n \mu(y_t \,|\, y_1, \ldots, y_{t-1})$ makes $\mu(\cdot)$ into a probability distribution on $[d]^n$. The regret compares the learner's performance relative to the best expert in $\mathcal{M}$ under the logarithmic loss:

$$R_n = \max_{\mu \in \mathcal{M}} \sum_{t=1}^n \log\left(\frac{\mu(y_t \,|\, y_1, \ldots, y_{t-1})}{\xi(y_t \,|\, y_1, \ldots, y_{t-1})} \right) = \max_{\mu \in \mathcal{M}} \log\left(\frac{\mu(y_1, \ldots, y_n)}{\xi(y_1, \ldots, y_n)} \right).$$

A Bayesian approach to this problem is to assume that $y_1, \ldots, y_n$ is sampled from some unknown $\mu \in \mathcal{M}$ and choose a prior distribution $Q \in \mathcal{P}(\mathcal{M})$ over the experts. Then predict to minimise the Bayesian expected loss, which you will show in Exercise 34.6 leads to

$$\xi(\cdot \mid y_1, \ldots, y_{t-1}) = \sum_{\mu \in \mathcal{M}} \overbrace{\mu(\cdot \mid y_1, \ldots, y_{t-1})}^{\text{predictive dist. of } \mu} \underbrace{\frac{\mu(y_1, \ldots, y_{t-1}) Q(\mu)}{\sum_{\nu \in \mathcal{M}} \nu(y_1, \ldots, y_{t-1}) Q(\nu)}}_{\text{posterior } Q_{t-1}(\mu)} . \tag{34.10}$$

You will also show that when Q is taken to be the uniform distribution, the regret is bounded by $R_n \leq \log(k)$ for all sequences $y_1, \ldots, y_n$. Simple algebraic manipulations show that the posterior is

$$Q_t(\mu) = \frac{\exp\left(-\sum_{s=1}^{t} \log\left(\frac{1}{\mu(y_s \mid y_1, \ldots, y_{s-1})}\right)\right)}{\sum_{\nu \in \mathcal{M}} \exp\left(-\sum_{s=1}^{t} \log\left(\frac{1}{\nu(y_s \mid y_1, \ldots, y_{s-1})}\right)\right)},$$

which is precisely the exponential weights distribution with learning rate $\eta = 1$. The analogy should not be taken too seriously, however. That this algorithm controls the regret for all sequences $y_1, \ldots, y_n$ does not hold for more general loss functions. For this, the learning rate must be chosen much more conservatively. For more on the online learning approach to learning under the logarithmic loss, see chapter 9 of the book by Cesa-Bianchi and Lugosi [2006]. The Bayesian approach is covered in the book by Hutter [2004].

6 Sion's minimax theorem provides a connection between minimax optimal regret and the maximum Bayesian optimal regret over all priors. Let Π be the space of all policies and $\mathcal{P}$ be a convex space of probability measures over policies and $\mathcal{Q}$ be a convex space of probability measures on $(\mathcal{E}, \mathcal{G})$. Define $\mathcal{L} : \mathcal{P} \times \mathcal{Q} \to \mathbb{R}$ by

$$\mathcal{L}(S, Q) = \int_{\Pi} \int_{\mathcal{E}} R_n(\pi, \nu) Q(d\nu) S(d\pi),$$

which is linear in both arguments because integrals are linear as a function of the measure. Suppose that $\mathcal{L}$ is continuous in both arguments and at least one of $\mathcal{P}$ and $\mathcal{Q}$ is compact. Then, by Sion's minimax theorem (Theorem 28.12),

$$\sup_{Q \in \mathcal{Q}} \inf_{S \in \mathcal{P}} \mathcal{L}(S, Q) = \inf_{S \in \mathcal{P}} \sup_{Q \in \mathcal{Q}} \mathcal{L}(S, Q). \tag{34.11}$$

Usually $\mathcal{P}$ and $\mathcal{Q}$ include all Dirac measures:

$$\{\delta_\pi : \pi \in \Pi_D\} \subseteq \mathcal{P} \quad \text{and} \quad \{\delta_\nu : \nu \in \mathcal{E}\} \subseteq \mathcal{Q},$$

where Π_D is the space of deterministic policies. Then the left-hand side of Eq. (34.11) is $\sup_{Q \in \mathcal{Q}} \mathrm{BR}_n^*(Q)$, and the right-hand side is the minimax regret $R_n^*(\mathcal{E})$. Choosing $\mathcal{P}$, $\mathcal{Q}$ and a measurable structure on Π is not always easy. Examples may be found in Exercises 34.16 and 36.11.

7 The issue of conditioning on measure zero sets has been described in many places. We do not know of a practical situation where things go awry. Sensible choices yield sensible posteriors. The curious reader could probably burn a few weeks reading through the literature on the **Borel–Kolmogorov paradox** [Jaynes, 2003, §15.7].

8 Suppose that $(P_\theta : \theta \in \Theta)$ is a probability kernel from $(\Theta, \mathcal{G})$ to $(\mathbb{R}, \mathfrak{B}(\mathbb{R}))$ for which there exists measure λ on $(\mathbb{R}, \mathfrak{B}(\mathbb{R}))$ such that $P_\theta \ll \lambda$ for all $\theta \in \Theta$. Then there exists a family of densities $p_\theta : \mathbb{R} \to [0, \infty)$ such that $p_\theta(x)$ is jointly measurable as a $(\theta, x) \mapsto p_\theta(x)$ map and

$p_\theta = dP_\theta/d\lambda$ for all $\theta \in \Theta$. See the proof of Lemma 1.2 in Ghosal and van der Vaart [2017] or sections 1.3 and 1.4 of the book by Strasser [2011].

9 The notion of a **sufficient statistic** is more general than its role in exponential families. Let X and Y be random elements on the same measurable space taking values in $\mathcal{X}$ and $\mathcal{Y}$ respectively. The random element Y is a sufficient statistic for X given a family of distributions $(\mathbb{P}_\theta)_{\theta \in \Theta}$ over the probability space carrying both X and Y if *(i)* Y is $\sigma(X)$-measurable and *(ii)* for all $\theta \in \Theta$, the conditional distribution $\mathbb{P}_\theta(X \in \cdot | Y)$ is independent of the value of θ. Formally, *(ii)* means there exists a probability kernel P from $\mathcal{Y}$ to $\mathcal{X}$ such that for any $\theta \in \Theta$, $\mathbb{P}_\theta(X \in \cdot | Y) = P(Y, \cdot)$ holds $\mathbb{P}_\theta$-almost surely. Informally, this means, that given Y, there is no information left about θ in X. Denoting by $\mathbb{P}_{X,\theta}$ the distribution of X under $\mathbb{P}_\theta$ and without loss of generality letting $Y = y(X)$ for some $y : \mathcal{X} \to \mathcal{Y}$ measurable map (recall Lemma 2.5), and assuming that X, Y take values in Borel spaces, with the help of the disintegration theorem (Theorem 3.12), it is not hard to see that if $(\mathbb{P}_{X,\theta})_\theta$ have a common dominating σ-finite measure μ and for any $\theta \in \Theta$, $\frac{d\mathbb{P}_{X,\theta}}{d\mu}(x) = h(x)g_\theta(y(x))$ holds μ-almost surely for all $x \in \mathcal{X}$ for some some $h : \mathcal{X} \to [0, \infty)$ and $g_\theta : \mathcal{Y} \to [0, \infty)$ Borel measurable maps, then Y is a sufficient statistic for X. The **Fisher–Neyman factorisation theorem** states that the converse also holds. With some creative matching of concepts, we can see that in single-parameter exponential families, what we called a sufficient statistic satisfies the more general definition.

34.8 Bibliographic Remarks

The original essay by Thomas Bayes is remarkably readable [Bayes, 1763]. There are many texts on Bayesian statistics. For an introduction to the applied side, there is the book by Gelman et al. [2014]. This book offers lots of discussions and examples. A more philosophical book that takes a foundational look at probability theory from a Bayesian perspective is by Jaynes [2003]. The careful definition of the posterior can be found in several places, but the recent book by Ghosal and van der Vaart [2017] does an impeccable job. A worthy mention goes to the article by Chang and Pollard [1997], which uses disintegration (Theorem 3.12) to formalise the 'private calculations' that probabilists so frequently make before writing

Thomas Bayes

everything carefully using Radon–Nikodym derivatives and regular versions. Theorem 34.1 is a specification of the theorem guaranteeing the existence of regular conditional probability measures (Theorem 3.11). For a detailed presentation of exponential families, see the book by Lehmann and Casella [2006]. A compendium of conjugate priors is by Fink [1997].

34.9 Exercises

34.1 (POSTERIOR CALCULATIONS) Evaluate the posteriors for each pair of conjugate priors in Section 34.3.

34.2 (UNIQUENESS OF BETA/BERNOULLI POSTERIOR) Explain why the posterior for the Bernoulli model with a beta prior is unique.

34.3 Use the tower rule to prove the identity in Eq. (34.5).

34.4 (POSTERIOR IN TERMS OF DENSITY) Let $P = (P_\theta : \theta \in \Theta)$ be a probability kernel from $(\Theta, \mathcal{G})$ to $(\mathcal{X}, \mathcal{H})$ and Q be a probability measure on Θ and $\mathbb{P} = Q \otimes P$ on $\Theta \times \mathcal{X}$. As usual, let θ and X be the coordinate projections on $\Theta \times \mathcal{X}$. Let ν and μ be probability measures on $(\Theta, \mathcal{G})$ and $(\mathcal{X}, \mathcal{H})$ such that $Q \ll \nu$ and $P_\theta \ll \mu$ for all $\theta \in \Theta$, and define

$$q(\theta \mid x) = \frac{p_\theta(x)q(\theta)}{\int_\Theta p_\psi(x)q(\psi)d\nu(\psi)},$$

where $p_\theta(x) = dP_\theta/d\mu$ and $q(\theta) = dQ/d\nu$. You may assume that $p_\theta(x)$ is jointly measurable in θ and x (see Note 8).

(a) Let $N = \{x : \int_\Theta p_\psi(x)q(\psi)d\nu(\psi) = 0\}$ and show that $\mathbb{P}_X(N) = 0$.
(b) Define $Q(A \mid x) = \int_A q(\theta \mid x)d\nu(\theta)$ for $x \notin N$ and $Q(A \mid x)$ be an arbitrary fixed probability measure for $x \in N$. Show that $Q(\cdot \mid X)$ is a regular version of $\mathbb{P}(\theta \in \cdot \mid X)$.

HINT   The 'sections' lemma may prove useful (Lemma 1.26 in Kallenberg 2002), along with the properties of the Radon–Nikodym derivative.

34.5 (EXPONENTIAL FAMILIES) Let A, T, h, η and Θ be as in Section 34.3.1.

(a) Prove that P_θ is indeed a probability measure.
(b) Let $\mathbb{E}_\theta$ denote expectations with respect to P_θ. Show that $A'(\theta) = \mathbb{E}_\theta[T]$.
(c) Let $\theta \in \Theta$ and $X \sim P_\theta$. Show that for all λ with $\lambda + \theta \in \Theta$,

$$\mathbb{E}_\theta[\exp(\lambda T(X))] = \exp(A(\lambda + \theta) - A(\theta)).$$

(d) Given $\theta, \theta' \in \Theta$, show that

$$d(\theta, \theta') = \mathbb{E}_\theta\left[\log\left(\frac{p_\theta(X)}{p_{\theta'}(X)}\right)\right] = A(\theta') - A(\theta) - (\theta' - \theta)A'(\theta). \tag{34.12}$$

(e) Let $\theta, \theta' \in \Theta$ be such that $A'(\theta') \geq A'(\theta)$ and $X_1, \ldots, X_n$ be independent and identically distributed and $\hat{T} = \frac{1}{n}\sum_{t=1}^n T(X_t)$. Show that

$$\mathbb{P}\left(\hat{T} \geq A'(\theta')\right) \leq \exp\left(-nd(\theta', \theta)\right).$$

Curiously, the function d of Eq. (34.12) is both the relative entropy $D(P_\theta, P_{\theta'})$ and the Bregman divergence between θ' and θ induced by the convex function A. See Section 26.3 for the definition of Bregman divergence.

34.6 (EXPONENTIAL WEIGHTS ALGORITHM) Consider the setting of Note 5.

(a) Prove the claim in Eq. (34.10).
(b) Prove that when $Q(\mu) = 1/k$ is the uniform prior, then the regret is bounded by $R_n \leq \log(k)$ for any $y_1, \ldots, y_n$.

34.7 (MEASURABILITY OF THE REGRET) Let $(\mathcal{E}, \mathcal{G}, Q, P)$ be a Bayesian bandit environment and π a policy. Prove that $R_n(\pi, \nu)$, defined in Eq. (34.8), is $\mathcal{G}$-measurable as a function of ν.

34.8 (BAYESIAN OPTIMAL REGRET CAN BE POSITIVE) Construct an example demonstrating that for some priors over finite-armed stochastic bandits, the Bayesian regret is strictly positive: $\inf_\pi \mathrm{BR}_n(\pi, Q) > 0$.

HINT   The key is to observe that under appropriate conditions, $\mathrm{BR}_n(\pi, Q) = 0$ would mean that π needs to know the identity of the optimal action under ν from round one, which is impossible when ν is random and the model is rich enough.

34.9 (CANONICAL MODEL) Prove the existence of a probability space carrying the random variables satisfying the conditions in Section 34.4.

34.10 (SUFFICIENCY OF DETERMINISTIC POLICIES) Let Π_D be the set of all deterministic policies and Π the space of all policies. Prove that for any k-armed Bayesian bandit environment $(\mathcal{E}, \mathcal{G}, Q, P)$,

$$\inf_{\pi \in \Pi} \mathrm{BR}_n(\pi, Q) = \inf_{\pi \in \Pi_D} \mathrm{BR}_n(\pi, Q).$$

34.11 Prove that the denominator in Eq. (34.7) is almost surely non-zero.

34.12 (BAYESIAN OPTIMAL POLICIES CAN BE DOMINATED) Consider the set-up in Example 34.2. A Bayesian learner observes $X \sim P_\theta$ and should choose an action $A_t \in [0, 1]$ that is $\sigma(X)$-measurable. Their loss is $\mathbb{I}\{A_t \neq \theta\}$.

(a) Show that the optimal choice is $A_t = X_t$.
(b) Give a Bayesian optimal algorithm with $A_t \neq X_t$ on some non-empty (measure zero) event.
(c) Give a Bayesian optimal algorithm and θ such that the loss when θ is true (and so $X \sim P_\theta$) is not zero.

34.13   (ADMISSIBLE   POLICIES   ARE   BAYESIAN   FOR   FINITE   ENVIRONMENTS)   Let $\mathcal{E} = \{\nu_1, \ldots, \nu_N\}$ and Π be sets. Call the elements of $\mathcal{E}$ environments, and the elements of Π policies (this is just to help to make connection to the rest of the material). Let $\ell : \Pi \times \mathcal{E} \to [0, \infty)$ be a positive loss function. Given a policy π, let $\ell(\pi) = (\ell(\pi, \nu_1), \ldots, \ell(\pi, \nu_N))$ be the loss vector resulting from policy π. Define $S = \{\ell(\pi) : \pi \in \Pi\} \subset \mathbb{R}^N$ and

$$\lambda(S) = \{x \in \mathrm{cl}(S) : y \not< x \text{ for all } y \in S\},$$

where $y \not< x$ is defined to mean it is not true that $y_i \leq x_i$ for all i with strict inequality for at least one i ($\lambda(S)$ is the Pareto frontier of set S, and its elements are the non-dominated loss-outcome vectors in $\mathrm{cl}(S)$). Prove that if $\lambda(S) \subseteq S$ and S is convex, then for every $\pi^* \in \Pi$ such that $\ell(\pi^*) \in \lambda(S)$, there exists a prior $q \in \mathcal{P}(\mathcal{E})$ such that

$$\sum_{\nu \in \mathcal{E}} q(\nu)\ell(\pi^*, \nu) = \min_{\pi \in \Pi} \sum_{\nu \in \mathcal{E}} q(\nu)\ell(\pi, \nu).$$

HINT   Use the supporting hyperplane theorem, stated in the hint after Exercise 26.2.

By identifying elements of $\mathcal{E}$ as 'criteria', the interpretation of the result of the exercise in multi-criteria optimisation is that for non-empty, convex, closed loss sets, solutions on the Pareto frontier (policies π such that $\ell(\pi) \in \lambda(S)$) can be obtained by minimizing a convex combination of the individual criteria. There is also a connection to constrained optimisation where the constraints are expressed as a bounds on linear combinations of the losses.

34.14 (UNIQUELY BAYES OPTIMAL POLICIES ARE ADMISSIBLE) Let $(\mathcal{E}, \mathcal{G})$ be a measurable space and Π an arbitrary set of the elements that we call policies. Let $\ell : \Pi \times \mathcal{E} \to \mathbb{R}$ be a function with $\ell(\pi, \cdot)$ being $\mathcal{G}$-measurable. Given a probability measure Q on $(\mathcal{E}, \mathcal{G})$, a policy is called Bayesian optimal with respect to Q if

$$\int_{\mathcal{E}} \ell(\pi, \nu) dQ(\nu) = \inf_{\pi' \in \Pi} \int_{\mathcal{E}} \ell(\pi', \nu) dQ(\nu).$$

Prove the following:

(a) If π is the unique Bayesian optimal policy given prior Q, then π is admissible.
(b) There is an example when π is a Bayesian optimal policy and π is inadmissible.
(c) If $\mathcal{E}$ is countable and $\text{Supp}(Q) = \mathcal{E}$, then any Bayes optimal policy π is admissible.
(d) If π is Bayesian optimal with respect to prior Q, then it is admissible on $\text{Supp}(Q) \subseteq \mathcal{E}$.

34.15 (ADMISSIBLE POLICIES ARE BAYESIAN FOR BERNOULLI BANDITS) Let $\mathcal{E}$ be the set of k-armed Bernoulli bandits. Prove that every admissible policy is Bayesian optimal for some prior.

HINT   Argue that all policies can be written as convex combinations of deterministic policies using an appropriate linear structure. Then identify the spaces of environments and policies with compact metric spaces. Let $(\nu_j)_{j=1}^{\infty}$ be a dense subset of $\mathcal{E}$ and repeat the argument in the previous exercise with each finite subset $\{\nu_1, \dots, \nu_j\}$, and then take the limit as $j \to \infty$. You will probably find Theorem 2.14 useful.

34.16 Let $\mathcal{E} = \mathcal{E}_B^k$ be the space of k-armed stochastic Bernoulli bandits. Endow $\mathcal{E}$ with a topology via the natural bijection to $[0, 1]^k$, and let $\mathcal{Q}$ be the space of all probability measures on $(\mathcal{E}, \mathfrak{B}(\mathcal{E}))$ with the weak* topology. Prove that

$$\max_{Q \in \mathcal{Q}} \text{BR}_n^*(Q) = R_n^*(\mathcal{E}).$$

HINT   Use Theorem 2.14 and Sion's theorem (Theorem 28.12).

35 Bayesian Bandits

The first section of this chapter provides simple bounds on the Bayesian optimal regret, which are obtained by integrating the regret guarantees for frequentist algorithms studied in Part II. This is followed by a short interlude on the basic theory of optimal stopping, which we will need later. The next few sections are devoted to special cases where computing the Bayesian optimal policy is tractable. We start with the finite horizon Bayesian one-armed bandit problem where the existence of a tractable solution is reduced to the computation of a sequence of functions on the sufficient statistics of the arm with the unknown pay-off. Next, the k-armed setting is considered. The main question is whether there exists a solution that avoids considering joint sufficient statistics over all arms, which would be intractable in the lack of further structure (see Note 2). Avoiding the joint sufficient in general is not possible, but in the remarkable case of the problem of maximising the total expected discounted reward over an infinite horizon, where John C. Gittins's celebrated result shows that the Bayesian optimal policy takes the form of an 'index' policy that keeps statistics for each arm separately (updated based on the arm's observations only) to compute a value ('index') for each arm, in each round choosing the arm with the highest index.

35.1 Bayesian Optimal Regret for k-Armed Stochastic Bandits

Even in relatively benign set-ups, the computation of the Bayesian optimal policy appears hopelessly intractable. Nevertheless, one can investigate the value of the Bayesian optimal regret by proving upper and lower bounds.

For simplicity, we restrict our attention to Bernoulli bandits, but the arguments generalise to other models. Let $(\mathcal{E}, \mathcal{G}) = ([0, 1]^k, \mathfrak{B}([0, 1]^k))$, and for $v \in [0, 1]^k$ let $P_{vj} = \mathcal{B}(v_j)$. Choose some prior Q on $(\mathcal{E}, \mathcal{G})$. The Bayesian optimal regret is necessarily smaller than the minimax regret, which by Theorem 9.1 means that

$$\mathrm{BR}_n^*(Q) \leq C\sqrt{kn},$$

where $C > 0$ is a universal constant. The proof of the lower bound in Exercise 15.2 shows that for each n, there exists a prior Q for which

$$\mathrm{BR}_n^*(Q) \geq c\sqrt{kn},$$

where $c > 0$ is a universal constant. These two together show that the $\sup_Q \mathrm{BR}_n^*(Q) = \Theta(\sqrt{kn})$.

Turning to the asymptotics for a fixed distribution, recall that that for any fixed Bernoulli bandit environment, the asymptotic growth rate of regret is $\Theta(\log(n))$. In stark contrast to this, the best we can say in the Bayesian case is that the asymptotic growth rate of $\mathrm{BR}_n^*(Q)$ is slower than $\sqrt{n}$, but for some priors, $\sqrt{n}$ is almost a lower bound on the growth rate. In particular, we ask you to prove the following theorem in Exercise 35.1:

THEOREM 35.1. *For any prior Q,*

$$\limsup_{n\to\infty} \frac{\mathrm{BR}_n^*(Q)}{n^{1/2}} = 0.$$

Furthermore, there exists a prior Q such that for all $\varepsilon > 0$,

$$\liminf_{n\to\infty} \frac{\mathrm{BR}_n^*(Q)}{n^{1/2-\varepsilon}} = \infty.$$

The lower bound has a worst-case flavour in the sense it holds for a specific prior. The prior that yields the lower bound is a little unnatural because it assigns the overwhelming majority of its mass to bandits with small suboptimality gaps. In particular, $Q(\{v \in \mathcal{E} : \Delta_{\min}(v) \leq \Delta\}) \geq c/\log(1/\Delta)$ for some constant $c > 0$. For more regular priors, the Bayesian optimal regret satisfies $\mathrm{BR}_n^*(Q) = \Theta(\log^2(n))$. See the bibliographic remarks for pointers to the literature.

35.2 Optimal Stopping (✦)

We now make a detour to show some results of optimal stopping, which will be used in the next sections to find tractable solutions to certain Bayesian bandit problems.

The first setting we consider will be useful for the one-armed bandit problem. Let $(U_t)_{t=1}^n$ be a sequence of random variables adapted to filtration $\mathbb{F} = (\mathcal{F}_t)_{t=1}^n$. Optimal stopping is concerned with finding solutions to optimisation problems of the following form:

$$\sup_{\tau \in \mathfrak{R}_1^n} \mathbb{E}[U_\tau], \tag{35.1}$$

where $\mathfrak{R}_1^n$ is the set of $\mathbb{F}$-stopping times τ with $1 \leq \tau \leq n$. When n is finite, the situation is conceptually straightforward. The idea is to use **backwards induction** to define the expected optimal utility conditioned on the information in $\mathcal{F}_t$ starting from $t = n$ and working backwards to $t = 1$. The **Snell envelope** is a sequence of random variables $(E_t)_{t=1}^n$ defined by

$$E_t = \begin{cases} U_n, & \text{if } t = n; \\ \max\left\{U_t, \mathbb{E}[E_{t+1} \mid \mathcal{F}_t]\right\}, & \text{otherwise.} \end{cases}$$

Intuitively, E_t is the optimal expected value one can guarantee provided that stage t was reached.

THEOREM 35.2. *Assume that n is finite and U_t is integrable for all $t \in [n]$. Then the stopping time $\tau = \min\{t \in [n] : U_t = E_t\} \in \mathfrak{R}_1^n$ achieves the supremum in Eq. (35.1).*

Backwards induction is not directly applicable when the horizon is infinite. There are several standard ways around this problem. For our purposes, the most convenient workaround is to introduce a Markov structure. The connection to the Bayesian bandit setting is that in the Bayesian setting, posteriors follow a Markov process. The connection will be made explicit in a few examples in later sections.

Let $(\mathcal{S}, \mathcal{G})$ be a Borel space and $(P_x : x \in \mathcal{S})$ be a probability kernel from $\mathcal{S}$ to itself and $u : \mathcal{S} \to \mathbb{R}$ be $\mathcal{S}/\mathcal{B}(\mathbb{R})$-measurable. A **Markov reward process** is a Markov chain $(S_t)_{t=1}^{\infty}$ evolving according to P and a sequence of random variables $(U_t)_{t=1}^{\infty}$ with $U_t = u(S_t)$. Define the filtration $\mathbb{F} = (\mathcal{F}_t)_{t=1}^{\infty}$ with $\mathcal{F}_t = \sigma(S_1, \ldots, S_t)$. The (Markov) optimal stopping problem is

$$\sup_{\tau \in \mathfrak{R}_1} \mathbb{E}[U_\tau],$$

where $\mathfrak{R}_1$ is the set of $\mathbb{F}$-adapted stopping times, and the initial distribution of S_1 is arbitrary. Inspired by the solution of the finite horizon problem define the **value function** $v : \mathcal{S} \to \mathbb{R}$ by

$$v(x) = \sup_{\tau \in \mathfrak{R}_1} \mathbb{E}_x[U_\tau], \tag{35.2}$$

where $\mathbb{P}_x$ is the probability measure on the space carrying $(S_t)_{t=1}^{\infty}$ for which $\mathbb{P}_x(S_1 = x) = 1$ and $\mathbb{E}_x$ be the expectation with respect to $\mathbb{P}_x$. As before, the idea is to stop when U_t is above $\int_{\mathcal{S}} v(y) P_{S_t}(dy)$, the predicted optimal value of continuing. Note that ties can be resolved in any way (depending on S_t, one may or may not stop when the predicted optimal value of continuation is equal to U_t). The next result gives sufficient conditions under which stopping rules of this form are indeed optimal.

THEOREM 35.3. *Assume for all $x \in \mathcal{S}$ that $U_\infty = \lim_{n\to\infty} U_n$ exists $\mathbb{P}_x$-a.s. and $\sup_{n \geq 1} |U_n|$ is $\mathbb{P}_x$-integrable. Then v satisfies the **Wald–Bellman equation**,*

$$v(x) = \max\{u(x), \int_{\mathcal{S}} v(y) P_x(dy)\} \qquad \text{for all } x \in \mathcal{S}.$$

Furthermore, $\lim_{n\to\infty} v(S_n) = U_\infty$ $\mathbb{P}_x$-a.s., and the supremum in Eq. (35.2) is achieved by any stopping time τ such that for all t,

(a) *$\tau \leq t$ on the event that $U_t > \int_{\mathcal{S}} v(y) P_{S_t}(dy)$; and*
(b) *$\tau > t$ on the event that $U_t < \int_{\mathcal{S}} v(y) P_{S_t}(dy)$ and $\tau \geq t$.*

The conditions are satisfied in many practical applications, e.g. if the Markov chain is ergodic and the utility function is bounded over the state space. In our application, U_n will be an accumulation of discounted rewards, which in all standard situations converges very fast.

A natural choice of stopping time satisfying conditions (a) and (b) in Theorem 35.3 is $\tau = \min\{t \geq 1 : v(S_t) = U_t\}$. The conditions express that in the indifference region $\{x \in \mathcal{S} : u(x) = \int_{\mathcal{S}} v(y) P_x(dy)\}$, both stopping and continuing are acceptable.

The proof of Theorem 35.2 is straightforward (Exercise 35.2). Measurability issues make the proof of Theorem 35.3 more technical (Exercise 35.3). Pointers to the literature are given in the notes, and a solution to the exercise is available.

35.3 One-armed bandits

The one-armed Bayesian bandit problem is a special case where the Bayesian optimal policy has a simple form that can often be computed efficiently. Before reading on, you might like to refresh your memory by looking at Exercises 4.10 and 8.2. Let $(\mathcal{E}, \mathcal{G}, Q, P)$ be a two-armed Bayesian bandit environment, where $P_{\nu 2} = \delta_{\mu_2}$ is a Dirac at fixed constant $\mu_2 \in \mathbb{R}$ for all $\nu \in \mathcal{E}$. Because the mean of the second arm is known in advance, we call this a one-armed Bayesian bandit problem. In Part (a) of Exercise 4.10, you showed that when the horizon is known, retirement policies that choose the first arm until some random time before switching to the second arm until the end of the game (pointwise over ν) dominate all other policies in terms of regret. Since we care about Bayesian optimal policies, the result of Exercise 34.10 allows us to restrict our attention to deterministic retirement policies.

Figure 35.1 When will *you* stop playing? A one-armed Bayesian bandit.

These facts allow us to frame the Bayesian one-armed bandit problem in terms of optimal stopping. Define a probability space $(\Omega, \mathcal{F}, \mathbb{P})$ carrying random elements $\nu \in \mathcal{E}$ and $Z = (Z_t)_{t=1}^n$ where

(a) the law of ν is $\mathbb{P}_\nu = Q$; and
(b) $\mathbb{P}(Z \in \cdot \,|\, \nu) = P_{\nu 1}^n(\cdot)$, which means that after conditioning on ν, the sequence $(Z_t)_{t=1}^n$ is independent and identically distributed according to $P_{\nu 1}$.

Given a deterministic retirement policy $\pi = (\pi_t)_{t=1}^n$, define the random variable

$$\tau = \min\{t \geq 1 : \pi_t(2\,|\,1, Z_1, \dots, 1, Z_{t-1}) = 1\},$$

where the minimum of an empty set in this case is $n + 1$. Clearly τ is an $\mathbb{F}$-stopping time, where $\mathbb{F} = (\mathcal{F}_t)_{t=1}^{n+1}$ with $\mathcal{F}_t = \sigma(Z_1, \dots, Z_{t-1})$. In fact, this correspondence between deterministic retirement policies and $\mathbb{F}$-stopping times is a bijection. The Bayesian expected reward when following the policy associated with stopping time τ is

$$\mathbb{E}\left[\sum_{t=1}^{\tau-1} Z_t + \sum_{t=\tau}^{n} \mu_2\right] = \mathbb{E}[U_\tau],$$

where $U_t = \sum_{s=1}^{t-1} Z_s + (n-t+1)\mu_2$. Since minimizing the Bayesian regret is equivalent to maximising the Bayesian expected cumulative reward, the problem of finding the Bayesian optimal policy has been reduced to an optimal stopping problem.

PROPOSITION 35.4. *If Z_1 is integrable, then the Bayesian regret is minimised by the retirement policy associated with stopping time $\tau = \min\{t \geq 1 : U_t = E_t\}$, where*

$$E_t = \begin{cases} U_t, & \text{if } t = n+1; \\ \max\{U_t, \mathbb{E}[E_{t+1} \mid \mathcal{F}_t]\}, & \text{otherwise.} \end{cases}$$

The interpretation of E_t is that it is the total expected optimal value conditioned on the information available at the start of round t. The proposition is an immediate corollary of Theorem 35.2 and the fact that integrability of Z_1 is equivalent to integrability of $(U_t)_{t=1}^{n+1}$. The optimal stopping time in Proposition 35.4 can be rewritten in a more convenient form. For $1 \leq t \leq n+1$, define $W_t = E_t - \sum_{s=1}^{t-1} Z_s$, which can be seen as the optimal value to go for the last $n - t + 1$ rounds. The definition of E_t shows that $W_{n+1} = 0$ and for $t \leq n$,

$$W_t = \max\left((n-t+1)\mu_2, \mathbb{E}[E_{t+1} \mid \mathcal{F}_t] - \sum_{s=1}^{t-1} Z_s\right)$$

$$= \max\left((n-t+1)\mu_2, \mathbb{E}\left[Z_t + W_{t+1} \mid \mathcal{F}_t\right]\right). \tag{35.3}$$

Hence the optimal stopping time can be rewritten as

$$\tau^* = \min\{t : U_t = E_t\} = \min\{t : W_t = (n-t+1)\mu_2\}.$$

This should make intuitive sense. It is optimal to continue only if the expected future reward from doing so is at least as large as what can be obtained by stopping immediately. The difficulty is that $\mathbb{E}[Z_t + W_{t+1} \mid \mathcal{F}_t]$ can be quite a complicated object. We now give two examples where $\mathbb{E}[Z_t + W_{t+1} \mid \mathcal{F}_t]$ has a simple representation and thus computing the optimal stopping rule becomes practical. The idea is to find a sequence of sufficient statistics $(S_t)_{t=0}^n$ so that $S_t \in \mathcal{S}$ is $\mathcal{F}_t$-measurable and $\mathbb{P}_{\nu 1}(Z_1, \ldots, Z_t \in \cdot \mid S_t)$ is independent of ν. Then E_t is $\sigma(S_t)$-measurable, and by Lemma 2.5 it follows that $E_t = \upsilon_t(S_t)$ for an appropriately measurable function $\upsilon_t : \mathcal{S} \to \mathbb{R}$. For more on this, read the next two subsections, and then do Exercise 35.4.

35.3.1 Bernoulli Rewards

Let $\mathcal{E} = [0, 1]$, $\mathcal{G} = \mathfrak{B}([0, 1])$ and for $\nu \in \mathcal{E}$, let $P_{\nu 1} = \mathcal{B}(\nu)$ and $P_{\nu 2} = \delta_{\mu_2}$: the first arm is Bernoulli, and the second is a Dirac at some fixed value $\mu_2 \in [0, 1]$. For the prior, choose $Q = \text{Beta}(\alpha, \beta)$, a Beta prior. By the argument in Example 34.6 the posterior at the start of round t is a Beta distribution $\text{Beta}(\alpha + S_t, \beta + t - 1 - S_t)$ where $S_t = \sum_{s=1}^{t-1} Z_s$. Letting $p_t(s) = (\alpha + s)/(\alpha + \beta + t - 1)$, it follows that

$$\mathbb{E}[Z_t \mid \mathcal{F}_t] = \frac{\alpha + S_t}{\alpha + \beta + t - 1} = p_t(S_t),$$

$$\mathbb{P}(S_{t+1} = S_t + 1 \mid S_t) = p_t(S_t),$$

$$\mathbb{P}(S_{t+1} = S_t \mid S_t) = 1 - p_t(S_t).$$

Now let $w_{n+1}(s) = 0$ for all s and

$$w_t(s) = \max\{(n-t+1)\mu_2, p_t(s) + p_t(s)w_{t+1}(s+1) + (1 - p_t(s))w_{t+1}(s)\}.$$

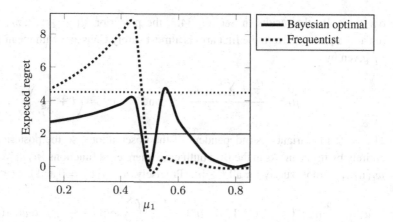

Figure 35.2 The plot shows the expected regret for the Bayesian optimal algorithm compared to the 'frequestist' algorithm in Eq. (35.4) on the Bernoulli 1-armed bandit where $\mu_2 = 1/2$ and μ_1 varies on the x-axis. The horizontal lines show the average regret for each algorithm with respect to the prior, which is uniform.

Then $W_t = w_t(S_t)$, and hence the optimal policy can be computed by evaluating $w_t(s)$ for all $s \in \{0, \ldots, t\}$ starting with $t = n$, then $n - 1$ and so on until $t = 1$. The total computation for this backwards induction is $O(n^2)$, and the output is a policy that can be implemented over all n rounds. By contrast, the typical frequentist stopping rule requires only $O(n)$ computations, so the overhead is quite severe. The improvement in terms of the Bayes regret is not insignificant, however, as illustrated by the following experiment.

EXPERIMENT 35.1   The horizon is set to $n = 500$ and $\mu_2 = 1/2$. The stopping rules we compare are the Bayesian optimal policy with a $\text{Beta}(1,1)$ prior and the 'frequentist' stopping rule given by

$$\tau = \min\left\{t \geq 2 : \hat{\mu}_{t-1} < \mu_2 \text{ and } d(\hat{\mu}_{t-1}, \mu_2) \geq \frac{\log(n/t)}{t-1}\right\}, \qquad (35.4)$$

where $d(p, q)$ is the binary relative entropy and $\hat{\mu}_t = \sum_{s=1}^{t} X_s / t$ is the empirical estimate of μ_1 based on the first t observations. Fig. 35.2 shows the expected regret for different values of μ, with horizontal dotted lines indicating the expected regret averaged over the prior. Note that although the prior is symmetric, the one-armed bandit problem is not, which explicates the asymmetric behaviour of the Bayesian optimal algorithm. The frequentist algorithm is even more asymmetric with very small regret for $\mu_1 > 1/2$, but large regret for $\mu_1 < 1/2$. This is caused by a conservative confidence interval in Eq. (35.4), which makes it stop consistently later than its Bayesian counterpart, which makes it 'win' for $\mu_1 > 1/2$, but it also makes it 'lose' when $\mu_1 < 1/2$, with an overall loss (naturally) when considering the average over all environments.

35.3.2 Gaussian Rewards

Let $(\mathcal{E}, \mathcal{G}) = (\mathbb{R}, \mathfrak{B}(\mathbb{R}))$, where for $v \in \mathbb{R}$, we let $P_{v1} = \mathcal{N}(v, 1)$ and $P_{v2} = \delta_{\mu_2}$ for $\mu_2 \in \mathbb{R}$ fixed. Choose a Gaussian prior $Q = \mathcal{N}(\mu_P, \sigma_P^2)$ with mean $\mu_P \in \mathbb{R}$ and variance

$\sigma_P^2 > 0$. By the results in Section 34.3, the posterior $Q(\cdot \mid x_1, \ldots, x_t)$ after observing rewards $x_1, \ldots, x_t$ from the first arm is almost surely Gaussian with mean μ_t and variance σ_t^2 given by

$$\mu_t = \frac{\frac{\mu_P}{\sigma_P^2} + \sum_{s=1}^{t} x_s}{1 + \sigma_P^{-2}} \quad \text{and} \quad \sigma_t^2 = \left(t + \frac{1}{\sigma_P^2}\right)^{-1}. \tag{35.5}$$

The posterior variance is independent of the observations, so the posterior is determined entirely by its mean. As in the Bernoulli case, there exist functions $(w_t)_{t=1}^{n+1}$ such that $W_t = w_t(\mu_{t-1})$ almost surely for all $t \in [n]$. Precisely, $w_{n+1}(\mu) = 0$ and for $t \leq n$,

$$w_t(\mu) = \max\left((n - t + 1)\mu_2, \; \mu + \frac{1}{\sqrt{2\pi}} \int_{-\infty}^{\infty} \exp\left(-\frac{x^2}{2\sigma_{t-1}^2}\right) w_{t+1}(\mu + x) dx\right). \tag{35.6}$$

The integral on the right-hand side does not have a closed-form solution, which forces the use of approximate methods. Fortunately w_t is a well-behaved function and can be efficiently approximated. The favourable properties are summarised in the next lemma, the proof of which is left to Exercise 35.5.

LEMMA 35.5. *The following hold:*

(a) *The function w_t is increasing.*

(b) *The function w_t is convex.*

(c) $\lim_{\mu \to \infty} w_t(\mu)/\mu = n - t + 1$ *and* $\lim_{\mu \to -\infty} w_t(\mu) = (n - t + 1)\mu_2$.

There are many ways to approximate a function, but in order to propagate the approximation using Eq. (35.6), it is convenient to choose a form for which the integral in Eq. (35.6) can be computed analytically. Given the properties in Lemma 35.5, a natural choice is to approximate w_t using piecewise quadratic functions. Let $\tilde{w}_{n+1}(\mu) = 0$ and

$$\bar{w}_t(\mu) = \max\left\{(n - t + 1)\mu_2, \; \mu + \frac{1}{\sqrt{2\pi}} \int_{-\infty}^{\infty} \exp\left(-\frac{x^2}{2\sigma_t^2}\right) \tilde{w}_{t+1}(\mu + x) dx\right\}.$$

Then let $-\infty < x_1 \leq x_2 \leq \ldots \leq x_N < \infty$, and for $\mu \in [x_i, x_{i+1}]$, define $\tilde{w}_t(\mu) = a_i\mu^2 + b_i\mu + c_i$ to be the unique quadratic approximation of $\bar{w}_t(\mu)$ such that

$$\tilde{w}_t(x_i) = \bar{w}_t(x_i),$$
$$\tilde{w}_t(x_{i+1}) = \bar{w}_t(x_{i+1}),$$
$$\tilde{w}_t((x_i + x_{i+1})/2) = \bar{w}_t((x_i + x_{i+1})/2).$$

For $\mu < x_1$, we approximate $w_t(\mu) = (n - t + 1)\mu_2$, and for $\mu > x_N$, the linear approximation $\tilde{w}_t(\mu) = (n - t + 1)\mu$ is reasonable by Lemma 35.5. The computation time for calculating the coefficients a_i, b_i, c_i for all t and $i \in [N]$ is $O(Nn)$. We encourage the reader to implement this algorithm and compare it to its natural frequentist competitors (Exercise 35.11).

35.4 Gittins Index

Generalising the analysis in the previous section to multiple actions is mathematically straightforward, but computationally intractable. The computational complexity of backwards induction increases exponentially with the number of arms, which is impractical unless the number of arms and horizon are both small.

An **index policy** is a policy that in each round computes a real-valued **index** for each arm and plays the arm with the largest index, while the index of an arm is restricted to depend on statistics collected for that arm only (the time horizon can also be used). Many policies we met earlier are index policies. For example, most variants of the upper confidence bound algorithm introduced in Part II are index policies. Sadly, however, the Bayesian optimal policy for finite horizon bandits is not usually an index policy (see Note 6). John C. Gittins proved that if one is prepared to modify the objective to a special kind of infinite horizon problem, then the Bayesian optimal policy becomes an index policy. In the remainder of this chapter, we explore his ideas.

35.4.1 A Discounted Retirement Game

We start by describing the discounted setting with one action and then generalise to multiple actions. Besides discounting, another change is that the reward-generating process is made into a Markov reward process, a strict generalisation of the previous case. The motivation is that, as hinted on before, the posterior of the arm with the unknown payoff evolves as a Markov process.

Let $(S_t)_{t=1}^\infty$ be a Markov chain on Borel space $(\mathcal{S}, \mathcal{G})$ evolving according to probability kernel $(P_x : x \in \mathcal{S})$. As in Section 35.2, let $(\Omega, \mathcal{F}, \mathbb{P}_x)$ be a probability space carrying $(S_n)_{n=1}^\infty$ with $S_n \in \mathcal{S}$ such that

(a) $\mathbb{P}_x(S_1 = x) = 1$; and
(b) $\mathbb{P}_x(S_{n+1} \in \cdot \mid S_n) = P_{S_n}(\cdot)$ with $\mathbb{P}_x$-probability one.

Expectations with respect to $\mathbb{P}_x$ are denoted by $\mathbb{E}_x$. Next, let $\gamma \in \mathbb{R}$ and $r : \mathcal{S} \to \mathbb{R}$ be a $\mathcal{G}/\mathcal{B}(\mathbb{R})$-measurable function, both of which are known to the learner. In each round $t = 1, 2, \ldots$, the learner observes the state S_t and chooses one of two options: *(a)* to retire and end the game or *(b)* pay the fixed cost γ to receive a reward of $r(S_t)$ and continue for another round. The policy of a learner in this game corresponds to choosing a $\mathbb{F}$-stopping time τ with $\mathbb{F} = (\mathcal{F}_t)_t$ and $\mathcal{F}_t = \sigma(S_1, \ldots, S_t)$, where $\tau = t$ means that the learner retires after observing S_t at the start of round t. The α-discounted value of the game when starting in state $S_1 = x$ is

$$v_\gamma(x) = \sup_{\tau \geq 1} \mathbb{E}_x \left[\sum_{t=1}^{\tau-1} \alpha^{t-1}(r(S_t) - \gamma) \right], \tag{35.7}$$

where $\alpha \in (0, 1)$ is the **discount factor**. To ensure that this is well defined, we need the following assumption:

ASSUMPTION 35.6. For all $x \in \mathcal{S}$, it holds that $\mathbb{E}_x \left[\sum_{t=1}^\infty \alpha^{t-1} |r(S_t)| \right] < \infty$.

If the rewards are bounded, the assumption will hold. When the rewards are unbounded, the assumption restricts the rate of growth of rewards over time.

The presence of discounting encourages the learner to obtain large rewards earlier rather than later and is one distinction between this model and the finite-horizon model studied for most of this book. A brief discussion of discounting is left for the notes.

Fix a state $x \in S$. The map $\gamma \mapsto v_\gamma(x)$ is decreasing and is always non-negative. In fact, if γ is large enough, it is easy to see that retiring immediately ($\tau = 1$) achieves the supremum in the definition of $v_\gamma(x)$, and thus $v_\gamma(x) = 0$. The **Gittins index**, or **fair charge**, of a state x is the smallest value of γ for which the learner is indifferent between retiring immediately and playing for at least one round:

$$g(x) = \inf \left\{ \gamma \in \mathbb{R} : v_\gamma(x) = 0 \right\}. \tag{35.8}$$

Straightforward manipulation (Exercise 35.6) shows that

$$g(x) = \sup_{\tau \geq 2} \frac{\mathbb{E}_x \left[\sum_{t=1}^{\tau-1} \alpha^{t-1} r(S_t) \right]}{\mathbb{E}_x \left[\sum_{t=1}^{\tau-1} \alpha^{t-1} \right]}. \tag{35.9}$$

The form in (35.9) will be useful for computation. It is not immediately clear that a stopping time attaining the supremum in (35.9) exists. The following lemma shows that it does and gives an explicit form.

LEMMA 35.7. *Let $x \in S$ be arbitrary. The following hold under Assumption 35.6:*

(a) $v_\gamma(x) = \max\{0, r(x) - \gamma + \alpha \int_S v_\gamma(y) P_x(dy)\}$ *for all $\gamma \in \mathbb{R}$.*
(b) *If $\gamma \leq g(x)$, then $v_\gamma(x) = r(x) - \gamma + \alpha \int_S v_\gamma(y) P_x(dy)$.*
(c) *The stopping time $\tau = \min\{t \geq 2 : g(S_t) \leq \gamma\}$ attains the supremum in Eq. (35.9).*

The result is relatively intuitive. The Gittins index represents the price the learner should be willing to pay for the privilege of continuing to play. The optimal policy continues to play as long as the actual value of the game is not smaller than this price was at the start. The proof of Lemma 35.7 uses Theorem 35.3 and is left for the reader in Exercise 35.7.

35.4.2 Discounted Bandits and the Index Theorem

The generalisation of the discounted retirement game to multiple arms is quite straightforward. As we will see, this will lead to a solution to the infinite horizon discounted Bayesian k-armed bandit problem where the prior factorises over the arms.

There are now k independent Markov chains sharing the same state space S. We are also given a reward function $r : S \to \mathbb{R}$. In each round t, the learner first observes the state of all chains $S_1(t), \dots, S_k(t)$ and then chooses an action $A_t \in [k]$ to receive a reward $r(S_{A_t}(t))$ and to make the state of the chain underlying arm k move according to a fixed transition kernel that is common to all chains. The states of the other chains do not move. The goal is still to maximise the total expected discounted reward. The interaction protocol is illustrated on Fig. 35.3.

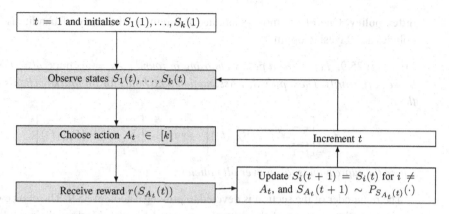

Figure 35.3 Interaction protocol for discounted bandits with Markov pay-offs

The assumption that the Markov chains evolve on the same state space with the same transition kernel is non-restrictive since the state space can always be taken to be the union of k state spaces and the transition kernel defined with k disconnected components.

Because the learner observes the state of all chains in each round, a policy π now is a collection $(\pi_t)_{t=1}^{\infty}$, where π_t is a probability kernel from $(\mathcal{S}^k \times [k])^{t-1} \times \mathcal{S}^k$ (history, including past observed states and actions) to $[k]$. Given a discount rate $\alpha \in (0,1)$, the objective is to find the policy maximising the cumulative discounted reward:

$$\operatorname{argmax}_\pi \mathbb{E}_\pi \left[\sum_{t=1}^{\infty} \alpha^{t-1} r(S_{A_t}(t)) \right],$$

where the expectation is taken with respect to the distribution on state/action sequences induced by the interaction of π and the k Markov chains.

EXAMPLE 35.8 (Bayesian k-armed Bernoulli bandits in the Markov framework). To see the relation to Bayesian bandits with discounted rewards, consider the following set-up. Let $\mathcal{S} = [0,\infty) \times [0,\infty)$ and $\mathcal{G} = \mathfrak{B}(\mathcal{S})$. Then let the initial state of each Markov chain be $S_i(1) = (1,1)$, and define probability kernel $(P_s : s \in \mathcal{S})$ from $(\mathcal{S}, \mathcal{G})$ to itself by

$$P_{(x,y)}(A) = \frac{x}{x+y} \mathbb{I}_A((x+1,y)) + \frac{y}{x+y} \mathbb{I}_A((x,y+1)).$$

The reward function is $r(x,y) = x/(x+y)$. The reader should check that this corresponds to a Bernoulli bandit with $\mathrm{Beta}(1,1)$ prior on the mean reward of each arm (Exercise 35.8). The role of the state space is to maintain a sufficient statistic for the posterior while the reward function is the expected reward given the posterior.

Returning to the general problem, let g be the Gittins index function as defined in Eq. (35.8) associated with the probability kernel $(P_x : x \in \mathcal{S})$ and reward function r. A policy π^* that chooses in round t the arm $A_t \in \operatorname{argmax}_{i \in [k]} g(S_i(t))$ is called a **Gittins**

index policy. One of the most celebrated theorems in the study of bandits is that these policies are Bayesian optimal.

THEOREM 35.9. *Let π^* be a policy choosing in round t $A_t = \text{argmax}_i\, g(S_i(t))$ with ties broken arbitrarily. Then, provided Assumption 35.6 holds for all Markov chains $(S_{iu})_{u=1}^\infty$, then*

$$\mathbb{E}_{\pi^*}\left[\sum_{t=1}^\infty \alpha^{t-1} r(S_{A_t}(t))\right] = \sup_\pi \mathbb{E}_\pi\left[\sum_{t=1}^\infty \alpha^{t-1} r(S_{A_t}(t))\right],$$

where the supremum is taken over all policies.

The remainder of the section is devoted to proving Theorem 35.9. The choice of actions produces an interleaving of the rewards generated by each Markov chain, and it will be useful to have a notation for these interleavings. For each $i \in [k]$, let $g_i = (g_{it})_{t=1}^\infty$ be a real-valued sequence and $g = (g_1, \ldots, g_k)$ be the tuple of these sequences.

> While this notation breaks our convention of putting the time index first in the reward sequences of a multi-armed bandit, we prefer this notation here as we need to consider reward sequences underlying individual arms.

Given an infinite sequence $(a_t)_{t=1}^\infty$, taking values in $[k]$, define the interleaving sequence $I(g, a) = (I_t(g, a))_{t=1}^\infty$ by

$$I_t(g, a) = g_{a_t, 1+n_{a_t}(a, t-1)} \qquad \text{with} \qquad n_i(a, t-1) = \sum_{s=1}^{t-1} \mathbb{I}\{a_s = i\}.$$

Note that this is the same as the 'reward-stack model' of bandits mentioned on page 53 in Chapter 4 except that here we have fixed sequences. The next lemma follows from the Hardy–Littlewood inequality, a generalisation of the trivial observation that the identical ordering of two sequences of numbers maximises their inner product. We leave the proof to Exercise 35.9.

LEMMA 35.10. *Suppose that g_i is decreasing for all $i \in [k]$ and $(a_t^*)_{t=1}^\infty$ is defined recursively by $a_t^* = \text{argmax}_i\, g_{i, 1+n_i(a^*, t-1)}$ and $I^*(g) = I(g, a^*)$. Then, for any $\alpha \in (0, 1)$,*

$$\sum_{t=1}^\infty \alpha^{t-1} I_t^*(g) = \sup_{a \in [k]^{\mathbb{N}}} \sum_{t=1}^\infty \alpha^{t-1} I_t(g, a).$$

Proof of Theorem 35.9   Given a policy $\pi = (\pi_t)_{t=1}^\infty$, let $(\Omega, \mathcal{F}, \mathbb{P}_\pi)$ be a probability space carrying random elements $S_1, \ldots, S_k$, where $S_i = (S_{iu})_{u=1}^\infty$ is a sequence of states and $(A_t)_{t=1}^\infty$ is a sequence of actions such that

(a) $\mathbb{P}_\pi(S_{i,u+1} \in \cdot \mid S_{i1}, S_{i2}, \ldots, S_{iu}) = P_{S_{iu}}(\cdot)$;
(b) The sequences $(S_{iu})_{u=1}^\infty$ and $(S_{ju})_{u=1}^\infty$ are independent for all $i \neq j$; and
(c) $\mathbb{P}_\pi(A_t \in \cdot \mid S(1), A_1, \ldots, A_{t-1}, S(t)) = \pi_t(\cdot \mid S(1), A_1, \ldots, A_{t-1}, S(t))$, where $S_i(t) = S_{i,(1+T_i(t-1))}$ is the state of machine i observed by the learner at the start of round t with $T_i(t) = \sum_{s=1}^t \mathbb{I}\{A_s = i\}$.

Let $\mathcal{F}_t = \sigma(S(1), A_1, S(2), \ldots, A_{t-1}, S(t), A_t)$ be the σ-algebra containing information available to the learner after choosing their action in round t. As usual, $\mathbb{E}_\pi$ denotes the expectation with respect to $\mathbb{P}_\pi$.

Given an arm i and round t, the **prevailing charge** is a random variable $\underline{G}_i(t) = \min_{s \leq t} g(S_i(s))$. The name comes from one of the early proofs of Gittins theorem that constructed a game in which the prevailing charge was the fee paid by the learner to play arm i in round t. The proof is decomposed into two steps. In the first step, we relate the prevailing charge to the discounted cumulative reward. The second step completes the proof by combining the first with an interleaving argument using Lemma 35.10.

Part 1: The Prevailing Charge
Fix an arm i. We claim that

$$\mathbb{E}_\pi \left[\sum_{t=1}^\infty \alpha^{t-1} r(S_i(t)) \mathbb{I}\{A_t = i\} \right] \leq \mathbb{E}_\pi \left[\sum_{t=1}^\infty \alpha^{t-1} \underline{G}_i(t) \mathbb{I}\{A_t = i\} \right].$$

Furthermore, equality holds for $\pi = \pi^*$. To prove this claim, let $\tau_1, \tau_2, \ldots$ be a sequence of stopping times defined recursively by

$$\tau_1 = \min\{t \geq 1 : A_t = i\} \quad \text{and}$$

$$\tau_{j+1} = \min\{t > \tau_j : A_t = i \text{ and } g(S_i(t)) \leq \underline{G}_i(\tau_j)\},$$

where the minimum of the empty set is defined to be infinite. Next, let

$$T_j = \{t : A_t = i \text{ and } \tau_j \leq t < \tau_{j+1}\} \quad \text{and} \quad \gamma_j = \underline{G}_i(\tau_j).$$

Note that on the event $\{\tau_j < \infty\}$, $\underline{G}_i(t) = \gamma_j$ for all $t \in T_j$. Furthermore, $g(S_i(\tau_j)) = \gamma_j$. By definition, we have

$$\mathbb{E}_\pi \left[\sum_{t=1}^\infty \alpha^{t-1} (r(S_i(t)) - \underline{G}_i(t)) \mathbb{I}\{A_t = i\} \right] = \sum_{j=1}^\infty \mathbb{E}_\pi \left[\sum_{t \in T_j} \alpha^{t-1} (r(S_i(t)) - \gamma_j) \right].$$

The claim follows by showing the term inside the sum on the right-hand side vanishes for the Gittins index policy and is not positive for any other policy.

Fix $j \geq 1$. By definition, for $t \in T_j$ it holds that $g_i(S_i(t)) \geq \underline{G}_i(t) = \gamma_j$. Combining this with Part (b) of Lemma 35.7, on $\{t \in T_j\}$, thanks to $\{t \in T_j\} \in \mathcal{F}_t$,

$$v_{\gamma_j}(S_i(t)) + \gamma_j - r(S_i(t)) = \alpha \int_S v_{\gamma_j}(y) P_{S_i(t)}(dy) = \alpha \mathbb{E}_\pi[v_{\gamma_j}(S_i(t+1)) \mid \mathcal{F}_t].$$

From this it follows that

$$\mathbb{E}_\pi \left[\sum_{t \in T_j} \alpha^{t-1} (r(S_i(t)) - \gamma_j) \right] = \mathbb{E}_\pi \left[\sum_{t \in T_j} \alpha^{t-1} \left(v_{\gamma_j}(S_i(t)) - \alpha v_{\gamma_j}(S_i(t+1)) \right) \right]$$

$$\leq 0,$$

where the final inequality holds since v_{γ_j} is non-negative, $v_{\gamma_j}(S_i(\tau_j)) = 0$ and by telescoping the sum, which is possible because whenever t' is the smallest element larger than t in T_j, then $S_i(t') = S_i(t+1)$. We now argue that the inequality is replaced by an equality for the Gittins index policy. The key observation is that having played $A_{\tau_j} = i$, the Gittins index policy continues playing arm i until $g(S_i(t)) \leq \gamma_j$, which means that $T_j = \{\tau_j, \tau_j + 1, \ldots, \kappa_j - 1\}$, where $\kappa_j = \min\{t > \tau_j : g(S_i(t)) \leq \gamma_j\}$, which by Part (c) of Lemma 35.7 means that

$$\mathbb{E}_{\pi^*}\left[\sum_{t \in T_j} \alpha^{t-1}(r(S_i(t)) - \gamma_j) \mid \mathcal{F}_{\tau_j}\right] = v_{\gamma_j}(S_i(\tau_j)) = 0.$$

Part 2: Interleaving Prevailing Charges
Let $H_{iu} = \min_{v \leq u} g(S_{iv})$. The key point is that the distribution of $H = (H_{iu})$ does not depend on the choice of policy, and clearly H_{iu} is decreasing in u for each i. For the Gittins index policy π^*,

$$\mathbb{E}_{\pi^*}\left[\sum_{t=1}^{\infty} \alpha^{t-1} r(S_{A_t}(t))\right] = \mathbb{E}_{\pi^*}\left[\sum_{t=1}^{\infty} \alpha^{t-1}\underline{G}_{A_t}(t)\right]$$

$$= \mathbb{E}_{\pi^*}\left[\sum_{t=1}^{\infty} \alpha^{t-1} I_t(H, A)\right]$$

$$= \mathbb{E}_{\pi^*}\left[\sum_{t=1}^{\infty} \alpha^{t-1} I_t^*(H)\right],$$

where the first equality follows from part 1, the second by the definition of I_t and H and the third by the definitions of I_t^* from Lemma 35.10 and that of the Gittins index policy, which always chooses an action that maximises the prevailing charge. On the other hand, for any policy π,

$$\mathbb{E}_{\pi}\left[\sum_{t=1}^{\infty} \alpha^{t-1} r(S_{A_t}(t))\right] \leq \mathbb{E}_{\pi}\left[\sum_{t=1}^{\infty} \alpha^{t-1}\underline{G}_{A_t}(t)\right]$$

$$= \mathbb{E}_{\pi}\left[\sum_{t=1}^{n} \alpha^{t-1} I_t(H, A)\right]$$

$$\leq \mathbb{E}_{\pi}\left[\sum_{t=1}^{n} \alpha^{t-1} I_t^*(H)\right],$$

where the last line follows from Lemma 35.10. Finally, note that the law of H under $\mathbb{P}_\pi$ does not depend on π, and hence

$$\mathbb{E}_{\pi}\left[\sum_{t=1}^{n} \alpha^{t-1} I_t^*(H)\right] = \mathbb{E}_{\pi^*}\left[\sum_{t=1}^{n} \alpha^{t-1} I_t^*(H)\right].$$

Therefore, for all π,

$$\mathbb{E}_{\pi^*}\left[\sum_{t=1}^{\infty} \alpha^{t-1} r(S_{A_t}(t))\right] \geq \mathbb{E}_{\pi}\left[\sum_{t=1}^{\infty} \alpha^{t-1} r(S_{A_t}(t))\right],$$

which completes the proof. □

35.5 Computing the Gittins Index

We describe a simple approach that depends on the state space being finite. References to more general methods are given in the bibliographic remarks. Assume without loss of generality that $S = \{1, 2, \ldots, |S|\}$ and $\mathcal{G} = 2^S$. The matrix form of the transition kernel is $P \in [0, 1]^{|S| \times |S|}$ and is defined by $P_{ij} = P_i(\{j\})$. We also let $r \in [0, 1]^{|S|}$ be the vector of rewards so that $r_i = r(i)$. The standard basis vector is $e_i \in \mathbb{R}^{|S|}$, and $1 \in \mathbb{R}^{|S|}$ is the vector with one in every coordinate. For $C \subset S$, let Q_C be the transition matrix with $(Q_C)_{ij} = P_{ij}\mathbb{I}_C(j)$. For each $i \in S$, the goal is to find

$$g(i) = \sup_{\tau \geq 2} \frac{\mathbb{E}_i\left[\sum_{t=1}^{\tau-1} \alpha^{t-1} r(S_t)\right]}{\mathbb{E}_i\left[\sum_{t=1}^{\tau-1} \alpha^{t-1}\right]},$$

where $\mathbb{E}_i$ is the expectation with respect to the measure $\mathbb{P}_i$ for which the initial state is $S_1 = i$. Lemma 35.7 shows that the stopping time $\tau = \min\{t \geq 2 : g(S_t) \leq g(i)\}$ attains the supremum in the above display. The set $C_i = \{j : g(j) > g(i)\}$ is called the continuation region, and $S_i = S \setminus C_i$ is the stopping region. Then the Gittins index can be calculated as

$$g(i) = \frac{\mathbb{E}_i\left[\sum_{t=1}^{\tau-1} \alpha^{t-1} r(S_t)\right]}{\mathbb{E}_i\left[\sum_{t=1}^{\tau-1} \alpha^{t-1}\right]} = \frac{\sum_{t=1}^{\infty} \alpha^{t-1} e_i^\top Q_{C_i}^{t-1} r}{\sum_{t=1}^{\infty} \alpha^{t-1} e_i^\top Q_{C_i}^{t-1} 1} = \frac{e_i^\top (I - \alpha Q_{C_i})^{-1} r}{e_i^\top (I - \alpha Q_{C_i})^{-1} 1}.$$

All this suggests an induction approach where the Gittins index is calculated for each state in decreasing order of their indices. To get started, note that the maximum possible Gittins index is $\max_i r_i$ and that this is achievable for state $i = \operatorname{argmax}_j r_j$ with the deterministic stopping time $\tau = 2$. For the induction step, assume that $g(i)$ is known for the j states $C = \{i_1, i_2, \ldots, i_j\}$ with the largest Gittins indices. Then i_{j+1} is given by

$$i_{j+1} = \operatorname{argmax}_{i \notin C} \frac{e_i^\top (I - \alpha Q_C)^{-1} r}{e_i^\top (I - \alpha Q_C)^{-1} 1}.$$

If Gauss–Jordan elimination is used for matrix inversion, then the computational complexity of this algorithm is $O(|S|^4)$. A more sophisticated inversion algorithm would reduce the complexity to $O(|S|^{3+\varepsilon})$ for some $\varepsilon \leq 0.373$, but these are seldom practical. When α is relatively small, the inversion can be replaced by directly calculating the sums to some truncated horizon with little loss in accuracy.

35.6 Notes

1 Bayesian methods automatically and optimally exploit the assumptions encoded in their prior. If we think of the prior as a way of enriching and refining the standard formulation of bandits, this is an advantage. However, this blessing can also be a curse. A policy that exploits its assumptions too heavily can be brittle when those assumptions turn out to be wrong. This can have a devastating effect in bandits where the cost of overly aggressive confidence intervals is large.

2 We claimed that computing the Bayesian optimal policy is generally intractable without discounting. This is a widely held belief, but we are not aware of any lower-bound on the computation

complexity. A good place to start might be to lower bound the computation complexity of finding the optimal action for k-armed Bayesian bandits when the prior is a product of Beta distributions, but without discounting.

3 The solution to optimal stopping problems is essentially a form of **dynamic programming**, which is a method that trades memory for computation by introducing recursively defined value functions that suffice for reconstructing an optimal policy. In the one-armed bandit optimal stopping problem, thanks to the factorisation lemma (Lemma 2.5), for any $0 \leq t \leq n$, there exists a function $w_t : \mathbb{R}^t \to \mathbb{R}$ such that $W_t = w_t(X_1, \ldots, X_t)$ almost surely. This function can be seen as the value function that captures the optimal value-to-go from stage t on, and (35.3) gives a recursive construction for it, $w_n(x_1, \ldots, x_n) = 0$, and for $t < n$,

$$
w_t(x_1, \ldots, x_t) = \max\left((n-t)\mu_2, \int x_{t+1} + w_{t+1}(x_1, \ldots, x_t, x_{t+1}) dP_t(x_{t+1})\right),
$$

where P_t is the distribution of X_{t+1} given $X_1, \ldots, X_t$. The problem with this general recursion is that the computation is prohibitive. The example with Bernoulli rewards shows that sometimes a similar recursion holds on a reduced 'state space' that avoids the combinatorial explosion that typically arises. For Gaussian rewards, even the reduced 'state space' was uncountably large, and a piecewise quadratic approximation was suggested. When this kind of approximation is used, we get an instance of **approximate dynamic programming**.

4 Discounted bandits with Markov pay-offs (Fig. 35.3) are a special case of discounted Markov decision processes on which there is a large literature. More details are in the bibliographic remarks in Chapter 38.

5 Economists have long recognised the role of time in the utility people place on rewards. Most people view a promise of pizza (freshly made) a year from today as less valuable than the same pizza tomorrow. Discounting rewards is one way to model this kind of preference. The formal model is credited to renowned American economist Paul Samuelson [1937], who, according to Frederick et al. [2002], had serious reservations about both the normative and descriptive value of the model. While discounting is not very common in the frequentist bandit literature, it appears often in **reinforcement learning**, where it offers certain technical advantages [Sutton and Barto, 1998].

6 Theorem 35.9 only holds for geometric discounting. If α^{t-1} is replaced by $\alpha(t)$, where $\alpha(\cdot)$ is not an exponential, then one can construct Markov chains for which the optimal policy is not an index policy. The intuition behind this result is that when $\alpha(t)$ is not an exponential function, then the Gittins index of an arm can change even in rounds you play a different arm, and this breaks the interleaving argument [Berry and Fristedt, 1985, chapter 6]. The Gittins index theorem is brittle in other ways. For example, it no longer holds in the multiple-play setting, where the learner can choose multiple arms in each round [Pandelis and Teneketzis, 1999].

7 The previous note does not apply to one-armed bandits for which the interleaving argument is not required. Given a Markov chain $(S_t)_t$ and horizon n, the undiscounted Gittins index of state s is

$$
g_n(s) = \sup_{2 \leq \tau \leq n} \frac{\mathbb{E}_s\left[\sum_{t=1}^{\tau-1} r(S_t)\right]}{\mathbb{E}_s[\tau - 1]}.
$$

If the learner receives reward μ_2 by retiring, then the Bayesian optimal policy is to retire in the first round t when $g_{n-t+1}(S_t) \leq \mu_2$. A reasonable strategy for undiscounted k-armed bandits is to play the arm A_t that maximises $g_{n-t+1}(S_i(t))$. Although this strategy is not Bayesian optimal anymore, it nevertheless performs well in practice. In the Gaussian case, it even enjoys frequentist regret guarantees similar to UCB [Lattimore, 2016c].

8 The form of the undiscounted Gittins index was analysed asymptotically by Burnetas and Kate-hakis [1997b], who showed the index behaves like the upper confidence bound provided by KL-UCB. This should not be especially surprising and explains the performance of the algorithm in the previous note. The asymptotic nature of the result does not make it suitable for proving regret guarantees, however.

9 We mentioned that computing the Bayesian optimal policy in finite horizon bandits is compu-tationally intractable. But this is not quite true if n is small. For example, when $n = 50$ and $k = 5$, the dynamic program for computing the exact Bayesian optimal policy for Bernoulli noise and Beta prior has approximately 10^{11} states. A big number to be sure, but not so large that the table cannot be stored on disk. And this is without any serious effort to exploit symmetries. For mission-critical applications with small horizon, the benefits of exact optimality might make the computation worth the hassle.

10 The algorithm in Section 35.5 for computing Gittins index is called **Varaiya's algorithm**. In the bibliographic remarks, we give some pointers on where to look for more sophisticated methods. The assumption that $|\mathcal{S}|$ is finite is less severe than it may appear. When the discount rate is not too close to one, then for many problems the Gittins index can be approximated by removing states that are not reachable from the start state before the discounting means they becomes close to irrelevant. When the state space is infinite, there is often a topological structure that makes a discretisation possible.

35.7 Bibliographical Remarks

The classic text on optimal stopping is by Robbins et al. [1971], while a more modern text is by Peskir and Shiryaev [2006], which includes a proof of Theorem 35.2 (see theorem 1.2). With a little extra work, you can also extract the proof of Theorem 35.3 from section 1.2 of that book. We are not aware of a reference for Theorem 35.1, but Lai [1987] has shown that for sufficiently regular priors and noise models, the asymptotic Bayesian optimal regret is $\mathrm{BR}_n^* \sim c \log(n)^2$ for some constant $c > 0$ that depends on the prior/model (see theorem 3 of Lai [1987]). The Bayesian approach dominated research on bandits from 1960 to 1980, with Gittins's result (Theorem 35.9) receiving the most attention [Gittins, 1979]. Gittins et al. [2011] has written a whole book on Bayesian bandits. Another book that focusses mostly on the Bayesian problem is by Berry and Fristedt [1985]. Although it is now more than 30 years old, this book is still a worthwhile read and presents many curious and unintuitive results about exact Bayesian policies. The book by Presman and Sonin [1990] also considers the Bayesian case. As compared to the other books, here the emphasis is on a case that is more similar to partial monitoring, the subject of Chapter 37 (in the adversarial setting). As far as we know, the earliest fully Bayesian analysis is by Bradt et al. [1956], who studied the finite horizon Bayesian one-armed bandit problem, essentially writing down the optimal policy using backwards induction, as presented here in Section 35.3. More general 'approximation results' are shown by Burnetas and Katehakis [2003], who show that under weak assumptions the Bayesian optimal strategy for one-armed bandits is asymptotically approximated by a retirement policy reminiscent of Eq. (35.4). The very specific approach to approximating the Bayesian strategy for Gaussian one-armed bandits is by one of the authors [Lattimore, 2016a], where a precise approximation for this special case is also given. There are at least four proofs of Gittins's theorem [Gittins, 1979, Whittle, 1980, Weber, 1992, Tsitsiklis, 1994]. All are summarised in the review by Frostig and Weiss [1999]. There is a line of work on computing and/or approximating the Gittins index, which we cannot do justice to. The approach presented here for finite state spaces is due to Varaiya et al. [1985], but more sophisticated algorithms exist with better guarantees. A nice survey is by Chakravorty and Mahajan [2014], but see also the articles by Chen and Katehakis [1986], Kallenberg [1986], Sonin [2008], Niño-Mora [2011] and Chakravorty and Mahajan [2013]. There is also a line of work on approximations of the Gittins index, most of which are based on approximating the discrete time stopping problem with continuous time and applying free boundary methods [Yao, 2006, and references therein]. The Gittins index has been generalised to continuous time, where the challenge is to ensure the existence of solutions to the resulting stochastic differential equations [Karoui and Karatzas, 1994]. We mentioned restless bandits in Chapter 31 on non-stationary bandits, but they are usually studied in the Bayesian context [Whittle, 1988, Weber and Weiss, 1990]. The difference is that now the Markov chains for all actions evolve regardless of the action chosen, but the learner only gets to observe the new state for the action they chose.

35.8 Exercises

35.1 (BOUNDING THE BAYESIAN OPTIMAL REGRET) Prove Theorem 35.1.

HINT   For the first part, you should use the existence of a policy for Bernoulli bandits such that

$$R_n(\pi, \nu) \le C \min \left\{ \sqrt{kn}, \frac{k \log(n)}{\Delta_{\min}(\nu)} \right\},$$

where $C > 0$ is a universal constant and $\Delta_{\min}(\nu)$ is the smallest positive suboptimality gap. Then let $\mathcal{E}_n$ be a set of bandits for which there exists a small enough positive suboptimality gap and integrate the above bound on $\mathcal{E}_n$ and $\mathcal{E}_n^c$. The second part is left as a challenge, though the solution is available.

35.2 (FINITE HORIZON OPTIMAL STOPPING) Prove Theorem 35.2.

HINT   Prove that $(E_t)_{t=1}^n$ is a $\mathbb{F}$-adapted supermartingale and that for stopping time τ satisfying the conditions of the theorem that $(M_t)_{t=1}^n$ defined by $M_t = E_{t \wedge \tau}$ is a martingale. Then apply the optional stopping theorem (Theorem 3.8).

35.3 (INFINITE HORIZON OPTIMAL STOPPING) Prove Theorem 35.3.

HINT   This is a technical exercise. Use theorem 1.7 of Peskir and Shiryaev [2006], and pass to the limit using the almost-sure convergence of $(U_t)_t$ as $t \to \infty$. You may find the ideas in the proof of theorem 1.11 of the same book useful. Be careful, Peskir and Shiryaev adopt the convention that stopping times are almost surely finite, while here we permit infinite stopping times.

35.4 This exercise uses the notation and setting of Section 35.3. Suppose that $(S_t)_{t=0}^n$ is a sequence of random elements taking values in measurable space $(\mathcal{S}, \mathcal{H})$ and with S_t being $\mathcal{F}_t/\mathcal{H}$-measurable and $\mathbb{P}_{\nu1}(Z_1, \ldots, Z_t \in \cdot \mid S_t)$ is independent of ν. Show that E_t is $\sigma(S_t)$-measurable, and there exists a $\mathcal{H}/\mathfrak{B}(\mathbb{R})$-measurable function $v_t : \mathcal{S} \to \mathbb{R}$ such that $E_t = v_t(S_t)$. You may assume that $(\mathcal{E}, \mathcal{G})$ is Borel.

35.5 Prove Lemma 35.5.

35.6 (EQUIVALENCE OF GITTINS DEFINITIONS) Prove that the definitions of the Gittins index given in Eq. (35.8) and Eq. (35.9) are equivalent.

35.7 Prove Lemma 35.7.

HINT   Find a way to apply Theorem 35.3.

35.8 Consider that the discounted bandit with Markov pay-offs described in Example 35.8. Show that there is a one-to-one correspondence ϕ between the policies for this problem and the discounted Bayesian bandit with $\text{Beta}(1, 1)$ on the mean reward of each arm such that the total expected discounted reward (value) is invariant under ϕ.

35.9 Prove Lemma 35.10.

HINT   Use the Hardy–Littlewood inequality, which for infinite sequences states that for any real, increasing sequences $(x_n)_{n=1}^\infty, (y_n)_{n=1}^\infty$ and any bijection $\sigma : \mathbb{N}^+ \to \mathbb{N}^+$ it holds that $\sum_{n=1}^\infty x_n y_n \geq \sum_{n=1}^\infty x_n y_{\sigma(n)}$.

35.10 (CORRECTNESS OF VARAIYA'S ALGORITHM) Prove the correctness of Varaiya's algorithm, as explained in Section 35.5.

35.11 In this exercise, you will implement some Bayesian (near-)optimal 1-armed bandit algorithms.

(a) Reproduce the experimental results in Experiment 1.
(b) Implement an approximation of the optimal policy for one-armed Gaussian bandits and compare its performance to the stopping rule τ_α defined below for a variety of different choices of $\alpha > 0$.

$$\tau_\alpha = \min \left\{ t \geq 2 : \hat{\mu}_{t-1} + \sqrt{\frac{2\max\{0, \log(\alpha n/t)\}}{t - 1}} \leq \mu_2 \right\}.$$

36 Thompson Sampling

"As all things come to an end, even this story, a day came at last when they were in sight of the country where Bilbo had been born and bred, where the shapes of the land and of the trees were as well known to him as his hands and toes." – Tolkien [1937].

Like Bilbo, as the end nears, we return to where it all began, to the first algorithm for bandits proposed by Thompson [1933]. The idea is a simple one. Before the game starts, the learner chooses a prior over a set of possible bandit environments. In each round, the learner samples an environment from the posterior and acts according to the optimal action in that environment. Thompson only gave empirical evidence (calculated by hand) and focused on Bernoulli bandits with two arms. Nowadays these limitations have been eliminated, and theoretical guarantees have been proven demonstrating the approach is often close to optimal in a wide range of settings. Perhaps more importantly, the resulting algorithms are often quite practical both in terms of computation and empirical performance. The idea of sampling from the posterior and playing the optimal action is called **Thompson sampling**, or **posterior sampling**.

The exploration in Thompson sampling comes from the randomisation. If the posterior is poorly concentrated, then the fluctuations in the samples are expected to be large and the policy will likely explore. On the other hand, as more data is collected, the posterior concentrates towards the true environment and the rate of exploration decreases. We focus our attention on finite-armed stochastic bandits and linear stochastic bandits, but Thompson sampling has been extended to all kinds of models, as explained in the bibliographic remarks.

> Randomisation is crucial for adversarial bandit algorithms and can be useful in stochastic settings (see Chapters 23 and 32 for examples). We should be wary, however, that injecting noise into our algorithms might come at a cost in terms of variance. What is gained or lost by the randomisation in Thompson sampling is still not clear, but we leave this cautionary note as a suggestion to the reader to think about some of the costs and benefits.

36.1 Finite-Armed Bandits

Recalling the notation from Section 34.5, let $k > 1$ and $(\mathcal{E}, \mathfrak{B}(\mathcal{E}), Q, P)$ be a k-armed Bayesian bandit environment. The learner chooses actions $(A_t)_{t=1}^n$ and receives rewards

$(X_t)_{t=1}^n$, and the posterior after t observations is a probability kernel $Q(\cdot \mid \cdot)$ from $([k] \times \mathbb{R})^t$ to $(\mathcal{E}, \mathfrak{B}(\mathcal{E}))$. Denote the mean of the ith arm in bandit $\nu \in \mathcal{E}$ by $\mu_i(\nu) = \int_{\mathbb{R}} x dP_{\nu i}(x)$. In round t, Thompson sampling samples a bandit environment ν_t from the posterior of Q given $A_1, X_1, \dots, A_{t-1}, X_{t-1}$ and then chooses the arm with the largest mean (Algorithm 23). A more precise definition is that Thompson sampling is the policy $\pi = (\pi_t)_{t=1}^\infty$ with

$$\pi_t(a \mid a_1, x_1, \dots, a_{t-1}, x_{t-1}) = Q(B_a \mid a_1, x_1, \dots, a_{t-1}, x_{t-1}),$$

where $B_a = \{\nu \in \mathcal{E} : \mu_a(\nu) = \mathrm{argmax}_b \, \mu_b(\nu)\} \in \mathfrak{B}(\mathcal{E})$, with ties in the argmax are resolved in an arbitrary, but systematic fashion.

1: **Input** Bayesian bandit environment $(\mathcal{E}, \mathfrak{B}(\mathcal{E}), Q, P)$
2: **for** $t = 1, 2, \dots, n$ **do**
3:     Sample $\nu_t \sim Q(\cdot \mid A_1, X_1, \dots, A_{t-1}, X_{t-1})$
4:     Choose $A_t = \mathrm{argmax}_{i \in [k]} \, \mu_i(\nu_t)$
5: **end for**

Algorithm 23: Thompson sampling.

Thompson sampling has been analysed in both the frequentist and the Bayesian settings. We start with the latter where the result requires almost no assumptions on the prior. In fact, after one small observation about Thompson sampling, the analysis is almost the same as that of UCB.

THEOREM 36.1. *Let $(\mathcal{E}, \mathfrak{B}(\mathcal{E}), Q, P)$ be a k-armed Bayesian bandit environment such that for all $\nu \in \mathcal{E}$ and $i \in [k]$, the distribution $P_{\nu i}$ is 1-subgaussian (after centering) with mean in $[0, 1]$. Then the policy π of Thompson sampling satisfies*

$$\mathrm{BR}_n(\pi, Q) \leq C\sqrt{kn \log(n)},$$

where $C > 0$ is a universal constant.

Proof Abbreviate $\mu_i = \mu_i(\nu)$ and let $A^* = \mathrm{argmax}_{i \in [k]} \, \mu_i$ be the optimal arm, which depends on ν and is a random variable. When there are ties, we use the same tie-breaking rule as in the algorithm in the definition of A^*. For each $t \in [n]$ and $i \in [k]$, let

$$U_t(i) = \mathrm{clip}_{[0,1]} \left(\hat{\mu}_i(t-1) + \sqrt{\frac{2\log(1/\delta)}{1 \vee T_i(t-1)}} \right),$$

where $\hat{\mu}_i(t-1)$ is the empirical estimate of the reward of arm i after $t-1$ rounds and we assume $\hat{\mu}_i(t-1) = 0$ if $T_i(t-1) = 0$. Let E be the event that for all $t \in [n]$ and $i \in [k]$,

$$|\hat{\mu}_i(t-1) - \mu_i| < \sqrt{\frac{2\log(1/\delta)}{1 \vee T_i(t-1)}}.$$

In Exercise 36.2, we ask you to prove that $\mathbb{P}(E^c) \leq 2nk\delta$. Let $\mathcal{F}_t = \sigma(A_1, X_1, \dots, A_t, X_t)$ be the σ-algebra generated by the interaction sequence by the end of round t. Note that $U_t(i)$ is $\mathcal{F}_{t-1}$-measurable. The Bayesian regret is

$$\mathrm{BR}_n = \mathbb{E}\left[\sum_{t=1}^n (\mu_{A^*} - \mu_{A_t})\right] = \mathbb{E}\left[\sum_{t=1}^n \mathbb{E}\left[\mu_{A^*} - \mu_{A_t} \mid \mathcal{F}_{t-1}\right]\right].$$

The key insight (Exercise 36.3) is to notice that the definition of Thompson sampling implies the conditional distributions of A^* and A_t given $\mathcal{F}_{t-1}$ are the same:

$$\mathbb{P}\left(A^* = \cdot \mid \mathcal{F}_{t-1}\right) = \mathbb{P}\left(A_t = \cdot \mid \mathcal{F}_{t-1}\right) \quad \text{a.s.} \tag{36.1}$$

Using the previous display,

$$
\begin{aligned}
\mathbb{E}\left[\mu_{A^*} - \mu_{A_t} \mid \mathcal{F}_{t-1}\right] &= \mathbb{E}\left[\mu_{A^*} - U_t(A_t) + U_t(A_t) - \mu_{A_t} \mid \mathcal{F}_{t-1}\right] \\
&= \mathbb{E}\left[\mu_{A^*} - U_t(A^*) + U_t(A_t) - \mu_{A_t} \mid \mathcal{F}_{t-1}\right] \quad \text{(Eq. (36.1))} \\
&= \mathbb{E}\left[\mu_{A^*} - U_t(A^*) \mid \mathcal{F}_{t-1}\right] + \mathbb{E}\left[U_t(A_t) - \mu_{A_t} \mid \mathcal{F}_{t-1}\right].
\end{aligned}
$$

Using the tower rule for expectation shows that

$$\mathrm{BR}_n = \mathbb{E}\left[\sum_{t=1}^{n}(\mu_{A^*} - U_t(A^*)) + \sum_{t=1}^{n}(U_t(A_t) - \mu_{A_t})\right]. \tag{36.2}$$

On the event E^c the terms inside the expectation are bounded by $2n$, while on the event E, the first sum is negative and the second is bounded by

$$
\mathbb{I}\{E\} \sum_{t=1}^{n}(U_t(A_t) - \mu_{A_t}) = \mathbb{I}\{E\} \sum_{t=1}^{n}\sum_{i=1}^{k} \mathbb{I}\{A_t = i\}\,(U_t(i) - \mu_i)
$$

$$
\leq \sum_{i=1}^{k}\sum_{t=1}^{n} \mathbb{I}\{A_t = i\} \sqrt{\frac{8\log(1/\delta)}{1 \vee T_i(t-1)}} \leq \sum_{i=1}^{k} \int_0^{T_i(n)} \sqrt{\frac{8\log(1/\delta)}{s}}\,ds
$$

$$
= \sum_{i=1}^{k} \sqrt{32 T_i(n)\log(1/\delta)} \leq \sqrt{32nk\log(1/\delta)}.
$$

The proof is completed by choosing $\delta = n^{-2}$ and the fact that $\mathbb{P}\left(E^c\right) \leq 2nk\delta$. $\qquad\square$

36.2   Frequentist Analysis

Bounding the frequentist regret of Thompson sampling is more technical than the Bayesian regret. The trouble is the frequentist regret does not have an expectation with respect to the prior, which means that A_t is not conditionally distributed in the same way as the optimal action (which is not random). Thompson sampling can be viewed as an instantiation of follow-the-perturbed-leader, which we already saw in action for adversarial combinatorial semi-bandits in Chapter 30. Here we work with the stochastic setting and consider the general form algorithm given in Algorithm 24.

Thompson sampling is recovered by choosing $F_1(1), \ldots, F_k(1)$ to be the cumulative distribution functions of the mean reward of each arm for a prior that is independent over the arms (a product prior). Then letting UPDATE be the function that updates the posterior for the played arm. There are, however, many alternatives ways to configure this algorithm.

The core property that we use in the analysis of Algorithm 24 (to be presented soon) is that $F_i(t+1) = F_i(t)$ whenever $A_t \neq i$. When UPDATE$(\cdot)$ is a Bayesian update this corresponds to choosing an independent prior on the distribution of each arm.

1: **Input** Cumulative distribution functions $F_1(1), \ldots, F_k(1)$
2: **for** $t = 1, \ldots, n$ **do**
3:    Sample $\theta_i(t) \sim F_i(t)$ independently for each i
4:    Choose $A_t = \operatorname{argmax}_{i \in [k]} \theta_i(t)$
5:    Observe X_t and update:

$$F_i(t+1) = F_i(t) \text{ for } i \neq A_t \quad \text{and} \quad F_{A_t}(t+1) = \text{UPDATE}(F_{A_t}(t), A_t, X_t)$$

6: **end for**

Algorithm 24: Follow-the-perturbed-leader

Let F_{is} be the cumulative distribution function used for arm i in all rounds t with $T_i(t-1) = s$. This quantity is defined even if $T_i(n) < s$ by using the reward-stack model from Section 4.6.

THEOREM 36.2. *Assume that arm 1 is optimal. Let $i > 1$ be an action and $\varepsilon \in \mathbb{R}$ be arbitrary. Then the expected number of times Algorithm 24 plays action i is bounded by*

$$\mathbb{E}[T_i(n)] \leq 1 + \mathbb{E}\left[\sum_{s=0}^{n-1}\left(\frac{1}{G_{1s}} - 1\right)\right] + \mathbb{E}\left[\sum_{s=0}^{n-1}\mathbb{I}\{G_{is} > 1/n\}\right], \tag{36.3}$$

where $G_{is} = 1 - F_{is}(\mu_1 - \varepsilon)$.

In applications, ε is normally chosen to be a small positive constant. In this case, the first sum in Eq. (36.3) measures the probability that the sample corresponding to the first arm is nearly optimistic and tends to be smaller when the variance of the perturbation is larger. The second sum measures the likelihood that the sample from arm i is close to μ_1 and is small when the variance of the perturbation is small. Balancing these two terms corresponds to optimising the exploration/exploitation trade-off.

Proof of Theorem 36.2 Let $\mathcal{F}_t = \sigma(A_1, X_1, \ldots, A_t, X_t)$ and $E_i(t) = \{\theta_i(t) \leq \mu_1 - \varepsilon\}$. By definition,

$$\mathbb{P}(\theta_1(t) \geq \mu_1 - \varepsilon \mid \mathcal{F}_{t-1}) = G_{1T_1(t-1)} \quad \text{a.s.}$$

We start with a straightforward decomposition:

$$\mathbb{E}[T_i(n)] = \mathbb{E}\left[\sum_{t=1}^{n}\mathbb{I}\{A_t = i\}\right]$$

$$= \mathbb{E}\left[\sum_{t=1}^{n}\mathbb{I}\{A_t = i, E_i(t)\}\right] + \mathbb{E}\left[\sum_{t=1}^{n}\mathbb{I}\{A_t = i, E_i^c(t)\}\right]. \tag{36.4}$$

In order to bound the first term, let $A_t' = \operatorname{argmax}_{i \neq 1} \theta_i(t)$. Then

$$\mathbb{P}(A_t = 1, E_i(t) \mid \mathcal{F}_{t-1}) \geq \mathbb{P}(A_t' = i, E_i(t), \theta_1(t) \geq \mu_1 - \varepsilon \mid \mathcal{F}_{t-1})$$

$$= \mathbb{P}(\theta_1(t) \geq \mu_1 - \varepsilon \mid \mathcal{F}_{t-1})\mathbb{P}(A_t' = i, E_i(t) \mid \mathcal{F}_{t-1})$$

$$\geq \frac{G_{1T_1(t-1)}}{1 - G_{1T_1(t-1)}}\mathbb{P}(A_t = i, E_i(t) \mid \mathcal{F}_{t-1}), \tag{36.5}$$

where in the first equality we used the fact that $\theta_1(t)$ is conditionally independent of A'_t and $E_i(t)$ given $\mathcal{F}_{t-1}$. In the second inequality, we used the definition of G_{1s} and the fact that

$$\mathbb{P}\left(A_t = i, E_i(t) \mid \mathcal{F}_{t-1}\right) \leq (1 - \mathbb{P}\left(\theta_1(t) > \mu_1 - \varepsilon \mid \mathcal{F}_{t-1}\right))\mathbb{P}\left(A'_t = i, E_i(t) \mid \mathcal{F}_{t-1}\right),$$

which is true since $\{A_t = i, E_i(t) \text{ occurs}\} \subseteq \{A'_t = i, E_i(t) \text{ occurs}\} \cap \{\theta_1(t) \leq \mu_1 - \varepsilon\}$, and the two intersected events are conditionally independent given $\mathcal{F}_{t-1}$. Therefore using Eq. (36.5), we have

$$\mathbb{P}\left(A_t = i, E_i(t) \mid \mathcal{F}_{t-1}\right) \leq \left(\frac{1}{G_{1T_1(t-1)}} - 1\right)\mathbb{P}\left(A_t = 1, E_i(t) \mid \mathcal{F}_{t-1}\right)$$

$$\leq \left(\frac{1}{G_{1T_1(t-1)}} - 1\right)\mathbb{P}\left(A_t = 1 \mid \mathcal{F}_{t-1}\right).$$

Substituting this into the first term in Eq. (36.4) leads to

$$\mathbb{E}\left[\sum_{t=1}^{n} \mathbb{I}\{A_t = i, E_i(t) \text{ occurs}\}\right] \leq \mathbb{E}\left[\sum_{t=1}^{n} \left(\frac{1}{G_{1T_1(t-1)}} - 1\right)\mathbb{P}\left(A_t = 1 \mid \mathcal{F}_{t-1}\right)\right]$$

$$= \mathbb{E}\left[\sum_{t=1}^{n} \left(\frac{1}{G_{1T_1(t-1)}} - 1\right)\mathbb{I}\{A_t = 1\}\right]$$

$$\leq \mathbb{E}\left[\sum_{s=0}^{n-1} \left(\frac{1}{G_{1s}} - 1\right)\right], \tag{36.6}$$

where in the last step we used the fact that $T_1(t - 1) = s$ is only possible for one round where $A_t = 1$. Let $\mathcal{T} = \{t \in [n] : 1 - F_{iT_i(t-1)}(\mu_1 - \varepsilon) > 1/n\}$. After some calculation (Exercise 36.5), we get

$$\mathbb{E}\left[\sum_{t=1}^{n} \mathbb{I}\{A_t = i, E_i^c(t) \text{ occurs}\}\right] \leq \mathbb{E}\left[\sum_{t \in \mathcal{T}} \mathbb{I}\{A_t = i\}\right] + \mathbb{E}\left[\sum_{t \notin \mathcal{T}} \mathbb{I}\{E_i^c(t)\}\right]$$

$$\leq \mathbb{E}\left[\sum_{s=0}^{n-1} \mathbb{I}\{1 - F_{is}(\mu_1 - \varepsilon) > 1/n\}\right] + \mathbb{E}\left[\sum_{t \notin \mathcal{T}} \frac{1}{n}\right]$$

$$\leq \mathbb{E}\left[\sum_{s=0}^{n-1} \mathbb{I}\{G_{is} > 1/n\}\right] + 1.$$

Putting together the pieces completes the proof.   □

By instantiating Algorithm 24 with different choices of perturbations, one can prove that Thompson sampling enjoys frequentist guarantees in a number of settings. The following theorem shows that Thompson sampling with an appropriate prior is asymptotically optimal for the set of Gaussian bandits. The reader is invited to prove this result by following the steps suggested in Exercise 36.6.

THEOREM 36.3. *Suppose that $F_i(1) = \delta_\infty$ is the Dirac at infinity and let* $\text{Update}(F_i(t), A_t,$ $X_t)$ *be the cumulative distribution function of the Gaussian $\mathcal{N}(\hat{\mu}_i(t), 1/t)$. Then the regret of Algorithm 24 on Gaussian bandit $v \in \mathcal{E}_{\mathcal{N}}^k(1)$ satisfies*

$$\lim_{n\to\infty} \frac{R_n}{\log(n)} = \sum_{i:\Delta_i>0} \frac{2}{\Delta_i}.$$

Furthermore, there exists a universal constant $C > 0$ such that $R_n \leq C\sqrt{nk\log(n)}$.

The choice of update and initial distributions in Theorem 36.3 correspond to Thompson sampling when the prior mean and variance are sent to infinity at appropriate rates. For this choice, a finite-time analysis is also possible (see the exercise).

EXPERIMENT 36.1   Empirically the algorithm described in Theorem 36.3 has a smaller expected regret than the version of UCB analysed in Chapter 7. Compared to more sophisticated algorithms, however, it has larger regret and larger variance. AdaUCB (which we briefly met in Section 9.3) and Thompson sampling were simulated on a two-armed Gaussian bandit with mean vector $\mu = (1/5, 0)$ and unit variance and a horizon of $n = 2000$. The expected regret as estimated over 100,000 independent runs was 23.8 for AdaUCB and 29.9 for Thompson sampling. The figure below shows that contribution of the second moment of $\hat{R}_n = \sum_i \Delta_i T_i(n)$ for each algorithm, which shows that Thompson sampling has a much larger variance than AdaUCB, despite its inferior expected regret.

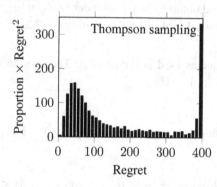
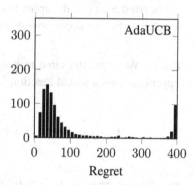

36.3   Linear Bandits

While the advantages of Thompson sampling in finite-armed bandits are relatively limited, in the linear setting there is much to be gained, both in terms of computation and empirical performance. Let $\mathcal{A} \subset \mathbb{R}^d$ and $(\mathcal{E}, \mathfrak{B}(\mathcal{E}), Q, P)$ be a Bayesian bandit environment where $\mathcal{E} \subset \mathbb{R}^d$ and for $\theta \in \mathcal{E}$ and $a \in \mathcal{A}$, $P_{\theta a}$ is 1-subgaussian with mean $\langle \theta, a \rangle$. Let $\theta : \mathcal{E} \to \mathbb{R}^d$ be the identity map, which is a random vector on $(\mathcal{E}, \mathfrak{B}(\mathcal{E}), Q)$.

1: **Input** Bayesian bandit environment $(\mathcal{E}, \mathfrak{B}(\mathcal{E}), Q, P)$
2: **for** $t \in 1, \ldots, n$ **do**
3:     Sample θ_t from the posterior
4:     Choose $A_t = \text{argmax}_{a \in \mathcal{A}} \langle a, \theta_t \rangle$
5:     Observe X_t
6: **end for**

Algorithm 25: Thompson sampling for linear bandits.

The Bayesian regret is controlled using the techniques from the previous section in combination with the concentration analysis in Chapter 20. A frequentist analysis is also possible under slightly unsatisfying assumptions, which we discuss in the notes and bibliographic remarks.

THEOREM 36.4. *Assume that* $\|\theta\|_2 \leq S$ *with Q-probability one and* $\sup_{a \in \mathcal{A}} \|a\|_2 \leq L$ *and* $\sup_{a \in \mathcal{A}} |\langle a, \theta \rangle| \leq 1$ *with Q-probability one. Then the Bayesian regret of Algorithm 25 is bounded by*

$$\mathrm{BR}_n \leq 2 + 2\sqrt{2dn\beta^2 \log\left(1 + \frac{nS^2L^2}{d}\right)},$$

where $\beta = 1 + \sqrt{2\log(n) + d\log\left(1 + \frac{nS^2L^2}{d}\right)}.$

For fixed S and L, the upper bound obtained here is of order $O(d\sqrt{n}\log(n)\log(n/d))$, which matches the upper bound obtained for Lin-UCB in Corollary 19.3.

Proof We apply the same technique as used in the proof of Theorem 36.1. Define the upper confidence bound function $U_t : \mathcal{A} \to \mathbb{R}$ by

$$U_t(a) = \langle a, \hat{\theta}_{t-1} \rangle + \beta \|a\|_{V_{t-1}^{-1}}, \quad \text{where } V_t = \frac{1}{S^2}I + \sum_{s=1}^{t} A_s A_s^\top.$$

By Theorem 20.5 and Eq. (20.9), $\mathbb{P}(\text{exists } t \leq n : \|\hat{\theta}_{t-1} - \theta\|_{V_{t-1}} > \beta) \leq 1/n$. Let E_t be the event that $\|\hat{\theta}_{t-1} - \theta\|_{V_{t-1}} \leq \beta$, $E = \bigcap_{t=1}^{n} E_t$ and $A^* = \mathrm{argmax}_{a \in \mathcal{A}} \langle a, \theta \rangle$. Note that A^* is a random variable because θ is random. Then

$$\mathrm{BR}_n = \mathbb{E}\left[\sum_{t=1}^{n} \langle A^* - A_t, \theta \rangle\right]$$

$$= \mathbb{E}\left[\mathbb{I}_{E^c} \sum_{t=1}^{n} \langle A^* - A_t, \theta \rangle\right] + \mathbb{E}\left[\mathbb{I}_E \sum_{t=1}^{n} \langle A^* - A_t, \theta \rangle\right]$$

$$\leq 2 + \mathbb{E}\left[\mathbb{I}_E \sum_{t=1}^{n} \langle A^* - A_t, \theta \rangle\right]$$

$$\leq 2 + \mathbb{E}\left[\sum_{t=1}^{n} \mathbb{I}_{E_t} \langle A^* - A_t, \theta \rangle\right]. \tag{36.7}$$

Let $\mathcal{F}_t = \sigma(A_1, X_1, \ldots, A_t, X_t)$ and let $\mathbb{E}_{t-1}[\cdot] = \mathbb{E}[\cdot \mid \mathcal{F}_{t-1}]$. As before, $\mathbb{P}(A^* = \cdot \mid \mathcal{F}_{t-1}) = \mathbb{P}(A_t = \cdot \mid \mathcal{F}_{t-1})$, and $U_t(a)$, for any fixed $a \in \mathcal{A}$, is $\mathcal{F}_{t-1}$-measurable, and so

$\mathbb{E}_{t-1}(U_t(A^*)) = \mathbb{E}_{t-1}(U_t(A_t))$. It follows that the second term in the above display is bounded by

$$
\begin{aligned}
\mathbb{E}_{t-1}\left[\mathbb{I}_{E_t}\langle A^* - A_t, \theta\rangle\right] &= \mathbb{I}_{E_t}\mathbb{E}_{t-1}\left[\langle A^*, \theta\rangle - U_t(A^*) + U_t(A_t) - \langle A_t, \theta\rangle\right] \\
&\leq \mathbb{I}_{E_t}\mathbb{E}_{t-1}\left[U_t(A_t) - \langle A_t, \theta\rangle\right] \\
&\leq \mathbb{I}_{E_t}\mathbb{E}_{t-1}\left[\langle A_t, \hat{\theta}_{t-1} - \theta\rangle\right] + \beta\|A_t\|_{V_t^{-1}} \\
&\leq \mathbb{I}_{E_t}\mathbb{E}_{t-1}\left[\|A_t\|_{V_t^{-1}}\|\hat{\theta}_{t-1} - \theta\|_{V_t}\right] + \beta\|A_t\|_{V_t^{-1}} \\
&\leq 2\beta\|A_t\|_{V_t^{-1}}.
\end{aligned}
$$

Substituting this combined with $\mathbb{I}_{E_t}\langle A^* - A_t, \theta\rangle \leq 2$ into the second term of Eq. (36.7), we get

$$
\begin{aligned}
\mathbb{E}\left[\sum_{t=1}^{n}\mathbb{I}_{E_t}\langle A^* - A_t, \theta\rangle\right] &\leq 2\beta\mathbb{E}\left[\sum_{t=1}^{n}(1 \wedge \|A_t\|_{V_t^{-1}})\right] \\
&\leq 2\sqrt{n\beta^2\mathbb{E}\left[\sum_{t=1}^{n}(1 \wedge \|A_t\|_{V_t^{-1}}^2)\right]} \qquad \text{(Cauchy-Schwarz)} \\
&\leq 2\sqrt{2dn\beta^2\mathbb{E}\left[\log\left(1 + \frac{nS^2L^2}{d}\right)\right]}. \qquad \text{(Lemma 19.4)}
\end{aligned}
$$

Putting together the pieces shows that

$$
\text{BR}_n \leq 2 + 2\sqrt{2dn\beta^2\log\left(1 + \frac{nS^2L^2}{d}\right)}. \qquad \square
$$

36.3.1 Computation

An implementation of Thompson sampling for linear bandits needs to sample θ_t from the posterior and then find the optimal action for the sampled parameter:

$$
A_t = \text{argmax}_{a \in \mathcal{A}}\langle a, \theta_t\rangle.
$$

For some priors and noise models, sampling from the posterior is straightforward. The most notable case is when Q is a multivariate Gaussian and the noise is Gaussian with a known variance. More generally, there is a large literature devoted to numerical methods for sampling from posterior distributions. Having sampled θ_t, finding A_t is a linear optimisation problem. By comparison, LinUCB needs to solve

$$
A_t = \text{argmax}_{a \in \mathcal{A}}\max_{\tilde{\theta} \in \mathcal{C}}\langle a, \tilde{\theta}\rangle,
$$

which for large or continuous action sets is often intractable.

36.4 Information Theoretic Analysis

We now examine a Bayesian version of the adversarial k-armed bandit. As we will see, the natural generalisation of Thompson sampling is still a reasonable algorithm. Recall that in the adversarial bandit model studied in Part III, the adversary secretly chooses a matrix $x \in [0,1]^{n \times k}$ at the start of the game and the reward in round t is x_{tA_t}. In the Bayesian set-up, there is a prior probability measure Q on $[0,1]^{n \times k}$ with the Borel σ-algebra. At the start of the game, a reward matrix X is sampled from Q, but not revealed. The learner then chooses actions $(A_t)_{t=1}^n$ and the reward in round t is X_{tA_t}. Formally, let $\pi = (\pi_t)_{t=1}^n$ be a policy and $X \in [0,1]^{n \times k}$ and $(A_t)_{t=1}^n$ be random elements on some probability space $(\Omega, \mathcal{F}, \mathbb{P})$ such that:

(a) the law of X is $\mathbb{P}_X = Q$; and
(b) $\mathbb{P}(A_t \in \cdot \mid X, H_{t-1}) = \pi_t(\cdot \mid H_{t-1})$ with $H_t = (A_1, X_{1A_1}, \ldots, A_t, X_{tA_t})$.

The inclusion of X in the conditional expectation in Part (b) implies that

$$\mathbb{P}(A_t \in \cdot \mid X, H_{t-1}) = \mathbb{P}(A_t \in \cdot \mid H_{t-1}),$$

which means that A_t and X are conditionally independent given H_{t-1}. This is consistent with our definition of the model where X is sampled first from Q and then A_t depends on X only through the history H_{t-1}. The optimal action is $A^* = \text{argmax}_{a \in [k]} \sum_{t=1}^n X_{ta}$ with ties broken arbitrarily. The Bayesian regret is

$$\text{BR}_n = \mathbb{E}\left[\sum_{t=1}^n (X_{tA^*} - X_{tA_t})\right].$$

Like in the previous sections, Thompson sampling is a policy $\pi = (\pi_t)_{t=1}^n$ that plays each action according to the conditional probability that it is optimal, which means the following holds almost surely:

$$\pi_t(\cdot \mid A_1, X_{1A_1}, \ldots, A_{t-1}, X_{t-1A_{t-1}}) = \mathbb{P}(A^* \in \cdot \mid A_1, X_{1A_1}, \ldots, A_{t-1}, X_{t-1A_{t-1}}).$$

The main result of this section is the following theorem:

THEOREM 36.5. *The Bayesian regret of Thompson sampling for Bayesian k-armed adversarial bandits satisfies*

$$\text{BR}_n \leq \sqrt{kn \log(k)/2}.$$

The proof is done through a generic theorem that is powerful enough to analyse a wide range of settings. For stating this result, we need some preparation. Let $\mathcal{F}_t = \sigma(A_1, X_{1A_1}, \ldots, A_t, X_{tA_t})$ and $\mathbb{E}_t[\cdot] = \mathbb{E}[\cdot \mid \mathcal{F}_t]$ and $\mathbb{P}_t(\cdot) = \mathbb{P}(\cdot \mid \mathcal{F}_t)$. Let $\Delta_t = X_{tA^*} - X_{tA_t}$ denote the immediate regret of round t.

The promised generic theorem bounds the regret in terms of an 'information ratio' that depends on the ratio of the squared expected instantaneous regret conditioned on the past and a Bregman divergence with respect to some convex function F to be chosen later.

THEOREM 36.6. *Let $F : \mathbb{R}^k \to \mathbb{R} \cup \{\infty\}$ be convex, and suppose there exists a constant $\beta \geq 0$ such that*

$$\mathbb{E}_{t-1}[\Delta_t] \leq \sqrt{\beta \mathbb{E}_{t-1}[D_F(\mathbb{P}_t(A^* = \cdot), \mathbb{P}_{t-1}(A^* = \cdot))]} \quad a.s.$$

Then $\text{BR}_n \leq \sqrt{n\beta \text{diam}_F(\mathcal{P}_{k-1})}.$

Proof Let $M_t = \mathbb{P}_t(A^* = \cdot) \in \mathcal{P}_{k-1}$. Using the directional derivative definition of the Bregman divergence combined with Fatou's lemma and convexity of F,

$$\mathbb{E}_{t-1}[D_F(M_t, M_{t-1})] = \mathbb{E}_{t-1}\left[F(M_t) - F(M_{t-1}) - \nabla_{M_t - M_{t-1}} F(M_{t-1})\right]$$

$$= \mathbb{E}_{t-1}\left[\liminf_{h \to 0+} \left(F(M_t) - F(M_{t-1}) - \frac{F((1-h)M_{t-1} + hM_t) - F(M_{t-1})}{h}\right)\right]$$

$$\leq \liminf_{h \to 0+} \left(\mathbb{E}_{t-1}\left[F(M_t) - F(M_{t-1}) - \frac{F((1-h)M_{t-1} + hM_t) - F(M_{t-1})}{h}\right]\right)$$

$$= \mathbb{E}_{t-1}[F(M_t)] - F(M_{t-1}) + \liminf_{h \to 0+} \frac{F(M_{t-1}) - \mathbb{E}_{t-1}[F((1-h)M_{t-1} + hM_t)]}{h}$$

$$\leq \mathbb{E}_{t-1}[F(M_t)] - F(M_{t-1}) + \liminf_{h \to 0+} \frac{F(M_{t-1}) - F(\mathbb{E}_{t-1}[(1-h)M_{t-1} + hM_t])}{h}$$

$$= \mathbb{E}_{t-1}[F(M_t)] - F(M_{t-1}), \tag{36.8}$$

where the first inequality follows from Fatou's lemma and the second from the convexity of F. The last equality is because $\mathbb{E}_{t-1}[M_t] = M_{t-1}$. Hence,

$$\mathrm{BR}_n = \mathbb{E}\left[\sum_{t=1}^n \Delta_t\right] \leq \mathbb{E}\left[\sum_{t=1}^n \sqrt{\beta \mathbb{E}_{t-1}[D_F(M_t, M_{t-1})]}\right]$$

$$\leq \sqrt{\beta n \mathbb{E}\left[\sum_{t=1}^n \mathbb{E}_{t-1}[D_F(M_t, M_{t-1})]\right]} \leq \sqrt{\beta n \mathrm{diam}_F(\mathcal{P}_{k-1})},$$

where the first inequality follows from the assumption in the theorem, the second by Cauchy–Schwarz, while the third follows by Eq. (36.8), telescoping and the definition of the diameter. $\square$

It remains to choose F and show that the condition of the previous result can be met. As you might have guessed, a good choice is the unnormalised negentropy potential $F(p) = \sum_{a=1}^k p_a \log(p_a) - p_a$. Remember that in this case the resulting Bregman divergence $D_F(p, q)$ is the relative entropy, $\mathrm{D}(p, q)$, between categorical distributions parameterised by p and q, respectively.

LEMMA 36.7. *If $X_{ti} \in [0, 1]$ almost surely for all $t \in [n]$ and $i \in [k]$ and A_t is chosen by Thompson sampling using any prior, then*

$$\mathbb{E}_{t-1}[\Delta_t] \leq \sqrt{\frac{k}{2} \mathbb{E}_{t-1}[\mathrm{D}(\mathbb{P}_t(A^* \in \cdot), \mathbb{P}_{t-1}(A^* \in \cdot))]}.$$

Proof Given a measure $\mathbb{P}$, we write $\mathbb{P}_{X|Y}(\cdot)$ for $\mathbb{P}(X \in \cdot \mid Y)$. In our application below, X is a random variable, and hence $\mathbb{P}(X \in \cdot \mid Y)$ can be chosen to be a probability measure by Theorem 3.11. When Y is discrete, we write $\mathbb{P}_{X|Y=y}(\cdot)$ for $\mathbb{P}(X \in \cdot \mid Y = y)$. The result follows by chaining Pinsker's inequality and Cauchy–Schwarz:

$$E_{t-1}[\Delta_t] = \sum_{a=1}^{k} \mathbb{P}_{t-1}(A_t = a) \left(\mathbb{E}_{t-1}[X_{ta} \mid A^* = a] - \mathbb{E}_{t-1}[X_{ta}]\right)$$

$$\leq \sum_{a=1}^{k} \mathbb{P}_{t-1}(A_t = a) \sqrt{\frac{1}{2} D(\mathbb{P}_{t-1,X_{ta}|A^*=a}, \mathbb{P}_{t-1,X_{ta}})}$$

$$\leq \sqrt{\frac{k}{2} \sum_{a=1}^{k} \mathbb{P}_{t-1}(A_t = a)^2 D(\mathbb{P}_{t-1,X_{ta}|A^*=a}, \mathbb{P}_{t-1,X_{ta}})}$$

$$\leq \sqrt{\frac{k}{2} \sum_{a=1}^{k} \mathbb{P}_{t-1}(A_t = a) \sum_{b=1}^{k} \mathbb{P}_{t-1}(A^* = a) D(\mathbb{P}_{t-1,X_{ta}|A^*=b}, \mathbb{P}_{t-1,X_{ta}})}$$

$$= \sqrt{\frac{k}{2} \mathbb{E}_{t-1}\left[D(\mathbb{P}_t(A^* \in \cdot), \mathbb{P}_{t-1}(A^* \in \cdot))\right]},$$

where the final equality follows from Bayes' law and is left as an exercise.   □

Proof of Theorem 36.5   The result follows by combining Lemma 36.7, Theorem 36.6 and the fact that the diameter of the unnormalised negentropy potential is $\text{diam}_F(\mathcal{P}_{k-1}) = \log(k)$.   □

> The reason for the name 'information-theoretic' is that historically Theorem 36.6 was specified to the unnormalised negentropy when the expected Bregman divergence is called the **information gain** or **mutual information**. In this, sense Theorem 36.6 shows that the Bayesian regret is well controlled if $\mathbb{E}_{t-1}[\Delta_t]$ can be bounded in terms of the information gain about the optimal action, which seems rather natural. Other potentials can be useful, however, as you will show in Exercise 36.10.

36.5   Notes

1 There are several equivalent ways to view Thompson sampling in stationary stochastic multi-armed bandits: *(a)* select an arm according to the posterior probability that the arm is optimal, or *(b)* sample an environment from the posterior and play the optimal action in that environment. When the mean rewards for each arm are independent under the posterior, then also equivalent is *(c)* sample the mean reward for each arm and choose the arm with the largest mean (Exercise 36.1). The algorithms in this chapter are based on *(b)*, but all are equivalent and simply correspond to sampling from different push-forward measures of the posterior. Historically it seems that Thompson [1933] had the form in *(a)* in mind, but there are reasons to remember the alternative views. Though we are not aware of an example, in some instances beyond finite-armed bandits, it might be more computationally efficient to sample from a push-forward of the posterior than the posterior itself. Furthermore, in more complicated situations like reinforcement learning, it may be desirable to 'approximate' Thompson sampling, and approximating a sample from each of the above three choices may lead to different algorithms. It is also good to keep in mind that in the

non-Bayesian setting there can be cheaper ways of inducing sufficient exploration than sampling from a posterior, especially in the context of structured bandit problems.

2 Thompson sampling is known to be asymptotically optimal in a variety of settings – most notably, when the noise model follows a single-parameter exponential family and the prior is chosen appropriately [Kaufmann et al., 2012b, Korda et al., 2013]. Unfortunately, Thompson sampling is not a silver bullet. The linear variant in Section 36.3 is not asymptotically optimal by the same argument we presented for optimism in Chapter 25. Characterising the conditions under which Thompson sampling is close to optimal remains an open challenge.

3 For the Gaussian noise model, it is known that Thompson sampling is not minimax optimal. Its worst-case regret is $R_n = \Theta(\sqrt{nk\log(k)})$ [Agrawal and Goyal, 2013a].

4 An alternative to sampling from the posterior is to choose in each round the arm that maximises a **Bayesian upper confidence bound**, which is a quantile of the posterior. The resulting algorithm is called **BayesUCB** and has excellent empirical and theoretical guarantees [Kaufmann et al., 2012a, Kaufmann, 2018].

5 The prior has a significant effect on the performance of Thompson sampling. In classical Bayesian statistics, a poorly chosen prior is quickly washed away by data. This is not true in (stochastic, non-Bayesian) bandits because if the prior underestimates the quality of an arm, then Thompson sampling may never play that arm with high probability and no data is ever observed. We ask you to explore this situation in Exercise 36.16.

6 An instantiation of Thompson sampling for stochastic contextual linear bandits is known to enjoy near-optimal frequentist regret. In each round the algorithm samples $\theta_t \sim \mathcal{N}(\hat{\theta}_{t-1}, rV_{t-1})$, where $r = \Theta(d)$ is a constant and

$$
V_t = I + \sum_{s=1}^{t} A_s A_s^\top \quad \text{and} \quad \hat{\theta}_t = V_t^{-1} \sum_{s=1}^{t} X_s A_s.
$$

Then $A_t = \operatorname{argmax}_{a \in \mathcal{A}_t} \langle \theta_t, a \rangle$. This corresponds to assuming the noise is Gaussian with variance r and choosing prior $Q = \mathcal{N}(0, I)$. Provided the rewards are conditionally 1-subgaussian, the frequentist regret of this algorithm is $R_n = \tilde{O}(d^{3/2}\sqrt{n})$, which is worse than LinUCB by a factor of $\sqrt{d}$. The increased regret is caused by the choice of noise model, which assumes the variance is $r = \Theta(d)$ rather than $r = 1$. The reason to do this comes from the analysis, which works by showing the algorithm is 'optimistic' with reasonable probability. Very recently, an example was constructed showing that the blowup of the variance is necessary, though the example heavily relies on the contextual nature of the problem with changing action sets [Hamidi and Bayati, 2020]. Empirically, $r = 1$ leads to superior performance on many instances.

7 The analysis in Section 36.4 can be generalised to structured settings such as linear bandits [Russo and Van Roy, 2016]. For linear bandits with an infinite action set, the entropy of the optimal action may be infinite. The analysis can be corrected in this case by discretising the action set and comparing to a near-optimal action. This leads to a trade-off between the fineness of the discretisation and its size, and when the trade-off is resolved in an optimal fashion, one obtains an upper bound of order $O(d\sqrt{n\log(1 + n/d)})$ on the Bayesian regret, slightly improving previous analysis. The reader is referred to the recent article by Dong and Van Roy [2018] for this analysis.

8 The information-theoretic ideas in Section 36.4 suggest that rather than sampling A_t from the posterior on A^*, one can sample A_t from the distribution P_t given by

$$
P_t = \operatorname{argmin}_{p \in \mathcal{P}_{k-1}} \frac{\sum_{a=1}^{k} p_a \left(\mathbb{E}_{t-1}[X_{ta} \mid A^* = a] - \mathbb{E}_{t-1}[X_{ta}] \right)}{\sum_{a=1}^{k} p_a \mathbb{E}_{t-1}\left[D_F(\mathbb{P}_{t-1}(A^* = \cdot \mid X_{ta}), \mathbb{P}_{t-1}(A^* = \cdot)) \right]}.
$$

When F is the unnormalised negentropy, the resulting policy is called **information-directed sampling**. Bayesian regret analysis for this algorithm follows along similar lines to what was presented in Section 36.4. See Exercise 36.9 or the paper by Russo and Van Roy [2014a] for more details.

9 The proof of Theorem 36.6 only used the fact that $M_t = \mathbb{P}_t(A^* = \cdot)$ is a martingale. The posterior is just one possible choice, but in some cases an alternative martingale leads to improved bounds.

10 Replacing the unnormalised negentropy potential with $F(p) = -2\sum_{i=1}^{k} \sqrt{p_i}$ leads to a bound of $\mathrm{BR}_n \leq \sqrt{2nk}$ for any prior for finite-armed bandits [Lattimore and Szepesvári, 2019c]. You will prove this in Exercise 36.10. The same potential also led to minimax bounds for adversarial bandits in Exercise 28.15, which suggests there is some kind of connection. This was explored by Zimmert and Lattimore [2019], who show that the same techniques used to bound the dual norm 'stability' terms in the analysis of mirror descent also control the information ratio for a version of Thompson sampling.

11 Let $\mathcal{E} = [0,1]^{n \times k}$ be the set of all adversarial bandits and Π the set of all randomised policies and $\mathcal{Q}$ be the set of all finitely supported distributions on $\mathcal{E}$, which means that $Q \in \mathcal{Q}$ is a function $Q : \mathcal{E} \to [0,1]$ with $\mathrm{Supp}(Q) = \{x : Q(x) > 0\}$ a finite set and $\sum_{x \in \mathrm{Supp}(Q)} Q(x) = 1$. Given $x \in \mathcal{E}$ and $\pi \in \Pi$, let $\mathbb{E}_{x\pi}$ be the expectation with respect to the interaction between policy π and environment x. Then,

$$
R_n^*(\mathcal{E}) = \min_{\pi \in \Pi} \sup_{x \in \mathcal{E}} \mathbb{E}_{x\pi} \underbrace{\left[\max_{i \in [k]} \sum_{t=1}^{n} (x_{ti} - x_{tA_t}) \right]}_{\text{Adversarial regret}}
$$

$$
= \sup_{Q \in \mathcal{Q}} \min_{\pi \in \Pi} \underbrace{\sum_{x \in \mathrm{Supp}(Q)} Q(x) \mathbb{E}_{x\pi} \left[\max_{i \in [k]} \sum_{t=1}^{n} (x_{ti} - x_{tA_t}) \right]}_{\text{Bayesian optimal regret}} \tag{36.9}
$$

$$
\leq \sqrt{nk \log(k)/2},
$$

where the second equality follows from Sion's minimax theorem (Exercise 36.11) and the inequality follows from Theorem 36.5. This bound is a factor of two better than what we gave in Theorem 11.2 and can be improved to $\sqrt{2nk}$ using the argument from the previous note and Exercise 36.10. The approach has been used in more sophisticated settings, like the first near-optimal analysis for adversarial convex bandits [Bubeck et al., 2015a, Bubeck and Eldan, 2016] or partial monitoring [Lattimore and Szepesvári, 2019c]. As noted earlier, the main disadvantage is that the technique does not lead to algorithms for the adversarial setting.

36.6 Bibliographic Remarks

Thompson sampling has the honor of being the first bandit algorithm and is named after its inventor [Thompson, 1933], who considered the Bernoulli case with two arms. Thompson provided no theoretical guarantees, but argued intuitively and gave hand-calculated empirical analysis. It would be wrong to say that Thompson sampling was entirely ignored for the next eight decades, but it was definitely not popular until recently, when a large number of authors independently rediscovered the article/algorithm [Graepel et al., 2010, Granmo, 2010, Ortega and Braun, 2010, Chapelle and Li, 2011, May et al., 2012]. The surge in interest was mostly empirical, but theoreticians followed soon with regret guarantees. For the frequentist analysis, we followed the proofs by Agrawal and Goyal [2012,

2013a], but the setting is slightly different. We presented results for the 'realisable' case where the pay-off distributions are actually Gaussian, while Agrawal and Goyal use the same algorithm but prove bounds for rewards bounded in $[0, 1]$. Agrawal and Goyal [2013a] also analyse the Beta/Bernoulli variant of Thompson sampling, which for rewards in $[0, 1]$ is asymptotically optimal in the same way as KL-UCB (see Chapter 10). This result was simultaneously obtained by Kaufmann et al. [2012b], who later showed that for appropriate priors, asymptotic optimality also holds for single-parameter exponential families [Korda et al., 2013]. For Gaussian bandits with unknown mean and variance, Thompson sampling is asymptotically optimal for some priors, but not others – even quite natural ones [Honda and Takemura, 2014]. The Bayesian analysis of Thompson sampling based on confidence intervals is due to Russo and Van Roy [2014b]. Recently the idea has been applied to a wide range of bandit settings [Kawale et al., 2015, Agrawal et al., 2017] and reinforcement learning [Osband et al., 2013, Gopalan and Mannor, 2015, Leike et al., 2016, Kim, 2017]. The BayesUCB algorithm is due to Kaufmann et al. [2012a], with improved analysis and results by Kaufmann [2018]. The frequentist analysis of Thompson sampling for linear bandits is by Agrawal and Goyal [2013b], with refined analysis by Abeille and Lazaric [2017a] and a spectral version by Kocák et al. [2014]. A recent paper analyses the combinatorial semi-bandit setting [Wang and Chen, 2018]. The information-theoretic analysis is by Russo and Van Roy [2014a, 2016], while the generalising beyond the negentropy potential is by Lattimore and Szepesvári [2019c]. As we mentioned, these ideas have been applied to convex bandits [Bubeck et al., 2015a, Bubeck and Eldan, 2016] and also to partial monitoring [Lattimore and Szepesvári, 2019c]. There is a tutorial on Thompson sampling by Russo et al. [2018] that focuses mostly on applications and computational issues. We mentioned there are other ways to configure Algorithm 24, for example the recent article by Kveton et al. [2019].

36.7 Exercises

36.1 (EQUIVALENT VIEWS) Prove the claimed equivalences in Note 1.

36.2 (FILLING IN STEPS IN THE PROOF OF THEOREM 36.1 (I)) Consider the event E defined in Theorem 36.1, and prove that $\mathbb{P}(E^c) \leq 2nk\delta$.

36.3 (FILLING IN STEPS IN THE PROOF OF THEOREM 36.1 (II)) Prove Eq. (36.1).

36.4 (REMOVING LOGARITHMIC FACTORS) Improve the bound in Theorem 36.1 to show that $\mathrm{BR}_n \leq C\sqrt{kn}$ where $C > 0$ is a universal constant.

HINT   Replace the naive confidence intervals used in the proof of Theorem 36.1 by the more refined confidence bounds used in Chapter 9. The source for this result is the paper by Bubeck and Liu [2013].

36.5 (FILLING IN STEPS IN THE PROOF OF THEOREM 36.2) Let $G_i(s) = 1 - F_{is}(\mu_1 - \varepsilon)$. Show that

(a) $\displaystyle \sum_{t \in \mathcal{T}} \mathbb{I}\{A_t = i\} \leq \sum_{s=1}^{n} \mathbb{I}\{G_i(s-1) > 1/n\}$; and

(b) $\displaystyle \mathbb{E}\left[\sum_{t \notin \mathcal{T}} \mathbb{I}\{E_i^c(t)\}\right] \leq \mathbb{E}\left[\sum_{t \notin \mathcal{T}} 1/n\right]$.

36.6 (FREQUENTIST BOUND FOR THOMPSON SAMPLING) In this exercise you will prove Theorem 36.3.

(a) Show that there exists a universal constant $c > 0$ such that

$$\mathbb{E}\left[\sum_{t=1}^{\infty}\left(\frac{1}{G_{1s}(\varepsilon)} - 1\right)\right] \leq \frac{c}{\varepsilon^2}\log\left(\frac{1}{\varepsilon}\right).$$

(b) Show that

$$\mathbb{E}\left[\sum_{s=1}^{n}\mathbb{I}\{G_{is} > 1/n\}\right] \leq \frac{2\log(n)}{(\Delta_i - \varepsilon)^2} + o(\log(n)).$$

(c) Use Theorem 36.2 and the fundamental regret decomposition (Lemma 4.5) to prove Theorem 36.3.

HINT   For (a) you may find it useful to know that for $y \geq 0$,

$$1 - \Phi(y) \geq \frac{\exp(-y^2/2)}{y + \sqrt{y^2 + 4}},$$

where $\Phi(y) = \frac{1}{\sqrt{2\pi}}\int_{-\infty}^{y}\exp(-x^2/2)dx$ is the cumulative distribution function of the standard Gaussian [Abramowitz and Stegun, 1964, §7.1.13].

36.7 Prove the final equality in the proof of Lemma 36.7.

36.8 (PREDICTION WITH EXPERT ADVICE) Consider the adversarial Bayesian framework from Section 36.4, but assume the learner observes the whole vector X_t rather than just X_{tA_t}, which corresponds to the prediction with expert advice setting. Prove that Thompson sampling in this setting has a Bayesian regret of at most

$$\mathrm{BR}_n \leq \sqrt{n\log(k)/2}.$$

36.9 (INFORMATION-DIRECTED SAMPLING) Prove that for any prior such that $X_{ti} \in [0, 1]$ almost surely, the Bayesian regret of information-directed sampling (see Note 8) satisfies

$$\mathrm{BR}_n \leq \sqrt{kn\log(k)/2}.$$

36.10 (MINIMAX BAYESIAN REGRET FOR THOMPSON SAMPLING) Prove that for any prior over adversarial k-armed bandits such that $X_{ti} \in [0, 1]$ almost surely, the Bayesian regret of Thompson sampling satisfies $\mathrm{BR}_n \leq \sqrt{2kn}$.

HINT   Use the potential $F(p) = -2\sum_{i=1}^{k}\sqrt{p_i}$ and the fact that the total variation distance is upper-bounded by the Hellinger distance.

36.11 (FROM BAYESIAN TO ADVERSARIAL REGRET) Let $\mathcal{E} = \{0, 1\}^{n\times k}$ and $\mathcal{Q}$ be the space of probability measures on $\mathcal{E}$. Prove that

$$R_n^*(\mathcal{E}) = \sup_{Q\in\mathcal{Q}} \mathrm{BR}_n^*(Q).$$

HINT   Repeat the argument in the solution to Exercise 34.16, noting that $\mathcal{Q}$ is finite dimensional. Take care to adapt the result in Exercise 4.4 to the adversarial setting.

36.12 (FROM BAYESIAN TO ADVERSARIAL REGRET) Let $\mathcal{E} = [0, 1]^{n\times k}$. Prove that

$$R_n^*(\mathcal{E}) = \sup_{Q\in\mathcal{Q}} \mathrm{BR}_n^*(Q),$$

where $\mathcal{Q}$ is the set of probability measures on $(\mathcal{E}, 2^{\mathcal{E}})$ with finite support.

HINT   That $\mathcal{E}$ is uncountably large introduces some challenges. Like in the previous exercise, the idea is to express the regret of a policy as an integral over the regret of deterministic policies, which can be viewed as functions $\pi : \cup_{t=1}^{n}[0,1]^{t-1} \rightarrow [k]$. Use Tychonoff's theorem to argue that the space of all deterministic policies is compact with respect to the product topology. Then the space of regular probability measures over deterministic policies is compact with the weak* topology by Theorem 2.14. Then carefully check continuity and linearity of the Bayesian regret, and apply Sion's theorem. Details are by Lattimore and Szepesvári [2019c].

36.13 (BINARY IS THE WORST CASE) Prove that $R_n^*(\{0,1\}^{n \times k}) = R_n^*([0,1]^{n \times k})$.

HINT   Think about how to use a minimax optimal policy for $\{0,1\}^{n \times k}$ for bandits in $[0,1]^{n \times k}$.

36.14 (IMPLEMENTATION (I)) In this exercise, you will reproduce the results in Experiment 1.

(a) Implement Thompson sampling as described in Theorem 36.3 as well as UCB and AdaUCB.
(b) Reproduce the figures in Experiment 1 as well as UCB.
(c) How consistent are these results across different bandits? Run a few experiments and report the results.
(d) Explain your findings. Which algorithm do you prefer and why.

36.15 (IMPLEMENTATION (II)) Implement linear Thompson sampling with a Gaussian prior as defined in Note 6 as well as LinUCB from Chapter 19 and Algorithm 12. Compare these algorithms in a variety of regimes, report your results, and tell an interesting story. Discuss the pros and cons of different choices of r.

36.16 (MISSPECIFIED PRIOR) Fix a Gaussian bandit with unit variance and mean vector $\mu = (0, 1/10)$ and horizon $n = 1000$. Now consider Thompson sampling with a Gaussian model with known unit covariance and a prior on the unknown mean of each arm given by a Gaussian distribution with mean μ_P and covariance $\sigma_P^2 I$.

(a) Let the prior mean be $\mu_P = (0,0)$, and plot the regret of Thompson sampling as a function of the prior variance σ_P^2.
(b) Repeat the above with $\mu_P = (0, 1/10)$ and $(0, -1/10)$ and $(2/10, 1/10)$.
(c) Explain your results.

Part VIII

Beyond Bandits

37 Partial Monitoring

While in a bandit problem, the feedback that the learner receives from the environment is the loss of the chosen action, in **partial monitoring** the coupling between the loss of the action and the feedback received by the learner is loosened.

Consider the problem of learning to match pennies when feedback is costly. Let $c > 0$ be a known constant. At the start of the game, the adversary secretly chooses a sequence $i_1, \ldots, i_n \in \{\text{HEADS}, \text{TAILS}\}$. In each round, the learner chooses an action $A_t \in \{\text{HEADS}, \text{TAILS}, \text{UNCERTAIN}\}$. The loss for choosing action a in round t is

$$
y_{ta} = \begin{cases} 0, & \text{if } a = i_t; \\ c, & \text{if } a = \text{UNCERTAIN}; \\ 1, & \text{otherwise.} \end{cases}
$$

Figure 37.1 Spam filtering is a potential application of partial monitoring. The turtle (called Spam) was inherited by one of the authors.

So far this looks like a bandit problem. The difference is that the learner never directly observes y_{tA_t}. Instead, the learner observes nothing unless $A_t = \text{UNCERTAIN}$, in which case they observe the value of i_t. As usual, the goal is to minimise the (expected) regret, which is

$$
R_n = \max_{a \in [k]} \mathbb{E}\left[\sum_{t=1}^{n} (y_{tA_t} - y_{ta}) \right].
$$

How should a learner act in problems like this, where the loss is not directly observed? Can we find a policy with sublinear regret? In this chapter we give a more or less complete answer to these questions for finite adversarial partial monitoring games, which include the above problems as a special case.

Matching pennies with costly feedback seems like an esoteric problem. But think about adding contextual information and replace the pennies with emails to be classified as spam or otherwise. The true label is only accessible by asking a human, which replaces the third action. While the chapter does not cover the contextual version, some pointers to the literature are added at the end.

37.1   Finite Adversarial Partial Monitoring Problems

A finite, k-action, d-outcome **adversarial partial monitoring problem** is specified by a **loss matrix** $\mathcal{L} \in \mathbb{R}^{k \times d}$ and a **feedback matrix** $\Phi \in \Sigma^{k \times d}$, where Σ is called the set of **signals**. We let m be the maximum number of distinct symbols in any row of Φ. At the beginning of the game, the learner is given $\mathcal{L}$ and Φ, and the environment secretly chooses n outcomes $i_1, \ldots, i_n$ with $i_t \in [d]$. The loss of action $a \in [k]$ in round t is $y_{ta} = \mathcal{L}_{ai_t}$. In each round t, the learner chooses $A_t \in [k]$ and receives feedback $\sigma_t = \Phi_{A_t i_t}$. Given a partial monitoring problem $G = (\Phi, \mathcal{L})$, the regret of policy π when the adversary chooses $i_{1:n} = (i_t)_{t=1}^n$ is

$$R_n(\pi, i_{1:n}, G) = \max_{a \in [k]} \mathbb{E}\left[\sum_{t=1}^n (y_{tA_t} - y_{ta})\right].$$

We omit the arguments of R_n when they can be inferred from the context.

To reduce clutter, we slightly abuse notation by using (e_i) to denote the standard basis vectors of Euclidean spaces of potentially different dimensions.

37.1.1   Examples

The partial monitoring framework is rich enough to model a wide variety of problems, a few of which are illustrated in the examples that follow. Many of the examples are quite artificial and are included only to highlight the flexibility of the framework and challenges of making the regret small.

EXAMPLE 37.1 (Hopeless problem). Some partial monitoring problems are completely hopeless in the sense that one cannot expect to make the regret small. A simple example occurs when $k = d = 2$, $m = 1$ and

$$\mathcal{L} = \begin{pmatrix} 0 & 1 \\ 1 & 0 \end{pmatrix}, \qquad \Phi = \begin{pmatrix} \perp & \perp \\ \perp & \perp \end{pmatrix}. \tag{37.1}$$

Note that rows/columns correspond to choices of the learner/adversary, respectively. In both rows, the feedback matrix has identical entries for both columns. As the learner has no way of distinguishing between different sequences of outcomes, there is no way to learn and avoid linear regret. The reader is encouraged to think of generalisations of this example where the game is still hopeless.

Two feedback matrices $\Phi \in \Sigma^{k \times d}$ and $\tilde{\Phi} \in \tilde{\Sigma}^{k \times d}$ encode the same information if the pattern of identical entries in each row match. For example,

$$\Phi = \begin{pmatrix} \perp & 4 & \perp \\ 1 & 2 & 2 \\ 3 & 1 & 1 \end{pmatrix} \qquad \text{and} \qquad \tilde{\Phi} = \begin{pmatrix} \diamondsuit & \spadesuit & \diamondsuit \\ \clubsuit & \heartsuit & \heartsuit \\ \clubsuit & \heartsuit & \heartsuit \end{pmatrix}$$

both encode the same information. Note that for these matrices $m = 2$ since in any row there are at most two distinct symbols.

EXAMPLE 37.2 (Trivial problem). Just as there are hopeless problems, there are also trivial problems. This happens when one action dominates all others as in the following problem:

$$L = \begin{pmatrix} 0 & 0 \\ 1 & 1 \end{pmatrix}, \qquad \Phi = \begin{pmatrix} \perp & \perp \\ \perp & \perp \end{pmatrix}.$$

In this game the learner can safely ignore the second action and suffer zero regret, regardless of the choices of the adversary.

EXAMPLE 37.3 (Matching pennies). The penny-matching problem mentioned in the introduction has $k = 3$ actions $d = 2$ outcomes and is described by

$$L = \begin{pmatrix} 0 & 1 \\ 1 & 0 \\ c & c \end{pmatrix}, \qquad \Phi = \begin{pmatrix} \perp & \perp \\ \perp & \perp \\ H & T \end{pmatrix}. \tag{37.2}$$

Matching pennies is a hard game for $c > 1/2$ in the sense that the adversary can force the regret of any policy to be at least $\Omega(n^{2/3})$. To see this, consider the randomised adversary that chooses the first outcome with probability p and the second with probability $1 - p$. Let $\varepsilon > 0$ be a small constant to be chosen later and assume p is either $1/2 + \varepsilon$ or $1/2 - \varepsilon$. The techniques in Chapter 13 show that the learner can only distinguish between these environments by playing the third action about $1/\varepsilon^2$ times. If the learner does not choose to do this, then the regret is expected to be $\Omega(n\varepsilon)$. Taking these together shows the regret is lower-bounded by $R_n = \Omega(\min(n\varepsilon, (c - 1/2 + \varepsilon)/\varepsilon^2))$. Choosing $\varepsilon = n^{-1/3}$ leads to a bound of $R_n = \Omega((c - 1/2)n^{2/3})$. Notice that the argument fails when $c \leq 1/2$. We encourage you to pause for a minute to convince yourself about the correctness of the above argument and to consider what might be the situation when $c \leq 1/2$.

EXAMPLE 37.4 (Bandits). Finite-armed adversarial bandits with binary losses can be represented in the partial monitoring framework. When $k = 2$, this is possible with the following matrices:

$$L = \begin{pmatrix} 0 & 1 & 0 & 1 \\ 0 & 0 & 1 & 1 \end{pmatrix}, \qquad \Phi = L = \begin{pmatrix} 0 & 1 & 0 & 1 \\ 0 & 0 & 1 & 1 \end{pmatrix}.$$

The number of columns for this game is 2^k. For non-binary rewards, you would need even more columns. A partial monitoring problem where $\Phi = L$ can be called a bandit problem because the learner observes the loss of the chosen action. In bandit games, Exp3 from Chapter 11 guarantees a regret of $O(\sqrt{kn \log(k)})$, and as noted there, a more sophisticated algorithm will also remove the $\log(k)$ factor. If you completed Exercise 15.4 then you will know that, up to a constant factor, $\sqrt{kn}$ is also the best possible regret in adversarial bandits with binary losses.

EXAMPLE 37.5 (Full information problems). One can also represent problems where the learner observes all the losses. With binary losses and two actions, we have

$$L = \begin{pmatrix} 0 & 1 & 0 & 1 \\ 0 & 0 & 1 & 1 \end{pmatrix}, \qquad \Phi = \begin{pmatrix} 1 & 2 & 3 & 4 \\ 1 & 2 & 3 & 4 \end{pmatrix}.$$

Like for bandits, the size of the game grows quickly as more actions/outcomes are added. A partial monitoring game where $\Phi_{ai} = i$ for all $a \in [k]$ and $i \in [d]$ can be called full information because the signal reveals the losses for all actions.

EXAMPLE 37.6 (Dynamic pricing). A charity worker is going door to door selling calendars. The marginal cost of a calendar is close to zero, but the wages of the door knocker represents a fixed cost of $c > 0$ per occupied house. The question is how to price the calendar. Each round corresponds to an attempt to sell a calendar, and the action is the seller's asking price from one of d choices. The potential buyer will purchase the calendar if the asking price is low enough. Below we give the corresponding matrices for case where both the candidate asking prices and the possible values for the buyer's private valuations are $\{\$1, \$2, \$3, \$4\}$:

$$\mathcal{L} = \begin{pmatrix} c-1 & c-1 & c-1 & c-1 \\ c & c-2 & c-2 & c-2 \\ c & c & c-3 & c-3 \\ c & c & c & c-4 \end{pmatrix}, \qquad \Phi = \begin{pmatrix} Y & Y & Y & Y \\ N & Y & Y & Y \\ N & N & Y & Y \\ N & N & N & Y \end{pmatrix}.$$

Notice that observing the feedback is sufficient to deduce the loss so the problem could be tackled with a bandit algorithm. But there is additional structure in the losses here because the learner knows that if a calendar did not sell for \$3, then it would not sell for \$4.

37.2 The Structure of Partial Monitoring

The minimax regret of partial monitoring problem $G = (\mathcal{L}, \Phi)$ is

$$R_n^*(G) = \inf_\pi \max_{i_{1:n}} R_n(\pi, i_{1:n}, G).$$

One of the core questions in partial monitoring is to understand the growth of $R_n^*(G)$ as a function of n for different games. We have seen examples where

$$R_n^*(G) = 0 \qquad\qquad\qquad \text{(Example 37.2)}$$
$$R_n^*(G) = \Theta(n^{1/2}) \qquad\qquad \text{(Example 37.4)}$$
$$R_n^*(G) = \Theta(n^{2/3}) \qquad\qquad \text{(Example 37.3)}$$
$$R_n^*(G) = \Omega(n). \qquad\qquad\quad \text{(Example 37.1)}$$

The main result of this chapter is that there are no other options. A partial monitoring game is called **trivial** if $R_n^*(G) = 0$, **easy** if $R_n^*(G) = \Theta(n^{1/2})$, **hard** if $R_n^*(G) = \Theta(n^{2/3})$ and **hopeless** if $R_n^*(G) = \Omega(n)$. Furthermore, we will show that any game can be classified using elementary linear algebra.

What makes matching pennies hard and bandits easy? To get a handle on this, we need a geometric representation of partial monitoring games. The next few paragraphs introduce a lot of new terminology that can be hard to grasp all at once. At the end of the section, there is an example illustrating the concepts (Example 37.10).

37.2.1 The Geometry of Losses and Actions

The geometry underlying partial monitoring comes from viewing the problem as a linear prediction problem, where the adversary plays on the $(d-1)$-dimensional probability simplex and the learner plays on the rows of $\mathcal{L}$. Define a sequence of vectors $(u_t)_{t=1}^n$ by

$u_t = e_{i_t}$ and let $\ell_a \in \mathbb{R}^d$ be the ath row of matrix $\mathcal{L}$. The loss suffered in round t when choosing action a is $y_{ta} = \langle \ell_a, u_t \rangle$.

Let $\bar{u}_t = \frac{1}{t} \sum_{s=1}^{t} u_s \in \mathcal{P}_{d-1}$ be the probability vector of proportions of the adversary's choices over t rounds. An action a is optimal in hindsight if $\langle \ell_a, \bar{u}_n \rangle \leq \min_{b \neq a} \langle \ell_b, \bar{u}_n \rangle$. The **cell** of an action a is the subset of $\mathcal{P}_{d-1}$ on which it is optimal:

$$C_a = \left\{ u \in \mathcal{P}_{d-1} : \max_{b \in [k]} \langle \ell_a - \ell_b, u \rangle \leq 0 \right\},$$

which is a convex polytope. The collection $\{C_a : a \in [k]\}$ is called the **cell decomposition** of $\mathcal{P}_{d-1}$. Actions with $C_a = \emptyset$ are called **dominated** because they are never optimal, no matter how the adversary plays. For non-dominated actions we define the **dimension** of an action to be the dimension of the **affine hull** of C_a. Readers unfamiliar with the affine hull should read Note 4 at the end of the chapter. A non-dominated action is called **Pareto optimal** if it has dimension $d-1$, and **degenerate** otherwise. Actions a and b are **duplicates** if $\ell_a = \ell_b$. The set of all Pareto optimal actions is denoted by $\Pi \subseteq [k]$. A partial monitoring game is called degenerate if it has any degenerate or duplicate actions.

Dominated and degenerate actions can never be uniquely optimal in hindsight, but their presence can make the difference between a hard game and a hopeless one. Consider the matching pennies game (Example 37.3). When $c > 1/2$, the third action is dominated, but without it the learner would suffer linear regret. Duplicate actions are only duplicate in the sense that they have the same loss. They may have different feedback structures and so cannot be trivially combined.

Neighbourhood relation

Pareto optimal actions a and b are **neighbours** if $C_a \cap C_b$ has dimension $d - 2$. Note that if a and b are Pareto optimal duplicates, then $C_a \cap C_b$ has dimension $d - 1$, and the definition means that a and b are not neighbours. For Pareto optimal action a we let $\mathcal{N}_a$ be the set consisting of a and its neighbours. Given a pair of neighbours $e = (a, b)$, we let $\mathcal{N}_e = \mathcal{N}_{ab} = \{c \in [k] : C_a \cap C_b \subseteq C_c\}$ to be the set of actions that are **incident** to e. The neighbourhood relation defines an undirected graph over $[k]$ with edges $E = \{(a, b) : a \text{ and } b \text{ are neighbours}\}$, which is called the neighbourhood graph.

The next result, which shows the connectedness of the neighborhood graph induced by a set of actions whose cells cover the whole simplex, will play an important role in subsequent proofs:

LEMMA 37.7. *Suppose that S is any set of Pareto optimal actions such that $\cup_{a \in S} C_a = \mathcal{P}_{d-1}$. Then the graph with vertices S and edges from E is connected.*

Let $e = (a, b) \in E$. The next lemma characterises actions in $\mathcal{N}_e$ as either a, b, duplicates of a, b or degenerate actions c for which ℓ_c is a convex combination of ℓ_a and ℓ_b. The situation is illustrated when $d = 2$ in Fig. 37.2.

LEMMA 37.8. *Let $e = (a, b) \in E$ be neighbouring actions and $c \in \mathcal{N}_e$ be an action such that $\ell_c \notin \{\ell_a, \ell_b\}$. Then*

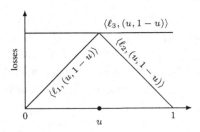

Figure 37.2   The figure shows the situation when $d = 2$ and $\ell_1 = (1, 0)$ and $\ell_2 = (0, 1)$ and $\ell_3 = (1/2, 1/2)$. The x axis corresponds to $\mathcal{P}_1 = [0, 1]$, the y axis to the losses. Then $C_1 = [0, 1/2]$ and $C_2 = [1/2, 1]$, which both have dimension $1 = d - 1$. Then $C_3 = \{1/2\} = C_1 \cap C_2$, which has dimension 0.

(a) *there exists an* $\alpha \in (0, 1)$ *such that* $\ell_c = \alpha \ell_a + (1 - \alpha)\ell_b$;
(b) $C_c = C_a \cap C_b$; *and*
(c) *c has dimension* $d - 2$.

Proof   We use the fact that if $\mathcal{X} \subseteq \mathcal{Y} \subseteq \mathbb{R}^d$ and $\dim(\mathcal{X}) = \dim(\mathcal{Y})$, then $\mathrm{aff}(\mathcal{X}) = \mathrm{aff}(\mathcal{Y})$ (Exercise 37.2). Introduce $\ker'(x) = \{u \in \mathbb{R}^d : u^\top x = 0, u^\top \mathbf{1} = 1\}$. Clearly, $C_a \cap C_b \subseteq C_a \cap C_c$ and $\mathrm{aff}(C_a \cap C_b) = \ker'(\ell_a - \ell_b)$ and $\mathrm{aff}(C_a \cap C_c) = \ker'(\ell_a - \ell_c)$. By assumption $\dim(C_a \cap C_b) = d - 2$. Since $C_a \cap C_b \subseteq C_a \cap C_c$, it holds that $\dim(C_a \cap C_c) \geq d - 2$. Furthermore, $\dim(C_a \cap C_c) \leq d - 2$, since otherwise $\ell_c = \ell_a$. Hence $\dim(C_a \cap C_c) = d - 2$ and thus by the fact mentioned and our earlier findings, $\ker'(\ell_a - \ell_b) = \ker'(\ell_a - \ell_c)$. This implies (Exercise 37.3) that $\ell_a - \ell_b$ is proportional to $\ell_a - \ell_c$ so that $(1 - \alpha)(\ell_a - \ell_b) = \ell_a - \ell_c$ for some $\alpha \neq 1$. Rearranging shows that

$$\ell_c = \alpha \ell_a + (1 - \alpha)\ell_b.$$

Now we show that $\alpha \in (0, 1)$. First note that $\alpha \notin \{0, 1\}$ since otherwise $\ell_c \in \{\ell_a, \ell_b\}$. Let $u \in C_a$ be such that $\langle \ell_a, u \rangle < \langle \ell_b, u \rangle$, which exists since $\dim(C_a) = d - 1$ and $\dim(C_a \cap C_b) = d - 2$. Then

$$\langle \ell_a, u \rangle \leq \langle \ell_c, u \rangle = \alpha \langle \ell_a, u \rangle + (1 - \alpha)\langle \ell_b, u \rangle = \langle \ell_a, u \rangle + (\alpha - 1)\langle \ell_a - \ell_b, u \rangle,$$

which by the negativity of $\langle \ell_a - \ell_b, u \rangle$ implies that $\alpha \leq 1$. A symmetric argument shows that $\alpha > 0$. For (b), it suffices to show that $C_c \subset C_a \cap C_b$. By de Morgan's law, for this it suffices to show that $\mathcal{P}_{d-1} \backslash (C_a \cap C_b) \subset \mathcal{P}_{d-1} \backslash C_c$. Thus, pick some $u \in \mathcal{P}_{d-1} \backslash (C_a \cap C_b)$. The goal is to show that $u \notin C_c$. The choice of u implies that there exists an action e such that $\langle \ell_a - \ell_e, u \rangle \geq 0$ and $\langle \ell_b - \ell_e, u \rangle \geq 0$ with a strict inequality for either a or b (or both). Therefore, using the fact that $\alpha \in (0, 1)$, we have

$$\langle \ell_c, u \rangle = \alpha \langle \ell_a, u \rangle + (1 - \alpha)\langle \ell_b, u \rangle > \langle \ell_e, u \rangle,$$

which by definition means that $u \notin C_c$, completing the proof of (b). Finally, (c) is immediate from (b) and the definition of neighbouring actions. $\square$

37.2.2 Estimating Loss Differences

In order to achieve small regret, the learner needs to identify an optimal action. How efficiently this can be done depends on the loss and feedback matrices. An initial observation is that since the loss matrix is known, the learner can restrict the search for the optimal action to the Pareto optimal actions. Furthermore, by Lemma 37.7, it suffices to estimate the loss differences between neighbours and then chain the estimates together along a connecting path. The second important point is that to minimise the regret the learner only needs to estimate the differences in losses between Pareto optimal actions and not the actual losses themselves. In fact, there exist games for which estimating the actual losses is impossible, but estimating the differences is straightforward:

EXAMPLE 37.9. Consider the partial monitoring game with

$$\mathcal{L} = \begin{pmatrix} 0 & 1 & 10 & 11 \\ 1 & 0 & 11 & 10 \end{pmatrix}, \qquad \Phi = \begin{pmatrix} \heartsuit & \clubsuit & \heartsuit & \clubsuit \\ \clubsuit & \heartsuit & \clubsuit & \heartsuit \end{pmatrix}.$$

The learner can never tell if the environment is playing in the first two columns or the last two, but the differences between the losses of actions are easily deduced from the feedback no matter the outcome and the action.

> Only the loss differences between Pareto optimal actions need to be estimated. There are games that are easy, but where some loss differences cannot be estimated. For example, there is never any need to estimate the losses of a dominated action.

Having decided we need to estimate the loss differences between neighbouring Pareto optimal actions, the next question is how the learner can do this. Focusing our attention on a single round, suppose the adversary secretly chooses an outcome $i \in [d]$ and the learner samples an action A from distribution $p \in \mathrm{ri}(\mathcal{P}_{k-1})$ and observes $\sigma = \Phi_{Ai}$. We are interested in finding an unbiased estimator of $\mathcal{L}_{ai} - \mathcal{L}_{bi}$ for neighbouring actions a and b. Without loss of generality, the estimator can be in the form of $f(A, \sigma)/p_A$ with some function $f : [k] \times \Sigma \to \mathbb{R}$. Then, the unbiasedness requirement takes the convenient form

$$\mathbb{E}\left[\frac{f(A, \sigma)}{p_A}\right] = \sum_{c=1}^{k} f(c, \Phi_{ci}).$$

In other words, $f(A, \sigma)/p_A$ is an unbiased estimator of $\mathcal{L}_{ai} - \mathcal{L}_{bi}$ regardless of the adversaries' choice if and only if

$$\sum_{c=1}^{k} f(c, \Phi_{ci}) = \mathcal{L}_{ai} - \mathcal{L}_{bi} \qquad \text{for all } i \in [d]. \tag{37.3}$$

A pair of neighbours a and b are called **globally observable** if there exists a function f satisfying Eq. (37.3). The set of all functions $f : [k] \times \Sigma \to \mathbb{R}$ satisfying Eq. (37.3) is denoted by $\mathcal{E}_{ab}^{\mathrm{glo}}$. A pair of neighbours a and b are **locally observable** if f can be chosen satisfying Eq. (37.3) with $f(c, \sigma) = 0$ whenever $c \notin \mathcal{N}_{ab}$. The set of functions satisfying this additional requirement are $\mathcal{E}_{ab}^{\mathrm{loc}}$. A partial monitoring problem is called globally/locally observable if all pairs of neighbouring actions are globally/locally observable. The global/local observability conditions formalise the idea introduced in Example 37.3. Games that are globally observable but not locally observable are hard because the learner cannot identify the optimal action by playing near-optimal actions only. Instead it has to play badly suboptimal actions to gain information, and this increases the minimax regret.

$$\mathcal{L} = \begin{pmatrix} 0 & 1 & 1 \\ 1 & 0 & 1 \\ 1/2 & 1/2 & 1/2 \\ 3/4 & 1/4 & 3/4 \\ 1 & 1/2 & 1/2 \\ 1 & 1/4 & 3/4 \end{pmatrix} \qquad \Phi = \begin{pmatrix} 1 & 2 & 3 \\ \perp & \perp & \perp \\ \perp & \perp & \perp \\ 1 & 2 & 3 \\ \perp & \perp & \perp \\ \perp & \perp & \perp \end{pmatrix}$$

Figure 37.3   Partial monitoring game with $k = 6$ and $d = 3$ and $m = 3$.

EXAMPLE 37.10. The partial monitoring problem illustrated in Fig. 37.3 has six actions, three feedbacks and three outcomes. The cell decomposition is shown on the right with the 2-simplex parameterised by its first two coordinates u_1 and u_2 so that $u_3 = 1 - u_2 - u_1$. Actions 1, 2 and 3 are Pareto optimal. There are no dominated actions while actions 4 and 5 are 1-dimensional and action 6 is 0-dimensional. The neighbours are $(1, 3)$ and $(2, 3)$, which are both locally observable, and so the game is locally observable. Note that $(1, 2)$ are not neighbours because the intersection of their cells is $(d - 3)$-dimensional. Finally, $\mathcal{N}_3 = \{1, 2, 3\}$ and $\mathcal{N}_1 = \{1, 3\}$ and $\mathcal{N}_{23} = \{2, 3, 4\}$. Think about how we decided on what losses to use to get the cell decomposition shown in Fig. 37.3.

37.3 Classification of Finite Adversarial Partial Monitoring

The terminology in the last section finally allows us to state the main theorem of this chapter that classifies finite adversarial partial monitoring games.

THEOREM 37.11. *The minimax regret of partial monitoring problem* $G = (\mathcal{L}, \Phi)$ *falls into one of four categories:*

$$R_n^*(G) = \begin{cases} 0, & \textit{if } G \textit{ has no pairs of neighbouring actions;} \\ \Theta(n^{1/2}), & \textit{if } G \textit{ is locally observable and has neighbouring actions;} \\ \Theta(n^{2/3}), & \textit{if } G \textit{ is globally observable, but not locally observable;} \\ \Omega(n), & \textit{otherwise.} \end{cases}$$

 The Landau notation is used in the traditional mathematical sense and obscures dependence on k, d, m and the finer structure of $G = (\mathcal{L}, \Phi)$.

The proof is split into parts by proving upper and lower bounds for each part. First up is the lower bounds. We then describe a policy and analyse its regret.

37.4 Lower Bounds

Like for bandits, the lower bounds are most easily proven using a stochastic adversary. In stochastic partial monitoring, we assume that $u_1, \dots, u_n$ are chosen independently at

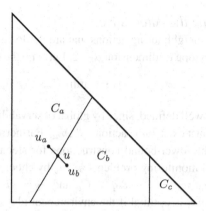

Figure 37.4 Lower-bound construction for hard partial monitoring problems. Shown is $\mathcal{P}_{d-1}$, the cells C_a and C_b of two Pareto optimal actions, and two alternatives $u_a \in C_a$ and $u_b \in C_b$ that induce the same distributions on the outcomes under both a and b.

random from the same distribution. To emphasise the randomness, we switch to capital letters. Given a partial monitoring game $G = (\mathcal{L}, \Phi)$ and probability vector $u \in \mathcal{P}_{d-1}$, the stochastic partial monitoring environment associated with u samples a sequence of independently and identically distributed random variables $I_1, \ldots, I_n$ with $\mathbb{P}(I_t = i) = u_i$ and $U_t = e_{I_t}$. In each round t, a policy chooses action A_t and receives feedback $\sigma_t = \Phi_{A_t I_t}$. The regret is

$$R_n(\pi, u) = \max_{a \in [k]} \mathbb{E}\left[\sum_{t=1}^{n} \langle \ell_{A_t} - \ell_a, U_t \rangle\right] = \max_{a \in [k]} \mathbb{E}\left[\sum_{t=1}^{n} \langle \ell_{A_t} - \ell_a, u \rangle\right].$$

The reader should check that $R_n^*(G) \geq \inf_\pi \max_{u \in \mathcal{P}_{d-1}} R_n(\pi, u)$, which allows us to restrict our attention to stochastic partial monitoring problems. Given $u, q \in \mathcal{P}_{d-1}$, let $D(u, q)$ be the relative entropy between categorical distributions with parameters u and q respectively:

$$D(u, q) = \sum_{i=1}^{d} u_i \log\left(\frac{u_i}{q_i}\right) \leq \sum_{i=1}^{d} \frac{(u_i - q_i)^2}{q_i}, \tag{37.4}$$

where the second inequality follows from the fact that for measures P, Q we have $D(P, Q) \leq \chi^2(P, Q)$ (see Note 5 in Chapter 13).

THEOREM 37.12. *Let $G = (\mathcal{L}, \Phi)$ be a globally observable partial monitoring problem that is not locally observable. Then there exists a constant $c_G > 0$ such that $R_n^*(G) \geq c_G n^{2/3}$.*

Proof The proof involves several steps. Roughly, we need to define two alternative stochastic partial monitoring problems. We then show these environments are hard to distinguish without playing an action associated with a large loss. Finally we balance the cost of distinguishing the environments against the linear cost of playing randomly. Without loss of generality assume that $\Sigma = [m]$.

Step 1: Defining the Alternatives

Let a, b be a pair neighbouring actions that are not locally observable. Then, by definition, $C_a \cap C_b$ is a polytope of dimension $d - 2$. Let u be the centroid of $C_a \cap C_b$ and

$$\varepsilon = \min_{c \notin \mathcal{N}_{ab}} \langle \ell_c - \ell_a, u \rangle. \tag{37.5}$$

The value of ε is well defined, since by global observability of G, but nonlocal observability of (a, b), there must exist some action $c \notin \mathcal{N}_{ab}$. Furthermore, since $c \notin \mathcal{N}_{ab}$, it follows that $\varepsilon > 0$. As in the lower-bound constructions for stochastic bandits, we now define two stochastic partial monitoring problems u_a, u_b by choosing a direction $q \in \mathbb{R}^d$ and a small value Δ such that $u_a = u - \Delta q \in C_a$ and $u_b = u + \Delta q \in C_b$ (see Fig. 37.4). This means that action a is optimal if the environment plays u_a on average and b is optimal if the environment plays u_b on average. The direction q will be chosen so that using a and b alone it is not possible to distinguish between u_a and u_b.

The vector q is chosen as follows: Since (a, b) are not locally observable, $\mathcal{E}_{ab}^{loc} = \emptyset$. Equivalently, there does not exist a function $f : [k] \times \Sigma \to \mathbb{R}$ such that for all $i \in [d]$,

$$\sum_{c \in \mathcal{N}_{ab}} f(c, \Phi_{ci}) = \ell_{ai} - \ell_{bi}. \tag{37.6}$$

In this form, it does not seem obvious what the next step should be. To clear things up, we introduce some linear algebra. Let $S_c \in \{0, 1\}^{m \times d}$ be the matrix with $(S_c)_{\sigma i} = \mathbb{I}\{\Phi_{ci} = \sigma\}$, which is chosen so that $S_c e_i = e_{\Phi_{ci}}$. Define the linear map $S : \mathbb{R}^d \to \mathbb{R}^{|\mathcal{N}_{ab}|m}$ by

$$S = \begin{pmatrix} S_a \\ S_b \\ \vdots \\ S_c \end{pmatrix},$$

which is the matrix formed by stacking the matrices $\{S_c : c \in \mathcal{N}_{ab}\}$. Then, an elementary argument shows that there exists a function f satisfying Eq. (37.6) if and only if there exists a $w \in \mathbb{R}^{|\mathcal{N}_{ab}|m}$ such that

$$\ell_a - \ell_b = S^\top w.$$

In other words, actions (a, b) are locally observable if and only if $\ell_a - \ell_b \in \mathrm{im}(S^\top)$. Since we have assumed that (a, b) are not locally observable, we must have $\ell_a - \ell_b \notin \mathrm{im}(S^\top)$. Let $z \in \mathrm{im}(S^\top)$ and $w \in \ker(S)$ be such that $\ell_a - \ell_b = z + w$, which is possible since $\mathrm{im}(S^\top) \oplus \ker(S) = \mathbb{R}^d$. Since $\ell_a - \ell_b \notin \mathrm{im}(S^\top)$, it holds that $w \neq 0$ and $\langle \ell_a - \ell_b, w \rangle = \langle z + w, w \rangle = \langle w, w \rangle \neq 0$. Note also that $\mathbf{1} \in \mathrm{im}(S^\top)$ and hence $\langle \mathbf{1}, w \rangle = 0$. Finally, let $q = w / \langle \ell_a - \ell_b, w \rangle$. By construction, $q \in \mathbb{R}^d$, $q \neq 0$ while $Sq = 0$, $\langle \ell_a - \ell_b, q \rangle = 1$ and $\langle \mathbf{1}, q \rangle = 0$. Let $\Delta > 0$ be some small constant to be chosen subsequently. With this, we define $u_a = u - \Delta q$ and $u_b = u + \Delta q$ so that

$$\langle \ell_b - \ell_a, u_a \rangle = \Delta \quad \text{and} \quad \langle \ell_a - \ell_b, u_b \rangle = \Delta. \tag{37.7}$$

We note that if Δ is sufficiently small, then $u_a \in C_a$ and $u_b \in C_b$ because a and b are Pareto optimal.

Step 2: Calculating the Relative Entropy

Given action c and $r \in \mathcal{P}_{d-1}$, let $\mathbb{P}_{cr}$ be the distribution on the feedback observed by the learner when playing action c in stochastic partial monitoring environment determined by r. That is $\mathbb{P}_{cr}(\sigma) = (S_c r)_{\sigma}$. Further, let $\mathbb{P}_r$ be the distribution on the histories $H_n = (A_1, \Phi_1, \ldots, A_n, \Phi_n)$ arising from the interaction of the learner's policy with the stochastic environment determined by r. Expectations with respect to $\mathbb{P}_r$ are denoted by $\mathbb{E}_r$. A modification of Lemma 15.1 shows that

$$D(\mathbb{P}_{u_a}, \mathbb{P}_{u_b}) = \sum_{c \in [k]} \mathbb{E}_{u_a}[T_c(n)] D(\mathbb{P}_{cu_a}, \mathbb{P}_{cu_b}). \tag{37.8}$$

By the definitions of u_a and u_b, we have $S_c u_a = S_c u_b$ for all $c \in \mathcal{N}_{ab}$. Therefore, $\mathbb{P}_{cu_a} = \mathbb{P}_{cu_b}$ and $D(\mathbb{P}_{cu_a}, \mathbb{P}_{cu_b}) = 0$ for all $c \in \mathcal{N}_{ab}$. On the other hand, if $c \notin \mathcal{N}_{ab}$, then by the data processing inequality (Exercise 14.9) and Eq. (37.4), for $\Delta \leq \min_{i: q_i \neq 0} u_i / (2|q_i|)$,

$$D(\mathbb{P}_{cu_a}, \mathbb{P}_{cu_b}) \leq D(u_a, u_b) \leq \sum_{i=1}^{d} \frac{(u_{ai} - u_{bi})^2}{u_{bi}} \leq 4\Delta^2 \sum_{i=1}^{k} \frac{q_i^2}{u_i - \Delta|q_i|} \leq \tilde{C}_u \Delta^2,$$

where we used that $u \in C_a \cap C_b$ is not on the boundary of $\mathcal{P}_{d-1}$, so $u_i > 0$ for all i and we defined $\tilde{C}_u$ as a suitably large constant that depends on u (q is entirely determined by a and b). Therefore,

$$D(\mathbb{P}_{u_a}, \mathbb{P}_{u_b}) \leq \tilde{C}_u \sum_{c \notin \mathcal{N}_{ab}} \mathbb{E}[T_c(n)] \Delta^2. \tag{37.9}$$

Step 3: Comparing the Regret

By Eq. (37.5) and Hölder's inequality, for $c \notin \mathcal{N}_{ab}$ we have $\langle \ell_c - \ell_a, u_a \rangle \geq \varepsilon - \langle \ell_c - \ell_a, \Delta q \rangle \geq \varepsilon - \Delta \|q\|_1$ and $\langle \ell_c - \ell_b, u_b \rangle \geq \varepsilon - \Delta \|q\|_1$, where, for simplicity and without the loss of generality, we assumed that the losses lie in $[0, 1]$. Define $\tilde{T}(n)$ to be the number of times an arm not in $\mathcal{N}_{ab}$ is played:

$$\tilde{T}(n) = \sum_{c \notin \mathcal{N}_{ab}} T_c(n).$$

By Lemma 37.8, for each action $c \in \mathcal{N}_{ab}$, there exists an $\alpha \in [0, 1]$ such that $\ell_c = \alpha \ell_a + (1 - \alpha) \ell_b$. Therefore, by Eq. (37.7),

$$\langle \ell_c - \ell_a, u_a \rangle + \langle \ell_c - \ell_b, u_b \rangle = (1 - \alpha)\langle \ell_b - \ell_a, u_a \rangle + \alpha \langle \ell_a - \ell_b, u_b \rangle = \Delta, \tag{37.10}$$

which means that $\max(\langle \ell_c - \ell_a, u_a \rangle, \langle \ell_c - \ell_b, u_b \rangle) \geq \Delta/2$. Define $\bar{T}(n)$ as the number of times an arm in $\mathcal{N}_{ab}$ is played that is at least $\Delta/2$ suboptimal in u_a:

$$\bar{T}(n) = \sum_{c \in \mathcal{N}_{ab}} \mathbb{I}\left\{ \langle \ell_c - \ell_a, u_a \rangle \geq \frac{\Delta}{2} \right\} T_c(n).$$

It also follows from (37.10) that if $c \in \mathcal{N}_{ab}$ and $\langle \ell_c - \ell_a, u_a \rangle < \frac{\Delta}{2}$, then $\langle \ell_c - \ell_b, u_b \rangle \geq \frac{\Delta}{2}$. Hence, under u_b, the random pseudo-regret, $\sum_c T_c(n)\langle \ell_c - \ell_b, u_b \rangle$, is at least $(n - \bar{T}(n))\Delta/2$. Assume that Δ is chosen sufficiently small so that $\Delta \|q\|_1 \leq \varepsilon/2$. By the above,

$$R_n(\pi, u_a) + R_n(\pi, u_b)$$

$$= \mathbb{E}_{u_a} \left[\sum_{c \in [k]} T_c(n) \langle \ell_c - \ell_a, u_a \rangle \right] + \mathbb{E}_{u_b} \left[\sum_{c \in [k]} T_c(n) \langle \ell_c - \ell_b, u_b \rangle \right]$$

$$\geq \frac{\varepsilon}{2} \mathbb{E}_{u_a} \left[\tilde{T}(n) \right] + \frac{n\Delta}{4} \left(\mathbb{P}_{u_a}(\bar{T}(n) \geq n/2) + \mathbb{P}_{u_b}(\bar{T}(n) < n/2) \right)$$

$$\geq \frac{\varepsilon}{2} \mathbb{E}_{u_a} \left[\tilde{T}(n) \right] + \frac{n\Delta}{8} \exp\left(- D(\mathbb{P}_{u_a}, \mathbb{P}_{u_b}) \right)$$

$$\geq \frac{\varepsilon}{2} \mathbb{E}_{u_a} \left[\tilde{T}(n) \right] + \frac{n\Delta}{8} \exp\left(-\tilde{C}_u \Delta^2 \mathbb{E}_{u_a} \left[\tilde{T}(n) \right] \right),$$

where the second inequality follows from the Bretagnolle–Huber inequality (Theorem 14.2) and the third from Eqs. (37.8) and (37.9). The bound is completed by choosing

$$\Delta = \min \left(\min_{i:q_i \neq 0} \frac{u_i}{2|q_i|}, \frac{\varepsilon}{2\|q\|_1 n^{1/3}} \right),$$

which is finite since $q \neq 0$. Straightforward calculation concludes the result (Exercise 37.7). $\qquad\square$

We leave the following theorems as exercises for the reader (Exercises 37.8 and 37.9):

THEOREM 37.13. *If G is not globally observable and has at least two non-dominated actions, then there exists a constant $c_G > 0$ such that $R_n^*(G) \geq c_G n$.*

Proof sketch Since G is not globally observable, there exists a pair of neighbouring actions (a, b) that are not globally observable. Let u be the centroid of $C_a \cap C_b$. Let $S \in \mathbb{R}^{km \times d}$ be the stack of matrices from $\{S_c : c \in [k]\}$. Then, using the same argument as the previous proof, we have $\ell_a - \ell_b \notin \mathrm{im}(S^\top)$. Now define $q \in \mathbb{R}^d$ such that $\langle 1, q \rangle = 0$, $\langle \ell_a - \ell_b, q \rangle = 1$ and $Sq = 0$. Let $\Delta > 0$ be sufficiently small and $u_a = u - \Delta q$ and $u_b = u + \Delta q$. Show that $D(\mathbb{P}_{u_a}, \mathbb{P}_{u_b}) = 0$ for all policies and complete the proof in the same fashion as the proof of Theorem 37.12. $\qquad\square$

THEOREM 37.14. *Let $G = (\mathcal{L}, \Phi)$ be locally observable and have at least one pair of neighbours. Then there exists a constant $c_G > 0$ such that for all large enough n the minimax regret satisfies $R_n^*(G) \geq c_G \sqrt{n}$.*

Proof sketch By assumption, there exists a pair of neighbouring actions (a, b). Define u as the centroid of $C_a \cap C_b$ and u_a and u_b be the centroids of C_a and C_b respectively. For sufficiently small $\Delta > 0$, let $v_a = (1 - \Delta)u - \Delta u_a$ and $v_b = (1 - \Delta)u + \Delta u_b$. Then

$$D(\mathbb{P}_{v_a}, \mathbb{P}_{v_b}) \leq n \sum_{i=1}^{d} \frac{(v_{ai} - v_{bi})^2}{v_{bi}} \leq c_G n \Delta^2,$$

where $c_G > 0$ is a game-dependent constant. Let $\Delta = 1/\sqrt{n}$ and apply the ideas in the proof of Theorem 37.12. $\qquad\square$

37.5 Policy and Upper Bounds

We now describe a policy for globally and locally observable games, and prove its regret is $O(n^{1/2})$ for locally observable games and $O(n^{2/3})$ otherwise. For the remainder of this section, fix a globally observable game $G = (\mathcal{L}, \Phi)$. The estimation functions in $\mathcal{E}_{ab}^{glo}$ and $\mathcal{E}_{ab}^{loc}$ are designed to combine with importance-weighting to estimate the loss differences between actions a and b. For this section, it is more convenient to define estimation functions for the whole loss vector up to constant shifts. Let $\mathcal{E}^{vec}$ be the set of all functions $f : [k] \times \Sigma \to \mathbb{R}^k$ such that:

(a) $f(a, \sigma)_b = 0$ for all $b \notin \Pi$; and
(b) for each outcome $i \in [d]$, there exists a constant $c \in \mathbb{R}$ with

$$\sum_{a=1}^{k} f(a, \Phi_{ai})_b = \mathcal{L}_{bi} + c \text{ for all } b \in \Pi.$$

The intuition is that $\mathcal{E}^{vec}$ is the set of functions that serve as unbiased loss difference estimators in the sense that when $A \sim p \in \text{ri}(\mathcal{P}_{k-1})$, then

$$\mathbb{E}\left[\frac{\langle e_a - e_b, f(A, \Phi_{Ai})\rangle}{p_A}\right] = \langle \ell_a - \ell_b, e_i\rangle \quad \text{for all Pareto optimal } a, b \text{ and } i \in [d].$$

As we will see in the proof of Theorem 37.16, if G is globally observable, then $\mathcal{E}^{vec}$ is nonempty. By identifying functions and vectors, $\mathcal{E}^{vec} \subset \mathbb{R}^{k(km)}$, a view that will be useful later.

The policy for partial monitoring combines exponential weights with a careful exploration strategy. A little reminder about exponential weights and some new notation will be useful. Given a probability vector $q \in \mathcal{P}_{k-1}$, define a function $\Psi_q : \mathbb{R}^k \to \mathbb{R}$ by

$$\Psi_q(z) = \langle q, \exp(-z) + z - 1\rangle,$$

where the exponential function is applied component-wise. You might recognise Ψ_q as the Bregman divergence

$$\Psi_q(z) = D_{F^*}(\nabla F(q) - z, \nabla F(q)),$$

where F is the unnormalised negentropy potential. Suppose that $(\hat{y}_t)_{t=1}^n$ is an arbitrary sequence of vectors with $\hat{y}_t \in \mathbb{R}^k$, $\eta > 0$ and

$$Q_{ta} = \frac{\exp\left(-\eta \sum_{s=1}^{t-1} \hat{y}_{sa}\right)}{\sum_{b=1}^{k} \exp\left(-\eta \sum_{s=1}^{t-1} \hat{y}_{sb}\right)}, \qquad t \in [n].$$

Recall from Theorem 28.4 that for any $a^* \in [k]$,

$$\sum_{t=1}^{n}\sum_{a=1}^{k} Q_{ta}(\hat{y}_{ta} - \hat{y}_{ta^*}) \leq \frac{\log(k)}{\eta} + \frac{1}{\eta}\sum_{t=1}^{n} \Psi_{Q_t}(\eta \hat{y}_t). \tag{37.11}$$

Exp3 is derived by defining $\hat{y}_t$ as the importance-weighted loss estimator and sampling A_t from Q_t. We will do something similar in partial monitoring, but with two significant differences: (a) the importance-weighted estimator must depend on the feedback and loss matrices, and (b) the algorithm will sample A_t from an alternative distribution P_t that is optimised to balance the regret suffered relative to Q_t and the information gained.

> The definition of global observability does not imply that loss differences between dominated and degenerate actions can be estimated. Consequentially, the distribution Q_t used by the new algorithm will be supported on Pareto optimal actions only. The actual distribution P_t used when choosing an action may also include degenerate actions, however.

The optimisation problem for balancing information and regret explicitly optimises a worst case upper bound on the right-hand side of Eq. (37.11). For $\eta > 0$ and $q \in \mathcal{P}_{k-1}$ with $\mathrm{Supp}(q) \subseteq \Pi$, let

$$\mathrm{opt}_q(\eta) = \inf_{\substack{f \in \mathscr{E}^{\mathrm{vec}} \\ p \in \mathrm{ri}(\mathcal{P}_{k-1})}} \max_{i \in [d]} \left[\frac{1}{\eta}(p - q)^\top \mathcal{L}e_i + \frac{1}{\eta^2} \sum_{a=1}^{k} p_a \Psi_q \left(\frac{\eta f(a, \Phi_{ai})}{p_a} \right) \right]. \quad (37.12)$$

Of course, $\mathrm{opt}_q(\eta)$ depends on the game G, which is hidden from the notation to reduce clutter. The first term in the right-hand side of Eq. (37.12) measures the additional regret when playing p rather than q, while the second corresponds to the expectation of the second term in Eq. (37.11) when the algorithm uses importance-weighting using estimation function f. The optimisation problem is convex and hence amenable to efficient computation (see Note 9 for some details). The worst-case value over all q is

$$\mathrm{opt}^*(\eta) = \sup\{\mathrm{opt}_q(\eta) : q \in \mathcal{P}_{k-1}, \ \mathrm{Supp}(q) \subseteq \Pi\}.$$

The function $q \mapsto \mathrm{opt}_q(\eta)$ is generally not convex, so $\mathrm{opt}^*(\eta)$ may be hard to compute. This causes a minor problem when setting the learning rate, which can be mitigated by adapting the learning rate online as discussed in Note 7.

> We say that $f \in \mathscr{E}^{\mathrm{vec}}$ and $p \in \mathrm{ri}(\mathcal{P}_{k-1})$ solve Eq. (37.12) with precision $\varepsilon \geq 0$ if
>
> $$\max_{i \in [d]} \left[\frac{1}{\eta}(p - q)^\top \mathcal{L}e_i + \frac{1}{\eta^2} \sum_{a=1}^{k} p_a \Psi_q \left(\frac{\eta f(a, \Phi_{ai})}{p_a} \right) \right] \leq \mathrm{opt}_q(\eta) + \varepsilon. \quad (37.13)$$
>
> Such approximately optimal solutions exist for any $\varepsilon > 0$, but may not exist for $\varepsilon = 0$ because the constraint on p is not compact.

> The convexity of the inner maximum in Eq. (37.12) can be checked using the following construction. The **perspective** of a convex function $f : \mathbb{R}^d \to \mathbb{R}$ is a function $g : \mathbb{R}^{d+1} \to \mathbb{R}$ given by
>
> $$g(x, u) = \begin{cases} uf(x/u), & \text{if } u > 0; \\ \infty, & \text{otherwise.} \end{cases} \quad (37.14)$$
>
> The perspective is known to be convex (Exercise 37.1). Since Ψ_q is convex and the max of convex functions is convex, it follows that the term inside of the infimum of Eq. (37.12) is convex.

1: **Input:** η, ε, $\mathcal{L}$ and Φ

2: **for** $t \in 1, \ldots, n$ **do**

3:     Compute exponential weights distribution $Q_t \in \mathcal{P}_{k-1}$ by:

$$Q_{ta} = \frac{\mathbb{I}_\Pi(a) \exp\left(-\eta \sum_{s=1}^{t-1} \hat{y}_{sa}\right)}{\sum_{b \in \Pi} \exp\left(-\eta \sum_{s=1}^{t-1} \hat{y}_{sb}\right)}.$$

4:     Solve Eq. (37.12) with $q = Q_t$ and precision ε to find $P_t \in \mathcal{P}_{k-1}$ and $f_t \in \mathcal{E}^{\text{vec}}$

5:     Sample $A_t \sim P_t$ and observe σ_t

6:     Set $\hat{y}_t = f_t(A_t, \sigma_t)/P_{tA_t}$

7: **end for**

Algorithm 26: Exponential weights for partial monitoring. Recall that Π denotes the set of Pareto optimal actions.

The full algorithm is given as Algorithm 26.

THEOREM 37.15. *For any $\eta > 0$ and $\varepsilon > 0$, the regret of Algorithm 26 is bounded by*

$$R_n \leq \frac{\log(k)}{\eta} + n\eta(\text{opt}^*(\eta) + \varepsilon).$$

Proof The result follows from the definitions of $\mathcal{E}^{\text{vec}}$ and the regret, and the bound for exponential weights in Eq. (37.11). Let $a^* = \operatorname{argmin}_{a \in \Pi} \sum_{t=1}^n \langle \ell_a, u_t \rangle$. Then,

$$R_n = \mathbb{E}\left[\sum_{t=1}^n \mathcal{L}_{A_t i_t} - \mathcal{L}_{a^* i_t}\right]$$

$$= \mathbb{E}\left[\sum_{t=1}^n \sum_{a=1}^k P_{ta}(\mathcal{L}_{a i_t} - \mathcal{L}_{a^* i_t})\right]$$

$$= \mathbb{E}\left[\sum_{t=1}^n \sum_{a=1}^k Q_{ta}(\mathcal{L}_{a i_t} - \mathcal{L}_{a^* i_t})\right] + \mathbb{E}\left[\sum_{t=1}^n \sum_{a=1}^k (P_{ta} - Q_{ta})\mathcal{L}_{a i_t}\right]$$

$$= \mathbb{E}\left[\sum_{t=1}^n \sum_{a=1}^k Q_{ta}(\hat{y}_{ta} - \hat{y}_{ta^*})\right] + \mathbb{E}\left[\sum_{t=1}^n \sum_{a=1}^k (P_{ta} - Q_{ta})\mathcal{L}_{a i_t}\right].$$

The first expectation is bounded using the definition of Q_t and Eq. (37.11) by

$$\mathbb{E}\left[\sum_{t=1}^n \sum_{a=1}^k Q_{ta}(\hat{y}_{ta} - \hat{y}_{ta^*})\right] \leq \frac{\log(k)}{\eta} + \frac{1}{\eta}\mathbb{E}\left[\sum_{t=1}^n \Psi_{Q_t}(\eta \hat{y}_t)\right]$$

$$= \frac{\log(k)}{\eta} + \frac{1}{\eta}\mathbb{E}\left[\sum_{t=1}^n \sum_{a=1}^k P_{ta}\Psi_{Q_t}\left(\frac{\eta f_t(a, \Phi_{a i_t})}{P_{ta}}\right)\right].$$

Combining the two displays, using the definitions of P_t, f_t and ε_t, and substituting the definition of $\text{opt}_{Q_t}(\eta) \leq \text{opt}^*(\eta)$ completes the proof. ☐

The extent to which this result is useful depends on the behaviour of $\text{opt}^*(\eta)$ for different classes of games. The following two theorems bound the value of the optimisation problem for globally observable and locally observable games respectively. An apparently important quantity in the regret upper bounds for both globally and locally observable games is the minimum magnitude of the estimation functions. Let

$$v_{\text{glo}} = \max_{e \in E} \min_{f \in \mathscr{E}_e^{\text{glo}}} \|f\|_\infty \quad \text{and} \quad v_{\text{loc}} = \max_{e \in E} \min_{f \in \mathscr{E}_e^{\text{loc}}} \|f\|_\infty.$$

In the remainder of this chapter we assume that the losses are between zero and one $\mathcal{L} \in [0,1]^{k \times d}$.

THEOREM 37.16. *For all globally observable games,* $\text{opt}^*(\eta) \le 2v_{\text{glo}}k^2/\sqrt{\eta}$ *for all* $\eta \le 1/\max\{1, v_{\text{glo}}^2 k^4\}$.

THEOREM 37.17. *For all locally observable games,* $\text{opt}^*(\eta) \le 9k^3 \max(1, v_{\text{loc}}^2)$ *for all* $\eta \le 1/(2k^2 \max(1, v_{\text{loc}}))$.

The proofs follow in subsequent sections. Combining Theorem 37.15 with Theorem 37.17 shows that for an appropriately tuned learning rate, the regret of Algorithm 26 on locally observable games is bounded by

$$R_n = O\left(v_{\text{loc}}k^{3/2}\sqrt{n\log(k)}\right).$$

By using Theorem 37.16, it follows that for globally observable games the regret is bounded by

$$R_n = O\left((v_{\text{glo}}kn)^{2/3}(\log(k))^{1/3}\right).$$

These results establish the upper bounds in the classification theorem for locally and globally observable games. The quantities v_{glo} and v_{loc} only depend on G but may be exponentially large in d. We walk you through the proof of the following proposition in Exercise 37.12.

PROPOSITION 37.18. *The following hold:*

(a) *If G is globally observable, then* $v_{\text{glo}} \le d^{1/2}k^{d/2}$.
(b) *If G is locally observable, then* $v_{\text{loc}} \le d^{1/2}k^{d/2}$.
(c) *If G is locally observable and non-degenerate, then* $v_{\text{loc}} \le m$.

The only property of non-degenerate games used in Part (c) is that $|\mathcal{N}_e| = 2$ for all $e \in E$. It is illustrative to bound $\text{opt}^*(\eta)$ for well-known games. The next proposition shows that Algorithm 26 recovers the usual bounds for bandits and the full information setting.

PROPOSITION 37.19. *The following hold:*

(a) *For bandit games ($\Phi = \mathcal{L}$),* $\text{opt}^*(\eta) \le k/2$.
(b) *For full information games ($\Phi_{ai} = i$ for all a and i),* $\text{opt}^*(\eta) \le 1/2$.

You will prove this proposition in Exercise 37.14 by making explicit choices of $p \in \text{ri}(\mathcal{P}_{k-1})$ and $f \in \mathscr{E}^{\text{vec}}$.

37.6   Proof of Theorem 37.16

The definition of global (and local) observability is defined in terms of the existence of functions serving as unbiased loss estimators between pairs of neighbouring actions. To make a connection between $\mathscr{E}^{\mathrm{vec}}$ and $\mathscr{E}^{\mathrm{glo}}$ (and $\mathscr{E}^{\mathrm{loc}}$) we need the concept of an **in-tree** on the neighbourhood graph. Let S be a subset of Pareto optimal actions with no duplicate actions and $\cup_{a \in S} C_a = \mathcal{P}_{d-1}$. An in-tree on the graph (S, E) is a set of edges $\mathcal{T} \subset E$ such that $(S, \mathcal{T})$ is a directed tree with all edges pointing towards a special vertex called the root, denoted by $\mathrm{root}_{\mathcal{T}}$ and such that $V(\mathcal{T})$, the set of vertices underlying $\mathcal{T}$, is the same as S. Provided the game is non-trivial, then such a tree exists by Lemma 37.7. Given a Pareto optimal action b, let $\mathrm{path}_{\mathcal{T}}(b) \subseteq \mathcal{T}$ denote the path from b to the root. The path is empty when b is the root. When b is not the root, we let $\mathrm{par}_{\mathcal{T}}(b)$ denote the unique Pareto optimal action such that $(b, \mathrm{par}_{\mathcal{T}}(b)) \in \mathcal{T}$.

Abbreviate $v = v_{\mathrm{glo}}$ and let $\mathcal{T} \subset E$ be an arbitrary in-tree over the Pareto optimal actions. For each $e \in E$, let $f_e \in \mathscr{E}_e^{\mathrm{glo}}$ be such that $\|f_e\|_\infty \leq v$. Then define $f : [k] \times \Sigma \to \mathbb{R}^k$ by

$$f(a, \sigma)_b = \sum_{e \in \mathrm{path}_{\mathcal{T}}(b)} f_e(a, \sigma).$$

By the triangle inequality, $\max_{a \in [k], \sigma \in \Sigma} \|f(a, \sigma)\|_\infty \leq kv$. Furthermore, $f \in \mathscr{E}^{\mathrm{vec}}$, since for any outcome i,

$$\sum_{a=1}^k f(a, \Phi_{ai})_b = \sum_{a=1}^k \sum_{e \in \mathrm{path}_{\mathcal{T}}(b)} f_e(a, \Phi_{ai}) = \mathcal{L}_{bi} - \mathcal{L}_{\mathrm{root}(\mathcal{T})i}.$$

Let $p = (1 - \gamma)q + \gamma \mathbf{1}/k$ with $\gamma = vk^2\sqrt{\eta}$. By the condition in the theorem that $\eta \leq 1/\max\{1, v^2 k^4\}$, it holds that $\gamma \leq 1$ and hence $p \in \mathrm{ri}(\mathcal{P}_{k-1})$. The next step is to bound the minimum possible value of the loss estimator. For actions a and b and outcome i,

$$\frac{\eta f(a, \Phi_{ai})_b}{p_a} \geq -\frac{\eta v k^2}{\gamma} = -\sqrt{\eta} \geq -1,$$

where in the final inequality we used the fact that $\eta \leq 1$. Next, using the fact that $\exp(-x) \leq x^2 + 1 - x$ for $x \geq -1$, it follows that for any $z \geq -1$,

$$\Psi_q(z) \leq \sum_{b=1}^k q_b z_b^2, \tag{37.15}$$

which is the inequality we have used long ago in Chapter 11. Using this,

$$\frac{1}{\eta^2} \sum_{a=1}^k p_a \Psi_q\left(\frac{\eta f(a, \Phi_{ai})}{p_a}\right) \leq \sum_{a=1}^k \sum_{b \in \Pi} \frac{q_b}{p_a} f(a, \Phi_{ai})_b^2 \leq \frac{k^4 v^2}{\gamma} = \frac{k^2 v}{\sqrt{\eta}},$$

where we used that $\|f(a, \sigma)\|_\infty \leq kv$ and $p \geq \gamma/k\mathbf{1}$ and that $q \in \mathcal{P}_{k-1}$. For the other component of the objective,

$$\frac{1}{\eta}(p - q)^\top \mathcal{L}e_i = \frac{\gamma}{\eta}(\mathbf{1}/k - q)^\top \mathcal{L}e_i = \frac{vk^2}{\sqrt{\eta}}(\mathbf{1}/k - q)^\top \mathcal{L}e_i \leq \frac{vk^2}{\sqrt{\eta}}.$$

Combining the previous two displays shows that for any $i \in [d]$,

$$\frac{1}{\eta}(p-q)^\top \mathcal{L}e_i + \frac{1}{\eta^2}\sum_{a=1}^{k} p_a \Psi_q \left(\frac{\eta f(a, \Phi_{ai})}{p_a}\right) \leq \frac{2vk^2}{\sqrt{\eta}},$$

which is the desired result.

37.7 Proof of Theorem 37.17

Exploiting local observability is not straightforward. To gain some insight let us consider the matching pennies game with $c = 1/4$:

$$\mathcal{L} = \begin{pmatrix} 0 & 1 \\ 1 & 0 \\ 1/4 & 1/4 \end{pmatrix} \qquad \Phi = \begin{pmatrix} \bot & \bot \\ \bot & \bot \\ H & T \end{pmatrix} \qquad \overset{\bullet}{1} \overset{\textbf{---}}{\underset{\textbf{3}}{\bullet}} \overset{\textbf{---}}{\underset{\textbf{2}}{\bullet}}$$

The figure on the right-hand side is the neighbourhood graph. Notice that the third action is revealing and also separates the first two actions in the neighbourhood graph. Clearly, loss differences can be estimated between all pairs of neighbours in this graph, and hence the game is locally observable. Let's suppose now that $q = (1/2 - \varepsilon/2, 1/2 - \varepsilon/2, \varepsilon)$ and $p = q$. The obvious estimation function $f \in \mathscr{E}^{\text{vec}}$ is given by

$$f(a, \sigma) = \begin{cases} (0, 1, 1/4)^\top, & \text{if } a = 3 \text{ and } \sigma = 1; \\ (1, 0, 1/4)^\top, & \text{if } a = 3 \text{ and } \sigma = 2; \\ 0, & \text{otherwise.} \end{cases}$$

Examining the second term in Eq. (37.12) and using a second order Taylor approximation,

$$\frac{1}{\eta^2}\sum_{a=1}^{3} p_a \Psi_q \left(\frac{\eta f(a, \Phi_{ai})}{p_a}\right) \approx \frac{1}{2}\sum_{b=1}^{3} \frac{q_b}{p_3} \mathcal{L}_{bi}^2 = \frac{1}{32} + \frac{1-\varepsilon}{4\varepsilon},$$

which holds for both $i = 1$ and $i = 2$. This is bad news. The appearance of $p_3 = q_3$ in the denominator means the objective can be arbitrarily large when ε is small. Taylor's theorem shows that the approximation is not to blame, provided that η is suitably small. The main issue is that q and p assign most of their mass to two actions that are not neighbours and hence cannot be distinguished without playing a third action. Now suppose that p is constructed by transferring mass from the first two actions to the third by:

$$p = q - \min(q_1, q_2)(e_1 + e_2) + 2\min(q_1, q_2)e_3.$$

The first observation is that this can only decrease the expected loss:

$$(p-q)^\top \mathcal{L} = -\frac{3}{4}\min(q_1, q_2)\mathbf{1} \leq 0.$$

This takes care of the first term in the objective. Let us assume without loss of generality that $p_1 = \max(p_1, p_2, p_3)$, and let

$$f(a, \sigma) = \begin{cases} (0, 1, 1/4)^\top, & \text{if } a = 3 \text{ and } \sigma = 1; \\ (0, -1, -3/4)^\top, & \text{if } a = 3 \text{ and } \sigma = 2; \\ 0, & \text{otherwise.} \end{cases}$$

Using again a Taylor approximation suggests the second term in the objective is now well behaved:

$$\frac{1}{\eta^2} \sum_{a=1}^k p_a \Psi_q \left(\frac{\eta f(a, \Phi_{ai})}{p_a} \right) \approx \frac{1}{2} \sum_{b=1}^k \frac{q_b}{p_3} f(3, \Phi_{3i})_b^2$$

$$\leq \frac{1}{2} \left(\frac{q_2}{p_3} + \frac{q_3}{p_3} \right) \leq \frac{1}{2} \left(\frac{1}{2} + 1 \right).$$

Things are starting to look more promising. By transferring the mass in q towards the revealing action and shifting the loss estimators to be zero on the most played action, we have gained control of the stability term and simultaneously decreased the expected loss of p relative to q.

37.7.1 Duality and the Water Transfer Operator

The water transfer operator, which we will introduce momentarily, provides the generalisation of the specific argument just given. The first step is an application of Sion's minimax theorem (Theorem 28.12) to Eq. (37.12), which shows that

$$\mathrm{opt}_q(\eta) = \max_{\lambda \in \mathcal{P}_{d-1}} \inf_{\substack{f \in \mathscr{E}^{\mathrm{vec}} \\ p \in \mathcal{P}_{k-1}}} \left[\frac{(p-q)^\top \mathcal{L}\lambda}{\eta} + \frac{1}{\eta^2} \sum_{i=1}^d \lambda_i \sum_{a=1}^k p_a \Psi_q \left(\frac{\eta f(a, \Phi_{ai})}{p_a} \right) \right].$$

$$(37.16)$$

By exchanging the max and the inf, we free ourselves from finding a distribution p and estimation function f such that the objective is controlled for all choices of the adversary. Now we only need to find a p and f for each distribution over outcomes $\lambda \in \mathcal{P}_{d-1}$.

Fix therefore an arbitrary distribution $\lambda \in \mathcal{P}_{d-1}$. Let S be an arbitrary subset of Pareto optimal actions containing no duplicates and for which $\cup_{a \in S} C_a = \mathcal{P}_{d-1}$ and let $T \subset E$ be an in-tree over S. Given an edge $e = (a, b) \in E$, let $\alpha_e : \mathcal{N}_e \to [0, 1]$ be the mapping such that $\ell_c = (1 - \alpha_e(c))\ell_a + \alpha_e(c)\ell_b$ for all $c \in \mathcal{N}_e$, which exists by Lemma 37.8. Note that $\alpha_e(c) = 0$ when c is a duplicate of a and $\alpha_e(c) = 1$ when it is a duplicate of b. A vector $y \in \mathbb{R}^k$ is called T-increasing if for all $e = (a, b) \in T$ and $c, d \in \mathcal{N}_e$ with $\alpha_e(d) \geq \alpha_e(c)$, it holds that $y_d \geq y_c$. A vector y is called T-decreasing if $-y$ is T-increasing. This concept is illustrated in Fig. 37.5.

LEMMA 37.20. *Given an in-tree $T \subset E$ and distribution $q \in \mathcal{P}_{k-1}$ there exists a distribution $r \in \mathcal{P}_{k-1}$ such that*

(a) $r \geq q/k$;

(b) *r is T-increasing; and*

(c) $\langle r - q, y \rangle \leq 0$ *for all T-decreasing vectors $y \in \mathbb{R}^k$.*

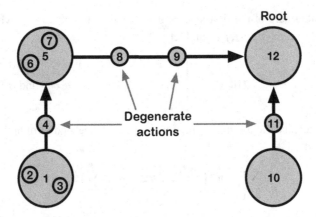

Root

Figure 37.5 The large nodes are Pareto optimal actions in $\mathcal{S}$. The smaller nodes inside are their duplicates, which are not part of $\mathcal{S}$. The remaining nodes are degenerate actions that are linear combinations of Pareto optimal actions. The arrows indicate the in-tree. A vector $y \in \mathbb{R}^k$ is $\mathcal{T}$-increasing if it is constant on duplicate actions and otherwise increasing in the direction of the arrows. In this case, the constraint is that $y_1 = y_2 = y_3 \leq y_4 \leq y_5 = y_6 = y_7 \leq y_8 \leq y_9 \leq y_{12}$ and $y_{10} \leq y_{11} \leq y_{12}$.

Proof For simplicity, we give the proof for the special case that all actions are Pareto optimal and there are no duplicates, in which case $\mathcal{S} = [k]$. The proof is generalised in Exercise 37.11. Given an action $a \in [k]$, let $\mathrm{anc}_{\mathcal{T}}(a) = \cup_{e \in \mathrm{path}_{\mathcal{T}}(a)} \mathcal{N}_e \cup \{a\}$ be the set of ancestors of a, including a and $\mathrm{desc}_{\mathcal{T}}(a) = \{b : a \in \mathrm{anc}_{\mathcal{T}}(b)\}$ be the set of descendants of a. Define r by

$$r_a = \sum_{b \in \mathrm{desc}_{\mathcal{T}}(a)} \frac{q_b}{|\mathrm{anc}_{\mathcal{T}}(b)|}.$$

Let us first confirm that $r \in \mathcal{P}_{k-1}$. That $r \geq 0$ is obvious and

$$\sum_{a=1}^{k} r_a = \sum_{a=1}^{k} \sum_{b \in \mathrm{desc}_{\mathcal{T}}(a)} \frac{q_b}{|\mathrm{anc}_{\mathcal{T}}(b)|} = \sum_{b=1}^{k} \sum_{a \in \mathrm{anc}_{\mathcal{T}}(b)} \frac{q_b}{|\mathrm{anc}_{\mathcal{T}}(b)|} = 1.$$

For Part (a), the definition means that $r_a \geq q_a/|\mathrm{anc}_{\mathcal{T}}(a)| \geq q_a/k$. That r is $\mathcal{T}$-increasing follows immediately from the definition. (c) follows because

$$\langle r, y \rangle = \sum_{a=1}^{k} y_a \sum_{b \in \mathrm{desc}_{\mathcal{T}}(a)} \frac{q_b}{|\mathrm{anc}_{\mathcal{T}}(b)|} \geq \sum_{a=1}^{k} \sum_{b \in \mathrm{desc}_{\mathcal{T}}(a)} \frac{y_b q_b}{|\mathrm{anc}_{\mathcal{T}}(b)|} = \langle q, y \rangle. \qquad \square$$

The existence of the mapping $q \mapsto r$ given by Lemma 37.21 was originally proven using a 'water flowing' argument and was called the water transfer operator.

LEMMA 37.21. *Let $\mathcal{S}$ as before. Then, for any $\lambda \in \mathcal{P}_{d-1}$, there exists an in-tree $\mathcal{T} \subset E$ over vertices $\mathcal{S}$ such that $\mathcal{L}\lambda$ is $\mathcal{T}$-decreasing.*

Proof Again, we outline the argument for games with no degenerate or duplicate actions, leaving the complete proof for Exercise 37.11. Let a be an action such that $\lambda \in C_a$. First, assume that $\lambda \in \mathrm{ri}(C_a)$. The root of our tree will be a (the reader may find helpful to check Fig. 37.6). Next, for $b \neq a$, define $\mathrm{par}(b) = \mathrm{argmin}_{c \in \mathcal{N}_b} e_c^\top \mathcal{L}\lambda$ and then let

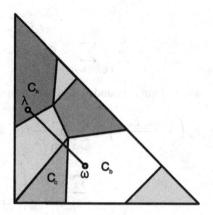

Figure 37.6 The core argument used in the proof of Lemma 37.21.

$\mathcal{T} = \{(b, \mathrm{par}(b)) : b \neq a\}$. Clearly, $V(\mathcal{T}) = [k]$. Provided that $\mathcal{T}$ really is a tree, the fact that $\mathcal{L}\lambda$ is $\mathcal{T}$-decreasing is obvious from the definition of the parent function. That $\mathcal{T}$ is a tree follows by showing that for any $(b, d) \in \mathcal{T}$, $e_d^\top \mathcal{L}\lambda < e_b^\top \mathcal{L}\lambda$, which we will prove now. For this, let $\omega \in \mathrm{ri}(C_b)$ and $c \in \mathcal{N}_b$ such that $C_c \cap [\omega, \lambda] \neq \emptyset$. These exist by Exercise 37.10 (see also Fig. 37.6). We now show that $e_c^\top \mathcal{L}\lambda < e_b^\top \mathcal{L}\lambda$ from which the desired result follows. To show this let

$$f(\alpha) = (e_b - e_c)^\top \mathcal{L}((1 - \alpha)\omega + \alpha\lambda).$$

It suffices to show that $f(1) > 0$. The following hold: (a) f is linear; (b) $f(0) < 0$, since $\omega \in \mathrm{ri}(C_b)$; and (c) there exists an $\alpha \in (0, 1)$ such that $f(\alpha) = 0$, which holds because $C_c \cap [\omega, \lambda] \neq \emptyset$ and $\lambda \in \mathrm{ri}(C_a)$. Thus $f(1) > 0$, establishing the result for $\lambda \in \mathrm{ri}(C_a)$. When λ is on the boundary of C_a, let $(\lambda^{(i)})_{i=1}^\infty$ be a sequence in $\mathrm{ri}(C_a)$ so that $\lim_{i \to \infty} \lambda^{(i)} \to \lambda$. For each i, let $\mathcal{T}^{(i)} \subset E$ be an in-tree such that $\mathcal{L}\lambda^{(i)}$ is $\mathcal{T}^{(i)}$-decreasing. Since there are only finitely many trees, by selecting a subsequence we conclude that there exists an in-tree $\mathcal{T} \subset E$ such that $\mathcal{L}\lambda^{(i)}$ is $\mathcal{T}$-decreasing for all i. The result follows by taking the limit. □

This concludes the building of the tools needed to control $\mathrm{opt}_q(\eta)$ for locally observable games.

Proof of Theorem 37.17 Abbreviate $v = v_{\mathrm{loc}}$ and let $\lambda \in \mathcal{P}_{d-1}$ be arbitrary. By Lemma 37.21, there exists an in-tree $\mathcal{T} \subset E$ over S such that $\mathcal{L}\lambda$ is $\mathcal{T}$-decreasing. Hence, by Lemma 37.20, there exists a $\mathcal{T}$-increasing $r \in \mathcal{P}_{k-1}$ such that $r \geq q/k$ and $(r - q)^\top \mathcal{L}\lambda \leq 0$. Let $p = (1 - \gamma)r + \gamma 1/k$ with $\gamma = \eta v k^2$ and

$$f(a, \sigma)_b = \sum_{e \in \mathrm{path}_\mathcal{T}(b)} f_e(a, \sigma),$$

where $f_e \in \mathcal{E}_e^{\mathrm{loc}}$ has $\|f_e\|_\infty \leq v$. The same argument as in the proof of Theorem 37.17 shows that $f \in \mathcal{E}^{\mathrm{vec}}$. Moving to the objective in Eq. (37.16), we lower-bound the loss estimates:

$$\frac{\eta f(a, \sigma)_b}{p_a} = \frac{\eta}{p_a} \sum_{e \in \text{path}_{\mathcal{T}}(b)} f_e(a, \sigma) \geq -\frac{\eta v k^2}{\gamma} = -1. \tag{37.17}$$

Fix $i \in [k]$. The stability term is bounded using the properties of p and f as follows:

$$\frac{1}{\eta^2} \sum_{a=1}^{k} p_a \Psi_q \left(\frac{\eta f(a, \Phi_{ai})}{p_a} \right) \leq \sum_{a=1}^{k} \sum_{b \in \Pi} \frac{q_b}{p_a} f(a, \Phi_{ai})_b^2$$

$$= \sum_{a=1}^{k} \sum_{b \in \Pi} \frac{q_b}{p_a} \left(\sum_{e \in \text{path}_{\mathcal{T}}(b)} f_e(a, \Phi_{ai}) \right)^2$$

$$\leq 2v^2 \sum_{a=1}^{k} \sum_{b \in \Pi} \frac{q_b}{r_a} \left(\sum_{e \in \text{path}_{\mathcal{T}}(b)} \mathbb{I}\{a \in \mathcal{N}_e\} \right)^2$$

$$\leq 8v^2 \sum_{a=1}^{k} \sum_{b \in \Pi} \frac{q_b}{r_a} \mathbb{I}\{a \in \cup_{e \in \text{path}_{\mathcal{T}}(b)} \mathcal{N}_e\}$$

$$\leq 8v^2 \sum_{a=1}^{k} \sum_{b \in \Pi} \frac{q_b}{r_b}$$

$$\leq 8k^3 v^2.$$

Here, in the first inequality we used Eq. (37.15) and Eq. (37.17). The second inequality follows by the definition of $v = v_{\text{loc}}$ and the choice of $f_e \in \mathscr{E}_e^{\text{loc}}$, and also because $p_a \geq r_a/2$ by the condition on η in the theorem statement. The third since any action a is in $\mathcal{N}_e$ for at most two edges in $e \in \text{path}_{\mathcal{T}}(b)$ (because $V(\mathcal{T}) \subset \Pi$ and it has no duplicates). The fourth inequality is true since r is $\mathcal{T}$-increasing and the fifth because $r \geq q/k$. Finally, by Part (c) of Lemma 37.20 and the fact that $\mathcal{L}\lambda$ is $\mathcal{T}$-decreasing,

$$\frac{1}{\eta}(p - q)^\top \mathcal{L}\lambda = \frac{1 - \gamma}{\eta}(r - q)^\top \mathcal{L}\lambda + \frac{\gamma}{\eta}(1/k - q)^\top \mathcal{L}\lambda \leq k^2 v \leq k^3 \max(1, v^2).$$

Combining the previous two displays shows that

$$\frac{(p - q)^\top \mathcal{L}\lambda}{\eta} + \frac{1}{\eta^2} \sum_{i=1}^{d} \lambda_i \sum_{a=1}^{k} p_a \Psi_q \left(\frac{\eta f(a, \Phi_{ai})}{p_a} \right) \leq 9k^3 \max(1, v^2).$$

Since the right-hand side is independent of λ, the result follows from Eq. (37.16). □

37.8 Proof of the Classification Theorem

Almost all the results are now available to prove Theorem 37.11. In Section 37.4, we showed that if G is globally observable and not locally observable, then $R_n^*(G) = \Omega(n^{2/3})$. We also proved that if G is locally observable and has neighbours, then $R_n^*(G) = \Omega(\sqrt{n})$. This last result is complemented by the policy and analysis in Sections 37.5 to 37.7, where we showed that for globally observable games $R_n^*(G) = O(n^{2/3})$ and for locally observable games $R_n^*(G) = O(\sqrt{n})$. Finally we proved that if G is not globally observable, then $R_n^*(G) = \Omega(n)$. All that remains is to prove that if G has no neighbouring actions, then $R_n^*(G) = 0$.

THEOREM 37.22. *If G has no neighbouring actions, then $R_n^*(G) = 0$.*

Proof Since G has no neighbouring actions, there exists an action a such that $C_a = \mathcal{P}_{d-1}$ and the policy that chooses $A_t = a$ for all rounds suffers no regret.   □

37.9 Notes

1 The next three notes are covering some basic definitions and facts in linear algebra. There are probably hundreds of introductory texts on linear algebra. A short and intuitive exposition is by Axler [1997].

2 A non-empty set $L \subseteq \mathbb{R}^n$ is a **linear subspace** of $\mathbb{R}^n$ if $\alpha v + \beta w \in L$ for all $\alpha, \beta \in \mathbb{R}$ and $v, w \in L$. If L and M are linear subspaces of $\mathbb{R}^n$, then $L \oplus M = \{v + w : L \in L, w \in M\}$. The **orthogonal complement** of linear subspace L is $L^\perp = \{v \in \mathbb{R}^n : \langle u, v \rangle = 0 \text{ for all } u \in L\}$. The following properties are easily checked: *(i)* $L^\perp$ is a linear subspace, *(ii)* $(L^\perp)^\perp = L$ and *(iii)* $(L \cap M)^\perp = L^\perp \oplus M^\perp$.

3 Let $A \in \mathbb{R}^{m \times n}$ be a matrix and recall that matrices of this form correspond to linear maps from $\mathbb{R}^n \to \mathbb{R}^m$ where the function $A : \mathbb{R}^n \to \mathbb{R}^m$ is given by matrix multiplication, $A(x) = Ax$. The **image** of A is $\mathrm{im}(A) = \{Ax : x \in \mathbb{R}^n\}$, and the **kernel** is $\ker(A) = \{x \in \mathbb{R}^n : Ax = 0\}$. Notice that $\mathrm{im}(A) \subseteq \mathbb{R}^m$ and $\ker(A) \subseteq \mathbb{R}^n$. One can easily check that $\mathrm{im}(A)$ and $\ker(A^\top)$ are linear subspaces, and an elementary theorem in linear algebra says that $\mathrm{im}(A) \oplus \ker(A^\top) = \mathbb{R}^m$ for any matrix $A \in \mathbb{R}^{m \times n}$. Finally, if $u \in \mathrm{im}(A)$ and $v \in \ker(A^\top)$, then $\langle u, v \rangle = 0$.

4 Given a set $A \subseteq \mathbb{R}^d$, the **affine hull** is the set

$$\mathrm{aff}(A) = \left\{ \sum_{i=1}^{j} \alpha_i x_i : j > 0,\ \alpha \in \mathbb{R}^j,\ x_i \in A \text{ for all } i \in [j] \text{ and } \sum_{i=1}^{j} \alpha_i = 1 \right\}.$$

Its dimension is the smallest m such that there exist vectors $v_1, \ldots, v_m \in \mathbb{R}^d$ such that $\mathrm{aff}(A) = x_\circ + \mathrm{span}(v_1, \ldots, v_m)$ for any $x_\circ \in A$.

5 We introduced the stochastic variant of partial monitoring to prove our lower bounds. Of course our upper bounds also apply to this setting, which means the classification theorem also holds in the stochastic case. The interesting question is to understand the problem-dependent regret, which for partial monitoring problem $G = (\mathcal{L}, \Phi)$ is

$$R_n(\pi, u) = \max_{a \in [k]} \mathbb{E}\left[\sum_{t=1}^{n} \langle \ell_{A_t} - \ell_a, U_t \rangle \right],$$

where $U, U_1, \ldots, U_n$ is a sequence of independent and identically distributed random vectors with $U_t \in \{e_1, \ldots, e_d\}$ and $\mathbb{E}[U] = u \in \mathcal{P}_{d-1}$. Provided G is not hopeless, one can derive an algorithm for which the regret is logarithmic, and like in bandits there is a sense of asymptotic optimality. The open research question is to understand the in-between regime where the horizon is not yet large enough that the asymptotically optimal logarithmic regret guarantees become meaningful, but not so small that minimax is acceptable.

6 More generally, a **stochastic partial monitoring problem** by a probability kernel $(P_{\theta,a} : \theta \in \Theta, a \in \mathcal{A})$ from $(\Theta \times \mathcal{A}, \mathcal{F} \otimes \mathcal{G})$ to $(\Sigma \times \mathbb{R}, \mathcal{H} \otimes \mathcal{B}(\mathbb{R}))$. The environment chooses $\theta \in \Theta$, and the learner chooses $(A_t)_{t=1}^n$ with $A_t \in A$ and observes $(\sigma_t)_{t=1}^n$ in a sequential manner, where $(\sigma_t, X_t) \sim P_{\theta,A_t}(\cdot)$. The reward X_t of round t is unobserved. As before, the learner's goal is to maximise the total expected reward or, equivalently, to minimise regret. The special case of the previous note is has been studied under the name of finite stochastic partial monitoring.

7 The optimal tuning of the bound for Algorithm 26 depends on $\mathrm{opt}^*(\eta)$, which may be hard to compute. A simple way to address this problem is to use an adaptive learning rate:

$$\eta_t = \min\left\{\frac{1}{B}, \sqrt{\frac{\log(k)}{1 + \sum_{s=1}^{t-1} V_s}}\right\},$$

where $V_t = \max\{0, \mathrm{opt}_{Q_t}(\eta_t)\}$ and B is chosen large enough that η_1 is sufficiently small to satisfy the conditions needed in either Theorem 37.16 or Theorem 37.17. An excessively large B only affects the regret in an additive fashion. The adaptive algorithm only needs to solve the optimisation in Eq. (37.12) and not $\mathrm{opt}^*(\eta)$. Another benefit of the adaptive algorithm is that it only depends on the game through the constant B. Furthermore, the bound depends on $(V_t)_{t=1}^n$, rather than $\mathrm{opt}^*(\eta)$, which may sometimes be beneficial. The analysis of the algorithm uses the same techniques as developed in Exercise 28.13 and is given by Lattimore and Szepesvári [2019d].

8 Algorithm 26 can be modified in several ways. One enhancement is to drop the constraint that $f \in \mathscr{E}^{\mathrm{vec}}$ in the optimisation problem and introduce the worst case bias of f as a penalty. Certainly this does not make the bounds worse. A more significant change is to introduce a moment-generating function into the optimisation problem, which leads to high-probability bounds [Lattimore and Szepesvári, 2019d].

9 The optimisation problem in Algorithm 26 is convex and can be solved using standard solvers when k and d are small and η is not too small. When η is small and/or k or d is large, then numerical instability is a real challenge. One way to address this issue is to approximate the exponential in the definition of Ψ_q with a quadratic and add constraints on p and f that ensure the approximation is reasonable. Since the analysis uses p and f satisfying these conditions, none of the theory changes. What is bought by this approximation is that the resulting optimisation problem becomes a second order cone program, rather than an exponential cone program, and these are better behaved. More details are in our paper: [Lattimore and Szepesvári, 2019d].

10 Partial monitoring has many potential applications. We already mentioned dynamic pricing and spam filtering. In the latter case, acquiring the true label comes at a price, which is a typical component of hard partial monitoring problems. In general, there are many set-ups where the learner can pay extra for high-quality information. For example, in medical diagnosis the doctor can request additional tests before recommending a treatment plan, but these cost time and money. Yet another potential application is quality testing in factory production where the quality control team can choose which items to test (at great cost).

11 There are many possible extensions to the partial monitoring framework. We have only discussed problems where the number of actions/feedbacks/outcomes is potentially infinite, but nothing prevents studying a more general setting. Suppose the learner chooses a sequence of real-valued outcomes $i_1, \ldots, i_n$ with $i_t \in [0, 1]$. In each round, the learner chooses $A_t \in [k]$ and observes $\Phi_{A_t}(i_t)$, where $\Phi_a : [0, 1] \to \Sigma$ is a known feedback function. The loss is determined by a collection of known functions $\mathcal{L}_a : [0, 1] \to [0, 1]$. We do not know of any systematic study of this setting. The reader can no doubt imagine generalising this idea to infinite action sets or introducing a linear structure for the loss.

12 A pair of Pareto-optimal actions (a, b) are called **weak neighbours** if $C_a \cap C_b \neq \emptyset$ and **pairwise observable** if there exists a function g satisfying Eq. (37.3) and with $g(c, f) = 0$ whenever $c \notin \{a, b\}$. A partial monitoring problem is called a **point-locally observable game** if all weak neighbours are pairwise observable. All point-locally observable games are locally observable, but the converse is not true. Bartók [2013] designed a policy for this type of game for which

$$R_n \leq \frac{1}{\varepsilon_G} \sqrt{k_{\text{loc}} n \log(n)},$$

where $\varepsilon_G > 0$ is a game-dependent constant and k_{loc} is the size of the largest $A \subseteq [k]$ of Pareto optimal actions such that $\cap_{a \in A} C_a \neq \emptyset$. Using a different policy, Lattimore and Szepesvári [2019a] have shown that as the horizon grows, the game-dependence diminishes so that

$$\limsup_{n \to \infty} \frac{R_n}{\sqrt{n}} \leq 8(2 + m) \sqrt{2 k_{\text{loc}} \log(k)}.$$

13 Linear regret is unavoidable in hopeless games, but that does not mean there is nothing to play for. Rustichini [1999] considered a version of the regret that captures the performance of policies in this harsh setting. Given $p \in \mathcal{P}_{d-1}$ define set $\mathcal{I}(p) \subseteq \mathcal{P}_{d-1}$ by

$$\mathcal{I}(p) = \left\{ q \in \mathcal{P}_{d-1} : \sum_{i=1}^{d} (p_i - q_i) \mathbb{I}\{\Phi_{ai} = f\} = 0 \text{ for all } a \in [k] \text{ and } f \in [m] \right\}.$$

This is the set of distributions over the outcomes that are indistinguishable from p by the learner using any actions. Then define

$$f(p) = \max_{q \in \mathcal{I}(p)} \min_{a \in [k]} \sum_{i=1}^{d} q_i \mathcal{L}_{ai}.$$

Rustichini [1999] proved there exist policies such that

$$\lim_{n \to \infty} \max_{i_{1:n}} \mathbb{E}\left[\frac{1}{n} \sum_{t=1}^{n} \mathcal{L}_{A_t i_t} - f(\bar{u}_n) \right] = 0,$$

where $\bar{u}_n = \frac{1}{n} \sum_{t=1}^{n} e_{i_t} \in \mathcal{P}_{d-1}$ is the average outcome chosen by the adversary. Intuitively this means the learner does not compete with the best action in hindsight with respect to the actual outcomes. Instead, the learner competes with the best action in hindsight with respect to an outcome sequence that is indistinguishable from the actual outcome sequence. Rustichini did not prove rates on the convergence of the limit. This has been remedied recently, and we give some references in the bibliographic remarks.

14 Partial monitoring is still quite poorly understood. With some exceptions, we do not know how the regret should depend on d, k, m or the structure of G. Lower bounds that depend on these quantities are also missing, and the lower bounds proven in Section 37.4 are surely very conservative. We hope this chapter inspires more activity in this area. The setting described in Note 13 is even more wide open, where the dependence on n is still not nailed down.

37.10 Bibliographical Remarks

The first work on partial monitoring is by Rustichini [1999], who focussed on finding Hannan consistent policies in the adversarial setting. Rustichini shows how to reduce the problem to Blackwell approachability (see Cesa-Bianchi and Lugosi [2006]) and uses this to deduce the existence of a Hannan consistent strategy. Rustichini also used a refined notion of regret that allows one to distinguish between learners even in the case of hopeless games (see Note 13). The first non-asymptotic result in the setting of this chapter is due to Piccolboni and Schindelhauer [2001], who derive a policy with regret $O(n^{3/4})$ for globally observable games. Cesa-Bianchi et al. [2006] reduced the dependence to $O(n^{2/3})$ and proved a wide range of other results for specific classes of problems. The first $O(n^{1/2})$ bound for non-degenerate locally observable games is due to Foster and Rakhlin [2012]. The classification theorem when $d = 2$ is due to Bartók et al. [2010] (extended version: Antos et al. [2013]). With the exception of degenerate games, the classification of adversarial partial monitoring games is by Bartók et al. [2014]. The case of degenerate games was resolved by the present authors [Lattimore and Szepesvári, 2019a]. The policies mentioned in Note 12 are due to Bartók [2013] and Lattimore and Szepesvári [2019a]. We warn the reader that neighbours are defined differently by Foster and Rakhlin [2012] and Bartók [2013], which can lead to confusion. Additionally, although both papers are largely correct, in both cases the core proofs contain errors that cannot be resolved without changing the policies [Lattimore and Szepesvári, 2019a]. Algorithm 26 and its analysis is also by the present authors [Lattimore and Szepesvári, 2019d], which is a followup on an earlier information-theoretic analysis [Lattimore and Szepesvári, 2019c].

There is a growing literature on the stochastic setting where it is common to study both minimax and asymptotic bounds. In the latter case, one can obtain asymptotically optimal logarithmic regret for games that are not hopeless. We refer the reader to papers by Bartók et al. [2012], Vanchinathan et al. [2014] and Komiyama et al. [2015b] as a good starting place. As we mentioned, partial monitoring can model problems that lie between bandits and full information. There are now several papers on this topic, but in more restricted settings and consequentially with more practical algorithms and bounds. One such model is when the learner is playing actions corresponding to vertices on a graph and observes the losses associated with the chosen vertex and its neighbours [Mannor and Shamir, 2011, Alon et al., 2013]. A related result is in the finite-armed Gaussian setting where the learner selects an action $A_t \in [k]$ and observes a Gaussian sample from each arm, but with variances depending on the chosen action. Like partial monitoring, this problem exhibits many challenges and is not yet well understood [Wu et al., 2015]. We mentioned in Note 13 that for hopeless games, the definition of the regret can be refined. A number of authors have studied this setting and proved sublinear regret guarantees. As usual, the price of generality is that the bounds are correspondingly a bit worse [Mannor and Shimkin, 2003, Perchet, 2011, Mannor et al., 2014]. There has been some work on infinite partial monitoring games. Lin et al. [2014] study a stochastic setting with finitely many actions, but infinitely many outcomes and a particular linear structure for the feedback. Chaudhuri and Tewari [2016] also consider a linear setting with global observability and prove $O(n^{2/3} \log(n))$ regret using an explore-then-commit algorithm. Kirschner et al. [2020] study a version of information-directed sampling in partial monitoring setting with a linear feedback structure and finitely or infinitely many actions.

One can also add context, as usual. The special case of stochastic finite contextual partial monitoring has been considered by Bartók and Szepesvári [2012]. In this version, the learner is still given the matrices $(\mathcal{L}, \Phi)$, but also a set of functions $\mathcal{F}$ that map a sequence $(x_t)_t$ of contexts to outcome distributions, with the assumption that the outcome in round t is generated from $f(x_t)$ with $f \in \mathcal{F}$ unknown to the learner. A special case, apple tasting with context (equivalently, matching pennies with context) is the subject of the paper of Helmbold et al. [2000]. The aforementioned paper by Kirschner et al. [2020] also studies the contextual partial monitoring problem in a linear setting.

37.11 Exercises

37.1 (PERSPECTIVE) Prove that the perspective as defined in Eq. (37.14) is convex.

37.2 (AFFINE SETS AND DIMENSION) Let $\mathcal{X} \subseteq \mathcal{Y} \subseteq \mathbb{R}^d$ and $\dim(\mathcal{X}) = \dim(\mathcal{Y})$. Prove that $\mathrm{aff}(\mathcal{X}) = \mathrm{aff}(\mathcal{Y})$.

37.3 (MODIFIED KERNEL) Recall that $\ker'(x) = \{u : u^\top x = 0 \text{ and } u^\top \mathbf{1} = 1\}$. Show that if $\ker'(x) = \ker'(y) \neq \emptyset$ then x and y are proportional.

37.4 (STRUCTURE OF EXAMPLES) Calculate the neighbourhood structure, cell decomposition and action classification for each of the examples in this chapter.

37.5 (APPLE TASTING) Apples arrive sequentially from the farm to a processing facility. Most apples are fine, but occasionally there is a rotten one. The only way to figure out whether an apple is good or rotten is to taste it. For some reason customers do not like bite marks in the apples they buy, which means that tested apples cannot be sold. Good apples yield a unit reward when sold, while the sale of a bad apple costs the company $c > 0$.

(a) Formulate this problem as a partial monitoring problem: determine $\mathcal{L}$ and Φ.

(b) What is the minimax regret in this problem?

(c) What do you think about this problem? Will actual farmers be excited about your analysis?

37.6 (TWO-ACTION PARTIAL MONITORING GAMES ARE TRIVIAL, HOPELESS OR EASY) Let $G = (\mathcal{L}, \Phi)$ be a partial monitoring game with $k = 2$ actions. Prove that G is either trivial, hopeless or easy.

37.7 (COMPLETE LOWER BOUND FOR HARD GAMES) Complete the last step in the proof of Theorem 37.12.

37.8 (LOWER BOUND FOR EASY GAMES) Prove Theorem 37.14.

37.9 (LOWER BOUND FOR HOPELESS GAMES) Prove Theorem 37.13.

37.10 Let a and b be non-duplicate Pareto optimal actions and $\lambda \in \mathrm{ri}(C_a)$. Show there exists an $\omega \in \mathrm{ri}(C_b)$ and neighbour c of b such that $C_c \cap [\omega, \lambda] \neq \emptyset$.

HINT   It may be useful to look at Fig. 37.6 to get some tips. The figure depicts a slightly different situation, but is still useful when it is changed a little.

37.11 Generalise the proofs of Lemma 37.20 and Lemma 37.21 to handle duplicate and degenerate actions.

37.12 Prove Proposition 37.18.

HINT   For Part (a), let $S \in \mathbb{R}^{km \times d}$ be obtained by stacking $(S_c)_{c=1}^k$, defined as in the proof of Theorem 37.12. Then argue that for globally observable games, $\sqrt{d}$ times the reciprocal of the smallest non-zero singular value of S is an upper bound on v_{glo} and then use the fact that $S^\top S$ has integer-valued coefficients. Part (b) follows in a similar fashion. For Part (c), use a graph-theoretic argument.

37.13 Let $m = |\Sigma| = 2$ and $d = 2k - 1$ and construct a globally observable game for which there exists a pair of neighbouring actions a, b for which

$$\min_{f \in \mathscr{E}_{ab}^{glo}} \|f\| \geq C2^{d/2},$$

where $C > 0$ is a universal constant.

37.14 Prove Proposition 37.19.

HINT Find choices of p and f that reduce the algorithm to Exp3 and exponential weights respectively.

37.15 (LOWER BOUND DEPENDING ON THE NUMBER OF FEEDBACKS) Consider $G = (\mathcal{L}, \Phi)$ given by

$$\mathcal{L} = \begin{pmatrix} 1 & 0 & 1 & 0 & \cdots & 1 & 0 \\ 0 & 1 & 0 & 1 & \cdots & 0 & 1 \end{pmatrix} \quad \text{and}$$

$$\Phi = \begin{pmatrix} 1 & 2 & 2 & 3 & 3 & 4 & \cdots & m-1 & m-1 & m \\ 1 & 1 & 2 & 2 & 3 & 3 & \cdots & m-2 & m-1 & m-1 \end{pmatrix}.$$

(a) Show this game is locally observable.

(b) Prove that for $n \geq m$, there exists a universal constant $c > 0$ such that $R_n^*(G) \geq c(m-1)\sqrt{n}$.

> The source for previous exercise is the paper by the authors [Lattimore and Szepesvári, 2019a].

37.16 (DIVERGENCE DECOMPOSITION FOR PARTIAL MONITORING) Complete the necessary modification of Lemma 15.1 to show that Eq. (37.8) is true.

37.17 (ALGORITHM FOR CLASSIFYING GAMES) Write a program that accepts as input matrices $\mathcal{L}$ and Φ and outputs the classification of the game.

37.18 (IMPLEMENTATION (I)) Implement a solver for the optimisation problem in Eq. (37.12). Consider the matching pennies problem (Example 37.3). Let $\eta = 1/100$ and plot $\text{opt}^*(\eta)$ as a function of the cost c. Explain your results.

HINT The convex optimisation problem in Eq. (37.12) seems to cause problems for some solvers (see Note 9 for some mitigating strategies). We assume that many libraries can be made to work. Our implementation used the splitting cone solver by O'Donoghue et al. [2016, 2017]. Your plot should resemble Fig. 37.7.

37.19 (IMPLEMENTATION (II)) In this exercise you will compare empirically or otherwise Algorithm 26 to exponential weights and Exp3 on full information and bandit games. Specifically:

(a) For full information games, exponential weights behaves like Algorithm 26 except that $\hat{y}_t = y_t$ and $P_t = Q_t$. Does the solution to the optimisation problem used by Algorithm 26 lead to the same loss estimators and distribution P_t?

(b) For bandits, Exp3 uses $\hat{y}_{ta} = y_{ta}\mathbb{I}\{A_t = a\}/P_{ta}$. Does Algorithm 26 end up using the same loss estimators? Does $P_t = Q_t$?

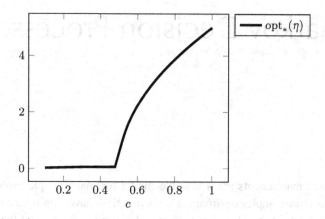

Figure 37.7   The value of opt*(η) as a function of c in matching pennies (Example 37.3).

HINT   You can approach this problem by using your solution to Exercise 37.18 and comparing values empirically. Alternatively, you can theoretically analyse Eq. (37.12) in these special cases. Some of these questions are answered by Lattimore and Szepesvári [2019d].

38 Markov Decision Processes

Bandit environments are a sensible model for many simple problems, but they do not model more complex environments where actions have long-term consequences. A brewing company needs to plan ahead when ordering ingredients, and the decisions made today affect their position to brew the right amount of beer in the future. A student learning mathematics benefits not only from the immediate reward of learning an interesting topic but also from their improved job prospects.

A **Markov decision process** (MDP) is a simple way to incorporate long-term planning into the bandit framework. Like in bandits, the learner chooses actions and receives rewards. But they also observe a **state**, and the rewards for different actions depend on the state. Furthermore, the actions chosen affect which state will be observed next.

38.1 Problem Set-Up

An MDP is defined by a tuple $M = (\mathcal{S}, \mathcal{A}, P, r, \mu)$. The first two items $\mathcal{S}$ and $\mathcal{A}$ are sets called the **state space** and **action space**, and $S = |\mathcal{S}|$ and $A = |\mathcal{A}|$ are their sizes, which may be infinite. An MDP is finite if $S, A < \infty$. The quantity $P = (P_a : a \in \mathcal{A})$ is called the **transition function** with $P_a : \mathcal{S} \times \mathcal{S} \to [0, 1]$ so that $P_a(s, s')$ is the probability that the learner transitions from state s to s' when taking action a. The fourth element of the tuple is $r = (r_a : a \in \mathcal{A})$, which is a collection of **reward functions** with $r_a : \mathcal{S} \to [0, 1]$. When the learner takes action a in state s, it receives a deterministic reward of $r_a(s)$. The last element is $\mu \in \mathcal{P}(\mathcal{S})$, which is a distribution over the states that determines the starting state. The transition and reward functions are often represented by vectors or matrices. When the state space is finite, we may assume without loss of generality that $\mathcal{S} = [S]$. We write $P_a(s) \in [0, 1]^S$ as the probability vector with s'th coordinate given by $P_a(s, s')$. In the same way, we let $P_a \in [0, 1]^{S \times S}$ be the right stochastic matrix with $(P_a)_{s,s'} = P_a(s, s')$. Finally, we view r_a as a vector in $[0, 1]^S$ in the natural way.

The interaction protocol is similar to bandits. Before the game starts, the initial state S_1 is sampled from μ. In each round t, the learner observes the state $S_t \in \mathcal{S}$, chooses an action $A_t \in \mathcal{A}$ and receives reward $r_{A_t}(S_t)$. The environment then samples S_{t+1} from the probability vector $P_{A_t}(S_t)$, and the next round begins (Fig. 38.1).

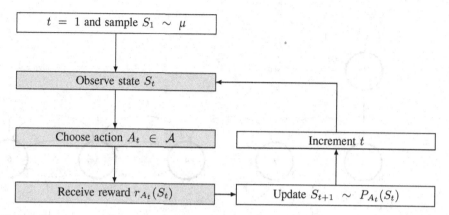

Figure 38.1   Interaction protocol for Markov decision processes.

Although the action set is the same in all states, this does not mean that $P_a(s)$ or $r_a(s)$ has any relationship to $P_a(s')$ or $r_a(s')$ for states $s \neq s'$. In this sense, it might be better to use an entirely different set of actions for each state, which would not change the results we present. And while we are at it, of course one could also allow the number of actions to vary over the state space.

Histories and Policies

Before considering the learning problem, we explain how to act in a known MDP. Because there is no learning going on, we call our protagonist the 'agent' rather than 'learner'. In a stochastic bandit, the optimal policy given knowledge of the bandit is to choose the action with the largest expected reward in every round. In an MDP, the definition of optimality is less clear.

The **history** $H_t = (S_1, A_1, \ldots, S_{t-1}, A_{t-1}, S_t)$ in round t contains the information available before the action for the round is to be chosen. Note that state S_t is included in H_t. The actions are also included because the agent may randomise. For simplicity the rewards are omitted because the all-knowing agent can recompute them if needed from the state-action pairs.

A **policy** is a (possibly randomised) map from the set of possible histories to actions. Simple policies include **memoryless policies**, which choose actions based on only the current state, possibly in a randomised manner. The set of such policies is denoted by Π_M, and its elements are identified with maps $\pi : \mathcal{A} \times \mathcal{S} \rightarrow [0,1]$ with $\sum_{a \in \mathcal{A}} \pi(a \mid s) = 1$ for any $s \in \mathcal{S}$ so that $\pi(a \mid s)$ is interpreted as the probability that policy π takes action a in state s.

A memoryless policy that does not randomise is called a **memoryless deterministic policy**. To reduce clutter, such policies are written as $\mathcal{S} \rightarrow \mathcal{A}$ maps, and the set of all such policies is denoted by Π_{DM}. A policy is called a **Markov policy** if the actions are randomised and depend only on the round index and the previous state. These policies are represented by fixed sequences of memoryless policies. Under a Markov policy, the sequence of states $(S_1, S_2, \ldots)$ evolve as a Markov chain (see Section 3.2). If the Markov policy is memoryless, this chain is homogeneous.

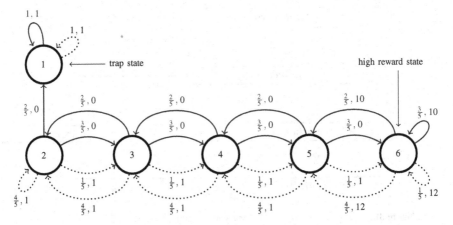

Figure 38.2 A Markov decision process with six states and two actions represented by solid and dashed arrows, respectively. The numbers next to each arrow represent the probability of transition and reward for the action respectively. For example, taking the solid action in state 3 results in a reward of 0, and the probability of moving to state 4 is 3/5, and the probability of moving to state 3 is 2/5. For human interpretability only, the actions are given consistent meaning across the states (blue/solid actions 'increment' the state index, black/dashed actions decrement it). In reality there is no sense of similarity between states or actions built into the MDP formalism.

Probability Spaces

It will be convenient to allow infinitely long interactions between the learner and the environment. In line with Fig. 38.1, when the agent or learner follows a policy π in MDP $M = (\mathcal{S}, \mathcal{A}, P, r, \mu)$, such a never-ending interaction gives rise to a random process $(S_1, A_1, S_2, A_2, \ldots)$ so that for any $s, s' \in \mathcal{S}$, $a \in \mathcal{A}$ and $t \geq 1$,

(a) $\mathbb{P}(S_1 = s) = \mu(s)$;
(b) $\mathbb{P}(S_{t+1} = s' \mid H_t, A_t) = P_{A_t}(S_t, s')$; and
(c) $\mathbb{P}(A_t = a \mid H_t) = \pi(a \mid H_t)$.

Meticulous readers may wonder whether there exists a probability space $(\Omega, \mathcal{F}, \mathbb{P})$ holding the infinite sequence of random variables $(S_1, A_1, S_2, A_2, \ldots)$ that satisfy (a)–(c). The Ionescu–Tulcea theorem (Theorem 3.3) furnishes us with a positive answer (Exercise 38.1). Item (b) above is known as the **Markov property**. Of course the measure $\mathbb{P}$ depends on the policy, Markov decision process and the initial distribution. For most of the chapter, these quantities will be fixed and the dependence is omitted from the notation. In the few places where disambiguation is necessary, we provide additional notation. In addition to this, to minimise clutter, we allow ourselves to write $\mathbb{P}(\cdot \mid S_1 = s)$, which just means the probability distribution that results from the interconnection of π and M, while replacing μ with an alternative initial state distribution that is a Dirac at s.

Traps and the Diameter of a Markov Decision Process

A significant complication in MDPs is the potential for traps. A trap is a subset of the state space from which there is no escape. For example, the MDP in Fig. 38.2 has a trap state. If being in the trap has a suboptimal yield in terms of the reward, the learner should avoid the trap. But since the learner can only discover that an action leads to a trap by trying that action, the problem of learning while competing with a fully informed agent is hopeless (Exercise 38.28).

To avoid this complication, we restrict our attention to MDPs with no traps. An MDP is called **strongly connected** or **communicating** if for any pair of states $s, s' \in \mathcal{S}$, there exists a policy such that when starting from s there is a positive probability of reaching s' some time in the future while following the policy. One can also define a real-valued measure of the connectedness of an MDP called the **diameter**. MDPs with smaller diameter are usually easier to learn because a policy can recover from mistakes more quickly.

DEFINITION 38.1. The diameter of an MDP M is

$$D(M) = \max_{s \neq s'} \min_{\pi \in \Pi_{\mathrm{DM}}} \mathbb{E}^{\pi}\left[\min\{t \geq 1 : S_t = s\} \mid S_1 = s'\right] - 1,$$

where the expectation is taken with respect to the law of Markov chain $(S_t)_{t=1}^{\infty}$ induced by the interaction between π and M.

A number of observations are in order about this definition. First, the order of the maximum and minimum means that for any pair of states a different policy may be used. Second, travel times are always minimised by deterministic memoryless policies, so the restriction to these policies in the minimum is inessential (Exercise 38.3). Finally, the definition only considers distinct states. We also note that when the number of states is finite, it holds that $D(M) < \infty$ if and only if M is strongly connected (Exercise 38.4). The diameter of an MDP with S states and A actions cannot be smaller than $\log_A(S) - 3$ (Exercise 38.5).

For the remainder of this chapter, unless otherwise specified, all MDPs are assumed to be strongly connected.

38.2 Optimal Policies and the Bellman Optimality Equation

We now define the notion of an optimal policy and outline the proof that there exists a deterministic memoryless optimal policy. Along the way, we define what is called the Bellman optimality equation. Methods that solve this equation are the basis for finding optimal policies in an efficient manner and also play a significant role in learning algorithms. Throughout, we fix a strongly connected MDP M.

The **gain** of a policy π is the long-term average reward expected from using that policy when starting in state s:

$$\rho_s^{\pi} = \lim_{n \to \infty} \frac{1}{n} \sum_{t=1}^{n} \mathbb{E}^{\pi}[r_{A_t}(S_t) \mid S_1 = s],$$

where $\mathbb{E}^{\pi}$ denotes the expectation on the interaction sequence when policy π interacts with MDP M. In general, the limit need not exist, so we also introduce

$$\bar{\rho}_s^{\pi} = \limsup_{n \to \infty} \frac{1}{n} \sum_{t=1}^{n} \mathbb{E}^{\pi}[r_{A_t}(S_t) \mid S_1 = s],$$

which exists for any policy. Of course, whenever ρ_s^π exists we have $\rho_s^\pi = \bar{\rho}_s^\pi$. The **optimal gain** is a real value

$$\rho^* = \max_{s \in \mathcal{S}} \sup_\pi \bar{\rho}_s^\pi,$$

where the supremum is taken over all policies. A π policy is an **optimal policy** if $\rho^\pi = \rho^* \mathbf{1}$. For strongly connected MDPs, an optimal policy is guaranteed to exist. This is far from trivial, however, and we will spend the next little while outlining the proof.

 MDPs that are not strongly connected may not have a constant optimal gain. This makes everything more complicated, and we are lucky not to have to deal with such MDPs here.

Before continuing, we need some new notation. For a memoryless policy π, define

$$P_\pi(s, s') = \sum_{a \in \mathcal{A}} \pi(a \mid s) P_a(s, s') \qquad \text{and} \qquad r_\pi(s) = \sum_{a \in \mathcal{A}} \pi(a \mid s) r_a(s). \tag{38.1}$$

We view P_π as an $S \times S$ **transition matrix** and r_π as a vector in $\mathbb{R}^S$. With this notation, P_π is the transition matrix of the homogeneous Markov chain $S_1, S_2, \ldots$ when $A_t \sim \pi(\cdot \mid S_t)$. The gain of a memoryless policy π satisfies

$$\rho^\pi = \lim_{n \to \infty} \frac{1}{n} \sum_{t=1}^{n} P_\pi^{t-1} r_\pi = P_\pi^* r_\pi, \tag{38.2}$$

where $P_\pi^* = \lim_{n \to \infty} \frac{1}{n} \sum_{t=1}^{n} P_\pi^{t-1}$ is called the **stationary transition matrix**, the existence of which you will prove in Exercise 38.7. For each $k \in \mathbb{N}$, define

$$v_\pi^{(k)} = \sum_{t=1}^{k} P_\pi^{t-1} (r_\pi - \rho^\pi).$$

For $s \in \mathcal{S}$, $v_\pi^{(k)}(s)$ gives the total expected excess reward collected by π when the process starts at state s and lasts for k time steps. The **(differential) value function** of a policy is a function $v_\pi : \mathcal{S} \to \mathbb{R}$ defined as the **Cesàro sum** of the sequence $(P_\pi^t (r_\pi - \rho^\pi))_{t \geq 0}$,

$$v_\pi = \lim_{n \to \infty} \frac{1}{n} \sum_{k=1}^{n} v_\pi^{(k)} = ((I - P_\pi + P_\pi^*)^{-1} - P_\pi^*) r_\pi. \tag{38.3}$$

Note, the second equality above is non-trivial (Exercise 38.7). The definition implies that $v_\pi(s) - v_\pi(s')$ is the 'average' long-term advantage of starting in state s relative to starting in state s' when following policy π. These quantities are only defined for memoryless policies where they are also guaranteed to exist (Exercise 38.7). The definition of P_π^* implies that $P_\pi^* P_\pi = P_\pi^*$, which in turn implies that $P_\pi^* v_\pi = 0$. Combining this with Eqs. (38.2) and (38.3) shows that for any memoryless policy π,

$$\rho^\pi + v_\pi = r_\pi + P_\pi v_\pi. \tag{38.4}$$

A **value function** is a function $v : \mathcal{S} \to \mathbb{R}$, and its **span** is given by

$$\operatorname{span}(v) = \max_{s \in \mathcal{S}} v(s) - \min_{s \in \mathcal{S}} v(s).$$

As with other quantities, value functions are associated with vectors in $\mathbb{R}^S$. A **greedy policy** with respect to value function v is a deterministic memoryless policy π_v given by

$$\pi_v(s) = \operatorname{argmax}_{a \in A} r_a(s) + \langle P_a(s), v \rangle.$$

There may be many policies that are greedy with respect to some value function v due to ties in the maximum. Usually the ties do not matter, but for consistency and for the sake of simplifying matters, we assume that ties are broken in a systematic fashion. In particular, this makes π_v well defined for any value function.

One way to find the optimal policy is as the greedy policy with respect to a value function that satisfies the **Bellman optimality equation**, which is

$$\rho + v(s) = \max_{a \in A} \left(r_a(s) + \langle P_a(s), v \rangle \right) \qquad \text{for all } s \in S. \tag{38.5}$$

This is a system of S nonlinear equations with unknowns $\rho \in \mathbb{R}$ and $v \in \mathbb{R}^S$. The reader will notice that if $v : S \to \mathbb{R}$ is a solution to Eq. (38.5), then so is $v + c\mathbf{1}$ for any constant $c \in \mathbb{R}$, and hence the Bellman optimality equation lacks unique solutions. It is *not* true that the optimal value function is unique up to translation, even when M is strongly connected (Exercise 38.11). The v-part of a solution pair (ρ, v) of Eq. (38.5) is called an **optimal (differential) value function**.

THEOREM 38.2. *The following hold:*

(a) *There exists a pair (ρ, v) that satisfies the Bellman optimality equation.*
(b) *If (ρ, v) satisfies the Bellman optimality equation, then $\rho = \rho^*$ and π_v is optimal.*
(c) *There exists a deterministic memoryless optimal policy.*

Proof sketch The proof of part (a) is too long to include here, but we guide you through it in Exercise 38.10. For part (b), let (ρ, v) satisfy the Bellman equation and $\pi^* = \pi_v$ be the greedy policy with respect to v. Then, by Eq. (38.2),

$$\rho^{\pi^*} = \lim_{n \to \infty} \frac{1}{n} \sum_{t=1}^{n} P_{\pi^*}^{t-1} r_{\pi^*} = \lim_{n \to \infty} \frac{1}{n} \sum_{t=1}^{n} P_{\pi^*}^{t-1} (\rho\mathbf{1} + v - P_{\pi^*} v) = \rho\mathbf{1}.$$

Next, let π be an arbitrary Markov policy. We show that $\bar{\rho}^{\pi} \leq \rho\mathbf{1}$. The result is then completed using the result of Exercise 38.2, where you will prove that for any policy π, there exists a Markov policy with the same expected rewards. Denote by π_t the memoryless policy used at time $t = 1, 2, \ldots$ when following the Markov policy π, and for $t \geq 1$, let $P_\pi^{(t)} = P_{\pi_1} \cdots P_{\pi_t}$, while for $t = 0$, let $P_\pi^{(0)} = I$. Thus, $P_\pi^{(t)}(s, s')$ is the probability of ending up in state s' while following π from state s for t time steps. It follows that $\bar{\rho}^{\pi} = \limsup_{n \to \infty} \frac{1}{n} \sum_{t=1}^{n} P_\pi^{(t-1)} r_{\pi_t}$. Fix $t \geq 1$. Using the fact that π^* is the greedy policy with respect to v gives

$$P_\pi^{(t-1)} r_{\pi_t} = P_\pi^{(t-1)} (r_{\pi_t} + P_{\pi_t} v - P_{\pi_t} v)$$
$$\leq P_\pi^{(t-1)} (r_{\pi^*} + P_{\pi^*} v - P_{\pi_t} v)$$
$$= P_\pi^{(t-1)} (\rho\mathbf{1} + v - P_{\pi_t} v)$$
$$= \rho\mathbf{1} + P_\pi^{(t-1)} v - P_\pi^{(t)} v.$$

Taking the average of both sides over $t \in [n]$ and then taking the limit shows that $\bar{\rho}^{\pi} \leq \rho \mathbf{1}$, finishing the proof. Part (c) follows immediately from the first two parts.   □

The theorem shows that there exist solutions to the Bellman optimality equation and that the greedy policy with respect to the resulting value function is an optimal policy. We need one more result about solutions to the Bellman optimality equation, the proof of which you will provide in Exercise 38.13.

LEMMA 38.3. *Suppose that (ρ, v) satisfies the Bellman optimality equation. Then* $\mathrm{span}(v) \leq D(M)$.

The map $T : \mathbb{R}^S \to \mathbb{R}^S$ defined by $(Tv)(s) = \max_{a \in A} r_a(s) + \langle P_a(s), v \rangle$ is called the **Bellman operator**. The Bellman optimality equation can be written as $\rho \mathbf{1} + v = Tv$.

38.3 Finding an Optimal Policy (✦)

There are many ways to find an optimal policy, including value iteration, policy iteration and enumeration. These ideas are briefly discussed in Note 12. Here we describe a two-step approach based on linear programming. Consider the following constrained linear optimisation problem:

$$\underset{\rho \in \mathbb{R}, v \in \mathbb{R}^S}{\text{minimise}} \quad \rho \tag{38.6}$$

$$\text{subject to} \quad \rho + v(s) \geq r_a(s) + \langle P_a(s), v \rangle \text{ for all } s, a.$$

Recall that a constrained optimisation problem is said to be **feasible** if the set of values that satisfy the constraints are non-empty.

THEOREM 38.4. *The optimisation problem in Eq. (38.6) is feasible, and if (ρ, v) is a solution, then $\rho = \rho^*$ is the optimal gain.*

Solutions (ρ, v) to the optimisation problem in Eq. (38.6) need not satisfy the Bellman optimality equation (Exercise 38.12).

Proof of Theorem 38.4   Theorem 38.2 guarantees the existence of a pair (ρ^*, v^*) that satisfies the Bellman optimality equation:

$$\rho^* + v^*(s) = \max_{a \in A} r_a(s) + \langle P_a(s), v^* \rangle \text{ for all } s, a.$$

Hence the pair (ρ^*, v^*) satisfies the constraints in Eq. (38.6) and witnesses feasibility. Next, let (ρ, v) be a solution of Eq. (38.6). Since (ρ^*, v^*) satisfies the constraints, $\rho \leq \rho^*$ is immediate. It remains to prove that $\rho \geq \rho^*$. Let $\pi = \pi_v$ be the greedy policy with respect to v and π^* be greedy with respect to v^*. By Theorem 38.2, $\rho^* = \rho^{\pi^*}$. Furthermore,

$$P_{\pi^*}^t r_{\pi^*} \leq P_{\pi^*}^t (r_\pi + P_\pi v - P_{\pi^*} v) \leq P_{\pi^*}^t (\rho \mathbf{1} + v - P_{\pi^*} v) = \rho \mathbf{1} + P_{\pi^*}^t v - P_{\pi^*}^{t+1} v.$$

Summing over t shows that $\rho^*\mathbf{1} = \lim_{n\to\infty} \frac{1}{n}\sum_{t=0}^{n-1} P_{\pi^*}^t r_{\pi^*} \leq \rho\mathbf{1}$, which completes the proof.   ☐

Having found the optimal gain, the next step is to find a value function that satisfies the Bellman optimality equation. Let $\tilde{s} \in \mathcal{S}$, and consider the following linear program:

$$\underset{v\in\mathbb{R}^S}{\text{minimise}} \quad \langle v, 1\rangle \tag{38.7}$$

$$\text{subject to} \quad \rho^* + v(s) \geq r_a(s) + \langle P_a(s), v\rangle \text{ for all } s, a$$

$$v(\tilde{s}) = 0.$$

The second constraint is crucial in order for the minimum to exist, since otherwise the value function can be arbitrarily small.

THEOREM 38.5. *There exists a state $\tilde{s} \in \mathcal{S}$ such that the solution v of Eq. (38.7) satisfies the Bellman optimality equation.*

Proof The result follows by showing that $\varepsilon = v + \rho^*\mathbf{1} - Tv = 0$. The first constraint in Eq. (38.7) ensures that $\varepsilon \geq 0$. It remains to show that $\varepsilon \leq 0$. Let π^* be an optimal policy and π be the greedy policy with respect to v. Then

$$P_{\pi^*}^t r_{\pi^*} \leq P_{\pi^*}^t (r_\pi + P_\pi v - P_{\pi^*}v) = P_{\pi^*}^t(\rho^*\mathbf{1} + v - \varepsilon - P_{\pi^*}v).$$

Hence $\rho^*\mathbf{1} = \rho^{\pi^*}\mathbf{1} \leq \rho^*\mathbf{1} - P_{\pi^*}^*\varepsilon$ and $P_{\pi^*}^*\varepsilon \leq 0$. Since $\varepsilon \geq 0$ and $P_{\pi^*}^*$ is right stochastic, $P_{\pi^*}^*\varepsilon = 0$. Choose $\tilde{s}$ to be a state such that $P_{\pi^*}^*(s, \tilde{s}) > 0$ for some $s \in \mathcal{S}$, which exists because $P_{\pi^*}^*$ is right stochastic. Then $0 = (P_{\pi^*}^*\varepsilon)(s) \geq P_{\pi^*}^*(s, \tilde{s})\varepsilon(\tilde{s})$ and hence $\varepsilon(\tilde{s}) = 0$. It follows that $\tilde{v} = v - \varepsilon$ also satisfies the constraints in Eq. (38.7). Because v is a solution to Eq. (38.7), $\langle \tilde{v}, 1\rangle \geq \langle v, 1\rangle$, implying that $\langle \varepsilon, 1\rangle \leq 0$. Since we already showed that $\varepsilon \geq 0$, it follows that $\varepsilon = 0$.   ☐

The theorem only demonstrates the existence of a state $\tilde{s}$ for which the solution of Eq. (38.7) satisfies the Bellman optimality equation. There is a relatively simple procedure for finding such a state using the solution to Eq. (38.6), but its analysis depends on the basic theory of duality from linear programming, which is beyond the scope of this text. More details are in Note 11 at the end of the chapter. Instead we observe that one can simply solve Eq. (38.7) for all choices of $\tilde{s}$ and take the first solution that satisfies the Bellman optimality equation.

38.3.1 Efficient Computation

The linear programs in Eq. (38.6) and Eq. (38.7) can be solved efficiently under assumptions that will be satisfied in subsequent applications.

The algorithm proposed in this subsection is guaranteed to run in polynomial time, which is a standard objective in theoretical computer science. Its practical performance, however, is usually much worse than alternatives that suffer from exponential running time in the worst case. These issues are discussed in Note 12 at the end of the chapter.

The general form of a linear program is an optimisation problem of the form

$$\underset{x \in \mathbb{R}^n}{\text{minimise}} \;\; \langle c, x \rangle$$

$$\text{subject to } Ax \geq b,$$

where $c \in \mathbb{R}^n$ and $A \in \mathbb{R}^{m \times n}$ and $b \in \mathbb{R}^m$ are parameters of the problem. This general problem can be solved in time that depends polynomially on n and m. When m is very large or infinite, these algorithms may become impractical, but nevertheless one can often still solve the optimisation problem in time polynomial in n only, provided that the constraints satisfy certain structural properties. Let $\mathcal{K} \subset \mathbb{R}^n$ be convex, and consider the optimisation problem

$$\underset{x \in \mathbb{R}^n}{\text{minimise}} \;\; \langle c, x \rangle \tag{38.8}$$

$$\text{subject to } x \in \mathcal{K}.$$

Algorithms for this problem generally have a slightly different flavour because $\mathcal{K}$ may have no corners. Suppose the following holds:

(a) There exists a known $R > 0$ such that $\mathcal{K} \subset \{x \in \mathbb{R}^n : \|x\|_2 \leq R\}$.
(b) There exists a separation oracle, which we recall from Chapter 27, is a computational procedure to evaluate some function ϕ on $\mathbb{R}^n$ with $\phi(x) = \text{TRUE}$ for $x \in \mathcal{K}$, and otherwise $\phi(x) = u$ with $\langle y, u \rangle > \langle x, u \rangle$ for all $y \in \mathcal{K}$ (see Fig. 27.1).
(c) There exists a $\delta > 0$ and $x_0 \in \mathbb{R}^d$ such that $\{x \in \mathbb{R}^n : \|x - x_0\|_2 \leq \delta\} \subset \mathcal{K}$.

Under these circumstances, the ellipsoid method accepts as input the size of the bounding sphere R, the separation oracle and an accuracy parameter $\varepsilon > 0$. Its output is a point x in time polynomial in n and $\log(R/(\delta\varepsilon))$ such that $x \in \mathcal{K}$ and $\langle c, x \rangle \leq \langle c, x^* \rangle + \varepsilon$, where x^* is the minimiser of Eq. (38.8). The reader can find references to this method at the end of the chapter.

The linear programs in Eq. (38.6) and Eq. (38.7) do not have bounded feasible regions because if v is feasible, then $v + c\mathbb{1}$ is also feasible for any $c \in \mathbb{R}$. For strongly connected MDPs with diameter D, however, Lemma 38.3 allows us to add the constraint that $\|v\|_\infty \leq D$. If the rewards are bounded in $[0, 1]$, then we may also add the constraint that $0 \leq \rho \leq 1$. Together these imply that for (v, ρ) in the feasible region,

$$\|(\rho, v)\|_2^2 = \rho^2 + \|v\|_2^2 \leq 1 + S\|v\|_\infty^2 \leq 1 + SD^2.$$

Then set $R = \sqrt{1 + D^2 S}$. When the diameter is unknown, one may use a doubling procedure. In order to guarantee the feasible region contains a small ball, we add some slack to the constraints. Let $\varepsilon > 0$, and consider the following linear program:

$$\underset{\rho \in \mathbb{R}, v \in \mathbb{R}^S}{\text{minimise}} \quad \rho \tag{38.9}$$

subject to $\quad \varepsilon + \rho + v(s) \geq r_a(s) + \langle P_a(s), v \rangle$ for all s, a.

$$v(s) \geq -D \text{ for all } s$$
$$v(s) \leq D \text{ for all } s$$
$$\rho \leq 1 + \varepsilon \text{ for all } s$$
$$\rho \geq -\varepsilon \text{ for all } s.$$

Note that for any x in the feasible region of Eq. (38.9), there exists a y that is feasible for Eq. (38.6) with $\|x - y\|_\infty \leq \varepsilon$. Furthermore, the solution to the above linear program is at most ε away from the solution to Eq. (38.6). What we have bought by adding this slack is that now the linear program in Eq. (38.9) satisfies the conditions (a) and (c) above. The final step is to give a condition when a separation oracle exists for the convex set determined by the constraints in the above program. Define convex set $\mathcal{K}$ by

$$\mathcal{K} = \{(\rho, v) \in \mathbb{R}^{d+1} : \varepsilon + \rho + v(s) \geq r_a(s) + \langle P_a(s), v \rangle \text{ for all } s, a\}. \tag{38.10}$$

Assuming that

$$\text{argmax}_{a \in \mathcal{A}}(r_a(s) + \langle P_a(s), v \rangle) \tag{38.11}$$

can be solved efficiently, Algorithm 27 provides a separation oracle for $\mathcal{K}$. For the specialised case considered later, Eq. (38.11) is trivial to compute efficiently. The feasible region defined by the constraints in Eq. (38.9) is the intersection of $\mathcal{K}$ with a small number of half-spaces. In Exercise 38.15, you will show how to efficiently extend a separation oracle for arbitrary convex set $\mathcal{K}$ to $\bigcap_{i=1}^n H_k \cap \mathcal{K}$, where $(H_k)_{k=1}^n$ are half-spaces. You will show in Exercise 38.14 that approximately solving Eq. (38.7) works in the same way as above, as well as the correctness of Algorithm 27.

In Theorem 38.2, we assumed an exact solution of the Bellman optimality equation, which may not be possible in practice. Fortunately, approximate solutions to the Bellman optimality equation with approximately greedy policies yield approximately optimal policies. Details are deferred to Exercise 38.16.

1: **function** SEPARATIONORACLE(ρ, v)
2:      For each $s \in \mathcal{S}$ find $a_s^* \in \text{argmax}_a(r_a(s) + \langle P_a(s), v \rangle)$
3:      **if** $\varepsilon + \rho + v(s) \geq r_{a_s^*}(s) + \langle P_{a_s^*}(s), v \rangle$ for all $s \in \mathcal{S}$ **then**
4:          **return** TRUE
5:      **else**
6:          Find state s with $\varepsilon + \rho + v(s) < r_{a_s^*}(s) + \langle P_{a_s^*}(s), v \rangle$
7:          **return** $(1, e_s - P_{a_s^*}(s))$
8:      **end if**
9: **end function**

Algorithm 27: Separation oracle for Eq. (38.6).

38.4   Learning in Markov Decision Processes

The problem of finding an optimal policy in an unknown MDP is no longer just an optimisation problem, and the notion of regret is introduced to measure the price of the uncertainty. For simplicity we assume that only the transition matrix is unknown while the reward function is given. This assumption is not especially restrictive as the case where the rewards are also unknown is easily covered using either a reduction or a simple generalisation, as we explain in the notes. The regret of a policy π is the deficit of rewards suffered relative to the expected average reward of an optimal policy:

$$\hat{R}_n = n\rho^* - \sum_{t=1}^{n} r_{A_t}(S_t).$$

The reader will notice we are comparing the non-random $n\rho^*$ to the random sum of rewards received by the learner, which was also true in the study of stochastic bandits. The difference is that ρ^* is an asymptotic quantity while for stochastic bandits the analogous quantity was $n\mu^*$. The definition stills makes sense, however, because for MDPs with finite diameter D the optimal expected cumulative reward over n rounds is at least $n\rho^* - D$ so the difference is negligible (Exercise 38.17). The main result of this chapter is the following:

THEOREM 38.6. *Let* S, A *and* n *be natural numbers and* $\delta \in (0, 1)$. *There exists an efficiently computable policy* π *that when interacting with any MDP* $M = (\mathcal{S}, \mathcal{A}, P, r)$ *with* S *states,* A *actions, rewards in* $[0, 1]$ *and any initial state distribution satisfies with probability at least* $1 - \delta$,

$$\hat{R}_n < CD(M)S\sqrt{An\log(nSA/\delta)},$$

where C *is a universal constant.*

In Exercise 38.18, we ask you to use the assumption that the rewards are bounded to find a choice of $\delta \in (0, 1)$ such that

$$\mathbb{E}[\hat{R}_n] \leq 1 + CD(M)S\sqrt{2An\log(n)}. \tag{38.12}$$

This result is complemented by the following lower bound:

THEOREM 38.7. *Let* $S \geq 3$, $A \geq 2$, $D \geq 6 + 2\log_A S$ *and* $n \geq DSA$. *Then for any policy* π *there exists a Markov decision process with* S *states,* A *actions and diameter at most* D *such that*

$$\mathbb{E}[\hat{R}_n] \geq C\sqrt{DSAn},$$

where $C > 0$ *is again a universal constant.*

The upper and lower bounds are separated by a factor of at least $\sqrt{DS}$, which is a considerable gap. Recent work has made progress towards closing this gap as we explain in the notes.

38.5 Upper Confidence Bounds for Reinforcement Learning

Reinforcement learning is the subfield of machine learning devoted to designing and studying algorithms that learn to maximise long-term reward in sequential context. The algorithm that establishes Theorem 38.6 is called UCRL2 because it is the second version of the 'upper confidence bounds for reinforcement learning' algorithm. Its pseudocode is shown in Algorithm 28.

At the start of each phase, UCRL2 computes an optimal policy for the statistically plausible MDP with the largest optimal gain. The details of this computation are left to the next section. This policy is then implemented until the number of visits to some state-action pair doubles when a new phase starts and the process begins again. The use of phases is important, not just for computational efficiency. Recalculating the optimistic policy in each round may lead to a dithering behaviour in which the algorithm frequently changes its plan and suffers linear regret (Exercise 38.19).

To complete the specification of the algorithm, we must define confidence sets on the unknown quantity, which in this case is the transition matrix. The confidence sets are centered at the empirical transition probabilities defined by

$$\hat{P}_{t,a}(s, s') = \frac{\sum_{u=1}^{t} \mathbb{I}\{S_u = s, A_u = a, S_{u+1} = s'\}}{1 \vee T_t(s, a)},$$

where $T_t(s, a) = \sum_{u=1}^{t} \mathbb{I}\{S_u = s, A_u = a\}$ is the number of times action a was taken in state s. As before, we let $\hat{P}_{t,a}(s)$ be the vector whose s'th entry is $\hat{P}_{t,a}(s, s')$. Given a state-action pair s, a, define

$$C_t(s, a) = \left\{ P \in \mathcal{P}(S) : \|P - \hat{P}_{t-1,a}(s)\|_1 \leq \sqrt{\frac{SL_{t-1}(s, a)}{1 \vee T_{t-1}(s, a)}} \right\}, \qquad (38.13)$$

where for $T_t(s, a) > 0$ we set

$$L_t(s, a) = 2 \log\left(\frac{4SAT_t(s, a)(1 + T_t(s, a))}{\delta} \right),$$

and for $T_t(s, a) = 0$ we set $L_t(s, a) = 1$. Note that in this case $C_{t+1}(s, a) = \mathcal{P}(S)$. Then define

$$C_t = \{P = (P_a(s))_{s,a} : P_a(s) \in C_t(s, a) \text{ for all } s, a \in S \times \mathcal{A}\}. \qquad (38.14)$$

Clearly $T_t(s, a)$ cannot be larger than the total number of rounds n, so

$$L_t(s, a) \leq L = 2 \log\left(\frac{4SAn(n + 1)}{\delta} \right). \qquad (38.15)$$

The algorithm operates in phases $k = 1, 2, 3, \ldots$ with the first phase starting in round $\tau_1 = 1$ and the $(k + 1)$th phase starting in round τ_{k+1} defined inductively by

$$\tau_{k+1} = 1 + \min \{t : T_t(S_t, A_t) \geq 2T_{\tau_k - 1}(S_t, A_t)\},$$

which means that the next phase starts once the number of visits to some state-action pair at least doubles.

1: **Input** $S, A, r, \delta \in (0, 1)$
2: $t = 0$
3: **for** $k = 1, 2, \ldots$ **do**
4:     $\tau_k = t + 1$
5:     Find π_k as the greedy policy with respect to v_k satisfying Eq. (38.16)
6:     **do**
7:         $t \leftarrow t + 1$, observe S_t and take action $A_t = \pi_k(S_t)$
8:     **while** $T_t(S_t, A_t) < 2T_{\tau_k - 1}(S_t, A_t)$
9: **end for**

Algorithm 28: UCRL2.

38.5.1 The Extended Markov Decision Process

The confidence set C_t defines a set of plausible transition probability functions at the start of round t. Since the reward function is known already, this corresponds to a set of plausible MDPs. The algorithm plays according to the optimal policy in the plausible MDP with the largest gain. There is some subtlety because the optimal policy is not unique, and what is really needed is to find a policy that is greedy with respect to a value function satisfying the Bellman optimality equation in the plausible MDP with the largest gain. Precisely, at the start of the kth phase, the algorithm must find a value function v_k, gain ρ_k and MDP $M_k = (S, A, P_k, r)$ with $P_k \in C_{\tau_k}$ such that

$$\rho_k + v_k(s) = \max_{a \in A} r_a(s) + \langle P_{k,a}(s), v_k \rangle \text{ for all } s \in S \text{ and } a \in A,$$

$$\rho_k = \max_{s \in S} \max_{\pi \in \Pi_{DM}} \max_{P \in C_{\tau_k}} \rho_s^\pi(P),$$

(38.16)

where $\rho_s^\pi(P)$ is the gain of deterministic memoryless policy π starting in state s in the MDP with transition probability function P. The algorithm then plays according to π_k defined as the greedy policy with respect to v_k. There is quite a lot hidden in these equations. The gain is only guaranteed to be constant when M_k has a finite diameter, but this may not hold for all plausible MDPs. As it happens, however, solutions to Eq. (38.16) are guaranteed to exist and can be found efficiently. To see why this is true we introduce the **extended MDP** $\tilde{M}_k$, which has state space S and state-dependent action space $\tilde{A}_s$ given by

$$\tilde{A}_s = \{(a, P) : a \in A, P \in C_{\tau_k}(s, a)\}.$$

The reward function of the extended MDP is $\tilde{r}_{(a,P)}(s) = r_a(s)$, and the transitions are $\tilde{P}_{a,P}(s) = P_a(s)$. The action space in the extended MDP allows the agent to choose both $a \in A$ and a plausible transition vector $P_a(s) \in C_{\tau_k}(s, a)$. By the definition of the confidence sets, for any pair of states s, s' and action $a \in A$, there always exists a transition vector $P_a(s) \in C_{\tau_k}(s, a)$ such that $P_a(s, s') > 0$, which means that $\tilde{M}_k$ is strongly connected. Hence solving the Bellman optimality equation for $\tilde{M}_k$ yields a value function v_k and constant gain $\rho_k \in \mathbb{R}$ that satisfy Eq. (38.16). A minor detail is that the extended action sets are infinite, while the analysis in previous sections only demonstrated existence of solutions to the Bellman optimality equation for finite MDPs. You should convince yourself that $C_t(s, a)$ is convex and has finitely many extremal points. Restricting the confidence sets to these points makes the extended MDP finite without changing the optimal policy.

38.5.2 Computing the Optimistic Policy (✦)

Here we explain how to efficiently solve the Bellman optimality equation for the extended MDP. The results in Section 38.3 show that the Bellman optimality equation for $\tilde{M}_k$ can be solved efficiently provided that for any value function $v \in \mathbb{R}^S$ computing

$$\text{argmax}_{a \in \mathcal{A}} \left(r_a(s) + \max_{P \in \mathcal{C}_{\tau_k}(s,a)} \langle P, v \rangle \right) \tag{38.17}$$

can be carried out in an efficient manner. The inner optimisation is another linear program with S variables and $O(S)$ constraints and can be solved in polynomial time. This procedure is repeated for each $a \in \mathcal{A}$ to compute the outcome of (38.17). In fact the inner optimisation can be solved more straightforwardly by sorting the entries of v and then allocating P coordinate by coordinate to be as large as allowed by the constraints in decreasing order of v. The total computation cost of solving Eq. (38.17) in this way is $O(S(A + \log S))$. Combining this with Algorithm 27 gives the required separation oracle.

The next problem is to find an R such that the set of feasible solutions to the linear programs in Eq. (38.6) and Eq. (38.7) are contained in the set $\{x : \|x\| \leq R\}$. As discussed in Section 38.3.1, a suitable value is $R = \sqrt{1 + D^2 S}$, where D is an upper bound on the diameter of the MDP. It turns out that $D = \sqrt{n}$ works because for each pair of states s, s', there exists an action a and $P \in \mathcal{C}_{\tau_k}(s, a)$ such that $P(s, s') \geq 1 \wedge (1/\sqrt{n})$ so $D(\tilde{M}_k) \leq \sqrt{n}$. Combining this with the tools developed in Section 38.3 shows that the Bellman optimality equation for $\tilde{M}_k$ may be solved using linear programming in polynomial time. Note that the additional constraints require a minor adaptation of the separation oracle, which we leave to the reader.

38.6   Proof of Upper Bound

The proof is developed in three steps. First we decompose the regret into phases and define a failure event where the confidence intervals fail. In the second step, we bound the regret in each phase, and in the third step we sum over the phases. Recall that $M = (\mathcal{S}, \mathcal{A}, P, r)$ is the true Markov decision process with diameter $D = D(M)$. The initial state distribution is $\mu \in \mathcal{P}(\mathcal{S})$, which is arbitrary.

Step 1: Failure Events and Decomposition
Let K be the (random) number of phases, and for $k \in [K]$, let $E_k = \{\tau_k, \tau_k+1, \ldots, \tau_{k+1}-1\}$ be the set of rounds in the kth phase, where τ_{K+1} is defined to be $n + 1$. Let $T_{(k)}(s, a)$ be the number of times state-action pair s, a is visited in the kth phase:

$$T_{(k)}(s, a) = \sum_{t \in E_k} \mathbb{I}\{S_t = s, A_t = a\}.$$

Define F as the failure event that $P \notin \mathcal{C}_{\tau_k}$ for some $k \in [K]$.

LEMMA 38.8. $\mathbb{P}(F) \leq \delta/2$.

The proof is based on a concentration inequality derived for categorical distributions and is left for Exercise 38.21. When F does not hold, the true transition kernel is in $\mathcal{C}_{\tau_k}$ for all k, which means that $\rho^* \leq \rho_k$ and

$$\hat{R}_n = \sum_{t=1}^n (\rho^* - r_{A_t}(S_t)) \leq \sum_{k=1}^K \underbrace{\sum_{t \in E_k} (\rho_k - r_{A_t}(S_t))}_{\tilde{R}_k}.$$

In the next step, we bound $\tilde{R}_k$ under the assumption that F does not hold.

Step 2: Bounding the Regret in Each Phase

Assume that F does not occur and fix $k \in [K]$. Recall that v_k is a value function satisfying the Bellman optimality equation in the optimistic MDP M_k and ρ_k is its gain. Hence

$$\rho_k = r_{\pi_k}(s) - v_k(s) + \langle P_{k,\pi_k}(s), v_k \rangle \quad \text{for all } s \in \mathcal{S}. \tag{38.18}$$

As noted earlier, solutions to the Bellman optimality equation remain solutions when translated, so we may assume without loss of generality that v_k is such that $\|v_k\|_\infty \leq \text{span}(v_k)/2$, which means that

$$\|v_k\|_\infty \leq \frac{1}{2} \text{span}(v_k) \leq \frac{D}{2}, \tag{38.19}$$

where the second inequality follows from Lemma 38.3 and the fact that when F does not hold, the diameter of the extended MDP $\tilde{M}_k$ is at most D and v_k also satisfies the Bellman optimality equation in this MDP. By the definition of the policy, we have $A_t = \pi_k(S_t)$ for $t \in E_k$, which implies that

$$\rho_k = r_{A_t}(S_t) - v_k(S_t) + \langle P_{k,A_t}(S_t), v_k \rangle \quad \text{for all } t \in E_k.$$

Rearranging and substituting yields

$$\tilde{R}_k = \sum_{t \in E_k} (-v_k(S_t) + \langle P_{k,A_t}(S_t), v_k \rangle)$$

$$= \sum_{t \in E_k} (-v_k(S_t) + \langle P_{A_t}(S_t), v_k \rangle) + \sum_{t \in E_k} \langle P_{k,A_t}(S_t) - P_{A_t}(S_t), v_k \rangle$$

$$\leq \underbrace{\sum_{t \in E_k} (-v_k(S_t) + \langle P_{A_t}(S_t), v_k \rangle)}_{\text{(A)}} + \underbrace{\frac{D}{2} \sum_{t \in E_k} \|P_{k,A_t}(S_t) - P_{A_t}(S_t)\|_1}_{\text{(B)}}, \tag{38.20}$$

where the inequality follows from Hölder's inequality and Eq. (38.19). Let $\mathbb{E}_t[\cdot]$ denote the conditional expectation with respect to $\mathbb{P}$ conditioned on $\sigma(S_1, A_1, \ldots, S_{t-1}, A_{t-1}, S_t)$. To bound (A), we reorder the terms and use the fact that $\text{span}(v_k) \leq D$ on the event F^c. We get

$$(A) = \sum_{t \in E_k} (v_k(S_{t+1}) - v_k(S_t) + \langle P_{A_t}(S_t), v_k \rangle - v_k(S_{t+1}))$$

$$= v_k(S_{\tau_{k+1}}) - v_k(S_{\tau_k}) + \sum_{t \in E_k} (\langle P_{A_t}(S_t), v_k \rangle - v_k(S_{t+1}))$$

$$\leq D + \sum_{t \in E_k} (\mathbb{E}_t[v_k(S_{t+1})] - v_k(S_{t+1})),$$

where the second equality used that $\max E_k = \tau_{k+1} - 1$ and $\min E_k = \tau_k$. We leave this here for now and move on to term (B) in Eq. (38.20). The definition of the confidence intervals and the assumption that F does not occur shows that

$$(B) \leq \frac{D\sqrt{LS}}{2} \sum_{(s,a) \in \mathcal{S} \times \mathcal{A}} \frac{T_{(k)}(s,a)}{\sqrt{1 \vee T_{\tau_k - 1}(s,a)}}.$$

Combining the bounds (A) and (B) yields

$$\tilde{R}_k \leq D + \sum_{t \in E_k} (\mathbb{E}_t[v_k(S_{t+1})] - v_k(S_{t+1})) + \frac{D\sqrt{LS}}{2} \sum_{(s,a) \in \mathcal{S} \times \mathcal{A}} \frac{T_{(k)}(s,a)}{\sqrt{1 \vee T_{\tau_k - 1}(s,a)}}.$$

Step 3: Bounding the Number of Phases and Summing
Let K_t be the phase in round t so that $t \in E_{K_t}$. By the work in the previous two steps, if F does not occur, then

$$\hat{R}_n \leq \sum_{k=1}^{K} \tilde{R}_k \leq KD + \sum_{t=1}^{n} (\mathbb{E}_t[v_{K_t}(S_{t+1})] - v_{K_t}(S_{t+1}))$$

$$+ \frac{D\sqrt{LS}}{2} \sum_{(s,a) \in \mathcal{S} \times \mathcal{A}} \sum_{k=1}^{K} \frac{T_{(k)}(s,a)}{\sqrt{1 \vee T_{\tau_k - 1}(s,a)}}.$$

The first sum is bounded using a version of Hoeffding–Azuma (Exercise 20.7):

$$\mathbb{P}\left(F^c \text{ and } \sum_{t=1}^{n} (\mathbb{E}_t[v_{K_t}(S_{t+1})] - v_{K_t}(S_{t+1})) \geq D\sqrt{\frac{n \log(2/\delta)}{2}} \right) \leq \frac{\delta}{2}.$$

For the second term, we note that $T_{(k)}(s,a)/\sqrt{1 \vee T_{\tau_k - 1}(s,a)}$ cannot be large too often. A continuous approximation often provides intuition for the correct form. Recalling the thousands of integrals you did at school, for any differentiable $f : [0, \infty) \to \mathbb{R}$,

$$\int_0^K \frac{f'(k)}{\sqrt{f(k)}} dk = 2\sqrt{f(K)} - 2\sqrt{f(0)}. \tag{38.21}$$

Here we are thinking of $f(k)$ as the continuous approximation of $T_{\tau_k - 1}(s,a)$ and its derivative as $T_{(k)}(s,a)$. In Exercise 38.22, we ask you to make this argument rigourous by showing that

$$\sum_{k=1}^{K} \frac{T_{(k)}(s,a)}{\sqrt{1 \vee T_{\tau_k - 1}(s,a)}} \leq (\sqrt{2} + 1) \sqrt{T_n(s,a)}.$$

Then by Cauchy–Schwarz and the fact that $\sum_{s,a \in \mathcal{S} \times \mathcal{A}} T_n(s,a) = n$,

$$\sum_{s \in \mathcal{S}} \sum_{a \in \mathcal{A}} \sqrt{T_n(s,a)} \le \sqrt{\mathrm{SA}n}.$$

It remains to bound the number of phases. A new phase starts when the visit count for some state-action pair doubles. Hence K cannot be more than the number of times the counters double in total for each of the states. It is easy to see that $1 + \log_2 T_n(s,a)$ gives an upper bound on how many times the counter for this pair may double (the constant 1 is there to account for the counter changing from zero to one). Thus $K \le K' = \sum_{s,a} 1 + \log_2 T_n(s,a)$. Noting that $0 \le T_n(s,a)$ and $\sum_{s,a} T_n(s,a) = n$ and relaxing $T_n(s,a)$ to take real values, we find that the value of K' is the largest when $T_n(s,a) = n/(\mathrm{SA})$, which shows that

$$K \le \mathrm{SA}\left(1 + \log_2\left(\frac{n}{\mathrm{SA}}\right)\right).$$

Putting everything together gives the desired result.

38.7 Proof of Lower Bound

The lower bound is proven by crafting a difficult MDP that models a bandit with approximately SA arms. This is a cumbersome endeavour, but intuitively straightforward, and the explanations that follow should be made clear in Fig. 38.3. Given S and A, the first step is to construct a tree of minimum depth with at most A children for each node using exactly $S-2$ states. The root of the tree is denoted by s_o and transitions within the tree are deterministic, so in any given node, the learner can simply select which child to transition to. Let L be the number of leaves, and label these states $s_1, \ldots, s_L$. The last two states are s_g and s_b

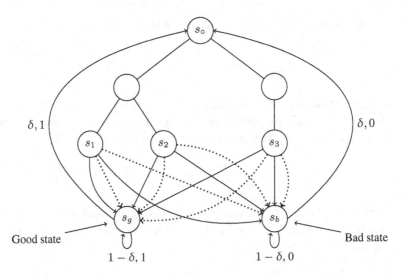

Figure 38.3 Lower-bound construction for A = 2 and S = 8. The resulting MDP is roughly equivalent to a bandit with six actions.

('good' and 'bad' respectively). For each $i \in [L]$, the learner can take any action $a \in \mathcal{A}$ and transitions to either the good state or the bad state according to

$$P_a(s_i, s_g) = \frac{1}{2} + \varepsilon(a, i) \qquad \text{and} \qquad P_a(s_i, s_b) = \frac{1}{2} - \varepsilon(a, i).$$

The function ε will be chosen so that $\varepsilon(a, i) = 0$ for all (a, i) pairs except one. For this special state-action pair, we let $\varepsilon(a, i) = \Delta$ for appropriately tuned $\Delta > 0$. The good state and the bad state have the same transitions for all actions:

$$P_a(s_g, s_g) = 1 - \delta, \qquad\qquad P_a(s_g, s_o) = \delta,$$
$$P_a(s_b, s_b) = 1 - \delta, \qquad\qquad P_a(s_b, s_o) = \delta.$$

Choosing $\delta = 4/D$, which under the assumptions of the theorem is guaranteed to be in $(0, 1]$, ensures that the diameter of the described MDP is at most D, regardless of the value of Δ. The reward function is $r_a(s) = 1$ if $s = s_g$ and $r_a(s) = 0$ otherwise.

   The connection to finite-armed bandits is straightforward. Each time the learner arrives in state s_o, it selects which leaf to visit and then chooses an action from that leaf. This corresponds to choosing one of $k = LA = \Omega(SA)$ meta actions. The optimal policy is to select the meta action with the largest probability of transitioning to the good state. The choice of δ means the learner expects to stay in the good/bad state for approximately D rounds, which also makes the diameter of this MDP about D. This means the learner expects to make about n/D decisions and the rewards are roughly in $[0, D]$, so we should expect the regret to be $\Omega(D\sqrt{kn/D}) = \Omega(\sqrt{nDSA})$.

   One could almost claim victory here and not bother with the proof. As usual, however, there are some technical difficulties, which in this case arise because the number of visits to the decision state s_o is a random quantity. For this reason we give the proof, leaving as exercises the parts that are both obvious and annoying.

Proof of Theorem 38.7   The proof follows the path suggested in Exercise 15.2. We break things up into two steps. Throughout we fix an arbitrary policy π.

Step 1: Notation and Facts about the MDP

Let d be the depth of the tree in the MDP construction, L the number of leaves and $k = LA$. Define the set of state–action pairs for which the state is a leaf of the tree by

$$\{(s, a) : a \in \mathcal{A} \text{ and } s \text{ is a leaf of the tree}\}.$$

By definition, this has k elements. Let M_0 be the MDP with $\varepsilon(s, a) = 0$ for all $(s, a)L$. Then let M_j be the MDP with $\varepsilon(s, a) = \Delta$ for the jth state-action pair in the above set. Define stopping time τ by

$$\tau = n \wedge \min\left\{t : \sum_{u=1}^{t} \mathbb{I}\{S_u = s_o\} \geq \frac{n}{D} - 1\right\},$$

which is the first round when the number of visits to state s_o is at least $n/D - 1$, or n if s_o is visited fewer times than n/D. Next, let T_j be the number of visits to state-action pair $j \in [k]$ until stopping time τ and $T_\sigma = \sum_{j=1}^{k} T_j$. For $0 \leq j \leq k$, let $\mathbb{P}_j$ be the law of $T_1, \ldots, T_k$ induced by the interaction of π and M_j. And let $\mathbb{E}_j[\cdot]$ be the expectation with respect to $\mathbb{P}_j$. None of the following claims is surprising, but they are all tiresome to prove to some extent. The claims are listed in increasing order of difficulty and left to the reader in Exercise 38.24.

CLAIM 38.9. *For all $j \in [k]$, the diameter is bounded by $D(M_j) \leq D$.*

CLAIM 38.10. *There exist universal constants $0 < c_1 < c_2 < \infty$ such that*

$$D\mathbb{E}_0[T_\sigma]/n \in [c_1, c_2].$$

CLAIM 38.11. *Let R_{nj} be the expected regret of policy π in MDP M_j over n rounds. There exists a universal constant $c_3 > 0$ such that*

$$R_{nj} \geq c_3 \Delta D\, \mathbb{E}_j[T_\sigma - T_j].$$

Step 2: Bounding the Regret

Notice that M_0 and M_j only differ when state-action pair j is visited. In Exercise 38.30, you are invited to use this fact and the chain rule for relative entropy given in Exercise 14.12 to prove that

$$D(\mathbb{P}_0, \mathbb{P}_j) = \mathbb{E}_0[T_j]d(1/2, 1/2 + \Delta), \tag{38.22}$$

where $d(p, q)$ is the relative entropy between Bernoulli distributions with means p and q, respectively. Now Δ will be chosen to satisfy $\Delta \leq 1/4$. It follows from the entropy inequalities in Eq. (14.16) that

$$D(\mathbb{P}_0, \mathbb{P}_j) \leq 4\Delta^2 \mathbb{E}_0[T_j]. \tag{38.23}$$

Using the fact that $0 \leq T_\sigma - T_j \leq T_\sigma \leq n/D$, Exercise 14.4 and Pinsker's inequality (Eq. (14.12)) and (38.23),

$$\mathbb{E}_j[T_\sigma - T_j] \geq \mathbb{E}_0[T_\sigma - T_j] - \frac{n}{D}\sqrt{\frac{D(\mathbb{P}_0, \mathbb{P}_j)}{2}} \geq \mathbb{E}_0[T_\sigma - T_j] - \frac{n\Delta}{D}\sqrt{2\mathbb{E}_0[T_j]}.$$

Summing over j and applying Cauchy–Schwarz yields

$$\sum_{j=1}^{k} \mathbb{E}_j[T_\sigma - T_j] \geq \sum_{j=1}^{k} \mathbb{E}_0[T_\sigma - T_j] - \frac{n\Delta}{D}\sum_{j=1}^{k}\sqrt{2\mathbb{E}_0[T_j]}$$

$$\geq (k-1)\mathbb{E}_0[T_\sigma] - \frac{n\Delta}{D}\sqrt{2k\mathbb{E}_0[T_\sigma]}$$

$$\geq \frac{c_1 n(k-1)}{D} - \frac{n\Delta}{D}\sqrt{\frac{2c_2 nk}{D}}$$

$$\geq \frac{c_1 n(k-1)}{2D}, \tag{38.24}$$

where the last inequality follows by choosing

$$\Delta = \frac{c_1(k-1)}{2}\sqrt{\frac{D}{2c_2 nk}}.$$

By Eq. (38.24), there exists a $j \in [k]$ such that

$$\mathbb{E}_j[T_\sigma - T_j] \geq \frac{c_1 n(k-1)}{2Dk}.$$

Then, for the last step, apply Claim 38.11 to show that

$$R_{nj} \geq c_3 D \Delta \mathbb{E}_j[T_\sigma - T_j] \geq \frac{c_1^2 c_3 n(k-1)^2}{4k} \sqrt{\frac{D}{2c_2 nk}}.$$

Naive bounding and simplification concludes the proof.   □

38.8 Notes

1 MDPs in applications can have millions (or 'billions and billions') of states, which should make the reader worried that the bound in Theorem 38.6 could be extremely large. The takeaway should be that learning in large MDPs without additional assumptions is hard, as attested by the lower bound in Theorem 38.7.

2 The key to choosing the state space is that the state must be observable and sufficiently informative that the Markov property is satisfied. Blowing up the size of the state space may help to increase the fidelity of the approximation (the entire history always works), but will almost always slow down learning.

3 We simplified the definition of MDPs by making the rewards a deterministic function of the current state and the action chosen. A more general definition allows the rewards to evolve in a random fashion, jointly with the next state. In this definition, the mean reward functions are dropped and the transition kernel P_a is replaced with an $\mathcal{S} \to \mathcal{S} \times \mathbb{R}$ stochastic kernel, call it, $\tilde{P}_a$. Thus, for every $s \in \mathcal{S}$, $\tilde{P}_a(s)$ is a probability measure over $\mathcal{S} \times \mathbb{R}$. The meaning of this is that when action a is chosen in state s, a random transition, $(S, R) \sim \tilde{P}_a(s)$ happens to state S, while reward R is received. Note that the mean reward along this transition is $r_a(s) = \int x \tilde{P}_a(s, ds', dx)$.

4 A state $s \in \mathcal{S}$ is **absorbing** if $P_a(s, s) = 1$ for all $a \in \mathcal{A}$. An MDP is **episodic** if there exists an absorbing state that is reached almost surely by any policy. The average reward criterion is meaningless in episodic MDPs because all policies are optimal. In this case the usual objective is to maximise the expected reward until the absorbing state is reached without limits or normalisation, sometimes with discounting. An MDP is **finite-horizon** if it is episodic and the absorbing state is always reached after some fixed number of rounds. The simplification of the setting eases the analysis and preserves most of the intuition from the general setting.

5 A **partially observable MDP** (POMDP) is a generalisation where the learner does not observe the underlying state. Instead they receive an observation that is a (possibly random) function of the state. Given a fixed (known) initial state distribution, any POMDP can be mapped to an MDP at the price of enlarging the state space. A simple way to achieve this is to let the new state space be the space of all histories. Alternatively you can use any sufficient statistic for the hidden state as the state. A natural choice is the posterior distribution over the hidden state given the interaction history, which is called the **belief space**. While the value function over the belief space has some nice structure, in general even computing the optimal policy is hard [Papadimitriou and Tsitsiklis, 1987].

6 We called the all-knowing entity that interacts with the MDP an **agent**. In operations research the term is **decision maker** and in control theory it is **controller**. In control theory the environment would be called the **controlled system** or the **plant** (for power-plant, not a biological plant). Acting in an MDP is studied in control theory under **stochastic optimal control**, while in operations research the area is called **multistage decision making under uncertainty** or **multistage stochastic programming**. In the control community the infinite horizon setting with the average

cost criterion is perhaps the most common, while in operations research the episodic setting is typical.

7 The definition of the optimal gain that is appropriate for MDPs that are not strongly connected is a vector $\rho^* \in \mathbb{R}^S$ given by $\rho_s^* = \sup_\pi \bar{\rho}_s^\pi$. A policy is optimal if it achieves the supremum in this definition and such a policy always exists as long as the MDP is finite. In strongly connected MDPs, the two definitions coincide. For infinite MDPs, everything becomes more delicate and a large portion of the literature on MDPs is devoted to this case.

8 In applications where the asymptotic nature of gain optimality is unacceptable, there are criteria that make finer distinctions between the policies. A memoryless policy π^* is **bias optimal** if it is gain optimal and $v_{\pi^*} \geq v_\pi$ for all memoryless policies π. Even more sensitive criteria exist. Some keywords to search for are **Blackwell optimality** and n-discount optimality.

9 The **Cesàro sum** of a real-valued sequence $(a_n)_n$ is the asymptotic average of its partial sums. Let $s_n = a_0 + \cdots + a_{n-1}$ be the nth partial sum. The Cesàro sum of this sequence is $A = \lim_{n\to\infty} \frac{1}{n}(s_1 + \cdots + s_n)$ when this limit exists. The idea is that Cesàro summation smoothes out periodicity, which means that for certain sequences the Cesàro sum exists while s_n does not converge. For example, the alternating sequence $(+1, -1, +1, -1, \ldots)$ is Cesàro summable, and its Cesàro sum is easily seen to be $1/2$, while it is not summable in the normal sense. If a sequence is summable, then its sum and its Cesàro sum coincide. The differential value of a policy is defined as a Cesàro sum so that it is well defined even if the underlying Markov chain has periodic states.

10 For $\gamma \in (0,1)$, the γ-discounted average of sequence $(a_n)_n$ is $A_\gamma = (1-\gamma)\sum_{n=0}^\infty \gamma^n a_n$. An elementary argument shows that if A_γ is well defined, then $A_\gamma = (1-\gamma)^2 \sum_{n=1}^\infty \gamma^{n-1} s_n$. Suppose the Cesàro sum $A = \lim_{n\to\infty} \frac{1}{n}\sum_{t=1}^n s_t$ exists, then using the fact that $1 = (1-\gamma)^2 \sum_{n=1}^\infty \gamma^{n-1} n$, we have $A_\gamma - A = (1-\gamma)^2 \sum_{n=1}^\infty \gamma^{n-1}(s_n - nA)$. It is not hard to see that $|\sum_{n=1}^\infty \gamma^{n-1}(s_n - nA)| = O(1/(1-\gamma))$, and thus $A_\gamma - A = O(1-\gamma)$ as $\gamma \to 1$, which means that $\lim_{\gamma\to 1} A_\gamma = A$. The value $\lim_{\gamma\to 1} A_\gamma$ is called the **Abel sum** of $(a_n)_n$. Put simply, the Abel sum of a sequence is equal to its Cesàro sum when the latter exists. Abel summation is stronger in the sense that there are sequences that are Abel summable but not Cesàro summable. The approach of approximating Cesàro sums through γ-discounted averages, and taking the limit as $\gamma \to 1$ is called the **vanishing discount approach** and is one of the standard ways to prove that the (average reward) Bellman equation has a solution (see Exercises 38.9 and 38.10). As an aside, the systematic study of how to define the 'sum' of a divergent series is a relatively modern endeavour. An enjoyable historical account is given in the first chapter of the book on the topic by Hardy [1973].

11 Given a solution (ρ, v) to Eq. (38.6), we mentioned a procedure for finding a state $\tilde{s} \in \mathcal{S}$ that is recurrent under some optimal policy. This works as follows. Let $C_0 = \{(s,a) : \rho + v(s) = r_a(s) + \langle P_a(s), v\rangle\}$ and $I_0 = \{s : (s,a) \in C_0$ for some $a \in \mathcal{A}\}$. Then define C_{k+1} and I_{k+1} inductively by the following algorithm. First find an $(s,a) \in C_k$ such that $P_a(s,s') > 0$ for some $s' \notin I_k$. If no such pair exists, then halt. Otherwise let $C_{k+1} = C_k \setminus \{(s,a)\}$ and $I_{k+1} = \{s : (s,a) \in C_{k+1}$ for some $a \in \mathcal{A}\}$. Now use the complementary slackness conditions of the dual program to Eq. (38.6) to prove that the algorithm halts with some non-empty I_k and that these states are recurrent under some optimal policy. For more details, have a look at Exercise 4.15 of the second volume of the book by Bertsekas [2012].

12 We mentioned enumeration, value iteration and policy iteration as other methods for computing optimal policies. Enumeration just means enumerating all deterministic memoryless policies and selecting the one with the highest gain. This is obviously too expensive. **Policy iteration** is an iterative process that starts with a policy π_0. In each round, the algorithm computes π_{k+1} from π_k by

computing v_{π_k} and then choosing π_{k+1} to be the greedy policy with respect to v_{π_k}. This method may not converge to an optimal policy, but by slightly modifying the update process, one can prove convergence. For more details, see chapter 4 of volume 2 of the book by Bertsekas [2012]. **Value iteration** works by choosing an arbitrary value function v_0 and then inductively defining $v_{k+1} = Tv_k$, where $(Tv)(s) = \max_{a \in \mathcal{A}} r_a(s) + \langle P_a(s), v \rangle$ is the Bellman operator. Under certain technical conditions, one can prove that the greedy policy with respect to v_k converges to an optimal policy. Note that $v_{k+1} = \Omega(k)$, which can be a problem numerically. A simple idea is to let $v_{k+1} = Tv_k - \delta_k$ where $\delta_k = \max_{s \in \mathcal{S}} v_k(s)$. Since the greedy policy is the same for v and $v + c\mathbf{1}$, this does not change the mathematics, but improves the numerical situation. The aforementioned book by Bertsekas is again a good source for more details. Unfortunately, none of these algorithms have known polynomial time guarantees on the computation complexity of finding an optimal policy without stronger assumptions than we would like. In practice, however, both value and policy iteration work quite well, while the ellipsoid method for solving linear programs should be avoided at all costs. Of course there are other methods for solving linear programs, and these can be effective.

13 Theorem 38.6 is vacuous when the diameter is infinite, but you might wonder if the bound continues to hold in certain 'nice' cases. Unfortunately, the algorithm is rather brittle. UCRL2 suffers linear regret if there is a single unreachable state with reward larger than the optimal gain (Exercise 38.27).

14 One can modify the concept of regret to allow for MDPs that have traps. We restrict our attention to policies with sublinear regret in strongly connected MDPs, which must try and explore the whole state space and hence almost surely become trapped in a strongly communicating subset of the state space. The regret is redefined by 'restarting the clock' at the time when the policy gets trapped. For details, see Exercise 38.29.

15 The assumption that the reward function is known can be relaxed without difficulty. It is left as an exercise to figure out how to modify algorithm and analysis to the case when r is unknown and reward observed in round t is bounded in $[0, 1]$ and has conditional mean $r_{A_t}(S_t)$. See Exercise 38.23.

16 Although it has not been done yet in this setting, the path to removing the spurious $\sqrt{S}$ from the bound is to avoid the application of Cauchy–Schwarz in Eq. (38.20). Instead one should define confidence intervals directly on $\langle \hat{P}_k - P, v_k \rangle$, where the dependence on the state and action has been omitted. Of course, the algorithm must be changed to use the improved confidence intervals. At first sight, it seems that one could apply Hoeffding's bound directly to the inner product, but there is a subtle problem that has spoiled a number of attempts: v_k and $\hat{P}_k$ are not independent. This non-independence is unfortunately quite pernicious and appears from many angles. We advise extreme caution. Some references for guidance are given in the bibliographic remarks.

38.9 Bibliographical Remarks

The study of sequential decision-making has a long history, and we recommend the introduction of the book by Puterman [2009] as a good starting point. One of the main architects in modern times is Richard Bellman, who wrote an influential book [Bellman, 1954]. His autobiography is so entertaining that reading it slowed the writing of this chapter: *The Eye of the Hurricane* [Bellman, 1984]. As a curiosity, Bellman knew about bandit problems after accidentally encountering a paper by Thompson [1935]. For the tidbit, see page 260 of the aforementioned biography.

MDPs are studied by multiple research communities, including control, operations research and artificial intelligence. The two-volume book by Bertsekas [2012] provides a thorough and formal introduction to the basics. The perspective is quite interdisciplinary, but with a slight (good) bias towards the control literature. The perspective of an operations researcher is most precisely conveyed in the comprehensive book by Puterman [2009]. A very readable shorter introductory book is by Ross [1983]. Arapostathis et al. [1993] surveyed existing analytical results (existence, uniqueness of optimal policies, validity of the Bellman optimality equation) for average-reward MDPs with an emphasis on continuous state and action space models. The online lecture notes of Kallenberg [2016] are a recent comprehensive alternative account for the theory of discrete MDPs.

Richard Bellman

There are many texts on linear/convex optimisation and the ellipsoid method. The introductory book on linear optimisation by Bertsimas and Tsitsiklis [1997] is a pleasant read, while the ellipsoid method is explained in detail by Grötschel et al. [2012].

The problem considered in this chapter is part of a broader field called reinforcement learning (RL), which has recently seen a surge of interest. The books by Sutton and Barto [2018] and Bertsekas and Tsitsiklis [1996] describe the foundations. The first book provides an intuitive introduction aimed at computer scientists, while the second book focuses on the theoretical results of the fundamental algorithms. A book by one of the present authors focuses on cataloguing the range of learning problems encountered in reinforcement learning and summarising the basic ideas and algorithms [Szepesvári, 2010].

The UCRL algorithm and the upper and lower regret analysis is due to Auer et al. [2009] and Jaksch et al. [2010]. Our proofs differ in minor ways. A more significant difference is that these works used value iteration for finding the optimistic policy and hence cannot provide polynomial time computation guarantees. In practice this may be preferable to linear programming anyway.

The number of rigourous results for bounding the regret of various algorithms is limited. One idea is to replace the optimistic approach with Thompson sampling, which was first adapted to reinforcement learning by Strens [2000] under the name PSRL (posterior sampling reinforcement learning). Agrawal and Jia [2017] recently made an attempt to improve the dependence of the regret on the state space. The proof is not quite correct, however, and at the time of writing the holes have not yet been patched. Azar et al. [2017] also improve upon the UCRL2 bound, but for finite-horizon episodic problems, where they derive an optimistic algorithm with regret $\tilde{O}(\sqrt{HSAn})$, which after adapting UCRL to the episodic setting improves on its regret by a factor of $\sqrt{SH}$. The main innovation is to use Freedman's Bernstein-style inequality for computing bonuses directly while computing action values using backwards induction from the end of the episode rather than keeping confidence estimates for the transition probabilities. An issue with both of these improvements is that lower-order terms in the bounds mean they only hold for large n. It remains to be seen if these terms arise from the analysis or if the algorithms need modification. UCRL2 will fail in MDPs with infinite diameter, even if the learner starts in a subset of the states that is strongly connected from which it cannot escape. This limitation was recently overcome by Fruit et al. [2018], who provide an algorithm with roughly the same regret as UCRL2, but where the dependence on the diameter and state space are replaced with those of the sub-MDP in which the learner starts and from which it is assumed there is no escape.

Tewari and Bartlett [2008] use an optimistic version of linear programming to obtain finite-time logarithmic bounds with suboptimal instance-dependent constants. Note this paper mistakenly drops some constants from the confidence intervals, which after fixing would make the constants even worse and seems to have other problems, as well [Fruit et al., 2018]. Similar results are also available for UCRL2 [Auer and Ortner, 2007]. Burnetas and Katehakis [1997a] prove asymptotic guarantees with optimal constants, but with the crucial assumption that the support of the next-state distributions $P_a(s)$ are known. Lai and Graves [1997] also consider asymptotic optimality. However, they consider general state spaces where the set of transition probabilities is smoothly parameterised with a known parameterisation but under the weakened goal of competing with the best of finitely many memoryless policies given to the learner as black boxes.

Finite-time regret for large state and action space MDPs under additional structural assumptions are also considered by Abbasi-Yadkori and Szepesvári [2011], Abbasi-Yadkori [2012] and Ortner and Ryabko [2012]. Abbasi-Yadkori and Szepesvári [2011] and Abbasi-Yadkori [2012] give algorithms with $O(\sqrt{n})$ regret for linearly parameterised MDP problems with quadratic cost (linear quadratic regulation, or LQR), while Ortner and Ryabko [2012] give $O(n^{(2d+1)/(2d+2)})$ regret bounds under a Lipschitz assumption, where d is the dimensionality of the state space. The algorithms in these works are not guaranteed to be computationally efficient because they rely on optimistic policies. In theory, this could be addressed by Thompson sampling, which is considered by Abeille and Lazaric [2017b], who obtain partial results for the LQR setting. Thompson sampling has also been studied in the Bayesian framework by Osband et al. [2013], Abbasi-Yadkori and Szepesvári [2015], Osband and Van Roy [2017] and Theocharous et al. [2017], of which Abbasi-Yadkori and Szepesvári [2015] and Theocharous et al. [2017] consider general parametrisations, while the other papers are concerned with finite state-action MDPs. Learning in MDPs has also been studied in the probability approximately correct (PAC) framework introduced by Kearns and Singh [2002], where the objective is to design policies for which the number of badly suboptimal actions is small with high probability. The focus of these papers is on the discounted reward setting rather than average reward. The algorithms are again built on the optimism principle. Algorithms that are known to be PAC-MDP include R-max [Brafman and Tennenholtz, 2003, Kakade, 2003], MBIE [Strehl and Littman, 2005, 2008], delayed Q-learning [Strehl et al., 2006], the optimistic-initialisation-based algorithm of Szita and Lőrincz [2009], MorMax by Szita and Szepesvári [2010], and an adaptation of UCRL by Lattimore and Hutter [2012], which they call UCRLγ. The latter work presents optimal results (matching upper and lower bounds) for the case when the transition structure is sparse, while the optimal dependence on the number of state-action pairs is achieved by delayed Q-learning and Mormax [Strehl et al., 2006, Szita and Szepesvári, 2010], though the Mormax bound is better in its dependency on the discount factor. The idea to incorporate the uncertainty in the transitions into the action space to solve the optimistic optimisation problem appeared in the analysis of MBIE [Strehl and Littman, 2008]. A hybrid between stochastic and adversarial settings is when the reward sequence is chosen by an adversary, while transitions are stochastic. This problem has been introduced by Even-Dar et al. [2004]. State-of-the-art results for the bandit case are due to Neu et al. [2014], where the reader can also find further pointers to the literature. The case when the rewards and the transitions probability distributions are chosen adversarially is studied by [Abbasi-Yadkori et al., 2013].

38.10 Exercises

38.1 (EXISTENCE OF PROBABILITY SPACE) Let $M = (\mathcal{S}, \mathcal{A}, P)$ be a finite **controlled Markov environment**, which is a finite MDP without the reward function. A policy $\pi = (\pi_t)_{t=1}^{\infty}$ is a sequence of probability kernels where π_t is from $(\mathcal{S} \times \mathcal{A})^{t-1} \times \mathcal{S}$ to $\mathcal{A}$. Given a policy π and initial state distribution $\mu \in \mathcal{P}(\mathcal{S})$, show there exists a probability space $(\Omega, \mathcal{F}, \mathbb{P})$ and an infinite sequence of random elements $S_1, A_1, S_2, A_2, \ldots$ such that for any $s \in \mathcal{S}, a \in \mathcal{A}$ and $t \in \mathbb{N}$,

(a) $\mathbb{P}(S_1 = s) = \mu(s)$;
(b) $\mathbb{P}(S_{t+1} = s \mid S_1, A_1, \ldots, S_t, A_t) = P_{A_t}(S_t, s)$; and
(c) $\mathbb{P}(A_t = a \mid S_1, A_1, \ldots, S_t) = \pi_t(a \mid S_1, A_1, \ldots, S_{t-1}, A_{t-1}, S_t)$.

HINT   Use Theorem 3.3.

38.2 (SUFFICIENCY OF MARKOV POLICIES) Let $M = (\mathcal{S}, \mathcal{A}, P)$ be a finite controlled Markov environment, π be an arbitrary policy and $\mu \in \mathcal{P}(\mathcal{S})$ an arbitrary initial state distribution. Denote by $\mathbb{P}_\mu^\pi$ the probability distribution that results from the interconnection of π and M, while the initial state distribution is μ.

(a) Show there exists a Markov policy π' such that

$$\mathbb{P}_\mu^\pi(S_t = s, A_t = a) = \mathbb{P}_\mu^{\pi'}(S_t = a, A_t = a).$$

for all $t \geq 1$ and $s, a \in \mathcal{S} \times \mathcal{A}$.

(b) Conclude that for any policy π there exists a Markov policy π' such that for any $s \in \mathcal{S}, \bar{\rho}_s^\pi = \bar{\rho}_s^{\pi'}$.

HINT   Define π' in an inductively starting at $t = 1$. Puterman [theorem 5.5.1 2009] proves this result and credits Strauch [1966].

38.3 (DETERMINISTIC POLICIES MINIMISE TRAVEL TIME) Let P be some transition structure over some finite state space $\mathcal{S}$ and some finite action space $\mathcal{A}$. Show that the expected travel time between two states s, s' of $\mathcal{S}$ is minimised by a deterministic policy.

HINT   Let $\tau^*(s, s')$ be the shortest expected travel time between some arbitrary pairs of states, which for $s = s'$ is defined to be zero. Show that τ^* satisfies the fixed point equation

$$\tau^*(s, s') = \begin{cases} 0, & \text{if } s = s'; \\ 1 + \min_a \sum_{s''} P_a(s, s'') \, \tau^*(s'', s'), & \text{otherwise.} \end{cases}$$

38.4 (STRONGLY CONNECTED $\Leftrightarrow$ FINITE DIAMETER) Let M be a finite MDP. Prove that $D(M) < \infty$ is equivalent to M being strongly connected.

38.5 (DIAMETER LOWER BOUND) Let $M = (\mathcal{S}, \mathcal{A}, P, r)$ be any MDP. Show that $D(M) \geq \log_A(S) - 3$.

HINT   Denote by $d^*(s, s')$ the minimum expected time it takes to reach state s' when starting from state s. The definition of d^* can be extended to arbitrary initial distributions μ_0 over states and sets $U \subset \mathcal{S}$ of target states: $d^*(\mu_0, U) = \sum_s \mu_0(s) \sum_{s' \in U} d^*(s, s')$. Prove by induction on the size of U that

$$d^*(\mu_0, U) \geq \min \left\{ \sum_{k \geq 0} k n_k \,\Big|\, 0 \leq n_k \leq A^k, k \geq 0, \sum_{k \geq 0} n_k = |U| \right\} \tag{38.25}$$

and then conclude that the proposition holds by choosing $U = \mathcal{S}$ [Jaksch et al., 2010, corollary 15].

38.6 (STATE VISITATION PROBABILITIES AND CUMULATIVE REWARD) Let $M = (\mathcal{S}, \mathcal{A}, P, r)$ be an MDP and π a memoryless policy and $i, j \in [S]$.

(a) Show that $e_i^\top P_\pi^t e_j$ is the probability of arriving in state j from state i in t rounds using policy π.

(b) Show that $e_i^\top \sum_{t=1}^n P_\pi^t r_\pi$ is the expected cumulative reward collected by policy π over n rounds when starting in state i.

38.7 (STOCHASTIC MATRICES) Let P be any $S \times S$ right stochastic matrix. Show that the following hold:

(a) $A_n = \frac{1}{n} \sum_{t=0}^{n-1} P^t$ is right stochastic.

(b) $A_n + \frac{1}{n}(P^n - I) = A_n P = P A_n$.

(c) $P^* = \lim_{n \to \infty} \frac{1}{n} \sum_{t=0}^{n-1} P^t$ exists and is right stochastic.

(d) $P^* P = P P^* = P^* P^* = P^*$.

(e) The matrix $H = (I - P + P^*)^{-1}$ is well defined.

(f) Let $U = H - P^*$. Then $U = \lim_{n \to \infty} \frac{1}{n} \sum_{i=1}^n \sum_{k=0}^{i-1} (P^k - P^*)$.

(g) Let $r \in \mathbb{R}^S$ and $\rho = P^* r$. Then $v = \lim_{n \to \infty} \frac{1}{n} \sum_{i=1}^n \sum_{k=0}^{i-1} P^k(r - \rho)$ is well defined and satisfies (38.3).

(h) With the notation of the previous part, $v + \rho = r + Pv$.

HINT   Note that the first four parts of this exercise are the same as in Chapter 37. For parts (c) and (d), you will likely find it useful that the space of right stochastic matrices is compact. Then show that all cluster points of (A_n) are the same. For (g), show that $v = Ur$.

> The previous exercise shows that the gain and differential value function of any memoryless policy in any MDP are well defined. The matrix H is called the **fundamental matrix**, and U is called the **deviation matrix**.

38.8 (DISCOUNTED MDPs) Let $\gamma \in (0, 1)$, and define the operator $T_\gamma : \mathbb{R}^S \to \mathbb{R}^S$ by

$$(T_\gamma v)(s) = \max_{a \in \mathcal{A}} r_a(s) + \gamma \langle P_a(s), v \rangle.$$

(a) Prove that T_γ is a contraction with respect to the supremum norm:

$$\|T_\gamma v - T_\gamma w\|_\infty \le \gamma \|v - w\|_\infty \text{ for any } v, w \in \mathbb{R}^S.$$

(b) Prove that there exists a $v \in \mathbb{R}^S$ such that $T_\gamma v = v$.

(c) Let π be the greedy policy with respect to v. Show $v = r_\pi + \gamma P_\pi v$.

(d) Prove that $v = (I - \gamma P_\pi)^{-1} r$.

(e) Define the γ-discounted value function v_γ^π of a policy π as the function that for any given state $s \in \mathcal{S}$ gives the total expected discounted reward of the policy when it is started from state s. Let $v_\gamma^* \in \mathbb{R}^S$ be defined by $v_\gamma^*(s) = \max_\pi v_\gamma^\pi(s)$, $s \in \mathcal{S}$. We call π γ-discount optimal if $v_\gamma^* = v_\gamma^\pi$. Show that if π is greedy with respect to v from part (b), then π is a γ-optimal policy.

HINT   For (b), you should use the contraction mapping theorem (or Banach fixed point theorem), which says that if $(\mathcal{X}, d)$ is a complete metric space and $T : \mathcal{X} \to \mathcal{X}$ satisfies $d(T(x), T(y)) \le \gamma d(x, y)$ for $\gamma \in [0, 1)$, then there exists an $x \in \mathcal{X}$ such that $T(x) = x$. For (e), use (d) and Exercise 38.2 to show that it suffices to check that $v_\gamma^\pi \le v$ for any Markov policy π. Verify this by using the fact that T_γ is monotone ($f \le g$ implies that $T_\gamma f \le T_\gamma g$) and showing that $v_{\gamma,n}^\pi \le T_\gamma^n 0$ holds for any n, where $v_{\gamma,n}^\pi(s)$ is the total expected discounted reward of the policy when it is started from state s and is followed for n steps.

38.9 (FROM DISCOUNTING TO AVERAGE REWARD) Recall that $H = (I - P + P^*)^{-1}, U = H - P^*$. For $\gamma \in [0, 1)$, define $P_\gamma^* = (1 - \gamma)(I - \gamma P)^{-1}$. Show that

(a) $\lim_{\gamma \to 1-} P_\gamma^* = P^*$;

(b) $\lim_{\gamma \to 1-} \frac{P_\gamma^* - P^*}{1 - \gamma} = U$.

HINT   For (a) start by manipulating the expressions $P_\gamma^* P$ and $(P_\gamma^*)^{-1} P^*$. For (b) consider $H^{-1}(P_\gamma^* - P^*)$.

38.10 (SOLUTION TO BELLMAN OPTIMALITY EQUATION) In this exercise you will prove part (a) of Theorem 38.2.

(a) Prove there exists a deterministic stationary policy π and increasing sequence of discount rates (γ_n) with $\gamma_n < 1$ and $\lim_{n \to \infty} \gamma_n = 1$ such that π is a greedy policy with respect to the fixed point v_n of T_{γ_n} for all n.

(b) For the remainder of the exercise, fix a policy π whose existence is guaranteed by part (a). Show that $\rho^\pi = \rho \mathbf{1}$ is constant.

(c) Let $v = v_\pi$ be the value function and $\rho = \rho_\pi$ the gain of policy π. Show that (ρ, v) satisfies the Bellman optimality equation.

HINT   For (a), use the fact that for finite MDPs there are only finitely many memoryless deterministic policies. For (b) and (c), use Exercise 38.9.

38.11 (COUNTERINTUITIVE SOLUTIONS TO THE BELLMAN EQUATION) Consider the deterministic MDP shown below with two states and two actions. The first action, STAY, keeps the state, the same and the second action, GO, moves the learner to the other state while incurring a reward of -1. Show that in this example, solutions (ρ, v) to the Bellman optimality equations (Eq. (38.5)) are exactly the elements of the set

$$\{(\rho, v) \in \mathbb{R} \times \mathbb{R}^2 : \rho = 0, \ v(1) - 1 \le v(2) \le v(1) + 1\}.$$

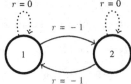

38.12 (DANGERS OF LINEAR PROGRAM RELAXATION) Give an example of an MDP and a solution (ρ, v) to the linear program in Eq. (38.6) such that v does not satisfy the Bellman optimality equation and the greedy policy with respect to v is not optimal.

38.13 (BOUND ON SPAN IN TERMS OF DIAMETER) Let M be a strongly connected MDP and (ρ, v) be a solution to the Bellman optimality equation. Show that $\mathrm{span}(v) \le (\rho^* - \min_{s,a} r_a(s)) D(M)$.

HINT   Note that by Theorem 38.2, $\rho = \rho^*$. Fix some states $s_1 \ne s_2$ and a memoryless policy π. Show that

$$v(s_2) - v(s_1) \le (\rho^* - \min_{s,a} r_a(s)) \mathbb{E}^\pi [\tau_{s_2} \mid S_1 = s_1].$$

Note for the sake of curiosity that the above display continues to hold for weakly communicating MDPs.

The proof of Theorem 4 in the paper by Bartlett and Tewari [2009] is incorrect. The problem is that the statement needs to hold for any solution v of the Bellman optimality equation. The proof uses an argument that hinges on the fact that in an aperiodic strongly connected MDP, v is in the set $\{c\mathbf{1} + \lim_{n\to\infty} T^n\mathbf{0} - n\rho^* : c \in \mathbb{R}\}$. However, Exercise 38.11 shows that there exist strongly connected MDPs where this does not hold.

38.14 (SEPARATION ORACLES) Solve the following problems:

(a) Prove that Algorithm 27 provides a separation oracle for convex set $\mathcal{K}$ defined in Eq. (38.10).

(b) Assuming that Algorithm 27 can be implemented efficiently, explain how to find an approximate solution to Eq. (38.7).

38.15 (COMBINING SEPARATION ORACLES) Let $\mathcal{K} \subset \mathbb{R}^d$ be a convex set and ϕ be a separation oracle for $\mathcal{K}$. Suppose that $a_1, \ldots, a_n$ is a collection of vectors with $a_k \in \mathbb{R}^d$ and $b_1, \ldots, b_k$ be a collection of scalars. Let $H_k = \{x \in \mathbb{R}^d : \langle a_k, x \rangle \geq b_k\}$. Devise an efficient separation oracle for $\bigcap_{k=1}^n \mathcal{K} \cap H_k$.

38.16 (APPROXIMATE SOLUTIONS TO BELLMAN EQUATION) Consider a strongly connected MDP, and suppose that ρ and v approximately satisfy the Bellman optimality equation in the sense that there exists an $\varepsilon > 0$ such that

$$\left| \rho + v(s) - \max_{a\in\mathcal{A}} r_a(s) + \langle P_a(s), v \rangle \right| \leq \varepsilon \qquad \text{for all state-action pairs } s, a. \qquad (38.26)$$

(a) Show that $\rho \geq \rho^* - \varepsilon$.

(b) Let $\tilde{\pi}$ be the greedy policy with respect to v. Assume that $\tilde{\pi}$ is ε'-greedy with respect to v in the sense that $r_{\tilde{\pi}(s)}(s) + \langle P_{\tilde{\pi}(s)}(s), v \rangle \geq \max_{a\in\mathcal{A}} r_a(s) + \langle P_a(s), v \rangle - \varepsilon'$ holds for all $s \in \mathcal{S}$. Show that $\tilde{\pi}$ is $2\varepsilon + \varepsilon'$ optimal: $\rho^{\tilde{\pi}} \geq \rho^* - (2\varepsilon + \varepsilon')$.

(c) Suppose that ρ^* in Eq. (38.7) is replaced with $\rho \in [\rho^*, \rho^* + \delta]$. Show that the linear program remains feasible and the solution (ρ, v) satisfies Eq. (38.26) with $\varepsilon \leq |\mathcal{S}|^2\delta$.

38.17 (AVERAGE-OPTIMAL IS NEARLY FINITE-TIME OPTIMAL) Let M be a strongly connected MDP with rewards in $[0, 1]$, diameter $D < \infty$ and optimal gain ρ^*. Let $v_n^*(s)$ be the maximum total expected reward in n steps when the process starts in state s. Prove that $v_n^*(s) \leq n\rho^* + D$.

38.18 (HIGH PROBABILITY $\Rightarrow$ EXPECTED REGRET) Prove that (38.12) follows from Theorem 38.6.

38.19 (NECESSITY OF PHASES) The purpose of this exercise is to show that without phases, UCRL2 may suffer linear regret. For convenience, we consider the modified version of UCRL2 in Exercise 38.23 that does not know the reward. Now suppose we further modify this algorithm to re-solve the optimistic MDP in every round ($\tau_k = k$ for all k). We make use of the following deterministic MDP with two actions $\mathcal{A} = \{\text{STAY}, \text{GO}\}$ represented by dashed and solid arrows respectively.

(a) Find all memoryless optimal policies for the MDP in Fig. 38.4.

(b) Prove that the version of UCRL2 given in Exercise 38.23 modified to re-solve the optimistic MDP in every round suffers linear regret on this MDP.

HINT   Since UCRL2 and the environment are both deterministic you can examine the behaviour of the algorithm on the MDP. You should aim to prove that eventually the algorithm will alternate between actions STAY and GO.

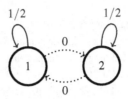

Figure 38.4   Transitions and rewards are deterministic. Numbers indicate the rewards.

38.20 (EXTENDED MDP IS STRONGLY CONNECTED) Let $\tilde{M}_k$ be the extended MDP defined in Section 38.5.1 and $\mathcal{C}_{\tau_k}$ be the confidence set defined in Eq. (38.13). Prove that $P \in \mathcal{C}_{\tau_k}$ implies that $\tilde{M}_k$ is strongly connected.

38.21 (CONFIDENCE SETS) Prove Lemma 38.8.

HINT   Use the result of Exercise 5.17 and apply a union bound over all state-action pairs and the number of samples. Use the Markov property to argue that the independence assumption in Exercise 5.17 is not problematic.

38.22 Let (a_k) and (A_k) be non-negative numbers so that for any $k \geq 0$, $a_{k+1} \leq A_k = 1 \vee (a_1 + \cdots + a_k)$. Prove that for any $m \geq 1$,

$$\sum_{k=1}^{m} \frac{a_k}{\sqrt{A_{k-1}}} \leq \left(\sqrt{2}+1\right)\sqrt{A_m}.$$

HINT   The statement is trivial if $\sum_{k=1}^{m-1} a_k \leq 1$. If this does not hold, use induction based on $m = n, n+1, \ldots$, where n is the first integer such that $\sum_{k=1}^{n-1} a_k > 1$.

38.23 (UNKNOWN REWARDS) In this exercise, you will modify the algorithm to handle the situation where r is unknown and rewards are stochastic. More precisely, assume there exists a function $r_a(s) \in [0, 1]$ for all $a \in \mathcal{A}$ and $s \in \mathcal{S}$. Then, in each round, the learner observes S_t, chooses an action A_t and receives a reward $X_t \in [0, 1]$ with

$$\mathbb{E}[X_t \mid A_t, S_t] = r_{A_t}(S_t).$$

In order to accommodate the unknown reward function, we modify UCRL2 in the following way. First, define the empirical reward at the start of the kth phase by

$$\hat{r}_{k,a}(s) = \sum_{u=1}^{\tau_k-1} \frac{\mathbb{I}\{S_u = s, A_u = a\}\, X_u}{1 \vee T_{\tau_k-1}(s,a)}.$$

Then, let $\tilde{r}_{t,a}(s)$ be an upper confidence bound given by

$$\tilde{r}_{k,a}(s) = \hat{r}_{t,a}(s) + \sqrt{\frac{L}{2(1 \vee T_{\tau_k-1}(s,a))}},$$

where L is as in the proof of Theorem 38.6. The modified algorithm operates exactly like Algorithm 28, but replaces the unknown $r_a(s)$ with $\tilde{r}_{k,a}(s)$ when solving the extended MDP. Prove that with probability at least $1 - 3\delta/2$, the modified policy in the modified setting has regret at most

$$\hat{R}_n \leq CD(M)\mathrm{S}\sqrt{n\mathrm{A}\log\left(\frac{n\mathrm{SA}}{\delta}\right)},$$

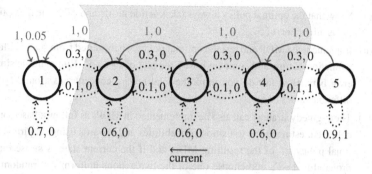

Figure 38.5 The RiverSwim MDP when S = 5. Solid arrows correspond to action left and dashed ones to action right. The right-hand bank is slippery, so the learner sometimes falls back into the river.

where $C > 0$ is a universal constant.

38.24 (LOWER BOUND) In this exercise, you will prove the claims to complete the proof of the lower bound.

(a) Prove Claim 38.9.

(b) Prove Claim 38.10.

(c) Prove Claim 38.11.

38.25 (CONTEXTUAL BANDITS AS MDPS) Consider the MDP $M = (S, A, P, r)$, where $P_a(s) = p$ for some fixed categorical distribution p for any $(s, a) \in S \times A$, where $\min_{s \in S} p(s) > 0$. Assume that the rewards for action a in state s are sampled from a distribution supported on $[0, 1]$ (see Note 3). An MDP like this defines nothing but a contextual bandit.

(a) Derive the optimal policy and the average optimal reward.

(b) Show an optimal value function that solves the Bellman optimality equation.

(c) Prove that the diameter of this MDP is $D = \max_s 1/p(s)$.

(d) Consider the algorithm that puts one instance of an appropriate version of UCB into every state (the same idea was explored in the context of adversarial bandits in Section 18.1). Prove that the expected regret of your algorithm will be at most $O(\sqrt{SAn})$.

(e) Does the scaling behaviour of the upper bound in Theorem 38.6 match the actual scaling behaviour of the expected regret of UCRL2 in this example? Why or why not?

(f) Design and run an experiment to confirm your claim.

38.26 (IMPLEMENTATION) This is a thinking and coding exercise to illustrate the difficulty of learning in MDPs. The RiverSwim environment is originally due to Strehl and Littman [2008]. The environment has two actions $A = \{\text{LEFT}, \text{RIGHT}\}$ and $S = [S]$ with $S \geq 2$. In all states $s > 1$, action LEFT deterministically leads to state $s - 1$ and provides no reward. In state 1, action LEFT leaves the state unchanged and yields a reward of 0.05. The action RIGHT tends to make the agent move right but not deterministically (the learner is swimming against a current). With probability 0.3, the state is incremented, with a probability 0.6, the state is left unchanged, while with probability of 0.1 the state is decremented. This action incurs a reward of zero in all states except in state S, where it receives a reward of 1. The situation when $S = 5$ is illustrated in Fig. 38.5.

(a) Show that the optimal policy always takes action RIGHT and calculate the optimal average reward ρ^* as a function of S.

(b) Implement the MDP and test the optimal policy when started from state 1. Plot the total reward as a function of time and compare it with the plot of $t \mapsto t\rho^*$. Run multiple simulations to produce error bars. How fast do you think the total reward concentrates around $t\rho^*$? Experiment with different values of S.

(c) The ε-greedy strategy can also be implemented in MDPs as follows: based on the data previously collected, estimate the transition probabilities and rewards using empirical means. Find the optimal policy π^* of the resulting MDP, and if the current state is s, use the action $\pi^*(s)$ with probability $1 - \varepsilon$ and choose one of the two actions uniformly at random with the remaining probability. To ensure the empirical MDP has a well-defined optimal policy, mix the empirical estimate of the next state distributions $P_a(s)$ with the uniform distribution with a small mixture coefficient. Implement this strategy and plot the trajectories it exhibits for various MDP sizes. Explain what you see.

(d) Implement UCRL2 and produce the same plots. Can you explain what you see?

(e) Run simulations in RiverSwim instances of various sizes to compare the regret of UCRL2 and ε-greedy. What do you conclude?

38.27 (UCRL2 AND UNREACHABLE STATES) Show that UCRL2 suffers linear regret if there is a single unreachable state with reward larger than the optimal gain.

HINT   Think about the optimistic MDP and the optimistic transitions to the unreachable state. The article by Fruit et al. [2018] provides a policy that mitigates the problem.

38.28 (MDPs WITH TRAPS (I)) Fix state space $\mathcal{S}$, action space $\mathcal{A}$ and reward function r. Let π be a policy with sublinear regret in all strongly connected MDPs $(\mathcal{S}, \mathcal{A}, r, P)$. Now suppose that $(\mathcal{S}, \mathcal{A}, r, P)$ is an MDP that is not strongly connected such that for all $s \in \mathcal{S}$, there exists a state s' that is reachable from s under some policy and where $\rho^*_{s'} < \max_u \rho^*_u$. Finally, assume that $\rho^*_{s_1} = \max_u \rho^*_u$ almost surely. Prove that π has linear regret on this MDP.

38.29 (MDPs WITH TRAPS (II)) This exercise develops the ideas mentioned in Note 14. First, we need some definitions: fix $\mathcal{S}$ and $\mathcal{A}$ and define Π_0 as the set of policies (learner strategies) for MDPs with state space $\mathcal{S}$ and action space $\mathcal{A}$ that achieve sublinear regret in any strongly connected MDP with state space $\mathcal{S}$ and action space $\mathcal{A}$. Now consider an arbitrary finite MDP $M = (\mathcal{S}, \mathcal{A}, P, r)$. A state $s \in \mathcal{S}$ is reachable from state $s' \in \mathcal{S}$ if there is a policy that when started in s' reaches state s with positive probability after one or more steps. A set of states $C \subset \mathcal{S}$ is a **strongly connected component** (SCC) if every state $s \in U$ is reachable from every other state $s' \in C$, including $s = s'$. A set $C \subseteq \mathcal{S}$ is **maximal** if we cannot add more states to C and still maintain the SCC property. A SCC C is called a **maximal end component** if there does not exist another SCC C' with $C \subset C'$. Show the following:

(a) There exists at least one MEC and two MECs C_1 and C_2, are either equal or disjoint.

(b) Let $C_1, \ldots, C_k$ be all the distinct MECs of an MDP. The MDP structure defines a connectivity over $C_1, \ldots, C_k$ as follows: for $i \neq j$, we say that C_i is connected to C_j if from some state in C_i, it is possible to reach some state of C_j with positive probability under some policy. Show that this connectivity structure defines a directed graph, which must be acyclic.

(c) Let $C_1, \ldots, C_m$ with $m \leq k$ be the sinks (the nodes with no out edges) of this graph. Show that if M is strongly connected, then $m = 1$ and $C_1 = \mathcal{S}$.

(d) Show that for any $i \in [m]$ and for any policy $\pi \in \Pi_0$, it holds that π will reach C_i in finite time with positive probability if the initial state distribution assigns positive mass to the non-trap states $\mathcal{S} \setminus \cup_{i \in [m]} C_i$.

(e) Show that for $i \leq m$, for any $s \in C_i$ and any action $a \in \mathcal{A}$, $P_a(s, s') = 0$ for any $s' \in \mathcal{S} \setminus C_i$, i.e., C_i is **closed**.

(f) Show that the restriction of M to C_i defined as

$$M_i = (C_i, \mathcal{A}, (P_a(s))_{s \in C_i, a \in \mathcal{A}}, (r_a(s))_{s \in C_i, a \in \mathcal{A}})$$

is an MDP.

(g) Show that M_i is strongly connected.

(h) Let τ be the time when the learner enters one of $C_1, \ldots, C_m$ and let $I \in [m]$ be the index of the class that is entered at time τ. That is, $S_\tau \in C_I$. Show that if M is strongly connected, then $\tau = 1$ with probability one.

(i) We redefine the regret as follows:

$$R'_n = \mathbb{E}\left[\sum_{t=\tau}^{\tau+n-1} r_{A_t}(S_t) - n\rho^*(M_I) \right].$$

Show that if M is strongly connected, then $R_n = R'_n$.

(j) Can you design a policy with $R'_n = O(\mathbb{E}[D(M_I)|C_I|]\sqrt{An\log(n)})$? Will UCRL2 already satisfy this?

> The logic of the regret definition in part (i) is that by part (d), reasonable policies cannot control which trap they fall into in an MDP that has more than one traps. As such, policies should not be penalised for what trap they fall into. However, once a policy falls into some trap, we expect it to start to behave near optimally. What this definition is still lacking is that it is insensitive to how fast a policy gets trapped. The last part is quite subtle [Fruit et al., 2018].

38.30 (CHAIN RULE FOR RELATIVE ENTROPY) Prove the claim in Eq. (38.22).

HINT   Make use of the result in Exercise 14.12.

Bibliography

Y. Abbasi-Yadkori. *Forced-exploration based algorithms for playing in bandits with large action sets.* PhD thesis, University of Alberta, 2009a. [213]

Y. Abbasi-Yadkori. Forced-exploration based algorithms for playing in bandits with large action sets. Master's thesis, University of Alberta, Department of Computing Science, 2009b. [79]

Y. Abbasi-Yadkori. *Online Learning for Linearly Parametrized Control Problems.* PhD thesis, University of Alberta, 2012. [214, 475]

Y. Abbasi-Yadkori and Cs. Szepesvári. Regret bounds for the adaptive control of linear quadratic systems. In *Proceedings of the 24th Conference on Learning Theory*, pages 1–26, Budapest, Hungary, 2011. JMLR.org. [475]

Y. Abbasi-Yadkori and Cs. Szepesvári. Bayesian optimal control of smoothly parameterized systems. In *Proceedings of the 31st Conference on Uncertainty in Artificial Intelligence*, pages 2–11, Arlington, VA, United States, 2015. AUAI Press. [475]

Y. Abbasi-Yadkori, A. Antos, and Cs. Szepesvári. Forced-exploration based algorithms for playing in stochastic linear bandits. In *COLT Workshop on On-line Learning with Limited Feedback*, 2009. [79, 213]

Y. Abbasi-Yadkori, D. Pál, and Cs. Szepesvári. Improved algorithms for linear stochastic bandits. In *Advances in Neural Information Processing Systems*, pages 2312–2320. Curran Associates, Inc., 2011. [213]

Y. Abbasi-Yadkori, D. Pál, and Cs. Szepesvári. Online-to-confidence-set conversions and application to sparse stochastic bandits. In *Proceedings of the 15th International Conference on Artificial Intelligence and Statistics*, pages 1–9, La Palma, Canary Islands, 2012. JMLR.org. [249]

Y. Abbasi-Yadkori, P. L. Bartlett, V. Kanade, Y. Seldin, and Cs. Szepesvári. Online learning in Markov decision processes with adversarially chosen transition probability distributions. In *Advances in Neural Information Processing Systems*, pages 2508–2516, USA, 2013. Curran Associates Inc. [475]

Y. Abbasi-Yadkori, P. Bartlett, V. Gabillon, A. Malek, and M. Valko. Best of both worlds: Stochastic & adversarial best-arm identification. In *Proceedings of the 31st Conference on Learning Theory*, 2018. [365]

N. Abe and P. M. Long. Associative reinforcement learning using linear probabilistic concepts. In *Proceedings of the 16th International Conference on Machine Learning*, pages 3–11, San Francisco, CA, USA, 1999. Morgan Kaufmann Publishers Inc. [213]

M. Abeille and A. Lazaric. Linear Thompson sampling revisited. In *Proceedings of the 20th International Conference on Artificial Intelligence and Statistics*, pages 176–184, Fort Lauderdale, FL, USA, 2017a. JMLR.org. [417]

M. Abeille and A. Lazaric. Thompson sampling for linear-quadratic control problems. In *Proceedings of the 20th International Conference on Artificial Intelligence and Statistics*, pages 1246–1254, Fort Lauderdale, FL, USA, 2017b. JMLR.org. [475]

J. D. Abernethy and A. Rakhlin. Beating the adaptive bandit with high probability. In *Proceedings of the 22nd Conference on Learning Theory*, 2009. [149, 301]

J. D. Abernethy, E. Hazan, and A. Rakhlin. Competing in the dark: An efficient algorithm for bandit linear optimization. In *Proceedings of the 21st Conference on Learning Theory*, pages 263–274. Omnipress, 2008. [301]

J. D. Abernethy, E. Hazan, and A. Rakhlin. Interior-point methods for full-information and bandit online learning. *IEEE Transactions on Information Theory*, 58(7):4164–4175, 2012. [148, 299]

J. D. Abernethy, C. Lee, A. Sinha, and A. Tewari. Online linear optimization via smoothing. In *Proceedings of the 27th Conference on Learning Theory*, pages 807–823, Barcelona, Spain, 2014. JMLR.org. [328]

J. D. Abernethy, C. Lee, and A. Tewari. Fighting bandits with a new kind of smoothness. In *Advances in Neural Information Processing Systems*, pages 2197–2205. Curran Associates, Inc., 2015. [301, 328]

M. Abramowitz and I. A. Stegun. *Handbook of mathematical functions: with formulas, graphs, and mathematical tables*, volume 55. Courier Corporation, 1964. [158, 418]

M. Achab, S. Clémençon, A. Garivier, A. Sabourin, and C. Vernade. Max k-armed bandit: On the extremehunter algorithm and beyond. In *Joint European Conference on Machine Learning and Knowledge Discovery in Databases*, pages 389–404. Springer, 2017. [365]

L. Adelman. Choice theory. In Saul I. Gass and Michael C. Fu, editors, *Encyclopedia of Operations Research and Management Science*, pages 164–168. Springer US, Boston, MA, 2013. [54]

A. Agarwal, D. P. Foster, D. J. Hsu, S. M. Kakade, and A. Rakhlin. Stochastic convex optimization with bandit feedback. In *Advances in Neural Information Processing Systems*, pages 1035–1043. Curran Associates, Inc., 2011. [315]

A. Agarwal, D. P. Foster, D. Hsu, S. M. Kakade, and A. Rakhlin. Stochastic convex optimization with bandit feedback. *SIAM Journal on Optimization*, 23(1):213–240, 2013. [364]

A. Agarwal, D. Hsu, S. Kale, J. Langford, L. Li, and R. Schapire. Taming the monster: A fast and simple algorithm for contextual bandits. In *Proceedings of the 31st International Conference on Machine Learning*, pages 1638–1646, Bejing, China, 2014. JMLR.org. [201, 202]

A. Agarwal, S. Bird, M. Cozowicz, L. Hoang, J. Langford, S. Lee, J. Li, D. Melamed, G. Oshri, and O. Ribas. Making contextual decisions with low technical debt. arXiv:1606.03966, 2016. [11]

R. Agrawal. Sample mean based index policies with O($\log n$) regret for the multi-armed bandit problem. *Advances in Applied Probability*, pages 1054–1078, 1995. [92, 100]

S. Agrawal and N. R. Devanur. Bandits with concave rewards and convex knapsacks. In *Proceedings of the 15th ACM conference on Economics and computation*, pages 989–1006. ACM, 2014. [315]

S. Agrawal and N. R. Devanur. Linear contextual bandits with knapsacks. In *Advances in Neural Information Processing Systems*, pages 3458–3467. Curran Associates Inc., 2016. [315]

S. Agrawal and N. Goyal. Analysis of Thompson sampling for the multi-armed bandit problem. In *Proceedings of the 25th Conference on Learning Theory*, 2012. [416]

S. Agrawal and N. Goyal. Further optimal regret bounds for Thompson sampling. In *Proceedings of the 16th International Conference on Artificial Intelligence and Statistics*, pages 99–107, Scottsdale, Arizona, USA, 2013a. JMLR.org. [415, 417]

S. Agrawal and N. Goyal. Thompson sampling for contextual bandits with linear payoffs. In *Proceedings of the 30th International Conference on Machine Learning*, pages 127–135, Atlanta, GA, USA, 2013b. JMLR.org. [417]

S. Agrawal and R. Jia. Optimistic posterior sampling for reinforcement learning: worst-case regret bounds. In *Advances in Neural Information Processing Systems*, pages 1184–1194. Curran Associates, Inc., 2017. [474]

S. Agrawal, V. Avadhanula, V. Goyal, and A. Zeevi. Thompson sampling for the MNL-bandit. In *Proceedings of the 2017 Conference on Learning Theory*, pages 76–78, Amsterdam, Netherlands, 2017. JMLR.org. [417]

N. Ailon, Z. Karnin, and T. Joachims. Reducing dueling bandits to cardinal bandits. In *Proceedings of the 31st International Conference on Machine Learning*, pages II–856–II–864. JMLR.org, 2014. [315]

J. Aldrich. "but you have to remember P. J. Daniell of Sheffield". *Electronic Journal for History of Probability and Statistics*, 3(2), 2007. [42]

C. Allenberg, P. Auer, L. Györfi, and G. Ottucsák. Hannan consistency in on-line learning in case of unbounded losses under partial monitoring. In *Proceedings of the 17th International Conference on Algorithmic Learning Theory*, pages 229–243, Berlin, Heidelberg, 2006. Springer-Verlag. [135, 148, 299]

N. Alon, Y. Matias, and M. Szegedy. The space complexity of approximating the frequency moments. In *Proceedings of the 28th annual ACM symposium on theory of computing*, pages 20–29. ACM, 1996. [96]

N. Alon, N. Cesa-Bianchi, C. Gentile, and Y. Mansour. From bandits to experts: A tale of domination and independence. In *Advances in Neural Information Processing Systems*, pages 1610–1618. Curran Associates, Inc., 2013. [316, 448]

N. Alon, N. Cesa-Bianchi, O. Dekel, and T. Koren. Online learning with feedback graphs: Beyond bandits. In *Proceedings of the 28th Conference on Learning Theory*, pages 23–35, Paris, France, 2015. JMLR.org. [316]

V. Anantharam, P. Varaiya, and J. Walrand. Asymptotically efficient allocation rules for the multi-armed bandit problem with multiple plays-part i: Iid rewards. *IEEE Transactions on Automatic Control*, 32(11):968–976, 1987. [214]

J. R. Anderson, J. L. Dillon, and J. E. Hardaker. *Agricultural decision analysis*. Monographs: Applied Economics. Iowa State University Press, 1977. [xiii]

F. J. Anscombe. Sequential medical trials. *Journal of the American Statistical Association*, 58(302): 365–383, 1963. [79]

A. Antos, G. Bartók, D. Pál, and Cs. Szepesvári. Toward a classification of finite partial-monitoring games. *Theoretical Computer Science*, 473:77–99, 2013. [448]

A. Arapostathis, V. S. Borkar, E. Fernandez-Gaucherand, M. K. Ghosh, and S. I. Marcus. Discrete-time controlled Markov processes with average cost criterion: a survey. *SIAM Journal of Control and Optimization*, 31(2):282–344, 1993. [474]

R. Arora, O. Dekel, and A. Tewari. Online bandit learning against an adaptive adversary: From regret to policy regret. In *Proceedings of the 29th International Conference on Machine Learning*, Madison, WI, USA, 2012. Omnipress. [136]

B. Ashwinkumar, J. Langford, and A. Slivkins. Resourceful contextual bandits. In *Proceedings of the 27th Conference on Learning Theory*, pages 1109–1134, Barcelona, Spain, 2014. JMLR.org. [315]

J.-V. Audibert and S. Bubeck. Regret bounds and minimax policies under partial monitoring. *Journal of Machine Learning Research*, 11:2785–2836, 2010a. [136]

J.-Y. Audibert and S. Bubeck. Minimax policies for adversarial and stochastic bandits. In *Proceedings of the 22nd Conference on Learning Theory*, pages 217–226, 2009. [108, 136, 305]

J.-Y. Audibert and S. Bubeck. Best arm identification in multi-armed bandits. In *Proceedings of the 23rd Conference on Learning Theory*, 2010b. [338, 364]

J.-Y. Audibert, R. Munos, and Cs. Szepesvári. Tuning bandit algorithms in stochastic environments. In *Proceedings of the 18th International Conference on Algorithmic Learning Theory*, pages 150–165, Berlin, Heidelberg, 2007. Springer Berlin Heidelberg. [56, 70, 92, 95, 183]

J.-Y. Audibert, R. Munos, and Cs. Szepesvári. Exploration-exploitation tradeoff using variance estimates in multi-armed bandits. *Theoretical Computer Science*, 410(19):1876–1902, 2009. [56]

J.-Y. Audibert, S. Bubeck, and G. Lugosi. Regret in online combinatorial optimization. *Mathematics of Operations Research*, 39(1):31–45, 2013. [301]

P. Auer. Using confidence bounds for exploitation-exploration trade-offs. *Journal of Machine Learning Research*, 3:397–422, 2002. [213, 238]

P. Auer and C. Chiang. An algorithm with nearly optimal pseudo-regret for both stochastic and adversarial bandits. In *Proceedings of the 29th Annual Conference on Learning Theory*, pages 116–120, New York, NY, USA, 2016. JMLR.org. [136]

P. Auer and R. Ortner. Logarithmic online regret bounds for undiscounted reinforcement learning. In *Advances in Neural Information Processing Systems*, pages 49–56. MIT Press, 2007. [475]

P. Auer and R. Ortner. UCB revisited: Improved regret bounds for the stochastic multi-armed bandit problem. *Periodica Mathematica Hungarica*, 61(1-2):55–65, 2010. [82, 108]

P. Auer, N. Cesa-Bianchi, Y. Freund, and R. E. Schapire. Gambling in a rigged casino: The adversarial multi-armed bandit problem. In *Foundations of Computer Science, 1995. Proceedings., 36th Annual Symposium on*, pages 322–331. IEEE, 1995. [81, 125, 137, 174]

P. Auer, N. Cesa-Bianchi, and P. Fischer. Finite-time analysis of the multiarmed bandit problem. *Machine Learning*, 47:235–256, 2002a. [79, 92]

P. Auer, N. Cesa-Bianchi, Y. Freund, and R. E. Schapire. The nonstochastic multiarmed bandit problem. *SIAM Journal on Computing*, 32(1):48–77, 2002b. [148, 149, 175, 201, 338]

P. Auer, R. Ortner, and Cs. Szepesvári. Improved rates for the stochastic continuum-armed bandit problem. In *International Conference on Computational Learning Theory*, pages 454–468. Springer, 2007. [314]

P. Auer, T. Jaksch, and R. Ortner. Near-optimal regret bounds for reinforcement learning. In *Advances in Neural Information Processing Systems*, pages 89–96, 2009. [474]

P. Auer, P. Gajane, and R. Ortner. Adaptively tracking the best arm with an unknown number of distribution changes. In *European Workshop on Reinforcement Learning 14*, 2018. [338]

P. Auer, P. Gajane, and R. Ortner. Adaptively tracking the best bandit arm with an unknown number of distribution changes. In *Proceedings of the 32nd Conference on Learning Theory*, 2019. [337, 338]

B. Awerbuch and R. Kleinberg. Adaptive routing with end-to-end feedback: Distributed learning and geometric approaches. In *Proceedings of the 36th annual ACM symposium on theory of computing*, pages 45–53. ACM, 2004. [328]

S. J. Axler. *Linear algebra done right*, volume 2. Springer, 1997. [445]

M. G. Azar, I. Osband, and R. Munos. Minimax regret bounds for reinforcement learning. In *Proceedings of the 34th International Conference on Machine Learning*, pages 263–272, Sydney, Australia, 06–11 Aug 2017. JMLR.org. [474]

A. Badanidiyuru, R. Kleinberg, and A. Slivkins. Bandits with knapsacks. In *Foundations of Computer Science (FOCS), 2013 IEEE 54th Annual Symposium on*, pages 207–216. IEEE, 2013. [315]

P. L. Bartlett and A. Tewari. Regal: A regularization based algorithm for reinforcement learning in weakly communicating MDPs. In *Proceedings of the 25th Conference on Uncertainty in Artificial Intelligence*, pages 35–42, Arlington, VA, United States, 2009. AUAI Press. [479]

G. Bartók. A near-optimal algorithm for finite partial-monitoring games against adversarial opponents. In *Proceedings of the 26th Conference on Learning Theory*, pages 696–710. JMLR.org, 2013. [447, 448]

G. Bartók and Cs. Szepesvári. Partial monitoring with side information. In *Proceedings of the 23rd International Conference on Algorithmic Learning Theory*, pages 305–319, 2012. [448]

G. Bartók, D. Pál, and Cs. Szepesvári. Toward a classification of finite partial-monitoring games. In *Proceedings of the 21st International Conference on Algorithmic Learning Theory*, pages 224–238. Springer, 2010. [448]

G. Bartók, N. Zolghadr, and Cs. Szepesvári. An adaptive algorithm for finite stochastic partial monitoring. In *Proceedings of the 29th International Conference on Machine Learning*, pages 1779–1786, USA, 2012. Omnipress. [448]

G. Bartók, D. P. Foster, D. Pál, A. Rakhlin, and Cs. Szepesvári. Partial monitoring—classification, regret bounds, and algorithms. *Mathematics of Operations Research*, 39(4):967–997, 2014. [448]

H. Bastani and M. Bayati. Online decision making with high-dimensional covariates. *Operations Research*, 68(1):276–294, 2020. [249]

J. A. Bather and H. Chernoff. Sequential decisions in the control of a spaceship. In *Fifth Berkeley Symposium on Mathematical Statistics and Probability*, volume 3, pages 181–207, 1967. [10]

T. Bayes. LII. An essay towards solving a problem in the doctrine of chances. by the late Rev. Mr. Bayes, FRS communicated by Mr. Price, in a letter to John Canton, AMFR S. *Philosophical transactions of the Royal Society of London*, 53:370–418, 1763. [382]

R. Bellman. The theory of dynamic programming. Technical report, RAND CORP SANTA MONICA CA, 1954. [473]

R. E. Bellman. *Eye of the Hurricane*. World Scientific, 1984. [473]

D. Berend and A. Kontorovich. On the concentration of the missing mass. *Electronic Communications in Probability*, 18(3):1–7, 2013. [69]

J. O. Berger. *Statistical Decision Theory and Bayesian Analysis*. Springer Science & Business Media, 1985. [380]

D. Bernoulli. Exposition of a new theory on the measurement of risk. *Econometrica: Journal of the Econometric Society*, pages 23–36, 1954. [54]

A. C. Berry. The accuracy of the Gaussian approximation to the sum of independent variates. *Transactions of the American mathematical society*, 49(1):122–136, 1941. [64]

D. Berry and B. Fristedt. *Bandit problems : sequential allocation of experiments*. Chapman and Hall, London ; New York, 1985. [11, 400, 401]

D. A. Berry, R. W. Chen, A. Zame, D. C. Heath, and L. A. Shepp. Bandit problems with infinitely many arms. *The Annals of Statistics*, 25(5):2103–2116, 1997. [314]

D. Bertsekas and J. N. Tsitsiklis. *Neuro-Dynamic Programming*. Athena Scientific, 1st edition, 1996. [474]

D. P. Bertsekas. *Dynamic Programming and Optimal Control*, volume 1-2. Athena Scientific, Belmont, MA, 4 edition, 2012. [472, 473, 474]

D. P. Bertsekas. *Convex optimization algorithms*. Athena Scientific Belmont, 2015. [329]

D. Bertsimas and J. N. Tsitsiklis. *Introduction to linear optimization*, volume 6. Athena Scientific Belmont, MA, 1997. [474]

O. Besbes, Y. Gur, and A. Zeevi. Stochastic multi-armed-bandit problem with non-stationary rewards. In *Advances in Neural Information Processing Systems*, pages 199–207. Curran Associates, Inc., 2014. [338]

L. Besson and E. Kaufmann. What doubling tricks can and can't do for multi-armed bandits. arXiv:1803.06971, 2018. [81]

A. Beygelzimer, J. Langford, L. Li, L. Reyzin, and R. E. Schapire. An optimal high probability algorithm for the contextual bandit problem. arXiv:1002.4058, 2010. [148]

A. Beygelzimer, J. Langford, L. Li, L. Reyzin, and R. Schapire. Contextual bandit algorithms with supervised learning guarantees. In *Proceedings of the 14th International Conference on Artificial Intelligence and Statistics*, pages 19–26, Fort Lauderdale, FL, USA, 2011. JMLR.org. [201, 204]

P. Billingsley. *Probability and measure*. John Wiley & Sons, 2008. [32, 42]

D. Blackwell. Controlled random walks. In *Proceedings of the International Congress of Mathematicians*, volume 3, pages 336–338, 1954. [125]

V. I. Bogachev. *Measure theory*, volume 2. Springer Science & Business Media, 2007. [33, 277]

T. Bonald and A. Proutiere. Two-target algorithms for infinite-armed bandits with bernoulli rewards. In *Advances in Neural Information Processing Systems*, pages 2184–2192, 2013. [314]

L. Bottou, J. Peters, J. Quiñonero-Candela, D. X. Charles, D. M. Chickering, E. Portugaly, D. Ray, P. Simard, and E. Snelson. Counterfactual reasoning and learning systems: The example of computational advertising. *The Journal of Machine Learning Research*, 14(1):3207–3260, 2013. [149]

S. Boucheron, G. Lugosi, and P. Massart. *Concentration inequalities: A nonasymptotic theory of independence*. OUP Oxford, 2013. [66, 300]

D. Bouneffouf and I. Rish. A survey on practical applications of multi-armed and contextual bandits. arXiv:1904.10040, 2019. [11]

G. E. P. Box. Science and statistics. *Journal of the American Statistical Association*, 71(356):791–799, 1976. [125]

G. E. P. Box. Robustness in the strategy of scientific model building. *Robustness in statistics*, 1:201–236, 1979. [125]

S. Boyd and L. Vandenberghe. *Convex optimization*. Cambridge University Press, 2004. [275]

R. N. Bradt, S. M. Johnson, and S. Karlin. On sequential designs for maximizing the sum of n observations. *The Annals of Mathematical Statistics*, pages 1060–1074, 1956. [401]

R. Brafman and M. Tennenholtz. R-MAX – a general polynomial time algorithm for near-optimal reinforcement learning. *Journal of Machine Learning Research*, 3:213–231, 2003. [475]

J. Bretagnolle and C. Huber. Estimation des densités: risque minimax. *Zeitschrift für Wahrscheinlichkeitstheorie und verwandte Gebiete*, 47(2):119–137, 1979. [167]

S. Bubeck and N. Cesa-Bianchi. Regret analysis of stochastic and nonstochastic multi-armed bandit problems. *Foundations and Trends in Machine Learning*, 5(1):1–122, 2012. [10, 92, 136, 301, 327]

S. Bubeck and R. Eldan. The entropic barrier: a simple and optimal universal self-concordant barrier. In *Proceedings of the 28th Conference on Learning Theory*, pages 279–279, Paris, France, 2015. JMLR.org. [284]

S. Bubeck and R. Eldan. Multi-scale exploration of convex functions and bandit convex optimization. In *Proceedings of the 29th Conference on Learning Theory*, pages 583–589, New York, NY, USA, 2016. JMLR.org. [315, 416, 417]

S. Bubeck and C. Liu. Prior-free and prior-dependent regret bounds for Thompson sampling. In *Advances in Neural Information Processing Systems*, pages 638–646. Curran Associates, Inc., 2013. [417]

S. Bubeck and A. Slivkins. The best of both worlds: Stochastic and adversarial bandits. In *Proceedings of the 25th Conference on Learning Theory*, pages 42.1–42.23, 2012. [136]

S. Bubeck, R. Munos, and G. Stoltz. Pure exploration in multi-armed bandits problems. In *International conference on Algorithmic learning theory*, pages 23–37. Springer, 2009. [364]

S. Bubeck, R. Munos, G. Stoltz, and Cs. Szepesvári. X-armed bandits. *Journal of Machine Learning Research*, 12:1655–1695, 2011. [314]

S. Bubeck, N. Cesa-Bianchi, and S. Kakade. Towards minimax policies for online linear optimization with bandit feedback. In *Proceedings of the 25th Conference on Learning Theory*, pages 41–1. Microtome, 2012. [238, 283, 301]

S. Bubeck, N. Cesa-Bianchi, and G. Lugosi. Bandits with heavy tail. *IEEE Transactions on Information Theory*, 59(11):7711–7717, 2013a. [96]

S. Bubeck, V. Perchet, and P. Rigollet. Bounded regret in stochastic multi-armed bandits. In *Proceedings of the 26th Annual Conference on Learning Theory*, pages 122–134, Princeton, NJ, USA, 2013b. JMLR.org. [174]

S. Bubeck, O. Dekel, T. Koren, and Y. Peres. Bandit convex optimization: $\sqrt{T}$ regret in one dimension. In *Proceedings of the 28th Conference on Learning Theory*, pages 266–278, Paris, France, 2015a. JMLR.org. [315, 416, 417]

S. Bubeck, R. Eldan, and J. Lehec. Finite-time analysis of projected Langevin Monte Carlo. In *Advances in Neural Information Processing Systems*, pages 1243–1251. Curran Associates, Inc., 2015b. [284, 299]

S. Bubeck, Y.T. Lee, and R. Eldan. Kernel-based methods for bandit convex optimization. In *Proceedings of the 49th Annual ACM SIGACT Symposium on Theory of Computing*, STOC 2017, pages 72–85, New York, NY, USA, 2017. ACM. ISBN 978-1-4503-4528-6. [315]

S. Bubeck, M. Cohen, and Y. Li. Sparsity, variance and curvature in multi-armed bandits. In *Proceedings of the 29th International Conference on Algorithmic Learning Theory*, pages 111–127. JMLR.org, 07–09 Apr 2018. [148, 298, 301]

A. N. Burnetas and M. N. Katehakis. Optimal adaptive policies for sequential allocation problems. *Advances in Applied Mathematics*, 17(2):122–142, 1996. [100, 119, 181]

A. N. Burnetas and M. N. Katehakis. Optimal adaptive policies for Markov decision processes. *Mathematics of Operations Research*, 22(1):222–255, 1997a. [475]

A. N. Burnetas and M. N. Katehakis. On the finite horizon one-armed bandit problem. *Stochastic Analysis and Applications*, 16(1):845–859, 1997b. [401]

A. N. Burnetas and M. N. Katehakis. Asymptotic Bayes analysis for the finite-horizon one-armed-bandit problem. *Probability in the Engineering and Informational Sciences*, 17(1):53–82, 2003. [401]

R. R. Bush and F. Mosteller. A stochastic model with applications to learning. *The Annals of Mathematical Statistics*, pages 559–585, 1953. [10]

O. Cappé, A. Garivier, O. Maillard, R. Munos, and G. Stoltz. Kullback–Leibler upper confidence bounds for optimal sequential allocation. *The Annals of Statistics*, 41(3):1516–1541, 2013. [100, 119, 120, 181]

A. Carpentier and A. Locatelli. Tight (lower) bounds for the fixed budget best arm identification bandit problem. In *Proceedings of the 29th Conference on Learning Theory*, pages 590–604, New York, NY, USA, 2016. JMLR.org. [364]

A. Carpentier and R. Munos. Bandit theory meets compressed sensing for high dimensional stochastic linear bandit. In *Proceedings of the 15th International Conference on Artificial Intelligence and Statistics*, pages 190–198, La Palma, Canary Islands, 2012. JMLR.org. [249, 311]

A. Carpentier and M. Valko. Extreme bandits. In *Advances in Neural Information Processing Systems*, pages 1089–1097. Curran Associates, Inc., 2014. [365]

A. Carpentier and M. Valko. Simple regret for infinitely many armed bandits. In *Proceedings of the 32nd International Conference on Machine Learning*, pages 1133–1141, Lille, France, 2015. PMLR. [314]

O. Catoni. Challenging the empirical mean and empirical variance: a deviation study. *Annales de l'Institut Henri Poincaré, Probabilités et Statistiques*, 48(4):1148–1185, 2012. [96]

N. Cesa-Bianchi and G. Lugosi. *Prediction, learning, and games.* Cambridge University Press, 2006. [10, 136, 301, 338, 381, 448]

N. Cesa-Bianchi and G. Lugosi. Combinatorial bandits. *Journal of Computer and System Sciences*, 78(5):1404–1422, 2012. [327]

N. Cesa-Bianchi, G. Lugosi, and G. Stoltz. Regret minimization under partial monitoring. *Mathematics of Operations Research*, 31:562–580, 2006. [448]

N. Cesa-Bianchi, C. Gentile, Y. Mansour, and A. Minora. Delay and cooperation in nonstochastic bandits. In *Proceedings of the 29th Conference on Learning Theory*, pages 605–622, New York, NY, USA, 2016. JMLR.org. [316]

N. Cesa-Bianchi, C. Gentile, G. Lugosi, and G. Neu. Boltzmann exploration done right. In *Advances in Neural Information Processing Systems*, pages 6284–6293. Curran Associates, Inc., 2017. [79]

J. Chakravorty and A. Mahajan. Multi-armed bandits, Gittins index, and its calculation. *Methods and Applications of Statistics in Clinical Trials: Planning, Analysis, and Inferential Methods*, 2:416–435, 2013. [402]

J. Chakravorty and A. Mahajan. Multi-armed bandits, Gittins index, and its calculation. *Methods and Applications of Statistics in Clinical Trials: Planning, Analysis, and Inferential Methods*, 2:416–435, 2014. [402]

H. P. Chan and T. L. Lai. Sequential generalized likelihood ratios and adaptive treatment allocation for optimal sequential selection. *Sequential Analysis*, 25:179–201, 2006. [365]

J. T. Chang and D. Pollard. Conditioning as disintegration. *Statistica Neerlandica*, 51(3):287–317, 1997. [382]

O. Chapelle and L. Li. An empirical evaluation of Thompson sampling. In *Advances in Neural Information Processing Systems*, pages 2249–2257. Curran Associates, Inc., 2011. [416]

S. Chaudhuri and A. Tewari. Phased exploration with greedy exploitation in stochastic combinatorial partial monitoring games. In *Advances in Neural Information Processing Systems*, pages 2433–2441, 2016. [448]

C-H. Chen, J. Lin, E. Yücesan, and S. E. Chick. Simulation budget allocation for further enhancing the efficiency of ordinal optimization. *Discrete Event Dynamic Systems*, 10(3):251–270, 2000. [365]

S. Chen, T. Lin, I. King, M. R. Lyu, and W. Chen. Combinatorial pure exploration of multi-armed bandits. In *Advances in Neural Information Processing Systems*, pages 379–387. Curran Associates, Inc., 2014. [364]

W. Chen, Y. Wang, and Y. Yuan. Combinatorial multi-armed bandit: General framework and applications. In *Proceedings of the 30th International Conference on Machine Learning*, pages 151–159, Atlanta, Georgia, USA, 17–19 Jun 2013. PMLR. [328]

W. Chen, W. Hu, F. Li, J. Li, Y. Liu, and P. Lu. Combinatorial multi-armed bandit with general reward functions. In *Advances in Neural Information Processing Systems*, pages 1659–1667. Curran Associates, Inc., 2016a. [328]

W. Chen, Y. Wang, Y. Yuan, and Q. Wang. Combinatorial multi-armed bandit and its extension to probabilistically triggered arms. *Journal of Machine Learning Research*, 17(50):1–33, 2016b. URL http://jmlr.org/papers/v17/14-298.html. [328]

Y. Chen, C-W. Lee, H. Luo, and C-Y. Wei. A new algorithm for non-stationary contextual bandits: Efficient, optimal, and parameter-free. arXiv:1902.00980, 2019. [337, 338]

Y. R. Chen and M. N. Katehakis. Linear programming for finite state multi-armed bandit problems. *Mathematics of Operations Research*, 11(1):180–183, 1986. [402]

H. Chernoff. Sequential design of experiments. *The Annals of Mathematical Statistics*, 30(3):755–770, 1959. [11, 364]

H. Chernoff. A career in statistics. *Past, Present, and Future of Statistical Science*, page 29, 2014. [119]

W. Cheung, D. Simchi-Levi, and R. Zhu. Learning to optimize under non-stationarity. In *Proceedings of the 22nd International Conference on Artificial Intelligence and Statistics*, pages 1079–1087. PMLR, 16–18 Apr 2019. [338]

W. Chu, L. Li, L. Reyzin, and R. Schapire. Contextual bandits with linear payoff functions. In *Proceedings of the 14th International Conference on Artificial Intelligence and Statistics*, pages 208–214, Fort Lauderdale, FL, USA, 2011. JMLR.org. [238]

A. Chuklin, I. Markov, and M. de Rijke. *Click Models for Web Search*. Morgan & Claypool Publishers, 2015. [351]

V. A. Cicirello and S. F. Smith. The max k-armed bandit: A new model of exploration applied to search heuristic selection. In *AAAI*, pages 1355–1361, 2005. [365]

A. Cohen and T. Hazan. Following the perturbed leader for online structured learning. In *Proceedings of the 32nd International Conference on Machine Learning*, pages 1034–1042, Lille, France, 07–09 Jul 2015. JMLR.org. [328, 330]

A. Cohen, T. Hazan, and T. Koren. Tight bounds for bandit combinatorial optimization. In *Proceedings of the 2017 Conference on Learning Theory*, pages 629–642, Amsterdam, Netherlands, 2017. JMLR.org. [326]

R. Combes, S. Magureanu, A. Proutiere, and C. Laroche. Learning to rank: Regret lower bounds and efficient algorithms. In *Proceedings of the 2015 ACM SIGMETRICS International Conference on Measurement and Modeling of Computer Systems*, pages 231–244. ACM, 2015a. ISBN 978-1-4503-3486-0. [351]

R. Combes, M. Shahi, A. Proutiere, and M. Lelarge. Combinatorial bandits revisited. In *Advances in Neural Information Processing Systems*, pages 2116–2124. Curran Associates, Inc., 2015b. [327, 328]

R. Combes, S. Magureanu, and A. Proutière. Minimal exploration in structured stochastic bandits. In *Advances in Neural Information Processing Systems*, pages 1761–1769, 2017. [213, 215, 264, 314]

A. R. Conn, K. Scheinberg, and L. N. Vicente. *Introduction to Derivative-Free Optimization*. SIAM, 2009. [364]

T. M. Cover. Universal portfolios. *Mathematical Finance*, 1(1):1–29, 1991. [284]

T. M. Cover and J. A. Thomas. *Elements of information theory*. John Wiley & Sons, 2012. [167]

W. Cowan and M. N. Katehakis. An asymptotically optimal policy for uniform bandits of unknown support. arXiv:1505.01918, 2015. [181]

W. Cowan, J. Honda, and M. N. Katehakis. Normal bandits of unknown means and variances. *Journal of Machine Learning Research*, 18(154):1–28, 2018. [181]

K. Crammer and C. Gentile. Multiclass classification with bandit feedback using adaptive regularization. *Machine learning*, 90(3):347–383, 2013. [249]

N. Craswell, O. Zoeter, M. Taylor, and B. Ramsey. An experimental comparison of click position-bias models. In *Proceedings of the 2008 International Conference on Web Search and Data Mining*, pages 87–94. ACM, 2008. [351]

V. Dani and T. P. Hayes. Robbing the bandit: Less regret in online geometric optimization against an adaptive adversary. In *17th Annual ACM-SIAM Symposium on Discrete Algorithms*, pages 937–943, 2006. [328]

V. Dani, T. P. Hayes, and S. M. Kakade. Stochastic linear optimization under bandit feedback. In *Proceedings of the 21st Conference on Learning Theory*, pages 355–366, 2008. [213, 257]

V. H. de la Peña, T. L. Lai, and Q. Shao. *Self-normalized processes: Limit theory and Statistical Applications*. Springer Science & Business Media, 2008. [66, 71, 226]

R. Degenne and W. M. Koolen. Pure exploration with multiple correct answers. In *Advances in Neural Information Processing Systems*, pages 14591–14600. Curran Associates, Inc., 2019. [364]

R. Degenne and V. Perchet. Anytime optimal algorithms in stochastic multi-armed bandits. In *Proceedings of the 33rd International Conference on Machine Learning*, pages 1587–1595, New York, NY, USA, 20–22 Jun 2016. JMLR.org. [108]

R. Degenne, W. M. Koolen, and P. Ménard. Non-asymptotic pure exploration by solving games. In *Advances in Neural Information Processing Systems*, pages 14492–14501. Curran Associates, Inc., 2019. [364]

O. Dekel, C. Gentile, and K. Sridharan. Robust selective sampling from single and multiple teachers. In *Proceedings of the 23rd Conference on Learning Theory*, pages 346–358, 2010. [249]

O. Dekel, C. Gentile, and K. Sridharan. Selective sampling and active learning from single and multiple teachers. *Journal of Machine Learning Research*, 13:2655–2697, 2012. [249]

A. Dembo and O. Zeitouni. *Large deviations techniques and applications*, volume 38. Springer Science & Business Media, 2009. [68]

E. V. Denardo, H. Park, and U. G. Rothblum. Risk-sensitive and risk-neutral multiarmed bandits. *Mathematics of Operations Research*, 32(2):374–394, 2007. [56]

T. Desautels, A. Krause, and J. W. Burdick. Parallelizing exploration-exploitation tradeoffs in gaussian process bandit optimization. *Journal of Machine Learning Research*, 15:4053–4103, 2014. [316]

R. L. Dobrushin. Eine allgemeine formulierung des fundamentalsatzes von shannon in der informationstheorie. *Usp. Mat. Nauk*, 14(6(90)):3–104, 1959. [167]

S. Dong and B. Van Roy. An information-theoretic analysis for Thompson sampling with many actions. In *Advances in Neural Information Processing Systems*, Red Hook, NY, USA, 2018. Curran Associates Inc. [415]

J. L. Doob. *Stochastic processes*. Wiley, 1953. [43]

M. Dudík, D. Hsu, S. Kale, N. Karampatziakis, J. Langford, L. Reyzin, and T. Zhang. Efficient optimal learning for contextual bandits. In *Proceedings of the 27th Conference on Uncertainty in Artificial Intelligence*, pages 169–178. AUAI Press, 2011. [202]

M. Dudík, K. Hofmann, R. E. Schapire, A. Slivkins, and M. Zoghi. Contextual dueling bandits. In *Proceedings of the 28th Conference on Learning Theory*, pages 563–587, Paris, France, 2015. JMLR.org. [315]

R. M. Dudley. *Uniform central limit theorems*, volume 142. Cambridge University Press, 2014. [66, 300]

C. G. Esseen. *On the Liapounoff limit of error in the theory of probability*. Almqvist & Wiksell, 1942. [64]

E. Even-Dar, S. Mannor, and Y. Mansour. PAC bounds for multi-armed bandit and Markov decision processes. In *Computational Learning Theory*, pages 255–270. Springer, 2002. [364, 368]

E. Even-Dar, S. M. Kakade, and Y. Mansour. Experts in a Markov decision process. In *Advances in Neural Information Processing Systems*, pages 401–408, Cambridge, MA, USA, 2004. MIT Press. [475]

E. Even-Dar, S. Mannor, and Y. Mansour. Action elimination and stopping conditions for the multi-armed bandit and reinforcement learning problems. *Journal of Machine Learning Research*, 7: 1079–1105, 2006. [364]

V. V. Fedorov. Theory of optimal experiments. *Academic Press, New York*, 1972. [235]

S. Filippi, O. Cappé, A. Garivier, and Cs. Szepesvári. Parametric bandits: The generalized linear case. In *Advances in Neural Information Processing Systems*, pages 586–594. Curran Associates, Inc., 2010. [213]

D. Fink. A compendium of conjugate priors, 1997. [382]

D. Foster and A. Rakhlin. No internal regret via neighborhood watch. In *Proceedings of the 15th International Conference on Artificial Intelligence and Statistics*, pages 382–390, La Palma, Canary Islands, 2012. JMLR.org. [448]

D. J. Foster and A. Rakhlin. Beyond UCB: Optimal and efficient contextual bandits with regression oracles. arXiv:2002.04926, 2020. [256]

M. Frank and P. Wolfe. An algorithm for quadratic programming. *Naval Research Logistics Quarterly*, 3(1-2):95–110, 1956. [235]

S. Frederick, G. Loewenstein, and T. O'donoghue. Time discounting and time preference: A critical review. *Journal of Economic Literature*, 40(2):351–401, 2002. [400]

E. Frostig and G. Weiss. Four proofs of Gittins' multiarmed bandit theorem. *Applied Probability Trust*, 70, 1999. [401]

R. Fruit, M. Pirotta, and A. Lazaric. Near optimal exploration-exploitation in non-communicating markov decision processes. In *Advances in Neural Information Processing Systems*, pages 2997–3007, 2018. [474, 475, 482, 483]

Y. Gai, B. Krishnamachari, and R. Jain. Combinatorial network optimization with unknown variables: Multi-armed bandits with linear rewards and individual observations. *IEEE/ACM Transactions on Networking*, 20(5):1466–1478, 2012. [328]

P. Gajane, R. Ortner, and P. Auer. A sliding-window algorithm for Markov decision processes with arbitrarily changing rewards and transitions. arXiv:1805.10066, 2018. [338]

A. Garivier. Informational confidence bounds for self-normalized averages and applications. arXiv:1309.3376, 2013. [93, 108]

A. Garivier and O. Cappé. The KL-UCB algorithm for bounded stochastic bandits and beyond. In *Proceedings of the 24th Conference on Learning Theory*, 2011. [118, 119]

A. Garivier and E. Kaufmann. Optimal best arm identification with fixed confidence. In *Proceedings of the 29th Conference on Learning Theory*, pages 998–1027, New York, NY, USA, 2016. JMLR.org. [364]

A. Garivier and E. Moulines. On upper-confidence bound policies for switching bandit problems. In *Proceedings of the 22nd International Conference on Algorithmic Learning Theory*, pages 174–188, Berlin, Heidelberg, 2011. Springer Berlin Heidelberg. [338]

A. Garivier, E. Kaufmann, and W. M. Koolen. Maximin action identification: A new bandit framework for games. In *Proceedings of the 29th Conference on Learning Theory*, pages 1028–1050, New York, NY, USA, 2016a. JMLR.org. [364]

A. Garivier, T. Lattimore, and E. Kaufmann. On explore-then-commit strategies. In *Advances in Neural Information Processing Systems*, pages 784–792. Curran Associates, Inc., 2016b. [79, 100, 181]

A. Garivier, P. Ménard, and G. Stoltz. Explore first, exploit next: The true shape of regret in bandit problems. *Mathematics of Operations Research*, 44(2):377–399, 2019. [181]

A. Gelman, J. B. Carlin, H. S. Stern, D. B. Dunson, A. Vehtari, and D. B. Rubin. *Bayesian data analysis*, volume 2. CRC Press Boca Raton, FL, 2014. [382]

C. Gentile and F. Orabona. On multilabel classification and ranking with partial feedback. In *Advances in Neural Information Processing Systems*, pages 1151–1159. Curran Associates, Inc., 2012. [249]

C. Gentile and F. Orabona. On multilabel classification and ranking with bandit feedback. *Journal of Machine Learning Research*, 15(1):2451–2487, 2014. [249]

S. Gerchinovitz. Sparsity regret bounds for individual sequences in online linear regression. *Journal of Machine Learning Research*, 14(Mar):729–769, 2013. [249]

S. Gerchinovitz and T. Lattimore. Refined lower bounds for adversarial bandits. In *Advances in Neural Information Processing Systems*, pages 1198–1206. Curran Associates, Inc., 2016. [174, 190]

S. Ghosal and A. van der Vaart. *Fundamentals of nonparametric Bayesian inference*, volume 44. Cambridge University Press, 2017. [382]

A. Ghosh, S. R. Chowdhury, and A. Gopalan. Misspecified linear bandits. In *31st AAAI Conference on Artificial Intelligence*, 2017. [238]

J. Gittins. Bandit processes and dynamic allocation indices. *Journal of the Royal Statistical Society. Series B (Methodological)*, 41(2):148–177, 1979. [337, 401]

J. Gittins, K. Glazebrook, and R. Weber. *Multi-armed bandit allocation indices*. John Wiley & Sons, 2011. [11, 337, 401]

D. Glowacka. Bandit algorithms in information retrieval. *Foundations and Trends® in Information Retrieval*, 13:299–424, 01 2019. [351]

P. Glynn and S. Juneja. Ordinal optimization – empirical large deviations rate estimators, and stochastic multi-armed bandits. arXiv:1507.04564, 2015. [365]

D. Goldsman. Ranking and selection in simulation. In *15th conference on Winter Simulation*, pages 387–394, 1983. [365]

A. Gopalan and S. Mannor. Thompson sampling for learning parameterized Markov decision processes. In *Proceedings of the 28th Conference on Learning Theory*, pages 861–898, Paris, France, 2015. JMLR.org. [417]

G. J. Gordon. Regret bounds for prediction problems. In *Proceedings of the 12th Conference on Learning Theory*, pages 29–40, 1999. [301]

T. Graepel, J. Q. Candela, T. Borchert, and R. Herbrich. Web-scale Bayesian click-through rate prediction for sponsored search advertising in microsoft's bing search engine. In *Proceedings of the 27th International Conference on Machine Learning*, pages 13–20, USA, 2010. Omnipress. [416]

O. Granmo. Solving two-armed bernoulli bandit problems using a Bayesian learning automaton. *International Journal of Intelligent Computing and Cybernetics*, 3(2):207–234, 2010. [416]

R. M. Gray. *Entropy and information theory*. Springer Science & Business Media, 2011. [167]

K. Greenewald, A. Tewari, S. Murphy, and P. Klasnja. Action centered contextual bandits. In *Advances in Neural Information Processing Systems*, pages 5977–5985. Curran Associates, Inc., 2017. [11]

M. Grötschel, L. Lovász, and A. Schrijver. *Geometric algorithms and combinatorial optimization*, volume 2. Springer Science & Business Media, 2012. [235, 327, 474]

F. Guo, C. Liu, and Y. M. Wang. Efficient multiple-click models in web search. In *Proceedings of the 2nd ACM International Conference on Web Search and Data Mining*, pages 124–131. ACM, 2009. [351]

A. György and Cs. Szepesvári. Shifting regret, mirror descent, and matrices. In *Proceedings of the 33rd International Conference on Machine Learning*, pages 2943–2951, New York, NY, USA, 20–22 Jun 2016. JMLR.org. [338]

A. György, T. Linder, G. Lugosi, and G. Ottucsák. The on-line shortest path problem under partial monitoring. *Journal of Machine Learning Research*, 8(Oct):2369–2403, 2007. [328, 329]

A. György, D. Pál, and Cs. Szepesvári. *Online learning: Algorithms for Big Data*. 2019. [338]

P. R. Halmos. *Measure Theory*. Graduate Texts in Mathematics. Springer New York, 1976. [42]

N. Hamidi and M. Bayati. A general framework to analyze stochastic linear bandit. arXiv:2002.05152, 2020. [415]

M. Hanawal, V. Saligrama, M. Valko, and R. Munos. Cheap bandits. In *Proceedings of the 32nd International Conference on Machine Learning*, pages 2133–2142, Lille, France, 07–09 Jul 2015. JMLR.org. [315]

J. Hannan. Approximation to Bayes risk in repeated play. *Contributions to the Theory of Games*, 3: 97–139, 1957. [125, 301, 328]

B. Hao, T. Lattimore, and Cs. Szepesvári. Adaptive exploration in linear contextual bandit. In *Proceedings of the 23rd International Conference on Artificial Intelligence and Statistics*, 2020. [213, 264]

G. H. Hardy. *Divergent Series*. Oxford University Press, 1973. [472]

E. Hazan. Introduction to online convex optimization. *Foundations and Trends® in Optimization*, 2 (3-4):157–325, 2016. [300, 301]

E. Hazan and S. Kale. A simple multi-armed bandit algorithm with optimal variation-bounded regret. In *Proceedings of the 24th Conference on Learning Theory*, pages 817–820. JMLR.org, 2011. [148]

E. Hazan, Z. Karnin, and R. Meka. Volumetric spanners: an efficient exploration basis for learning. *Journal of Machine Learning Research*, 17(119):1–34, 2016. [235, 284]

D. P. Helmbold, N. Littlestone, and P. M. Long. Apple tasting. *Information and Computation*, 161(2): 85–139, 2000. [448]

M. Herbster and M. K. Warmuth. Tracking the best expert. *Machine Learning*, 32(2):151–178, 1998. [338]

M. Herbster and M. K. Warmuth. Tracking the best linear predictor. *Journal of Machine Learning Research*, 1(Sep):281–309, 2001. [338]

Y-C. Ho, R. S. Sreenivas, and P. Vakili. Ordinal optimization of DEDS. *Discrete Event Dynamic Systems*, 1992. [365]

J. Honda and A. Takemura. An asymptotically optimal bandit algorithm for bounded support models. In *Proceedings of the 23rd Conference on Learning Theory*, pages 67–79, 2010. [100, 109, 119, 181]

J. Honda and A. Takemura. An asymptotically optimal policy for finite support models in the multiarmed bandit problem. *Machine Learning*, 85(3):361–391, 2011. [100]

J. Honda and A. Takemura. Optimality of Thompson sampling for Gaussian bandits depends on priors. In *Proceedings of the 17th International Conference on Artificial Intelligence and Statistics*, pages 375–383, Reykjavik, Iceland, 2014. JMLR.org. [417]

J. Honda and A. Takemura. Non-asymptotic analysis of a new bandit algorithm for semi-bounded rewards. *Journal of Machine Learning Research*, 16:3721–3756, 2015. [119, 181]

X. Hu, Prashanth L.A., A. György, and Cs. Szepesvári. (Bandit) convex optimization with biased noisy gradient oracles. In *AISTATS*, pages 819–828, 2016. [315, 364]

R. Huang, M. M. Ajallooeian, Cs. Szepesvári, and M. Müller. Structured best arm identification with fixed confidence. In *Proceedings of the 28th International Conference on Algorithmic Learning Theory*, pages 593–616, Kyoto, Japan, 2017a. JMLR.org. [364]

R. Huang, T. Lattimore, A. György, and Cs. Szepesvári. Following the leader and fast rates in online linear prediction: Curved constraint sets and other regularities. *Journal of Machine Learning Research*, 18:1–31, 2017b. [300]

W. Huang, J. Ok, L. Li, and W. Chen. Combinatorial pure exploration with continuous and separable reward functions and its applications. In *IJCAI*, pages 2291–2297, 2018. [364]

M. Hutter. *Universal artificial intelligence: Sequential decisions based on algorithmic probability*. Springer Science & Business Media, 2004. [381]

M. Hutter and J. Poland. Adaptive online prediction by following the perturbed leader. *Journal of Machine Learning Research*, 6:639–660, 2005. [328]

E. L. Ionides. Truncated importance sampling. *Journal of Computational and Graphical Statistics*, 17(2):295–311, 2008. [149]

V. I. Ivanenko and V. A. Labkovsky. On regularities of mass random phenomena. arXiv:1204.4440, 2013. [125]

T. Jaksch, P. Auer, and R. Ortner. Near-optimal regret bounds for reinforcement learning. *Journal of Machine Learning Research*, 99:1563–1600, August 2010. ISSN 1532-4435. [474, 476]

K. Jamieson and R. Nowak. Best-arm identification algorithms for multi-armed bandits in the fixed confidence setting. In *Information Sciences and Systems (CISS), 2014 48th Annual Conference on*, pages 1–6. IEEE, 2014. [364]

K. Jamieson and A. Talwalkar. Non-stochastic best arm identification and hyperparameter optimization. In *Proceedings of the 19th International Conference on Artificial Intelligence and Statistics*, pages 240–248, 2016. [365]

K. Jamieson, S. Katariya, A. Deshpande, and R. Nowak. Sparse dueling bandits. In *Proceedings of the 18th International Conference on Artificial Intelligence and Statistics*, pages 416–424, San Diego, CA, USA, 2015. JMLR.org. [315]

E. T. Jaynes. *Probability theory: the logic of science*. Cambridge University Press, 2003. [381, 382]

A. Jefferson, L. Bortolotti, and B. Kuzmanovic. What is unrealistic optimism? *Consciousness and Cognition*, 50:3–11, 2017. [92]

P. Joulani, A. György, and Cs. Szepesvári. Online learning under delayed feedback. In *Proceedings of the 30th International Conference on Machine Learning*, pages 1453–1461, Atlanta, GA, USA, 2013. JMLR.org. [316]

P. Joulani, A. György, and Cs. Szepesvári. A modular analysis of adaptive (non-) convex optimization: Optimism, composite objectives, and variational bounds. In *Proceedings of the 28th International Conference on Algorithmic Learning Theory*, pages 681–720, Kyoto University, Kyoto, Japan, 2017. JMLR.org. [298]

K. Jun, A. Bhargava, R. Nowak, and R. Willett. Scalable generalized linear bandits: Online computation and hashing. In *Advances in Neural Information Processing Systems*, pages 99–109. Curran Associates, Inc., 2017. [213]

L. P. Kaelbling. *Learning in embedded systems*. MIT Press, 1993. [92]

D. Kahneman and A. Tversky. Prospect theory: An analysis of decision under risk. *Econometrica*, 47 (2):263–91, 1979. [54]

S. Kakade. *On The Sample Complexity Of Reinforcement Learning*. PhD thesis, University College London, 2003. [475]

S. M. Kakade, S. Shalev-Shwartz, and A. Tewari. Efficient bandit algorithms for online multiclass prediction. In *Proceedings of the 25th International Conference on Machine Learning*, pages 440–447, 2008. [202]

A. Kalai and S. Vempala. Geometric algorithms for online optimization. Technical Report MIT-LCS-TR-861, MIT, 2002. [301, 328]

A. Kalai and S. Vempala. Efficient algorithms for online decision problems. *Journal of Computer and System Sciences*, 71(3):291–307, 2005. [328]

L. Kallenberg. A note on M.N. Katehakis' and Y.-R. Chen's computation of the Gittins index. *Mathematics of Operations Research*, 11(1):184–186, 1986. [402]

L. Kallenberg. Markov decision processes: Lecture notes, 2016. [474]

O. Kallenberg. *Foundations of modern probability*. Springer-Verlag, 2002. [32, 33, 41, 42, 43, 168, 228, 383]

Z. Karnin, T. Koren, and O. Somekh. Almost optimal exploration in multi-armed bandits. In *Proceedings of the 30th International Conference on Machine Learning*, pages 1238–1246, Atlanta, GA, USA, 2013. JMLR.org. [364]

N. El Karoui and I. Karatzas. Dynamic allocation problems in continuous time. *The Annals of Applied Probability*, pages 255–286, 1994. [402]

S. Katariya, B. Kveton, Cs. Szepesvári, and Z. Wen. DCM bandits: Learning to rank with multiple clicks. In *Proceedings of the 33rd International Conference on Machine Learning*, pages 1215–1224, 2016. [351]

S. Katariya, B. Kveton, Cs. Szepesvári, C. Vernade, and Z. Wen. Bernoulli rank-1 bandits for click feedback. In *Proceedings of the 26th International Joint Conference on Artificial Intelligence*, 2017a. [351]

S. Katariya, B. Kveton, Cs. Szepesvári, C. Vernade, and Z. Wen. Stochastic rank-1 bandits. In *Proceedings of the 20th International Conference on Artificial Intelligence and Statistics*, 2017b. [351]

M. N. Katehakis and H. Robbins. Sequential choice from several populations. *Proceedings of the National Academy of Sciences of the United States of America*, 92(19):8584, 1995. [92, 100]

V. Ya Katkovnik and Yu Kulchitsky. Convergence of a class of random search algorithms. *Automation Remote Control*, 8:1321–1326, 1972. [364]

E. Kaufmann. On Bayesian index policies for sequential resource allocation. *The Annals of Statistics*, 46(2):842–865, 04 2018. [100, 109, 415, 417]

E. Kaufmann, O. Cappé, and A. Garivier. On Bayesian upper confidence bounds for bandit problems. In *Proceedings of the 15th International Conference on Artificial Intelligence and Statistics*, pages 592–600, La Palma, Canary Islands, 2012a. JMLR.org. [415, 417]

E. Kaufmann, N. Korda, and R. Munos. Thompson sampling: An asymptotically optimal finite-time analysis. In *Proceedings of the 23rd International Conference on Algorithmic Learning Theory*, volume 7568 of *Lecture Notes in Computer Science*, pages 199–213. Springer Berlin Heidelberg, 2012b. ISBN 978-3-642-34105-2. [100, 415, 417]

J. Kawale, H. H. Bui, B. Kveton, L. Tran-Thanh, and S. Chawla. Efficient Thompson sampling for online matrix-factorization recommendation. In *Advances in Neural Information Processing Systems*, pages 1297–1305. Curran Associates, Inc., 2015. [417]

A. Kazerouni, M. Ghavamzadeh, Y. Abbasi, and B. Van Roy. Conservative contextual linear bandits. In *Advances in Neural Information Processing Systems*, pages 3910–3919. Curran Associates, Inc., 2017. [315]

M. Kearns and L. Saul. Large deviation methods for approximate probabilistic inference. In *Proceedings of the 14th Conference on Uncertainty in Artificial Intelligence*, page 311–319. Morgan Kaufmann Publishers Inc., 1998. [69]

M. Kearns and S. Singh. Near-optimal reinforcement learning in polynomial time. *Machine Learning*, 49(2-3):209–232, 2002. [475]

M. J. Kearns and U. V. Vazirani. *An introduction to computational learning theory*. MIT Press, 1994. [202]

J. Kiefer and J. Wolfowitz. The equivalence of two extremum problems. *Canadian Journal of Mathematics*, 12(5):363–365, 1960. [235]

G-S. Kim and M. C. Paik. Doubly-robust lasso bandit. In *Advances in Neural Information Processing Systems*, pages 5877–5887. Curran Associates, Inc., 2019. [249]

M. J. Kim. Thompson sampling for stochastic control: The finite parameter case. *IEEE Transactions on Automatic Control*, 62(12):6415–6422, 2017. [417]

J. Kirschner and A. Krause. Information directed sampling and bandits with heteroscedastic noise. In *Proceedings of the 31st Conference On Learning Theory*, pages 358–384. PMLR, 06–09 Jul 2018. [72, 213]

J. Kirschner, T. Lattimore, and A. Krause. Information directed sampling for linear partial monitoring. arXiv:2002.11182, 2020. [448]

R. Kleinberg. Nearly tight bounds for the continuum-armed bandit problem. In *Advances in Neural Information Processing Systems*, pages 697–704. MIT Press, 2005. [314]

R. Kleinberg, A. Slivkins, and E. Upfal. Multi-armed bandits in metric spaces. In *Proceedings of the 40th Annual ACM Symposium on Theory of Computing*, pages 681–690. ACM, 2008. [314]

T. Kocák, G. Neu, M. Valko, and R. Munos. Efficient learning by implicit exploration in bandit problems with side observations. In *Advances in Neural Information Processing Systems*, pages 613–621. Curran Associates, Inc., 2014. [148, 149, 316]

T. Kocák, M. Valko, R. Munos, and S. Agrawal. Spectral Thompson sampling. In *AAAI*, pages 1911–1917, 2014. [417]

L. Kocsis and Cs. Szepesvári. Discounted UCB. In *2nd PASCAL Challenges Workshop*, pages 784–791, 2006. [11, 338]

H. Komiya. Elementary proof for Sion's minimax theorem. *Kodai Mathematical Journal*, 11(1):5–7, 1988. [301]

J. Komiyama, J. Honda, H. Kashima, and H. Nakagawa. Regret lower bound and optimal algorithm in dueling bandit problem. In *Proceedings of the 28th Conference on Learning Theory*, pages 1141–1154, Paris, France, 2015a. JMLR.org. [315]

J. Komiyama, J. Honda, and H. Nakagawa. Regret lower bound and optimal algorithm in finite stochastic partial monitoring. In *Advances in Neural Information Processing Systems*, pages 1792–1800. Curran Associates, Inc., 2015b. [448]

W. M. Koolen, M. K. Warmuth, and J. Kivinen. Hedging structured concepts. In *Proceedings of the 23rd Conference on Learning Theory*, pages 93–105. Omnipress, 2010. [328]

N. Korda, E. Kaufmann, and R. Munos. Thompson sampling for 1-dimensional exponential family bandits. In *Advances in Neural Information Processing Systems*, pages 1448–1456. Curran Associates, Inc., 2013. [100, 120, 415, 417]

J. Kujala and T. Elomaa. On following the perturbed leader in the bandit setting. In *Proceedings of the 16th International Conference on Algorithmic Learning Theory*, pages 371–385, 2005. [328]

J. Kujala and T. Elomaa. Following the perturbed leader to gamble at multi-armed bandits. In *Proceedings of the 18th International Conference on Algorithmic Learning Theory*, pages 166–180. Springer, 2007. [328]

S. R. Kulkarni and G. Lugosi. Finite-time lower bounds for the two-armed bandit problem. *IEEE Transactions on Automatic Control*, 45(4):711–714, 2000. [181]

B. Kveton, Cs. Szepesvári, Z. Wen, and A. Ashkan. Cascading bandits: Learning to rank in the cascade model. In *Proceedings of the 32nd International Conference on Machine Learning*, pages 767–776. JMLR.org, 2015a. [351]

B. Kveton, Z. Wen, A. Ashkan, and Cs. Szepesvári. Tight regret bounds for stochastic combinatorial semi-bandits. In *Proceedings of the 18th International Conference on Artificial Intelligence and Statistics*, pages 535–543, San Diego, CA, USA, 2015b. JMLR.org. [328]

B. Kveton, Z. Wen, Z. Ashkan, and Cs. Szepesvári. Combinatorial cascading bandits. In *Advances in Neural Information Processing Systems*, pages 1450–1458. Curran Associates Inc., 2015c. [351]

B. Kveton, Cs. Szepesvári, S. Vaswani, Z. Wen, T. Lattimore, and M. Ghavamzadeh. Garbage in, reward out: Bootstrapping exploration in multi-armed bandits. In *Proceedings of the 36th International Conference on Machine Learning*, pages 3601–3610, Long Beach, California, USA, 09–15 Jun 2019. PMLR. [417]

P. Lagree, C. Vernade, and O. Cappé. Multiple-play bandits in the position-based model. In *Advances in Neural Information Processing Systems*, pages 1597–1605. Curran Associates Inc., 2016. [351]

T. L. Lai. Adaptive treatment allocation and the multi-armed bandit problem. *The Annals of Statistics*, pages 1091–1114, 1987. [92, 100, 109, 119, 401]

T. L. Lai. Martingales in sequential analysis and time series, 1945–1985. *Electronic Journal for history of probability and statistics*, 5(1), 2009. [226]

T. L. Lai and T. Graves. Asymptotically efficient adaptive choice of control laws in controlled Markov chains. *SIAM Journal on Control and Optimization*, 35(3):715–743, 1997. [475]

T. L. Lai and H. Robbins. Asymptotically efficient adaptive allocation rules. *Advances in applied mathematics*, 6(1):4–22, 1985. [56, 92, 100, 119, 181, 230]

J. Langford and T. Zhang. The epoch-greedy algorithm for multi-armed bandits with side information. In *Advances in Neural Information Processing Systems*, pages 817–824. Curran Associates, Inc., 2008. [204]

P. Laplace. *Pierre-Simon Laplace Philosophical Essay on Probabilities: Translated from the fifth French edition of 1825 With Notes by the Translator*, volume 13. Springer Science & Business Media, 2012. [33]

T. Lattimore. The Pareto regret frontier for bandits. In *Advances in Neural Information Processing Systems*, pages 208–216. Curran Associates, Inc., 2015a. [136, 257]

T. Lattimore. Optimally confident UCB: Improved regret for finite-armed bandits. arXiv:1507.07880, 2015b. [108]

T. Lattimore. Regret analysis of the finite-horizon Gittins index strategy for multi-armed bandits. In *Proceedings of the 29th Annual Conference on Learning Theory*, pages 1214–1245, New York, NY, USA, 2016a. JMLR.org. [100, 401]

T. Lattimore. Regret analysis of the anytime optimally confident ucb algorithm. arXiv:1603.08661, 2016b. [108]

T. Lattimore. Regret analysis of the finite-horizon Gittins index strategy for multi-armed bandits. In *Proceedings of the 29th Conference on Learning Theory*, pages 1214–1245, 2016c. [400]

T. Lattimore. A scale free algorithm for stochastic bandits with bounded kurtosis. In *Advances in Neural Information Processing Systems*, pages 1584–1593. Curran Associates, Inc., 2017. [96, 181]

T. Lattimore. Refining the confidence level for optimistic bandit strategies. *Journal of Machine Learning Research*, 2018. [82, 108, 110, 181]

T. Lattimore and M. Hutter. PAC bounds for discounted MDPs. In *Proceedings of the 23th International Conference on Algorithmic Learning Theory*, volume 7568 of *Lecture Notes in Computer Science*, pages 320–334. Springer Berlin / Heidelberg, 2012. [475]

T. Lattimore and R. Munos. Bounded regret for finite-armed structured bandits. In *Advances in Neural Information Processing Systems*, pages 550–558. Curran Associates, Inc., 2014. [214]

T. Lattimore and Cs. Szepesvári. The end of optimism? An asymptotic analysis of finite-armed linear bandits. In *Proceedings of the 20th International Conference on Artificial Intelligence and Statistics*, pages 728–737, Fort Lauderdale, FL, USA, 2017. JMLR.org. [213, 264]

T. Lattimore and Cs. Szepesvári. Cleaning up the neighbourhood: A full classification for adversarial partial monitoring. In *Proceedings of the 30th International Conference on Algorithmic Learning Theory*, 2019a. [447, 448, 450]

T. Lattimore and Cs. Szepesvári. Learning with good feature representations in bandits and in RL with a generative model. arXiv:1911.07676, 2019b. [238, 256]

T. Lattimore and Cs. Szepesvári. An information-theoretic approach to minimax regret in partial monitoring. In *Proceedings of the 32nd Conference on Learning Theory*, pages 2111–2139, Phoenix, USA, 2019c. PMLR. [416, 417, 419, 448]

T. Lattimore and Cs. Szepesvári. Exploration by optimisation in partial monitoring. arXiv:1907.05772, 2019d. [446, 448, 451]

T. Lattimore, K. Crammer, and Cs. Szepesvári. Linear multi-resource allocation with semi-bandit feedback. In *Advances in Neural Information Processing Systems*, pages 964–972. Curran Associates, Inc., 2015. [249]

T. Lattimore, B. Kveton, S. Li, and Cs. Szepesvári. Toprank: A practical algorithm for online stochastic ranking. In *Advances in Neural Information Processing Systems*, pages 3949–3958. Curran Associates, Inc., 2018. [230, 330, 351]

B. Laurent and P. Massart. Adaptive estimation of a quadratic functional by model selection. *Annals of Statistics*, pages 1302–1338, 2000. [66]

A. Lazaric and R. Munos. Hybrid stochastic-adversarial on-line learning. In *Proceedings of the 22nd Conference on Learning Theory*, 2009. [202]

T. Le, Cs. Szepesvári, and R. Zheng. Sequential learning for multi-channel wireless network monitoring with channel switching costs. *IEEE Transactions on Signal Processing*, 62(22):5919–5929, 2014. [11]

L Le Cam. Convergence of estimates under dimensionality restrictions. *The Annals of Statistics*, 1(1): 38–53, 1973. [174]

Y. T. Lee, A. Sidford, and S. S. Vempala. Efficient convex optimization with membership oracles. In *Proceedings of the 31st Conference On Learning Theory*, pages 1292–1294. JMLR.org, 06–09 Jul 2018. [327]

E. L. Lehmann and G. Casella. *Theory of point estimation*. Springer Science & Business Media, 2006. [382]

H. Lei, A. Tewari, and S. A. Murphy. An actor-critic contextual bandit algorithm for personalized mobile health interventions. arXiv:1706.09090, 2017. [11]

J. Leike, T. Lattimore, L. Orseau, and M. Hutter. Thompson sampling is asymptotically optimal in general environments. In *Proceedings of the 32nd Conference on Uncertainty in Artificial Intelligence*, pages 417–426. AUAI Press, 2016. [417]

H. R. Lerche. *Boundary crossing of Brownian motion: Its relation to the law of the iterated logarithm and to sequential analysis*. Springer, 1986. [110]

D. A. Levin and Y. Peres. *Markov chains and mixing times*, volume 107. American Mathematical Soc., 2017. [42]

L. A. Levin. On the notion of a random sequence. *Soviet Mathematics Doklady*, 14(5):1413–1416, 1973. [125]

L. Li, K. Jamieson, G. DeSalvo, A. Rostamizadeh, and A. Talwalkar. Hyperband: A novel bandit-based approach to hyperparameter optimization. *Journal of Machine Learning Research*, 18(185): 1–52, 2018. [365]

S. Li, B. Wang, S. Zhang, and W. Chen. Contextual combinatorial cascading bandits. In *Proceedings of the 33rd International Conference on Machine Learning*, pages 1245–1253, 2016. [351]

S. Li, T. Lattimore, and Cs. Szepesvári. Online learning to rank with features. In *Proceedings of the 36th International Conference on Machine Learning*, pages 3856–3865, Long Beach, California, USA, 09–15 Jun 2019a. PMLR. [350]

Y. Li, Y. Wang, and Y. Zhou. Nearly minimax-optimal regret for linearly parameterized bandits. In *Proceedings of the 32nd Conference on Learning Theory*, pages 2173–2174, Phoenix, USA, 2019b. JMLR.org. [212]

T. Liang, H. Narayanan, and A. Rakhlin. On zeroth-order stochastic convex optimization via random walks. arXiv:1402.2667, 2014. [364]

T. Lin, B. Abrahao, R. Kleinberg, J. Lui, and W. Chen. Combinatorial partial monitoring game with linear feedback and its applications. In *Proceedings of the 31st International Conference on Machine Learning*, pages 901–909, Bejing, China, 22–24 Jun 2014. PMLR. [448]

T. Lin, J. Li, and W. Chen. Stochastic online greedy learning with semi-bandit feedbacks. In *Advances in Neural Information Processing Systems*, pages 352–360. Curran Associates, Inc., 2015. [328]

N. Littlestone and M. K. Warmuth. The weighted majority algorithm. *Information and Computation*, 108(2):212–261, 1994. [125, 137]

L. Lovász and S. Vempala. The geometry of logconcave functions and sampling algorithms. *Random Structures & Algorithms*, 30(3):307–358, 2007. [284]

H. Luo, C-Y. Wei, A. Agarwal, and J. Langford. Efficient contextual bandits in non-stationary worlds. In *Proceedings of the 31st Conference On Learning Theory*, pages 1739–1776. JMLR.org, 06–09 Jul 2018. [338]

D. MacKay. *Information theory, inference and learning algorithms*. Cambridge University Press, 2003. [167]

S. Magureanu, R. Combes, and A. Proutière. Lipschitz bandits: Regret lower bound and optimal algorithms. In *Proceedings of the 27th Conference on Learning Theory*, pages 975–999, 2014. [215, 314]

O. Maillard. Robust risk-averse stochastic multi-armed bandits. In *Proceedings of the 24th International Conference on Algorithmic Learning Theory*, pages 218–233. Springer, Berlin, Heidelberg, 2013. [56]

O. Maillard, R. Munos, and G. Stoltz. Finite-time analysis of multi-armed bandits problems with Kullback-Leibler divergences. In *Proceedings of the 24th Conference on Learning Theory*, 2011. [119]

S. Mannor and O. Shamir. From bandits to experts: On the value of side-observations. In *Advances in Neural Information Processing Systems*, pages 684–692. Curran Associates, Inc., 2011. [316, 448]

S. Mannor and N. Shimkin. On-line learning with imperfect monitoring. In *Learning Theory and Kernel Machines*, pages 552–566. Springer, 2003. [448]

S. Mannor and J. N. Tsitsiklis. The sample complexity of exploration in the multi-armed bandit problem. *Journal of Machine Learning Research*, 5:623–648, December 2004. [364]

S. Mannor, V. Perchet, and G. Stoltz. Set-valued approachability and online learning with partial monitoring. *The Journal of Machine Learning Research*, 15(1):3247–3295, 2014. [448]

H. Markowitz. Portfolio selection. *The Journal of Finance*, 7(1):77–91, 1952. [55]

M. E. Maron and J. L. Kuhns. On relevance, probabilistic indexing and information retrieval. *Journal of the ACM*, 7(3):216–244, 1960. [352]

P. Martin-Löf. The definition of random sequences. *Information and Control*, 9(6):602–619, 1966. [125]

A. Maurer and M. Pontil. Empirical Bernstein bounds and sample variance penalization. arXiv:0907.3740, 2009. [70, 95]

B. C. May, N. Korda, A. Lee, and D. S. Leslie. Optimistic Bayesian sampling in contextual-bandit problems. *The Journal of Machine Learning Research*, 13(1):2069–2106, 2012. [416]

C. McDiarmid. Concentration. In *Probabilistic methods for algorithmic discrete mathematics*, pages 195–248. Springer, 1998. [66, 71, 228]

H. B. McMahan and A. Blum. Online geometric optimization in the bandit setting against an adaptive adversary. In *Proceedings of the 17th Conference on Learning Theory*, volume 3120, pages 109–123. Springer, 2004. [328]

H. B. McMahan and M. J. Streeter. Tighter bounds for multi-armed bandits with expert advice. In *Proceedings of the 22nd Conference on Learning Theory*, 2009. [201]

P. Ménard and A. Garivier. A minimax and asymptotically optimal algorithm for stochastic bandits. In *Proceedings of the 28th International Conference on Algorithmic Learning Theory*, pages 223–237, Kyoto University, Kyoto, Japan, 15–17 Oct 2017. JMLR.org. [100, 108, 119]

S. P. Meyn and R. L. Tweedie. *Markov chains and stochastic stability*. Springer Science & Business Media, 2012. [41, 42]

V. Mnih, Cs. Szepesvári, and J.-Y. Audibert. Empirical Bernstein stopping. In *Proceedings of the 25th International Conference on Machine Learning*, pages 672–679, New York, NY, USA, 2008. ACM. [70, 95]

S. Mukherjee, KP. Naveen, N. Sudarsanam, and B. Ravindran. Efficient-UCBV: An almost optimal algorithm using variance estimates. In *32nd AAAI Conference on Artificial Intelligence*, 2018. [108]

J. A. Nelder and R. W. M. Wedderburn. Generalized linear models. *Journal of the Royal Statistical Society. Series A (General)*, 135(3):370–384, 1972. [213]

A. S. Nemirovsky. Efficient methods for large-scale convex optimization problems. *Ekonomika i Matematicheskie Metody*, 15, 1979. [301]

A. S. Nemirovsky and D. B. Yudin. *Problem Complexity and Method Efficiency in Optimization*. Wiley, 1983. [301, 364, 365]

G. Neu. Explore no more: Improved high-probability regret bounds for non-stochastic bandits. In *Advances in Neural Information Processing Systems*, pages 3168–3176. Curran Associates, Inc., 2015a. [148, 149, 201, 328]

G. Neu. First-order regret bounds for combinatorial semi-bandits. In *Proceedings of the 28th Conference on Learning Theory*, pages 1360–1375, Paris, France, 2015b. JMLR.org. [148, 299]

G. Neu, A. György, Cs. Szepesvári, and A. Antos. Online Markov decision processes under bandit feedback. *IEEE Transactions on Automatic Control*, 59(3):676–691, December 2014. [475]

J. Von Neumann and O. Morgenstern. *Theory of Games and Economic Behavior*. Princeton University Press, Princeton, 1944. [55]

J. Niño-Mora. Computing a classic index for finite-horizon bandits. *INFORMS Journal on Computing*, 23(2):254–267, 2011. [402]

B. O'Donoghue, E. Chu, N. Parikh, and S. Boyd. Conic optimization via operator splitting and homogeneous self-dual embedding. *Journal of Optimization Theory and Applications*, 169(3): 1042–1068, 2016. [450]

B. O'Donoghue, E. Chu, N. Parikh, and S. Boyd. SCS: Splitting conic solver, version 2.1.1. https://github.com/cvxgrp/scs, November 2017. [450]

J. Ok, A. Proutiere, and D. Tranos. Exploration in structured reinforcement learning. In *Advances in Neural Information Processing Systems*, Red Hook, NY, USA, 2018. Curran Associates Inc. [213, 264]

P. A. Ortega and D. A. Braun. A minimum relative entropy principle for learning and acting. *Journal of Artificial Intelligence Research*, pages 475–511, 2010. [416]

R. Ortner and D. Ryabko. Online regret bounds for undiscounted continuous reinforcement learning. In *Advances in Neural Information Processing Systems*, pages 1763–1771, USA, 2012. Curran Associates Inc. [475]

R. Ortner, D. Ryabko, P. Auer, and R. Munos. Regret bounds for restless Markov bandits. In *Proceedings of the 23rd International Conference on Algorithmic Learning Theory*, pages 214–228, Berlin, Heidelberg, 2012. Springer Berlin Heidelberg. [337]

I. Osband and B. Van Roy. Why is posterior sampling better than optimism for reinforcement learning? In *Proceedings of the 34th International Conference on Machine Learning*, pages 2701–2710, Sydney, Australia, 06–11 Aug 2017. JMLR.org. [475]

I. Osband, D. Russo, and B. Van Roy. (more) efficient reinforcement learning via posterior sampling. In *Advances in Neural Information Processing Systems*, pages 3003–3011. Curran Associates, Inc., 2013. [417, 475]

E. Ostrovsky and L. Sirota. Exact value for subgaussian norm of centered indicator random variable. arXiv:1405.6749, 2014. [69]

D. G. Pandelis and D. Teneketzis. On the optimality of the gittins index rule for multi-armed bandits with multiple plays. *Mathematical Methods of Operations Research*, 50(3):449–461, 1999. [400]

C. H. Papadimitriou and J. N. Tsitsiklis. The complexity of Markov decision processes. *Mathematics of Operations Research*, 12(3):441–450, 1987. [471]

C. H. Papadimitriou and S. Vempala. On the approximability of the traveling salesman problem. *Combinatorica*, 26(1):101–120, 2006. [328]

V. Perchet. Approachability of convex sets in games with partial monitoring. *Journal of Optimization Theory and Applications*, 149(3):665–677, 2011. [448]

V. Perchet and P. Rigollet. The multi-armed bandit problem with covariates. *The Annals of Statistics*, 41(2):693–721, 04 2013. [215]

G. Peskir and A. Shiryaev. *Optimal stopping and free-boundary problems*. Springer, 2006. [43, 401, 402]

A. Piccolboni and C. Schindelhauer. Discrete prediction games with arbitrary feedback and loss. In *Computational Learning Theory*, pages 208–223. Springer, 2001. [448]

C. Pike-Burke, S. Agrawal, Cs. Szepesvári, and S. Grünewälder. Bandits with delayed, aggregated anonymous feedback. In *Proceedings of the 35th International Conference on Machine Learning*, volume 80, pages 4102–4110. JMLR.org, 10–15 Jul 2018. [316]

J. Poland. FPL analysis for adaptive bandits. In O. B. Lupanov, O. M. Kasim-Zade, A. V. Chaskin, and K. Steinhöfel, editors, *Stochastic Algorithms: Foundations and Applications*, pages 58–69, Berlin, Heidelberg, 2005. Springer Berlin Heidelberg. [328]

D. Pollard. *A user's guide to measure theoretic probability*, volume 8. Cambridge University Press, 2002. [32]

E. L. Presman and I. N. Sonin. *Sequential control with incomplete information. The Bayesian approach to multi-armed bandit problems*. Academic Press, 1990. [11, 401]

M. Puterman. *Markov decision processes: discrete stochastic dynamic programming*, volume 414. Wiley, 2009. [473, 474, 476]

C. Qin, D. Klabjan, and D. Russo. Improving the expected improvement algorithm. In *Advances in Neural Information Processing Systems*, pages 5381–5391. Curran Associates, Inc., 2017. [364]

F. Radlinski, R. Kleinberg, and T. Joachims. Learning diverse rankings with multi-armed bandits. In *Proceedings of the 25th International Conference on Machine Learning*, pages 784–791. ACM, 2008. [350, 351, 352]

A. N. Rafferty, H. Ying, and J. J. Williams. Bandit assignment for educational experiments: Benefits to students versus statistical power. In *Artificial Intelligence in Education*, pages 286–290. Springer, 2018. [11]

A. Rakhlin and K. Sridharan. BISTRO: An efficient relaxation-based method for contextual bandits. In *Proceedings of the 33rd International Conference on Machine Learning*, pages 1977–1985, 2016. [202]

A. Rakhlin and K. Sridharan. On equivalence of martingale tail bounds and deterministic regret inequalities. In *Proceedings of the 30th Conference on Learning Theory*, pages 1704–1722, Amsterdam, Netherlands, 2017. JMLR.org. [249]

A. Rakhlin, O. Shamir, and K. Sridharan. Making gradient descent optimal for strongly convex stochastic optimization. In *Proceedings of the 29th International Conference on Machine Learning*, 2012. [365]

L. M. Rios and N. V. Sahinidis. Derivative-free optimization: a review of algorithms and comparison of software implementations. *Journal of Global Optimization*, 56(3):1247–1293, Jul 2013. [364]

H. Robbins. Some aspects of the sequential design of experiments. *Bulletin of the American Mathematical Society*, 58(5):527–535, 1952. [10, 56, 78, 79]

H. Robbins and D. Siegmund. Boundary crossing probabilities for the wiener process and sample sums. *The Annals of Mathematical Statistics*, pages 1410–1429, 1970. [226]

H. Robbins and D. Siegmund. A class of stopping rules for testing parametric hypotheses. In *Proceedings of the Sixth Berkeley Symposium on Mathematical Statistics and Probability*, pages 37–41. University of California Press, 1972. [230]

H. Robbins, D. Sigmund, and Y. Chow. Great expectations: the theory of optimal stopping. *Houghton-Nifflin*, 7:631–640, 1971. [401]

S. Robertson. The probability ranking principle in IR. *Journal of Documentation*, 33(4):294–304, 1977. [352]

R. T. Rockafellar. *Convex analysis*. Princeton university press, 2015. [275, 329]

R. T. Rockafellar and S. Uryasev. Optimization of conditional value-at-risk. *Journal of Risk*, 2:21–42, 2000. [55]

C. A. Rogers. *Packing and covering*. Cambridge University Press, 1964. [226]

S. M. Ross. *Introduction to Stochastic Dynamic Programming*. Academic Press, New York, 1983. [474]

P. Rusmevichientong and J. N. Tsitsiklis. Linearly parameterized bandits. *Mathematics of Operations Research*, 35(2):395–411, 2010. [79, 213, 257]

D. Russo. Simple Bayesian algorithms for best arm identification. In *Proceedings of the 29th Annual Conference on Learning Theory*, pages 1417–1418, New York, NY, USA, 2016. JMLR.org. [364]

D. Russo and B. Van Roy. Eluder dimension and the sample complexity of optimistic exploration. In *Advances in Neural Information Processing Systems*, pages 2256–2264. Curran Associates, Inc., 2013. [214]

D. Russo and B. Van Roy. Learning to optimize via information-directed sampling. In *Advances in Neural Information Processing Systems*, pages 1583–1591. Curran Associates, Inc., 2014a. [213, 416, 417]

D. Russo and B. Van Roy. Learning to optimize via posterior sampling. *Mathematics of Operations Research*, 39(4):1221–1243, 2014b. [417]

D. Russo and B. Van Roy. An information-theoretic analysis of Thompson sampling. *Journal of Machine Learning Research*, 17(1):2442–2471, 2016. ISSN 1532-4435. [328, 415, 417]

D. J. Russo, B. Van Roy, A. Kazerouni, I. Osband, and Z. Wen. A tutorial on Thompson sampling. *Foundations and Trends in Machine Learning*, 11(1):1–96, 2018. [417]

A. Rustichini. Minimizing regret: The general case. *Games and Economic Behavior*, 29(1):224–243, 1999. [447, 448]

A. Salomon, J. Audibert, and I. Alaoui. Lower bounds and selectivity of weak-consistent policies in stochastic multi-armed bandit problem. *Journal of Machine Learning Research*, 14(Jan):187–207, 2013. [181]

P. Samuelson. A note on measurement of utility. *The Review of Economic Studies*, 4(2):pp. 155–161, 1937. [400]

A. Sani, A. Lazaric, and R. Munos. Risk-aversion in multi-armed bandits. In *Advances in Neural Information Processing Systems*, pages 3275–3283. Curran Associates, Inc., 2012. [56]

Y. Seldin and G. Lugosi. An improved parametrization and analysis of the EXP3++ algorithm for stochastic and adversarial bandits. In *Proceedings of the 2017 Conference on Learning Theory*, pages 1743–1759, Amsterdam, Netherlands, 2017. JMLR.org. [136]

Y. Seldin and A. Slivkins. One practical algorithm for both stochastic and adversarial bandits. In *Proceedings of the 31st International Conference on Machine Learning*, pages 1287–1295, Bejing, China, 2014. JMLR.org. [136]

S. Shalev-Shwartz. *Online learning: Theory, algorithms, and applications*. PhD thesis, The Hebrew University of Jerusalem, 2007. [301]

S. Shalev-Shwartz. Online learning and online convex optimization. *Foundations and Trends in Machine Learning*, 4(2):107–194, 2012. [300, 301]

S. Shalev-Shwartz and S. Ben-David. *Understanding Machine Learning: From Theory to Algorithms*. Cambridge University Press, 2014. [201, 202, 204]

S. Shalev-Shwartz and Y. Singer. A primal-dual perspective of online learning algorithms. *Machine Learning*, 69(2-3):115–142, 2007. [301]

O. Shamir. On the complexity of bandit and derivative-free stochastic convex optimization. In *Proceedings of the 26th Conference on Learning Theory*, pages 3–24. JMLR.org, 2013. [315, 364]

O. Shamir. On the complexity of bandit linear optimization. In *Proceedings of the 28th Conference on Learning Theory*, pages 1523–1551, Paris, France, 2015. JMLR.org. [257, 311]

T. Sharot. The optimism bias. *Current Biology*, 21(23):R941–R945, 2011a. [91, 92]

T. Sharot. *The optimism bias: A tour of the irrationally positive brain*. Pantheon/Random House, 2011b. [92]

D. Silver, A. Huang, C. J. Maddison, A. Guez, L. Sifre, G. Van Den Driessche, J. Schrittwieser, I. Antonoglou, V. Panneershelvam, and M. Lanctot. Mastering the game of go with deep neural networks and tree search. *Nature*, 529(7587):484–489, 2016. [11]

S. D. Silvey and B. Sibson. Discussion of Dr. Wynn's and of Dr. Laycock's papers. *Journal of Royal Statistical Society (B)*, 34:174–175, 1972. [235]

M. Sion. On general minimax theorems. *Pacific Journal of mathematics*, 8(1):171–176, 1958. [300]

A. Slivkins. Contextual bandits with similarity information. *Journal of Machine Learning Research*, 15(1):2533–2568, 2014. [314]

A. Slivkins. Introduction to multi-armed bandits. *Foundations and Trends in Machine Learning*, 12 (1-2):1–286, 2019. ISSN 1935-8237. [10, 314]

A. Slivkins and E. Upfal. Adapting to a changing environment: the Brownian restless bandits. In *Proceedings of the 21st Conference on Learning Theory*, pages 343–354, 2008. [338]

M. Soare, A. Lazaric, and R. Munos. Best-arm identification in linear bandits. In *Advances in Neural Information Processing Systems*, pages 828–836. Curran Associates, Inc., 2014. [264, 364]

I. M. Sonin. A generalized Gittins index for a Markov chain and its recursive calculation. *Statistics and Probability Letters*, 78(12):1526–1533, 2008. [402]

N. Srebro, K. Sridharan, and A. Tewari. On the universality of online mirror descent. In *Advances in neural information processing systems*, pages 2645–2653, 2011. [299]

K. Sridharan and A. Tewari. Convex games in banach spaces. In *Proceedings of the 23rd Conference on Learning Theory*, pages 1–13. Omnipress, 2010. [301]

N. Srinivas, A. Krause, S. Kakade, and M. Seeger. Gaussian process optimization in the bandit setting: No regret and experimental design. In *Proceedings of the 27th International Conference on Machine Learning*, page 1015–1022, Madison, WI, USA, 2010. Omnipress. [214]

G. Stoltz. *Incomplete information and internal regret in prediction of individual sequences*. PhD thesis, Université Paris Sud-Paris XI, 2005. [137]

H. Strasser. *Mathematical theory of statistics: statistical experiments and asymptotic decision theory*, volume 7. Walter de Gruyter, 2011. [382]

R. E. Strauch. Negative dynamic programming. *The Annals of Mathematical Statistics*, 37(4):871–890, 08 1966. [476]

M. J. Streeter and S. F. Smith. A simple distribution-free approach to the max k-armed bandit problem. In *International Conference on Principles and Practice of Constraint Programming*, pages 560–574. Springer, 2006a. [365]

M. J Streeter and S. F. Smith. An asymptotically optimal algorithm for the max k-armed bandit problem. In *Proceedings of the National Conference on Artificial Intelligence*, pages 135–142, 2006b. [365]

A. Strehl and M. Littman. A theoretical analysis of model-based interval estimation. In *Proceedings of the 22nd International Conference on Machine learning*, pages 856–863, New York, NY, USA, 2005. ACM. [475]

A. Strehl and M. Littman. An analysis of model-based interval estimation for Markov decision processes. *Journal of Computer and System Sciences*, 74(8):1309–1331, 2008. [475, 481]

A. Strehl, L. Li, E. Wiewiora, J. Langford, and M. Littman. PAC model-free reinforcement learning. In *Proceedings of the 23rd international conference on Machine learning*, pages 881–888, New York, NY, USA, 2006. ACM. [475]

M. J. A. Strens. A Bayesian framework for reinforcement learning. In *Proceedings of the 17th International Conference on Machine Learning*, pages 943–950, San Francisco, CA, USA, 2000. Morgan Kaufmann Publishers Inc. [474]

Y. Sui, A. Gotovos, J. Burdick, and A. Krause. Safe exploration for optimization with gaussian processes. In *Proceedings of the 32nd International Conference on Machine Learning*, pages 997–1005, Lille, France, 07–09 Jul 2015. JMLR.org. [315]

Q. Sun, W. Zhou, and J. Fan. Adaptive huber regression: Optimality and phase transition. arXiv:1706.06991, 2017. [96]

R. Sutton and A. Barto. *Reinforcement Learning: An Introduction*. MIT Press, 1998. [79, 400]

R. Sutton and A. Barto. *Reinforcement Learning: An Introduction*. MIT Press, second edition, 2018. [474]

J.M. Swart. Large deviation theory, January 2017. URL http://staff.utia.cas.cz/swart/lecture_notes/LDP8.pdf. [68]

V. Syrgkanis, A. Krishnamurthy, and R. Schapire. Efficient algorithms for adversarial contextual learning. In *Proceedings of the 33rd International Conference on Machine Learning*, pages 2159–2168, New York, NY, USA, 2016. JMLR.org. [202]

Cs. Szepesvári. *Algorithms for Reinforcement Learning*. Synthesis Lectures on Artificial Intelligence and Machine Learning. Morgan & Claypool Publishers, 2010. [474]

I. Szita and A. Lőrincz. Optimistic initialization and greediness lead to polynomial time learning in factored MDPs. In *Proceedings of the 26th International Conference on Machine Learning*, pages 1001–1008, New York, USA, 2009. ACM. [475]

I. Szita and Cs. Szepesvári. Model-based reinforcement learning with nearly tight exploration complexity bounds. In *Proceedings of the 27th International Conference on Machine Learning*, pages 1031–1038, USA, 2010. Omnipress. [475]

E. Takimoto and M. K. Warmuth. Path kernels and multiplicative updates. *Journal of Machine Learning Research*, 4:773–818, 2003. [329]

M. Talagrand. The missing factor in Hoeffding's inequalities. *Annales de l'IHP Probabilités et Statistiques*, 31(4):689–702, 1995. [65]

G. Taraldsen. Optimal learning from the Doob-Dynkin lemma. arXiv:1801.00974, 2018. [30]

J. Teevan, S. T. Dumais, and E. Horvitz. Characterizing the value of personalizing search. In *Proceedings of the 30th Annual International ACM SIGIR Conference on Research and Development in Information Retrieval*, pages 757–758, New York, NY, USA, 2007. ACM. [352]

A. Tewari and P. L. Bartlett. Optimistic linear programming gives logarithmic regret for irreducible MDPs. In *Advances in Neural Information Processing Systems*, pages 1505–1512. Curran Associates, Inc., 2008. [474]

A. Tewari and S. A. Murphy. From ads to interventions: Contextual bandits in mobile health. In *Mobile Health*, pages 495–517. Springer, 2017. [201]

G. Theocharous, Z. Wen, Y. Abbasi-Yadkori, and N. Vlassis. Posterior sampling for large scale reinforcement learning. arXiv:1711.07979, 2017. [475]

W. Thompson. On the likelihood that one unknown probability exceeds another in view of the evidence of two samples. *Biometrika*, 25(3/4):285–294, 1933. [10, 55, 79, 404, 414, 416]

W. R. Thompson. On the theory of apportionment. *American Journal of Mathematics*, 57(2):450–456, 1935. [473]

M. J. Todd. *Minimum-volume ellipsoids: Theory and algorithms*. SIAM, 2016. [235]

J. R. R. Tolkien. *The Hobbit*. Ballantine Books, 1937. [404]

L. Tran-Thanh, A. Chapman, E. Munoz de Cote, A. Rogers, and N. R. Jennings. Epsilon–first policies for budget–limited multi-armed bandits. In *Proceedings of the 24th AAAI Conference on Artificial Intelligence*, AAAI, pages 1211–1216, 2010. [315]

L. Tran-Thanh, A. Chapman, A. Rogers, and N. R. Jennings. Knapsack based optimal policies for budget-limited multi-armed bandits. In *Proceedings of the 26th AAAI Conference on Artificial Intelligence*, AAAI'12, pages 1134–1140. AAAI Press, 2012. [315]

J. A. Tropp. An introduction to matrix concentration inequalities. *Foundations and Trends® in Machine Learning*, 8(1-2):1–230, 2015. [66]

J. N. Tsitsiklis. A short proof of the Gittins index theorem. *The Annals of Applied Probability*, pages 194–199, 1994. [401]

A. B. Tsybakov. *Introduction to nonparametric estimation*. Springer Science & Business Media, 2008. [167]

C. Ionescu Tulcea. Mesures dans les espaces produits. *Atti Accademia Nazionale Lincei Rend*, 7: 208–211, 1949–50. [43]

E. Uchibe and K. Doya. Competitive-cooperative-concurrent reinforcement learning with importance sampling. In *Proceedings of the International Conference on Simulation of Adaptive Behavior: From Animals and Animats*, pages 287–296, 2004. [149]

M. Valko. Bandits on graphs and structures, 2016. [217, 316]

M. Valko, A. Carpentier, and R. Munos. Stochastic simultaneous optimistic optimization. In *Proceedings of the 30th International Conference on Machine Learning*, pages 19–27, Atlanta, GA, USA, 2013a. JMLR.org. [364]

M. Valko, N. Korda, R. Munos, I. Flaounas, and N. Cristianini. Finite-time analysis of kernelised contextual bandits. In *Proceedings of the 29th Conference on Uncertainty in Artificial Intelligence*, pages 654–663, Arlington, VA, USA, 2013b. AUAI Press. [214]

M. Valko, R. Munos, B. Kveton, and T. Kocák. Spectral bandits for smooth graph functions. In *Proceedings of the 31st International Conference on Machine Learning*, pages 46–54, Bejing, China, 2014. JMLR.org. [214, 217, 238]

S. van de Geer. *Empirical Processes in M-estimation*, volume 6. Cambridge University Press, 2000. [66, 226, 300]

D. van der Hoeven, T. van Erven, and W. Kotłowski. The many faces of exponential weights in online learning. In *Proceedings of the 31st Conference on Learning Theory*, pages 2067–2092, 2018. [284]

A. W. van der Vaart and J. A. Wellner. *Weak Convergence and Empirical Processes*. Springer, New York, 1996. [300]

H. P. Vanchinathan, G. Bartók, and A. Krause. Efficient partial monitoring with prior information. In *Advances in Neural Information Processing Systems*, pages 1691–1699. Curran Associates, Inc., 2014. [448]

V. Vapnik. *Statistical learning theory. 1998*, volume 3. Wiley, New York, 1998. [204]

P. Varaiya, J. Walrand, and C. Buyukkoc. Extensions of the multiarmed bandit problem: The discounted case. *IEEE Transactions on Automatic Control*, 30(5):426–439, 1985. [402]

C. Vernade, O. Cappé, and V. Perchet. Stochastic bandit models for delayed conversions. In *Proceedings of the 33rd Conference on Uncertainty in Artificial Intelligence*. AUAI Press, 2017. [316]

C. Vernade, A. Carpentier, G. Zappella, B. Ermis, and M. Brueckner. Contextual bandits under delayed feedback. arXiv:1807.02089, 2018. [316]

S. Villar, J. Bowden, and J. Wason. Multi-armed bandit models for the optimal design of clinical trials: benefits and challenges. *Statistical science: a review journal of the Institute of Mathematical Statistics*, 30(2):199–215, 2015. [11]

W. Vogel. An asymptotic minimax theorem for the two armed bandit problem. *The Annals of Mathematical Statistics*, 31(2):444–451, 1960. [174]

J. von Neumann. Zur theorie der gesellschaftsspiele. *Mathematische annalen*, 100(1):295–320, 1928. [301]

V. G. Vovk. Aggregating strategies. *Proceedings of Computational Learning Theory*, 1990. [125, 137]

S. Wang and W. Chen. Thompson sampling for combinatorial semi-bandits. In *Proceedings of the 35th International Conference on Machine Learning*, pages 5114–5122, Stockholmsmässan, Stockholm Sweden, 10–15 Jul 2018. JMLR.org. [328, 417]

Y. Wang, J-Y. Audibert, and R. Munos. Algorithms for infinitely many-armed bandits. In *Advances in Neural Information Processing Systems*, pages 1729–1736, 2009. [314]

M. K. Warmuth and A. Jagota. Continuous and discrete-time nonlinear gradient descent: Relative loss bounds and convergence. In *Electronic Proceedings of the 5th International Symposium on Artificial Intelligence and Mathematics*, 1997. [301]

P. L Wawrzynski and A. Pacut. Truncated importance sampling for reinforcement learning with experience replay. In *Proceedings of the International Multiconference on Computer Science and Information Technology*, pages 305–315, 2007. [149]

R. Weber. On the Gittins index for multiarmed bandits. *The Annals of Applied Probability*, 2(4):1024–1033, 1992. [401]

R. Weber and G. Weiss. On an index policy for restless bandits. *Journal of Applied Probability*, 27 (3):637–648, 1990. [402]

C-Y. Wei and H. Luo. More adaptive algorithms for adversarial bandits. In *Proceedings of the 31st Conference On Learning Theory*, pages 1263–1291. JMLR.org, 06–09 Jul 2018. [299, 301, 304]

M. J. Weinberger and E. Ordentlich. On delayed prediction of individual sequences. In *Information Theory, 2002. Proceedings. 2002 IEEE International Symposium on*, page 148. IEEE, 2002. [316]

Z. Wen, B. Kveton, and A. Ashkan. Efficient learning in large-scale combinatorial semi-bandits. In *Proceedings of the 32nd International Conference on Machine Learning*, volume 37, pages 1113–1122, Lille, France, 2015. JMLR.org. [328]

P. Whittle. Multi-armed bandits and the Gittins index. *Journal of the Royal Statistical Society (B)*, pages 143–149, 1980. [401]

P. Whittle. Restless bandits: Activity allocation in a changing world. *Journal of applied probability*, 25(A):287–298, 1988. [337, 402]

D. Williams. *Probability with martingales*. Cambridge University Press, 1991. [32]

H. Wu and X. Liu. Double Thompson sampling for dueling bandits. In *Advances in Neural Information Processing Systems*, pages 649–657. Curran Associates, Inc., 2016. [315]

Y. Wu, A. György, and Cs. Szepesvári. Online learning with gaussian payoffs and side observations. In *Advances in Neural Information Processing Systems*, pages 1360–1368. Curran Associates Inc., 2015. [448]

Y. Wu, R. Shariff, T. Lattimore, and Cs. Szepesvári. Conservative bandits. In *Proceedings of the 33rd International Conference on Machine Learning*, pages 1254–1262, New York, NY, USA, 20–22 Jun 2016. JMLR.org. [315]

H. P. Wynn. The sequential generation of D-optimum experimental designs. *The Annals of Mathematical Statistics*, pages 1655–1664, 1970. [235]

Y. Xia, H. Li, T. Qin, N. Yu, and T.-Y. Liu. Thompson sampling for budgeted multi-armed bandits. In *Proceedings of the 24th International Conference on Artificial Intelligence*, IJCAI, pages 3960–3966. AAAI Press, 2015. [315]

Y. Yao. Some results on the Gittins index for a normal reward process. In *Time Series and Related Topics*, pages 284–294. Institute of Mathematical Statistics, 2006. [402]

B. Yu. Assouad, Fano, and Le Cam. In D. Pollard, E. Torgersen, and G. L. Yang, editors, *Festschrift for Lucien Le Cam: Research Papers in Probability and Statistics*, pages 423–435. Springer, 1997. [174, 175]

Y. Yue and T. Joachims. Interactively optimizing information retrieval systems as a dueling bandits problem. In *Proceedings of the 26th International Conference on Machine Learning*, pages 1201–1208. ACM, 2009. [315]

Y. Yue and T. Joachims. Beat the mean bandit. In *Proceedings of the 28th International Conference on Machine Learning*, pages 241–248, New York, NY, USA, June 2011. ACM. [315]

Y. Yue, J. Broder, R. Kleinberg, and T. Joachims. The *k*-armed dueling bandits problem. In *Proceedings of the 22nd Conference on Learning Theory*, 2009. [315]

J. Zimmert and T. Lattimore. Connections between mirror descent, thompson sampling and the information ratio. In *Advances in Neural Information Processing Systems*, pages 11973–11982. Curran Associates, Inc., 2019. [416]

J. Zimmert and Y. Seldin. An optimal algorithm for stochastic and adversarial bandits. In *AISTATS*, pages 467–475, 2019. [136, 305, 315]

J. Zimmert, H. Luo, and C-Y. Wei. Beating stochastic and adversarial semi-bandits optimally and simultaneously. In *Proceedings of the 36th International Conference on Machine Learning*, pages 7683–7692, Long Beach, California, USA, 09–15 Jun 2019. JMLR.org. [305]

M. Zinkevich. Online convex programming and generalized infinitesimal gradient ascent. In *Proceedings of the 20th International Conference on Machine Learning*, pages 928–935. AAAI Press, 2003. [301]

M. Zoghi, S. Whiteson, R. Munos, and M. Rijke. Relative upper confidence bound for the *k*-armed dueling bandit problem. In *Proceedings of the 31st International Conference on Machine Learning*, pages 10–18, Bejing, China, 2014. JMLR.org. [315]

M. Zoghi, Z. Karnin, S. Whiteson, and M. Rijke. Copeland dueling bandits. In *Advances in Neural Information Processing Systems*, pages 307–315. Curran Associates, Inc., 2015. [315]

M. Zoghi, T. Tunys, M. Ghavamzadeh, B. Kveton, Cs. Szepesvári, and Z. Wen. Online learning to rank in stochastic click models. In *Proceedings of the 34th International Conference on Machine Learning*, JMLR.org, pages 4199–4208, 2017. [351]

S. Zong, H. Ni, K. Sung, R. N. Ke, Z. Wen, and B. Kveton. Cascading bandits for large-scale recommendation problems. In *Proceedings of the 32nd Conference on Uncertainty in Artificial Intelligence*, 2016. [350, 351]

Index